MILITARY LAW

UNDER THE UNIFORM CODE OF

MILITARY JUSTICE

MILITARY LAW
UNDER THE UNIFORM CODE OF
MILITARY JUSTICE

BY

WILLIAM B. AYCOCK

AND

SEYMOUR W. WURFEL

1955

THE UNIVERSITY OF NORTH CAROLINA PRESS

CHAPEL HILL

Manufactured in the United States of America

DEDICATION

This book is dedicated to the overwhelming majority of soldiers, sailors, marines and airmen, law-abiding Americans, who do not get into trouble.

Preface

On May 31, 1951, the effective date of the Uniform Code of Military Justice and THE MANUAL FOR COURTS-MARTIAL, UNITED STATES, 1951, new and significant changes were introduced in the field of military justice. An important feature of the new Code is a provision for a Court of Military Appeals composed of three civilian judges. The nature and extent of many of the changes could not be ascertained fully until this new Court had time to provide judicial interpretation to a substantial number of provisions in the Code and MANUAL. During the past three years the Court has rendered more than five hundred opinions in which it has dealt with many of the Code and MANUAL provisions. One purpose of this book is to collect this fundamental body of military case law. All opinions of the Court from its inception through August 13, 1954 have received consideration.

This material is essentially practical. It is designed to afford a ready reference to the military lawyer, or the civilian practitioner with a military justice case, whether his problem is trial, appellate or post-appellate, and whether his client is the Government or the accused. It should also prove useful to teachers and students of military law either in law school courses, in service schools or in reserve judge advocate and legal specialist training programs.

The Code and MANUAL have been freely quoted when necessary to portray adequately the impact of the Court's decisions on them. Generally, MANUAL provisions which have not yet been subject to judicial review are not repeated. In a number of instances the same case has been discussed in two or more places. When this occurs the purpose is to give complete topical coverage without cumbersome cross-referencing.

Chapter I "Historical Introduction" was published originally in 49 MICHIGAN LAW REVIEW 493 (1951). Chapters 2-6 first appeared in

32 NORTH CAROLINA LAW REVIEW 1 (1953). They have been revised and extended. This material is a definitive treatment of the subject of "Jurisdiction" and includes decisions of service boards of review and federal civilian courts in addition to those of the Court of Military Appeals. Chapters 7-14 are concerned with the work of the Court of Military Appeals on all matters except those involving questions of jurisdiction covered in Chapters 2 through 6. Chapter 10 on *"Prejudicial Error vs. 'Military Due Process'"* was initially published in 6 VANDERBILT LAW REVIEW 251 (1953) under the title *"'Military Due Process'—What Is It?"* A few additions have been made since original publication. Some of the material included in Chapters 7 through 9, and 11 through 14 originally appeared in articles in 31 NORTH CAROLINA LAW REVIEW 1 (1952) and 2 JOURNAL OF PUBLIC LAW 254 (1954). Chapter 15 includes a detailed discussion of habeas corpus—and the relationship between the federal civilian judiciary and the military system of justice. This chapter first appeared in 49 MICHIGAN LAW REVIEW 493, 699 (1951). It has been revised to include significant developments in the last three years and expanded to cover Selective Service cases. The authors acknowledge the generous consent of the editors of these publications to the present publication of this material.

Thanks are due to Dean Henry P. Brandis, Jr. and Professor M. T. Van Hecke of the Law School of the University of North Carolina for providing helpful suggestions and comments on many parts of the manuscript. Lieutenants Zane Finkelstein, Hurshell H. Keener, John G. Golding and Willis D. Brown, Judge Advocate General's Corps, United States Army Reserve, and Private William W. Smith assisted materially in verifying citations and in the task of proof-reading. Mr. Thomas W. Steed, former Editor-in-Chief of THE NORTH CAROLINA LAW REVIEW prepared the Table of Articles and the Table of Cases and assisted in the preparation of the Index.

The authors alone contrived whatever errors are detected and matters of opinion herein expressed are their personal views.

WILLIAM B. AYCOCK
SEYMOUR W. WURFEL

Introduction

The enactment of the Uniform Code of Military Justice marks the first time in the history of the nation that the members of the armed services, whether land, sea, or air, have been subjected, except in minor detail, to exactly the same provisions for trial and punishment for offenses against the laws of the United States. To revise, reduce to an acceptable and harmonious working basis, and modify the widely divergent views and practices of over a century and a half in the several services was a monumental undertaking.

To put the provisions of the Code into operation was likewise a great task. It was somewhat akin to raising an infant who, during its earlier life, is frequently the cause of so much worry, care, and annoyance that its parents sometimes wonder whether it is an asset or a liability. At about the age of three the child begins to show signs of perhaps growing into something useful and sensible.

The Uniform Code of Military Justice, now three and a half years old, has gone through this first stage. From a groping start in a new world of conflicting ideas and interests it is emerging as a distinctive creature in its own right. Whether, like some of its human guardians, it is adapted to perform its function and survive in the world of A and H bombs and supersonic speeds, or whether, like many of them, it is too weighted down with outworn convention and Alice-in-Wonderland theory, is an open question.

In attempting to describe the Code as it is and as it operates, the authors have performed a magnificent service to those who labor in the field of rendering justice as between the United States and its occasional wayward uniformed son. They have provided a definitive and scholarly work to serve as a guide line in solving the perplexing issues which will continue to arise, for a long time to come, in the administration of the comparatively new Code.

EUGENE M. CAFFEY
Major General, USA
The Judge Advocate General

Washington
November 20, 1954

Contents

Chapter 3

JURISDICTION OF THE PERSON

Chapter 4

JURISDICTION OF THE OFFENSE

Chapter 5

JURISDICTION OF THE SENTENCE

Chapter 6

Chapter 7

LAW OFFICER

Chapter 8

TRIAL AND RELATED MATTERS

Chapter 11

Sufficiency of the Evidence as a Matter of Law

Chapter 12

Punishments

MILITARY LAW

UNDER THE UNIFORM CODE OF

MILITARY JUSTICE

CHAPTER I

Historical Background

A. *Early Military Law and Tribunals*

"Richard, by the grace of God, King of England, Duke of Normandy and Aquitaine, and Earl of Anjou, to all his subjects about to proceed by sea to Jerusalem, greeting. Know ye, that we, with common consent of fit and proper men, have made the enactments, underwritten. Whoever shall slay a man on ship-board, he shall be bound to the dead man and thrown into the sea. If he shall slay him on land he shall be bound to the dead man and buried in the earth. If any one shall be convicted, by means of lawful witnesses, of having drawn out a knife with which to strike another, or shall strike another so as to draw blood, he shall lose his hand. If, also, he shall give a blow with his hand, without shedding blood, he shall be plunged in the sea three times. If any man shall utter disgraceful language or abuse, or shall curse his companion, he shall pay him an ounce of silver for every time he has so abused him. A robber who shall be convicted of theft shall have his head cropped after the manner of a champion,* [*Champions hired to fight legal duels, in cases of murder and homicides, had their hair clipped close to their heads. (Note by Samuel)] and boiling pitch shall be poured thereon, and then the feathers of a cushion shall be shaken out upon him, so that he may be known, and at the first land at which the ship shall touch, he shall be set on shore. Witness myself, at Chinon."[1]

The above ordinance of Richard I, promulgated in the year 1190, was "Chiefly meant to prevent disputes between the soldiers and sailors in their voyage to the holy land"[2] during the third crusade. It should have been efficacious in achieving that purpose. Richard's approach

[1] ORDINANCE OF RICHARD I—A. D. 1190. Reprinted in 2 WINTHROP, MILITARY LAW, appendix 3 (1886).
[2] 2 GROSE, HIST. ENG. ARMY 83.

to a specific problem of "unification" in a joint operation possessed the merits of vigor and simplicity.

Lest one fall into the easy error of ascribing such barbarity to the machinations of "the military mind," as distinguished from "the civilian mind," a quick glance at the impact of contemporary criminal law upon civilians under the common law of the twelfth century is necessary. In the England of Justiciar Ranulph De Glanville and Archbishop Hubert Walter all felonies were punishable by mutilation or death and "treasons" by disembowling and quartering.[3] The only safe conclusion seems to be that, with the passage of some eight centuries, both the military and civilian systems of justice have benefited from the emergence of a more humanitarian jurisprudence.

A primary purpose of this chapter is to establish the historical, and continuing, separation of military and civil courts. Legal systems predicated upon military organizations are of ancient origin. The feudal law was made known to the Romans in the first century B. C. by the Teutons and was utilized by the Roman Emperor, Alexander Severus. Upon the decline of the Roman Empire the Goths, Huns, Franks, Vandals and Lombards borrowed the feudal law and carried it into Europe as an instrument of their military policy. It became the "law of nations" of the western world of that time. The hard core of feudal law was predicated upon a military society in which a state of war was the normal condition.[4] By the eleventh century, feudal law had been codified in Lombardy as the *Libri Feudorum*.[5] This well-developed continental feudal system was brought to England by William the Conqueror in 1066 and imposed upon the simpler feudal system already existing in Britain.[6]

It is of considerable academic interest that at least one creditable legal scholar maintains the primary purpose of the magnates and the barons in 1215 in the Magna Carta was to preserve their feudal law prerogatives against encroachment by the Crown rather than to establish a declaration of the rights of free men.[7] The Court Baron of the feudal lord, which was also known as the earl's court, exercised both criminal and civil feudal law jurisdiction over knights, tenants, and vassals from before Magna Carta until well into the sixteenth century during the reign of Elizabeth.[8]

The Court of the Constable existed in medieval England apart from

[3] RADIN, ANGLO-AMERICAN LEGAL HISTORY, 236, 237, 278, 279.
[4] 2 BLACKSTONE, COMMENTARIES, Cooley ed., 45-46 (1899).
[5] RADIN, ANGLO-AMERICAN LEGAL HISTORY 145 (1936).
[6] *Id.* at 119, 152. Also, DAVIS, A TREATISE ON THE MILITARY LAW OF THE UNITED STATES, 3d ed., 13 (1915).
[7] RADIN, ANGLO-AMERICAN LEGAL HISTORY 152-155 (1936).
[8] *Id.* at 139-140.

and in addition to the common law, equity, canon and admiralty courts.[9] From the time of William the Conqueror, the Constable, under the direction of the king, was commander of the Royal Army. He presided over a court assisted by the Marshal and three doctors of the civil law, and by a clerk who was the trial counsel of that day since his duty was to prosecute all delinquents brought before the court for trial.[10] The Constable's Court exercised criminal jurisdiction over offenses of soldiers and others against Articles of War promulgated by the king for the government of his Army on expeditions to the continent. It also had jurisdiction of the acts of rebels within the realm and in civil contract matters growing out of war beyond the realm.[11] As a Court of Chivalry it decided questions of injury to honor, of pedigree, precedent, and heraldry.[12] In 1384 Parliament imposed legislative restraint upon the civil jurisdiction of the Constable's Court[13] and in 1399 upon its criminal jurisdiction.[14]

Dating back to the Conquest, the Earl Marshal was the high officer next in rank to the Constable. His original duties were those of marshaling the king's army and resembled those now performed by the Adjutant General. The office of Constable ceased to exist in 1521[15] when it reverted to the Crown upon the attainder of the incumbent Edward, Duke of Buckingham, for high treason. Thereafter the Constable's duties devolved upon the Earl Marshal, and the Constable's Court became the Marshal's Court from which is derived the present term court-martial.[16] The last case tried before the Marshal was in 1737 but the function persisted, and as early as 1642 the House of Lords and the Commons had concurred in legislation authorizing military commanders to punish soldiers by martial law.[17] Gradually the place of the Marshal and his assistants had been taken by military officers detailed for the purpose and the court came to be convened in pursuance of a commission issued by the Crown to a proper military commander.[18] When armies were sent abroad authority was delegated

[9] FAIRMAN, THE LAW OF MARTIAL RULE, 2d ed., 1-2 (1943).

[10] DAVIS, A. TREATISE OF THE MILITARY LAW OF THE UNITED STATES, 3d ed., 13-14 (1915).

[11] FAIRMAN, THE LAW OF MARTIAL RULE, 2d ed., 3 (1943).

[12] DAVIS, A TREATISE ON THE MILITARY LAW OF THE UNITED STATES, 3d ed., 2, 14, footnote 3 (1915). For a history of the Court of Chivalry, see THE ENGLISH MANUAL OF MILITARY LAW 7.

[13] 8 Richard II, c. 5.

[14] 1 Henry IV, c. 14.

[15] This was the thirteenth year of the reign of Henry VIII.

[16] DAVIS, A TREATISE ON THE MILITARY LAW OF THE UNITED STATES, 3d ed., 13-14 (1915).

[17] FAIRMAN, THE LAW OF MARTIAL RULE, 2d ed., 6, 12 (1943).

[18] DAVIS, A. TREATISE ON THE MILITARY LAW OF THE UNITED STATES, 3d ed., 15 (1915).

to the commander "to execute marshall law, and, upon trial by an orderly court, . . . to inflict punishment. . . ."[19]

Originally the Articles of War were framed by the king and proclaimed solely by his authority. This procedure must be contrasted with the later British practice, and that which has always prevailed in the American service, whereby the Articles of War are exclusively statutory enactments of the legislative body.[20]

Following the 1190 classic pronouncement of Richard I, successive Articles of War were issued by royal fiat or royal delegation as occasion required. Only a few of these need be noted. In 1385 Richard II proclaimed Articles of War comprising twenty-four paragraphed items governing not only the conduct of soldiers but providing in detail for the division of the arms and mounts of those taken prisoner.[21]

Similar military codes establishing separate military tribunals are to be found in other European countries at an early date. The first French ordinance of military law dated back to 1378 and the first German Kriegsartikel to 1487. Other celebrated Articles of War were those of the Franks under Emperor Charles V in 1532, of the Netherlands in 1590, of Louis XIV in 1651 and 1665, of Peter the Great in 1715 and of Empress Maria Theresa in 1768.[22] Perhaps the most famous were the elaborate Articles of War issued in 1621 by King Gustavus Adolphus of Sweden. These contained one hundred and sixty-seven articles, a number of which, by their careful provision for court procedure, indicated concern for what currently would be characterized as "due process of law."[23] Early British interest in the rudiments of

[19] Commission to Sir Thomas Baskerville, June 10, 1597. CAMDEN SOCIETY, THE EGERTON PAPERS 246, from FAIRMAN, THE LAW OF MARTIAL RULE, 2d ed., 6 (1943).

[20] FAIRMAN, THE LAW OF MARTIAL RULE, 2d ed., 6 (1943).

[21] Reprinted in 2 WINTHROP, MILITARY LAW, appendix 4-7 (1886). The preamble recites:

"These are the Statutes, Ordinances, and Customs, to be observed in the Army, ordained and made by good consultation and deliberation of our Most Excellent Lord the King Richard, John Duke of Lancaster, Seneschall of England, Thomas Earl of Essex and Buckingham, Constable of England, and Thomas de Mowbray, Earl of Notingham, Mareschall of England, and other Lords, Earls, Barons, Baneretts, and experienced Knights, whom they have thought proper to call unto them; then being at Durham the 17th day of the Month of July, in the ninth year of the Reign of our Lord the King Richard II." Representative of its Articles is: "III. Item, that none be so hardy as to rob and pillage the church, nor to destroy any man belonging to holy church, religious or otherwise, nor any woman, nor to take them prisoners if not bearing arms; nor to force any woman, upon pain of being hanged."

[22] MUNSON, MILITARY LAW 5 (1923).

[23] Reprinted in 2 WINTHTOP, MILITARY LAW, appendix 8-23 (1886). Illustrative are:

"142. In our highest Marshall Court, shall our General be President; in his absence our Field Marshall; when our Generall is present his associates shall be our Field Marshall first, next him our Generall of the Ordnance, Sergeant Major

military "due process" was evidenced by some of the provisions in the Prince Rupert Articles of 1672,[24] in the English Military Discipline of James II of 1686,[25] and in the Articles of James II of 1688.[26]

The English Parliament first directly entered the field of military law with the passage of the Mutiny Act.[27] It was initially adopted in

---

Generall; Generall of the Horse, Quartermaster Generall; next to them shall sit our Muster-Masters and all our Colonells, and in their absence their Lieutenant Colonells, and these shall sit together when there is any matter of great importance in controversie. . . .

"144. All these Judges both of higher and lower Courts, shall under the blue Skies thus sweare before Almighty God, that they will inviolably keep this following oath unto us: I.R.W. doe here promise before God upon his holy Gospell, that I both will and shall judge uprightly in all things according to the Lawes of God, of our Nation, and these Articles of Warre, so farre forth as it pleaseth Almighty God to give me understanding; neither will I for favour nor for hatred, for good will, feare, ill will, anger, or any gift or bribe whatsoever, judge wrongfully; but judge him free that ought to be free, and doom him guilty, that I finde guilty; as the Lord of Heaven and Earth shall help my soule and body at the last day, I shall hold this oath truly."

[24] Reprinted in DAVIS, A TREATISE ON THE MILITARY LAW OF THE UNITED STATES, 3d ed., appendix A, 567-580 (1915). The 74th and last Article thereof reads:

"Whatever is to be published or generally made known, shall be done by beat of drum or the sound of trumpet, that so no man may pretend ignorance thereof.

"And after that whoever shall be found disobedient, or faulty, against what is thus published shall be punish'd according to these Articles, or the quality of the fact."

[25] Reprinted in 2 WINTHROP, MILITARY LAW, appendix 24-25 (1886). The following is a typical excerpt:

"If the Councel of War, or Court-martial be held to judge a Criminal, the President and Captains having taken their places, and the prisoner being brought before them, And the Informations read, the President Interrogates the Prisoner about all the Facts whereof he is accused, and having heard his Defence, and the Proof made or alleged against him, He is ordered to withdraw, being remitted to the care of the Marshal or Jaylor. Then every one judges according to his Conscience, and the Ordnances of the Articles of War. The Sentence is framed according to the Plurality of Votes, and the Criminal being brought in again, The Sentence is Pronounced to him in the name of the Councel of War, or Court-Martial.

"When a Criminal is Condemned to any Punishment, the Provost Martial causes the sentence to be put in execution; And if it be a publick Punishment, the Regiment ought to be drawn together to see it, that thereby the Soldiers may be deterred from offending. Before a Soldier be punished for any infamous Crime, he is to be publickly Degraded from his Arms, and his coat stript over his ears."

[26] Reprinted in 2 WINTHROP, MILITARY LAW, appendix 26-37 (1886), Article LXI thereof provides:

"If any Person be committed by the Provost Martial's own Authority without other Command, he shall acquaint the General or other Chief Commander with the Cause within twenty-four hours, and the Provost-Martial shall thereupon dismiss him unless he have Order to the contrary."

[27] Statutes of the Realm 55, 1 W & M, c. 5, Reprinted in 2 WINTHROP, MILITARY LAW, appendix 38-39 (1886). Paragraph 10 directs:

"And noe Sentence of Death shall be given against any offender in such case by any Court Martiall unless nine of thirteene Officers present shall concur therein. And if there be a greater number of officers present, then the judgment shall passe by the concurrence of the greater part of them soe sworne, and not otherwise; and noe Proceedings, Tryall or Sentence of Death shall be had or given against any offender, but betweene the houres of eight in the morning and one in the afternoone."

the time of William III in 1689 as a result of the mutiny and desertion of Scotch troops adhering to the Stuart cause in the rebellion of 1686. Its purpose was to deprive the crown of any army for more than one year at a time by limiting army appropriations and the authority to define and punish military offenses to one year. Thereafter, annual mutiny acts were passed which made mutiny and desertion punishable by court-martial, but left all other matters affecting discipline to regulation by royal prerogative as before, thus sanctioning the then existing Articles for the government of the British Army. Not until 1881 were the Mutiny Act and the Articles of War consolidated by Parliament into the Army Annual Act.[28] Thus military law in time of peace did not come into existence in statutory form until the passage of the Mutiny Act. The system of governing troops in time of war by Articles of War issued under the prerogative power of the Crown continued from the conquest until superseded by corresponding statutory power[29] in 1803.[30] All earlier British ordinances and Articles of War remained in force only during the service of the troops for whose government they were issued and ceased to operate upon the conclusion of peace.[31] Since 1881 Parliament each year passes the Army Annual Act which includes the Articles of War and British military justice is dependent upon this annual parliamentary approval.[32]

The various Articles of War and other military laws herein mentioned are illustrative only and do not by any means comprise a complete list. A comparative law treatment of military justice is beyond the scope of this book.[33] Although remaining substantially unchanged in matters essential to discipline, new editions of Articles were issued from time to time, especially during the last half of the eighteenth century. For example from 1766 to 1775 seven sets of British Articles were issued.[34]

It is clear that throughout British history in time of war, from the

[28] GLENN AND SCHILLER, THE ARMY AND THE LAW, rev. ed., 34-35 (1943) and WINTHROP, MILITARY LAW AND PRECEDENT, 2d ed., 19-20 (1920).

[29] 43 Geo. III, c. 20.

[30] DAVIS, A TREATISE ON THE MILITARY LAW OF THE UNITED STATES, 3d ed., 339 (1915).

[31] MUNSON, MILITARY LAW 6 (1923).

[32] A single Army and Air Force Annual Act prescribes the basic system of justice for both services although the British Air Force has been separate since 1917. British naval justice, at the trial level, continues to be a separate system. For an interesting discussion of the current system of British military justice, see PASLEY, A COMPARATIVE STUDY OF MILITARY JUSTICE REFORMS IN BRITAIN AND AMERICA, 6 VAND. L. REV. 305 (1953).

[33] French military justice is ably surveyed in GAYNOR, THE FRENCH CODE OF MILITARY JUSTICE: A COMPARISON WITH THE UNIFORM CODE OF MILITARY JUSTICE, 22 GEO. WASH. L. REV. 318 (1954).

[34] DAVIS, A TREATISE ON THE MILITARY LAW OF THE UNITED STATES, 3 ed., 340 (1915).

Conquest to the American Revolution, and down to the present, military laws and tribunals entirely separate from civilian laws and courts have been employed to administer justice in the armed forces.[35] It is important to keep this in mind while examining the history of American military law and in considering the applicability of ordinary civilian legal principles to military tribunal proceedings.

B. *American Military Law and Tribunals*

The substance of the original American Articles of War has been traced to the Code of Gustavus Adolphus of 1621 and to the British Articles of 1774.[36] The first Articles of War drafted on American soil for American troops were those adopted by the Provisional Congress of Massachusetts Bay on April 5, 1775, for observance by Massachusetts troops.[37] They consisted of fifty-three articles and spoke of ". . . the duty we owe . . . to the king." These were followed by

[35] Dynes v. Hoover, 20 How. (61 U. S.) 65, 83 (1857).

[36] DAVIS, A TREATISE OF THE MILITARY LAW OF THE UNITED STATES, 3d ed., 340-1 and 581-601, appendix B, at which the British Articles of 1774 are reprinted. Also WINTHROP, MILITARY LAW AND PRECEDENT, 2d ed., 19 (1920).

[37] Reprinted in 2 WINTHROP, MILITARY LAW, appendix 61-67 (1886). Its preamble reads in part:

"Whereas the lust of power which of old oppressed, persecuted and exiled our pious and virtuous ancestors from their fair possessions in Britain, now pursues with ten-fold severity us, their guileless children, who are unjustly and wickedly charged with licentiousness, sedition, treason and rebellion; and being deeply impressed with a sense of the almost incredible fatigues and hardships our venerable progenitors encountered, who fled from oppression for the sake of civil and religious liberty for themselves and their offspring, and began a settlement here on bare creation at their own expense; and having seriously considered the duty we owe to God, to the memory of such invincible worthies, to the King, to Great Britain, our country, ourselves, and posterity, do think it our indispensable duty, by all lawful ways and means in our power, to recover, maintain, defend and preserve the free exercise of all those civil and religious rights and liberties, for which many of our forefathers fought, bled, and died, and to hand them down entire for the free enjoyment of the latest posterity. . . .

"And whereas the great law of self-preservation may suddenly require our raising and keeping an Army of observation and defense, in order to prevent or repel any further attempt to force the late cruel and oppressive Acts of the British Parliament, which are evidently designed to subject us and the whole Continent to the most ignominious slavery. And whereas, in case of raising and keeping such an Army, it will be necessary that the Officers and Soldiers in the same be fully acquainted with their duty and that the Articles, Rules and Regulations thereof be made as plain as possible; and having great confidence in the honour and public virtue of the inhabitants of this Colony that they will readily obey the officers chosen by themselves, and will cheerfully do their duty when known, without any such severe Articles and Rules (except in capital cases) and cruel punishments as are usually practiced in Standing Armies, and will submit to all such Rules and Regulations as are founded in Reason, honor and virtue. It is, therefore,

"*Resolved,* That the following Articles, Rules and Regulations for the Army, that may be raised for the defense and security of our lives, liberties, and estates be, and are hereby earnestly recommended to be, strictly adhered to, by all Officers, Soldiers, and others concerned, as they regard their own honour and the publick good."

Articles enacted June 30, 1775, by the second Continental Congress[38] consisting of sixty-nine articles. The preamble recited that "His Majesty's most faithful subjects . . . are reduced to a dangerous . . . situation by . . . the British minister . . . and oppressive acts of the British Parliament. . . ." Sixteen additional articles were enacted November 7, 1775.[39]

On September 20, 1776, American Articles of War consisting of eighteen sections each containing from two to seventeen articles were enacted by the Continental Congress. This revision was made at the suggestion of General Washington.[40] The work of revision was performed by a congressional committee composed of John Adams, Thomas Jefferson, John Rutledge, James Wilson, and R. R. Livingston.[41] This document was the first to speak of ". . . the respective Armies of the United States" and omitted all reference to the Crown.[42]

In a period of eighteen months patriots of the Revolution had transformed the British military legal system into an American institution

[38] George Washington was a member of the legislative committee. WINTHROP, MILITARY LAW AND PRECEDENT, 2d ed., 21 (1920). These articles are reprinted in 2 WINTROP, MILITARY LAW, appendix 68-76 (1886). The preamble reads:

"*Whereas* His Majesty's most faithful subjects in these colonies are reduced to a dangerous and critical situation by the attempts of the British minister to carry into execution by force of arms several unconstitutional and oppressive acts of the British parliament for laying taxes in America, to enforce the collection of those taxes, and for altering and changing the constitution and internal police of some of these colonies in violation of the natural and civil rights of the colonies;

"*And whereas* hostilities have been actually commenced in Massachusetts Bay by the British troops under the command of General Gage, and the lives of a number of the inhabitants of that colony destroyed; the town of Boston not only having been long occupied as a garrisoned town in an enemy's country, but the inhabitants thereof treated with a severity and cruelty not to be justified even towards declared enemies;

"*And whereas* large reinforcements have been ordered, and are soon expected, for the declared purpose of compelling these colonies to submit to the operation of the said acts; which hath rendered it necessary, and an indispensable duty, for the express purpose of securing and defending these colonies, and preserving them in safety against all attempts to carry the said acts into execution, that an armed force be raised sufficient to defeat such hostile designs, and preserve and defend the lives, liberties and immunities of the colonists; for the due regulating and well ordering of which;

"*Resolved,* That the following Rules and Articles be attended to and observed by such forces as are or may hereafter be raised for the purposes aforesaid."

[39] Reprinted in WINTHROP, MILITARY LAW, appendix 76-78 (1886). DAVIS, A TREATISE ON THE MILITARY LAWS OF THE UNITED STATES, 3d ed., 342 (1915).

[40] DAVIS, A TREATISE ON THE MILITARY LAWS OF THE UNITED STATES, 3d ed., 342 (1915).

[41] WINTHROP, MILITARY LAW AND PRECEDENT, 2d ed., 22 (1920).

[42] Art. 1, §XIV of these Articles in WINTHROP, MILITARY LAW AND PRECEDENT, 2d ed., 79-92 (1920), provides:

"A general court-martial in the United States shall not consist of less than thirteen commissioned officers, and the president of such court-martial shall not be the commander-in-chief or commandant of the garrison where the offender shall be tried, nor be under the degree of a field officer."

considered to be appropriate for the government of an Army of freemen fighting for freedom. American courts-martial had already become recognized agencies of American justice. John Marshall, then a twenty-two year old captain-lieutenant of infantry, was, at Valley Forge in the bitter fall of 1777, appointed "Deputy Judge Advocate in the Army of the United States," in addition to his other duties.[43] Thus John Marshall was a party to the shaping of American military law more than ten years before there was a Supreme Court of the United States and more than twenty years before he became Chief Justice of the United States.

Other pre-constitutional developments in the Articles of War are worthy of note. By Congressional resolution of May 27, 1777, the general or commander-in-chief was given power to pardon or mitigate punishments authorized by the Articles of War.[44] The most important of other amendments made was that accomplished by congressional resolution on May 31, 1786, reducing the required membership of courts-martial.[45] It was the Articles of 1776 plus these amendments which continued in force at and after the adoption of the Constitution.[46] It should be observed that from the very beginning American Articles of War have been wholly statutory products of congressional exercise of legislative power[47] and that the jurisdiction of American courts-martial has always been exclusively criminal.[48]

In approaching the constitutional treatment of military law and tribunals it should be remembered that military men were active in the Constitutional Convention and as constitutional advocates. General Washington was unanimously elected to serve as president of the Constitutional Convention.[49] It was largely due to the vast influence of Washington[50] and the active oratorical espousal of Federalist leader John Marshall[51] that the Virginia convention in June 1788 gave its

[43] 1 BEVERIDGE, THE LIFE OF JOHN MARSHALL 119, 138 (1916).

[44] DAVIS, A TREATISE ON THE MILITARY LAWS OF THE UNITED STATES, 3d ed., 342 (1915).

[45] WINTHROP, MILITARY LAW AND PRECEDENT, 2d ed., 23 (1920) says:

"The occasion of this Amendment, as expressed in the preamble of the Resolution of Congress, was the fact that the pre-existing Articles failed to make adequate provision for the trial of offenders 'serving with small detachments,' those articles requiring that a general court-martial should consist of thirteen members, and a regimental or garrison court of five members; in the new section the number of the inferior court was fixed at three, and the minimum of the general court at five—limitations which have subsisted to the present time." The same minimum court membership is currently required by Article 6 of the Uniform Code of Military Justice, 50 U. S. C. § 576 (1951).

[46] WINTHROP, MILITARY LAW AND PRECEDENT, 2d ed., 22 (1920).

[47] *Id.* at 21.

[48] *Id.* at 107.

[49] VAN DOREN, THE GREAT REHEARSAL 24 (1948).

[50] *Id.* at 218.

[51] *Id.* at 224.

sorely-needed ratification to the Constitution.[52] How then did this infant instrument of government deal with the ancient yet virile institution of military law and its tribunals?

The Constitution vested in Congress power "To define and punish . . . Offenses against the Law of Nations";[53] "To declare War . . . and make Rules concerning Captures on Land and Water";[54] "To raise and support Armies . . .";[55] "To provide and maintain a Navy";[56] "To make Rules for the Government and Regulation of the land and naval Forces";[57] "To provide for calling forth the Militia to execute the Laws of the Union, suppress Insurrections and repel Invasions";[58] and "To provide for organizing, arming, and disciplining, the Militia, and for governing such Part of them as may be employed in the Service of the United States. . . ."[59] As to the President, the Constitution provided that he ". . . shall be Commander in Chief of the Army and Navy of the United States, and of the Militia of the several States, when called into the actual service of the United States";[60] ". . . and shall Commission all the Officers of the United States."[61]

The Third Amendment provided: "No soldier shall, in time of peace be quartered in any house, without the consent of the Owner, nor in time of war, but in a manner to be prescribed by law."[62] Pursuant to the Fifth Amendment, "No person shall be held to answer for a capital, or otherwise infamous crime unless on a presentment or indictment of a Grand Jury, except in cases arising in the land or naval forces, or in the Militia, when in actual service in time of War or public danger."

In *Houston v. Moore,* Justice Washington, in 1820, writing for an unanimous Supreme Court, declared:

> "But military offenses are not included in the act of Congress conferring jurisdiction upon the circuit and district courts; no person has ever contended that such offenses are cognizable before the common law courts. The militia laws have, therefore, provided, that the offence of disobedience to the president's call upon the militia, shall be cognizable by a court-martial of the United States; but an exclusive cognizance is not conferred upon that court, as it had been upon the common law courts, as to other offences by the judiciary act. It follows, then, as I con-

[52] *Id.* at 230.
[53] Art. I, § 8, cl. 10.
[54] Art. I, § 8, cl. 11.
[55] Art. I, § 8, cl. 12.
[56] Art. I, § 8, cl. 13.
[57] Art. I, § 8, cl. 14.
[58] Art. I, § 8, cl. 15.
[59] Art. I, § 8, cl. 16.
[60] Art. II, § 2, cl. 1.
[61] Art. II, § 3.
[62] See WURFEL, QUARTERING OF TROOPS: THE UNLITIGATED THIRD AMENDMENT, 21 TENN. L. REV. 723 (1951).

ceive, that jurisdiction over this offense remains to be concurrently exercised by the national and state courts-martial, since it is authorized by the laws of the state and not prohibited by those of the United States."[63]

In 1857, in *Dynes v. Hoover,* the Court, after citing the pertinent constitutional provisions, held:

"These provisions show that Congress has the power to provide for the trial and punishment of military and naval offences in the manner then and now practiced by civilized nations; and that the power to do so is given without any connection between it and the 3d article of the Constitution defining the judicial power of the United States; indeed, that the two powers are entirely independent of each other."[64]

It is significant that since the Bill of Rights no constitutional amendment has dealt with a military subject. Apparently, the American people have continued satisfied with the views expressed in this field by the founding fathers.

Under its power "to make Rules for the Government and Regulation of the land and naval Forces" Congress has perpetuated and from time to time changed the Articles of War. The first United States Congress by Act of September 29, 1789,[65] recognized the existing military establishment and provided that the troops thus recognized should "be governed by the rules and articles of war which have been established by the United States in Congress assembled, or by such rules and articles of war, as may hereafter by law be established."

The Articles of War of 1806[66] consisting of 101 articles superseded all other enactments on the subject and reverted to consecutive numbering without division into sections. These Articles, except for minor amendments, remained in force until 1874,[67] thus withstanding the tests of the War of 1812, the Mexican War, the Civil War and part of the Indian Wars. During the War of 1812 four articles were amended, during the Seminole wars three were amended and one added and in the Civil War seventeen articles were amended and eight added.[68]

The Confederate States supplemented these Articles of 1806 by a Congressional Act of October 9, 1862,[69] establishing, for each Corps,

[63] 5 Wheat. (18 U. S.) 1, 27 (1820).
[64] 20 How. (61 U. S.) 65, 79 (1857).
[65] 1 Stat. L. 95-96 (1789).
[66] 2 Stat. L. 359 (1806). Reprinted in 2 WINTHROP, MILITARY LAW, appendix 98-111 (1886).
[67] WINTHROP, MILITARY LAW AND PRECEDENT, 2d ed., 23 (1920) and DAVIS, A TREATISE ON THE MILITARY LAW OF THE UNITED STATES, 3d ed., 343 (1915).
[68] MUNSON, MILITARY LAW 7 (1923).
[69] Reprinted in 2 WINTHROP, MILITARY LAW, appendix 318-320 (1886).

a separate court of three civilian judges appointed by the president of the Confederacy with jurisdiction over all offenses cognizable by courts-martial. These tribunals were entirely separate from the civil courts.[70]

The Articles of War of 1874[71] consisted of 128 Articles[72] and were essentially a restatement of the Articles of 1806.[73] The Articles of War of 1916[74] which became effective March 1, 1917, were the first complete revision of military law in one hundred and ten years and eliminated much obsolete material. These, in turn, were amended but not completely revised by the Articles of 1920.[75] The 1920 Articles consisting of 121 articles embraced certain changes considered desirable as a result of World War I experience and are of importance since, with minor amendments in 1937[76] and 1942,[77] they were the Articles which governed the Army throughout World War II. Accordingly these Articles of 1920 have been subjected to the scrutiny of the federal civil courts in the habeas corpus litigation of recent years. It was the Army system of justice prevailing under these Articles of 1920 of which the War Department Advisory Committee on Military Justice[78] spoke when it said: ". . . that the innocent are almost never convicted and the guilty seldom acquitted."[79]

Based upon World War II experience and the recommendations of the Advisory Committee, the Articles of 1920 were, without change in total number, substantially amended in 1948,[80] effective February 1, 1949. A new provision of these 1948 articles which has been construed by the federal courts is Article of War 53, which will be discussed in Chapter 15.

[70] For an interesting account of courts-martial and military courts in the Confederacy see ROBINSON, JUSTICE IN GREY 362-382 (1941).

[71] U. S. Rev. Stat. passed at the first session of the 43d Congress, 1873-74, 2d ed., Tit. XIV, § 1342, p. 230-242 (1878).

[72] Reprinted in 2 WINTHROP, MILITARY LAW, appendix, 112-125 (1886).

[73] MUNSON, MILITARY LAW 7 (1923).

[74] 39 Stat. L. 619 at 650-670 (1916).

[75] 41 Stat. L. 787 (1920), 10 U.S.C. (1946) §§ 1471-1593a.

[76] 50 Stat. L. 724 (1937), 10 U.S.C. (1946) §§ 1522, 1542, amending arts. 50½ and 70.

[77] 56 Stat. L. 732 (1942), 10 U.S.C. (1946) §1522, amending art. 50½; 56 Stat. L. 1050 (1942), 10 U.S.C. (1946) § 1586 (1942), amending art. 114; and 56 Stat. L. 1051 (1942), 10 U.S.C. (1946) § 1524, amending art. 52.

[78] The members of this Committee popularly known as the "Vanderbilt Committee" were, at the request of the Secretary of War, nominated by the American Bar Association in 1946 to hold hearings and to formulate recommendations for the improvement of the system of military justice. The chairman was Chief Justice Arthur T. Vanderbilt of New Jersey and its distinguished membership included Judge Morris A. Soper of the United States Court of Appeals for the Fourth Circuit, Justice Alexander Holtsoff of Washington, D. C., and Judge Frederick E. Crane of New York.

[79] REPORT OF ADVISORY COMMITTEE ON MILITARY JUSTICE, p. 3.

[80] 62 Stat. L. 604 at 627-644 (1948), 10 U.S.C. (1950 Supp.) c. 36. Commonly known as the Elston Act.

Public Law 506 (81st Congress, 2d session), approved May 5, 1950, established a "Uniform Code of Military Justice" for the Army, Air Force, Navy, Marine Corps and Coast Guard. Its 140 articles made substantial revisions in both trial and appellate review procedure, especially so far as the Navy, Marine Corps and Coast Guard are concerned. This act, which became effective May 31, 1951, was drafted by a Department of Defense committee ably chairmanned by Professor Edmund M. Morgan, Jr.[81]

Finally, it is important to distinguish courts-martial from the administrative agency tribunals which have sprung up since Congress created the Interstate Commerce Commission. Almost without exception the decisions of these late-comers in the field of adjudication are subject to direct appellate review by the federal courts, either under their individual basic acts or pursuant to section 10 of the Administrative Procedure Act.[82] Not so courts-martial, which, under both the Articles of War and the Uniform Code,[83] had and have their own appellate procedure wholly apart from the Federal Courts. This "complete system of review within the military system" has been expressly recognized by the Supreme Court.[84] In the Administrative Procedure Act, Congress went to great pains in section 2(a) to provide, ". . . there shall be excluded from the operation of this Act . . . (2) courts martial and military commissions. . . ."[85] This serves to underscore the basic legal proposition that the federal courts have no appellate jurisdiction over courts-martial and that the court-martial system is a separate jurisdiction wholly apart from the civil federal judiciary.[86]

[81] See MORGAN, THE BACKGROUND OF THE UNIFORM CODE OF MILITARY JUSTICE, 6 VAND. L. REV. 169 (1953).

[82] 60 Stat. L. 237 (1946), 5 U.S.C. (1950 Supp.) c. 19.

[83] Articles 64-76 inclusive, 50 U.S.C. §§ 651-663 (1951). This was also true under Articles of War 47, 48, 49, 50, 51; 10 U.S.C. (1950 Supp.) §§ 1518, 1519, 1520, 1523.

[84] Burns v. Wilson, 346 U.S. 137, 73 S. Ct. 1045 (1953), rehearing den. 346 U.S. 844, 74 S. Ct. 3 (1953).

[85] Immunity of courts-martial proceedings from the provisions of the Administrative Procedure Act is judicially recognized in Goldstein v. Johnson 184 F. (2d) 342 (D. C. Cir. 1950).

[86] That federal civil courts have no jurisdiction to exercise appellate review in courts-martial cases has been affirmed in Shaw and Begalke v. United States 209 F. 2d 811 (D. C. Cir. 1954).

CHAPTER 2

Jurisdiction of Courts-Martial

I. General

The modest pretension of this discussion is to collect the more important pronouncements of the United States Court of Military Appeals[1] during its first three years of operation[2] and of the Boards of Review[3] on the fundamental subject of jurisdiction. No attempt is made to review the centuries-long development of foreign and American military court jurisdiction[4] beyond the basic statement that Congress in enacting the Uniform Code of Military Justice[5] merely exercised once more its express constitutional power "to make Rules for the Government and Regulation of the land and naval forces."[6] The considerable body of

[1] The court of last resort in the system of military law as prescribed by Art. 67 of the Uniform Code of Military Justice, 64 Stat. 129 (1950), 50 U. S. C. § 654 (Supp. 1952).

[2] Although the Uniform Code became effective on May 31, 1951 pursuant to Pub. L. No. 506, 81st Cong., § 5, c. 169 (May 5, 1950), the first decision by the Court of Military Appeals was not rendered until November 8, 1951 in United States v. McCrary, 1 USCMA 1, 1 CMR 1 (1951). Accordingly, the actual period of productivity to May 31, 1954 is slightly less than thirty-one months. Decisions through May 31, 1954 are considered herein.

The Court has held it is without jurisdiction to review cases received in the office of a Judge Advocate General for appellate review prior to May 31, 1951. United States v. Musick, 3 USCMA 440, 12 CMR 196 (1953). For a general survey and analysis of the decisions of the Court of Military Appeals up to July 25, 1952, see Aycock, *The Court of Military Appeals—The First Year*, 31 N. C. L. Rev. 1 (1952). Mr. Aycock extends this analysis to the decisions rendered by the Court of Military Appeals during its second year in an article appearing in 2 Journal of Public Law 254 (1953).

[3] Army, Navy, Coast Guard and Air Force Boards of Review are the intermediate appellate tribunals in the military justice system. They are provided for by Art. 66 of the Uniform Code, 50 U. S. C. § 653 (Supp. 1952).

[4] For a brief treatment of the history of the jurisdiction of military tribunals, see Chapter 1.

[5] Act of May 5, 1950, 64 Stat. 108 (1950), 50 U. S. C. §§ 551-736 (Supp. 1952).

[6] U. S. Const. Art. I, § 8, cl. 14. An Air Force Board of Review has had occasion to hold that the words "land and naval forces" in the Constitution refer not only to the Army and Navy but equally to the Air Force. This was done in United States v. Naar (ACM 4215), 2 CMR 739, 745 (1951) in rejecting the contention of an Air Force lieutenant that since he was not in the land or naval forces he was

textual[7] and periodic[8] material treating military jurisdiction in the era before the Uniform Code will not be surveyed. Pre-Code Board of Review opinions[9] dealing with jurisdiction are not extensively discussed. No effort is made to consider all the facets presented in the Code's cluster of some fifteen essentially jurisdictional Articles.[10] The appellate jurisdiction vested in the Boards of Review by Article 66,[11] and in the Court of Military Appeals by Article 67,[12] is not explored. The versatile jurisdiction of military commissions to try law of war violations,[13] war crimes,[14] offenses under military government[15] and to sit as martial law courts[16] is beyond the ambit of this chapter. Also excluded, most reluctantly, are the inviting international law problems concerning the exercise of conflicting jurisdiction over members of visiting armed forces stationed in or passing through friendly foreign countries.[17]

---

entitled under the Fifth Amendment to grand jury indictment before being brought to trial. The same accused endeavored to raise the same issue by seeking an injunction to restrain the air force court-martial in a proceeding before a three judge federal court. On May 22, 1951 the District Court for the District of Columbia dismissed this complaint on the ground that it failed to state a cause of action. (Civil Action No. 2061-51).

[7] The outstanding text is WINTHROP, MILITARY LAW AND PRECEDENTS (2d ed. 1920). See c. VIII, pp. 81-109 on jurisdiction. Also significant is DAVIS, A TREATISE ON THE MILITARY LAW OF THE UNITED STATES (3d ed. 1915).

[8] Representative of the best law review articles of that period are Underhill, *Jurisdiction of Military Tribunals in the United States Over Civilians,* 12 CALIF. L. REV. 75, 159 (1924) and Morgan, *Court-Martial Jurisdiction Over Non-Military Persons Under the Articles of War,* 4 MINN. L. REV. 79 (1920).

[9] In the thirty years before the Code, Army Board of Review opinions alone ran into thousands of pages contained in some 141 volumes.

[10] Arts. 2, 3, 5, 17, 18, 19, 20, 21, 22, 23, 24, 25, 26, 27 and 56, which, respectively, are 50 U. S. C. §§ 552, 553, 555, 577, 578, 579, 580, 581, 586, 587, 588, 589, 590, 591, and 637 (Supp. 1952).

[11] 50 U. S. C. § 653 (Supp. 1952). For example, United States v. Bigger, 2 USCMA 297, 7 CMR 97 (1953) holding Boards of Review have jurisdiction to commute a death sentence when reducing the finding to unpremeditated murder. The case of United States v. Washington (CM 362541, 11 CMR 388 (1953) where a death sentence was similarly reduced without reduction of the finding has been certified to the Court, 11 CMR 397 (1953), and is now pending decision. See also United States v. Reeves, 1 USCMA 388, 3 CMR 122 (1953) and United States v. Weeden, 3 USCMA 405, 12 CMR 161 (1953) holding a Board of Review has power to entertain a motion for reconsideration of a decision rendered by it.

[12] 50 U. S. C. § 654 (Supp. 1952).

[13] Examined in the able opinion by Chief Justice Stone in *Ex parte* Quirin, 317 U. S. 1 (1942).

[14] *In re* Yamashita, 327 U. S. 1 (1946).

[15] Madsen v. Kinsella, 343 U. S. 341 (1952).

[16] *Ex parte* Milligan, 4 Wall. 2 (U. S. 1866) ; Duncan v. Kahanamoku, 327 U. S. 304 (1945). Fairman, *The Law of Martial Rule and the National Emergency,* 55 HARV. L. REV. 1253 (1942).

[17] This problem was first grappled with by Chief Justice John Marshall in Schooner Exchange v. M'Fadden, 7 Cranch 116 (U. S. 1812) in which he concluded that members of the visiting force remained exclusively subject to the criminal and civil jurisdiction of the sovereign by whom employed. It is case and treaty law of this type which Congress had in mind in prefacing both paragraphs (11) and (12) of Article 2, dealing with jurisdiction "without the continental limits of the

At this juncture the reader may well cry out, "With what area of jurisdiction are we here to cope?" The answer is, with the decisions of jurisdictional matters by the Court of Military Appeals and the Boards of Review[18] under the Uniform Code and the salient United States Supreme Court decisions in the field of military habeas corpus. That is to say, the current case law from which the military bar[19] must seek its enlightenment and direction in matters of courts-martial jurisdiction.

It must be remembered that jurisdiction is the only aspect of a court-martial proceeding which may be inquired into by the regular federal courts,[20] this only by habeas corpus collateral attack and not by appeal,[21] and then only after the petitioner has first exhausted all appellate and new trial remedies within the military law system.[22] The Supreme Court has thus defined the test of jurisdiction to be applied to military courts:

> " 'The single inquiry, the test is jurisdiction' . . . In this case the court-martial had jurisdiction of the person of accused and the offense charged, and acted within its lawful powers. The correction of any errors it may have committed is for the military authorities which are alone authorized to review its decisions."[23]

Boards of Review and the Court of Military Appeals monitor courts-martial jurisdiction in the exercise of their normal appellate functions. In doing so they concern themselves with four questions: (1) Was the court duly constituted? (2) Did it have jurisdiction of the person tried? (3) Did it have jurisdiction of the offense charged? (4) Was the sentence imposed within the prescribed maximum limit? It will be convenient to discuss the cases by classifying them under these headings.

United States" with the language, "Subject to the provisions of any treaty or agreement to which the United States is or may be a party or to any accepted rule of international law. . . ." See United States v. Weiman, 3 USCMA 216, 11 CMR 216 (1953).

[18] Board of Review opinions of the four services under the Uniform Code have burgeoned in the first fifteen volumes of Court-Martial Reports into a total of more than 10,500 pages and extend to hundreds of additional pages not yet published since 15 CMR includes decisions only through May 1954.

[19] In addition to the officer lawyers of the four armed services who have become members of the bar of the Court of Military Appeals, as early as November 1, 1952, 244 civilian attorneys had been admitted. Walker and Neibank, *The Court of Military Appeals—Its History, Organization and Operation,* 6 VAND. L. REV. 228, 236 (1953). By June of 1953 this bar had grown to 1219 members, a third of whom are civilian attorneys. Address, Judge Brosman, Army Judge Advocate General's School, Charlottesville, Va., June 15, 1953.

[20] *In re* Grimley, 137 U. S. 147, 150 (1890). See Chapter 15, *post.*

[21] *Ex parte* Reed, 100 U. S. 13, 23 (1879).

[22] Gusik v. Schilder, 340 U. S. 128 (1950); Burns v. Wilson, 346 U. S. 137 (1953); McKinney v. Finletter, 205 F. 2d 761 (10th Cir. 1953).

[23] Hiatt v. Brown, 339 U. S. 103, 111, *rehearing denied,* 339 U. S. 939 (1950), cited with approval by Justice Minton in his separate concurring opinion in Burns v. Wilson, 346 U. S. 137 (1953), *rehearing denied,* 74 S. Ct. 3 (1953).

II. Was the Court Duly Constituted?

In civil life the court is taken much for granted. Rarely is the appointment or election of a judge contested and by a liberal construction of de facto judicial powers it is even more rare to have purported judicial acts declared void because the court was not duly constituted. The judge is sworn in once for each term of office and enjoys a stabilized status.

Courts-martial, unlike ordinary civil courts, do not possess any high degree of permanence. They come into existence by express written direction of the convening authority[24] who is normally a commanding officer, and who so far as general courts-martial are concerned is usually of general officer rank. In the Army and Air Force this is done by a special order and in the Navy by an official letter addressed to the officer who is to be president of the court. In either case the document specifically names and identifies by their service numbers the officers who are to serve as members, trial counsel, defense counsel, assistant counsel, and, for general courts, the law officer. For a summary court a single summary court officer is appointed. Although a minimum of five members is sufficient to constitute a general court and three to constitute a special court,[25] it is customary to name nine or more members in an order appointing a general court and five or more for a special court since members may be excused from attendance by the covening authority to perform other military duties, and are subject to peremptory challenge and challenge for cause.[26] This principle of flexibility was carried to extreme in a general court case in which the order appointed fifty-one members, only seven of whom attended the trial.[27] The Army Board of Review, after condemning the administrative wisdom of appointing so large a court, rejected a defense contention that this was a jurisdictional defect pointing out that the minimum jurisdictional requirement was the presence of five members. The Court of Military Appeals has said that where the membership of a general court is reduced to less than five: "This would constitute a palpable jurisdictional defect."[28]

The exigencies of combat,[29] administrative transfer of units, and

[24] Arts. 22, 23, and 24, respectively, specify who may convene a general, special and summary court-martial. 50 U. S. C. §§ 586, 587 and 588 (Supp. 1952).

[25] Art. 16, 50 U. S. C. § 576 (Supp. 1952).

[26] Art. 41, 50 U. S. C. § 616 (Supp. 1952).

[27] Holt (CM 357002), 8 CMR 360 (1953). See, however, United States v. Moses (CM 363294) 11 CMR 281 (1953) where it was affirmatively shown that the trial counsel failed to notify eleven members of a thirty-one officer court and this was held to be prejudicial error.

[28] United States v. Padilla and Jacobs, 1 USCMA 603, 606, 5 CMR 31, 34 (1952). See also United States v. Tobita, 3 USCMA 267, 12 CMR 23 (1953).

[29] The discontinuance of a trial in its midst necessitated by enemy action in Europe during the Battle of the Bulge and the later trial of the case by another

orders transferring individual officers and enlisted men to new stations all combine to make it unusual, even in peacetime, for any one court-martial to be able to try cases for a period of as long as three months. Members can be relieved and others added by amending orders, but to curtail the number of orders pertaining to any one case it is administratively desirable to appoint an entirely new court at frequent intervals. Large "jurisdictions," that is commands with authority to convene courts, often have several different general and special courts operating at the same time. Normally a given case is referred by written indorsement for trial to a specified court identified by the number and date of the special order appointing it. Unarraigned cases may be re-referred to another court, this usually being done in the order appointing the new court.

The foregoing practical considerations involved in convening a court-martial, while routine to the military lawyer, are perhaps not so well known to the bar at large. Possibly this fluid medium in which courts-martial must operate is what repeatedly motivates Congress to require members of general and special courts-martial, as well as counsel, the law officer and the reporter, in each case, to take an oath "in the presence of the accused to perform their duties faithfully."[30] The Court of Military Appeals has said:

> "General courts-martial, being tribunals of special and limited jurisdiction, must be convened strictly in accordance with statutory requirements. . . . Members of a court-martial must have been lawfully appointed thereto in order that they may enjoy status as members."[31]

This factual and legal background lends great importance in courts-martial cases to the inquiry, "Was the court duly constituted?"

A. *Who Are Proper Court Members?*

Students of jurisdiction are primarily indebted to the Navy for the volume of current decisions dealing with the validity of courts-martial organization. Since the Articles for the Government of the Navy remained almost completely unchanged from 1862 until replaced by the Uniform Code in 1951[32] it is not surprising that the vessel of naval

general court convened by another command was held not to constitute double jeopardy in Wade v. Hunter, 336 U. S. 684, *rehearing denied,* 337 U. S. 921 (1949).

[30] Art. 42(a), 50 U. S. C. § 617 (Supp. 1952). This elaborate swearing of the various components of the court in each case is a time-consuming ingredient in the administration of military justice.

[31] United States v. Padilla and Jacobs, 1 USCMA 601, 603, 5 CMR 31, 34 (1952).

[32] Walker and Niebank, *The Court of Military Appeals—Its History, Organization and Operation,* 6 VAND. L. REV. 228, 230 (1953). It was in the Navy case of

justice has pitched a bit in the heavy seas of transition. Definitely a transition case was that of Seaman Apprentice Merritt[33] who was charged with the offense of absence after leave committed before the effective date of the Uniform Code. On June 6, 1951, he was arraigned, pleaded guilty and was sentenced before a navy summary court convened under the old Articles for the Government of the Navy, but not constituted as required for a special court-martial, its successor equivalent, under the Uniform Code. The Court of Military Appeals held that the navy summary court lacked jurisdiction.[34]

In the case of Ship's Serviceman Stephenson the special court which tried the accused simply was not sworn. The Navy Board of Review properly held:

> "The entire membership of the new court and the personnel of the prosecution and the defense not having been duly sworn, the newly appointed court was without jurisdiction to try this case, and such lack of jurisdiction was absolutely fatal to its proceedings. (Dynes v. Hoover, 61 US 65, 83, 15 L Ed 278. . . .)"[35]

The other services have also contributed cases illustrative of jurisdictional error in court membership. Corporal Heineman requested and received the services of Lieutenant Gillespie as his individual counsel at his Article 32[35a] pretrial investigation. Thereafter Lieutenant Gillespie was appointed and actually sat as a member of the court and was not challenged by the accused. An Army Board of Review held Gillespie

---

United States v. Pulliam, 3 USCMA 95, 96, 11 CMR 95, 96 (1953) that the question certified was: "Did the special court-martial lose jurisdiction . . . because a junior member acted as president?" The court held: ". . . the special court-martial did not, as a matter of law, lose jurisdiction . . . because a junior member acted as president. . . . there was no substantial prejudice to the rights of the accused."

[33] United States v. Merritt, 1 USCMA 56, 1 CMR 56 (1951).

[34] At page 63 of United States v. Merritt, *supra* note 33, the Court said:

"The next question posed is whether or not the error was jurisdictional, and we answer this in the affirmative. . . . The phases properly processed by the court ended with the serving of the charges on the accused, as the trial phase was clearly severable from the pre-trial proceedings. . . . The only act which could have retained jurisdiction of the court to hear the trial phase would have been an arraignment. . . . A court qualified to act under the new code should have been constituted by the convening authority."

[35] United States v. Stephenson (NCM 58), 2 CMR 571, 572 (1951). The members of the special court assembled to hear the case were sworn and the accused exercised a peremptory challenge which reduced the membership to two. The convening authority instead of adding new members to the old court by amendment elected to appoint a wholly new court composed of the same personnel as the old court, including counsel, except for a member appointed to replace the one who had been challenged. Only this replacement member was sworn when the newly appointed court proceeded to try the case. See also United States v. Anderson (CM 334145), 1 BR/JC 123 (1949).

[35a] 50 U. S. C. § 603(a) (Supp. 1952).

was clearly incompetent to sit as a member of the court, that the proceedings were therefore null and void, and that failure of the accused to challenge the member could not operate as a waiver of the jurisdictional defect.[36] Similarly, it has been held that tainted court membership is jurisdictional and cannot be waived where a member testified as a prosecution witness,[37] or was the officer who signed the original of a morning report placed in evidence,[38] or attested a record of previous convictions used in a case where the accused pleaded guilty.[39] However a member of the Judge Advocate General's Corps may properly serve as an ordinary member of a court-martial if he has not otherwise participated in the case.[39a]

Airman Trent was convicted by a court, a member of which had previously been appointed as assistant defense counsel of another court to which Trent's case was originally referred for trial. Trent did not challenge and the record did not disclose whether this member ever in fact served as his counsel. The Air Force Board of Review applied a *Manual* provision that under these circumstances a court member must "Unless the contrary appears of record, . . . be deemed to have acted as a member of . . . the defense,"[40] and reversed.[41] The Board did not call this situation jurisdictional error but elected instead to find in it a probability of specific material prejudice to the substantial rights of the accused. It said:

> "It is difficult to envision any case where the membership . . . during the trial includes an officer who was the accuser or a witness for the prosecution or has acted as investigating officer or as counsel in the same case in which a 'probability of specific prejudice against the accused' . . . will not be found."[42]

The Board here placed reliance on the decision of the Court of Military Appeals in the *Bound* case.[43] There a security watch officer on the

[36] United States v. Heineman (CM 350672), 2 CMR 517 (1952). The court relied on Article 25(d)(1) of the Code which provides: "No person shall be eligible to sit as a member of a general or special court-martial when he is the accuser or a witness for the prosecution or has acted as investigating officer or as counsel in the same case."

[37] United States v. Grant (CM 259563), 38 BR 369 (1944).

[38] United States v. Beeks (ACM S-5398), 9 CMR 743 (1953).

[39] United States v. Morris (ACM S-5374), 9 CMR 786 (1953); United States v. Moore, 4 USCMA 675, 16 CMR 249 (1954).

[39a] United States v. Glaze, 3 USCMA 168, 11 CMR 168 (1953). There is no requirement that the membership of a court-martial include personnel of the same race as the accused, nor was it improper that the court was composed of senior officers or "southerners." United States v. Bryson (CM 360557), 10 CMR 164 (1953).

[40] MANUAL FOR COURTS-MARTIAL, UNITED STATES, 1951, ¶ 6a, p. 10.

[41] United States v. Trent (ACM 5165), 5 CMR 574 (1952).

[42] *Id.* at 576.

[43] United States v. Bound, 1 USCMA 224, 2 CMR 130 (1952).

night of the offense made an investigation and later sat as a member of the special court that tried the accused. An Article 32[43a] pretrial investigation was never made, this not being a prerequisite to a special court-martial trial. The Court pointed out that the Code does not define the term "investigating officer" as used in Article 25(d)(2), but that Paragraph 64, *Manual for Courts-Martial, United States, 1951,* defines it as "a person who . . . as an investigating officer or otherwise, has conducted a personal investigation of a general matter involving the particular offense," and then found "a probability of specific prejudice" against the accused.[44] The Court did not treat the situation as jurisdictional but did hold that the prejudice was not waived by failure to challenge even though the accused had pleaded guilty.

These two different approaches to improper court membership may be reconciled by saying that where the court composition clearly violates a Code provision, as in the *Heineman, Grant, Beeks,* and *Morris* cases the defect is jurisdictional, but where the *Manual* elaboration must be resorted to to work out a defect in composition, as in *Trent* and *Bound,* then decision will rest on the "probability of specific prejudice." Actually, reconciliation is perhaps not so simple. Probably the situation reflects a lack of crystallization of thought as to precisely what is jurisdictional, as distinguished from what constitutes "a probability of specific prejudice" or "general prejudice."[45]

B. *Inter-Service Eligibility*

A service self-imposed[46] problem of court member eligibility is whether a member of one of the services other than that of the accused may sit. A unification-conscious Congress provided:

> ". . . Any officer on active duty with the armed forces shall be eligible to serve on all courts-martial for the trial of any person who may lawfully be brought before such courts for trial."[47]

The several armed forces, pursuing their monadic ways, prevailed in the

[43a] 50 U. S. C. § 603(a) (Supp. 1952).

[44] United States v. Bound, 1 USCMA 224, 230, 2 CMR 130, 136 (1952).

[45] United States v. Woods and Duffer, 2 USCMA 203, 8 CMR 3 (1953) illustrates the deep division of the court as to whether there is any such thing as "general prejudice." Chief Judge Quinn, writing the majority opinion, disposed of the case in less than a page. Judge Brosman in a separate concurring opinion, and Judge Latimer in a dissenting opinion, each eleven pages long, then proceeded warmly, not to say heatedly, to discuss the merits and demerits, respectively, of the doctrine of "general prejudice."

[46] See *Hearings Before a Subcommittee of the Committee on Armed Services on H. R. 2498,* 81st Cong., 1st Sess. 735, 754 and 1189 (1949); H. R. Rep. No. 491, 81st Cong., 1st Sess. 17 (1949) to accompany H. R. 4085; and Sen. Rep. No. 486, 81st Cong., 1st Sess. 14 (1949) to accompany H. R. 4080.

[47] Art. 25(a), 50 U. S. C. § 589 (Supp. 1952).

Manual[48] in prescribing a policy drastically curtailing this eligibility. Illustrative is the case of Army Private Caternolo who was tried by a special court-martial whose president was an Air Force Lieutenant assigned for duty with the 1st Infantry Division. The Board of Review reversed on another point, but said:

> "While it is clear that the appointment of an Air Force officer as a member of an Army court-martial is permitted by Article 25a, *supra,* and is therefore not fatal to the court's jurisdiction, it is equally clear that such action is contrary to the general policy set forth in paragraph 4g(1), *supra.* Unless the convening authority commands a joint command or exercises reciprocal jurisdiction (MCM, 1951, par 4g(2)), members of the Air Force should not be appointed to an Army court-martial."[49]

The Board was undoubtedly correct in its conclusion that disregard of the *Manual* restriction, superimposed on the clear Congressional grant, was only procedural error and not a jurisdictional defect.

C. *Enlisted Members*

Article 25(c)[50] permits the accused personally to request in writing that enlisted personnel serve on the court, in which case they shall compromise not less than one-third of the total membership and may not be members of the same unit as the accused. This particular aspect of court membership has not yet engaged the attention of the Court of Military Appeals. It has been ruled administratively that an accused, if fully advised, may in writing insert into the formal proceedings at the time of trial a withdrawal of a prior written request for enlisted members. Short of thus eliminating enlisted members entirely an accused may not waive the prescribed ratio of at least one-third of the membership being enlisted where his original request stands.[51] An Army Board of Review has held that a soldier who is only "attached," as distinguished from being regularly assigned, to the accused's unit may properly sit.[52] An Air Force Board has held that a court was not legally constituted where one of its members was an airman assigned to the same squadron as the accused and that this disqualification could not be waived.[53]

[48] MANUAL FOR COURTS-MARTIAL, UNITED STATES, 1951, ¶ 4g(1), states in part: "g.—Members of courts-martial should be members of the same armed force as the accused."

[49] United States v. Caternolo (Sp CM 4057), 2 CMR 385, 386 (1952). See discussion, p. 50.

[50] 50 U. S. C. § 589 (Supp. 1952).

[51] Ltr. JAG-J 1952 6970 (11 September 1952), cited in JAG CHRON. No. 40, p. 179 (3 October 1952).

[52] United States v. Quimbo (CM 335865), 2 BR/JC 297 (1949).

[53] United States v. Chilcoat (ACM S-1285), 4 CMR (AF) 486 (1951). This case involved Article of War 16 of the Act of June 24, 1948 [62 STAT. 630 (1948)]

D. *Appointment of Court*

A technical question which arises is whether a member is duly designated in the writing appointing the court. The Navy practice of convening courts by official letter addressed to the officer who is to serve as president has at least four times reached the Court of Military Appeals for decision.[54] These letters, in addition to the name of the addressee, contained a direction that the court be convened and an assignment of four designated officers, other than the addressee, to serve as members and designations of trial and defense counsel, but no reference to the president except as addressee in the official form. The Court of Military Appeals in upholding jurisdiction of courts so appointed said:

> ". . . courts-martial are tribunals of special and limited jurisdiction, and must, therefore, be convened strictly in accordance with statutory requirements. At the same time this admonition should not be carried to the absurd length that matters of sheer form take precedence over those of substance.
>
> "It should not be—and is not—an unyielding condition precedent to the lawful convention of a court-martial that the appropriate form be followed parrot-like in minute detail."[55]

Where court members are added by amendment there is always the possibility of administrative error.[56] The Court of Military Appeals has

which contained a requirement substantially the same as Art. 25(c), 50 U. S. C. § 589 (Supp. 1952).

[54] United States v. Beard, 2 USCMA 344, 8 CMR 144 (1953); United States v. Lawrence, 2 USCMA 348, 8 CMR 148 (1953); United States v. Swaim, 2 USCMA 347, 8 CMR 147 (1953), all decided March 24, 1953. United States v. Lee, 3 USCMA 109, 11 CMR 109 (1953). These cases involve the construction of § 0102 e, Navy Supplement to MANUAL FOR COURTS-MARTIAL, UNITED STATES, 1951.

[55] United States v. Beard, 2 USCMA 344, 346, 8 CMR 144, 146 (1953).

[56] Typical is United States v. Padilla, 1 USCMA 603, 5 CMR 31 (1952). The original court to which the case was referred for trial was appointed by Special Orders No. 116, Headquarters 1st Infantry Division. Thereafter, Special Order No. 124 appointed a new court and provided that all unarraigned cases in the hands of the trial counsel of the court appointed by Special Orders No. 116 "be brought to trial before the court hereby appointed." Thereafter two new members were appointed by Special Order No. 128 "to the General Court-Martial convened by Special Order Number 116 . . . as amended by . . . Special Orders Number 124. . . ." The two members so named actually sat. The convening authority reversed and remanded, holding the court was without jurisdiction because these two officers were not in fact named as members of the court appointed by Special Orders No. 124, and ordered another hearing as to both the accused Padilla who had been convicted and his co-accused Jacobs who was found not guilty. On appeal from the second hearing the Court of Military Appeals held the first court was properly constituted and had jurisdiction, that jeopardy attached to the acquitted accused Jacobs, and that as to Padilla the sentence imposed at the second hearing could not exceed the first.

held that technical error in this regard is not jurisdictional.[57]

A basic defect in the organization of a court, which destroys its jurisdiction, occurs if a person not in fact detailed thereto participates in its deliberations.[58]

E. *Law Officer Eligibility*

Not only must the status of court members be scrutinized with care but other components of the tribunal as well. The law officer must be a member of the bar and also certified to be qualified for law officer duty by The Judge Advocate General of the service of which he is a member.[59] It has been held, however, that mere clerical error in describing the law officer in the order appointing the court is not jurisdictional if he is in fact a lawyer and certified.[60] Failure of the record to show affirmatively that the law officer was sworn necessitates disapproval of a conviction.[61]

Where the same officer, as Acting Staff Judge Advocate, first wrote a "detailed and painstaking" pretrial advice[62] and then later served as

[57] In United States v. Padilla, 1 USCMA 603, 607, 5 CMR 31, 35, the court said:

> ". . . This language, however, inartificial, indicates with clarity that the user regarded the second court as a replacement for the first. . . . the language is strongly persuasive of the existence of an intention to appoint the two captains to the court-martial created by Special Orders No. 124."

[58] DIG. OP. JAG § 1351 (1912-30). Similarly, participation by an officer as assistant trial counsel who was not on orders as a member of the prosecution, and was not sworn, has been held by an Army Board of Review to constitute jurisdictional error. United States v. Taylor (CM 338217), 4 BR/JC 235 (1949).

[59] Art. 26(a), 50 U. S. C. § 590 (Supp. 1952).

[60] United States v. Hathaway (ACM 4183), 1 CMR 776, 778 (1951). It has been held that technical error in an order appointing a new trial counsel and adding, at the request of the accused, enlisted members to a general court already in existence by mistakenly referring to the original court as a special court is not jurisdictional. United States v. Barber (ACM 5097), 5 CMR 726 (1952).

[61] United States v. Pino (ACM 5274), 6 CMR 542 (1952). Here the record of trial stated: "the members of the court and the personnel of the prosecution and the defense were sworn," but not that the law officer was sworn. An Air Force Board found "the expression 'members of the court' does not include the law officer," and although it expressly held that failure to swear the law officer did not deprive the court-martial of jurisdiction ruled it was a "substantial error of procedure" requiring disapproval and rehearing. Since the Board did not examine the record for specific prejudice to the accused presumably it relied on either general prejudice or lack of "military due process." This Board appears to reflect the rather wary attitude the Court of Military Appeals has adopted toward at least some problems of jurisdiction. It is submitted on principle that failure to swear the law officer as required by Article 42 of the Code [50 U. S. C. § 617 (Supp. 1952)] constitutes fatal jurisdictional error. If here the law officer was in fact sworn, a certificate of correction could properly have been appended to the record and jurisdiction thus established. *Cf.* Givens v. Zerbst, 255 U. S. 11 (1921) and McRae v. Henkes, 273 Fed. 108 (8th Cir. 1921).

A statement in the record that "The court was then sworn" is not sufficient to show that the law officer, members, trial counsel and defense counsel were sworn. If they in fact were, a certificate of correction will be required. JAGU (CM 361274), March 23, 1953, cited in 2 JAG CHRON., No. 17, p. 74 (24 April 1953).

[62] Art. 34(a), 50 U. S. C. § 605 (Supp. 1952) in part requires: "Before directing

law officer at the trial of the case, an Army Board of Review ordered a rehearing finding this to be error materially prejudicial to the substantial rights of the accused.[63] Acting in this dual capacity is not prohibited by Article 26(a),[64] which specifies who may be law officers, and probably is not jurisdictional. However, the decision that it constitutes prejudicial error appears to be proper.

F. *Counsel Eligibility*

The Code provides that trial and defense counsel of general courts must be bar members and certified as qualified to serve as counsel by The Judge Advocate General of the service of which they are members.[65] Not only may counsel not change sides in a given case, but "no person who has acted as investigating officer, law officer, or court member in any case shall act subsequently as trial counsel, assistant trial counsel, or, unless expressly requested by the accused, as defense counsel or assistant defense counsel in the same case."[66] The Court of Military Appeals has held that an accuser, who made a preliminary investigation in that capacity, was not an investigating officer within the meaning of either Article 32 or Article 27(a) and that he was not disqualified from thereafter serving as trial counsel in the case.[67]

---

the trial of any charge by general court-martial, the convening authority shall refer it to his staff judge advocate or legal officer for consideration and advice."

[63] United States v. Thorpe (CM 360188), 9 CMR 351 (1953). *Accord,* United States v. Hentz (CM 347839), 1 CMR 422 (1951); *cf.* United States v. Nelson (CM 347000), 1 CMR 169 (1951) and United States v. Montez (CM 346677), 1 CMR 178 (1951); *contra,* United States v. St. Ours (CM 355349), 6 CMR 178 (1952). The problem has been treated as one of prejudicial error rather than jurisdiction.

[64] Art. 26(a), 50 U. S. C. § 590 (Supp. 1952) in pertinent part provides: "No person shall be eligible to act as law officer in a case when he is the accuser or a witness for the prosecution or has acted as investigating officer or as counsel in the same case." Thus it has been declared prejudicial error for the trial counsel of a general court to which a case of one of two joint offenders was referred to serve later as law officer at the trial of the other joint offender. This is so even though the law officer was relieved within four days in the first case and there was no showing that he participated therein as trial counsel. In accord are United States v. Tolbert (ACM 6751), 11 CMR 680 (1953) where the law officer had been appointed defense counsel but did not participate in the previous trial of an accomplice, and United States v. Gemelli (ACM 6695), 11 CMR 690 (1953) where the law officer had formerly been trial counsel of the same court-martial which tried accused but was relieved as trial counsel and appointed law officer one day after accused's case was referred.

[65] Article 27(b), 50 U. S. C. § 591 (Supp. 1952). Individual defense counsel, whether military or civilian, does not have to be certified as qualified, nor need he be appointed or otherwise designated in the order appointing the court. A ruling by a law officer that such appointment was necessary which caused an accused to withdraw his request for an officer, who was present, to be his individual defense counsel was held by an Air Force Board to render the proceeding void. United States v. Hanson (ACM 6062), 8 CMR 671 (1953).

[66] 27(a), 50 U. S. C. § 591 (Supp. 1952). See United States v. Kelsey (ACM 5228), 6 CMR 522 (1952) and United States v. Borner, 3 USCMA 313, 12 CMR 69 (1953).

[67] United States v. Lee, 1 USCMA 212, 2 CMR 118 (1952).

The Court has stated that it is only a custom of the service, and not an express requirement of the Code, that military counsel be officers. "[T]here is implicit in the Code the requirement of the Manual that appointed counsel of inferior courts-martial be an officer."[68] The Court held it was not jurisdictional error, nor prejudicial to the accused, to have appointed a non-lawyer noncommissioned pay clerk as trial counsel of a special court-martial and observed, "it is not every provision of the Code that reaches the level of a jurisdictional requirement."[69] Though this opinion appears to create a problem in order to solve it, the rule seems to emerge that the appointment of military personnel other than an officer as trial counsel of a special court is not in itself a jurisdictional defect. The special court before which Navy Airman Hutchison[70] pleaded guilty had officers appointed to it as trial and assistant trial counsel and defense counsel, and a noncommissioned warrant gunner as assistant defense counsel. None were lawyers. The Court of Military Appeals upheld jurisdiction, opining:

> "Congress has not . . . conferred upon an accused an explicit and absolute right to have any assistant defense counsel appointed, nor to have such counsel, if appointed, be an officer. . . .
>
> "There is here no violation of a mandatory requirement of the Code, and therefore no jurisdictional defect . . . nor . . . any reasonable possibility of prejudice under these circumstances."[71]

A general court case tried in May 1951 under the 1948 Articles of War which raised the question of whether there must be equality of experience between trial and defense counsel is of continued interest because of its current applicability to special court cases.[72] The trial counsel who tried Private Bartholomew[73] was a college and law school graduate with extensive legal experience in the Army, but not a lawyer nor a member of the Judge Advocate General's Corps. The defense

[68] United States v. Goodson, 1 USCMA 298, 3 CMR 32 (1952).
[69] *Id.* at 300, 3 CMR at 34.
[70] United States v. Hutchinson, 1 USCMA 291, 3 CMR 25 (1952).
[71] *Id.* at 292, 293, 3 CMR at 26, 27. Compare with United States v. Ness (Sp CM 1770), 6 BR/JC 345 (1950) where an Army Board of Review held it was jurisdictional error to appoint a warrant officer as defense counsel of a special court-martial and permit him to serve.
[72] Art. 27(c), 50 U. S. C. § 591 (Supp. 1952), provides:

"Sec. 591. Appointment of trial counsel and defense counsel (Article 27)
* * *
"(c) In the case of a special court-martial—

(1) If the trial counsel is qualified to act as counsel before a general court-martial, the defense counsel appointed by the convening authority shall be a person similarly qualified; and

(2) If the trial counsel is a judge advocate, or a law specialist or a member of the bar of a Federal court or the highest court of a State, the defense counsel appointed by the convening authority shall be one of the foregoing. . . ."

[73] United States v. Bartholomew 1 USCMA 307, 3 CMR 41 (1952).

counsel was a high school graduate with no professional education and relatively little Army legal experience. On appeal it was not contended that this disparity was jurisdictional but that it was prejudicial to the accused. Though charged with murder the accused was found guilty of voluntary manslaughter only. The Court affirmed the conviction saying:

> ". . . the disparity in legal qualifications of counsel disclosed in the case now before us is inconsistent with the spirit although not the letter, of the Articles of War. . . .
>
> ". . . we find here at least a literal and technical compliance with the command of Congress. . . .
>
> ". . . we find nothing whatever which would indicate that the accused was not accorded full, fair and competent representation by his counsel. This being the case, we cannot at all say that he was materially prejudiced in any substantial right. . . .
>
> ". . . the problem is in no sense an academic one . . . because of the possibility of its recurrence under the Uniform Code . . . in cases tried by special court-martial."[74]

This *Bartholomew* decision should not be pushed very far for even though disparity of training of counsel is not jurisdictional, it is most probable the Court in most cases would find wide disparity constituted material prejudice to the substantial rights of the accused requiring reversal.

An Air Force Board of Review has held a special court-martial improperly constituted and its proceedings void where at the time of its appointment both trial and defense counsel were lawyers but neither was certified and before trial the trial counsel only was certified by The Judge Advocate General of the Air Force as qualified to act as counsel.[75]

[74] *Id.* at 310, 311, 312, 3 CMR at 44, 45, 46.

[75] United States v. Klug (ACM S-5219), 8 CMR 664 (1953). Where the duly appointed defense counsel of a general court was relieved from that assignment and his duties, with the consent of the accused, were taken over by the assistant defense counsel who was also qualified and certified, but no amendatory order was issued redesignating him as defense counsel, Boards of Review have disagreed as to the effect. An Army Board held the absence of a duly appointed defense counsel at the time of trial constituted error in violation of Article 27 but that this error was neither jurisdictional nor prejudicial and affirmed the conviction. United States v. McCarthy (CM 357972), 8 CMR 329 (1953). Under similar circumstances an Air Force Board held that a court-martial which technically had no appointed defense counsel, as distinguished from assistant defense counsel, at the time of trial was without jurisdiction and declared its findings and sentence void even though the accused was also represented by counsel of his own choice. United States v. Butler (ACM 6164), 8 CMR 692 (1953). This same result was reached by an earlier Army Board of Review in United States v. Watson (CM 337855), 4 BR/JC 157 (1949). These latter opinions appear to exalt form unduly and to disregard substance. The Court of Military Appeals has not yet passed on this question.

Failure to swear an assistant defense counsel who participated in the trial has been held to constitute jurisdictional error. An Air Force Board of Review in reversing the conviction of Airman Nyman said:

> "... the record shows that Captain Mayo, an assistant defense counsel, entered the court room and seated himself at the defense table after the members of the court, personnel of the prosecution, and the other assistant defense counsel, Captain Wuhrman, had been sworn (R. 3-4). The record does not show that Captain Mayo was ever sworn, nor does it appear that he withdrew prior to the conclusion of the case. Captain Wuhrman signed the record as having examined it on behalf of the accused. The order appointing the court listed Captain Mayo as first and Captain Wuhrman as second assistant defense counsel.
>
> "...
>
> "... we feel that by whatever name it be known, the error of participation by unsworn defense counsel in a trial conducted after 31 May 1951 is one that is fundamentally prejudicial to the substantial rights of the accused. Otherwise stated, whether the error be termed a violation of military due process, a matter of general prejudice, or failure to meet a jurisdictional requirement, as those terms have been used by the Court of Military Appeals, we conclude, under the universality of holdings on the participation of unsworn counsel, that such participation constitutes error which is fatal to the legal efficacy of the findings and sentence arrived at in these proceedings.

It has been held to be jurisdictional error for an officer not appointed as an assistant trial counsel to sit at trial counsel table and assist the trial counsel. United States v. Taylor (CM 338217), 4 BR/JC 235 (1949). To permit the investigating officer to serve as assistant trial counsel is a jurisdictional defect which the accused cannot waive. United States v. Mullen (Sp CM 2576), 7 BR/JC 359 (1950).

An investigating officer may not serve as either defense counsel nor assistant defense counsel if the accused merely states that he has no objection, and such participation constitutes reversable error. United States v. Nelson (CM 335048), 2 BR/JC 7 (1949) and United States v. Henry (CM 319176), 68 BR 181 (1947). However, where from the record it affirmatively appeared that the accused expressly desired the investigating officer to serve as defense counsel and the accuser to serve as individual defense counsel, permitting them so to serve was held to be proper. United States v. Fleming (CM 320233), 69 BR 271 (1947). It is a question of fact which should be fully developed in each case since Article 27(a) in pertinent part provides: "No person who has acted as investigating officer, . . . in any case shall act subsequently . . . unless expressly requested by the accused, as defense counsel or assistant defense counsel in the same case."

Special court trial counsel may not prepare the review thereof as staff judge advocate. Such dual action constitutes prejudicial error. United States v. Coulter (No. 2786), 14 CMR 75 (1954). Contra, United States v. Carter (ACM S-4723), 7 CMR 785 (1953). It is prejudicial error for the law officer to prepare the staff judge advocate review of a case in which he served as law officer. United States v. Crunk, 4 USCMA 290, 15 CMR 290 (1954).

". . .

". . . We are not prepared, particularly in view of the complete unanimity of opinion hereinbefore referred to, to hold that this accused has by his plea of guilty to Charge II and its specification eliminated the necessity for compliance with this or any of the other provisions of Article 42. Past interpretations as to the administration of oaths appear to us to have been predicated upon the fact that these requirements were jurisdictional in nature and we see nothing in Article 42 as enacted which suggests a change in the fundamental nature of the requirements."[76]

Here the Board, though beset with legitimate doubts as to just which of at least three different approaches the Court of Military Appeals might take in reversing the case, at last manfully closed with the problem and held it to be "jurisdictional in nature." The Board is to be congratulated for so doing. Failure to swear individual civilian defense counsel has been held not jurisdictional and not to constitute prejudicial error.[76a]

G. *Reference of Case to Court*

Another court composition problem is whether a given case is properly before the court which in fact tries it. As already indicated, when a convening authority has determined a case should be tried the charges are forwarded by indorsement to the trial counsel of a specific existing court identified by the number and date of the special order appointing it and the case is usually tried by that court. It not infrequently is necessary to transfer unarraigned cases from the court to which they were originally referred to another court. This is usually done either by general language in the order appointing the new court to the effect that all unarraigned cases pending before the old court, specifying it by order number and date, are referred to the new court, or by transfer of individual cases from one court to another by an additional numbered indorsement to the charges so directing. The Code itself does not prescribe any procedure for referral but the *Manual* sets forth procedure for customary usage.[77] In the case of Commissary Seaman Emerson[78] which had been referred to one special court, but was actually tried without re-reference by another special court convened by the same convening authority, the Navy Board of Review held the latter was without jurisdiction. The Court of Military Appeals reversed the Board of Review, holding:

[76] United States v. Nyman (ACM S-3051), 5 CMR 598, 599, 601 (1952).
[76a] United States v. Danilson (ACM 6499), 11 CMR 692 (1953).
[77] See ¶ 33(j), MANUAL FOR COURTS-MARTIAL, UNITED STATES, 1951.
[78] United States v. Emerson, 1 USCMA 43, 1 CMR 43 (1951).

> "A failure to follow the procedure set out in the Manual for customary usage does not . . . constitute a defect of sufficient import to deprive the court of jurisdiction."[79]

In doing so it followed the earlier Army Board of Review rule on the point.[80] The same result has been reached under the Code by Army Boards of Review in two cases, each referred by the Commanding General of the 25th Division to a general court other than the one which tried it, but which latter court he had also appointed. The decisions were based on the ground that the action of the convening authority "approving the sentence amounts to a ratification of the actual reference of the case to the legally constituted court which tried it."[81] This doctrine is safely applicable only where the trial is by a court convened by the same commanding officer who referred the case for trial, or by his official successor in that command.

H. *Personnel from Other Commands*

Officers from other commands may properly be made available to a convening authority for the purpose of sitting as members of a court-martial. This was done in the trial of then Air Force Colonel Jack Durant in the Hesse crown jewels theft case in order to convene a court each member of which was senior to the accused. On habeas corpus attack the federal courts held this court was properly constituted and was proof against jurisdictional attack.[82]

I. *Convening Authority Competency*

Still pursuing the question "Was the court duly constituted?", we turn now from the competency of the court or its component elements to that of the convening authority which ordered the court into existence. Even where the officer appointing the court is one authorized to do so by Article 22 or 23 of the Code[83] there may be circumstances which so

[79] *Id.* at 45, 1 CMA 45.

[80] United States v. Casey (CM 198108), 3 BR 159, 163 (1932); United States v. Brandon (CM 232790), 19 BR 193, 207, 208 (1943); *Cf.* United States v. Anderson (CM 334145), 1 BR/JC 123 (1949). Also in accord see Hartley v. Malanophy, 81 F. Supp. 316 (E. D. N. Y. 1948).

[81] United States v. Clements (CM 346741), 1 CMR 164, 167 (1951), and United States v. Hofus (CM 348185), 4 CMR 356, 362 (1952).

[82] Durant v. Hiatt, 81 F. Supp. 948 (N. D. Ga. 1948), *aff'd,* 177 F. 2d 373 (5th Cir. 1949).

[83] Arts. 22(a) and 23(a), 50 U.S.C. §§ 586, 587 (Supp. 1952) specify in considerable detail who may convene general and special courts-martial respectively. United States v. Bunting, 4 USCMA 84, 88, 90, 15 CMR 84, 88, 90 (1954) held a general court convened in the absence of Admiral Joy, by Admiral Ofstie, Chief of Staff, was properly constituted, even though Admiral Ofstie was not the senior admiral remaining in the command. The Court said: "we conclude that Admiral Joy was absent from his command within the meaning of Article 1371 during the time that he was in Korea in the performance of his duties as Senior

contaminate him as to render jurisdictionally void, as to a specific accused, any court convened by him. The Code provides that when the normal convening authority "is an accuser, the court shall be convened by superior competent authority,"[84] and defines an accuser as: "a person who signs and swears to charges, . . . who directs that charges nominally be signed and sworn to by another, . . . (or) who has an interest other than an official interest in the prosecution of the accused."[85] Private Moseley[86] broke into the home of the Commanding General of Camp Campbell, Kentucky, larcenously took therefrom valuable property of the general's son, pawned it, and then went absent without leave. The General summoned Criminal Investigation Detachment agents, showed them incriminating evidence found in his garage, and thereafter convened the court which tried and convicted the accused. The charges were actually signed by a junior officer. The Army Board held the proceedings void and said:

> ". . . the conclusion is inescapable that Major General Lemnitzer could not but have had an interest other than an official interest in the prosecution. He was 'in fact' the accuser and thereby precluded by UCMJ, Article 22, from appointing a court-martial which could exercise jurisdiction over this accused."[87]

Confronted with a similar problem the Court of Military Appeals, without reference to the previously decided *Moseley* case, reached the same result by traveling a somewhat different road. Airman Gordon[88] at Bolling Field burglarized the house of Lieutenant General Edwards and four days later attempted to burglarize the quarters of Brigadier General Lee, the base commander. General and Mrs. Lee were interviewed as part of the investigation. Who actually swore to the charges does not appear. Ultimately the charge involving General Lee's quarters was dismissed and the accused tried for the offense at General Edwards' quarters by a court convened, after the event, by General Lee as base commander. Conviction and sentence to a dishonorable discharge and five years confinement was reviewed by General Lee as convening authority and the period of confinement was by him reduced to two years. The offense occurred in March of 1951 so that the applicable

United Nations Delegate. . . . Hence, . . . during the absence of Admiral Joy, Admiral Ofstie (Chief of Staff) had the power to convene a general court-martial in his own right." This case turns on construction of Naval Regulations and should not be relied upon by the other services.

[84] Arts. 22(b) and 23(b), 50 U. S. C. §§ 586, 587 (Supp. 1952).

[85] Art. 1(11), 50 U. S. C. § 551 (Supp. 1952).

[86] United States v. Moseley (CM 348127), 2 CMR 263 (1951).

[87] *Id.* at 265, 266.

[88] United States v. Gordon, 1 USCMA 255, 2 CMR 161 (1952).

law was Article of War 8[89] which contained language similar to that in Articles 22(b) and 23(b) of the Code[90] prohibiting an accuser from convening the court. The Court of Military Appeals held that: "General . . . Lee was disqualified to act as convening and reviewing authority in this case,"[91] and said:

> ". . . reasonable persons would impute to General Lee at the time he appointed the court a personal feeling or interest in the matter. . . .
>
> "While General Lee reduced the sentence, who can say what, if any, additional remission might have been made by one who had no interest in the matter.
>
> ". . . we find substantial rights of the accused were materially prejudiced. . . ."[92]

Judge Brosman, in a separate concurring opinion, wrote:

> "I do not understand Judge Latimer to evaluate the error . . . as jurisdictional . . . I do understand him to have concluded that the substantial rights of the accused were materially prejudiced. . . . I prefer to bottom my concurrence on the concept of general prejudice. . . ."[93]

The writer pauses to express preference for the forthright treatment given to this problem by the Army Board of Review in the *Moseley* case where it flatly held the defect to be jurisdictional. In view of the Court's lively concern for congressional intent it is difficult to understand how, having found that "General . . . Lee was disqualified to act as convening and reviewing authority in this case," it was able to stop short of declaring this error to be jurisdictional. Brushing aside legal niceties, commanding officers should be alert to refrain from convening courts to try cases in which they, by possibility, may be "accusers" within the broad meaning of that term.[94] The point at which to draw the line

[89] 41 STAT. 788 (1920).
[90] 50 U. S. C. §§ 586, 587 (Supp. 1952).
[91] United States v. Gordon, 1 USCMA 255, 262, 2 CMR 161, 168 (1952).
[92] *Id.* at 255, 261, 262, 2 CMR at 167, 168.
[93] *Id.* at 255, 262, 2 CMR at 168.
[94] In United States v. Bergin (ACM 4374), 7 CMR 501 (1952), an Air Force Board of Review held the Commanding General of Lackland Air Force Base to be an accuser, and hence the court convened by him to be without jurisdiction. The accused, the custodian of a consolidated base welfare fund, embezzled therefrom. He had been appointed custodian by the General who himself was president of the counsel for the Central Post Fund. The accused was under bond payable to the General in event of defalcation, and such payment was in fact made to and receipted for by the General. The Board found the convening authority had "not only an official, but more—a direct and personal interest and responsibility in the funds and in the loss sustained as the result of the alleged theft of the accused." It said, "The test should be whether the appointing authority is so closely connected

presents a difficult question of fact.[95]

J. *Reference Procedure Where Convening Authority Is Disqualified*

What procedure is jurisdictionally acceptable where the normal convening authority is disqualified? Articles 22(b) and 23(b) of the Code provide: "When . . . (a) commanding officer is an accuser, the court shall be convened by superior competent authority. . . ." The *Manual* states: ". . . superior competent authority . . . will convene the court or designate another competent convening authority to exercise jurisdiction."[96] A determination as to which of these divergent directions prevails became necessary in the case of Hospitalmen LaGrange and Clay.[97] These accused were charged personally by their commander, a Navy

---

to the offense that a reasonable person would conclude that he had a personal interest in the matter." See United States v. Self, 3 USCMA 568, 13 CMR 124, 130 (1953).

In United States v. Marsh, 3 USCMA 48, 52, 11 CMR 48, 52 (1953), the court reversed as to both specifications because it found that as to one of them the convening authority was in fact the accuser. It said "Congress concluded the probability of harm to an accused was sufficient to deny to an accuser the right to convene a court and if he elects to join specifications for trial all must fall as the court is disqualified to try any." *Cf.* United States v. Keith (No. 3293), 13 CMR 135, 140 (1953).

[95] In United States v. Sippel (ACM 5615), 8 CMR 698 (1953) an Air Force Board ruled that a convening authority, who had first recommended, upon the advice of his staff judge advocate, the acceptance of a resignation for the good of the service tendered by the accused, which tender was refused by higher authority, did not thereby become an accuser, and properly convened the court which thereafter tried the accused. The Board found the action of the convening authority was merely "a part of the necessary supervision which he must exercise over his command in order to preserve discipline." It was also contended that the court was without jurisdiction because the Staff Judge Advocate as well as the convening authority was disqualified. As to this the Board said: "the actions and state of mind of the convening authority and Staff Judge Advocate appear reasonable, dispassionate, and divorced from any personal interest in the matter." *Accord,* United States v. Jewson, 1 USCMA 652, 5 CMR 80 (1952); United States v. Grow, 3 USCMA 77, 11 CMR 77 (1953). Apparently *contra* United States v. Marsh, 3 USCMA 48, 11 CMR 48 (1953). The Court has distinguished *Marsh, supra,* and held, "The commanding general had only an official interest," and was not the accuser in United States v. Keith, 3 USCMA 579, 13 CMR 135 (1953); United States v. Tell, 4 USCMA 39, 15 CMR 39 (1954), and United States v. Noonan, 4 USCMA 297, 15 CMR 297 (1954). Boards of Review have distinguished *Marsh, supra,* in United States v. Barnes (ACM S-6846), 12 CMR 735 (1953) and United States v. Orso (CM 365475), 12 CMR 435 (1953).

In a case where the staff judge advocate of a command accompanied investigating officers to Rome and from time to time gave them legal advice during the course of the investigation the Court has held that this did not disqualify him from subsequently reviewing the record of trial for the convening authority. United States v. DeAngelis, 3 USCMA 298, 12 CMR 54 (1953). The Court said: "Since a staff judge advocate is the administrator of military justice and discipline, it would be incongruous in the extreme were we to assume that he is unable to function at all unless and until charges have been preferred and investigated. . . . His services were as necessary to the accused, as to the government, and in no way disqualified him in performing his impartial task of reviewing the record of trial."

[96] MANUAL FOR COURTS-MARTIAL, UNITED STATES, 1951, ¶ 5b(2).

[97] United States v. La Grange and Clay, 1 USCMA 342, 3 CMR 76 (1952). Distinguished in United States v. Pease, 3 USCMA 291, 12 CMR 47 (1953).

Captain, with violating regulations by misusing barbiturates and the charges were forwarded to his superior, the Commander, Naval Forces, Far East, who in turn referred the case for trial by special court to a Navy Commander commanding a naval base at Pusan, Korea. A commander is, of course, inferior in grade to a captain in the Navy. The Court of Military Appeals relying on the provision of Article 36 of the Code which provides that, "procedure . . . prescribed by the President by regulations . . . shall not be contrary to or inconsistent with the Code," ruled that only a "superior" could be a "competent convening authority" as used in the *Manual* provision, adverted to Congressional intent to adopt a procedure that would lessen command control, and held:

> "The provisions with which we deal require a superior to convene the court; and these provisions having been violated, the tribunal designated was not authorized by law to try these accused and render a judgment against them."[98]

The Court avoids the word "jurisdiction" itself, but paints a word picture adding up to lack of jurisdiction. The Court made it clear that the officer to appoint the court in such cases must be superior in rank to the accuser but does not squarely hold that he must also be superior in the sense of commanding an organization of which the unit commanded by the accuser is a component part. For example, suppose the commander of the Pusan Base had been a rear admiral. Since the Base and the ship commanded by the accuser both reported directly to the Commander, Naval Forces, Far East, the Base would be a command collateral, and not superior, to the accuser's ship. To avoid pitfalls prudence would dictate that where this problem is present the convening authority should be superior in both rank and command to the accuser.

An Air Force Board of Review confronted with substantially the same problem relied on the *LaGrange* and *Clay* case but frankly declared the defect to be jurisdictional. It said:

> ". . . the convening authority in the instant case, being junior in rank to the accuser and not in the chain of command, should not properly have assumed jurisdiction over the charges herein. . . . The defect being jurisdictional in nature, the proceedings are a nullity and the findings and sentence must be set aside."[99]

[98] *Id.* at 346, 3 CMR at 80.
[99] United States v. Burnette (ACM S-3033), 5 CMR 522, 524 (1952).

K. *Pretrial Investigations*

The United States Supreme Court has twice determined that neither a substantial nor a complete failure to comply with the pretrial investigative procedure required under former Article of War 70[100] is fatal error and has held such failure does not divest a court-martial of jurisdiction.[101] This rule has been perpetuated by Congress in the new Code by adding to Article 32,[102] the successor to old Article of War 70 as to pretrial investigations, paragraph (d) which expressly states: "The requirements of this article shall be binding on all persons administering this code, but failure to follow them in any case shall not constitute jurisdictional error."

L. *Caveat*

At least some of the foregoing may initially strike the civilian practitioner as bordering on hair-splitting. Upon reflection, however, it should be manifest that an active pursuit in military cases of the inquiry, "Was the court duly constituted?" may lead astute appellate defense counsel to legal pay dirt whether characterized as jurisdictional, or, simply, prejudicial error. Though the cause may be tried again,[103] as a practical matter it is even more difficult in the military system, plagued with worldwide distribution and constant personnel changes, to reassemble witnesses, than is the case in the civilian administration of justice. The clear caveat to those who must administer the system of military justice is that not only must evil, but even the appearance of evil, be avoided in the composition and convening of courts. A high degree of aseptic administrative care must be given to precluding the possibility of actual or constructive contamination of members, other component elements of courts-martial, and convening authorities if jurisdictional error is to be avoided.

[100] 41 STAT. 802 (1920).

[101] Humphrey v. Smith, 336 U. S. 695, 700, *rehearing denied,* 337 U. S. 934 (1949); Hiatt v. Brown, 339 U. S. 103, 110, *rehearing denied,* 339 U. S. 937 (1950).

[102] 50 U. S. C. § 603 (Supp. 1952).

[103] United States v. Padilla, 1 USCMA 603, 606, 5 CMR 31, 34 (1952).

CHAPTER 3

Jurisdiction of the Person

The second jurisdictional inquiry, "does the court have jurisdiction of the person," is similar to the first query already considered in that it is much more likely to be remunerative to the criminally accused before a military court than to one before a civilian court. With rare exceptions any person who commits any criminal offense within the geographical boundaries of a county or other judicial district of a state, or of a federal court district, is subject to the jurisdiction of the court of that district regardless of nationality, nature of employment or other status. True, Section 2 of Article III of the Constitution vests exclusive original jurisdiction in the Supreme Court of all cases affecting ambassadors and, normally, infants under seven are conclusively presumed to be incapable of crime, but such exceptions simply emphasize the general rule in civil life that exemption from criminal jurisdiction cannot be predicated upon the status of the person accused.

Under the civilian rule usually the locus of the offense is all important, the status of the accused not at all. Under military law quite the reverse is true. The traditional unlimited geographical jurisdiction of courts-martial[104] has not only received recent judicial approval[105] but express congressional sanction in Article 5 of the Uniform Code[106] which declares, with amazing conciseness: "This code shall be applicable in all places." This summary disposition of locus contrasts sharply with the

[104] WINTHROP, MILITARY LAW AND PRECEDENTS 81 (2d ed. 1923). Chief Justice Chase in *Ex parte* Milligan, 4 Wall. 2 (U. S. 1867) said, "And wherever our Army or Navy may go beyond our territorial limits neither can go beyond the authority of the President or the legislation of Congress."

[105] Durant v. Hiatt, 81 F. Supp. 948 (N. D. Ga. 1948), *aff'd,* 177 F. 2d 373 (5th Cir. 1949). In this case the court-martial originally convened in Germany, recessed and reconvened in Washington, D. C., recessed and again reconvened in Germany. This was expressly held to be within the proper jurisdiction of the court. Also, United States v. Solinsky, 2 USCMA 153, 7 CMR 29 (1953) where the accused was tried in the United States for forgeries committed in Germany.

[106] 50 U. S. C. § 555 (Supp. 1952).

elaborate Code provisions as to what persons in what status at what times are subject to military law.[107]

[107] Art. 2, 50 U. S. C. § 552 (Supp. 1952) provides:

"The following persons are subject to this chapter:

(1) All persons belonging to a regular component of the armed forces, including those awaiting discharge after expiration of their terms of enlistment; all volunteers from the time of their muster or acceptance into the armed forces of the United States; all inductees from the time of their actual induction into the armed forces of the United States, and all other persons lawfully called or ordered into, or to duty in or for training in, the armed forces, from the dates they are required by the terms of the call or order to obey the same;

(2) Cadets, aviation cadets, and midshipmen;

(3) Reserve personnel while they are on inactive duty training authorized by written orders which are voluntarily accepted by them, which orders specify that they are subject to this code;

(4) Retired personnel of a regular component of the armed forces who are entitled to receive pay;

(5) Retired personnel of a reserve component who are receiving hospitalization from an armed force;

(6) Members of the Fleet Reserve and Fleet Marine Corps Reserve;

(7) All persons in custody of the armed forces serving a sentence imposed by a court-martial;

(8) Personnel of the Coast and Geodetic Survey, Public Health Service, and other organizations, when assigned to and serving with the armed forces of the United States;

(9) Prisoners of war in custody of the armed forces;

(10) In time of war, all persons serving with or accompanying an armed force in the field;

(11) Subject to the provisions of any treaty or agreement to which the United States is or may be a party or to any accepted rule of international law, all persons serving with, employed by, or accompanying the armed forces without the continental limits of the United States and without the following territories: That part of Alaska east of longitude one hundred and seventy-two degrees west, the Canal Zone, the main group of the Hawaiian Islands, Puerto Rico, and the Virgin Islands;

(12) Subject to the provisions of any treaty or agreement to which the United States is or may be a party or to any accepted rule of international law, all persons within an area leased by or otherwise reserved or acquired for the use of the United States which is under the control of the Secretary of a Department and which is without the continental limits of the United States and without the following territories: That part of Alaska east of longitude one hundred and seventy-two degrees west, the Canal Zone, the main group of the Hawaiian Islands, Puerto Rico, and the Virgin Islands."

Art. 3, 50 U. S. C. § 553 (Supp. 1952) states:

"Sec. 553. Jurisdiction to try certain personnel (article 3)

(a) Subject to the provisions of section 618 of this title, any person charged with having committed, while in a status in which he was subject to this chapter, an offense against this chapter, punishable by confinement of five years or more and for which the person cannot be tried in the courts of the United States or any State or Territory thereof or of the District of Columbia, shall not be relieved from amenability to trial by courts-martial by reason of the termination of said status.

(b) All persons discharged from the armed forces subsequently charged with having fraudulently obtained said discharge shall, subject to the provisions of section 618 of this title, be subject to trial by court-martial on said charge and shall after apprehension be subject to this chapter while in the custody of the armed forces for such trial. Upon conviction of said charge they shall be subject to trial by court-martial for all offenses under this chapter committed prior to the fraudulent discharge.

(c) Any person who has deserted from the armed forces shall not be re-

Dangerously oversimplified, those persons subject to military law are: all on active federal armed forces service regardless of component or assigned duty; cadets and midshipmen; reserves on voluntary inactive duty training under an order expressly so stating; retired regular personnel entitled to receive pay; retired reserve personnel receiving armed force hospitalization; Fleet Reserve and Fleet Marine Corps Reserve personnel; prisoners sentenced by courts-martial and in armed forces custody; prisoners of war in armed forces custody; Coast and Geodetic Survey, Public Health Service and other organization personnel when assigned to and serving with the armed forces; without the continental limits of the United States, Alaska, Puerto Rico, Canal Zone and the Hawaiian and Virgin Islands all persons serving with, employed by, or accompanying the armed forces, or within an area under the control of the Secretary of a Department; and, in time of war, all persons serving with or accompanying an armed force in the field. From this hasty glance it becomes apparent that status is all important and that in some cases time and place are essential ingredients of status.

A. *Military Personnel*

Clarity will probably be promoted by discussing first jurisdictional problems regarding military persons only as distinguished from those of civilians subject to military law. The latter will be considered separately. As to military persons it should be remembered that in general they continue to be subject to civil court jurisdiction for transgressions of ordinary criminal law.[108] After prior trial by a court-martial former jeopardy may be asserted only where later civil prosecution is by federal authority[109] and not where later civil prosecution is by a state[110] except where a state statute expressly so provides.[111] Our concern here is, simply, does the court-martial have jurisdiction of the person, and need not be complicated by determining whether such jurisdiction is exclusive or concurrent.

(1) *When Is Military Status Acquired?*

A military person cannot be tried by court-martial for a criminal offense committed by him before he acquired military status, even though the offense is one prohibited by military law.[112] This necessitates a

lieved from amenability to the jurisdiction of this chapter by virtue of a separation from any subsequent period of service."

[108] Caldwell v. Parker, 252 U. S. 376 (1920).

[109] Grafton v. United States, 206 U. S. 333 (1907).

[110] State v. Rankin, 44 Tenn. (4 Cold.) 145 (1867).

[111] State *ex rel.* Cobb v. Mills, 82 Okl. Cr. 155, 163 P. 2d 558 (1945).

[112] United States v. Logan (CM 248867), 31 BR 363 (1944). In this case the accused who first entered the service in 1942 was tried for a bigamous marriage

precise rule for determining the instant at which a person ceases to be a civilian and acquires a military status. The number of cases of recalcitrance by selectees under the Selective Training and Service Act of 1940,[113] or crudely put, draft-dodging, while insignificant percentagewise, has caused this question to become one of more than mere academic interest. Fortunately the Supreme Court supplied the answer in *Billings v. Truesdale*.[114] Billings, a teacher at the University of Texas, who claimed to be a conscientious objector, was ordered by both his draft board and appeal board to report for induction at Fort Leavenworth, Kansas. He did so and the next morning was found physically and mentally qualified whereupon he refused to take the oath of induction and refused to submit to fingerprinting. For this latter refusal he was tried and convicted by court-martial for wilful disobedience of a lawful order. The Supreme Court on habeas corpus attack granted certiorari and held the court-martial was without jurisdiction since Billings had not taken the oath of induction and so had not been "actually inducted" into the Army. It pointed out that Billings was subject to criminal prosecution in the federal district court for a violation of the Selective Training and Service Act in refusing to be inducted. This was wholly consistent with a Supreme Court statement of 1890, "that the taking of the oath of allegiance is the pivotal fact which changes the status from that of civilian to that of soldier."[115] The Court of Military Appeals has applied the oath test in finding that a court-martial was without jurisdiction to convict an accused of desertion.[116] In another desertion

---

celebrated in 1934. It was held the continued illicit cohabitation did not make the bigamy a continuing offense and that the court-martial was without jurisdiction.

[113] 54 STAT. 894 (1940).

[114] 321 U. S. 542 (1944).

[115] *In re* Grimley, 137 U. S. 147, 156 (1890). *In re* Grimley was cited as controlling, in favor of jurisdiction, by a Navy Board of Review in a case in which the accused admitted that he had taken the oath. United States v. Perry (NCM 36), 1 CMR 516, 517 (1951).

[116] United States v. Ornelas, 2 USCMA 96, 6 CMR 96 (1952). While not itself strictly a jurisdictional problem, the military lawyer can scarcely pass by the procedural dilemma presented by the Court of Military Appeals in *Ornelas* and its companion case, United States v. Rodriguez, 2 USCMA 101, 6 CMR 101 (1952) decided the same day. In the face of the well-established rule that the law officer shall rule on interlocutory questions, save on a motion for a finding of not guilty or an accused's sanity, and that such rulings shall be final and shall constitute the ruling of the court [Article 51(b), 50 USC § 626 (Supp. 1952)] the Court in *Ornelas, supra,* at page 101, 6 CMR at 101, held:

> "We conclude that where an accused raises a defense or objection which should properly be considered by the court in its determination of guilt or innocence, and which resolves itself into a question of fact, that issue must be presented to and decided by the court pursuant to appropriate instructions. But where the issue is purely interlocutory or raises solely a question of law, it is within the sole cognizance of the law officer. It follows that the law officer in this case erred in making his decision on the issue of jurisdiction final. The accused was entitled to have the issue submitted to the court itself and decided by them under appropriate instructions. We should add that it

case it extended the rule in affirming jurisdiction by holding that the taking of the oath of allegiance was not necessary where the accused, a Mexican citizen, without objection reported for induction and remained in a military status for ten days before deserting.[117] This decision finds support in the federal courts;[118] in Army opinions;[119] in an Air Force opinion;[120] and in a Navy Board of Review case which held a Canadian citizen, who, under selective service, had filed an application for voluntary induction and had served in the Navy for over a year before deserting, was subject to naval jurisdiction for that offense.[121]

As to officers, military jurisdiction commences from the time the oath of office is taken accepting the commission.[122]

---

matters not, in our opinion, whether the issue is submitted at the time the motion is made or at the conclusion of the case when the court is required to deliberate on the evidence."

In *Rodriguez, supra,* at page 104, 6 CMR at 104, the Court said:

"The present case is readily distinguishable from United States v. Ornelas, *supra.* In that case, Ornelas testified that he did not at any time participate in an induction ceremony, and that he did not serve with the Army for any moment of time. Instead it was his contention that he merely took the required physical examination and returned immediately to his home in Mexico. Here, Rodriguez makes no claim that he did not participate in the induction ceremony, but only that he did not take the oath of allegiance. He did not object to service—in fact, he voluntarily entered upon the Army duty assigned. He proceeded to Fort MacArthur for basic training and remained in a military status, apparently without objection, for some ten days. Under such circumstances, he is in no position to claim that he was not lawfully inducted."

While the ultimate result in each case appears to be correct, the distinction in procedure required by the court to be followed depending on whether a motion to the jurisdiction "resolves itself into a question of fact" seems to impose upon the law officer the obligation of a well-nigh super-human clairvoyance in outguessing the Court. Clarification as to what is desired by the Court in this situation is essential, and until it is forthcoming law officers and Boards of Review must proceed at their peril in disposing of pleas raising jurisdiction. The Court in United States v. McNeill, 2 USCMA 383, 388, 9 CMR 13, 18 (1953) enlarged its position in this matter saying: "In United States v. Ornelas, . . . we held that if there was a factual dispute concerning jurisdiction which would have an effect on the ultimate guilt or innocence of the accused, it should be presented to the court-martial for determination. In the instant case there was no such question. The issue here raised was predicated on testimony which was undisputed and, therefore, involved only a question of law. When that is the posture of the case, the decision rests solely with the law officer." It is probable that the last word on this problem has not yet been spoken. See United States v. Grow, 3 USCMA 77, 11 CMR 77 (1953) which held the law officer alone properly passed on the interlocutory factual question as to whether the convening authority was an "accuser."

[117] United States v. Rodriguez, 2 USCMA 101, 6 CMR 101 (1952).

[118] Mayborn v. Heflebower, 145 F. 2d 864 (5th Cir. 1944), *cert. denied,* 325 U. S. 854 (1945); U. S. v. Mellis, 59 F. Supp. 682 (M. D. N. C. 1945).

[119] DIG. OPS. JAG § 467, p. 384 (1912-40), and SPJGA 325.34 (July 18, 1942), 1 BULL. JAG 165, 166.

[120] United States v. Patton (ACM 4272), 2 CMR 658, 662 (1951).

[121] United States v. Barlow (NCM 113), 3 CMR 440, 445 (1952).

[122] WINTHROP, MILITARY LAW AND PRECEDENTS 89 (2d ed. 1920). Under Art. 20, 50 U. S. C. § 580 (Supp. 1952), summary courts-martial have no jurisdiction over officers, warrant officers, cadets or midshipmen, nor, over objection, over anyone who has not first been offered and refused to accept non-judicial punishment under Art. 15, 50 U. S. C. § 575 (Supp. 1952).

(2) *When Does Military Status Terminate?*

The time element again becomes a significant status factor when a military person separates from the service. Reserve personnel who are no longer performing duty but who are continuing to draw active duty pay while in a terminal leave status remain subject to military jurisdiction, and prior to the expiration of such terminal leave may be recalled to active duty for the sole purpose of standing trial.[123] This is logical since their service was not in fact terminated.

Courts-martial jurisdiction over all military and other persons subject to the Code generally ceases upon termination of such status and, as to offenses committed prior to such termination, is not renewed by re-entry into the mililitary service or return to another status subject to the code.[124] This well-established rule was given spectacular application by the Supreme Court in *Hirshberg* v. *Cooke*[125] where a Navy court-martial was held to be without jurisdiction to try the accused for mistreating fellow-American personnel while held by the Japanese as a prisoner of war. This result was reached because the accused's period of enlistment expired after his liberation and his offense did not come to light until after he had re-enlisted. An Army Board of Review followed the *Hirshberg* case in holding a court-martial without jurisdiction to try an accused who had previously been given an undesirable discharge from the Army based upon his conviction by a civil court for a criminal offense.[126] This applied to two charges of desertion, one before the discharge, the other alleged to have been committed after the discharge. The technical point in issue was whether the discharge had become effective.

A striking application of this rule occurred in the case of former Sergeant Lo Dolce[127] where a confessed killer was permitted to go free. The murder and robbery were committed in Northern Italy in 1944 when that area was occupied by Germany as a hostile belligerent and after Italy had entered into an armistice with the United States. The accused, then on active duty as an American army sergeant, killed his commanding officer, an American major, and threw the body into a mountain lake. The offenses were not discovered until long after Lo Dolce had returned

[123] Hironimus v. Durant, 168 F. 2d 288 (4th Cir. 1948), *cert. denied,* 335 U. S. 818 (1948); Durant v. Hiatt, 81 F. Supp. 948 (N. D. Ga. 1949), *aff'd,* 177 F. 2d 373 (5th Cir. 1949). A reserve officer, whose commission expired while his petition for review of a conviction and sentence to dismissal was pending, continued to be subject to the jurisdiction of the Court of Military Appeals. United States v. Sippel, 4 USCMA 50, 15 CMR 50 (1954).

[124] MANUAL FOR COURTS-MARTIAL, UNITED STATES, 1951, ¶ 11a, p. 14.

[125] 336 U. S. 210 (1949).

[126] United States v. Santiago (CM 346819), 1 CMR 365, 368 (1951). *Cf. Ex parte* Wilson, 33 F. 2d 214 (E. D. Va. 1929) holding that a former officer administratively dropped from the rolls of the Navy by the President was not thereafter subject to military jurisdiction.

[127] *In re* Lo Dolce, 106 F. Supp 455 (W. D. N. Y. 1952).

to the United States, been discharged and reverted to civilian status. No attempt was made to try Lo Dolce by court-martial. The effort made by Italy to extradite was rejected by the federal district court upon dual grounds. First, that since at the time of the crimes Italy had capitulated and American forces were present as friendly visiting forces the rule of *Schooner Exchange* v. *M'Faddon*[128] vested jurisdiction of the offense in the military authorities of the United States, and not Italy. Second, that, following the rule of *Coleman* v. *Tennessee*,[129] even if a state of belligerency still existed between Italy and the United States, jurisdiction over its own forces vested exclusively in the United States as a hostile occupant. Since the exercise of this jurisdiction by the United States was impossible due to Lo Dolce's fortutious change of status from soldier to civilian, and because murder committed in Italy normally is not punishable by any American civil court, federal or state, a complete immunity bath emersion resulted for this confessed homocidist.[129a] This fantastic situation has arisen more than once. Several similar, but unpublicized, homicides were committed in Italy during the last year of World War II by merchant seamen employed on vessels chartered by the military. Requests for extradition made after they had completed their voyages, returned to the United States and been discharged were administratively denied.

Congress, most fortunately, has taken appropriate action to remedy, in large measure at least, this glaring jurisdictional hiatus. Article 3(a)[130] of the Code now provides:

> "Subject to the provisions of article 43 [statute of limitations], any person charged with having committed, while in a status in which he was subject to this code, an offense against this code, punishable by confinement of five years or more and for which the person cannot be tried in the courts of the United States or any State or Territory thereof or of the District of Columbia, shall not be relieved from amenability to trial by courts-martial by reason of the termination of said status."

Since under Article 43(a)[131] the statute of limitations never runs on wartime desertion or absence without leave, aiding the enemy, mutiny or murder, offenders in these respects remain indefinitely subject to court-

[128] 7 Cranch 116 (U. S. 1812).
[129] 97 U. S. 509 (1878).
[129a] Lo Dolce and a co-accused, Icardi, were tried in absentia for this offense by the Italian Government. On November 6, 1953 they were found guilty of murder by a trial court at Novara, Italy. Lo Dolce was sentenced to seventeen years confinement; Icardi, to life imprisonment. N. Y. Times, Nov. 8, 1953, p. 2 E.
[130] 50 U. S. C. § 553 (Supp. 1952). See note, 67 HARV. L. REV. 479 (1954).
[131] 50 U. S. C. § 618 (Supp. 1952).

martial jurisdiction where the offense is not triable in an American civil court. Those committing other military or civilian type offenses not triable in other American courts and punishable by confinement of five years or more remain subject to military jurisdiction during the three-year period of limitation[132] even though sooner separated from the service. As to offenses the maximum punishment for which is less than five years the jurisdictional hiatus still exists. Jurisdiction under Article 3(a) is not to be exercised without the prior consent of the Secretary of the Department concerned.[133] The constitutional prohibition against ex post facto applicability of law[134] precludes the use of this remedial legislation in any case occurring prior to May 31, 1951.[135]

(3) *Military Status Not Terminated by Desertion Nor Absence from Trial*

Within the wide ambit from oath to discharge a number of interesting problems of status arise to complicate military jurisdiction. An accused, otherwise subject thereto, may not terminate military jurisdiction by his own wrongful act. Thus, the contention of a Coast Guardsman accused that the expiration of the three-year period for which he enlisted, occurring while he was in desertion, divested the military of jurisdiction over that offense was rejected.[136] This obviously correct result in effect, applied to the Coast Guard the long-standing congressional requirement that soldiers must make up time lost, or "bad time," and that the enlistment extends until such time has been made good.[137]

[132] Art. 43(b), 50 U. S. C. § 618 (Supp. 1952).

[133] MANUAL FOR COURTS-MARTIAL, UNITED STATES, 1951, ¶ 11b, p. 15 Exercise of jurisdiction over a former airman for murder allegedly committed while in service in Korea was upheld as constitutional in Talbott v. Toth, 215 F. 2d 22, 31 (D. C. Cir. 1954), reversing 114 F. Supp. 468 (D. C. D. C. 1953). "The Constitution put the government of the land and naval forces in the hands of the legislative branch, not of the judicial branch."

[134] U. S. CONST. Art. I, § 9, cl. 3.

[135] PUB. L. No. 506, 81st Cong., c. 169, § 5, 64 STAT. 108 (1950).

[136] United States v. Meyer (CGCM 9737), 1 CMR 562 (1951), citing ¶ 11d, MANUAL FOR COURTS-MARTIAL, UNITED STATES, 1951. *Accord, Ex parte* Clark, 271 Fed. 533 (E. D. N. Y. 1921). See also, United States v. Klunk, 3 USCMA 92, 11 CMR 92(1953).

[137] 64 STAT. 145 (1950), 10 U. S. C. § 629 (Supp. 1952) continues in force old Article of War 107 [41 STAT. 809 (1920)]. It provides:

> "§ 629. Soldiers to make good time lost. Every soldier who in an existing or subsequent enlistment deserts the service of the United States or without proper authority absents himself from his organization, station, or duty for more than one day, or who is confined for more than one day under sentence, or while awaiting trial and disposition of his case, if the trial results in conviction, or through the intemperate use of drugs or alcoholic liquor, or through disease or injury the result of his own misconduct, renders himself unable for more than one day to perform duty, shall be liable to serve, after his return to a full-duty status, for such period as shall, with the time he may have served prior to such desertion, unauthorized absence, confinement, or inability to perform duty, amount to the full term of that part of his enlist-

Similarly, where an accused, after being arraigned, voluntarily absents himself from his trial the court-martial retains jurisdiction to complete the trial, arrive at findings and sentence the accused in his absence.[138] This rule, which applies to capital as well as non-capital cases, has received the approval of the Court of Military Appeals in a rape case.[139] This doctrine has been applied to a case where after the court was sworn the accused exercised his peremptory challenge, was arraigned, then before plea, requested and was granted a continuance, and thereafter wrongfully absented himself. When the court reconvened not only was the accused absent but two members of the original court who had been excused by the convening authority. Two members of the court who were not present at the first meeting were sworn and the proceedings of the previous meeting made known to them.[140] The defense counsel announced he had no challenge for cause. An Army Board held the findings and sentence imposed on the absent accused by this court-martial to be valid.[141]

(4) *Changes of Military Status Not Terminating Jurisdiction*

The rigor of the discharge rule has long been tempered by limiting it largely to those discharges occurring at the end of a full term of enlistment. Thus it is necessary to examine the nature of a given honor-

---

ment period which he is required to serve with his organization before being furloughed to the Army reserve. June 4, 1920, c. 277, Subch. II, § 1, 41 Stat. 809; May 5, 1950, c. 169, § 6(a), 64 Stat. 145."

[138] United States v. Hollings (Sp CM 1213), 5 BR/JC 465 (1950); MANUAL FOR COURTS-MARTIAL, UNITED STATES, 1951, ¶ 11c, p. 16.

[139] United States v. Houghtaling, 2 USCMA 230, 234, 8 CMR 30, 34 (1953). The Court, with considerable perspicacity, observed: "Of necessity military personnel are highly mobile, and on occasion are scattered to the four winds within a matter of hours. In oversea theaters, and particularly in combat areas, witnesses, both military and civilian, are exposed to uncommon hazards which make their assembly for trial difficult always and too often impossible. Certainly the degree of prosecution hardship sharply increases as the time of trial is delayed. The capital offense escapee may thus gain great advantage, which will vary directly with the length of time he is able to prolong his absence. This is, of course, true in all areas of law enforcement, but it is greatly intensified in that of military judicial administration. We discern no reason for impending (*sic*)—perhaps even defeating—the prosecution of those who choose not to be present for trial, regardless of the offense with which they are charged. This would, we believe, be distinctly in derogation of the just claims of the military society, an interest often disregarded in febrile evaluation of the rights of frequently undeserving individuals."

". . . In the civilian community there is no rigid rule demanding that a convicted man be sentenced only by the judge who presided over his trial. However, there is no provision in military criminal law procedure for the imposition of any sort of sentence save by the court which tried and convicted the accused. As a practical necessity, the court which convicts a man *in absentia* must have the power to sentence him as well, otherwise the conviction will have gone for naught. It will always be difficult, and usually impossible, ever to reassemble a court-martial—and the longer the delay, the greater the difficulty and threat of impossibility."

[140] This is required by Art. 29(b), 50 U. S. C. § 593 (Supp. 1952).

[141] United States v. Henkel (CM 356028), 9 CMR 172 (1952).

able discharge to determine its effect on jurisdiction. Where prior to the expiration of a term of enlistment an individual is given an honorable discharge for "the convenience of the Government" for the purpose of re-enlisting or accepting a commission jurisdiction is retained over offenses committed during the previous foreshortened enlistment.[142] The Court of Military Appeals, one judge dissenting, has subscribed to this jurisdictional principle. It upheld jurisdiction to try in 1951 a postal clerk sergeant for six money order forgeries and larcenies perpetrated in 1948, although the sergeant had been discharged in 1949 for "the convenience of the Government" to re-enlist for an indefinite period of time.[143] Here the discharge was delivered the following day after the re-enlistment had been effected.

An Air Force Board of Review has upheld jurisdiction over larcenies committed before a re-enlistment entered into in lieu of a one-year involuntary extension of the prior enlistment under Executive Order 10270 of July 9, 1951.[144] Jurisdiction has also been affirmed where the accused in writing first voluntarily extended a one-year enlistment to three years and later extended it for two more years without ever taking a new oath. Accused performed military duty, wore an airman's uniform and accepted pay up until he deserted during the fifth year of this extended service. Accused contended that since he had not taken a new oath he was not in the service at the time he deserted. The Air Force Board in rejecting this contention held that the extensions did not constitute either a reformation of the contract or a separate enlistment but a voluntary "holding over" in the military service effecting a constructive enlistment.[145] It should be noted this case did not involve the survival after the extension of the enlistment of jurisdiction as to offenses previously committed, but was directed to jurisdiction of an offense committed after the second extension.

A complicated status situation was presented in the larceny case of Airman Eaton,[146] who originally enlisted for three years on October 25, 1946. On October 24, 1949, he voluntarily extended his enlistment one year. Because of "bad time" his period of service continued until

[142] United States v. Aikens (CM 337089), 5 BR/JC 331 (1950). The offenses involved were murder, robbery and assault. See also A MANUAL FOR COURTS-MARTIAL, UNITED STATES ARMY, 1928, ¶ 10; MANUAL FOR COURTS-MARTIAL, UNITED STATES ARMY, 1949, ¶ 10; MANUAL FOR COURTS-MARTIAL, UNITED STATES, 1951, ¶ 11b.

[143] In United States v. Solinsky, 2 USCMA 153, 160, 7 CMR 29, 36 (1953), the majority of the court observed: "A momentary break in service does not necessarily break court-martial jurisdiction. Chief Judge Quinn dissented and would apply the *Hirshberg* case rule in all situations not expressly covered by statute.

[144] United States v. Isidore (ACM 5625), 7 CMR 595 (1952).

[145] United States v. Patton (ACM 4272), 2 CMR 658, 662 (1951).

[146] United States v. Eaton (ACM S-3519), 6 CMR 675 (1952).

April 19, 1951 and he was retained in service for one year thereafter pending decision whether his enlistment was subject to involuntary extension for one year. The offense in question was committed in this last year. The Board held the accused had not been officially discharged and was, therefore, a person "awaiting discharge" within the provision of Article 2(1) of the Code,[147] and, hence, subject to court-martial trial. On the question of sentence evidence of five previous convictions was introduced—one for an offense during the original enlistment, three during the one year voluntary extension and one during the involuntary holding over. The last four were held to be properly admitted, but the first was ruled to be inadmissible since the voluntary extension started the accused with a clean slate so far as prior convictions was concerned.

Jurisdiction exists over a person who fraudulently enlists and accepts pay or allowances. Such a person may be tried by court-martial at the same time for the fraudulent enlistment and for a subsequent desertion therefrom.[148]

(5) *Jurisdiction Over Military Prisoners*

A prisoner in the custody of an armed force though under an executed sentence of dishonorable[149] or bad conduct[150] discharge remains subject to military jurisdiction not only for offenses committed while a prisoner but for offenses perpetrated while in the service prior to such discharge. The Court of Military Appeals has not had occasion to pass upon this point.

[147] 50 U. S. C. § 552(1) (Supp. 1952). A similar result was reached by the Court in the Navy case of United States v. Downs, 3 USCMA 90, 11 CMR 90 (1953).

[148] United States v. Luce (ACM 4191), 2 CMR 734 (1951). At page 738, the Board said: "The Board of Review concludes that the accused was properly tried and convicted at one trial both for fraudulent enlistment and for desertion from the period of service thereunder. His status as a person subject to military law while serving under such enlistment was a fact which cannot, as to offenses punishable by court-martial committed during such period, be considered retroactively terminated by a subsequent execution of the discharge adjudged. Such service is 'void' in its civil aspect as to benefits for the accused, but it is not 'void' in its disciplinary aspect as to burdens of service imposed on him by virtue of his status therein as a member of the armed forces."

[149] The last sentence of ¶ 11b, MANUAL FOR COURTS-MARTIAL, UNITED STATES, 1951 in part reads: ". . . a dishonorably discharged prisoner in custody of an armed force may be tried for an offense committed while a member of the armed forces and prior to the execution of his dishonorable discharge." Presumably such a person, if not confined, or if confined in a civilian detention institution, would not continue subject to military jurisdiction other than in the exceptional cases provided for in Article 3 of the Code [50 U. S. C. § 553 (Supp. 1952)]. Military jurisdiction over a military prisoner was upheld in Mosher v. Hudspeth, 123 F. 2d 401 (10th Cir. 1941), *cert. denied,* 316 U. S. 670 (1942); and Mosher v. Hunter, 143 F. 2d 745 (10th Cir. 1944).

[150] United States v. Drummond (ACM 5243), 5 CMR 400 (1952).

(6) *Effect of Service in Another Armed Force*

Naval Reserve Fireman Hazeldine, while in the inactive naval reserve, enlisted in the Air Force and served therein for two months before receiving an undesirable discharge. Thereafter he was ordered to active duty with the Navy and was subsequently convicted of a series of four absences without leave. Accused contended his Air Force service had terminated his Naval status rendering him not subject to Naval jurisdiction. In rejecting this assertion the Navy Board of Review declared:[151]

> "The accused in this case, a naval reservist, was in and out of another military organization and had not been discharged from his de jure status in the Naval Reserve prior to reporting as such reservist for active duty. He was, therefore, a naval reservist on active duty at the time of the commission of the offenses alleged, and a person subject to the Code and the court which tried him."

This decision appears to reverse *sub silentio* a 1951 opinion of the Judge Advocate General of the Navy.[152] In this latter case the accused enlisted in the Naval Reserve in 1946 for a four-year term, then in 1948 enlisted in the regular navy and in 1949 received a bad conduct discharge therefrom. In 1950, prior to the expiration of his original naval reserve enlistment, accused signed an agreement extending this reserve enlistment an additional four years, later entered upon active duty thereunder and thereafter received a bad conduct discharge for absence without leave. The Judge Advocate General of the Navy said that the accused ceased to be a member of the naval establishment when discharged from the regular navy, stressed that he had not thereafter taken an oath of enlistment, and held that even though he had entered upon and performed active duty the accused could not be guilty of the offense of unauthorized absence. This opinion was rendered prior to the decision of the Court of Military Appeals in *Rodriguez*[153] which held that the taking of an oath was not indispensable to jurisdiction if the accused in fact voluntarily entered into service. Of these two Navy views, that expressed by the Board of Review in *Hazeldine* seems to be the correct one under present law.

(7) *Selective Service Induction*

Private McNeill who had previously served two years in the army and three years in the enlisted reserve corps would have been exempt

[151] United States v. Hazeldine (NCM 125), 4 CMR 429, 431 (1952).

[152] Op. JAGN 1951/22 (15 August 1951), digested in 1 Dig. Ops. JAG 143 (1951-52).

[153] United States v. Rodriguez, 2 USCMA 101, 6 CMR 101 (1952).

from selective service induction if he had disclosed these facts. Accused simply left blank the spaces provided on the form for showing prior service and six weeks after reporting for duty deserted. Accused contended that the law officer erred in overruling a motion to dismiss for lack of jurisdiction on the ground that accused was not subject to selective service. The Court, relying on federal court authority,[154] affirmed jurisdiction and said:

> ". . . when an accused fails to furnish a basis for an exemption he is subject to military law. . . . When he . . . does not appeal from his classification, but on the contrary reports for duty he cannot reverse the local board by concluding not to serve."[155]

(8) *Short Active Duty Tours by Reserve Personnel*

Reservists ordered to short tours of active duty, as distinguished from those on extended active duty, also come within the jurisdictional purview of Article 2(1)[156] in that they are "persons lawfully . . . ordered . . . to duty in or for training in, the armed forces, from the dates they are required by the terms of the . . . order to obey the same." The Army Judge Advocate General has rendered an opinion that both officer and enlisted reservists who fail to comply with orders to active duty for fifteen days or less, or who while engaged in such duty commit offenses, may be punished by court-martial; that military jurisdiction fully attaches to such individuals if proceedings with a view to trial by court-martial are commenced, such as by arrest or service of charges, prior to expiration of the period of active duty; and that such proceedings may then be prosecuted to their conclusion.[157]

(9) *Member of Another Armed Force*

Concerning military personnel, there remains for discussion the self-imposed inter-service difficulty as to whether courts of one service may try an accused of another service. Congress imposed no limitation whatever in this respect and expressly provided: "Each armed force shall

[154] Harris v. Ross, 146 F. 2d 355 (5th Cir. 1944); United States v. Graham, 57 F. Supp. 938 (E. D. Ark. 1944); United States v. Mitchell, 248 Fed. 997 (E. D. N. Y. 1918).

[155] United States v. McNeill, 2 USCMA 383, 386, 9 CMR 13, 16 (1953).

[156] 50 U. S. C. § 552 (Supp. 1952).

[157] JAGA 1951/7487 (4 December 1951), reported in 1 Dig. Ops. JAG 138 (1951-52). *In re* Schulz (D. C. Ariz. April 30, 1953) digested in JAG Chron. No. 22, p. 99 (29 May 1953), upheld military jurisdiction to try a former reserve officer for an offense committed while on active duty, where his active duty terminated and his commission had expired before the charges were served on him, but after the charges had been preferred and referred to a court-martial for trial. In denying the petition for habeas corpus the district court relied on Carter v. McClaughry, 183 U. S. 365 (1902).

have court-martial jurisdiction over all persons subject to this code."[158] Congress did, however, make possible the "segregation" which the services have adopted by adding the proviso: "The exercise of jurisdiction by one armed force over personnel of another armed force shall be in accordance with regulations prescribed by the President."[159] In the exercise of this authority the President approved the *Manual* provisions:[160] "In general, jurisdiction by one armed force over personnel of another should be exercised only when the accused cannot be delivered to the armed force of which he is a member without manifest injury to the service," and: "Cases involving two or more accused who are members of different armed forces should not be referred to a court-martial for a joint or common trial." The only exemptions authorized are in the case of "The commanding officer of a joint command or joint task force who has been specifically empowered by the President or the Secretary of Defense to exercise jurisdiction over personnel of another armed force,"[161] and isolated commanders of small units who have first been so authorized by the Secretary of the Department primarily concerned with the concurrence of the Secretary of the other Department.[162] Presidential authority to so empower a joint commander was delegated to the Secretary of Defense by Executive Order 10428 of January 17, 1953.[163]

The Judge Advocate General of the Army has rendered an opinion that a member of the Marine Corps may not be tried by a court-martial convened by an armed force other than the Navy where the accused can be delivered to the Navy without manifest injury to the service.[164] This result definitely changed the rule prescribed by the Articles of War prior to the Uniform Code that "Officers and soldiers of the Marine Corps when detached for service with the armies of the United States by Order of the President,"[165] were subject to army courts-martial jurisdiction. An Army Regulation[166] cautions that Naval medical and dental officers assigned for duty with the Army are not subject to Army courts-martial or to non-judicial punishment under Article 15[167] by an Army commanding officer unless the President or Secretary of Defense has specifically so empowered the Army commanding officer. Where disciplinary action

[158] Art. 17 (a), 50 U. S. C. § 577 (Supp. 1952).
[159] *Ibid.*
[160] MANUAL FOR COURTS-MARTIAL, UNITED STATES, 1951, ¶ 13, p. 17.
[161] *Id.* at ¶ 4g(2), p. 5.
[162] *Id.* at ¶ 4g(3), p. 6.
[163] 18 FED. REG. 408 (1953).
[164] JAGJ 1952/2903 (25 March 1952), cited in JAG CHRON. No. 18, p. 75 (2 May 1952).
[165] Article of War 2(c), 41 STAT. 787 (1920) and Article of War 2(c), 62 STAT. 628 (1948).
[166] ¶ 7, SR 605-145-25 (25 August 1952).
[167] 50 U. S. C. § 571 (Supp. 1952).

is deemed necessary a request should be made to the Chief of Naval Personnel through the Surgeon General, Department of the Army, to have the individual relieved from duty with the Army.

An Air Force Board of Review[168] has reversed a desertion conviction of an Air Force private imposed by an Army court-martial holding that its purported exercise of jurisdiction was "nugatory."[169] The Air Force Board said:

> ". . . it was the Congressional purpose that the exercise of reciprocal jurisdiction under Article 17 was conditioned upon compliance with Presidential regulations and that purported exercise of such jurisdiction without such compliance is nugatory. Accordingly, accused could not be tried by an Army court-martial for the offense of desertion (Specification 2 of the Charge), inception of which occurred after he had been transferred administratively to the Air Force without specific authority to do so."[170]

A case which arose at the United States Disciplinary Barracks at Camp Gordon, Georgia, resulted in an interesting application of the administrative prohibition against cross-service trials. Six army prisoners and one air force prisoner, all under courts-martial sentences including dishonorable discharge, engaged in a common offense within the Army operated confinement facility. The Code expressly provides that "all persons in custody of the armed forces serving a sentence imposed by a court-martial"[171] are subject to its jurisdiction, and does not concern itself with their source of origin. The Judge Advocate General of the Army, in response to a pretrial inquiry, rendered an opinion that prisoners confined at disciplinary barracks who at the time of their original conviction were Air Force members, and who commit offenses while in confinement, should be tried by an Air Force court-martial in the absence of a showing of manifest injury to the service.[172] Pursuant thereto separate courts were convened, one by the Army[173] and one by the Air Force.[174]

[168] Art. 17(b), 50 U. S. C. § 577 (Supp. 1952) reads: "In all cases, departmental review subsequent to that by the officer with authority to convene a general court-martial for the command which held the trial, where such review is required under the provisions of this code, shall be carried out by the armed force of which the accused is a member."

[169] United States v. Mack (ACM 4920), 4 CMR 536 (1952).

[170] *Id.* at 542.

[171] Art. 2(7), 50 U. S. C. § 552 (Supp. 1952).

[172] JAGJ 1952/8435 (5 November 1952) cited in JAG CHRON. No. 48, p. 211 (28 November 1952).

[173] United States v. Gomez, Duggan, Mendiola, Fowler, Comeaux and Simcox (CM 361674) 10 CMR 463 (1953). *Aff'd,* 4 USCMA 396, 15 CMR 396 (1954) and 4 USCMA 403, 15 CMR 403 (1954).

[174] United States v. Criswell (ACM 4815), (1953).

In these cases where the accused is of a service other than that of the convening authority it must be kept in mind that the impediment to the exercise of jurisdiction is administrative and not congressional, and that the administrative bar is to the exercise of existing jurisdiction and does not destroy jursdiction itself. If and when the President should elect to withdraw the administrative impediment, or the Secretary of Defense expressly empowers a joint commander to exercise such jurisdiction, the basic congressional grant thereof remains and could properly be exercised.[174a] The problem is not by any means wholly academic since there are many occasions where small groups from one service must perform duty with another of the services for extended periods of time. For example, so common are such assignments for some army men that their status has been officially alphabetized and they are characterized as ARWAF and SCARWAF personnel. Translated, these mean "Army with Air Force" and "Special Category Army with Air Force." Prompt administration of discipline, when occasion arises, encounters great administrative difficulty.

B. *Civilian Personnel*

Congress, with a lively concern for the basic principle of American government of separation of powers, has in general consistently limited the jurisdiction of military tribunals over ordinary civilians to situations where the civil courts are not functioning[175] or where no American civil court has jurisdiction to adjudicate the cause. This continued concern is evidenced by the limitation in Article 3(a)[176] upon the survival of jurisdiction after the termination of military status to those cases where "the person cannot be tried in the courts of the United States or of a State or Territory thereof or of the District of Columbia," and by the common provision in paragraphs (11) and (12) of Article 2[177] which limits the jurisdiction therein conferred over civilians to areas "without the continental limits of the United States and without the following territories: That part of Alaska east of longitude one hundred and seventy-two degrees west, the Canal Zone, the main group of the Hawaiian Islands, Puerto Rico, and the Virgin Islands." Thus, where American civil courts are available jurisdiction over civilians is reserved

[174a] The Secretary of Defense on July 20, 1953 elected under his delegated authority to empower the commanding officers of three joint commands, one in Greenland, one in Newfoundland, and one at Sandia Base, New Mexico, ". . . to refer for trial by courts-martial the cases of members of any of the armed forces assigned or attached to or on duty with such command." Dept. of Defense Directive No. 5510.2 (20 July 1953), and companion directives.

[175] *Ex parte* Milligan, 4 Wall. 2 (U. S. 1866). Duncan v. Kahanomoku, 327 U. S. 304 (1945).

[176] 50 U. S. C. § 503 (Supp. 1952).

[177] 50 U. S. C. § 554 (Supp. 1952).

to them except for the provision of paragraph (10) of Article 2[178] that "In time of war, all persons serving with or accompanying an armed force in the field" are subject to military jurisdiction. Only the above cited paragraphs (10), (11) and (12) of Article 2 confer jurisdiction over civilians, while the first nine paragraphs thereof are concerned with defining military personnel for jurisdictional purposes. The global nature of missions which during the past decade have been assigned to the military establishment of the United States has been productive of decisions which have enriched the law of military jurisdiction over civilians.

Most of the decisions deal with former Article of War 2(d),[179] in effect from 1920 to 1951, which subjected to military jurisdiction:

> "All retainers to the camp and all persons accompanying or serving with the armies of the United States without the territorial jurisdiction of the United States, and in time of war all such retainers and persons accompanying or serving with the armies of the United States in the field, both within and without the territorial jurisdiction of the United States, though not otherwise subject to these articles."

Most of these decisions continue to be of value in applying the current jurisdictional provisions regarding civilians. Many of the cases prior to 1945 are collected in a published opinion of The Judge Advocate General of the Army.[180]

Of historical interest are Civil and Indian War rulings holding the following civilians subject to military law: ambulance drivers employed by the army;[181] guides for the army during warfare with Indians;[182] conductor and engineer on a train running from Alexandria to Manassas;[183] pilots and crews employed in the "Ram Fleet" in western waters;[184] contract surgeons;[185] teamsters employed by the Quartermaster;[186] deputies appointed by district provost marshals;[187] paymaster's clerks;[188]

[178] *Ibid.* See, however, Chapter 4, C, *post,* p. 65.

[179] 41 STAT. 787 (1920) and 62 STAT. 628 (1948).

[180] SP-JGW 1945/4990 (23 June 1945 and 2 July 1945) published in 4 BULL. JAG No. 6, pp. 223-229 (1945).

[181] Record Book No. 9, p. 146 (May 1864).

[182] Record Book No. 36, p. 435 (May 1875), DIG. OPS. JAG 49 (1880).

[183] Record Book No. 7, p. 116 (February 1864), DIG. OPS. JAG 38 (1865).

[184] Record Book No. 2, p. 570 (June 1863), DIG. OPS. JAG 107 (1865).

[185] Record Book No. 11, p. 493 (March 1865), DIG. OPS. JAG 11 (1866); Record Book No. 12, p. 376 (March 1865); Record Book No. 13, p. 459 (March 1865).

[186] Record Book No. 9, p. 111 (May 1864). DIG. OPS. JAG 38 (1865).

[187] Record Book No. 8, p. 246, DIG. OPS. JAG 69 (1866).

[188] Record Book No. 3, p. 269, DIG. OPS. JAG 92 (1865).

civilian horse trader with the army;[189] and War Department employees serving with the army in the Indian country.[190]

During World War I civilians in the following categories were held to be subject to military jurisdiction: field auditor in Quartermaster office at Camp Jackson, South Carolina;[191] Port of Brooklyn storage office chauffeur[192] and laborers;[193] laborers employed by civilian contractors engaged in constructing facilities for the American Expeditionary Force in France;[194] cook employed by quartermaster at New Mexico camp;[195] scout in Texas;[196] quartermaster civilian employee laborers on docks at ports of embarkation[197] and at Camp Upton, New York;[198] civilian member of a labor unit in France;[199] stevedore employed by the Army in France;[200] clerks employed by the Quartermaster overseas[201] and at Camp Meade, Maryland;[202] civilian passengers on an army transport;[203] Red Cross personnel serving with the Army overseas;[204] Captain of an Army transport in the Port of New York;[205] chief cook on an Army transport carrying military cargo;[206] merchant seamen on Army transports at sea or in English, French, or American ports;[207] telephone operator employed by Army in France;[208] secretaries and other employees of the Young Men's Christian Association and Knights of Columbus in France;[209] the superintendent for the Quartermaster Corps in Texas;[210] and a caretaker employed by the Army in France.[211]

[189] Record Book No. 7, p. 511 (April 1864).

[190] 14 OP. ATT'Y GEN. 22 (1872); Record Book No. 32, p. 385.

[191] Rines v. Mikell, 259 F. 28 (4th Cir. 1919), *cert. denied,* 250 U. S. 645 (1919); JAG 205.4 (15 October 1918), DIG. OPS. JAG § 359(9) (1912-40).

[192] CM 133361 (1919).

[193] CM 133362 (1919); CM 133363 (1919).

[194] JAG 250.4 (4 April 1948), Op. JAG 246 (1918), DIG. OPS. JAG § 359(12) (1912-40); CM 117642 (1918); CM 127110 (1919); CM 127126 (1919); CM 115772 (1918).

[195] CM 111573 (1918).

[196] CM 136256 (1919).

[197] JAG 250.4 (3 April 1918), DIG. OPS. JAG § 359(9) (1912-40); CM 133364 (1919).

[198] CM 117909 (1918), DIG. OPS. JAG §359(12) (1912-40); CM 117910 (1918); CM 117911 (1918); CM 117912 (1918); CM 117914 (1918); CM 117915 (1918); CM 118055 (1918); CM 118120 (1918).

[199] CM 115773 (1918).

[200] CM 108605 (1918).

[201] CM 108116 (1917); CM 110496 (1918); CM 133032 (1919).

[202] CM 132707 (1919).

[203] *Ex parte* Gerlach, 247 Fed. 616 (S. D. N. Y. 1917).

[204] JAG 080 (3 February 1919), DIG. OPS. JAG § 359(14) (1912-40); JAG 250.4 (21, 29 December 1917), DIG. OPS. JAG 98 (April-December 1917); CM 128898 (1919); *cf.* United States v. Snyder (CM 330683), 79 BR 121 (1948).

[205] CM 110574 (1918).

[206] *Ex parte* Falls, 251 Fed. 415 (D. C. N. J. 1918).

[207] JAG 251 (5 February 1918); DIG. Op. JAG 79 (1918); and twenty-five courts-martial cases cited in 4 BULL. JAG No. 6, pp. 227-228 (1945).

[208] CM 120393 (1918).

[209] CM 118327 (1918); CM 118333 (1918); CM 119135 (1918); CM 120639 (1918); CM 122855 (1918); CM 127502 (1919); CM 130005 (1919); CM 132387 (1919); CM 132407 (1919); CM 132607 (1919); CM 133387 (1919); CM 133818 (1919); JAG 000.51 (1 February 1919).

[210] *Ex parte* Jochen, 257 Fed. 200 (S. D. Tex. 1919).

[211] CM 136620 (1919).

World War II cases in which military jurisdiction was exercised over civilian personnel were even more voluminous and included: employees of the Board of Economic Warfare sent overseas at the request of a Theater Commander to feed and clothe the civilian population;[212] decoding experts employed by the Signal Corps at installations in the United States;[213] employees of civilian contractors in overseas areas;[214] discharged employees of a contractor with the Army awaiting transportation to the United States;[215] electricians employed by the Corps of Engineers in the Caribbean Defense Command,[216] the British West Indies,[217] and Alaska;[218] laborers, construction and maintenance personnel employed by the Army overseas;[219] mechanics at overseas bases;[220] USO Camp Shows entertainers with troops overseas;[221] American newspaper correspondents overseas officially accredited to the Army;[222] em-

[212] SPJGW 1943/230 (1 March 1943); SPJGW 1943/6250 (14 May 1943), 2 BULL. JAG 235.

[213] SPJGW 1944/8675 (19 July 1944).

[214] *In re* Di Bartolo, 50 F. Supp. 929 (S. D. N. Y. 1943), 2 BULL. JAG 338 (occupied enemy territory); SPJGW 1943/14720 (4 November 1943) (airfield overseas); SPJGW 1943/4722 (13 April 1943) (West Africa); SPJGW 1944/11096 (9 September 1944) (Alaska); SPJGW 1943/7941 (10 June 1943) (Alaska); CM 269448 (1944) (Alaska); the following in the Northwest Service Command: CM 245670 (1943); CM 247236 (1944); CM 248244 (1944); 31 BR 203, 3 BULL. JAG 58; CM 248722 (1944); CM 248725 (1944); CM 249973 (1944); CM 250124 (1944); CM 259249 (1944); the following at United States Military installations on bases leased in British possessions: SPJGW 1942/5668 (1 December 1942), 1 BULL. JAG 357; CM 218308 (1941); CM 221982 (1942); CM 228677 (1942); CM 230704 (1943).

[215] Perlstein v. United States, 57 F. Supp. 123 (M. D. Penn. 1944); JAG 250.401 (27 December 1941); CM 254272 (1944). Distinguished in United States v. Guidry (CM 357066), 7 CMR 305 (1952) where a discharged merchant seaman, not entitled to, and not awaiting, transportation to the United States, was held not subject to military jurisdiction for offenses committed in Japan after termination of his employment.

[216] SPJGW 1941/12887 (17 September 1943).

[217] CM 269484 (1944). [218] CM 243080 (1943).

[219] SPJGW 1942/6245 (28 December 1942) (Engineer Corps workers on Pan-American Highway in Nicaragua and Costa Rica, not normally resident there); CM 279377 (1945) (caretaker at partially abandoned airfield in Costa Rica recruited from Canal Zone); CM 267338 (1944) and CM 272817 (1945) (Northwest Service Command); CM 254962 (1944) (laborer in Persian Gulf Command); CM 243309 (1943) (construction worker at leased base in a British possession); CM 241292 (1943) (engineer employed at base in British West Indies); CM 245662 (1943) (storekeeper); SPJGW 1943/12887 (17 September 1943) (Panama Canal Department).

In United States v. Weiman, 3 USCMA 216, 11 CMR 216 (1953) two Polish nationals, members of a Labor Service Company brought to France for service with United States forces there located, were convicted by court-martial. In upholding jurisdiction the Court said: ". . . we are here concerned with nationals of a country other than the United States, present in a foreign country friendly to the United States, solely as employees of the military forces of the United States. We are not here concerned with nationals of a host nation, employed by our forces within the borders of such a nation."

[220] CM 245165 (1943); CM 245661 (1943).

[221] SPJGA 1943/6116 (29 April 1943).

[222] SPJGW 1942/4281 (17 September 1942); 1 BULL. JAG 212.

ployees of Psychological Warfare Branch, Office of War Information, attached to the Army in Algiers;[223] civilian passengers on Army transports,[224] commercial vessels operated under Army control carrying troops and military cargo,[225] and on War Shipping Administration vessels allocated to the Army carrying military personnel and cargo;[226] employees of post exchanges at camps in the United States;[227] Treasury Department agents in North Africa on foreign fund control work;[228] firefighters at an air base within the United States;[229] Civil Service pilots with Air Corps Ferrying Command and subject to military orders;[230] pilots of Civil Air Patrol who receive some of their orders from Army theater commanders;[231] policemen and guards at installations in the United States important to the prosecution of war[232] and at overseas bases;[233] messman[234] and chief cook[235] on ships operated by private shipping corporation carrying military cargo; civilian seamen serving on ships under army control or with troops or army cargo aboard;[236] and civilian employees of army transports and mine planters.[237]

The foregoing cases all arose either without the territorial limits of the United States or in the field in time of war. Through all of the former group runs a hard core of common sense thinking, shared in by Congress, that those whose employment, either directly or indirectly for military purposes, carries them beyond the territorial jurisdiction of state and federal civil courts should be subject to the jurisdiction of the only American courts which can reach them, namely, military tribunals. The latter group of cases, confined to those who in time of war serve with or accompany an armed force in the field, include some arising within the United States as well as overseas. Normally this jurisdiction is sparingly exercised in the United States and is reserved for cases where the individual is not only serving with or accompanying the armed force in the

223 SPJGW 1944/977 (13 March 1944).

224 *Ex parte* Gerlach, 247 Fed. 616 (S. D. N. Y. 1917) (A World War I case).

225 SPJGW 1944/6511 (16 June 1944).

226 SPJGW 1944/9568 (18 August 1944).

227 CM 222383 (1942). A civilian employee of a post exchange concessionaire on Okinawa is subject to military jurisdiction. United States v. Biagini (ACM 6341), 10 CMR 682 (1953).

228 SPJGW 1943/7335 (26 May 1943).

229 SPJGW 1943/9505 (12 July 1943).

230 SPJGW 1942/318 (30 January 1942).

231 SPJGW 1942/1877 (8 May 1942), 1 BULL. JAG 12.

232 SPJGW 1943/9505 (12 July 1943); CM 248051 (1944); CM 276755 (1945).

233 SPJGW 1942/214 (21 January 1942), 1 BULL. JAG 12; CM 238012 (1943).

234 *In re* Berue, 54 F. Supp. 252 (S. D. Ohio 1944), 3 BULL. JAG 135, 139.

235 McCune v. Kilpatrick, 53 F. Supp. 80 (E. D. Va. 1943), 3 BULL. JAG 6.

236 SPJGW 1942/2777 (30 June 1942); CM 226362 (1942), 15 BR 95, 1 BULL. JAG 357; CM 260578 (1944); CM 276748 (1945). *Cf.* Forgione v. United States, 100 F. Supp. 239 (E. D. Penn. 1951).

237 Weber v. Squier (W. D. Wash., May 31, 1945) (No opinion filed); 4 BULL. JAG 229 (June 1945).

field but is also engaged in work essential to the war effort. The Attorney General has ruled that the words "in the field" imply military operations with a view to an enemy. The federal courts have held that the question of whether an armed force is "in the field" is to be determined by the activity in which it is engaged at the time rather than by the locality in which it may be. Thus a temporary training camp in the United States is "in the field."[238] So also is a merchant ship and crew engaged in transporting troops and supplies to a battle zone.[239]

The Judge Advocate General of the Army has administratively determined that the following classes of persons are not subject to military law: laborers, mechanics or professional personnel at industrial establishments in the United States;[240] employees of an independent contractor engaged in construction work on the Inter-American highway supervised by a few Army Engineer officers but where no troops were present;[241] War Department clerical employees in Washington or in a field office in the United States not located at a military camp;[242] and, armed civilian guards at an Office of Strategic Services installation in a foreign country.[243] The Attorney General in 1878 rendered an opinion that clerks employed by the quartermaster in time of peace in the United States were not subject to military law.[244]

The Court of Military Appeals has as yet had little occasion to consider military jurisdiction over civilians. It has affirmed the traditional jurisdiction of the military over its civilian employees in overseas areas in the case of *Marker,* a General Service-11, Department of Army civil service employee, who was the superintendent of a tire plant operated by the Army in Japan under a contract with a Japanese corporation. His conviction by court-martial for forcing from officials of the corporation substantial "gifts" and the construction of a residence for his personal use was approved by the court.[245]

A civilian, subject to the Code, who has been placed in arrest for an offense committed in an overseas area cannot by his own wrongful acts

[238] Hines v. Mikell, 259 Fed. 28, 34 (4th Cir. 1919).

[239] McCune v. Kilpatrick, 53 F. Supp. 80 (S. D. Va. 1943); *In re* Berue, 54 F. Supp. 252 (S. D. Ohio 1944); *Ex parte* Gerlach, 247 Fed. 616 (S. D. N. Y. 1917).

[240] SPJGW 1943/9505 (12 July 1943).

[241] SPJGW 1943/2645 (12 February 1943).

[242] SPJGW 1943/9505 (12 July 1943) and SPJGW 1944/5969 (22 May 1944).

[243] SPJGW 1944/12441 (19 October 1944).

[244] 16 Op. Att'y Gen. 13, 48 (1878), Dig. Ops. JAG 49, 50 (1880).

[245] In United States v. Marker, 1 USCMA 393, 398, 3 CMR 127 (1952). At page 132, the court stated: "Federal cases make it clear that . . . petitioner was 'accompanying or serving with the armies of the United States,' Perlstein v. United States, 151 F (2d) 167 (C. A. 3rd Cir.), *cert. dismissed,* 328 U. S. 822, 90 L. Ed. 1602, 66 S. Ct. 1358; Greive v. France, 75 F. Supp. 433; *Ex parte* Jochen, 257 Fed. 200; U. S. *ex rel.* Mobley v. Handy, 176 F (2d) 491 (C. A. 5th Cir.), *cert. den.,* 338 U. S. 904, 94 L. Ed. 556, 70 S. Ct. 306, Hines v. Mickell, 259 F. 28 (C. A. 4th Cir.)."

of breaching such arrest and returning to the United States divest the military of jurisdiction.[246]

By way of *dictum,* the Court has indicated that military personnel who are discharged and re-enlist in overseas areas continue subject to military jurisdiction during the interim as persons "accompanying the armed forces without the continental limits of the United States." It said:

> "If . . . accused's status changed, we would be faced with this factual situation. For an infinitesimal period of time the accused became a civilian without the territorial jurisdiction of the United States. During this period he was housed, maintained, paid, and otherwise serviced by the United States Army. He was transported overseas and he was returned to the United States by the Army. Between these two events he was always a soldier. Under these circumstances he would either be accompanying or serving with the Armies of the United States from the moment he left these shores until he returned. If, for a moment, he stepped from his uniform into civilian clothes and then back again, he never stepped into a category which was not subject to military law. . . ."[247]

C. *Dependents*

The problem of jurisdiction over "dependents," that is principally wives and children, of military and other personnel subject to military law does not appear to have arisen until the close of World War II. This is not surprising since such dependents while in the United States are subject to ordinary civil jurisdiction and while at typical overseas stations before World War II, such as Puerto Rico, the Canal Zone, Alaska and the Philippines were triable in United States territorial courts. Military attaché personnel in foreign countries were carefully selected, including close scrutiny of their families, and the question either did not arise or was settled administratively. Only after World War II were families in large numbers permitted to accompany, or to join, military or civilian employee heads of families in foreign countries. Where such dependents committed offenses in occupied enemy countries,

[246] United States *ex rel.* Mobley v. Handy, 176 F. 2d 491 (5th Cir. 1949). See also, United States v. Biagini (ACM 6341), 10 CMR 682 (1953). However, where an individual who was both a former officer and former civilian employee of an officer's club had completely severed all connection with the military and had been granted a permit to remain in occupied Japan as a civilian, the Court of Military Appeals held that he was not thereafter within the jurisdiction of the Uniform Code when charges were finally preferred for an earlier offense. United States v. Schultz, 1 USCMA 512, 4 CMR 104 (1952).

[247] United States v. Solinsky, 2 USCMA 153, 160, 7 CMR 29, 36 (1953).

under the laws of war, they were subject to trial by military commission, or other tribunals in the nature of military commissions, convened by the occupying power in the discharge of its obligation under international law to establish and maintain law and order in the occupied area.[248]

The Military Government Court solution was inapplicable to cases arising in friendly foreign countries such as England, France and the Philippine Republic after it acquired full sovereignty on July 4, 1946. Executive agreements with friendly foreign countries even where they accorded jurisdiction over dependents to the United States did not afford a complete answer, since the problem still remained as to whether American military jurisdiction extended to dependents who were otherwise not subject thereto. Of course, where a wife or grown child took civilian employment with one of the United States armed forces, as many in fact did, they thereby became subject to military jurisdiction. Still left in question was the status of those who did not become so employed. The Judge Advocate General of the Army in 1947 made a policy decision that military jurisdiction over such dependents would not be exercised in spite of the fact that they were "accompanying . . . the armies of the United States without the territorial jurisdiction of the United States."[249] Not until May 31, 1951 did the Congressional grant of military jurisdiction over "all persons within an area leased by or otherwise reserved or acquired for the use of the United States which is under the control of a Secretary of a Department and which is without the continental limits of the United States . . ." (and its territories)[250] become effective. This now covers all offenses committed by dependents while on such leased bases but is inapplicable to off base offenses.

Fortunately, it is probable that by a deft dictum, the United States Supreme Court has approved a simple solution which will hereafter be followed where dependents commit offenses in foreign countries, either friendly or hostile. Yvette Madsen killed her American Air Force lieutenant husband at their residence in Frankfurt, Germany in October 1949, was thereafter tried for and convicted of murder by a United States Court of the Allied High Commission for Germany, and after affirmance by the "Court of Appeals for the Allied High Commission for Germany" was confined in the Federal Reformatory for Women at Alderson, West Virginia, to serve a fifteen year sentence. She petitioned for habeas corpus relief contending that she should have been

[248] Madsen v. Kinsella, 343 U. S. 341 (1952).
[249] Article of War 2(d), 41 STAT. 787 (1920).
[250] Art. 2(12), 50 U. S. C. § 552 (Supp. 1952).

tried by a court-martial and that the tribunal which tried her was without jurisdiction. The Supreme Court granted certiorari, upheld the jurisdiction of the court which tried petitioner, denied relief and discussed petitioner's status and liability to trial by court-martial, as follows:

> "Petitioner is a native-born citizen of the United States who lawfully entered the American Zone of Occupied Germany in 1947 with her husband, Lieutenant Madsen of the United States Air Force. In 1949, she resided there, with him, in a house requisitioned for military use, furnished and maintained by military authority. She was permitted to use the facilities of the United States Army maintained there for persons in its service and for those serving with or accompanying the United States Armed Forces. In brief, her status was that of a civilian dependent wife of a member of the United States Armed Forces which were then occupying the United States Area of Control in Germany.[251]
>
> ". . . Article of War 2(d) further defined 'any person subject to military law' as including 'all persons accompanying or serving with the armies of the United States without the territorial jurisdiction of the United States . . .' . This included petitioner."[252]

In this concise manner the high court has stated, what on principle appears to be perfectly clear, that dependents overseas, "accompany" the Armies of the United States and so, under present Article 2(11),[253] may be tried by court-martial.

In 1952 in occupied Japan, Dorothy Krueger Smith killed her Army colonel husband in their military residence in Tokyo. An Army court-martial convicted her of premeditated murder and imposed a life sentence which action was affirmed by a Board of Review.[254] It was seriously contended that the accused upon the death of her husband ceased to be a dependent and so at the time of trial was not subject to court-martial jurisdiction. In rejecting this contention, the Board, in part, relied on the *Madsen* case, and said:

> ". . . her status as a spouse or dependent ceased to exist upon her husband's death; but . . . she remained a person 'accompanying' the armed forces of the United States within the meaning of the Code and subject to the jurisdiction thereof for all purposes herein considered."[255]

[251] Madsen v. Kinsella, 343 U. S. 341, 343 (1952).
[252] *Id.* at 361.
[253] 50 U. S. C. § 552 (Supp. 1952).
[254] United States v. Smith (CM 360857), 10 CMR 350 (1953).
[255] *Id.* at 363.

A point not raised by the Smith case is whether a court-martial convened by the Navy, Coast Guard or Air Force would have had jurisdiction. A reading of the Code would seem to impel an affirmative answer. Having in mind, however, the administrative ruling made as to the trial of dishonorably discharged military prisoners,[256] it is probable that the opinion of the respective Judge Advocates General on this point would be that jurisdiction should be exercised only by the service of which the dependent's sponsor is, or was, a member.

D. *Miscellaneous*

There remain for discussion a few problems of status of the person which do not fall within the three foregoing classifications. It should be noted that Congress has expressly preserved military jurisdiction in Article 3(b) over those who have fraudulently obtained their discharge from the armed forces, and in Article 3(c) over undetected deserters who have obtained a separation from any subsequent period of service.[257]

National Guard personnel, who have no other dual military status, are not in the armed forces of the United States except when called into the active federal service by direction of the President either as units or as individuals. Thus, such National Guard personnel while attending service schools in the United States under Section 99 of the National Defense Act[258] have been held to be not subject to trial by court-martial convened by the commanding officer of the service school.[259] Similarly

[256] See note 172, *supra*. See, however, United States v. Biagini (ACM 6341), 10 CMR 682 (1953) which held a civilian employee on Okinawa of a concessionaire of the central exchange, an army activity, was subject to the jurisdiction of an Air Force court-martial.

[257] The provisions of Article 3(b) and 3(c) are set forth in full in note 107 *supra*.

[258] 39 STAT. 207 (1916).

[259] DIG. OPS. JAG § 359(5) (1912-40) and Letter JAGJ 1953/2104 (4 March 1953), cited in 2 JAG CHRON. No. 14, p. 56 (April 3, 1953). See also Johnson v. Sayre, 158 U. S. 109 (1895). See, however, Armed Forces Reserve Act of July 9, 1952, 66 STAT. 481 (1952), 50 U. S. C. A. §§ 901-1124 (Supp. 1952). Section 1001 thereof provides: "There shall be no discrimination between and among members of the Regular and reserve components in the administration of laws applicable to both Regulars and Reserves." Section 1112 thereof in substance provides that the National Guard and Air National Guard of the United States shall consist of members who in addition to their status as such are Reserves of the Army and Air Force in the same grade they hold in the Guard. Section 1124 in part provides: "For the purpose of . . . benefits . . . full-time training or other full-time duty performed by members of the National Guard . . . or the Air National Guard of the United States . . . for which they are entitled to receive pay from the United States . . . shall be considered active duty for training in the Service of the United States as Reserve members of the Army or Air Force . . . ," and contains a similar provision as to inactive-duty training. The impact of this legislation, if any, in the area of federal courts-martial jurisdiction has not yet been tested. It might be urged that this legislation places National Guard personnel in the same jurisdictional status as other reserve personnel. On the other hand it could be argued that Congress would not extend Article 2 jurisdiction by implication. It is probable this question will ultimately engage the attention of the Court of Military Appeals.

National Guard personnel on garrison duty or at summer encampments while under state control, as distinguished from being in active federal service, are not normally subject to trial by a federally convened court-martial. While in a non-federal duty status such personnel are subject to trial by state courts-martial where the law of the state makes separate provision therefor. In a number of the states detailed legislative provision is made for all aspects of the government of the state militia or national guard when not in federal service.[260] The propriety of the exercise of such jurisdiction by the states was recognized by the Supreme Court at least as early as 1820.[261]

To the reader who has persisted thus far it becomes apparent that between those who obviously are and those who obviously are not subject to military jurisdiction there lies a large peripheral area containing persons whose status is such as to require discriminating evaluation by those charged with the enforcement of the military law, alert examination by defense counsel and measured judgment by all who discharge judicial duties within the system of military law.

[260] Typical are CAL. MIL. AND VET. CODE §§ 450-473 (Supp. 1949) and New York Laws 1953, c. 617, approved April 8, 1953.

[261] Houston v. Moore, 5 Wheat. 27 (U. S. 1820).

CHAPTER 4

Jurisdiction of the Offense

A. *Offenses Punishable Are Purely Statutory*

Although the authority for courts-martial does not stem from the Third or Judiciary Article of the Constitution,[262] courts-martial are analogous to other federal courts in that the offenses to which their jurisdiction extend are confined to those expressly denounced by Congress in the punitive articles.[263] This statement is subject to the qualification that Congress by Article 18 has specified: "General courts-martial shall also have jurisdiction to try any person who by the law of war is subject to trial by a military tribunal. . . ."[264] This derivative jurisdiction from the law of war widens the horizon of general courts-martial not only as to persons but as to offenses as well. As previously stated, the ramifications of this derivative jurisdiction are beyond the scope of this book. It should be remembered, however, that this law of war jurisdiction vests in general courts-martial, as distinguished from military commissions, only because Congress has expressly so provided. Courts-martial *per se* do not have any residual or common law jurisdiction as to either persons or offenses such as normally resides in state courts of general jurisdiction. Accordingly, the investigation by defense counsel as to jurisdiction of the offense is in the military system potentially more remunerative than is normally the case in state criminal proceedings.

B. *Only Military Personnel Can Commit Certain Offenses*

It should be observed that a few of the offenses denounced in the punitive articles are strictly military offenses and so can be committed

[262] Dynes v. Hoover, 20 How. 65 (U. S. 1857).

[263] Arts. 77 to 134 inclusive, 50 U. S. C. §§ 671-728 (Supp. 1952).

[264] 50 U. S. C. § 578 (Supp. 1952). Special and summary courts-martial do not possess this derivative jurisdiction, nor do they have jurisdiction over any capital offenses. Arts. 19 and 20, 50 U. S. C. §§ 579, 580 (Supp. 1952). However, a special court may try non-mandatory sentence capital offenses if a general court-martial convening authority has first directed that the case be treated as non-capital. MANUAL FOR COURTS-MARTIAL, UNITED STATES, 1951, ¶ 15(a)(3), p. 19.

only by military personnel, whereas the others are of such a nature that anyone subject to the Code, either military or civilian, may commit them. For example, desertion[265] cannot be committed by a civilian, nor can it be commited by a military prisoner with an executed dishonorable discharge.[266] On the other hand, the Court of Military Appeals has decided that a civilan employee overseas can commit under Article 134, the general article, the offense of "conduct of a nature to bring discredit upon the armed forces. . . ."[267] There the specific conduct found to be violative of the article was the coercing, from subordinate Japanese civilian employees manufacturing tires for the military, of substantial donations of both goods and services for the personal benefit of the accused.

The offenses of desertion,[268] absence without leave[269] and the nine separate offenses denounced under the collective heading of "Misbehavior before the enemy"[270] can be committed only by "Any member of the armed forces. . . ." The offenses of using contemptuous words against certain government officials can be commited only by an officer.[271] Conduct unbecoming an officer and a gentleman can be accomplished only by an officer, cadet or midshipman.[272] Insubordinate conduct towards warrant officers, noncommissioned officers or petty officers can be perpetrated only by warrant officers and enlisted persons.[273] The offenses of being drunk or sleeping upon his post, or leaving it before being regularly relieved, can be committed only by a person who has been posted as a sentinel or look-out.[274] All of the other punitive articles, presumptively at least, may be violated by any person subject to the Code whether civilian or military.

C. *Jurisdiction Unlimited As to Certain Offenses*

There are three offenses for which a court-martial may try any person, even though in all other respects such persons are not in any other manner subject to the Code. These are aiding the enemy,[275] spying,[276] and contempt of a court-martial by menacing words, signs or gestures

[265] Art. 85, 50 U. S. C. §§ 679 (Supp. 1952).
[266] United States v. Rushing (CM 272382), 46 BR 301 (1945). However, it has been held that a military prisoner with an executed dishonorable discharge can be guilty of the offense of assaulting a superior officer. [Art. 90, 50 U. S. C. § 684 (Supp. 1952)]. United States v. Scott (CM 252812), 34 BR 197, 201 (1944).
[267] United States v. Marker, 1 USCMA 393, 3 CMR 127 (1952).
[268] Art. 85, 50 U. S. C. § 679 (Supp. 1952).
[269] Art. 86, 50 U. S. C. § 680 (Supp. 1952).
[270] Art. 99, 50 U. S. C. § 693 (Supp. 1952).
[271] Art. 88, 50 U. S. C. § 682 (Supp. 1952).
[272] Art. 133, 50 U. S. C. § 727 (Supp. 1952).
[273] Art. 91, 50 U. S. C. § 685 (Supp. 1952).
[274] Art. 113, 50 U. S. C. § 707 (Supp. 1952).
[275] Art. 104, 50 U. S. C. § 698 (Supp. 1952).
[276] Art. 106, 50 U. S. C. § 700 (Supp. 1952).

in its presence, or by disturbing its proceedings by any riot or disorder.[277] This jurisdiction has been sparingly exercised, if at all. Where civilians, who are American citizens, engage in conduct which constitutes aiding the enemy, normally they are tried for treason[278] in a United States District Court.[279] Similarly, American civilians who engage in spying are tried in the United States District Court.[280]

D. *Jurisdiction Is a Question of Fact, Not Pleading*

Defects in pretrial procedure, not involving the composition of the court, generally will not divest a court-martial of jurisdiction.[281] Thus, although Article 30(a)[282] requires that, "Charges and specifications shall be signed by a person subject to this code under oath before an officer of the armed forces authorized to administer oaths . . . ," the Court of Military Appeals has held that, where the accused does not promptly object, a trial on unsworn charges is valid.[283] Similarly, Congress has confirmed previous decisions of the Supreme Court which held that defects in, or the complete absence of, a pretrial investigation did not divest a general court-martial of jurisdiction.[284] It has also been held that material changes made in charges after the investigation and without a new investigation being conducted is neither jurisdictional nor prejudicial error.[285]

Military pleading requires that the article, or articles, of the Code violated be set forth in the "Charge" or "Charges"[286] and that the "Specification," or specifications should include the name of the accused, his status subjecting him to the Code, where and when the offense was committed, and in simple concise language, the facts constituting the offense.[287] However, neither the designation of a wrong article[287a] in the

[277] Art. 48, 50 U. S. C. § 623 (Supp. 1952).

[278] 18 U. S. C. § 1 (Supp. 1952) based upon the definition of treason contained in U. S. CONST. Art. III § 3 providing: "Whoever, owing allegiance to the United States levies war against them or adheres to their enemies, giving them aid and comfort within the United States or elsewhere is guilty of treason."

[279] Typical is United States v. Kawakita, 343 U. S. 717 (1952).

[280] United States v. Rosenburg, 195 F. 2d 583 (2d Cir. 1952), *cert. denied*, 344 U. S. 838 (1952); *rehearing denied*, 344 U. S. 889 (1952); order dismissing petition for new trial affirmed, 200 F. 2d 666 (2d Cir. 1952); motion to vacate stay granted, 346 U. S. 273 (1953).

[281] United States v. Floyd (CM 229477), 17 BR 149 (1943).

[282] 50 U. S. C. § 601 (Supp. 1952).

[283] United States v. May, 1 USCMA 174, 2 CMR 80 (1952); United States v. Marcy, 1 USCMA 176, 2 CMR 82 (1952); United States v. Simpson (CM 310246), 61 BR 225 (1946). However, where prior to entering a plea the accused objected to being brought to trial on unsworn charges, it was prejudicial error for the law officer to overrule the objection. United States v. Olivieri (ACM 6055), 10 CMR 644 (1953).

[284] See notes 100-102, p. 37 *supra*. Cf. United States v. Taylor (CM 366209) 13 CMR 201 (1953); *pet. denied*, 14 CMR 228 (1954).

[285] United States v. Hawkins (CM ETO 4570), 13 BR ETO 57 (1945).

[286] MANUAL FOR COURTS-MARTIAL, UNITED STATES, 1951, ¶ 27, p. 30.

[287] *Id.* at ¶ 28, pp. 30, 31.

[287a] United States v. Deller, 3 USCMA 409, 12 CMR 165 (1953). Desertion with intent to shirk important service erroneously charged under Article 134.

charge nor the failure to designate any article is ordinarily material, so long as the specification states an offense subject to court-martial jurisdiction. Charging murder under the wrong article has been held on habeas corpus attack not to constitute jurisdictional error.[288] The Court of Military Appeals has gone further and ruled it to be immaterial that the charge recited a violation of Article of War 93,[289] when in fact the accused, having finally and completely separated from the service and all connection therewith, was not subject to the Articles of War. The conviction was affirmed because the specification stated a violation of the Japanese criminal code which had been continued in effect by military order and which a court-martial could enforce by reason of its derivative jurisdiction conferred by Article of War 12[290] to try offenses against the law of war. In upholding jurisdiction in the case the Court said:

> "Jurisdiction is neither vested nor divested by the formalities of pleading. . . . If a specification states an offense in violation of the law of war, categorizing it as a violation of military law is not a fatal error."[291]

The general rule as to the sufficiency of the wording of a specification is that it must fairly inform the accused of the offense with which he stands charged and must be sufficiently definite to prevent the accused from again being tried for the same offense, but it need not be framed in technical language nor with the exactitude of a common law indictment.[292] The Court has aptly observed in this regard, "Sight must not be lost of the fact that the prosecution of crime—military or civilian—is not a fox hunt, and that rather different ground rules should obtain."[293]

[288] Johnson v. Biddle, 12 F. 2d 366 (8th Cir. 1926).

[289] 41 Stat. 805 (1920) (involuntary manslaughter).

[290] 41 Stat. 789 (1920). The present equivalent provision is Art. 18, 50 U. S. C. § 578 (Supp. 1952).

[291] United States v. Schultz, 1 USCMA 512, 523, 4 CMR 104, 115 (1952), affirming (ACM 3786) 4 CMR 574. Reliance was placed on Givens v. Zerbst, 255 U. S. 11 (1921). *Accord,* United States v. Fleming (CM 347931), 2 CMR 312 (1951) (forgery), and United States v. Kaukoreit (CM 302791), 59 BR 7 (1946). See Williams v. United States, 168 U. S. 382 (1897). See, however, United States v. Bernard (ACM 6383) 10 CMR 718 (1953).

[292] United States v. Marker, 1 USCMA 393, 3 CMR 127 (1952); United States v. Snyder, 1 USCMA 423, 4 CMR 15 (1952); United States v. Aldridge, 2 USCMA 330, 333, 8 CMR 130, 133 (1953); United States v. Johnson, 3 USCMA 174, 176, 11 CMR 174, 176 (1953); United States v. Field, 3 USCMA 182, 185, 11 CMR 182, 185 (1953); United States v. Bunch, 3 USCMA 186, 188, 11 CMR 186, 189 (1953); United States v. Sell, 3 USCMA 202, 206, 11 CMR 202, 206 (1953); United States v. Cowan (CM 364954), 11 CMR 374 (1953); United States v. Karl, 3 USCMA 183, 12 CMR 183 (1953); United States v. Lawrence, 3 USCMA 628, 14 CMR 46 (1954). See, however, United States v. Fout, 3 USCMA 565, 13 CMR 121 (1953) and United States v. Hunter (CM 354897), 6 CMR 172 (1952).

[293] United States v. Aldridge, 2 USCMA 330, 333, 8 CMR 130, 133 (1953).

E. *Specific Offenses*

With this enlightened approach it is not surprising that only a few cases have reached the Court which challenge a specification as not stating an offense punishable under the Code. Article 121,[294] which prolixly combined common law larceny, embezzlement, and larceny by false pretense into the single offense of larceny and collectively characterized all three by the word "steals," has been examined. A specification drawn thereunder was found to state an offense though it did not contain language which would identify it as one of the common law offenses to the exclusion of the others. The specification in question alleged that the accused did "steal" specified sums of money from named individuals. The Court of Military Appeals found this properly pleaded the elements of this offense consisting of:

> ". . . two elements: (1) that the accused obtained possession of the property in question, of some value, (2) with an intent, then or thereafter conceived, permanently to deprive the true owner of its use and benefit."[295]

The Court has upheld a specification under Article 132[295a] which in essence alleged that the accused "did . . . by preparing a request for

[294] 50 U.S.C. ¶ 715 (Supp. 1952). Paragraph (a) thereof reads:
"Larceny and wrongful appropriation (article 121)
(a) Any person subject to this code who wrongfully takes, obtains, or withholds, by any means whatever, from the possession of the true owner or of any other person any money, personal property, or article of value of any kind—
(1) with intent permanently to deprive or defraud another person of the use and benefit of property or to appropriate the same to his own use or the use of any person other than the true owner, steals such property and is guilty of larceny; or
(2) with intent temporarily to deprive or defraud another person of the use and benefit of property or to appropriate the same to his own use or the use of any other person other than the true owner is guilty of wrongful appropriation . . ."
In a prosecution under Article 121 it is unnecessary to allege the false pretenses by which the property was obtained, but they must be proved. United States v. Beasley, 3 USCMA 111, 112, 11 CMR 110, 112 (1953). See also United States v. Buck, 3 USCMA 341, 12 CMR 97 (1953).

[295] United States v. Aldridge, 2 USCMA 330, 332, 8 CMR 130, 132 (1953). It has been held that a specification alleging the larceny of "the property of the Trailer Court Fund, Fort Benjamin Harrison, Indiana" is good since the owner need not be a legal entity. United States v. Wilkey (CM 358746), 10 CMR 334 (1953). See also United States v. Krawczyk, 4 USCMA 255, 15 CMR 255 (1954).
As to whether a larceny is single or multiple for the purpose of determining the value of the property taken see United States v. Florence 1 USCMA 620, 5 CMR 48 (1953).

[295a] 50 U. S. C. § 726 (Supp. 1952). Forging a signature to a payroll and obtaining money thereby constitutes presenting a claim and is fraud against the government properly chargeable under Article 132. United States v. Field, 3 USCMA 182, 11 CMR 182 (1952). *Cf.* United States v. Lawrence, 3 USCMA 628, 14 CMR 46 (1954).

commutation of rations for presentment to the commanding general . . . make a claim against the United States . . . which claim was false and fraudulent . . . in that he . . . did not then intend to so subsist with his family and was then known by the (accused) to be false and fraudulent."[296] Accused pleaded guilty to this specification but on appeal contended that it did not state an offense. Article 132 in pertinent part denounces as offenses, among others, the conduct of one "(1) who, knowing it to be false or fraudulent—(A) makes a claim against the United States . . . ; or (B) presents to any person in the civil or military service thereof, for approval or payment, any claim against the United States. . . ." Accused's appellate contention was that merely the preparation of a claim was alleged and nothing which carried the act of the accused beyond the preparatory stage. The Court pointed out that by motion before or during trial the accused could have required a more artful wording of the specification but that, as against jurisdictional attack, the specification as drawn alleged that the accused "did . . . make a claim," and that this stated an offense since it was "susceptible of an interpretation that a voucher was prepared by (accused) and placed in the hands of some individual who in the normal course of events would present it to the general."[297]

In a Navy case the Board of Review reversed a conviction for missing ship through neglect. This and the more serious act of missing ship through design are both declared to be offenses by Article 87.[298] The evidence showed the accused on June 7, 1952 acknowledged in writing the information that his ship was scheduled to sail for overseas duty on July 7, 1952, and that the ship so sailed. Accused pleaded guilty to unauthorized absence from June 17, 1952 until July 27, 1952. The Board based its reversal on the absence of evidence establishing causal connection between accused's neglect and the missing of the scheduled movement. Upon certification of the case by the Navy Judge Advocate General, the Court found this evidence established a prima facie case of missing ship through neglect, reversed the Board, and said:

> "Where a definite movement date is set and known to the accused, who thereupon remains absent without authority beyond the scheduled date of departure, we can see no necessity for any special proof of causal connection. Assuming knowledge, the only rational explanations are either deliberate avoidance or carelessness resulting in avoidance."[299]

[296] United States v. Steele, 2 USCMA 379, 380, 9 CMR 9, 10 (1953).
[297] *Id.* at 382, 9 CMR at 5.
[298] 50 U. S. C. § 681 (Supp. 1952).
[299] United States v. Thompson, 2 USCMA 460, 464, 9 CMR 90, 94 (1953). The accused need not be assigned to duty with the aircraft or ship involved in

There is a salty tang to the case of Seaman Simpson who, it was alleged, " having knowledge of a lawful order issued by the Commanding Officer . . . in part as follows: 'Liberty Uniform . . . white jumper is mandatory,' an order which it was his duty to obey, did, while at . . . Guam . . . fail to obey the same, to wit: not wearing the jumper."[300] Simpson pleaded guilty to this offense under Article 92,[301] but the Board of Review concluded the failure to allege that the accused was on liberty at the time the order was violated constituted a fatal defect. Upon certification the Court again reversed the Board, held the specification good and said:

> ". . . The accused could not disobey the order without being on liberty. There could not be a disobedience unless the accused was in that status as failure to wear it on other occasions would not be a violation of the order. We do not understand the rule governing pleading to go so far as to hold that every self-evident fact must be alleged. Neither do we understand that required implication cannot be considered in determining the sufficiency of a specification."[302]

---

the movement missed to constitute the offense of missing movement. United States v. Johnson, 3 USCMA 174, 11 CMR 174 (1953).

[300] United States v. Simpson, 2 USCMA 493, 494, 9 CMR 123, 124 (1953).

[301] 50 U. S. C. § 686 (Supp. 1952). United States v. Snyder, 1 USCMA 423, 428, 4 CMR 15, 19 (1953) held evidence supporting a specification that accused ". . . did . . . violate a lawful regulation, to wit, . . . camp regulations . . . 'Female civilians will not be permitted to enter the barracks . . .'; in that he did permit . . . to enter . . . and did accompany . . . Gertrude Williams into . . . building number BB-12," properly established the offense under Article 92 of violating a lawful general order or regulation. The court stated in substance that "general orders" are what were formerly referred to in the services as "standing orders" and include post regulations. The *Snyder* case, however, is no longer law so far as the naval service is concerned. After its decision the Naval Supplement to the MANUAL was published which defines a "commander," as used in paragraph 171(a) of the MANUAL as "an officer of flag or general rank." Based on this definition, the Court distinguished the *Snyder* case and held the allegation of the violation of a ship order, issued by a navy commander commanding a destroyer, did not state a violation of a general order under Article 92(1). United States v. Bunch, 3 USCMA 186, 11 CMR 186 (1953).

For a discussion of the limitation imposed on punishment of offenses charged under Article 92 by the provisions of MANUAL FOR COURTS-MARTIAL, UNITED STATES, 1951, ¶ 127c, p. 221, n. 5, see United States v. Buckmiller, 1 USCMA 504, 4 CMR 96 (1953). See also United States v. Sell, 3 USCMA 202, 11 CMR 202 (1953).

[302] United States v. Simpson, 2 USCMA 493, 495, 9 CMR 123, 125 (1953). Similarly, it has been held under Art. 108, 50 U. S. C. § 702 (Supp. 1952) that ". . . destruction of government property through neglect appears to be a lesser included offense of willful destruction of such property, whenever it is reasonably raised by the evidence without regard to its description in the specification." United States v. Wright, 3 USCMA 431, 12 CMR 187 (1953).

F. *Offenses Under the General Articles*

As might be expected, most attacks against the sufficiency of specifications to state, or evidence to establish, cognizable offenses have been launched in cases brought under the general Articles 133 or 134[303] or their predecessors. The punitive Articles from 80 to 132 inclusive,[304] though many of them state more than one offense in a single article, all deal with specific offenses the elements of which are precisely defined therein. In addition to these, however, Congress has again seen fit to denounce as offenses, in general terms in Articles 133 and 134, conduct which traditionally from the foundation of the Government has been prohibited by the Articles of War.[305] Thus under Article 133, "Any officer, cadet or midshipman who is convicted of conduct unbecoming an officer and a gentleman shall be punished as a court-martial may direct." What constitutes "conduct unbecoming an officer and a gentleman" is not defined by Congress. Article 134 may be violated by any person subject to the Code. It provides for punishment of, "Though not specifically mentioned in this code," (1) "all disorders and neglects to the prejudice of good order and discipline in the armed forces," (2) "all conduct of a nature to bring discredit upon the armed forces, and" (3) "crimes and offenses not capital, of which persons subject to this code may be guilty." This Article defines three distinct classes of offenses,[306] although Congress has not seen fit to set them off by number or paragraphing, but leaves to custom and case law the determination of precisely what specific acts constitute violations under each of these prohibitions. Actually the type of conduct which will be charged as violative of these general articles has become considerably rigidified. It is unusual to proceed under the general articles unless the conduct is of

[303] 50 U. S. C. §§ 727, 728 (Supp. 1952).

[304] 50 U. S. C. §§ 674-726 (Supp. 1952).

[305] The American Articles of War enacted by the Second Continental Congress on June 30, 1775 contained these provisions:

> "XLVII. Whatsoever commissioned officer shall be convicted before a general court-martial, of behaving in a scandalous, infamous manner such as is unbecoming the character of an officer and a gentleman, shall be discharged from the services."
>
> "L. All crimes, not capital, and all disorders and neglects, which officers and soldiers may be guilty of, to the prejudice of good order and military discipline, though not mentioned in the articles of war, are to be taken cognizance of by a general or regimental court-martial, according to the nature and degree of the offense, and be punished at their discretion."

Reprinted in WINTHROP, MILITARY LAW AND PRECEDENTS 957 (2d ed. 1920); see discussion at page 720.

[306] See United States v. Snyder, 1 USCMA 423, 4 CMR 15 (1952); United States v. Messenger, 2 USCMA 21, 6 CMR 21 (1952); United States v. Long, 2 USCMA 60, 6 CMR 60 (1952); and United States v. Frantz, 2 USCMA 161, 7 CMR 37 (1953).

a type expressly classified thereunder in the Manual[307] and for which sample specifications are provided.[308]

"Crimes and offenses not capital" include acts, not made punishable by another article, which are denounced as crimes by Congress or under authority of Congress and made triable in the Federal civil courts.[309] Examples of these are indecent assaults; assaults with intent to commit murder, voluntary manslaughter, rape, robbery, sodomy, arson, burglary and housebreaking which are not embraced within Article 128; counterfeiting; false swearing; bribery; offenses against the mail; and misprison of felony. This list, which is by no means exhaustive, indicates that Congress has been content to leave a number of offenses which it has denounced in the United States Criminal Code[310] to be enforced by military justice procedures, against those subject to the Code, under the general articles rather than duplicating them in specific articles of the Code. As to murder,[311] manslaughter,[312] rape,[313] larceny,[314] robbery,[315] forgery,[316] maiming,[317] sodomy,[318] arson,[319] extortion,[320] certain assaults,[321] burglary,[322] housebreaking,[323] perjury,[324] and making or presenting a false or fraudulent claim,[325] Congress has seen fit to duplicate its prohibition in both the Criminal Code and in separate articles of the Uniform Code. Generally, these offenses to which separate articles are devoted are the more serious ones, but why Congress persists in using both the method of express denunciation and incorporation by reference in solving essentially the same legislative problem remains an inscrutable Congressional prerogative. Perhaps the best answer is that each ap-

[307] MANUAL FOR COURTS-MARTIAL, UNITED STATES, 1951 ¶¶ 212, 213, pp. 380-387.
[308] *Id.* App. 6c, pp. 488-495.
[309] *Id.* ¶ 213c, p. 383. Included are offenses denounced by state law, as to federal reservations within any given state, as provided by the Assimilative Crimes Act, 18 U. S. C. § 13 (Supp. 1952). This is true, however, only to the extent that such state law does not conflict with federal law or regulation. Williams v. United States, 327 U. S. 711 (1946); and see Johnson v. Yellow Cab Co., 321 U. S. 383 (1944); Air Terminal Services Inc., v. Rentzel, 81 F. Supp. 611 (E. D. Va. 1949); Nash v. Air Terminal Services Inc., 85 F. Supp. 545 (E. D. Va. 1949).
[310] Title 18, U. S. C. (Supp. 1952).
[311] Art. 118, 50 U. S. C. § 712 (Supp. 1952).
[312] Art. 119, 50 U. S. C. § 713 (Supp. 1952).
[313] Art. 120, 50 U. S. C. § 714 (Supp. 1952).
[314] Art. 121, 50 U. S. C. § 715 (Supp. 1952).
[315] Art. 122, 50 U. S. C. § 716 (Supp. 1952).
[316] Art. 123, 50 U. S. C. § 717 (Supp. 1952).
[317] Art. 124, 50 U. S. C. § 718 (Supp. 1952).
[318] Art. 125, 50 U. S. C. § 719 (Supp. 1952).
[319] Art. 126, 50 U. S. C. § 720 (Supp. 1952).
[320] Art. 127, 50 U. S. C. § 721 (Supp. 1952).
[321] Art. 128, 50 U. S. C. § 722 (Supp. 1952).
[322] Art. 129, 50 U. S. C. § 723 (Supp. 1952).
[323] Art. 130, 50 U. S. C. § 724 (Supp. 1952).
[324] Art. 131, 50 U. S. C. § 725 (Supp. 1952).
[325] Art. 132, 50 U. S. C. § 726 (Supp. 1952).

proach is a proper exercise of its power, "To make Rules for the Government and Regulation of the land and naval Forces."[326]

The contention that the general articles are unconstitutional because of uncertainty, and hence that an offense cannot be stated thereunder, is a favorite one with defense counsel. It was urged upon the Court of Military Appeals in the case of Marine Private Frantz, whom under Article 134 it was charged "did . . . wrongfully have in his possession with intent to deceive, an armed forces liberty pass . . . well knowing the same to be false." The Navy Board of Review reversed a conviction holding that an allegation of "intent to deceive" did not state an "intent to defraud" which was required by 18 U. S. C. § 499 which renders criminal the possession of a military pass "with intent to defraud." On certification, the Court ruled that the Board erred in assuming that the specification was laid under the "crimes and offenses not capital" part of the Article and held that deceitful possession of a liberty card was conduct "to the prejudice of good order and discipline," and that it was unnecessary to decide whether it also was "conduct of a nature to bring discredit upon the armed forces."[327] Passing to the asserted unconstitutionality of Article 134, the Court rejected this contention and said:

> "Surely the third clause of the Article is not vague. However, we cannot ignore the conceivable presence of uncertainty in the first two clauses. Assuming that civilian precedents in the field are applicable in full force to the military community, we do not perceive in the Article vagueness or uncertainty to an unconstitutional degree. The provision as it appears in the Uniform Code is no novelty to service criminal law. . . . On the contrary it has been a part of our military law since 1775, and directly traces its origin to British sources. . . . It must be judged, therefore, not *in vacuo,* but in the context in which the years have placed it. . . . That the clauses under scrutiny have acquired the core of a settled and understandable content of meaning is clear from the no less than forty-seven different offenses cognizable thereunder explicitly included in the Table of Maximum Punishments of the Manual, . . . paragraph 127c, pages 224-227. Accordingly, we conclude that the Article establishes a standard 'well enough known to enable those within . . . (its) reach to correctly apply them.' "[328]

[326] U. S. CONST., Art. I, § 8, cl. 14.
[327] United States v. Frantz, 2 USCMA 161, 163, 7 CMR 37, 38 (1953). *Accord,* United States v. Tomes (ACM 6187), 9 CMR 679 (1953); United States v. Blue, 3 USCMA 550, 13 CMR 106 (1953).
[328] United States v. Frantz, 2 USCMA 161, 163, 7 CMR 37, 39 (1953).

WAC Sergeant First Class Long and other enlisted WAC's were charged with and convicted of a violation of Article 134, "In that (they) . . . did . . . violate Title 18, Section 241, United States Code . . . by commiting an assault and battery upon Private First Class Carol A. Kierce, on account of her having previously attended and testified as a witness in a court of the United States, namely a Summary Court-Martial."[329] The contention was made that this allegation and proof did not establish an offense under Title 18, Section 241 because a summary court-martial was not a "court of the United States." The Court affirmed the conviction and held it was unnecessary to decide this question since in any event, the assaulting of a witness because she had testified before a military court would constitute a disorder to the prejudice of good order and discipline of the armed forces and, hence, an offense under Article 134. As to the fact that the pleader patently had considered the offense not "a disorder," but rather an "offense not capital" the Court said:

> "The phrase in the specification which states 'violate Title 18, Section 241, United States Code . . .' may be deleted and a substantive offense contrary to Article 134 is sufficiently alleged. The quoted clause may, therefore, be considered redundant and unnecessary."[330]

The case of Navy Captain Schumacher involved Article I, Paragraph 1, Articles for the Government of the Navy,[331] the naval antecedent of general Article 134. Under it accused was charged with and convicted of, among other things, that he did in violation of Section 311 of the Penal Code of Guam, from on or about June 15, 1950 to on or about August 1, 1950, expose his person and private parts to a young girl, who was offended and annoyed thereby, and further that he did during the same period take indecent liberties with a fifteen-year-old girl by placing his hand on the leg and under the dress of the girl. The Court rejected a contention that the specifications were defective in that they failed to allege with particularity the time of the commission of the offenses specified and expressly approved the *Manual* provision that "When the acts specified extend over a considerable period of time it is proper to allege them as having occurred, for example, "from about 15 June 1951 to about 4 November 1951."[332] In affirming the sentence of dismissal the Court also rejected the contention that this evidence established no crimes. It found that the indecent exposure violated the Guam Penal

[329] United States v. Long, 2 USCMA 60, 64, 6 CMR 60, 64 (1953).
[330] *Id.* at 66, 4 CMR at 66.
[331] REV. STAT. § 1624 (1800), 34 U. S. C. § 1200 (1946).
[332] MANUAL FOR COURTS-MARTIAL, UNITED STATES, 1951, ¶ 7, app. 6a, p. 470.

Code and thus was an offense not capital, and that the indecent liberties taken by this commanding officer of a Naval Air Station constituted scandalous conduct which tended to the destruction of good morals and was also prejudicial to good order and military discipline.[333]

Naval Airman Messenger was convicted by a special court-martial of impersonating an officer in violation of Article 134. The Board of Review reversed because there was no evidence that by the impersonation the accused gained some advantage to the prejudice of the person counterfeited. In the absence of such evidence the Board felt the offense was so minor that it should have been disposed of by trial by a summary court or by non-judicial punishment under Article 15.[334] On certification the Court reversed the Board and declared that, except possibly in a clear case of abuse, a Board of Review could not interfere with the discretion of the convening authority in the selection of the type of court to try a case and that here there had been no abuse in selecting a special court. The Court further held that:

> "The gravamen of the military offense of impersonation does not depend upon the accused deriving a benefit from the deception or upon some third party being misled, but rather upon whether the acts and conduct would influence adversely the good order and discipline of the armed forces."[335]

Marine Sergeant Snyder was charged with and convicted of three different violations of Article 134 in that he "did at Camp Lejeune . . . attempt to entice (three different military persons) to engage in sexual intercourse with a female to be directed to him by . . . Snyder."[336] Apparently in all seriousness, appellate defense counsel urged that pandering was not an offense under the Code and the Navy Board of Review agreed. Again the Navy Judge Advocate General certified the case and

[333] United States v. Schumacher, 2 USCMA 134, 136, 7 CMR 10, 12 (1953).

[334] 50 U. S. C. § 571 (Supp. 1952).

[335] United States v. Messenger, 2 USCMA 21, 24, 6 CMR 21, 24 (1952). Cited with approval were United States v. Miller (CM 266137), 43 BR 135 (1944) and United States v. Yaroslowsky (CM 316932), 66 BR 121 (1947). See United States v. Gillispie (CM 360289) 9 CMR 299 (1953). Similarly, it has been held that the unauthorized sale of blank pass forms constitutes conduct prejudicial to the Naval service and that an intent to deceive or defraud is not an essential element of the offense. United States v. Karl, 3 USCMA 427, 12 CMR 183 (1953).

[336] United States v. Snyder, 1 USCMA 423, 424, 4 CMR 15, 16 (1952). It has been held that the mere act of a single man and single woman registering as husband and wife and occupying a room together for the night with no other circumstances shown does not amount to an offense in violation of Article 134. United States v. Walters (CM 362540), 11 CMR 355 (1953); United States v. Prater (CM 339731), 5 BR/JC 221, 229 (1950); United States v. Martin (CM 317233), 66 BR 259 (1947). Apparently *contra* is United States v. Andrews (ACM 6105), 9 CMR 667 (1953).

the Court held that such solicitation even though not shown to have been accompanied by an expectation of financial gain constituted the offense of conduct prejudicial to good order and military discipline under the general article.

Navy Lieutenant Herndon was found guilty of a violation of Article 134 under a specification charging that he did at "Yokosuka, Japan, . . . unlawfully receive about two hundred pounds of coffee, . . . the property of the United States Government, which property . . . he . . . then well knew, had been stolen."[337] The Board of Review assumed that the specification intended to allege a violation of 18 U. S. C. § 641 and fell short of doing so in that it failed to state that the receiving was "with intent to convert to his own use or gain." For this reason it held the proceedings fatally defective. The Navy Judge Advocate General certified the case and the Court, while agreeing with the Board that the specification did not state an offense under Title 18, found it did define an offense under Article 134 as a disorder and neglect to the prejudice of good order and discipline, and that the knowing receipt of stolen government property is such an offense regardless of the presence of an intent to "convert it to his own use or gain." Again the Board of Review was reversed. It is perhaps appropriate to observe here that since dismissal is no longer mandatory upon a conviction under Article 133 and may be imposed as a part of the sentence against an erring officer under Article 134, and since Article 134 is considerably broader than Article 133, there is a current trend away from the use of Article 133 and to Article 134 in officer cases. However Article 133 may still be used.[337a]

Basic Airman Shores' conviction under Article 134 for being disrespectful in language to an air policeman while in the exercise of police duties was upheld by an Air Force Board as a disorder to the prejudice of good order and discipline.[338] It referred to as analogous, but not controlling, Army Board of Review cases holding it to be an offense in violation of Article of War 95, the predecessor of Article 133, for an

[337] United States v. Herndon, 1 USCMA 461, 463, 4 CMR 53, 55 (1952).

[337a] In United States v. Gomes, 3 USCMA 232, 236, 11 CMR 232, 236 (1953) the Court held: ". . . an allegation that an officer of the armed forces who, with intent to deceive, gives a known false statement to a special agent of the Federal Bureau of Investigation making inquiry on acts touching upon the execution of his official duties while in the employ of the Government sufficiently charges conduct unbecoming an officer and gentleman."

A specification alleging that the accused officer "did . . . wrongfully, corruptly, and dishonorably solicit (Sgt K) to aid and assist him . . . to obtain from the United States a jacket, field, wool, OD, and a pair of trousers, wool, OD, for his own personal use, to which he . . . was not entitled" sufficiently alleges an offense in violation of Article 133. United States v. Love (CM 365501), 12 CMR 290 (1953).

[338] United States v. Shores (ACM S-4378), 8 CMR 636 (1953).

officer to be disrespectful toward a military policeman in the execution of his duties.[339]

It has been previously noted that a civilian employee of the military in an overseas area who requires subordinate employees to donate goods and services for his personal use thereby engages in conduct of a nature to bring discredit upon the armed forces and may be convicted under Article 134.[340]

From the foregoing collection of authorities it is apparent that the persistent assaults of defense counsel against the general article have been singularly unsuccessful.[340a] There remains for consideration the one small area in which their efforts have been rewarded with success. Army Private Norris was charged with larceny of a vehicle under Article 121[341] and pleaded guilty to "taking without authority" in violation of Article 134. The law officer instructed the court that the accused could not be found guilty of any offense other than larceny or wrongful appropriation but failed to instruct as to the possible effect of intoxication on intent. The Court found the accused guilty of wrongful appropriation. The Board of Review held the law officer erred in both respects and affirmed only a finding of wrongful taking under Article 134. Upon certification, the Court affirmed the ruling that it was prejudicial error not to instruct on intoxication, but held there was no such offense as wrongful taking without the specific intent either permanently or temporarily to deprive another of the property. The Court said:

[339] United States v. Grubb (CM 234008), 20 BR 213, 219 (1943); United States v. Brandt (CM 253339), 34 BR 359, 363 (1944); United States v. Warren (CM 263080), 41 BR 181, 196 (1944); United States v. Rippey (CM 327522), 76 BR 131, 142 (1948).

[340] United States v. Marker, 1 USCMA 393, 3 CMR 127 (1952). See notes 245 and 267 *supra.*

[340a] The acts of operating a house of prostitution and misuse of assigned government billets by permitting rooms therein to be used for the purpose of carrying on illicit sexual relations, though both arising out of the same general course of conduct, have been held to constitute separate violations of Article 134 for each of which punishment may be imposed. United States v. Butler (CM 363644), 12 CMR 445 (1953).

It has been held that the misappropriation of a government vehicle for the purpose of transportation of a Korean prostitute constituted not only a violation of Article 121 as charged, but also a separate violation of Article 134 as an act to the prejudice of good order and discipline in the armed forces under a specification charging that the accused did ". . . wrongfully and unlawfully accept . . . the sum of thirty dollars to transport a Korean female in a government vehicle." United States v. Alexander, 3 USCMA 346, 347, 12 CMR 102, 103 (1953). In this case it was found that this violation of Article 134 constituted the offense of "graft" as listed in the Table of Maximum Punishments and hence would support a sentence of confinement of up to three years.

[341] 50 U. S. C. § 715 (Supp. 1952). In pertinent part it provides: "Any person . . . who wrongfully takes . . . from the possession of . . . any other person . . . personal property . . . with intent temporarily to deprive or defraud another person of the use and benefit of property or to appropriate the same to his own use . . . is guilty of wrongful appropriation."

> "... we are convinced that the general article ... embraces no criminal conversion offense lesser than wrongful appropriation as defined by Article 121. ...
>
> "... Article 134 should generally be limited to military offenses and those crimes not specifically delineated by the punitive articles. ... We cannot grant to the services unlimited authority to eliminate vital elements from common law crimes and offenses expressly defined by Congress and permit the remaining elements to be punished as an offense under Article 134."[342]

In a separate concurring opinion Judge Brosman pointed out the need for a statutory offense of "wrongful taking" in the military service not predicated upon a specific intent to deprive, and in a later companion case said:

> "... under the Code as presently written, wrongful taking is not an offense punishable under Article 134. The remedy for this hiatus must rest with the Congress."[343]

An Air Force Board of Review has held that simple negligence in the operation of an automobile, thereby causing non-fatal injury to another person, in the absence of other circumstances, is not conduct of a nature to bring discredit upon the armed forces within the meaning of Article 134, and is not an offense under the Code.[344]

From the very nature of the problem, and as a result of the small encouragement to be drawn from the careful and correct decision in the *Norris* case, it is likely that defense counsel will avidly continue to assail the validity of offenses charged under the general articles. It is also likely that their batting average in this effort will be unimpressive.[344a]

[342] United States v. Norris, 2 USCMA 236, 239, 8 CMR 36, 39 (1953). Followed in United States v. Haywood, 2 USCMA 376, 9 CMR 6 (1953). See also, United States v. Holy Rock, (CM 362791) 10 CMR 479 (1953) and United States v. Johnson, 3 USCMA 174, 11 CMR 174 (1953).

[343] United States v. Haywood, *supra,* at 377; 7.

[344] United States v. Eagleson (ACM 5666), 11 CMR 893 (1953). This must be distinguished from the offense of negligent homicide which may be sustained by evidence of simple negligence. The Court of Military Appeals has held that negligent homicide is an offense under Article 134 and may be punished as conduct of a nature to bring discredit upon the armed forces or, alternatively, as a disorder and neglect to the prejudice of good order and discipline in the armed forces. United States v. Roman, 1 USCMA 244, 2 CMR 150 (1952); United States v. Clark, 1 USCMA 201, 2 CMR 107 (1952); United States v. Kirchner, 1 USCMA 477, 4 CMR 69 (1952).

[344a] United States v. Doyle, 3 USCMA 585, 14 CMR 3 (1954) (shortage in accounts of disbursing officer); United States v. Thompson, 3 USCMA 620, 14 CMR 38 (1954) (carrying concealed weapon); United States v. Bentley, 3 USCMA 625, 14 CMR 43 (1954) (carrying concealed weapon); United States v. Eagleson, 3 USCMA 685, 14 CMR 103 (1954) (leaving scene of accident); United States v. McElroy, 3 USCMA 606, 14 CMR 24 (1954) (failure to render accounts); United States v. Kautz (CM 362116), 10 CMR 227 (1953) (falsely altering a military pass).

CHAPTER 5

Jurisdiction of the Sentence

A. *The Framework of Authorized Punishments*

The framework of legally authorized punishment in the courts-martial system is somewhat more complicated than that prevailing in most civilian penal systems. The basic jurisdiction to punish is prescribed by Congress as an integral part of each of the punitive articles. The only wholly mandatory sentence prescribed is that of death for wartime spying.[345] A mandatory alternative is imposed for premeditated murder and murder committed "in the perpetration or attempted perpetration of burglary, sodomy, rape, robbery, or aggravated arson," which compels a sentence of "death or imprisonment for life as a court-martial may direct."[346] Those convicted of wartime desertion or attempted desertion,[347] mutiny or sedition,[348] misbehavior before the enemy,[349] compelling or attempting to compel a commander to surrender,[350] improper use of a countersign,[351] forcing a safeguard,[352] aiding the enemy,[353] misbehavior of a sentinel in time of war[354] and rape by force[355] "shall suffer death or such other punishment as a court-martial shall direct." This unlimited discretion is permitted only for the most serious military offenses and forceful rape. All other offenses, no matter how trivial, so far as the basic provision in the punitive articles is concerned, may "be punished as a court-martial may direct."[356] The

345 Art. 106, 50 U. S. C. § 700 (Supp. 1952).
346 Art. 118, 50 U. S. C. § 712 (Supp. 1952).
347 Art. 85, 50 U. S. C. § 679 (Supp. 1952).
348 Art. 94, 50 U. S. C. § 688 (Supp. 1952).
349 Art. 99, 50 U. S. C. § 693 (Supp. 1952).
350 Art. 100, 50 U. S. C. § 694 (Supp. 1952).
351 Art. 101, 50 U. S. C. § 695 (Supp. 1952).
352 Art. 102, 50 U. S. C. § 696 (Supp. 1952).
353 Art. 104, 50 U. S. C. § 698 (Supp. 1952).
354 Art. 113, 50 U. S. C. § 707 (Supp. 1952).
355 Art. 120, 50 U. S. C. § 714 (Supp. 1952).
356 The only deviation from this language is found in general Art. 134, 50 U. S. C. § 728 (Supp. 1952) where the wording is: "shall be taken cognizance of

effect is to permit up to life imprisonment to be imposed for any offense. Congress traditionally has vested in the military this very broad discretion so that it might adequately cope with the widely differing conditions and considerations involved, depending on whether an offense was committed in peace or in war, at home or abroad, in garrison, in the field or in combat.[357]

Also traditional in the system of military punishments is the drastic curtailment of this power by the President in what is known as the Table of Maximum Punishments. Congress has continued this practice, in the Uniform Code, by expressly providing: "The punishment which a court-martial may direct for an offense shall not exceed such limits as the President may prescribe for the offense."[358] This permits curtailment, but not enlargement, of the punishment authorized by the punitive articles. The President liberally exercised this power in the Table of Maximum Punishments, an integral part of the *Manual,*[359] prescribed by Executive Order 10214, February 8, 1951.[360] For example, a two-day absence without leave which could be punishable by life imprisonment, dishonorable discharge and total forfeitures under the literal terms of punitive Article 86, can under the Table of Maximum Punishments not be punished more severely than by six days' confinement at hard labor, forfeiture of four days' pay, reduction in grade and a reprimand.[361] The Table of Maximum Punishments in fact substantially curtails authorized punishments for all offenses except mutiny, sedition, misbehavior before the enemy, compelling surrender, improper use of a countersign, knowingly forcing a safeguard, aiding the enemy, misconduct as a prisoner, spying, murder, rape, and conduct unbecoming an officer and a gentleman.[362] In dealing with general Article 134, the Table expressly sets forth some sixty-seven different specific offenses thereunder and establishes maximum penalties for each, running from twenty years for assaulting with intent to commit murder or rape, down to one month for breach of restriction.[363]

---

by a general or special or summary court court-martial, according to the nature and degree of the offense, and punished at the discretion of such court." This occurs because of the express reference to the inferior military courts. This excludes from the power of a general court the death sentence only.

[357] *Hearing of Subcommittee of the Committee on Armed Services,* H. R. REP. No. 37, 81st Cong., 1st Sess., pp. 1087-1089 (1949).

[358] Art. 56, 50 U. S. C. § 637 (Supp. 1952). Exec. Order No. 10565, 19 FED. REG. — (1954) increased maximum punishment for absence without leave and missing movement.

[359] MANUAL FOR COURTS-MARTIAL, UNITED STATES, 1951, ¶ 127c, pp. 214-228.

[360] *Id.* at IX.

[361] *Id.* at 220. Under Exec. Order No. 10565 a maximum of one month confinement and forfeiture of two-thirds of one month's pay may now be imposed for this offense.

[362] *Id.* at 221-224.

[363] *Id.* at 224-227. The rule applicable to the other offenses chargeable under the general article is stated at page 214 of the MANUAL, as follows: "Offenses not listed in this table, and not included within an offense listed, or not closely related to either, remain punishable as authorized by the United States Code (see, gen-

Under Article 56 the President may at any time change the provisions of the Table of Maximum Punishments by executive order so long as such change does not exceed the limit prescribed by Congress in the punitive article itself. This power has been sparingly exercised. During World War II the Table was suspended as to desertion, advising or aiding desertion, absence without leave, and misbehavior of sentinels,[364] but was promptly reimposed shortly after the termination of actual hostilities.[365] On August 8, 1950, the President again suspended the Table as to desertion, advising or aiding desertion, absence without leave, assaulting or disobeying a superior officer, insubordination to a noncommissioned officer in the execution of his office and misbehavior of sentinels thereafter committed. This suspension, however, applied only to these offenses when committed in any area controlled by the Commander-in-Chief, Far East.[366] The automatic suspension of the Table provided for by the *Manual*[367] "upon a declaration of war" applies to soliciting either desertion, mutiny, sedition, or misbehavior before the enemy,[368] and to desertion,[369] absence without leave,[370] missing movement,[371] striking or wilfully disobeying an officer,[372] misbehavior of a sentinel[373] and malingering.[374] Since there has been no declaration of war after the Code became effective this provision has remained inoperative.

There can be no doubt that the maximum punishments prescribed by Congress in the punitive articles are jurisdictional and that any part of a sentence which is in excess thereof is void and unenforceable. This does not mean that the portion of an excessive sentence which is within the authorized maximum is void or unenforceable. This result is clearly contemplated by Congress in its legislative direction to the convening authority that he "shall approve only . . . such part or amount of the sentence as he finds correct in law and fact . . . ,"[375] and to the board

erally, Title 18) or the Code of the District of Columbia, whichever prescribed punishment is the lesser, or as authorized by the custom of the service." Applied in United States v. Long, 2 USCMA 60, 71, 6 CMR 60, 71 (1953).

[364] Exec. Order No. 9048, 7 FED. REG. 775 (1942) and Exec. Order No. 9267, 7 FED. REG. 9221 (1942).

[365] Exec. Order No. 9683, 11 FED. REG. 789 (1946) and Exec. Order No. 9772, 11 FED. REG. 9325 (1946).

[366] Exec. Order No. 1049, 15 FED. REG. 5149 (1950).

[367] MANUAL FOR COURTS-MARTIAL, UNITED STATES, 1951, ¶ 127c, p. 217.

[368] Art. 82, 50 U. S. C. § 676 (Supp. 1952).

[369] Art. 85, 50 U. S. C. § 679 (Supp. 1952).

[370] Art. 86, 50 U. S. C. § 680 (Supp. 1952).

[371] Art. 87, 50 U. S. C. § 681 (Supp. 1952).

[372] Art. 90, 50 U. S. C. § 684 (Supp. 1952).

[373] Art. 113, 50 U. S. C. § 707 (Supp. 1952).

[374] Art. 115, 50 U. S. C. § 709 (Supp. 1952).

[375] Art. 64, 50 U. S. C. § 651 (Supp. 1952).

of review that, "it shall affirm only . . . such part or amount of the sentence as it finds correct in law and fact. . . ."[376]

An academic problem arises as to the effect of the limits imposed by the Table of Maximum Punishments upon jurisdiction to punish. It seems clear that these limitations do not destroy it since by subsequent executive order, so providing, jurisdiction to punish may be exercised up to the maximum authorized by Congress. It is probably accurate to say that the provisions of the Table of Maximum Punishments impose binding limitations upon the *exercise* of jurisdiction to punish, as distinguished from destroying jurisdiction itself. This question would be reached for decision only in event all the military appellate tribunals should approve a sentence which, while within the maximum prescribed by Congress, was in excess of that authorized by the Table. On petition for habeas corpus it would then be necessary to determine whether the amount imposed in excess of the maximum prescribed by the Table was void for lack of jurisdiction. The Court of Military Appeals has clearly indicated that no case will be permitted to reach such a status, by its declaration that, "The general provisions of paragraph 127b (of the *Manual*) are limitations on punishment fully as much as are the specific limits set out in the Table of Maximum Punishments,"[377] and by its further statement, "we disclaim any intent to classify these (rights) as jurisdictional . . . we can reverse for errors of law which materially prejudice the substantial rights of the accused. . . ."[378] Relief would certainly be granted even if the error were held not to be jurisdictional.

B. *Limited Powers of Inferior Military Courts*

In dealing with problems of jurisdiction to sentence not only must resort be had to the punitive articles of the Code and the Table of Maximum Punishments of the *Manual,* but care must be exercised not to exceed the maximum punishment imposable by a summary or special court where their sentences are under consideration. Congress has provided:

> "Summary courts-martial may, under such limitations as the President may prescribe, adjudge any punishment not forbidden by this code except death, dismissal, dishonorable discharge or bad conduct discharge, confinement in excess of one month, hard labor without confinement in excess of forty-five days, restriction

[376] Art. 66(c), 50 U. S. C. § 653 (Supp. 1952). This comports with the rule in the federal civil courts that if the excess is separable from the residue the legal portion of the sentence will remain undisturbed. McKinney v. Finletter, 205 F. 2d 761 (10th Cir. 1953).

[377] United States v. Murgaw, 2 USCMA 369, 371, 8 CMR 169, 171 (1953).

[378] United States v. Clay, 1 USCMA 74, 78, 1 CMR 74, 78 (1951). See also United States v. Davis, 1 USCMA 102, 107, 2 CMR 8, 13 (1952).

to certain specified limits in excess of two months or forfeiture of pay in excess of two-thirds of one month's pay."[379]

Affirmatively stated, a summary court may sentence to confinement at hard labor for one month, or to forty-five days' hard labor without confinement, or restriction for two months, or to a proportional amount of the three.[380] For example, ten days' confinement, plus fifteen days' hard labor without confinement, plus twenty days' restriction would be permissible. In addition to the above, the forfeiture of two-thirds of one month's pay, a reduction in grade and a reprimand could also be imposed. As to noncommissioned and petty officers of the first three grades a summary court may not impose confinement, hard labor without confinement, nor reduction except to the next inferior grade.[381]

As to special courts, Congress has declared that they may:

> ". . . under such limitations as the President may prescribe, adjudge any punishment not forbidden by this code except death, dishonorable discharge, dismissal, confinement in excess of six months, hard labor without confinement in excess of three months, forfeiture of pay exceeding two-thirds pay per month, or forfeiture of pay for a period exceeding six months. A bad conduct discharge shall not be adjudged unless a complete record of the proceedings and testimony before the court has been made."[382]

[379] Art. 20, 50 U. S. C. § 580 (Supp. 1952).

[380] MANUAL FOR COURTS-MARTIAL, UNITED STATES, 1951, ¶ 127c, p. 215; Table of Equivalent Punishments. These equivalents may be applied to enlisted accused by either a summary or special court so long as the sentence does not include a punitive discharge.

[381] *Id.* ¶ 126c(2), p. 208.

[382] Art. 19, 50 U. S. C. § 579 (Supp. 1952). In United States v. Bancroft, 3 USCMA 3, 11 CMR 3 (1953) a Marine sentry was tried by a special court-martial for sleeping on post during the Korean conflict. The officer exercising general court-martial authority had not declared the offense to be non-capital. The Court of Military Appeals found that the Korean conflict, though not predicated upon any formal declaration of war, did constitute "time of war" within the meaning of the phrase as used in Art. 113, 50 U. S. C. § 707 (Supp. 1952), authorizing a death sentence. Accordingly, it held the offense was capital and that a special court-martial had no jurisdiction to try it.

In United States v. Whitman, 3 USCMA 179, 181, 11 CMR 179, 181 (1953) the record of trial in a navy special court case was in part a narrative summary and in part a verbatim account. The court said: "The punitive discharge . . . cannot stand without the support of a verbatim record. This portion of the sentence is, therefore, illegal."

Where a special court-martial imposed a sentence for bad conduct discharge, reduction in grade, and restriction to limits for three months and the convening authority suspended the bad conduct discharge, the Court has held it was proper to impose restriction as a less severe type of restraint than confinement and this without regard to the Table of Equivalent Punishments which is inapplicable where a punitive discharge is imposed. United States v. Benson, 3 USCMA 351, 12 CMR 107 (1953).

So far as the Army is concerned, the exercise of the jurisdiction to impose a bad conduct discharge has been prohibited in special courts by the issuance of a regulation by the Secretary of the Army forbidding the use of reporters in special court-martial cases, except with prior authority of the Secretary.[383] Such regulation is authorized by the *Manual* and was consistent with a recommendation made by the Court of Military Appeals and by The Judge Advocates General of the Army and Air Force, but from which The Judge Advocate General of the Navy and the General Counsel of the Treasury Department dissented.[384] No such administrative limitation has been imposed on special courts by any of the services except the Army.

C. *Miscellaneous Limitations on Punishments*

General courts are subject to no limitation on punishment except those contained in the punitive articles and the Table of Maximum Punishments.[384a] One further exception is that where a convening authority has directed that a non-mandatory capital case be treated as not capital to permit the use of depositions by the prosecution a death penalty may not be imposed.[385]

No military court upon a rehearing or a new trial may impose a sentence more severe than that originally adjudged by a lawful court in the same case unless the sentence prescribed for the offense is manda-

[383] Army Special Regulation 22-145-1 (1950), as amended by C-1 (March 6, 1952).

[384] MANUAL FOR COURTS-MARTIAL, UNITED STATES, 1951, ¶ 7, p. 12; ANNUAL REPORT OF THE UNITED STATES COURT OF MILITARY APPEALS AND JUDGE ADVOCATES GENERAL OF THE ARMED FORCES, 1952, p. 4.

[384a] Subject to certain limitations imposed by the MANUAL FOR COURTS-MARTIAL, UNITED STATES, 1951 ¶ 127c, § B, p. 228, a general court may, in addition to other authorized punishments, impose a fine. In United States v. DeAngelis, 3 USCMA 298, 12 CMR 54 (1953) the accused officer, convicted of larceny, was sentenced to dismissal, total forfeitures, confinement at hard labor for five years (the maximum confinement authorized by the Table of Maximum Punishments), and a fine of $10,000, "or further confinement until the fine is paid, but not exceeding two more years." Confronted with this interesting situation the Court stated the problem and disposed of it as follows: "The sole question is, whether the additional confinement provided in the event the accused fails to pay the imposed fine is excessive. . . . The provision for further confinement was not made as punishment for the offense, but merely as a means of coercing the collection of the fine imposed. While the accused may suffer further imprisonment as a result of this provision, it must be remembered that 'he carries the keys of his prison in his own pocket.' In re Nevitt, 177 F. 448, 461."

Loss of promotion rights is not an authorized punishment, at least for Army and Air Force personnel. MANUAL FOR COURTS-MARTIAL, UNITED STATES, 1951, ¶ 126i, p. 212. The inclusion in an Air Force sentence of a provision that the accused "not be considered for promotion" for twenty-four months is "illegal." United States v. Taylor (ACM 6458) 10 CMR 669 (1953). See United States v. Braden (ACM 7712) 14 CMR 617 (1954).

[385] Art. 49(f), 50 U. S. C. § 624 (Supp. 1952). See United States v. Gann and Sommer, 3 USCMA 12, 11 CMR 12 (1953).

tory.[386] This restriction of course goes far beyond any principle or requirement of constitutional due process.[387]

Executive Order No. 10214 promulgating the 1951 *Manual* expressly provided,

> "That the maximum punishment for an offense committed prior to May 31, 1951, shall not exceed the applicable limit in effect at the time of the commission of such offense."[388]

The Court of Military Appeals has had occasion to apply this rule. Lieutenant Colonel Downard was charged under Article of War 95[389] with conduct unbecoming an officer and a gentleman which involved assaulting and cursing his wife in the vicinity of the Fort Monroe Offi-

[386] Art. 63(b), 50 U. S. C. § 650 (Supp. 1952) and MANUAL FOR COURTS-MARTIAL, UNITED STATES, 1951, ¶ 109g(2), p. 179. Cf. United States v. Iverson (CM 362797), 11 CMR 306 (1953) and United States v. Castner, 3 USCMA 466, 13 CMR 22 (1953).

The same rule applies to action taken on a sentence by a convening authority. MANUAL FOR COURTS-MARTIAL, UNITED STATES, 1951, ¶ 88a, p. 147. Thus in United States v. White (ACM S-7152), 12 CMR 783 (1953) where a special court, as part of its sentence, imposed a forfeiture of sixty-five dollars per month for fifty-six days and the convening authority, as to this part of the sentence, approved a forfeiture of fifty-eight dollars per month for two months, the Board of Review held that, although the forfeiture approved was less than that adjudged, the increase in its duration increased the punishment and only a forfeiture of fifty-eight dollars per month for one month and twenty-six days was approved. In United States v. O'Shea, 3 USCMA 434, 12 CMR 190 (1953) it was held that a convening authority may properly reduce a sentence of confinement to hard labor for three months to sixty days restriction. *Accord,* United States v. Austin, 3 USCMA 433, 12 CMR 189 (1953).

The same prohibition against increasing a sentence also applies to a proceeding in revision before the original court-martial. Art. 62(b)(2), 50 U.S.C. § 649 (Supp. 1952). See, however, United States v. Bates (CM 365561), 12 CMR 395 (1953), a bigamy conviction in which the sentence announced by the court was dishonorable discharge, total forfeitures and confinement at hard labor for "not to exceed six months." The next day the court, on its own motion, convened in revision proceedings, the president stating that the previous announcement did not "correctly reflect the sentence that was determined." The court then closed, reopened, and announced the sentence as dishonorable discharge, total forfeitures and confinement at hard labor "for six months." Held: ". . . the correct announcement of the sentence in revision proceedings was not a modification of the sentence originally determined nor an increase in the punishment." *Cf.* United States v. Long, 4 USCMA 101, 15 CMR 101 (1954) and United States v. Robinson, 4 USCMA 12, 15 CMR 12 (1954).

The same prohibition applies to subsequent sentence action by a court-martial in the same proceeding, once it has announced a sentence lawful in part. United States v. Iverson (CM 362797), 11 CMR 306 (1953), in which the Board said: "Where a duly adjudicated and announced divisible sentence is legal in part and illegal in part, the maximum sentence which may be adjudicated by a court-martial upon reconsideration, where there is no mandatory sentence involved, is the legal portion of the sentence originally adjudicated and announced, and . . . any increase in the severable legal portion itself constitutes a prohibited increase in the severity of the sentence." See also United States v. Castner, 3 USCMA 446, 13 CMR 22 (1953).

[387] See Palko v. Connecticut, 302 U. S. 319, 322 (1937).

[388] MANUAL FOR COURTS-MARTIAL, UNITED STATES, 1951, p. IX.

[389] 41 STAT. 806 (1920).

cers' Club. The acts involved occurred prior to May 31, 1951, but the case was tried thereafter. The mandatory penalty upon conviction prescribed by Article of War 95 was dismissal, whereas the successor Article 133[390] prescribed that punishment shall be as a court-martial may direct. The law officer instructed that dismissal was mandatory and the court imposed that sentence. The Court of Military Appeals reversed, held this instruction constituted prejudicial error, and stated that a proper instruction would have been that the court might assess punishment at its discretion, not in excess of dismissal. It pointed out that anything in excess of dismissal would constitute an ex post facto application of the new Code, but that the accused was entitled to the benefit of the possibility of a lesser sentence under it.[391] Jurisdiction was not directly involved since under proper instruction the court could have imposed dismissal.

Another case raising essentially the same issue was that of Private Murgaw who was, after May 31, 1951, tried and convicted of a desertion committed before the effective date of the Code.[392] Under the previous law a general court could impose up to twelve months' confinement without also adjudging a punitive discharge,[393] whereas the present *Manual* prohibited confinement in excess of six months unless the sentence also included a punitive discharge.[394] In answer to a question by the court the law officer advised that a sentence of confinement in excess of six months could not be given without also imposing a punitive discharge. The court imposed a bad conduct discharge twelve months' confinement and partial forfeitures for twelve months. The convening authority not only suspended the discharge but ultimately completely remitted it as well as most of the confinement and forfeiture. The Court held remission of the discharge did not render the issue moot, since if improperly imposed the accused was entitled to have that fact affirmatively appear upon his service record. It then decided that the provision of the current *Manual* was more stringent than its predecessor and, therefore, the law officer should have instructed that confinement up to twelve months could be imposed without a punitive discharge. With one judge dissenting, the Court then proceeded to cure the prejudicial error by setting the bad conduct discharge aside. Again jurisdiction was not reached since the sentence imposed by the court was permissible had it been properly instructed.

390 50 U. S. C. § 727 (Supp. 1952).
391 United States v. Downard, 1 USCMA 346, 3 CMR 80 (1952).
392 United States v. Murgaw, 2 USCMA 369, 8 CMR 169 (1953).
393 MANUAL FOR COURTS-MARTIAL, UNITED STATES ARMY, 1949, ¶ 117b.
394 MANUAL FOR COURTS-MARTIAL, UNITED STATES, 1951, ¶ 127b, p. 214.

In the case of Electrician's Mate Second Class Flood, a Navy general court sitting under the Code sentenced the accused to a bad conduct discharge, confinement for ten months, forfeiture of ten months' pay and reduction to electrician's mate third class, having found him guilty of absence without leave for a period commencing before the Code was effective. The Court applied the rule that the sentence could not be greater than that authorized by the current *Manual* and held that so much of the sentence as extended to confinement and forfeitures in excess of six months was "illegal."[395] Here the Court was dealing with a clearly excessive sentence but simply characterized it as "illegal." As before noted, it makes little practical difference whether the Court treats such excess as jurisdictional or simply as prejudicial error so long as it grants relief. In this same case it was held that since Navy regulations permitted only one grade reductions where confinement was not in excess of three months and required reduction to the lowest enlisted grade where longer confinement was imposed the confinement must be further reduced to not to exceed three months since the sentence imposed had reduced accused only one grade. This result points up the necessity for care by courts in imposing sentences all parts of which are consistent, since any ambiguity will be resolved against the government and in favor of the accused. Judge Latimer dissented and agreed with the view taken by the Board of Review that the portion of the sentence reducing the accused only one grade should be treated as a nullity.

D. *Excessive Punishments Resulting from Other Errors of Law*

Since all concerned with the functioning of the military justice system are alert to prevent the imposition of unauthorized punishments it is not surprising that practically all cases reaching the Court of Military Appeals involving excessive sentences result from some collateral error of law which caused the court, the convening authority and the Board of Review to believe the sentence imposed was lawful. A number of such cases has arisen under what may be termed "the military habitual criminal act." This phrase, however, is misleading in that it is only as to relatively minor offenses that the proof of prior offenses increases permissible punishments. This authorization stems not from the Code but from Section B of the Table of Maximum Punishments which relaxes its other limitations so that:

> "If an accused is found guilty of an offense or offenses for none of which dishonorable or bad conduct discharge is author-

[395] United States v. Flood, 2 USCMA 114, 6 CMR 114 (1952) citing United States v. Emerson, 1 USCMA 43, 1 CMR 43 (1951) and United States v. Brasher, 2 USCMA 50, 6 CMR 50 (1952).

ized, proof of two or more previous convictions will authorize bad conduct discharge and forfeiture of all pay and allowances and, if the confinement otherwise authorized is less than three months, confinement at hard labor for three months. In such a case no forfeiture shall be imposed for any period in excess of the period of confinement so adjudged."[396]

The Navy has made considerable use of this provision in imposing bad conduct discharges. In a number of these cases the data as to the prior convictions was simply read to the court by trial counsel and the records themselves were neither marked for identification nor offered in evidence. The Court of Military Appeals held this state of the record did not constitute proof of prior convictions, found sentences imposed in reliance thereon excessive and remanded for rehearings.[397] The Court said, "That an excessive sentence is prejudicial is apparent,"[398] thus treating the problem as one of prejudicial error rather than jurisdiction.

A variant of the above situation arose in the trial of Fireman Apprentice Chapman for being absent without leave for twenty days. Of the three prior convictions admitted in evidence two, due to technical defects, were inadmissible. Upon rehearing the prior convictions were proved by competent evidence and the sentence imposed was a bad conduct discharge, confinement for three months and forfeiture of $36.00 per month for three months. Accused contended before the Board of Review that since sixty days' confinement was the maximum sentence properly imposable by the first court this could not be exceeded by the rehearing sentence. The Judge Advocate General of the Navy certified this question and the Court upheld the sentence announcing that where

[396] MANUAL FOR COURTS-MARTIAL, UNITED STATES, 1951, ¶ 127c, p. 228. Under this provision a summary court is authorized to sentence an accused to not to exceed thirty days confinement at hard labor upon a showing of two previous convictions when the maximum punishment for the offense of which the accused was convicted is less than thirty days. Letter, JAGJ 1953/3857 (5 May 1953).

To constitute an admissible "prior conviction" both the date of commission and the date of conviction must precede the date of commission of the offense being tried in the proceeding in which it is offered. United States v. Henson (ACM S-6725), 11 CMR 832 (1953). See also, United States v. Crusoe, 3 USCMA 793, 798, 14 CMR 211, 216 (1954). The court approved section B in United States v. Prescott, 2 USCMA 122, 6 CMR 122 (1952).

[397] United States v. Carter, 1 USCMA 108, 2 CMR 14 (1952); United States v. Zimmerman, 1 USCMA 160, 2 CMR 66 (1952); United States v. Trimiar, 1 USCMA 727, 2 CMR 169 (1952); United States v. Schabel, 1 USCMA 275, 3 CMR 9 (1952); United States v. Adams, 1 USCMA 275, 3 CMR 9 (1952); United States v. Hand, 1 USCMA 301, 3 CMR 35 (1952); United States v. Pruchniewski, 1 USCMA 328, 3 CMR 62 (1952); United States v. Deweese, 1 USCMA 400, 3 CMR 134 (1952); United States v. Townsend, 1 USCMA 411, 4 CMR 33 (1952). See United States v. Parker, 3 USCMA 272, 12 CMR 28 (1953).

[398] United States v. Carter, 1 USCMA 108, 114, 2 CMR 14, 20 (1952).

error extends to sentence only, the second court is not restricted by the error affecting the sentence of the first.[399]

Due to the express provision in Section B of the Table of Maximum Punishments that where prior convictions are necessary to the imposition of a bad conduct discharge "no forfeiture shall be imposed for any period in excess of the period of confinement so adjudged,"[400] the Court of Military Appeals held that a sentence imposed by a Navy special court for a two-day absence without leave of a $36.00 forfeiture and a suspended bad conduct discharge, but without confinement, was as to the forfeiture "excessive and therefore illegal."[401] The Court approved the suspended bad conduct discharge but did not make clear whether under these circumstances it would approve a forfeiture of two days' pay for each day of absence as provided by Paragraph 127c of the *Manual.* In civil life police court fines are not safeguarded with such elaborate appellate procedures. Perhaps it is cases of this kind which have evoked the recommendation of the Court of Military Appeals that the power to impose bad conduct discharges be denied to special courts-martial.[402]

Another provision of the Table of Maximum Punishments which has presented sentencing problems is the requirement that:

> "If an offense not listed in the table is included in an offense which is listed and is also closely related to some other listed offense, the lesser punishment prescribed for either the included or closely related offense will prevail as the maximum limit of punishment."[403]

Army Private Beach, a unit mail clerk, pleaded guilty to negligently permitting some three hundred pieces of mail to accumulate over a period of eight months without delivering it in violation of general Article 134.[404] The Board of Review approved a sentence to dishonorable dis-

[399] United States v. Chapman, 2 USCMA 138, 7 CMR 14 (1953). Pursuant to Article 44(b) until a prior conviction has been finally approved on appeal or review it is prejudicial error to offer it in evidence in another case. United States v. Drummon (ACM 5243), 5 CMR 400, 403, 404 (1952) and United States v. Engle, 3 USCMA 41, 45, 11 CMR 41, 45 (1953).

[400] MANUAL FOR COURTS-MARTIAL, UNITED STATES, 1951, ¶ 127c, p. 228.

[401] United States v. Watkins, 2 USCMA 287, 8 CMR 87 (1953).

[402] ANNUAL REPORT OF THE UNITED STATES COURT OF MILITARY APPEALS AND JUDGE ADVOCATES GENERAL OF THE ARMED FORCES, 1952, p. 4.

[403] MANUAL FOR COURTS-MARTIAL, UNITED STATES, 1951, ¶ 127c, p. 214. The "closely related" rule was applied where a specification under Article 134 alleged the accused "... a married man, did ... wrongfully cohabit with ... a woman not his wife." The law officer instructed that the sentence might be the same as that authorized for adultery. In rejecting a contention that the sentence could be no greater than that for a simple disorder under Article 134, the Board of Review held: ". . . if the offense here charged is not adultery, then it is so similar that the offense designated in the Table of Maximum Punishments by that name should control the punishment." United States v. Bailey (CM 365023), 12 CMR 564 (1953).

[404] 50 U. S. C. § 728 (Supp. 1952).

charge, total forfeitures and confinement for two years. On certification by The Judge Advocate General of the Army, the Court of Military Appeals[405] rejected the contention of the government that this offense was punishable as lesser included to that of obstructing the mail, which under the Table would authorize a dishonorable discharge and five years' confinement,[406] and found instead that this offense was "closely related" to a dereliction in performance of duty under Article 92.[407] Since this latter offense was punishable by a maximum sentence of only three months' confinement and forfeiture of two-thirds pay for three months[408] the Court held that portion of the sentence imposed in excess of these limits to be "illegal."

The opposite conclusion was reached in applying the "closely related" rule to the case of Marine Private Stewart who had pleaded guilty to desertion in violation of Article 8 of Articles for the Government of the Navy.[409] A Board of Review found the specification as worded stated only a desertion from "command" to the prejudice of good order and discipline and not desertion "from the Naval service." The absence had been for nearly three years and the sentence imposed was a dishonorable discharge and three years' confinement, the maximum authorized by the Table for a desertion terminated by apprehension.[410] Accused contended that his offense, as approved by the Board of Review, was "closely related" to simple absence without leave, the maximum punishment for which is dishonorable discharge and six months' confinement.[411] The Court of Military Appeals affirmed the sentence and said:

> "Patently, his absence from command for almost three years is hardly *closely* related to mere absence without leave. Thus, having concluded that the offense alleged here is at least included within desertion of a type other than to avoid hazardous duty or to shirk important service, and that it is not 'closely related' to another enumerated offense, the punishment for the former must govern."[412]

[405] United States v. Beach, 2 USCMA 172, 7 CMR 48 (1953).
[406] MANUAL FOR COURTS-MARTIAL, UNITED STATES, 1951, ¶ 127c, p. 226.
[407] 50 U. S. C. § 686 (Supp. 1952).
[408] MANUAL FOR COURTS-MARTIAL, UNITED STATES, 1951, ¶ 127c, p. 221.
[409] 34 U. S. C. § 1200 (1946).
[410] MANUAL FOR COURTS-MARTIAL, UNITED STATES, 1951, ¶ 127c, p. 220.
[411] *Ibid.*
[412] United States v. Stewart, 2 USCMA 321, 8 CMR 121 (1953). A similar problem is presented by footnote 5 to the Table of Maximum Punishments at page 221 of the MANUAL FOR COURTS-MARTIAL, UNITED STATES, 1951. It provides that the punishment prescribed for failure to obey a lawful general order "does not apply in those cases wherein the accused is found guilty of an offense which, although involving a failure to obey a lawful order, is specifically listed elsewhere in this table." Pursuant thereto it has been held that carrying a concealed weapon in violation of a post regulation though prosecuted under Article 92,

In the case of Corporal Grossman the question presented was what maximum controls where the offense proved by the evidence is more serious than the one charged in the specification. There the accused was charged, in addition to other offenses, with drunken driving under Article 111[413] with no allegation of personal injury resulting therefrom. The evidence in fact established such injury. The maximum provided by the Table for drunken driving resulting in personal injury is dishonorable discharge and one year's confinement but for drunk driving alone is bad conduct discharge and six months' confinement. Here the Court of Military Appeals found it was prejudicial error for the law officer to have instructed that the larger penalty might be imposed and said: "A sentence is limited by the facts alleged in the specification. . . ."[414]

A final example of excessive sentencing resulting from error of law as to another point occurred in the case of Private Cooper who, with his co-accused, was charged, among other things, with the offense of robbery and assault with intent to commit robbery. The evidence established that these two separate specifications each pertained to the same robbery but the law officer in effect instructed that each might be considered as separate offenses for sentencing purposes. The *Manual* provisions state that:

> "The maximum authorized punishment may be imposed for each of two or more separate offenses arising out of the same act or transaction. . . . An accused may not be punished for both a principal offense and for an offense included therein. . . ."[415]

cannot be punished more severely than is authorized under Article 134 for the offense of carrying a concealed weapon. United States v. Amato (CM 360145), 9 CMR 416 (1953). *Accord,* United States v. McGovern (CM 363388), 10 CMR 391 (1953).

[413] 50 U. S. C. § 705 (Supp. 1952).

[414] United States v. Grossman, 2 USCMA 406, 9 CMR 36 (1953).

[415] MANUAL FOR COURTS-MARTIAL, UNITED STATES, 1951, ¶ 76a(6), p. 123. It has been held that absence without leave upon a change of station from Brooklyn, New York to Newport, Rhode Island, which conduct also violated an express lawful order of a commanding officer to report to Newport, constituted two separate offenses for sentencing purposes. United States v. Larney, 2 USCMA 563, 10 CMR 61 (1953). Likewise the offenses of making a forged instrument and uttering that same forged instrument, even though occurring substantially in one transaction, are separate and the maximum punishment may be imposed for each. United States v. Parr (ACM 6326), 10 CMR 840 (1953). The offenses of desertion with intent to remain away permanently and desertion with intent to avoid important service embody separate and distinct elements, each requires proof of a fact not required in the other, and the maximum punishment may be imposed for each when the two arise out of one transaction. United States v. Greer (CM 366411), 12 CMR 499 (1953). However, under two specifications of a single conspiracy the maximum sentence for only one may be imposed. United States v. Crusoe, 3 USCMA 793, 796, 14 CMR 211, 214 (1954).

The Court of Military Appeals declared the instruction as given was prejudicial error, and opined:

> "Where, as here, the assault with intent to commit a robbery constitutes the force and violence laying (*sic*) at the core of the robbery charge, the former certainly is a lesser crime included within the latter. . . . The maximum punishment for each is . . . ten years. . . . This is the maximum which might be adjudged in this case under the two specifications here in question."[416]

E. *Cruel and Unusual Punishment*

Article 55 of the Code, in part, provides that "cruel or unusual punishment, shall not be adjudged by any court-martial. . . ."[417] However, Article 15(a)(2)(F) thereof expressly permits,

> "if imposed upon a person attached to or embarked in a vessel, confinement on bread and water or diminished rations for a period not to exceed three consecutive days."[418]

The *Manual* purported to prohibit Army and Air Force courts from imposing bread and water punishment and to authorize Navy and Coast Guard courts to adjudge confinement on bread and water for not to exceed thirty days,[419] in keeping with unbroken Navy practice. In the case of Marine Private Wappler, shore-based at Camp Pendleton, California, a special court in an absence without leave and missing movement case, as part of its sentence included a bad conduct discharge and thirty-day confinement on bread and water with a full ration every third day. This set the stage for one of the more spectacular decisions rendered by the Court of Military Appeals. It held confinement on bread and water was cruel and unusual punishment prohibited by Article 55 and that accordingly that part of the sentence "was illegal and void."[420] It further held that since confinement on bread and water was included in the Table of Equivalent Punishments[421] it could in no event be imposed as part of a sentence which also included a punitive discharge. The Court stated:

> "Although we do not believe that the proscription against punishments of this nature contained in the Constitution's Eighth Amendment—if applicable—would bar the punishment adjudged

[416] United States v. Cooper, 2 USCMA 333, 338, 8 CMR 133, 138 (1953).

[417] 50 U. S. C. § 636 (Supp. 1952). [418] 50 U. S. C. § 571 (Supp. 1952).

[419] MANUAL FOR COURTS-MARTIAL, UNITED STATES, 1951, ¶ 126a, p. 206. Medical certificate, that serious injury to health would not result, was required, and a full ration could not be deprived for more than three consecutive days.

[420] United States v. Wappler, 2 USCMA 393, 9 CMR 23 (1953).

[421] MANUAL FOR COURTS-MARTIAL, UNITED STATES, 1951, ¶ 125, p. 215.

here, it is to be noted that the Amendment does not necessarily define the limits of 'cruel and unusual' as used by Congress in Article 55. Use of the phrase by Congress, therefore, raises a problem of *legislative* rather than constitutional construction. Certainly Congress intended to confer as much protection as that afforded by the Eighth Amendment. . . . we believe it intended to grant protection covering even wider limits. Accordingly, we think Article 55 quite broad enough to bar confinement on bread and water, except to the extent permitted by Article 15.

". . .

"In the interest of clarity, a summary of our views is perhaps required. They are simply these: (1) No court-martial—Navy or otherwise—may adjudge confinement on bread and water for personnel other than those 'attached to or embarked in a vessel,' but (2) a court-martial of any service may impose confinement on bread and water in cases involving personnel 'attached to or embarked in a vessel' for a 'period not to exceed three consecutive days.' To the extent to which paragraphs 125 and 127c of the *Manual* are in conflict with this construction of the Code, they are without sanction of law and must fall.

". . . where punitive discharge is imposed, the court may not additionally sentence the accused to confinement on bread and water even though the latter course may otherwise be open to it under the view we have taken earlier in this opinion.

". . . The instant case . . . is quite unlike *United States* v. *Flood*. . . . Here the bread and water confinement aspect of the sentence was void *in toto*. Striking it thus leaves the punitive discharge effective in an entirely legal sentence, and certainly places the accused in no worse position than when the sentence left the court-martial."[422]

This decision no doubt came as a considerable shock to many a ward room. Something which for over one hundred and seventy-five years had not been "cruel and unusual," suddenly became so. Though some old salts may view the decision as an evidence of effete decadence its practical impact upon Navy discipline is likely to be minuscule. Comparable, would be the removal of most of a small benign wart from an inconspicuous portion of the anatomy of a healthy individual. After such minor surgery the patient might look a trifle better but his general health would not be affected one way or the other.

[422] United States v. Wappler, 2 USCMA 393, 396, 397, 9 CMR 23, 26, 27 (1953).

A curious consequence of the *Wappler* decision was promptly emphasized in the case of Seaman Apprentice Wyatt who was tried aboard the U. S. S. Bon Homme Richard and sentenced to a bad conduct discharge, twenty days' solitary confinement on bread and water and forfeitures for four months. The Court held since the accused was attached to a vessel three days of confinement on bread and water was proper, but that this punishment and a bad conduct discharge could not be approved in the same sentence. It then proceeded to declare "void" all that portion of the sentence in excess of three days on bread and water.[423] Some may feel that somewhere between *Wappler* and *Wyatt* logic and common sense parted company.

F. *Permissible Punishment for a Violation of the Law of War*

The Court of Military Appeals has had occasion to pass upon the extent of punishment that may be imposed by a general court-martial while in the exercise of its derivative jurisdiction under Article 18[424] to punish violations of the law of war. American civilian Schultz was tried and convicted for the offense of negligent homicide in occupied Japan and sentenced to one year of confinement and $1,000 fine. The conviction was upheld since the conduct of the accused was a violation of the Penal Code of Japan which in turn, by virtue of an order of the Supreme Commander of the Allied Powers in the Far East, was a violation of the law of war. Accused contended, since the maximum sentence authorized by the Japanese Penal Code for this offense was a fine of $140 at the prevailing rate of exchange, that to the extent the sentence imposed exceeded this amount it was illegal. The Court approved the sentence and said:

> ". . . SCAP Circular No. 17 . . . provides that a military commission in Japan may impose any sentence up to death, including fines in any amount or imprisonment up to life. . . . Under the law of war, General MacArthur had the power . . . to determine punishment policies for military tribunals. The sentence here does not exceed the limitations set out by him. . . . The sentence is therefore legal."[425]

This case simply recognized the well-established rule of international law that any violation of the law of war may, so far as jurisdiction is concerned, be punished by death by a military commission.[426] This

[423] United States v. Wyatt, 2 USCMA 647, 10 CMR 145 (1953).
[424] 50 U. S. C. § 578 (Supp. 1952).
[425] United States v. Schultz, 1 USCMA 512, 530, 4 CMR 104, 122 (1952).
[426] *Ex parte* Quirin, 317 U. S. 1 (1942); WAR DEPARTMENT FIELD MANUAL 27-10, Rules of Land Warfare ¶ 357, p. 89 (1940).

result, in the proper setting of Article 18,[427] is undoubtedly correct. It is hardly necessary to add that this law of war rule would never be invoked to support the punishment jurisdiction of a general court-martial when proceeding under any other article.

G. *The Approach of the Court of Military Appeals to Problems of Jurisdiction to Punish*

The Court has defined what agencies in the military justice system may take what action with regard to sentences. Thus it has held that a court-martial may not suspend a sentence; that such action may be taken by a convening authority;[427a] that a Board of Review, although it may entirely remit, may not suspend, a punitive discharge;[428] and that Boards of Review have power, in a proper case, to commute a death sentence to life imprisonment and a dishonorable discharge.[429] It has repeatedly held that under Article 67(d) the Court itself "shall take action only with respect to matters of law,"[430] and so may not modify sentences, but may return cases for rehearings or remand them to Boards of Review for appropriate sentence action consistent with directions as to matters of law given by the Court. This method of remand has been used even in dealing with void sentences.[431]

The Court of Military Appeals does not speak of jurisdiction in dealing with excessive punishments but uses instead the prejudicial error approach and talks of "illegal" sentences. Since the vast preponderance of questioned punishments exceed only the Table of Maximum Punishments limits and not the maximums prescribed by Congress in the punitive articles, it is in such cases technically correct for the Court to refrain from considering the problem as jurisdictional. In *Wappler,* where the Court found the "imposed confinement on bread and water, was illegal and void," it characterized a jurisdictional defect without using the word.

It seems clear that a punishment in excess of that authorized by Congress would, as to the excess, be treated by the United States Supreme Court as jurisdictional.[432]

[427] 50 U. S. C. § 578 (Supp. 1952).

[427a] United States v. Marshall, 2 USCMA 342, 8 CMR 142 (1953). A convening authority may also disapprove a sentence and order a rehearing. United States v. Freeman, 3 USCMA 71, 11 CMR 71 (1953).

[428] United States v. Simmons, 2 USCMA 105, 6 CMR 105 (1952).

[429] United States v. Bigger, 2 USCMA 297, 8 CMR 97 (1953).

[430] 50 U. S. C. § 654 (Supp. 1952).

[431] United States v. Wappler, 2 USCMA 393, 9 CMR 23 (1953); United States v. Wyatt, 2 USCMA 647, 10 CMR 145 (1953).

[432] United States v. Reed, 100 U. S. 13, 23 (1879); *Ex parte* Lange, 18 Wall. 163 (U. S. 1873).

CHAPTER 6

Due Process and Jurisdiction

There remains the interesting question whether procedural errors committed in trials before military courts can ever, either individually or collectively, reach the stature of a jurisdictional factor. On direct appeal within the military justice system it is unnecessary to decide this point since long before procedural error could conceivably be sufficiently aggravated to become jurisdictional it would certainly be "materially prejudicial to the substantial rights of the accused," and for this reason would require reversal by either a Board of Review or the Court of Military Appeals. Within the framework of the Congressional limitation imposed upon it, that "A finding or sentence of a court-martial shall not be held incorrect on the ground of an error of law unless the error materially prejudices the substantial rights of the accused,"[433] the Court of Military Appeals has in substance said that as it conceives military due process, certain procedural omissions or commissions will *per se* constitute "error materially prejudicial to the substantial rights of the accused."[434] This, of course, is quite a different thing from treating such procedural error as divesting a court-martial of jurisdiction. Reversal for prejudicial error fully protects the rights of the accused without ever reaching an issue of jurisdiction and the Court of Military Appeals has gone to some pains to point out that it distinguishes due process from jurisdiction.[435]

In collateral attack by habeas corpus procedural errors may not be considered,[436] nor may the evidence be reviewed to ascertain the guilt

[433] Article 59, 50 U. S. C. § 646 (Supp. 1952).

[434] United States v. Clay, 1 USCMA 74, 78, 1 CMR 74, 78 (1951). See Chapter 10, *post*.

[435] United States v. Davis, 1 USCMA 102, 107, 2 CMR 8, 13 (1952); United States v. Bartholomew, 1 USCMA 307, 311, 3 CMR 41, 45 (1952). In its most recent consideration of due process the court affirmed a death sentence murder case saying, "the accused was convicted without there being any error which materially prejudiced his substantial rights." United States v. Vigneault, 3 USCMA 247, 258, 12 CMR 3, 14 (1953).

[436] Hiatt v. Brown, 339 U. S. 103, 111, *rehearing denied*, 339 U. S. 939 (1950).

or innocence of the accused.[437] The inquiry has always been limited to whether the military court had jurisdiction.[438] Traditionally this inquiry has been confined to the four fundamental questions examined in the four preceding chapters. In recent years petitioners' counsel in military cases have repeatedly urged, by analogy to federal court habeas corpus review of criminal cases arising in state jurisdictions, that procedural error may be so gross as to deprive an accused of due process as guaranteed by the Fifth Amendment and, thus, become a jurisdictional defect which may be reached and remedied by habeas corpus. In a few instances inferior federal courts have tried, without success, to approve this concept.[439] If accepted, the next question raised is: "What kind of due process does the Constitution provide for those subject to military law, and what violates it?" The answer the Supreme Court has always given to this is, "To those in the military or naval service of the United States the military law is due process."[440]

The Supreme Court in recent years has had at least three different opportunities in military cases to put at rest this due process contention, but has not dealt with it conclusively. In both *Humphrey* v. *Smith*[441] and *Hiatt* v. *Brown*,[442] the Supreme Court reversed the courts of appeal; set forth an array of alleged procedural errors; held that they did not deprive the accused of due process although the courts of appeal had so found; and denied habeas corpus relief. In *Burns* v. *Wilson*,[443] the high Court again set forth some six specific allegations of procedural error which petitioners contended constituted a denial of due process; found that all these assignments of error had been passed upon and rejected by the military tribunals during the course of the appellate review of the case within the system of military courts; concluded that these same issues should not be reviewed by a civil federal court; and affirmed the orders of the district and circuit courts denying habeas corpus relief. In arriving at this result the Court split four ways. Six judges concurred

[437] *Ex parte* Quirin, 317 U. S. 1, 25 (1942); Humphrey v. Smith, 336 U. S. 695, 696, *rehearing denied*, 337 U. S. 934 (1949); Whelchel v. McDonald, 176 F. 2d 260, 262 (5th Cir. 1949), *aff'd*, 340 U. S. 122 (1950), *rehearing denied*, 340 U. S. 923 (1951).

[438] Hiatt v. Brown, 339 U. S. 103, 111, *rehearing denied*, 339 U. S. 939 (1950); *In re* Grimley, 137 U. S. 147 (1890); *Ex parte* Reed, 100 U. S. 13, 23 (1879).

[439] Smith v. Hiatt, 170 F. 2d 61 (3d Cir. 1948), *rev'd sub nom.* Humphrey v. Smith, 336 U. S. 695, *rehearing denied*, 337 U. S. 934 (1949); Hiatt v. Brown, 175 F. 2d 273 (5th Cir. 1949), *rev'd*, 339 U. S. 103, *rehearing denied*, 339 U. S. 939 (1950); Innes v. Hiatt, 141 F. 2d 664, 666 (3d Cir. 1944); Schita v. King, 133 F. 2d 283 (8th Cir. 1943), second appeal, 139 F. 2d 971 (8th Cir. 1944), *cert. denied sub nom.* Schita v. Pescor, 322 U. S. 761, *rehearing denied*, 323 U. S. 810 (1944). In both *Innes* and *Schita* the courts found due process had not been violated.

[440] Creary v. Weeks, 259 U. S. 336, 344 (1922); French v. Weeks, 259 U. S. 326, 335 (1922); Reeves v. Ainsworth, 219 U. S. 296, 304 (1911).

[441] 336 U. S. 695, *rehearing denied*, 337 U. S. 934 (1949).

[442] 339 U. S. 103, *rehearing denied*, 339 U. S. 939 (1950).

[443] 346 U. S. 137 (1953), *rehearing denied*, 346 U. S. 844 (1953).

in the denial of relief although only Justices Reed, Burton, and Clark joined in the prevailing opinion written by Chief Justice Vinson.[444] Justice Minton wrote a separate concurring opinion adhering to the traditional view of the Court that the sole test is jurisdiction.[445] Justice

[444] *Id.* at 139. This opinion, in part, read:

". . . But, in military habeas corpus the inquiry, the scope of matters open for review has always been more narrow than in civil cases. Hiatt v. Brown, 339 U. S. 103 (1950). Thus the law which governs a civil court in the exercise of its jurisdiction over military habeas corpus applications cannot simply be assimilated to the law which governs the exercise of that power in other instances. It is *sui generis;* it must be so, because of the peculiar relationship between the civil and military law.

"Military law, like state law, is a jurisprudence which exists separate and apart from the law which governs in our federal judicial establishment. This Court has played no role in its development; we have exerted no supervisory power over the courts which enforce it; the rights of men in the armed forces must perforce be conditioned to meet certain overriding demands of discipline and duty, and the civil courts are not the agencies which must determine the precise balance to be struck in this adjustment. The Framers expressly entrusted that task to Congress.

"Indeed, Congress has taken great care both to define the rights of those subject to military law, and to provide a complete system of review within the military system to secure those rights. . . .

"The military courts, like the state courts, have the same responsibilities as do the federal courts to protect a person from a violation of his constitutional rights. In military habeas corpus cases, even more than in state habeas corpus cases, it would be in disregard of the statutory scheme if the federal civil courts failed to take account of the prior proceedings—of the fair determinations of the military tribunals after all military remedies have been exhausted. Congress has provided that these determinations are "final" and "binding" upon all courts. We have held before that this does not displace the civil courts' jurisdiction over an application for habeas corpus from the military prisoner. Gusik v. Schilder, 340 U. S. 128 (1950). But these provisions do mean that when a military decision has dealt fully and fairly with an allegation raised in that application, it is not open to a federal civil court to grant the writ simply to re-evaluate the evidence. Whechel v. McDonald, 340 U. S. 122 (1950).

"These records make it plain that the military courts have heard petitioners out on every significant allegation which they now urge. Accordingly, it is not the duty of the civil courts simply to repeat that process—to reexamine and reweigh each item of evidence of the occurrence of events which tend to prove or disprove one of the allegations in the application for habeas corpus. It is the limited function of the civil courts to determine whether the military have given fair consideration to each of these claims. Whelchel v. McDonald, *supra.* We think they have.

"Petitioners have failed to show that this military review was legally inadequate to resolve the claims which they have urged upon the civil courts. They simply demand an opportunity to make a new record, to prove *de novo* in the District Court precisely what they failed to prove in the military court. We think, under the circumstances, that due regard for the limitations on a civil court's power to grant such relief precludes such action. We think that although the Court of Appeals may have erred in reweighing each item of evidence in the trial record, it certainly did not err in holding there was no need for a further hearing in the District Court. Accordingly its judgment must be affirmed."

[445] The forthright approach of Justice Minton is the one which the Supreme Court has heretofore consistently taken in military habeas corpus cases and possesses the old fashioned virtue of clarity. In part, in his separate concurring opinion at 147, he said:

". . . Due process of law for military personnel is what Congress has provided

Jackson concurred in the result reached by the Court. Justice Frankfurter cast no vote, feeling the case should be set down for reargument, but even so, wrote an opinion to the effect that due process in military courts is quite different from due process in civil courts.[446] Justices Black and Douglas dissented, asserting that the 5th Amendment due process clause is applicable and probably had been violated by the improper admission in evidence of a questioned confession. Earnest lawyers who have wrestled with the problem, while they will not find in this performance of the Court an absolute to which to cling, should draw solace from this striking testimonial to the highly divisive propensity of the legal enigma presented by the effort to isolate, identify and define the concept of due process applied to military law.

---

for them in the military hierarchy in courts established according to law. If the court is thus established, its action is not reviewable here. Such military court's jurisdiction is exclusive but for the exceptions contained in the statute, and the civil courts are not mentioned in the exceptions. 64 STAT. 115, 50 U. S. C. (Supp. V) Sec. 581.

"If error is made by the military courts, to which Congress has committed the protection of the rights of military personnel, that error must be corrected in the military hierarchy of courts provided by Congress. We have but one function, namely, to see that the military court has jurisdiction, not whether it has committed error in the exercise of that jurisdiction.

"The rule was clearly stated in the early case of *In re* Grimley, 137 U. S. 147, 150, . . .

". . . The single inquiry, the test, is jurisdiction."

[446] *Id.* at 148. Justice Frankfurter, in part, wrote:

". . . if imprisonment is the result of a denial of due process, it may be challenged no matter under what authority of the Government it was brought about. Congress itself in the exercise of the war power 'is subject to application of constitutional limitations.' Hamilton v. Kentucky Distilleries Co., 251 U. S. 146, 156. It is therefore not freed from the requirements of due process of the Fifth Amendment. But there is no table of weights and measures for ascertaining what constitutes due process. Indeed, it was common ground, in the majority and dissenting opinion below, that due process, in the language of Judge Bazelon, is not 'the same in a military setting as it is in a civil setting.' 202 Fed. at page 352.

"I cannot agree that the only inquiry that is open on an application for habeas corpus challenging a sentence of a military tribunal is whether that tribunal was legally constituted and had jurisdiction, technically speaking, over the person and the crime. Again, I cannot agree that the scope of inquiry is the same as that open to us on review of State convictions; the content of due process in civil trials does not control what is due process in military trials. Nor is the duty of the civil courts upon habeas corpus met simply when it is found that the military sentence has been reviewed by the military hierarchy, although in a debatable situation we should no doubt attach more weight to the conclusions reached on controversial facts by military appellate courts than those reached by the highest court of a State.

". . . I believe this case should be set down for reargument."

This "opinion," not backed by a vote in the case either way, is something of a legal oddity. To borrow partially from the words of Justice Frankfurter, "there is no table of weights and measures for ascertaining" its legal effect. It does make clear that the Justice feels that military due process and civilian due process are not by any means the same commodity. See, however, the further views of Justice Frankfurter expressed when the Supreme Court denied a petition for rehearing in the *Burns* case, 346 U. S. 844 (1953).

From the *Burns* case, a new rule seems to emerge for military cases. It is that federal civil courts in habeas corpus may look only to determine whether a military petitioner has received full and fair consideration of his contentions by the appellate tribunals of the military justice system. If so, the civil courts are closed to him, not only for direct appeal but for collateral habeas corpus relief as well. This rule seems to shift the inquiry along from, "Was the accused accorded due process by the court-martial?" to "Was the accused accorded a full and fair hearing by military justice appellate agencies either on appeal or on separate motion for a new trial?" It appears to infer that if the answer to the last question were "no," then habeas corpus relief might be granted even though jurisdiction were not involved. The rule certainly neither states nor infers that due process considerations are jurisdictional. The same Court has clearly ruled that all remedies within the military system must first be completely exhausted as a prerequisite to seeking habeas corpus relief in the civil courts.[447] This, of necessity, means a petitioner must have been heard *in extenso* by all military appellate tribunals before he may even seek a hearing in the federal civil courts. Since error in decision cannot be reached by habeas corpus,[448] it would follow that only provable wilful dishonesty of decision, either committed or approved, by the Court of Military Appeals, or its refusal to consider at all a case properly submitted to it under its appellate jurisdiction, would fit the test of a failure to afford the petitioner a full and fair consideration of his contentions by the appellate tribunals of the military justice system. While conceivable, such conduct is improbable almost to the point of impossibility. More within the realm of possibility would be a failure to pass upon a material issue raised in a case. However, in view of the vigorous activities of assigned appellate defense counsel in all cases this, too, is most unlikely. The rule, very properly, makes narrow the way and straight the course of the military petitioner seeking habeas corpus in the civil courts.

In any non-capital case not certified to it by a Judge Advocate General the Court of Military Appeals is authorized by law to deny the petition of an accused for a hearing by that court.[449] This petition jurisdiction of the Court of Military Appeals is analogous to the certiorari jurisdiction of the Supreme Court and is carefully exercised.[450]

[447] Gusik v. Schilder, 340 U. S. 128 (1950); Whelchel v. McDonald, 340 U. S. 122 (1950), *rehearing denied,* 340 U. S. 923 (1951). Followed in McKinney v. Finletter, 205 F. 2d 761 (10th Cir. 1953).

[448] See notes 436 and 437 *supra.*

[449] Article 67(b), (c), 50 U. S. C. § 654 (Supp. 1952).

[450] For authoritative accounts of the process by which the Court of Military Appeals exercises its petition jurisdiction see Latimer, *"Good Cause" in Petitions for Review,* 6 VAND. L. REV. 163-168 (1953) and Walker and Niebank, *The Court*

In testing to determine whether the military had in a certain case given full and fair consideration to the contentions of the military habeas corpus petitioner, what, if any, significance the Supreme Court may attach to the fact that a petition for hearing was denied by the Court of Military Appeals, must await the pronouncement of the high Court itself.[451]

It remains to be seen whether the Supreme Court, since the *Burns* case, would hold that a petitioner, who was not at all within the jurisdiction of military courts but whose case had been, on the jurisdictional issue, fully and fairly, but erroneously, decided against him by the Court of Military Appeals, was thereby wholly debarred from civil court relief. It is highly unlikely this case will arise. If it should, the Supreme Court probably would approve federal civil court habeas corpus intervention under its traditional doctrine, espoused in the *Burns* case by Justice Minton, that "the single . . . test, is jurisdiction."[452]

The Court of Military Appeals has said that due process considerations are not jurisdictional in nature.[453] The Supreme Court has adamantly refrained from saying that due process compliance in a military case is an element of jurisdiction. It is significant that in the only recent case in which the Supreme Court approved civil court habeas corpus relief for a military petitioner the clear ground was lack of jurisdiction of the person and due process was not an issue.[454] It seems safe to conclude that the according of civil due process is not, *per se,* an essential element of military jurisdiction. This is not meant to imply that courts-martial do not scrupulously adhere to all of the provisions of the Uniform Code of Military Justice which is the military "Law of the Land." They, in fact, earnestly endeavor to do just that. Where errors occur, in the exercise of granted jurisdiction, which materially prejudice the substantial rights of an accused,[455] they are corrected by the military appellate tribunals by granting rehearings, new trials, or other appropriate relief.[456]

---

of Military Appeals—Its History, Organization and Operations, 6 VAND. L. REV. 228, 232 (1953).

[451] Such pronouncement is not likely to be either brief or simple, if it should follow the lead of the 118 page Supreme Court decision setting forth the effect of its own previous denial of certiorari upon habeas corpus litigation by civilian prisoners. Brown v. Allen, 344 U. S. 443 (1953). This problem evoked no less than five separate opinions from the Justices.

[452] See note 445 *supra.*

[453] See note 435 *supra.*

[454] Hershberg v. Cooke, 336 U. S. 210 (1949). The same was true in Billings v. Truesdale, 321 U. S. 542 (1944).

[455] Article 59(a), 50 U. S. C. § 646 (Supp. 1952).

[456] In Easley v. Hunter, 209 F(2d) 483, 487 (10th Cir. 1953), the *Burns* case is thus analyzed, ". . . as we understand the Burns decision it does no more than hold that a military court must consider questions relating to the guarantees afforded an accused by the Constitution and when this is done, the civil courts will not review its action."

See 52 MICH. L. REV. 602 (1954).

CHAPTER 7

Law Officer

I. General

It is the aim of the Court, wherever possible, to assimilate the status of the law officer to that of a civilian judge in the federal system.[1] The president[2] of a special court-martial performs duties resembling those of a law officer in a general court-martial. But, unlike the law officer, he is a member of the court-martial and more often than not he is without legal training. It should be kept in mind that most of the developments relating to the duties of a law officer are also applicable to the president of a special court-martial.

II. Law officer's rulings on motions

A law officer must rule on interlocutory questions, other than challenges,[3] arising during trial. The Code[4] provides that the ruling of the law officer on interlocutory questions, other than a motion for a finding of not guilty[5] or the question of the accused's sanity, shall

[1] United States v. Biesak, 3 USCMA 714, 14 CMR 132 (1954). For a discussion of the duties of a law officer see United States v. Jackson, 3 USCMA 646, 14 CMR 64 (1954).

[2] Manual for Courts-Martial, United States, 1951, par. 57*c* discusses the rulings by the president of a special court-martial. Paragraph 73 requires the president of a special court-martial to instruct the court as to the elements of the offense, presumption of innocence, burden of proof and reasonable doubt. United States v. Pulliam, 3 USCMA 95, 11 CMR 95 (1953) discusses the duties and functions of the president of a special court-martial.

[3] *Cf.* United States v. Shaffer, 2 USCMA 75, 6 CMR 75 (1952); United States v. Stewart, 2 USCMA 78, 6 CMR 78 (1952). See Manual for Courts-Martial, United States, 1951, par. 62*h* for procedure when a challenge is exercised.

[4] Art. 51 (b). If a member of a special court-martial objects to any ruling of the president, the court will be closed and a vote will be taken in accordance with par. 57*f* of the Manual for Courts-Martial, United States, 1951.

[5] The Joint Committee composed of the Judges of the Court, The Judge Advocates General, and the General Counsel of the Department of the Treasury, hereafter referred to as the Code Committee, recommended that Article 51 (b) of the Code be amended to provide that the ruling of a law officer on a motion for a finding of not guilty be final. Annual Report of the United States Court of Mili-

be final. This provision, however, must be considered in connection with the decision of the Court in *Ornelas*.[6] In that case a factual issue was raised as to whether the accused had been inducted. The law officer denied a defense motion to dismiss. The motion was supported by an argument that the accused had not been inducted and therefore jurisdiction had not been acquired over the accused. The Court held that the law officer erred in making a final ruling on this motion. Instead, he also should have submitted the "factual" issue concerning the question of induction to the court-martial for decision. In this connection the Court stated:

> "We conclude that where an accused raises a defense or objection which should properly be considered by the court in its determination of guilt or innocence, and which resolves itself into a question of fact, that issue must be presented to and decided by the court pursuant to appropriate instructions. But where the issue is purely interlocutory or raises solely a question of law, it is within the sole cognizance of the law officer."[7]

If, therefore, as in *Ornelas,* there is a motion involving a defense which raises a question of fact,[8] it must be submitted to the court-martial either at the time the motion is made or at the conclusion of the trial when the court-martial deliberates on the evidence.

The law officer rules on an application for a continuance when the court-martial is in session. Such ruling is not subject to review until the trial has been completed.[8a] Several cases involving law officers' rulings on an application for continuance are discussed in Chapter 8, Section X.

III. LAW OFFICER AND EVIDENTIAL MATTERS

The Court adopted the federal rule, along with its limitations, which permits a judge to comment on the evidence.[9] This authority, however, must be exercised with caution. There should be no attempt

---

TARY APPEALS AND THE JUDGE ADVOCATES GENERAL OF THE ARMED FORCES AND THE GENERAL COUNSEL OF THE DEPARTMENT OF THE TREASURY, FOR THE PERIOD JUNE 1, 1952, TO DECEMBER 13, 1953, United States Government Printing Office, Washington (1954), p. 5. Hereafter cited as ANNUAL REPORT, FOR JUNE 1, 1952 TO DECEMBER 31, 1953.

[6] 2 USCMA 96, 6 CMR 96 (1952).

[7] *Id.* at 101.

[8] *Cf.* United States v. Rodriquez, 2 USCMA 101, 6 CMR 101 (1952); United States v. McNeill, 2 USCMA 383, 9 CMR 13 (1953) (no factual issue).

[8a] United States v. Knudson, 4 USCMA 587, 16 CMR 161 (1954).

[9] United States v. Andis, 2 USCMA 364, 8 CMR 164 (1953). He may also comment on his refusal to grant a motion for a finding of not guilty. United States v. Toms, 3 USCMA 435, 12 CMR 191 (1953).

to influence the members of the court-martial to adopt a construction advocated by the law officer. In applying the facts to the law, he may find it advisable, in the interest of caution, explicitly to inform the court-martial members that they should not regard any comments made by him on the evidence as binding on them.[10] The Court has warned that the line between proper and improper comment will be "thinly" drawn.

The law officer is permitted "great freedom" to enlighten the members of the court-martial regarding the inferences which they may draw from the evidence.[11] Likewise, he determines whether proffered evidence should be admitted or excluded. His rulings on the admissibility of evidence will not be reversed unless it is clear that he committed prejudicial error. This may be illustrated by a case in which the accused was prosecuted for instructing a subordinate to deny knowledge of certain lewd and obscene films alleged to have been shown to the unit. The law officer admitted one of the films in evidence. He erred in doing so because the issue in the case did not involve the content of the films. However, the Court concluded inasmuch as the film was not shown to the members of the court-martial, there was no "fair risk" of prejudice; consequently, the error was not sufficiently serious to require a reversal.[12] On another occasion a law officer permitted an assistant judge advocate, over objection, to testify regarding information he secured from the accused during an interview held after the accused had been tried for another offense. The Court assumed the admission of this testimony was error—and proceeded to test it for prejudice.[13] None was found because there was overwhelming evidence in the record apart from the challenged testimony that the accused had committed the alleged offense.[14]

The law officer's rulings in connection with the admission of confessions are discussed in Chapter 13.

The law officer is responsible for determining whether a witness is qualified to testify as an expert. His ruling on this question may

[10] United States v. Smith, 3 USCMA 25, 29, 11 CMR 25, 29 (1953).

[11] United States v. Biesak, 3 USCMA 714, 14 CMR 132 (1954). The law officer may also limit evidence in extenuation to those matters permitted by par. 75*c* (3) of the MANUAL FOR COURTS-MARTIAL, UNITED STATES, 1951. United States v. Tobita, 3 USCMA 267, 12 CMR 23 (1953).

[12] United States v. Stewart, 1 USCMA 648, 5 CMR 76 (1952); United States v. Hagen, 2 USCMA 324, 8 CMR 124 (1953) (letter expressing opinion of commanding general excluded).

[13] United States v. Fleming, 3 USCMA 461, 13 CMR 17 (1953) (see cases cited therein).

[14] *Ibid.*

be reviewed on appeal; however, the inquiry is limited to whether he abused his discretion in making his ruling.[15]

If evidence is improperly admitted, the law officer, in most instances, may cure the error by ordering it stricken from the record and advising the members of the court-martial that it should be disregarded.[16] The Court is not unmindful of the fact that the damaging effect cannot entirely be removed in this manner; however, it believes that sound judicial administration requires that the "lion's share" of such errors be regarded as fully reparable through proper instructions.

If a law officer strikes testimony which is unfavorable to the accused and it should have been admitted, such testimony cannot be considered by appellate authorities.[17] On the other hand, if he excludes evidence favorable to the accused which should have been admitted, it is an error which requires reversal if prejudice results.[18]

In the absence of a request, a law officer is not required to instruct the court-martial on the effect to be given character evidence presented on behalf of the accused.[19] But he cannot safely refuse a defense request for such an instruction.[20] Law officers commit prejudicial error[21] by ruling that general character evidence cannot be considered on the issue of guilt or innocence. Moreover, a failure of the defense counsel to object to this ruling is not a waiver and it may be considered on appeal.[22] The Court held[23] that in certain circumstances if requested, the law officer must instruct the court-martial that evidence of good character may be enough to raise a reasonable doubt of guilt.

[15] United States v. Hagelberger, 3 USCMA 259, 12 CMR 15 (1953).

[16] United States v. O'Briski, 2 USCMA 361, 8 CMR 161 (1953). See also United States v. Johnson, 3 USCMA 447, 13 CMR 3 (1953).

[17] United States v. Jones, 2 USCMA 80, 6 CMR 80 (1952) (law member).

[18] United States v. Allen, 2 USCMA 266, 8 CMR 66 (1953). According to the Court evidence that victim was suffering from an advanced stage of syphilis three days after the alleged rape and that accused was examined sixty days after alleged offense and found free of the disease should have been admitted.

[19] United States v. Schumacher, 2 USCMA 134, 7 CMR 10 (1953).

[20] *Ibid.* *Cf.* United States v. Dodge, 3 USCMA 158, 11 CMR 158 (1953) (accused admitted the offense).

[21] United States v. Browning, 1 USCMA 599, 5 CMR 27 (1952); United States v. Presley, 2 USCMA 414, 9 CMR 44 (1953); United States v. Johnson, 3 USCMA 709, 14 CMR 127 (1954).

[22] United States v. Presley, 2 USCMA 414, 9 CMR 44 (1953).

[23] United States v. Phillips, 3 USCMA 137, 11 CMR 137 (1953). The accused was charged with sodomy and he disputed the testimony of the pathic. The outcome of the case depended to a large extent on determination by the fact-finders as to who was telling the truth. Likewise, character evidence was extremely important on the issue as to whether an accused would commit such an offense. *Cf.* United States v. Dodge, 3 USCMA 158, 11 CMR 158 (1953).

The *Manual*[24] permits the prosecution to use deposition testimony in proof of a non-capital offense tried along with a capital offense in the same case. If the deposition is relevant to the capital as well as the non-capital offense, the law officer must instruct the members of the court-martial that the deposition may be considered only with respect to the non-capital offense. But where the deposition is not relevant to the capital offense, this instruction is not required.[25]

IV. LAW OFFICER'S INSTRUCTIONS—GENERAL

The statutory basis for the law relating to instructions is found in Article 51 (c) of the Code which provides:

> "Before a vote is taken on the findings, the law officer of a general court-martial and the president of a special court-martial shall, in the presence of the accused and counsel, instruct the court as to the elements of the offense and charge the court—
> (1) that the accused must be presumed to be innocent until his guilt is established by legal and competent evidence beyond reasonable doubt;
> (2) that in the case being considered, if there is a reasonable doubt as to the guilt of the accused, the doubt shall be resolved in favor of the accused and he shall be acquitted;
> (3) that if there is a reasonable doubt as to the degree of guilt, the finding must be in a lower degree as to which there is no reasonable doubt; and
> (4) that the burden of proof to establish the guilt of the accused beyond a reasonable doubt is upon the Government."

Paragraph 73 of the *Manual* goes further and requires that these instructions be given in those cases in which a plea of guilty has been entered.

The Court has observed that adopting, in part, the civilian practice of instructing the jury "opens up an extremely important, but difficult, field of law."[26] An analysis of the cases will serve to underscore this statement.

If the law officer fails to give instructions to the court-martial, it is error, whether the accused pleads guilty or not guilty. However, the consequences differ with the nature of the plea. If the accused pleads not guilty, a complete failure on the part of the law officer to instruct constitutes reversible error and violates the concept of "military

[24] Paragraph 145*a*. Depositions are discussed in Chapter 13.
[25] United States v. Gann, 3 USCMA 12, 11 CMR 12 (1953).
[26] United States v. Rhoden, 1 USCMA 193, 196, 2 CMR 99, 102 (1952).

due process."[27] On the other hand, a plea of guilty amounts to a waiver and eliminates the prejudicial effect of the failure to instruct.[28] In cases in which there is a total failure to instruct or in which the instructions are highly inadequate, the Court will consider such an error on appeal notwithstanding the absence of an objection at the trial.[29] In this area the Court has gone further to state that any error in the law officer's instructions will be noticed on appeal if it results in depriving the accused of a substantial right.[30]

It is rare for a law officer to offer no instructions at all; hence the sources of difficulty may be traced to inadequate and incorrect instructions. For instance, in *Rhoden*[31] one of the charges against the accused was that he willfully disobeyed the lawful command of a superior officer. The specification stated:

> "In that [the accused] having received a lawful command from 1st Lt. John H. Stopyro, his superior officer to stop talking and sit down did . . . *willfully*, disobey the same."

The instructions of the law officer were, in part, as follows:

> "The court is advised that the elements of the offense are . . . That the accused received a lawful command from a certain officer and that the accused *failed* to obey said command from his superior officer." (Emphasis supplied.)

The court-martial rendered a finding of guilty of willful disobedience—an offense greater than failure to obey. The verdict rendered carried no limit as to the period of confinement where the offense, as here, occurred in the Far East Command; whereas the maximum sentence for failure to obey was only six months. The law officer's incorrect instruction permitted the court-martial to find the accused guilty of willful disobedience on a showing of mere failure to obey. Unquestionably, this was a clear-cut example of specific prejudice and the Court reversed.[32]

The *Manual,* although frequently adequate, does not provide suf-

[27] United States v. Clay, 1 USCMA 74, 1 CMR 74 (1951) (president of a special court-martial); United States v. Slaughter, 2 USCMA 196, 7 CMR 72 (1953) (law officer); United States v. Keith, 1 USCMA 442, 4 CMR 34 (1952). The conviction was reversed as to one of two offenses because no instructions were given defining the elements of that offense.

[28] United States v. Lucas, 1 USCMA 19, 1 CMR 19 (1951).

[29] United States v. Cromartie, 1 USCMA 551, 4 CMR 143 (1952) (instructions were highly inadequate).

[30] United States v. Ransom, 4 USCMA 195, 15 CMR 195 (1954).

[31] 1 USCMA 193, 198-199, 2 CMR 99, 104-105 (1952).

[32] See United States v. Berry, 1 USCMA 235, 2 CMR 141 (1952) for a discussion of prejudice.

ficient information on which to base minimum instructions in all situations. For this reason the Court announced the correct test is not whether the *Manual* is followed but whether the instructions sufficiently define the elements which must be proved.[33] To fulfill this responsibility it is essential that a law officer, in some instances, give more adequate instructions than those which appear in the *Manual*. For example, many of the requirements for instructions on such matters as insanity, intoxication and character evidence do not appear in the instructions supplied by the *Manual*. For this reason it is necessary to refer to the opinions of the Court.

According to the Court the "only appropriate source of the law applicable to any case should come from the law officer." Consequently a law officer committed prejudicial error by referring the members of the court-martial to Board of Review opinions in order that they might determine the law for themselves.[34]

The law officer has a duty to give oral instructions, and merely referring the members of a court-martial to provisions in the *Manual*, even when such provisions supply a full and accurate discussion, does not constitute an adequate instruction and cannot cure an otherwise inadequate instruction.[35] A mere failure to object by defense counsel may not constitute a waiver to this method of instructing the court-martial. However, the Court held[36] objections were waived in a case in which the defense counsel read the elements of the offense to the court-martial and the law officer approved and adopted the language of the *Manual* as read by defense counsel. Further, defense counsel expressed satisfaction with the manner in which the law officer "covered the instructions" in the case.

Several sample instructions in the *Manual* contain the phrase "as alleged." This is intended to refer to the specification under which the accused was tried. The Court rejected a contention that the use of the term "as alleged" by a law officer would supply a missing element in an instruction even though the specification included all the elements of the offense.[37]

[33] United States v. Williams, 1 USCMA 231, 2 CMR 137 (1952); United States v. Grossman, 2 USCMA 406, 9 CMR 36 (1953). For example, MANUAL FOR COURTS-MARTIAL, UNITED STATES, 1951, p. 355 does not adequately distinguish between voluntary and involuntary manslaughter.

[34] United States v. Chaput, 2 USCMA 127, 7 CMR 3 (1953). See also United States v. Fair and Boyce, 2 USCMA 521, 10 CMR 19 (1953) (trial counsel reading law to court-martial).

[35] United States v. Gilbertson, 1 USCMA 465, 4 CMR 57 (1952) (Judge Latimer dissented); United States v. Strong, 1 USCMA 627, 5 CMR 55 (1952); United States v. Cline, 2 USCMA 411, 9 CMR 41 (1953).

[36] United States v. Smith, 2 USCMA 440, 9 CMR 70 (1953).

[37] United States v. Grossman, 2 USCMA 406, 9 CMR 36 (1953); United States v. White, 2 USCMA 439, 9 CMR 69 (1953).

The rule requiring the law officer to instruct on the elements of the offense charged means *every* element of the offense.[38] Inadequate instruction cases have caused the Court to discuss military due process, but it is probable that most instruction errors will be judged by the test of specific prejudice.[39] Ordinarily defects in instructions cannot be remedied by counsel's argument[40] to the court-martial.[41] The Court, on one occasion, found that an instruction in which two elements of the offense were omitted was not prejudicial inasmuch as the record revealed that the court-martial affirmatively found that these elements were proved by the government.[42]

In the absence of a request a law officer is not under a duty to define legal terms that have a meaning which is generally understood.[43] But when a specific request is made for clarifying instructions such as a definition of reasonable doubt—and particularly when accompanied by suggested language—it may be a clear abuse of discretion on the part of the law officer to reject the request.[44] This does not mean that the law officer must employ the suggested language; it is sufficient that he use language adequate to clarify the issue.[45] It is advisable for a law officer to define words with a technical meaning even in the absence of a request therefor.[45a]

V. INSTRUCTIONS ON PRINCIPAL OFFENSES

The opinions of the Court which discuss law officer's instructions on the principal offense charged appear in Chapter 14 which deals with the Punitive Articles. The elements of the offense and the content of

[38] United States v. Cromartie, 1 USCMA 551, 4 CMR 143 (1952) (intent not included in instructions on charge of assault with intent to do bodily harm with a dangerous weapon); United States v. Peterson, 2 USCMA 645, 10 CMR 143 (1953) (value not included in instructions on larceny).

[39] United States v. Howard, 2 USCMA 519, 521, 10 CMR 17, 19 (1953). The Court stated:

> "It is settled that the right of an accused to have the triers of facts instructed fairly, accurately and in full detail is one of the rights secured to him through the concept of military due process of law."

In United States v. White, 2 USCMA 439, 9 CMR 69 (1953) the facts were similar to those in *Howard.* The Court reversed but did not mention military due process. United States v. Cromartie, 1 USCMA 551, 4 CMR 143 (1952); United States v. Greenlee, 3 USCMA 284, 12 CMR 40 (1953). In the latter case the Court did not state whether it relied upon specific prejudice or military due process.

[40] United States v. Johnson, 1 USCMA 536, 4 CMR 128 (1952).

[41] *Cf.* United States v. Smith, 2 USCMA 440, 9 CMR 70 (1953).

[42] United States v. Kubel, 1 USCMA 645, 5 CMR 73 (1952). Value and intent to deprive permanently were the missing elements in a larceny prosecution.

[43] United States v. Soukup, 2 USCMA 141, 7 CMR 17 (1953).

[44] United States v. Offley, 3 USCMA 276, 12 CMR 32 (1953). See Judge Latimer's dissenting opinion.

[45] United States v. Beasley, 3 USCMA 111, 11 CMR 111 (1953).

[45a] United States v. Jones, 1 USCMA 276, 3 CMR 10 (1952) (dictum).

an instruction thereon cannot be disassociated. For this reason the two subjects are treated in a single chapter.

VI. LAW OFFICER'S INSTRUCTIONS ON LESSER INCLUDED OFFENSES

A. *When instructions required*

Law officers[46] are confronted frequently with the problem of giving proper instructions on lesser included offenses. First, it is essential to know the lesser offenses of the principal offense; and second, if there are lesser offenses, to determine which, if any, have been put in issue by the evidence in a given case. In *Clark*[47] the Court first considered the subject of instruction on lesser offenses. In that case the accused was charged with voluntary manslaughter. The law officer instructed the members of the court-martial on that offense. He did not instruct on any lesser offenses even though there was a reasonable basis in the evidence from which it could be inferred that a lesser crime had been committed. The court-martial, nevertheless, found the accused guilty of the lesser included offense of negligent homicide. A board of review affirmed this conviction. The Court reversed and made the following statement:

> "Correct procedure under military law requires that, unless the evidence excludes any reasonable inference that a lesser crime was committed, the duty of the law officer is to carve out instructions covering the offense. He is the judge in the military system and he must furnish to the court the legal framework of all offenses which the evidence tends to establish. Unless he does so the accused has been denied a right which we conclude was granted by Congress and error as a matter of law follows."[48]

The majority of the Court concluded in *Clark* that without instructions the court-martial may have considered negligence as different from or less than what an appropriate instruction would have required. For this reason there was a reasonable showing that the substantial rights of the accused were prejudiced. The purpose of the rule requiring instructions covering lesser included offenses, appropriately in issue,

[46] Although reference is made only to law officers, the same requirements apply to the president of a special court-martial. United States v. Sheehan, 1 USCMA 532, 4 CMR 124 (1952).

[47] 1 USCMA 201, 2 CMR 107 (1952).

[48] *Id.* at 205-206, 2 CMR at 111-112. The majority appeared to apply the prejudicial error rule. Judge Quinn dissented because he failed to find prejudice. Compare the view of the Court in two cases involving A. W. 92 in which it was held that under the circumstances an instruction on premeditated murder also included an instruction of the lesser offense of unpremeditated murder. United States v. Day, 2 USCMA 416, 9 CMR 46 (1953); United States v. Sechler, 3 USCMA 363, 12 CMR 119 (1953).

is to provide the triers of fact with a legal framework within which they must operate in deliberating on the findings.[49] Nevertheless, defense counsel by affirmative action can remove a lesser included offense from consideration by a court-martial and thereby waive the right to have instructions thereon.[49a]

A law officer should ask himself this question—will the reviewing authorities think that under the facts of this case there should be instructions on every lesser included offense, or on certain ones only or none? Included in the many cases that have been reversed because the law officer failed to instruct on appropriate lesser included offenses are ones involving voluntary manslaughter,[50] unpremeditated murder,[50a] assault with intent to commit murder,[51] larceny,[52] robbery,[53] desertion,[54] willful disobedience of a lawful command of a superior officer,[55] assault with intent to commit rape,[56] mutiny,[56a] and involuntary manslaughter.[57]

It is prejudicial error for a law officer to foreclose consideration of a lesser included offense by erroneously ruling that the offense charged does not have any lesser offenses.[58] Inadequate[59] instructions on lesser offenses as distinguished from none at all may also constitute a sufficient basis for reversal.

[49] United States v. Clark, 1 USCMA 201, 2 CMR 107 (1952).

[49a] United States v. Mundy, 2 USCMA 500, 9 CMR 130 (1953).

[50] United States v. Strong, 1 USCMA 627, 5 CMR 55 (1952). Instructions defining involuntary manslaughter and negligent homicide should have been given in this case.

[50a] United States v. Fox, 2 USCMA 465, 9 CMR 95 (1953).

[51] United States v. Warren, 2 USCMA 59, 6 CMR 59 (1952). Instructions defining assault with intent to commit voluntary manslaughter should have been given. United States v. Williams, 1 USCMA 231, 2 CMR 137 (1952). Instructions defining assault with a dangerous weapon should have been given.

[52] United States v. Burr, 2 USCMA 182, 7 CMR 58 (1953). Instructions defining wrongful appropriation should have been given.

[53] United States v. Richardson, 2 USCMA 88, 6 CMR 88 (1952); United States v. Cloutier, 2 USCMA 244, 8 CMR 44 (1953). Instructions defining assault and battery should have been given.

[54] United States v. Lowery, 2 USCMA 315, 8 CMR 115 (1953); United States v. Apple, 2 USCMA 592, 10 CMR 90 (1953); United States v. Oliver, 2 USCMA 613, 10 CMR 111 (1953). Instructions defining absence without leave should have been given in these cases.

[55] United States v. Simmons, 1 USCMA 691, 5 CMR 119 (1952). Instructions defining failure to obey should have been given.

[56] United States v. Burgess, 2 USCMA 542, 10 CMR 40 (1953). Instructions defining assault should have been given.

[56a] United States v. Watson, 4 USCMA 557, 16 CMR 131 (1954). Instructions defining riot should have been given.

[57] United States v. Moreash, 1 USCMA 616, 5 CMR 44 (1952). Instructions defining negligent homicide should have been given.

[58] United States v. Tubbs, 1 USCMA 588, 5 CMR 16 (1952).

[59] United States v. Cline, 2 USCMA 411, 9 CMR 41 (1953). *Cf.* United States v. Ransom, 4 USCMA 195, 15 CMR 195 (1954).

B. *When instructions not required*

The law officer is not required to instruct on lesser included offenses unless the evidence reasonably puts such offenses in issue. In *Banks*[60] the accused was convicted of an assault with intent to murder. The law officer refused to instruct the court-martial on the lesser included offense of an assault with intent to commit voluntary manslaughter. The accused was the aggressor throughout the encounter, which had terminated when the accused shot at another soldier three or four times without hitting him. The Court stated the test in regard to the necessity of instructions on lesser offenses is whether the lesser offense constitutes, under the evidence, a "reasonable alternative" to the offense charged. To constitute an assault with intent to commit voluntary manslaughter, the acts in question must have been done under such circumstances that, had death ensued, the offense would have been voluntary manslaughter. Here there was no basis to conclude the assault was for any offense less than murder—hence it was not error for the law officer to refuse such an instruction. The Court has upheld the judgment of the law officer in several cases in which he determined that it was not necessary to instruct on a lesser offense or offenses.[61] A proposal to adopt the practice in some civilian courts which would require the law officer to instruct on all degrees of homicide when the charge is murder and the evidence is circumstantial was rejected by the Court.[62]

C. *Instructions improper on principal offense but correct on lesser*

A verdict on the principal offense when the only correct instructions were on lesser offenses cannot stand. In such case a board of review[63] or the Court [64] may take corrective action by reducing the offense to the lesser one on which correct instructions were given.

[60] 1 USCMA 479, 4 CMR 71 (1952).

[61] The offenses in question are stated following each citation. United States v. Stout, 1 USCMA 639, 5 CMR 67 (1952); United States v. Smith, 3 USCMA 25, 11 CMR 25 (1953); United States v. Jackson, 4 USCMA 294, 15 CMR 294 (1954) (willful disobedience of an order of a superior officer). United States v. Quisenberry, 1 USCMA 670, 5 CMR 98 (1952) (unpremeditated murder). United States v. Cobb, 2 USCMA 339, 8 CMR 139 (1953) (involuntary manslaughter). United States v. Smith, 2 USCMA 312, 8 CMR 112 (1953) (larceny). United States v. Clark, 2 USCMA 437, 9 CMR 67 (1953); United States v. Henderson, 4 USCMA 268, 15 CMR 268 (1954) (rape). United States v. Fair, 2 USCMA 521, 10 CMR 19 (1953) (premeditated murder). United States v. Black, 3 USCMA 57, 11 CMR 57 (1953) (premeditated and unpremeditated murder). United States v. Dejewski, 3 USCMA 53, 11 CMR 53 (1953) (aggravated assault and assault and battery). United States v. Roman, 1 USCMA 244, 2 CMR 150 (1952) (unpremeditated murder).

[62] United States v. Riggins, 2 USCMA 451, 9 CMR 81 (1953).

[63] United States v. Cromartie, 1 USCMA 557, 4 CMR 143 (1952); United States v. Bigger, 2 USCMA 297, 8 CMR 97 (1953) (dictum).

[64] United States v. Hunter, 2 USCMA 37, 6 CMR 37 (1952); United States v. Mitchell, 2 USCMA 200, 7 CMR 77 (1953). United States v. Bentley, 3 USCMA 625, 14 CMR 43 (1954).

If the court-martial returns a verdict initially on the lesser offense, it should stand. In such case the Government has no way open in which to secure a correction of the error of the law officer in failing to instruct properly on the principal offense.

Although an accused is entitled to have a court-martial correctly instructed on all lesser included offenses properly in issue, an incorrect instruction is not always prejudicial. For instance in *Ransom*[65] the accused was charged with and found guilty of premeditated murder. The court-martial was correctly instructed on premeditated murder and incorrectly instructed on unpremeditated murder. The Court concluded that the accused was not harmed by the incorrect instruction on the lesser included offense.

D. *Action by reviewing authorities when there is failure to instruct on lesser offenses*

In *Baguex*[66] the accused was charged with premeditated murder. The law officer should have but did not instruct adequately on unpremeditated murder and voluntary manslaughter. The court-martial found the accused guilty of unpremeditated murder. The Court, instead of ordering a rehearing, decided to purge the instructional error by its own action. This was accomplished by affirming the conviction insofar as it involved guilt of the *lowest* of the lesser offenses raised by the evidence, in this case, voluntary manslaughter. The Court stated that in view of its lack of fact-finding powers it will exercise this authority sparingly and that it will reserve it for cases presenting a "clear and clean-cut difference between the offense of which the accused was found guilty and another as to which it may be said as a matter of law that the evidence indicates guilt."[67] There appears to be no reason why a board of review cannot take similar[68] corrective action instead of ordering a rehearing.[69] It is probable that the convening authority may also use this means to purge this type of error.[70]

E. *Action by the court-martial when there is failure to instruct on appropriate lesser offenses*

If a law officer fails to instruct on lesser offenses when he should have, may the *court-martial* cure this instructional error by returning

[65] United States v. Ransom, 4 USCMA 195, 15 CMR 195 (1954).

[66] 2 USCMA 306, 8 CMR 106 (1953); *accord,* United States v. Parker, 3 USCMA 541, 13 CMR 97 (1953).

[67] United States v. Baguex, 2 USCMA 306, 310, 8 CMR 106, 110 (1953).

[68] United States v. Arnovits, 3 USCMA 538, 13 CMR 94 (1953) (specifications 5, 6 of Charge IV).

[69] United States v. Burgess, 2 USCMA 542, 10 CMR 40 (1953) (rehearing ordered).

[70] United States v. Aldridge, 4 USCMA 107, 15 CMR 107 (1954).

a finding of guilty of the lowest of the lesser offenses raised by the evidence? The earlier[71] cases decided by the Court were in agreement that such action by a court-martial did not cure the error. A majority of the Court stated that Congress did not intend that a court-martial should frame its own instructions in secrecy and thereby deprive the accused of his right to know what elements were being considered. In *Gibson*[72] the Court expressly extended the *Baguex*[73] rule to action taken by a court-martial. The accused was tried for unpremeditated murder. The law officer did not instruct on voluntary manslaughter. The court-martial returned a finding of guilty of voluntary manslaughter. The Court held that voluntary manslaughter was fairly raised as an alternative to the offense charged and then stated:

> "It is likewise clear, from the recited facts, that no other lesser offense was raised—for the accused, in purposefully firing four rounds directly at his victim from a distance of only a few feet, must be deemed to have intended to kill him, or at least to do him great bodily harm."[74]

The Court decided in these circumstances the error of the law officer was deprived of its otherwise prejudicial effect by the action of the court-martial in returning a verdict of voluntary manslaughter. It must be emphasized that the rule of *Gibson* is limited to those situations in which the court-martial finds the accused guilty of the lowest of the lesser offenses raised by the evidence and *then* only where under proper instructions the court-martial was bound to find the accused guilty of at least the offense on which the finding was returned. If a properly instructed court-martial could have found the accused not guilty or guilty of an offense less than the one on which it rendered a verdict, the rule of *Gibson* is inapplicable. A rehearing is the appropriate action in the latter situation.[75]

Law officers can help reduce the number of instances in which a court-martial returns a verdict on a lesser offense without first having received instructions thereon by emphasizing in clear and unequivocal

[71] United States v. Clark, 1 USCMA 201, 2 CMR 107 (1952); United States v. Moreash, 1 USCMA 616, 5 CMR 44 (1952); United States v. Burden, 2 USCMA 547, 10 CMR 45 (1953); United States v. Burgess, 2 USCMA 542, 10 CMR 40 (1953). Judge Quinn dissented in these cases because he believed that the accused was guilty of the offense charged according to the evidence in the record and that therefore no prejudice had occurred.

[72] 3 USCMA 512, 13 CMR 68 (1953). Judge Latimer vigorously dissented. *Cf.* United States v. Lee, 3 USCMA 501, 13 CMR 57 (1953). The majority stated that even though the court-martial returned a finding on a lesser included offense, it did not mean it was in issue.

[73] 2 USCMA 306, 8 CMR 106 (1953).

[74] United States v. Gibson, 3 USCMA 512, 519, 13 CMR 68, 75 (1953).

[75] For example, United States v. Clark, 1 USCMA 201, 2 CMR 107 (1952).

language that the court-martial must not find the accused guilty on any lesser offense without first hearing proper instructions on such offense. Law officers should inform the members of a court-martial, that if doubts arise during a closed session, they should open court and request instructions regarding lesser offenses that they may believe to be in issue. This procedure should also preclude findings by a court-martial of guilt of a lesser offense when such lesser offense is not, in fact, in issue. An error of this kind by a court-martial is beneficial to an accused in a case in which the evidence supports the principal offense charged and there is no means by which it can be corrected.[76]

F. *Failure to instruct on lesser included offenses when there is a plea of guilty to a lesser offense*

The *Manual*[77] requires a law officer to instruct the court-martial in the elements of the offense charged including cases in which a *plea of guilty* has been entered. But as heretofore indicated the Court held[78] that a plea of guilty constitutes a waiver of this requirement. In *Glover*[79] the Court considered whether the principle of waiver should also apply when the accused pleads guilty to a lesser included offense. In this case the charge was larceny. The accused pleaded not guilty to this charge but guilty to the lesser included offense of wrongful appropriation. The law officer confined his instructions to larceny and the court-martial returned a finding of guilty on that offense. The lesser offense of wrongful appropriation was in issue. A board of review decided that the instructional requirement of *Clark*[80] applied and it was necessary to reduce the finding to wrongful appropriation. The Court disagreed[81] with the board of review and distinguished *Clark* on the ground that here, unlike *Clark,* the accused had pleaded guilty to the lesser offense. The failure to instruct on the lesser offense was not prejudicial because the principle of waiver announced in *Lucas* was applicable in this situation.

[76] United States v. Bartholomew, 1 USCMA 307, 3 CMR 41 (1952); United States v. Ginn, 1 USCMA 453, 4 CMR 45 (1952); United States v. Lee, 3 USCMA 501, 13 CMR 57 (1953).

[77] Par. 73*b*.

[78] United States v. Lucas, 1 USCMA 19, 1 CMR 19 (1951).

[79] 2 USCMA 164, 7 CMR 40 (1953).

[80] 1 USCMA 201, 2 CMR 107 (1952), *accord,* United States v. Estes, 2 USCMA 171, 7 CMR 47 (1953); United States v. Bryant, 2 USCMA 373, 9 CMR 3 (1953).

[81] Judge Brosman dissented in *Glover* because he found error and prejudice. He was not sure the members of the court-martial knew they might properly return a finding of guilty of the lesser offense. He further stated that the refusal of the law officer earlier in the trial to drop the larceny charge and accept a plea of guilty of wrongful appropriation may have misled the court-martial into thinking that it would be improper to find the accused guilty of that offense.

VII. AFFIRMATIVE DEFENSES

The requirement for instructions on affirmative defenses is in general the same as for lesser included offenses. There must be some evidence from which a reasonable inference can be drawn that the affirmative defense is in issue.[82] The testimony of the accused may be sufficient to raise an issue necessitating an instruction.[83] Further, the Court held that a pretrial statement of an accused introduced in evidence by the Government may contain sufficient exculpatory information to raise an issue.[84] If an affirmative defense is fairly raised by the evidence, the law officer must give appropriate instructions.[85] A request of defense counsel is not required. An improper instruction may constitute prejudicial error.[86] The Court agreed with the law officer in several cases[87] and held that self-defense was not in issue and hence no error was committed by the refusal of the law officer to instruct thereon.

VIII. INSTRUCTIONS ON INTOXICATION[88]

Law officers encounter difficulty in determining the necessity for instructing the court-martial on the effect of intoxication. These difficulties arise in many situations including those involving ques-

[82] United States v. Ginn, 1 USCMA 453, 4 CMR 45 (1952); United States v. Lee, 3 USCMA 501, 13 CMR 57 (1953). There was no evidence to raise issue of justification.

It is not altogether clear whether a law officer should take into consideration his own notion of the veracity of a witness in determining whether an issue is sufficiently raised to require an instruction. *Compare* United States v. Furney, 2 USCMA 270, 8 CMR 70 (1953), *with* United States v. Simmons, 1 USCMA 691, 5 CMR 119 (1952) (knowledge that the one issuing the order was a superior officer). See also United States v. Johnson, 3 USCMA 209, 11 CMR 209 (1953) for a statement by the Court that unless exculpatory statements in a pretrial statement of the accused are "inherently improbable and unworthy of belief," they should be accepted by the law officer to frame his issues.

[83] United States v. Simmons, 1 USCMA 691, 5 CMR 119 (1952) (lack of knowledge); United States v. Heims, 3 USCMA 418, 12 CMR 174 (1953) (physical incapacity). In the latter case there was some corroborating testimony. United States v. Lee, 3 USCMA 501, 13 CMR 57 (1953). The statement of the accused possibly could have raised an affirmative defense of justification but the defense counsel chose to rely on another theory.

[84] United States v. Johnson, 3 USCMA 209, 11 CMR 209 (1953); United States v. Henderson, 4 USCMA 268, 15 CMR 268 (1954).

[85] United States v. Heims, 3 USCMA 418, 12 CMR 174 (1953). The Court in an earlier case stated it had not specifically held that a law officer must instruct on affirmative defenses. United States v. Simmons, 1 USCMA 691, 5 CMR 119 (1952).

[86] United States v. Weems, 3 USCMA 469, 13 CMR 25 (1953) (excusable homicide).

[87] United States v. Ginn, 1 USCMA 453, 4 CMR 45 (1952); United States v. Amdahl, 3 USCMA 199, 11 CMR 199 (1953); United States v. Troglin, 3 USCMA 385, 12 CMR 141 (1953).

[88] Addiction to drugs also may be the basis for an inference that the accused did not entertain the necessary intent. United States v. Cirelli, 1 USCMA 568, 4 CMR 160 (1952).

tions of specific intent, knowledge or insanity. Cases concerned with a question of specific intent are discussed at this point. If the principal offense charged does not require a specific intent, the condition of an accused regarding sobriety is irrelevant.[89] However, where a specific intent is a necessary element of an offense, the accused, if sufficiently intoxicated so as to preclude the formation of such an intent, cannot lawfully be convicted of the offense. But under proper circumstances he may be found guilty of a lesser included offense not requiring a specific intent.[90] In *Backley* the Court summarized the law on the necessity for instructions on the effect of intoxication as follows:

> ". . . where the drunkenness of the accused at the time of the offense is fairly raised by evidence in such a posture as to suggest a reasonable possibility that the intoxication was of a kind and extent likely to affect the ability of accused to entertain a specific intent, the law officer is required to instruct (1) on the legal effect of intoxication in relation to specific intent, and (2) as to the elements of lesser offenses not involving such an intent, if any."[91]

The most difficult determination for the law officer is whether drunkenness was fairly raised by the evidence to the extent that there was a "reasonable possibility" that it affected the ability of the accused to entertain the specific intent charged. The Court has stated that the fact the accused "had been drinking" or that he was "under the influence of liquor" is clearly insufficient to require an unrequested instruction on intoxication. The intoxication of the accused must be of a degree and sort "characterized by a discernible relationship to the potential absence of a capacity to entertain specific intent."[92] A comparison of *Benavides*[93] with *Backley*[94] where intoxication was found in the latter but not in the former is helpful in understanding the degree of intoxication required by the Court in this area.

If a law officer finds that the offense charged requires a specific intent, and that intoxication was of such a degree that it had a reasonable possibility of affecting the ability of the accused to entertain the

[89] United States v. Backley, 2 USCMA 496, 9 CMR 126 (1953).

[90] United States v. Miller, 2 USCMA 194, 7 CMR 70 (1953). United States v. Olvera, 4 USCMA 134, 15 CMR 134 (1954).

[91] United States v. Backley, 2 USCMA 496, 498, 9 CMR 126, 128 (1953).

[92] *Ibid.*

[93] 2 USCMA 226, 8 CMR 26 (1953). *Compare* United States v. Miller, 2 USCMA 194, 7 CMR 70 (1953) (intoxication sufficient) *with* United States v. St. Pierre, 3 USCMA 33, 11 CMR 33 (1953) (intoxication insufficient). See also United States v. Christensen, 4 USCMA 22, 15 CMR 22 (1954) (intoxication insufficient).

[94] 2 USCMA 496, 9 CMR 126 (1953).

specific intent, he must then determine if there are any lesser included offenses which do *not* require a specific intent. If there are such, he must instruct both on the legal effect of intoxication and on appropriate lesser included offenses which the court-martial may consider. Instruction on one without the other under such circumstances is error.[95]

Several cases have been reversed because of a lack of instructions on either intoxication or lesser included offenses or both when intoxication was in issue. These cases involved an assault with intent to commit murder,[96] assault with intent to commit voluntary manslaughter,[97] robbery,[98] larceny,[99] assault in which grievous harm was intentionally inflicted with a weapon,[100] assault with intent to commit rape,[101] and wilfully damaging military property.[102]

Unpremeditated murder as defined in Article 118 does not require a specific intent but only a general criminal intent. Consequently, the Court held that voluntary intoxication may reduce premeditated murder to unpremeditated murder but it will not reduce murder to manslaughter.[103] In *Craig*[104] one of the charges was premeditated murder and there was evidence that the accused consumed large quantities of liquor. The law officer erred inasmuch as he failed to instruct the members of the court-martial that, if they found all other elements present but also found the accused was so intoxicated that he was unable to deliberate and premeditate and form a specific intent to kill, they could return a finding of guilty of unpremeditated murder.

[95] United States v. Backley, 2 USCMA 496, 9 CMR 126 (1953); United States v. Groves, 2 USCMA 541, 10 CMR 39 (1953).

[96] United States v. Avery, 1 USCMA 533, 4 CMR 125 (1952) (also failed to define murder); United States v. Lookinghorse, 1 USCMA 660, 5 CMR 88 (1952) (also failed to define murder); United States v. Wray, 2 USCMA 26, 6 CMR 26 (1952); United States v. Mitchell, 2 USCMA 200, 7 CMR 77 (1953).

[97] United States v. Drew, 1 USCMA 471, 4 CMR 63 (1952).

[98] United States v. Craig, 2 USCMA 650, 10 CMR 148 (1953).

[99] United States v. Norris, 2 USCMA 236, 8 CMR 36 (1953); United States v. Ferry, 2 USCMA 326, 8 CMR 126 (1953).

[100] United States v. Backley, 2 USCMA 496, 9 CMR 126 (1953).

[101] United States v. Burgess, 2 USCMA 542, 10 CMR 40 (1953); United States v. Burden, 2 USCMA 547, 10 CMR 45 (1953). In United States v. Wycliffe, 3 USCMA 38, 11 CMR 38 (1953) the Court held that it was not error for the law officer to refuse to instruct on indecent assault.

[102] United States v. Groves, 2 USCMA 541, 10 CMR 39 (1953).

[103] United States v. Roman, 1 USCMA 244, 2 CMR 150 (1952); United States v. Long, 2 USCMA 45, 6 CMR 45 (1952); United States v. Bowers, 3 USCMA 615, 14 CMR 33 (1954) (unless intoxication amounts to insanity).

[104] 2 USCMA 650, 10 CMR 148 (1953). *Cf.* United States v. Day, 2 USCMA 416, 9 CMR 46 (1953). The Court held that for all "practical" purposes an instruction on unpremeditated murder was given. This was under Article of War 92 and may not be permitted under Article 118 of the Code.

In two cases[105] the law officer's instructions on premeditated murder were as follows:

" 'a. That the victim named is dead;
'b. That his death resulted from the act or omission of the accused, as alleged; and
'c. Facts and circumstances showing that the accused had a premeditated design to kill, or intended to kill or inflict great bodily harm.' "

Although this instruction alone is sufficient to require a reversal because it permits a finding of guilty of premeditated murder upon the standard of proof required for the lesser offense of unpremeditated murder, the error is more serious in cases, as these, in which there is considerable proof of intoxication which would militate against a finding of premeditation.

The effect of intoxication on instructions concerned with the offense of willful disobedience of a lawful command of a superior officer has been considered by the Court in several cases. The basic difficulty stems from a lack of certainty as to whether knowledge that the person giving the orders is a superior officer is an essential element of this offense or only an affirmative defense.[106] Although the Court has not made a clear cut decision on this question,[107] it has, nevertheless, provided law officers with information regarding appropriate instructions where there is evidence of intoxication. The fundamental rule is that if intoxication is of a sufficient degree to put knowledge in issue then the law officer must instruct the members of the court-martial to consider knowledge in their deliberations.[108] If knowledge is conceded, or if the evidence compels a finding that the accused knew the order was given by a superior officer, or if the record is barren of any evidence from which it could be reasonably inferred the accused might

[105] United States v. Mitchell, 2 USCMA 200, 7 CMR 77 (1953). United States v. Mungo, 3 USCMA 18, 11 CMR 18 (1953).

[106] MANUAL FOR COURTS-MARTIAL, UNITED STATES, 1951, par. 169 in the discussion states that it is a defense. There is nothing in the requirements of "proof" of the offense concerning knowledge. The Court refers to the *Manual* provisions as being "ambiguous." United States v. St. Pierre, 3 USCMA 33, 11 CMR 33 (1953).

[107] In United States v. Simmons, 1 USCMA 691, 695, 5 CMR 119, 123(1952). The Court in a dictum stated ". . . we lean to the previously announced belief that knowledge is an element of the offense which must be proven by the Government." United States v. Miller, 2 USCMA 194, 7 CMR 70 (1953). This case appears to be a square holding that knowledge was an affirmative defense. United States v. St. Pierre, 3 USCMA 33, 11 CMR 33 (1953). The Court's dictum indicates it has not yet decided the question.

[108] United States v. Wallace, 2 USCMA 595, 10 CMR 93 (1953); United States v. Higgins, 4 USCMA 143, 15 CMR 143 (1954); United States v. Johnson, 4 USCMA 149, 15 CMR 149 (1954).

not know that a superior officer was issuing the order, the law officer does not commit reversible error by a failure to instruct on knowledge.[109]

A similar problem is presented in a prosecution for striking or assaulting a superior officer.[110] In *St. Pierre*[111] there was some evidence of intoxication but the evidence of sobriety was so overwhelming that an instruction by the law officer that if the accused did not know that the officer was his superior he "might" have a defense did not constitute prejudicial error.

Although inconsistent defenses are open to an accused, the "defense" of intoxication may be abandoned in favor of another. If such choice is intelligently and deliberately made, the "defense" of intoxication may be waived. If so, the law officer does not err when he fails to instruct on intoxication.[112]

There is no lesser included offense in the crime of wrongful appropriation. In a case involving this offense the law officer should have instructed the court-martial on the effect of intoxication but he failed to do so. If, on rehearing, it is found the accused was sufficiently intoxicated that he did not have the required intent, the finding should be for acquittal.[113]

IX. LAW OFFICER'S INSTRUCTIONS ON INSANITY

A. *Mental responsibility*

Paragraph 120 of the *Manual* provides that an accused is not mentally responsible unless he was, at the time of the offense, so far free from mental defect, disease, or derangement as to be able, concerning the particular act charged, both to distinguish right from wrong and to adhere to the right.[114]

An inquiry as to an accused's mental condition may be made prior to trial, during the hearing on the merits, and any time after conviction prior to final disposition of the case on appeal.[115] Any person con-

[109] *Ibid.*

[110] United States v. Field, 2 USCMA 278, 8 CMR 78 (1953).

[111] 3 USCMA 33, 11 CMR 33 (1953).

[112] United States v. Bowers, 3 USCMA 615, 14 CMR 33 (1954).

[113] United States v. Haywood, 2 USCMA 376, 9 CMR 6 (1953). There is no military offense of wrongful taking unaccompanied by an intent, permanently or temporarily, to deprive the owner of his property.

[114] The same paragraph further provides that an accused is required to have sufficient mental capacity to understand the nature of the proceedings against him and intelligently to conduct or cooperate in his defense. See generally for a discussion of insanity in military law: JAG JOURNAL (January, 1954), p. 3.

[115] United States v. Higgins, 4 USCMA 143, 15 CMR 143 (1954) (during trial). Insanity may also be the subject of a motion for a new trial if other conditions are met. United States v. Trede, 2 USCMA 581, 10 CMR 79 (1953); United States v. Walters, 3 USCMA 732, 14 CMR 150 (1954).

nected with the trial may suggest an inquiry into the sanity of the accused. The evidence necessary to make a preliminary determination whether to proceed with an inquiry need not meet the tests of admissibility required of evidence admitted on the merits. If a member of the court-martial objects to a ruling of the law officer denying an inquiry into the sanity of the accused, the question then becomes one for the court-martial. It is not prejudicial if the members of a court-martial are permitted to read a statement made by a board of medical officers which includes an opinion that the accused is sane before deciding whether to sustain or overrule the action of the law officer.[116]

If opinion evidence or other incompetent evidence is considered for the limited purpose of determining whether a further inquiry should be made into the sanity of the accused, the law officer should instruct the members of the court-martial that such incompetent evidence should not be considered by them in any determination by them of the issue of sanity.

The Court has held, contrary to the usual rule, that when evidence bearing on the sanity of the accused is secured after the trial, either at the direction of the convening authority or of a Judge Advocate General, such evidence may properly be considered by a board of review along with any evidence produced at the trial.[117]

If an accused pleads guilty, and subsequently evidence is introduced which is sufficient to raise an issue of sanity, the law officer should not let the plea stand. He should set aside the plea of guilty or permit it to be withdrawn. This is true even when the evidence of insanity comes to the attention of the court-martial after the findings and during the time it is considering matters in extenuation and mitigation.[118] After the plea is set aside or withdrawn, the issue of sanity should be considered on an interlocutory basis. If the accused is found to lack mental responsibility, the case should be dismissed. But if he was found to be sane the case should then proceed to trial on a plea of not guilty.[119]

An accused is presumed initially to be sane and to have been sane

[116] United States v. Concepcion-Velez, 4 USCMA 183, 15 CMR 183 (1954). The majority of the Court thus approved the provision in paragraph 122*c*, MANUAL FOR COURTS-MARTIAL, UNITED STATES, 1951. But *cf.* United States v. Bransetter, 1 USCMA 30, 1 CMR 30 (1951) (unsworn statement of accused under A. G. N.).

[117] United States v. Burns, 2 USCMA 400, 9 CMR 30 (1953). See Chapter 9, Section II.

[118] United States v. Trede, 2 USCMA 581, 10 CMR 79 (1953). Although the law officer failed to withdraw the plea, the Court did not test for prejudice because there was no substantial issue of sanity in the case.

[119] *Ibid.*

at the time of the alleged offense.[120] However, when evidence sufficient to place sanity in issue is produced, the law officer must instruct on this issue regardless of whether a request is made for such instructions.[121] It is, therefore, essential that a law officer know when the evidence is sufficient to raise the issue.

The Court has observed that the *Manual* provides for a "liberal" determination of the presence of an issue of sanity. However, mere assertion that one is insane is not in itself sufficient to impose any burden of inquiry on the court-martial or to raise the issue of sanity. Further, the Court has held that evidence that the accused was "an extremely nervous person suffering seriously from battle fatigue"[122] or that the accused was of low mentality[123] at the time of the alleged offense was insufficient to raise the issue of his sanity. Likewise, the mere fact that medical experts in psychiatry conclude in their testimony that an accused had an "irresistible impulse" at the time of the offense is not necessarily sufficient to raise the issue.

In *Trede*[124] the accused pleaded guilty to stealing a camera. Two medical experts agreed that the accused did not require hospitalization for a mental disease but they concluded that at the time of the offense he was actuated by an "irresistible impulse" which grew out of his immature reaction to prior false accusations of theft made against him. The Court conceded that "irresistible impluse" was a type of mental disease recognized as a defense under military law; however, the legal concept of this defense is more restricted than that employed by the expert witnesses in this case. The Court regarded the acts of the accused as "no more than a type of moral insanity or a retarded mental condition which is described as immaturity—something akin to an aggravated spoiled child act." Such conduct does not involve a mental disease within the legal definition of "irresistible impulse."

[120] MANUAL FOR COURTS-MARTIAL, UNITED STATES, 1951, par. 122. United States v. Biesak, 3 USCMA 714, 14 CMR 132 (1954).

[121] United States v. Burns, 2 USCMA 400, 9 CMR 30 (1953); United States v. Niolu, 2 USCMA 513, 10 CMR 11 (1953); United States v. Biesak, 3 USCMA 714, 14 CMR 132 (1954). In the latter case the Court stated: "It is not inappropriate to add parenthetically at this point that, in view of the liberal attitude of the Manual toward determining the presence of an issue of insanity in a trial by court-martial, there will be little inclination on our part to find in borderline cases an abuse of discretion by the law officer in instructing thereon." United States v. Larry, 2 USCMA 415, 9 CMR 45 (1953) (president of a special court-martial failed to instruct on insanity).

[122] United States v. Biesak, 3 USCMA 714, 14 CMR 132 (1954). In *United States v. Holman,* 3 USCMA 396, 12 CMR 152 (1953) the Court stated that the law officer in cases in which insanity is not in issue is not required to instruct that consideration be given the disturbed state of the accused's mind in regard to his ability to entertain a specific intent to the same extent that instructions might have been demanded had there been abundant evidence of intoxication.

[123] United States v. Vigneault, 3 USCMA 247, 12 CMR 3 (1953).

[124] 2 USCMA 581, 10 CMR 79 (1953).

In *Biesak*[125] the Court held that notwithstanding the fact that his statements were not a "model of consistency" the testimony of Hospitalman Phillips was sufficient to raise an issue of sanity. The Court related this testimony in the following manner:

> "After describing Biesak's symptoms on direct examination, the witness stated on cross-examination that he did not consider the accused to have been insane 'in the meaning of the word "insane" itself.' However, on redirect Phillips ventured the opinion that accused might have been 'partly insane.' The final question put to this witness came from a court member, who asked whether in the opinion of the witness the accused was 'so free from mental defects as to be able, concerning the particular actions charged, to distinguish right from wrong and to adhere to the right.' To this the witness replied, 'I don't feel that he was, sir, when I saw him at least.' "[126]

In *Burns*[127] the Court observed that a psychiatrist had testified substantially as follows:

> "That the accused was sane at the time of the trial; that, therefore, he was able to understand the nature of the proceedings against him and cooperate in his defense; that the accused had a personality defect described as a schizoid personality, verging into a latent schizophrenic reaction; and, that at the time the crime was committed the accused was legally insane in that he was unable to adhere to the right."

This was held to be sufficient to raise an issue of sanity.

What happens to the presumption of sanity after sufficient evidence to raise the issue of sanity has been introduced? Does it completely disappear and thereby require the prosecution to come forward with positive evidence of sanity? Although the *Manual* states that when sanity is in issue the prosecution must prove the sanity of the accused, it also appears to provide that the prosecution will be aided by the presumption of sanity. In several cases law officers have employed in substance the language of Paragraph 122*a* of the *Manual* and instructed, in part, as follows:

> "If, in the light of all the evidence, *including that supplied by the presumption of sanity,* the court has a reasonable doubt as to

[125] 3 USCMA 714, 14 CMR 132 (1954). Opinion testimony of a lay witness plus other evidence was sufficient to put sanity in issue. United States v. Looff, 4 USCMA 36, 15 CMR 36 (1954).

[126] 3 USCMA 714, 717, 14 CMR 132, 135 (1954).

[127] 2 USCMA 400, 401, 9 CMR 30, 31 (1953).

> the mental responsibility of the accused at the time of the alleged offense the court must find the accused not guilty of that offense."[128]

Defense counsel objected to the use of the emphasized words on the ground that in this context they constituted an improper attempt to denominate a "presumption" as legal and competent evidence. In *Biesak* the Court considered this objection. The conclusion reached was that the use of these words amounted to:

> ". . . no more than an inartful attempt to advise court members that, apart from the existence of the presumption of sanity, they are free to consider all of the evidence before them through the lens of general human experience—especially that which indicates that most men are sane and that insanity may be feigned with ease."[129]

The Court then suggested that because of the "inartful quality" of the italicized words, it would be preferable to omit them from future instructions. However, use of these words will not constitute error unless the defense counsel requests and fails to receive a clarification of meaning.

It is apparent that introducing sufficient evidence to put sanity in issue will not per se demand a finding of insanity in those cases in which the prosecution fails to produce any positive proof of the accused's sanity.[130] In *Johnson* the Court made the following statement:

> "Additionally we pointed out there [Biesak] that, although the instruction had been viewed as going further—which we do not feel to be the case either there or here—and informing court members that under certain circumstances they would be *bound* to find the accused sane, we would be unwilling to find prejudicial error. This view is based on our concept that the presumption of sanity, in the sense of a mandatory inference, cannot be dispelled by evidence which the finder of fact disbelieves, or which, under proper instructions, he does not regard as tending to show that the accused was insane within the meaning of military law. An instruction on the subject of this mandatory inference would not, we believe, constitute error provided any reasonable possibility exists that the finder of fact might dis-

[128] United States v. Biesak, 3 USCMA 714, 718-719, 14 CMR 132, 136-137 (1954); United States v. Johnson, 3 USCMA 725, 14 CMR 143 (1954); United States v. Walters, 3 USCMA 732, 14 CMR 150 (1954); United States v. Boykins, 3 USCMA 806, 14 CMR 224 (1954).

[129] United States v. Biesak, 3 USCMA 714, 721, 14 CMR 132, 139 (1954).

[130] United States v. Burns, 2 USCMA 400, 9 CMR 30 (1953).

believe the evidence adduced to show insanity, or might interpret it to have a different effect."[131]

Testimony relating to an accused's mental status as of a date prior to the commission of an offense is often highly relevant and generally admissible.[132] Although legal insanity once shown to exist is presumed to continue in effect, a law officer is not required to give such an instruction in the absence of a request.[133] The Court has indicated that a civil adjudication of insanity even though unrefuted would not require dismissal of charges unless it met the test of insanity employed in military law.[134]

The Court regards amnesia alone as a relatively neutral circumstance in its bearing on criminal responsibility.[135] It has observed that it can be the result of moral delinquency which may include no more than an intense desire to forget rather than a diseased mind. In regard to whether alcoholic amnesia may constitute a defense the Court stated:

> "When dealing with alcoholic amnesia, we prefer to adopt a pragmatic approach to the problem and fix the total defense line squarely on a showing that alcoholism has so affected the mind of the person asserting the defense that he cannot distinguish between right and wrong or he cannot adhere to the right. If the consistent use of alcohol has impaired the mental faculties to that extent it is a defense but otherwise it is not."[136]

As indicated in the following statement of the Court, a law officer must consider whether amnesia and other evidence, although not sufficient to require an instruction on mental responsibility, might, nevertheless, require an instruction on such elements as specific intent or premedita tion in appropriate cases.

> ". . . amnesia, plus *other evidence* of mental shortcomings, may require an instruction not only on insanity, but also on the possibility of partial criminal responsibility. In other words, we would consider that the existence of mental processes, such as intent or

[131] United States v. Johnson, 3 USCMA 725, 731-732, 14 CMR 143, 149-150 (1954).
[132] United States v. Walters, 3 USCMA 732, 14 CMR 150 (1954).
[133] United States v. Johnson, 3 USCMA 725, 14 CMR 143 (1954).
[134] *Ibid.*
[135] United States v. Olvera, 4 USCMA 134, 15 CMR 134 (1954) (leading case on amnesia). The Court drew heavily from PSYCHIATRY IN MILITARY LAW, TM 8-240, AFM 160-42. Head injury, alcoholism and hysteria were discussed in this case.
[136] United States v. Marriott, 4 USCMA 390, 395-396, 15 CMR 390, 395-396 (1954).

premeditation, necessary for conviction of certain crimes, may be negated by a showing that the accused's mind could not entertain those processes."[137]

The concept of "partial criminal responsibility" referred to by the Court can be illustrated by reference to the intoxication cases previously discussed.[138] An accused may be legally sane but evidence of intoxication may be sufficient in appropriate cases to put in issue the question of knowledge, or intent or premeditation. The presence of genuine alcoholic amnesia without more would not constitute a bar to a finding of intent, knowledge or premeditation.[139]

A legally sane accused, who is successful in showing that his mental state was such that he was incapable of having knowledge, or intent, or premeditation because of intoxication, or other reasons,[140] may be found guilty of an appropriate lesser included offense not requiring any of those elements.

B. *Mental capacity*

The *Manual*[141] provides that a person should not be tried unless he possesses sufficient mental capacity to understand the nature of the proceedings against him and intelligently to conduct or cooperate in his defense. It is essential for law officers to distinguish between mental responsibility and mental capacity.

As indicated in the previous section a motion to dismiss is proper if there is an issue of sanity at the time of the commission of the offense. Moreover, if this motion is denied as an interlocutory matter, a court-martial may consider the question of mental responsibility during its deliberations on the findings upon the general issue. And, if at this time, the court-martial entertains a reasonable doubt that the accused was mentally responsible, it will enter a finding of not guilty.

The procedure and consequences, however, are quite different if the accused was sane at the time of the offense but lacks mental capacity. In such case he is not entitled either to a dismissal on motion or to a finding of not guilty.[142] Proper procedure is to grant a continuance

[137] United States v. Higgins, 4 USCMA 143, 148, 15 CMR 143, 148 (1954). See United States v. Marriott, *supra* note 136 for an example of an instruction given on voluntary intoxication and specific intent.

[138] See Section VIII this chapter on intoxication.

[139] United States v. Johnson, 4 USCMA 149, 15 CMR 149 (1954); United States v. Olvera, 4 USCMA 134, 15 CMR 134 (1954).

[140] See United States v. Edwards, 4 USCMA 299, 15 CMR 299 (1954) for an indication that other factors would be considered by the Court. But mere loss of moral restraints was mentioned specifically as not sufficient to destroy premeditation.

[141] Par. 120*c*.

[142] United States v. Lopez-Malave, 4 USCMA 341, 15 CMR 341 (1954).

until his mental deficiency is corrected. If the condition is permanent, the case may be dismissed by appropriate administrative action but not by a court-martial.[143]

If there is a question of mental capacity, defense counsel should move for a continuance.[144] A motion to dismiss is not proper. Should a motion to dismiss be made the law officer may consider it as a motion for a continuance. After evidence is presented on the motion for a continuance, the law officer should rule on it. Since the sanity of the accused is involved, the ruling of the law officer is subject to an objection by any member of the court-martial. In the absence of an objection his ruling is final. But if a member of the court-martial objects, the court-martial must then determine the issue. This procedure is exactly the same as that on any motion involving the sanity of the accused.

If the accused is found to possess mental capacity as a result of action taken on the motion, the question is settled. Thereafter, the law officer should not give instructions on, and the court-martial should not consider, the issue of mental capacity.

Should a lack of mental capacity be caused by alcoholism or amnesia caused by hysteria the Court does not think it is improper to grant a continuance in those cases in which medical evidence shows the probability of an *early* recovery.[145] But the Court does not believe the wrongdoing of the accused should provide him with an escape hatch from ultimate prosecution. The Court made the following statement regarding the disposition it would make of a case involving a lack of mental capacity caused by alcoholism or hysterical amnesia:

> "Our test for dismissing a criminal prosecution for a mental deficiency, at the time of trial, will not be extended to those mental disorders arising out of alcoholism or hysteria which interfere only with a clear recollection of the facts surrounding the offense of those antedating its occurrence. The right to a dismissal of the charges must grow out of a permanent mental disturbance at the time of the trial which, in good conscience, would require the legal proceedings be stayed and the action disposed of through administrative channels."[146]

[143] *Ibid.*
[144] *Ibid.*
[145] *Ibid.*
[146] *Id.* at 347-348. Questions involving amnesia were previously discussed by the Court in United States v. Olvera, *supra* note 135.

CHAPTER 8

Trial and Related Matters

I. Specifications

The purpose of this chapter is to discuss those matters considered by the Court of Military Appeals not covered elsewhere in this book. The topics are arranged, in general, in the sequence in which they appear in the *Manual*. No effort has been made to duplicate the provisions in the *Manual* other than what is deemed essential to explain the work of the Court. Many provisions appearing in Chapters X, XI, and XII in the *Manual* dealing with the subject of "Trial" do not appear in this chapter.

The Court has stated that federal practice "applies to court-martial procedures if not incompatible with military law or with the special requirements of the military establishment."[1]

A specification should include the name, rank and organization of the accused; the time and place where the offense is alleged to have occurred; and a statement in simple and concise language of the facts constituting the offense.[1] It is necessary to allege every essential element of the offense either directly or by clear implication. However, the rigors of common law rules of pleading have yielded to the general principle that formal defects, not prejudicial, will be disregarded.[2] The rule applied by the Court in ascertaining the sufficiency of a specification follows:

> "The true test of the sufficiency of an indictment is not whether it could have been made more definite and certain, but whether it contains the elements of the offense intended to be charged, and sufficiently apprises the defendant of what he must be prepared to meet; and, in case any other proceedings are taken against him for a similar offense, whether the record shows with

[1] United Statse v. Knudson, 4 USCMA 587, 590, 16 CMR 161, 164 (1954).

[2] United States v. Marker, 1 USCMA 393, 3 CMR 127 (1952); United States v. Hoph, 1 USCMA 584, 5 CMR 12 (1952); United States v. Simpson, 2 USCMA 493, 9 CMR 123 (1953).

accuracy to what extent he may plead a former acquittal or conviction."[3]

The mere fact that a specification is laid under an incorrect Article of the Code does not render it invalid. The test is whether the facts alleged are sufficient to constitute a military offense. For example, an allegation that an accused "went absent without leave to avoid completion of basic training in violation of Article 134" is not fatally defective even though this misconduct in fact violates Article 85 rather than Article 134.[4]

If a specification states an offense but the defense counsel desires clarification, he can make his request by motion. The Court refused[5] to go further and require the preparation of a request for a bill of particulars. Such motion should be made before plea[6] and ordinarily must be made during trial or else there is a waiver.[7] On the other hand, if a specification fails to state an offense, the defect is not waived by a plea of guilty[8] or by a failure to attack[9] it during trial.

Whether an offense is stated depends on the specification and not on the Article under which it is laid. If an essential element is missing in the specification, it cannot be supplied by a reference in the specification to a proper Article in the Code. Thus an allegation that the *accused was absent in violation of Article 86* is fatally defective because the specification does not contain a statement that the absence was without authority.[10]

II. Investigations

All cases referred to a general court-martial for trial must be investigated in accordance with Article 32 of the Code unless an adequate investigation preceded the preferring of charges.[11] This formal type investigation although not required may be held for cases referred to

[3] United States v. Sell, 3 USCMA 202, 206, 11 CMR 202, 206 (1953). This is consistent with MANUAL FOR COURTS-MARTIAL, UNITED STATES, 1951, par. 87*a* (2).

[4] United States v. O'Neil, 3 USCMA 416, 12 CMR 172 (1953). The specification stated the offense of desertion with intent to shirk important service.

[5] United States v. Hemp, 1 USCMA 280, 3 CMR 14 (1952).

[6] MANUAL FOR COURTS-MARTIAL, UNITED STATES, 1951, par. 69.

[7] United States v. Karl, 3 USCMA 427, 12 CMR 183 (1953); United States v. Steele, 2 USCMA 379, 9 CMR 9 (1953).

[8] MANUAL FOR COURTS-MARTIAL, UNITED STATES, 1951, par. 68*b*; United States v. Fout, 3 USCMA 565, 13 CMR 121 (1953).

[9] United States v. Karl, 3 USCMA 427, 12 CMR 183 (1953).

[10] United States v. Fout, 3 USCMA 565, 13 CMR 121 (1953); *accord*, United States v. Rios, 4 USCMA 203, 15 CMR 203 (1954) (robbery).

[11] A formal investigation, such as a court of inquiry, held before charges are preferred, will suffice if the accused was afforded his rights under Article 32 of the Code and he does not demand further investigation. MANUAL FOR COURTS-MARTIAL, UNITED STATES, 1951, par. 33*e* (1).

trial before a special court-martial. The investigation held pursuant to Article 32 serves much the same purpose in the military judicial system as in the preliminary hearing in civilian practice.[12] This investigation is impartial in nature and any objection to its sufficiency must be raised at the trial stage or it is waived.[13]

An investigating officer is not defined in the Code but paragraph 64 of the *Manual* provides that an investigating officer is one who "has conducted a personal investigation of a general matter involving the particular offense." In *Lee*[14] the Court was confronted with the question whether a trial counsel (prosecutor) who made an informal preliminary investigation and then signed the charges as accuser was an investigating officer. If so, he was disqualified to act subsequently as trial counsel in the case.[15] The Court observed that prosecuting attorneys in civilian courts frequently investigate a probable offense, file an information and later act in the same case as prosecutor. The Court then explicitly held that the inquiry did not constitute the trial counsel an investigating officer. But an officer on security watch who made an informal investigation immediately after the occurrence of the alleged offense was deemed to be an investigating officer, and therefore, he was disqualified to sit as a member of the court-martial which tried the case.[16]

Occasionally, a formal type investigation is conducted before charges are preferred.[17] If so, the officer conducting the investigation is unquestionably an investigating officer within the meaning of paragraph 64 of the *Manual.*

III. Instructing personnel of court-martial

Article 37 of the Code is a Congressional expression of an intent to free court-martial members from improper and undue influence which might affect an honest and conscientious consideration of the guilt or innocence of the accused. It provides in part:

> "No authority convening a . . . court-martial nor any other commanding officer, shall censure, reprimand, or admonish such court or any member, law officer, or counsel thereof, with respect to the findings or sentence adjudged by the court. . . . No person

[12] United States v. Lee, 1 USCMA 212, 2 CMR 118 (1952); United States v. Bound, 1 USCMA 224, 2 CMR 130 (1952).
[13] United States v. McCormick, 3 USCMA 361, 12 CMR 117 (1953).
[14] 1 USCMA 212, 2 CMR 118 (1952).
[15] Art. 27.
[16] United States v. Bound, 1 USCMA 224, 2 CMR 130 (1952). See Chapter 2, for disqualification of an investigating officer to sit as a member of the court-martial.
[17] For example, United States v. Welch, 1 USCMA 402, 3 CMR 136 (1952).

subject to this code shall attempt to coerce or, by any unauthorized means, influence the action of a court-martial. . . ."

On the other hand the *Manual*[18] provides that a convening authority may give general instructions to the personnel of a court-martial. These instructions, among others, may include information as to the state of discipline in the command, the prevalence of offenses which have impaired efficiency and discipline, and command measures taken to prevent the offenses. Although the Code and the *Manual* are not necessarily inconsistent, their provisions present difficult problems for determination.

The basic question presented is as follows:

> "Did the instructions given by the . . . [commanding officer, staff judge advocate or legal officer] fall within the fair limits permitted by the Manual or were they of such coercive nature that there was a violation of the Code restriction against the exercise of improper influence upon the court-martial members?"[19]

In *Littrice*[20] the Court found command coercion resulted from the totality of facts present in that case. Just prior to the trial of an alleged thief, the members of the court-martial, already informed of the name of the accused and the nature of the offense, were assembled to hear instructions from the acting commanding officer. The Court described the situation, in part, as follows:

> "Involved in the dissertation were statements to the effect that sentences which permit one convicted of larceny to remain in the service are improper; that imposition of inadequate sentences brings the armed forces in disrepute; that prerogatives of the convening authority should not be usurped; that the court-martial's findings and sentence are relatively unimportant in view of the thorough review given by division headquarters; that failure to recognize that the Army is no place for thieves is a serious deficiency; that great care must be used in selecting officers to serve on courts-martial; and, that when individuals selected for that duty have verified by their performance that they have certain qualifications, appropriate notations will be made in their efficiency reports."[21]

The Court in concluding its observations stated:

> "With these admonitions ringing in their ears, the members

[18] Par. 38.
[19] United States v. Littrice, 3 USCMA 487, 492, 13 CMR 43, 48 (1953).
[20] *Ibid.*
[21] *Id.* at 495, 13 CMR at 51.

of the court-martial began to hear this case on its merits. It requires little imagination to arrive at the reason why a finding of guilty was returned and the maximum sentence imposed."[22]

In *Isbell*[23] a sharply divided Court reached a different result. The facts were different in several particulars. For instance, the information concerning the retention of thieves in the Army reached certain members of the court-martial in the form of an official communication rather than through a direct appearance of a commanding officer. Moreover, this information was distributed several weeks before the offense for which Private Isbell was tried had been committed. However, this communication included the following statement:

> ". . . the greatest care should be exercised in the selection of officers who are to be appointed as members of all courts martial. They must be the best qualified by reason of age, education, training, experience, length of service, and judicial temperament. Moreover, *when the individual members have verified by their performance that they have those qualities, it is proper that you recognize that fact by appropriate notation on their efficiency report or by other written communication.*" (Emphasis supplied.)

In addition to this communication the Staff Judge Advocate issued a bulletin in which he criticized the results of previous court-martial trials but without specifically identifying a particular court-martial or an accused. Conceding the instructional value of distributing information regarding previous trials together with a statement of policy opposing the retention of thieves in the Army, it is difficult to justify references to an officer's efficiency report in this setting.

Command influence appeared more directly in a case[24] in which the convening authority informed three members of a court-martial that, in his opinion, a previous trial had not resulted in sufficient punishment. And further, to employ the words of one who heard the statements, he "was suggesting or recommending or instructing what verdict should be given." On appeal the Government conceded that this pretrial conference materially prejudiced the substantial rights of the accused.

[22] *Ibid.*

[23] 3 USCMA 782, 14 CMR 200 (1954). For a discussion of the *Littrice* and *Isbell* cases see Note, *Judicial Checks on Command Influence Under the Uniform Code of Military Justice,* 63 YALE L. J. 880 (1954). The Code Committee has recommended that staff officers be specifically named in Article 37. ANNUAL REPORT June 1, 1952, to December 31, 1953, p. 6.

[24] United States v. Hunter, 3 USCMA 497, 13 CMR 53 (1953). See also United States v. Borner, 3 USCMA 313, 12 CMR 69 (1953).

IV. Trial Counsel

Counsel eligibility is discussed in Chapter 2. Although a prosecutor, the role of trial counsel is not that of a partisan advocate, but, rather his primary duty is to see that justice is done.[25] In the absence of a showing of hostility, it is permissible for an accuser subsequently to act as trial counsel in the same case.[26]

A trial counsel is permitted to offer evidence of doubtful competency,[27] but if he deliberately disregards the rules of evidence such misconduct may constitute reversible error.[28] For example, extensive use of hearsay testimony and leading questions has been the basis for a finding of prejudicial error.[29] The Court occasionally has found it necessary to admonish both trial and defense counsel for failure to demonstrate the degree of professional responsibility and diligence imposed on them by the Code. The main criticism made by the Court has been directed at a lack of development of the facts;[30] particularly, when readily available evidence, if introduced, would have made it unnecessary for the Court to grant the accused's petition for review.[31]

Paragraph 44*g* (2) of the *Manual* provides that after the pleas, the trial counsel will, to the extent required by the law officer, read the parts of the *Manual* or of authoritative precedents that are pertinent to the definition and proof of any offense charged and to the defense thereto. The Court stated[32] that the law officer should supervise the exercise of this duty by the trial counsel. He should examine legal materials proposed for reading to insure they are regarded as authoritative precedents and, if so, he should make a determination whether the reading of such material by the trial counsel will be helpful to the members of the court-martial in a proper understanding of the case.

V. Defense Counsel

The Court usually disagrees with contentions of the accused that he was not represented adequately by counsel.[33] However, there are

[25] United States v. Johnson, 3 USCMA 447, 13 CMR 3 (1953).
[26] United States v. Lee, 1 USCMA 212, 2 CMR 118 (1952).
[27] United States v. Johnson, 3 USCMA 447, 13 CMR 3 (1953).
[28] United States v. Valencia, 1 USCMA 415, 4 CMR 7 (1952); United States v. Russell, 3 USCMA 696, 14 CMR 114 (1954) (error not prejudicial).
[29] United States v. Smith, 3 USCMA 15, 11 CMR 15 (1953).
[30] United States v. Knoph, 2 USCMA 108, 6 CMR 108 (1952) (trial counsel and defense counsel); United States v. Squirrell, 2 USCMA 146, 7 CMR 22 (1952) (trial counsel and defense counsel); United States v. Marshall, 2 USCMA 54, 6 CMR 54 (1952) (defense counsel). In United States v. Apple, 2 USCMA 592, 10 CMR 90 (1953) one of the judges criticized trial counsel for failure to ask pertinent questions on cross-examination.
[31] United States v. Wilson, 4 USCMA 3, 15 CMR 3 (1954); United States v. Beninate, 4 USCMA 98, 15 CMR 98 (1954).
[32] United States v. Fair and Boyce, 2 USCMA 521, 10 CMR 19 (1953). See also United States v. Guest, 3 USCMA 147, 11 CMR 147 (1953).
[33] United States v. Hunter, 2 USCMA 37, 6 CMR 37 (1952); United States

exceptional cases. On one[34] occasion the individual defense counsel (selected by accused) defended on the theory the shooting was an accident—then the appointed defense counsel arose and invited the court-martial to convict the accused of "wrongful killing." The Court referred to this conduct as almost incomprehensible and decided it was prejudicial to the accused.

In another case defense counsel apparently thought at the time of the trial that members of the court-martial had been improperly influenced by the staff judge advocate. He failed to mention it during trial. Later, this defense counsel filed an affidavit in support of a petition for a new trial in which he set out the circumstances of the alleged undue influence. The Court was so disturbed at the initial inaction of the defense counsel it concluded an officer so lacking in appreciation of his duties was unworthy of belief.[35] A serious weakness in this reasoning is that it apparently precludes a negligent or perhaps overly timid defense counsel from subsequently taking effective action to assist in the correction of any injustice which may have resulted from his own inaction.

Defense counsel may request additional instructions and submit to the law officer specific proposals as to the language to be incorporated in them.[36] All avenues favorable to the accused may be explored by defense counsel. A vigorous defense is permissible, but flagrantly contemptuous conduct such as a threat to hold civilly liable the members of the court-martial should they announce judgment before the Government produced certain witnesses for the defense will not be tolerated.[37]

VI. Staff Judge Advocate or Legal Officer

A staff judge advocate or legal officer may advise investigating officers without becoming disqualified to review the record of trial.[38] When requested by trial counsel on behalf of a law officer or president of a special court-martial, a staff judge advocate or legal officer may

v. Soukup, 2 USCMA 141, 7 CMR 17 (1953); United States v. Wilson, 2 USCMA 248, 8 CMR 48 (1953); United States v. Bigger, 2 USCMA 297, 8 CMR 97 (1953).

[34] United States v. Walker, 3 USCMA 355, 12 CMR 111 (1953).

[35] United States v. Borner, 3 USCMA 313, 12 CMR 69 (1953). Defense counsel and assistant defense counsel were involved. No corroboration appeared in reply affidavits and none was furnished by the defense.

[36] United States v. Offley, 3 USCMA 276, 12 CMR 32 (1953).

[37] United States v. DeAngelis, 3 USCMA 298, 12 CMR 54 (1953) (civilian counsel). Swartz, *Legal Ethics of Defense Counsel,* JAG Journal (April 1953) p. 7.

[38] United States v. DeAngelis, 3 USCMA 298, 12 CMR 54 (1954).

render legal advice on matters arising during trial.[39] But the Court has condemned the giving of legal advice at the scene of the trial.[40] This does not preclude a staff judge advocate or legal officer from attending a trial as a spectator so long as he refrains from participating in the proceedings. While a staff judge advocate was attending trial, he conferred with the president of the court-martial during a time in which the law officer was hearing arguments on a motion to dismiss. The result of the conference between the president of the court-martial and the staff judge advocate was an agreement to get certain legal materials before the court-martial in an unauthorized manner. The Court penned a stinging rebuke which ended with a statement that it hoped in the future courts-martial will be "unmolested by self-appointed friends of the court."[41]

VII. Joint Trials and Common Trials

When a joint offense is charged, a joint trial is customary and proper practice. A separate trial is a privilege, not a right.[42] Although a pretrial statement of one accused may implicate his co-accused, this factor alone does not require a severance. Generally an instruction by the law officer that the statement may be considered as evidence only against the accused who made it will be considered sufficient to safeguard the rights of co-accused.[43] A severance should be ordered when good cause, such as conflicting defenses, is shown. To meet the requirement that good cause be shown, it may be necessary for the defendant to open a part of his case for inspection. However, this inquiry may be accomplished in an out-of-court hearing.[44]

Paragraph 33*l* of the *Manual* provides that

> "If two or more persons are charged with the commission of an offense or offenses which, although not jointly committed, were committed at the same time and place and are provable by the same evidence, the convening authority may in his discretion direct a common trial for such offenses only."

If these requirements are not met the accused should if he desires, move for a severance. A motion to sever will be liberally construed.[45] Ordinarily the accused will be deemed to have waived his rights for a sev-

[39] Manual for Courts-Martial, United States, 1951, par. 73*a*. (Only convening authority expressly mentioned.)
[40] United States v. Self, 3 USCMA 568, 13 CMR 124 (1953).
[41] United States v. Guest, 3 USCMA 147, 11 CMR 147 (1953).
[42] United States v. Evans and Parker, 1 USCMA 541, 4 CMR 133 (1952); United States v. Wilson and Harvey, 2 USCMA 248, 8 CMR 48 (1953).
[43] United States v. Borner, 3 USCMA 306, 12 CMR 62 (1953).
[44] United States v. Evans and Parker, 1 USCMA 541, 4 CMR 133 (1952).
[45] Par. 69*d*.

erance unless a timely motion is made.[46] The Court indicated it might refuse to find a waiver in a case in which a manifest miscarriage of justice would result from a strict adherence to the waiver rule.[47]

VIII. Witnesses

Any witness requested by the defense must be shown to be both material and necessary in those instances in which process to compel attendance is required. If a witness is more than one hundred miles from the place of trial, the defense counsel should establish the materiality of the proposed testimony and submit a request for obtaining his deposition, or show why a deposition would not answer the purpose.[48]

Paragraph 53*f* of the *Manual* provides that a law officer, upon his own motion or upon motion of counsel, may instruct a witness to refrain from discussing his testimony or prospective testimony with anyone except counsel or the accused in the case. Segregation of witnesses during trial is ordinarily not required. A law officer does not commit error if he denies a motion made during trial to segregate witnesses in the absence of a showing of an attempt by one of the witnesses to influence the testimony of the other.[49] Witnesses other than the accused are usually excluded from the courtroom except when they are testifying.

IX. Views and Inspections

Paragraph 54*e* of the *Manual* provides that in exceptional circumstances, the court-martial may proceed to view or inspect the premises or place or an article or object if such view or inspection is necessary to enable the members better to understand and apply the evidence in the case. Action upon a request for a view rests solely in the sound discretion of the law officer. In a case in which photographs of the house in question, and the surrounding area, as well as a sketch of the scene were received in evidence, the law officer did not abuse his discretion in denying a request to view the premises.[50]

X. Continuance

Article 40 of the Code provides that a court-martial may, for reasonable cause, grant a continuance to any party for such time and

[46] United States v. Bodenheimer, 2 USCMA 130, 7 CMR 6 (1953); United States v. Smith, 2 USCMA 312, 8 CMR 112 (1953).

[47] United States v. Bodenheimer, 2 USCMA 130, 7 CMR 6 (1953).

[48] United States v. DeAngelis, 3 USCMA 298, 12 CMR 54 (1953). The Court found it unnecessary to determine if compulsory process was available to compel the attendance of Italian nationals in a court-martial trial held in Rome either in late 1950 or in early 1951.

[49] United States v. Borner, 3 USCMA 306, 12 CMR 62 (1953).

[50] *Ibid.*

as often as may appear to be just. The question of granting a continuance except when lack of mental capacity is the basis therefor is one for the sound discretion of the law officer.[51] The Court held that a law officer abused his discretion when he denied defense counsel a ten minute recess.[52] In a prosecution for rape the law officer refused to grant an overnight continuance after the defense counsel was surprised by a ruling which excluded certain evidence. The defense counsel desired to secure another witness to testify concerning the matter excluded. The Court held[53] that under the circumstances the denial of a continuance was an abuse of discretion which resulted in an error that materially prejudiced the substantial rights of the accused.

XI. CHALLENGE

Paragraph 62*f* of the *Manual* lists some of the grounds of challenge for cause against members of a court-martial and the law officer. The first eight grounds listed include such matters as the challenged member is the accuser, or will be a witness for the prosecution, or that he was the investigating officer in the case. These grounds are of such importance that the Court has indicated[54] that a waiver of the right to challenge will not be readily decreed. On the other hand, the Court made a general statement that a challenge to a court-martial member which is based on facts known prior to the conclusion of a trial must be made at that time or it will be considered waived.[55] Notwithstanding the generality of the language of the Court, it is possible that the first eight grounds will not be subject to waiver under the same circumstances that will be deemed sufficient when there are less serious grounds for challenge.

The mere fact that a Provost Marshall prior to trial had received some information concerning the offense is not sufficient grounds to sustain a challenge for cause.[56]

XII. DEFENSES

A. *Statute of Limitations*

In peacetime most offenses under the Code are subject to either a

[51] United States v. Lopez-Malave, 4 USCMA 341, 15 CMR 341 (1954). MANUAL FOR COURTS-MARTIAL, UNITED STATES, 1951, par. 58*d*; United States v. Nichols, 2 USCMA 27, 6 CMR 27 (1952). There was no abuse of discretion in denying motion for continuance.

[52] United States v. Sizemore, 2 USCMA 572, 10 CMR 70 (1953).

[53] United States v. Plummer, 1 USCMA 373, 3 CMR 107 (1952). See also United States v. Olvera, 4 USCMA 134, 15 CMR 134 (1954). The Court indicated that temporary amnesia would be a good ground for continuance. See also United States v. Knudson, 4 USCMA 587, 16 CMR 161 (1954).

[54] United States v. Bound, 1 USCMA 224, 2 CMR 130 (1952). The investigating officer subsequently sat as a member of the special court-martial.

[55] United States v. Thomas, 3 USCMA 161, 11 CMR 161 (1953).

[56] United States v. Edwards, 4 USCMA 299, 15 CMR 299 (1954).

two or three year period of limitation.[57] For instance, in the absence of a state of war the period is two years for absence without leave and three years for desertion. Prosecution is barred if the prescribed period expires between the commission of the offense and the receipt of sworn charges and specifications by an officer exercising summary court-martial jurisdiction over the command.[58]

In time of war there is no limitation on the offenses of absence without leave and desertion.[59] In *Ayers*[60] the Court was concerned with the question of whether an absence without leave which occurred in the United States on December 23, 1950 was barred by the statute of limitations inasmuch as sworn charges and specifications were not received by the officer exercising summary court-martial authority until March 18, 1953. Previously, the Court held[61] that the hostilities in Korea constituted a state of war for our forces in the Korean zone of operation for purpose of applying the provisions of the Code. But these decisions did not deal with offenses which occurred in the United States. In the instant case the Court decided that the "in time of war" provision of Article 43 (a) applied to offenses committed in the United States during the existence of large-scale hostilities in Korea. However, the Court reserved decision as to whether the same result would be reached in construing the war clauses in other provisions in the Code.[62]

Article 43 (f) provides that for certain enumerated offenses, including frauds against the United States, the running of the statute of limitations will be suspended when the United States is at war until

[57] Code, Art. 43. Murder and some other offenses listed in Article 43 (a) do not have any time limitation. A period of limitations may be extended subsequent to the commission of a crime without violating proscriptions against ex post facto legislation. United States v. Ayers, 4 USCMA 220, 15 CMR 220 (1954). See also, United States v. Nichols, 2 USCMA 27, 6 CMR 27 (1952) for period of limitations for offenses committed prior to the Code.

[58] *Ibid;* MANUAL FOR COURTS-MARTIAL, UNITED STATES, par. 68*c*. The following statement appears in LEGAL AND LEGISLATIVE BASIS, MANUAL FOR COURTS-MARTIAL, UNITED STATES (1951), p. 85 regarding the *Manual* provision on the running of the statute of limitations:

> "In effect this may mean that there will be virtually no statute of limitations as to AWOL and desertion cases if departmental regulations will authorize the forwarding of charges to the various departments when the absentee is dropped from the unit as a deserter. When they are received by the Secretary of the Department (who exercises summary court-martial jurisdiction over the command which includes the accused) or his representative, the running of the statute is stopped."

[59] CODE, Art. 43 (a) provides: "A person charged with desertion or absence without leave in time of war, or with aiding the enemy, mutiny, or murder, may be tried and punished at any time without limitation."

[60] 4 USCMA 220, 15 CMR 220 (1954).

[61] United States v. Bancroft, 3 USCMA 3, 11 CMR 3 (1953) and cases cited in Chapter 12, Sec. II A.

[62] For instance, Art. 90 (assaulting or willfully disobeying officer), and Art. 106 (spies).

three years after the termination of hostilities as proclaimed by the President or by a joint resolution of Congress. The Court held that the Korean conflict was sufficient to invoke the suspension provisions of this section for frauds against the United States regardless of where the offense was committed.[63] Thus a fraudulent enlistment which occurred in the United States on February 20, 1951 was not barred from prosecution even though the peacetime statute of limitations period of two years expired before charges were received by the officer exercising summary court-martial jurisdiction.[64]

B. *Former jeopardy*

Article 44 of the Code provides that no person shall, without his consent, be tried a second time for the same offense.[65] Although the question has not been definitely decided, the Supreme Court of the United States indicated[66] that the double jeopardy provisions of the Fifth Amendment apply to courts-martial.

Congress established in Article 44 (b) the time when jeopardy will attach:

> "No proceeding in which an accused has been found guilty by a court-martial upon any charge or specification shall be held to be a trial in the sense of this article until the finding of guilty has become final after review of the case has been fully completed."[67]

An order publishing the result of trial has been held to constitute a prima facie showing of conviction in that trial.[68]

The Court has decided several other cases involving important questions of jeopardy. In *Zimmerman*[69] a board of review *dismissed*

[63] United States v. Taylor, 4 USCMA 232, 15 CMR 232 (1954).

[64] *Ibid.*

[65] United States v. Padilla and Jacobs, 1 USCMA 603, 5 CMR 31 (1952). Jacobs was acquitted at the first trial, and the second trial put him twice in jeopardy.

[66] Wade v. Hunter, 336 U. S. 684 (1949); *cf.* United States v. Zimmerman, 2 USCMA 12, 6 CMR 12 (1952). Thornton, *Double Jeopardy and the Court-Martial,* 19 BROOKLYN L. REV. 63 (1953).

[67] Article 44 (c) further provides: "A proceeding which, subsequent to the introduction of evidence but prior to a finding, is dismissed or terminated by the convening authority or on motion of the prosecution for failure of available evidence or witnesses without any fault of the accused shall be a trial in the sense of this article." See generally MANUAL FOR COURTS-MARTIAL, UNITED STATES, 1951, par. 68*d*. *But cf.* United States v. Chapman, 2 USCMA 138, 7 CMR 14 (1953).

[68] United States v. Tiedemann, 1 USCMA 595, 5 CMR 23 (1952).

[69] 2 USCMA 12, 6 CMR 12 (1952), 21 GEO. WASH. L. REV. 497 (1953); 26 TEMP. L. Q. 446. See also United States v. Messenger, 2 USCMA 21, 6 CMR 21 (1952). The United States Supreme Court held that a second trial granted on appeal of accused was not double jeopardy. Bryan v. United States, 338 U. S. 552 (1950).

the charges because several procedural errors were committed during trial. The Court reversed the conclusions of the board of review after considering the case on certificate of The Judge Advocate General of the Navy. However, the Court found error in the sentence because previous convictions of the accused were improperly considered by the trial court. The case was remanded by the Court with the idea that the board of review would affirm so much of the sentence as it deemed appropriate in the absence of the improperly considered previous convictions. Instead, the board, one member dissenting, ruled that its prior dismissal must stand because otherwise the accused would be twice put in jeopardy. On a second certification the Court differed with the board of review and held that jeopardy had not attached—the initial decision of the board was not final but only interlocutory. Appellate review is complete when a case such as this one is decided by the Court or the time in which it could be presented to the Court has expired.[70]

The Court in *Frisbee*[71] again reversed a board of review because the board incorrectly concluded that jeopardy had attached. The accused pleaded guilty in a special court-martial trial. The convening authority approved the findings and the bad conduct discharge but reduced the forfeitures adjudged by the court-martial. Later a rehearing was ordered by the officer exercising general court-martial jurisdiction (supervisory authority) because he believed the trial court had improperly considered previous convictions. A second trial was held and the accused again pleaded guilty. This time the convening authority *and* the officer exercising general court-martial jurisdiction approved the findings and sentence. The board of review concluded the second trial constituted double jeopardy. This conclusion was predicated on the reasoning that the officer exercising general court-martial jurisdiction did not have authority to order a rehearing, and when he disapproved the sentence it amounted to a final review and hence completion of the first trial. The Court reversed the action of the board of review after deciding that the officer exercising general court-martial jurisdiction in a review of a special court-martial case involving a bad conduct discharge has the same power as that of a convening authority in a general court-martial case. This included, among other things, the power to order a rehearing.[72]

[70] See Rules 22 and 23, *Rules of Practice and Procedure, United States Court of Military Appeals,* 1 USCMA pp. xxviii-xxix.

[71] 2 USCMA 293, 8 CMR 93 (1953).

[72] Judge Brosman concurred in the result in *Frisbee* because he wished to disassociate himself from the part of the majority opinion which indicated that the supervisory authority had the same power in a special or summary court-

A question of double jeopardy in connection with an amended specification was decided in *Wilson and Harvey*.[73] The accused were charged with premeditated murder. The specification under which the two accused were convicted alleged that:

> ". . . acting jointly, and in pursuance of a common intent, did, at . . . Korea, on or about 10 April 1951, *with malice aforethought,* willfully, *deliberately, feloniously,* unlawfully and with premeditation kill Hong Jae Gun, a human being, by shooting him with a carbine."[74]

At the inception of the trial, the specification did not include the emphasized words. On request of trial counsel these words were added to the specification after one witness had been heard. Defense counsel did not object to the amendment but he did request and was granted a continuance for one week. The accused were found guilty under the amended specification. The Court held the two accused had not been put in jeopardy at the time they were arraigned on the amended specification.

Jurisdiction to try the person and the offense is essential to a valid trial; therefore, a person has not been tried in the sense of Article 44 if the proceedings were void for a lack of jurisdiction.[75] However, if a convening authority incorrectly determines that a court-martial was without jurisdiction in a case in which the accused is found guilty and orders another trial, the second court-martial still has authority to try the case anew by virtue of the convening authority's power to direct further proceedings in such cases.[76] But the second court-martial cannot adjudge a sentence in excess of the one imposed in the first trial.

In *Niolu*[77] the defense of former jeopardy was invoked unsuccessfully. The convening authority ordered a rehearing because he received a memorandum from the president of the court-martial *after* the trial expressing the opinion of members of the court-martial, the investigating officer, and the accused's battery commander that accused was not mentally sound. During the rehearing a plea of former jeopardy based on the contention that the memorandum amounted to an acquittal at the first trial was made and rejected by the court-

---

martial case not involving a bad conduct discharge. In United States v. Watkins, 2 USCMA 287, 8 CMR 87 (1953), all judges agreed that this authority exists in a case in which the sentence includes a bad conduct discharge.

[73] 2 USCMA 248, 8 CMR 48 (1953).

[74] *Id.* at 252, 8 CMR at 52.

[75] MANUAL FOR COURTS-MARTIAL, UNITED STATES, 1951, par. 68*d*.

[76] United States v. Padilla and Jacobs, 1 USCMA 603, 5 CMR 31 (1952).

[77] 2 USCMA 513, 10 CMR 11 (1953).

martial rehearing the case. The Court held there was no double jeopardy inasmuch as no evidence concerning insanity was introduced in the first trial. Further there was no indication that the members of the court-martial had at the time of the findings in the first trial entertained a reasonable doubt as to the sanity of the accused.

Another aspect of the jeopardy problem arises from the fact that a commander of a military prison is given administrative powers to punish prisoners. This authority is in addition to and not in lieu of the authority of commanding officers to punish under Article 15. The Court held an exercise of these administrative powers to punish a prisoner for a major offense did not preclude a subsequent trial by a court-martial for the same conduct.[78]

The *Manual*[79] specifically provides that the defense of former jeopardy ordinarily should be asserted by motion to dismiss before a plea is entered. However, it can be raised anytime during trial. This defense is subject to waiver and is waived unless raised before the completion of the trial.[80]

C. *Constructive condonation of desertion*

If an officer exercising general court-martial jurisdiction unconditionally restores a deserter to duty without trial with knowledge of the alleged desertion, this action amounts to a constructive condonation of the desertion.[81] The Court emphasized the necessity that the restoration to duty be by an officer exercising general court-martial jurisdiction.[82] Since this is an affirmative defense, it must be raised at the trial level.[83] The Court held[84] condonation cannot be extended and used as a defense to a charge of misbehavior before the enemy. The Court has also expressed doubt whether absence without leave can be brought within this concept without legislative sanction.[85]

D. *Entrapment*

Historically, the defense of entrapment has been available only to those who have been induced to commit a crime because of proposals

[78] United States v. Vaughan, 3 USCMA 121, 11 CMR 121 (1953). Escape from confinement was considered a major offense under the facts of this case.

[79] Par. 67*a*.

[80] United States v. Kreitzer, 2 USCMA 284, 8 CMR 84 (1953).

[81] MANUAL FOR COURTS-MARTIAL, UNITED STATES, 1951, par. 68*f*.

[82] United States v. Minor, 1 USCMA 497, 4 CMR 89 (1952); United States v. Perkins, 1 USCMA 502, 4 CMR 94 (1952); United States v. Walker, 1 USCMA 501, 4 CMR 93 (1952).

[83] United States v. Squirrell, 2 USCMA 146, 7 CMR 22 (1953).

[84] United States v. Walker, 1 USCMA 501, 4 CMR 93 (1952).

[85] United States v. Minor, 1 USCMA 497, 4 CMR 89 (1952). The argument for applying this concept to absence without leave is that it is a lesser included offense.

made by the arresting officers. Therefore, setting the stage to discover the guilt of one who has conceived his own wrongful plan does not violate the rule against entrapment.[86] The Court considered but rejected[87] a theory of "permissive entrapment." This theory would require an officer, who is aware that a member of his command proposes to commit an offense, to stop the potential offender—and if the officer does not undertake to do so, the accused would have a defense based on such inaction.

E. *Res Judicata*

The *Manual*[88] provides that res judicata is a defense and that the doctrine cannot ordinarily be employed by the prosecution. In regard to this doctrine as a defense the *Manual* states:

> "The defense of *res judicata* is based on the rule that any issue of fact or law put in issue and finally determined by a court of competent jurisdiction cannot be disputed between the same parties in a subsequent trial even if the second trial is for another offense."

In *Smith*[89] the accused was first tried for larceny of two letters. The law officer incorrectly excluded the confession of the accused. The accused was thereafter acquitted upon a motion for a finding of not guilty based on an insufficiency of the evidence. The following month the accused was tried for larceny of a package.

The Government undertook to introduce in this trial the same confession which had been excluded in the previous trial. Defense counsel objected on the ground of res judicata. The Court agreed with the view of the defense counsel and reversed the board of review which had held the confession was admissible. The Court gave recognition to the broad definition of res judicata contained in the *Manual* in making the following statement:

> ". . . [it] makes no distinction as to issues directly involved or collaterally involved; it does not limit its application to issues arising out of one transaction; and we find no good reason to interpret the provision so narrowly as to require the accused again to litigate an issue which has been decided in his favor. While the fact that the general verdict returned in the military system may, on occasions, make it impossible to determine whether a

[86] United States v. Buck, 3 USCMA 341, 12 CMR 97 (1953).
[87] United States v. Jewson, 1 USCMA 652, 5 CMR 80 (1952).
[88] Par. 71*b*.
[89] 4 USCMA 369, 15 CMR 369 (1954).

particular issue was in fact decided in a prior trial, we are not faced with that difficulty in this instance."[90]

XIII. Pleas

In court-martial procedure, pleas include guilty, not guilty, and pleas corresponding to permissible findings of lesser included offenses.[90a]

Article 45 (a) of the Code provides in part that if an accused sets up a matter inconsistent with a prior plea of guilty, "a plea of not guilty shall be entered in the record, and the court shall proceed as though he had pleaded not guilty." The majority of the Court held[91] a statement made by an accused after findings that he intended to borrow the food (allegedly stolen) and replace it was not inconsistent with his plea of guilty to charges of larceny and wrongful appropriation. The Court in effect, upheld the *Manual* provision which states that an intention to pay for the property stolen or otherwise to replace it with an equivalent is not a defense.[92]

XIV. Conferences During Trial

A. *Conferences between counsel and law officer*

A law officer and counsel are permitted to hold unrecorded out-of-court conferences.[93] The Court regarded an unrecorded in-court conference between defense counsel and the law officer as a "doubtful" practice. In this connection the Court made the following general statement:

> "We believe that during the trial of a case the better practice is to record all matters which in any way affect the proceedings."[94]

Subsequently, the Court refused to find that prejudice resulted when the law officer and counsel for both sides held an unrecorded in-court conference.[95]

B. *Closed Conferences between the law officer and the court-martial*

Prior to the adoption of the Code the law member not only acted as legal adviser to the court-martial but he also participated fully in

[90] *Id.* at 374.

[90a] For more details see Par. 70, Manual for Courts-Martial, United States, 1951.

[91] United States v. Krull, 3 USCMA 129, 11 CMR 129 (1953).

[92] Par. 200*a* (6). See discussion of Punitive Article 121 in Chapter 14.

[93] Manual for Courts-Martial, United States, 1951, par. 57*g* (2); United States v. Ransom, 4 USCMA 195, 15 CMR 195 (1954).

[94] United States v. Lampkins, 4 USCMA 31, 33, 15 CMR 31, 33 (1954).

[95] United States v. Ransom, 4 USCMA 195, 15 CMR 195 (1954).

the court-martial proceedings as a member. Congress, however, as observed in the preceding chapter, determined that the law officer should function more like a judge—therefore, he is authorized to appear in a closed session of a court-martial only for the purpose of advising on the form of the findings.[96] This authority is further limited to occasions on which a request is made for such assistance. Moreover, it is required that a record be made of the proceedings.[97]

Beginning with *Keith*[98] the Court has decided a large number of closed conference cases. In the initial case to come before the Court the court-martial announced its findings, heard evidence in extentuation and mitigation and closed to deliberate on the sentence. Subsequently, the court-martial was opened and the president stated that advice from the law officer was desired. The law officer excused trial counsel, defense counsel and the accused, and proceeded to answer questions by members of the court-martial concerning the difference between a bad conduct discharge and a dishonorable discharge insofar as the possibilities of suspension and rehabilitation were involved. He further responded to questions regarding the application of the 1951 *Manual* and its predecessor in determining the maximum sentence which could be imposed. A verbatim report of this conference appeared in the record. Error was present because the conference violated the Code and the *Manual*. Was it prejudicial? The Court, Judge Latimer not participating, rejected the test of specific prejudice (i.e., a fair risk that the accused actually was prejudiced) in this setting and instead, applied the rule of general prejudice. This meant a rehearing without an inquiry into the possible prejudicial effect of the illegal conference. The Court stated it would adhere to the general prejudice rule in these cases until the tradition of non-participation was well established. However, it indicated at some future time that it may be possible "to assess the occasional lapses in terms of specific prejudice."

[96] CODE, Art. 39; United States v. Smith, 3 USCMA 680, 14 CMR 98 (1954) (three closed conferences all concerning the form of the findings).

[97] CODE, Art. 39. See United States v. Kupfer, 3 USCMA 478, 13 CMR 34 (1953).

[98] 1 USCMA 493, 4 CMR 85 (1952); *accord,* United States v. McConnell, 1 USCMA 508, 4 CMR 100 (1952) (conference on sentence); United States v. Cadena, 1 USCMA 534, 4 CMR 126 (1952) (conference before findings); United States v. Smith, 1 USCMA 531, 4 CMR 123 (1952) (conference before findings); United States v. Mann, 2 USCMA 261, 8 CMR 61 (1953) (conference on sentence); United States v. Jester, 2 USCMA 280, 8 CMR 80 (1953) (conference on sentence); United States v. Miller, 2 USCMA 272, 8 CMR 72 (1953) (conference before findings and the record did not contain an account thereof); United States v. Curtis, 2 USCMA 311, 8 CMR 111 (1953) (conference on sentence); United States v. Holland, 2 USCMA 314, 8 CMR 114 (1953) (conference on sentence).

In *Miskinis*[99] nine months later the Court began to relax its rigid policy of reversing in unauthorized closed conference cases. The law officer assisted the court-martial in putting the *sentence* in proper form *after* that body had decided on the sentence to be imposed. This was error but the Court distinguished it from prior cases and tagged it "harmless." In the opinion the following rule was announced by the Court:

> ". . . where the law officer appears before the court when it is in closed session without the presence of accused or his counsel in violation of Articles 26 (b) and 39 of the Code . . . and *participates in the deliberations* of the court, a finding of reversible error based upon the doctrine of general prejudice will result. We may also note that, if the record does not reflect what transpired during the conference, then we will be constrained to resolve the doubt in favor of the accused." (Emphasis supplied.)[100]

This rule makes it apparent that not every unauthorized closed conference will invoke the doctrine of general prejudice. Several cases[101] have not felt the impact of the general prejudice rule because the Court found that the law officer, although a party to a closed conference, did not participate in the deliberations of the court-martial. For example, merely answering procedural questions is not regarded as participating in the deliberations.

The Court further has held that general prejudice may be "cured" when the law officer repeats in open court the questions and answers dealt with in the closed conference.[102]

A closed conference may occur in the presence of the accused if the law officer confers with the members of the court-martial so quietly that the conversation cannot be heard by the accused or his counsel.[103]

The most recent cases[104] indicate the Court is now ready to resort

[99] 2 USCMA 273, 8 CMR 73 (1953); *accord,* United States v. Derosier, 2 USCMA 282, 8 CMR 82 (1953); United States v. Allen, 2 USCMA 276, 8 CMR 76 (1953).

[100] United States v. Miskinis, 2 USCMA 273, 275, 8 CMR 73, 75 (1953).

[101] United States v. Fields, 2 USCMA 278, 8 CMR 78 (1953); United States v. Reinking, 2 USCMA 360, 8 CMR 160 (1953); United States v. Headspeth, 2 USCMA 635, 10 CMR 133 (1953).

[102] United States v. Ferry, 2 USCMA 326, 8 CMR 126 (1953); United States v. Freeman, 2 USCMA 329, 8 CMR 129 (1953).

[103] United States v. Vaughan, 3 USCMA 121, 11 CMR 121 (1953) (specific prejudice was found).

[104] United States v. Taborn, 3 USCMA 61, 11 CMR 61 (1953); United States v. Vaughan, 3 USCMA 121, 11 CMR 121 (1953). The "Court Committee" (appointed by the Court and to be distinguished from the Code Committee) rejected a proposal submitted by the services that the law officer be permitted to enter and assist the court-martial in putting both findings and sentence in proper form. The Court supported the "Court Committee" "at least, to the extent

to the test of specific prejudice. The technique suggested by Judge Latimer in his dissenting opinion in *Woods and Duffer*[105] probably will receive the acceptance of the entire Court.

XV. Proving Previous Convictions

After a finding of guilty and before sentence, it is the duty of trial counsel to introduce evidence of any previous convictions of the accused by a court-martial which have occurred during the current enlistment[106] and during the three years[107] next preceding the commission of any offense of which the accused stands convicted. Proof of two previous convictions operates to increase the maximum authorized punishment which a court-martial may impose in certain cases.[108] For example, a punitive discharge is not ordinarily a permissible sentence if the accused has been convicted of an unauthorized absence for less than sixty days, but when there is proof of two previous convictions a bad conduct discharge is authorized.

Sworn testimony of trial counsel is a permissible method of proof of previous convictions.[109] If sworn testimony is confined to presenting the contents of documents it is necessary to show the documents

---

that the Judges are of the opinion that any difficulties in this regard are purely procedural in nature and do not warrant any change in the substantive law." Annual Report, for June 1, 1952, to December 31, 1953, p. 18.

[105] 2 USCMA 203, 8 CMR 3 (1953). Judge Latimer outlined his views in the following manner:

> ". . . divide the cases into two general categories, namely, those where the error crept into the case before a finding of guilt and those where the error affected only the sentence. . . . In the first category . . . if the record indicated the communication was prejudicial to the accused, I would reverse. If, on the contrary, it established that it was either to his benefit or did not prejudice materially his substantial rights, I would affirm. If the record was silent as to what transpired, I would presume it to be prejudicial to the accused and place the burden on the Government to establish that it was not to his detriment.
>
> Substantially the same rule would be adopted if the communication took place after a finding of guilty. . . . I would not reverse the findings of guilt as the error could not possibly influence the court-martial in its deliberations on the guilt or innocence of the accused."

[106] Manual for Courts-Martial, United States, 1951, par. 75*b*, provides: "The evidence must, however, relate to offenses committed during a current enlistment, voluntary extension of enlistment, appointment, or other engagement or obligation for service of the accused, and during the three years next preceding the commission of any offense of which the accused stands convicted."

[107] In a trial for an offense committed in January, 1952 it was improper for the court-martial to consider convictions for offenses which occurred in April, 1952. United States v. Crusoe, 3 USCMA 793, 14 CMR 211 (1954).

[108] Manual for Courts-Martial, United States, 1951, par. 127*c*, Section B. Paragraph 75*b* (2) refers to previous convictions by courts-martial and does not include non-judicial punishment. McDonald, *Trial Counsel and Records of Previous Convictions*, JAG Journal (July, 1952), p. 9.

[109] United States v. Carter, 1 USCMA 108, 2 CMR 14 (1952); United States v. Castillo, 1 USCMA 352, 3 CMR 86 (1952); United States v. Lowery, 2 USCMA 315, 8 CMR 115 (1953).

were executed in substantial compliance with the rules and regulations applicable to documentary evidence.[110] However, sworn testimony is not required by the Code or *Manual*. Proof of previous convictions, like other evidence, may be properly considered by a court-martial if presented by stipulation, by admissions in open court, or by written instrument.[111] If documentary evidence is employed, the service record of the accused or an admissible copy or extract will be sufficient if properly introduced. Moreover, it is permissible to resort to the order publishing the result of trial if the rules applicable to documentary evidence are followed.[112]

Correct practice requires that the defense be given an opportunity to inspect documentary evidence of prior convictions. But if the record does not reveal an explicit tender, it is a procedural irregularity and not reversible error.[113]

In *Carter*[114] the accused pleaded guilty to a charge of absence without leave for five days. After a finding of guilty, the trial counsel made a detailed unsworn statement concerning two previous convictions. In reply to a specific question the defense counsel stated that he had no objection. The court-martial accepted the oral statement of trial counsel and imposed a sentence which, unless the evidence of previous convictions was properly considered, was in excess of the maximum permitted by the *Manual* and accordingly prejudicial.[115]

The procedure outlined in the *Manual* for presenting this proof is susceptible to two interpretations. One would permit trial counsel, as in *Carter,* to relate the previous convictions to the court-martial and require no further proof unless the accused objects. Another interpretation would require, even when there is no objection, competent proof of previous convictions, such as the service record or the order publishing the result of trial, *after* trial counsel recited the previous convictions to the court-martial. The Court chose the latter interpretation

[110] United States v. Castillo, 1 USCMA 352, 3 CMR 86 (1952).

[111] United States v. Carter, 1 USCMA 108, 2 CMR 14 (1952).

[112] *Ibid.* See MANUAL FOR COURTS-MARTIAL, UNITED STATES, 1951, par. 143*a* for procedure in proving the contents of a writing.

[113] United States v. Castillo, 1 USCMA 352, 3 CMR 86 (1952).

[114] 1 USCMA 108, 2 CMR 14 (1952).

[115] *Ibid.* The Court has reversed the board of review in several cases in which the Court found prejudicial error. United States v. Trimiar, 1 USCMA 262, 2 CMR 169 (1952); United States v. Schabel, 1 USCMA 275, 3 CMR 9 (1952); United States v. Adams, 1 USCMA 275, 3 CMR 9 (1952); United States v. Pruchniewski, 1 USCMA 328, 3 CMR 62 (1952); United States v. DeWeese, 1 USCMA 400, 3 CMR 134 (1952); United States v. Townsend, 1 USCMA 441, 4 CMR 33 (1952); United States v. West, 1 USCMA 590, 5 CMR 18 (1952); United States v. Zimmerman, 1 USCMA 160, 2 CMR 66 (1952). See also United States v. Hand 1 USCMA 301, 3 CMR 35 (1952).

and held that in all cases the accused is entitled to have introduced in the record competent evidence of previous convictions.

In order to avoid any tendency on the part of the trial counsel to forget to offer the exhibit after he reads it, the Court suggested that it would be helpful to depart from the sequence of events outlined in the *Manual:*

> "As a matter of practice, it would appear to be more desirable to have the document marked as an exhibit, shown to the accused, its admissibility determined, and, if admitted in evidence, then permit the trial counsel to read it to the court."[116]

In *Zimmerman*[117] the Court held that merely attaching to the court-martial record a copy of a service record reflecting previous convictions did not correct a failure to introduce it in evidence inasmuch as the Court had no way of knowing the appended material was the source from which the trial counsel read to the court-martial. The Court further indicated that appending material marked as an exhibit does not sufficiently show it was introduced in evidence.[118]

A mere statement by defense counsel[119] or the accused[120] that there is no objection to a recitation of previous convictions by unsworn trial counsel does not constitute either a stipulation or a waiver of proof of previous convictions.[121]

Paragraph 75*b* (2) of the *Manual* provides that "unless the accused has been tried for an offense within the meaning of Article 44*b* [former jeopardy], evidence as to the offense is not admissible as evidence of a previous conviction." Article 44(b) states that "no proceeding in which an accused has been found guilty by a court-martial upon any charge or

[116] United States v. Carter, 1 USCMA 108, 113, 2 CMR 14, 19 (1952). In United States v. Castillo, 1 USCMA 352, 3 CMR 86 (1952) the Court approved the following procedure: (1) trial counsel asked that the pages of the accused's service record which reflected previous convictions be marked as exhibits; (2) each page was shown to defense counsel who was asked if there was any objection; and (3) when defense counsel informed the court he had none, the trial counsel read the contents of the extracts into evidence and requested that copies be appended to the record. *Accord,* United States v. Anderson, 2 USCMA 606, 10 CMR 104 (1953).

[117] 1 USCMA 160, 2 CMR 66 (1952).

[118] United States v. West, 1 USCMA 590, 5 CMR 18 (1952) (record did not recite the oral statements of trial counsel); United States v. Parker, 3 USCMA 272, 12 CMR 28 (1953) (error not prejudicial because of particular facts in the case). *Cf.* United States v. Walker, 1 USCMA 580, 5 CMR 8 (1952).

[119] United States v. Carter, 1 USCMA 108, 2 CMR 14 (1952); United States v. Zimmerman, 1 USCMA 160, 2 CMR 66 (1952); United States v. Parker, 3 USCMA 272, 12 CMR 28 (1953).

[120] United States v. West, 1 USCMA 590, 5 CMR 18 (1952).

[121] Proof of authenticity of the documents was waived by defense counsel in United States v. Castillo, 1 USCMA 352, 3 CMR 86 (1952).

specification shall be held to be a trial in the sense of this article until the *finding of guilty has become final after review of the case has been fully completed.*" (Emphasis supplied.) The Court was confronted with the question of whether this language required the prosecution to prove that appellate review had been completed in each instance in which a previous conviction was offered in evidence. In *Tiedemann*[122] the previous conviction involved was the result of a trial by a special court-martial. The convening authority issued the order promulgating the result of the trial. The sentence did not contain a bad conduct discharge; consequently, appellate review of this case was complete when it was approved by the supervisory authority. However, the evidence did not reveal that the supervisory authority had taken any action. The Court decided the order publishing the result of trial was sufficient to make out a prima facie showing of a conviction for purposes of establishing former jeopardy and of proving previous convictions.

If the sentence contains a bad conduct discharge, review would not be complete until thirty days after the accused is notified of the action by the board of review.[123] In *Larney*[124] the sentence included a bad conduct discharge and the record did not show that action had been taken by a board of review. The Court decided to extend the prima facie rule to cases involving a bad conduct discharge and stated:

> ". . . when an order publishing the result of trial or a service record entry showing conviction and the promulgation of the result of trial is admitted in evidence a prima facie showing of a former conviction has been established."[125]

This language is sufficiently broad to include previous convictions by general courts-martial.[126]

An accused is entitled to rebut the prima facie showing. In *Anderson*[127] the previous conviction carried a sentence which included a bad conduct discharge. The exhibit introduced in evidence revealed that only thirty-six days elapsed between the time the record was approved by the officer exercising general court-martial jurisdiction and the time

[122] 1 USCMA 595, 5 CMR 23 (1953).
[123] United States v. Anderson, 2 USCMA 606, 10 CMR 104 (1953).
[124] 2 USCMA 563, 10 CMR 61 (1953).
[125] *Id.* at 570, 10 CMR at 68.
[126] Conviction by a summary court-martial is final when action is taken by the supervisory authority. Navy regulations require that such action be recorded in the service record. If a Navy service record does not show the action of the supervisory authority, the conviction is not final. The prima facie rule is not applicable in this situation. United States v. Engle, 3 USCMA 41, 11 CMR 41 (1953); United States v. McKnight, 4 USCMA 190, 15 CMR 190 (1954).
[127] 2 USCMA 606, 10 CMR 104 (1953).

it was offered in evidence as proof of a previous conviction. The Court held the record contained "seeds of its own undoing" inasmuch as ". . . anyone familiar with military procedure would know that a board of review could not receive, review and act on a case in that short time." Subsequently, a period of eight weeks[128] was held sufficiently short to destroy the prima facie case established by the order publishing the result of trial.

If a court-martial erroneously admits evidence of previous convictions, the convening authority[129] or a board of review[130] may order a rehearing and thus enable the prosecution to introduce proper evidence, if any, of previous convictions. The error of the first court-martial does not prevent the rehearing court-martial from considering previous convictions when properly proved; however, the second sentence cannot be in excess of that adjudged at the first trial.[131]

The Court found prejudice in the sentence in cases in which the court-martial improperly considered previous convictions notwithstanding the sentence was within legal limits apart from any consideration of previous convictions.[132]

XVI. Reconsideration by a Court-martial of Findings and Sentence

A court-martial may reconsider its findings before they are formally announced in open court.[133] Once announced in open court a finding of not guilty may not be reconsidered.[134] But revealing the proposed findings to the law officer during a closed session in which he was helping to put the findings in proper form is not an announcement in open court.[135] The rule prohibiting reconsideration does not include correcting an error in the announcement of the findings. Thus if the president of a court-martial announces a finding of not guilty, when, in fact, the court-martial found the accused guilty of a lesser included offense, it is proper to recast the language and correctly announce the findings previously agreed upon.[136]

After a sentence has been announced in open court, the court-martial

[128] United States v. Reed, 2 USCMA 622, 10 CMR 120 (1953).

[129] *Ibid.*

[130] United States v. Chapman, 2 USCMA 138, 7 CMR 14 (1953). *Cf.* the curative measures employed in United States v. Jones, 1 USCMA 302, 3 CMR 36 (1952).

[131] Code, Art. 63 (b).

[132] United States v. McIntyre, 2 USCMA 559, 10 CMR 57 (1953); United States v. West, 1 USCMA 590, 5 CMR 18 (1952).

[133] Manual for Courts-Martial, United States, 1951, par. 74*d* (3); United States v. London, 4 USCMA 90, 15 CMR 90 (1954).

[134] United States v. Downs, 4 USCMA 8, 15 CMR 8 (1954).

[135] United States v. London, 4 USCMA 90, 15 CMR 90 (1954).

[136] United States v. Downs, 4 USCMA 8, 15 CMR 8 (1954).

cannot reconsider it with a view to increasing its severity unless the sentence prescribed for the offense of which the accused was convicted is mandatory.[137] This rule does not preclude changes in phraseology necessary to express the sentence agreed upon even though the true sentence is more severe than the one erroneously announced.[138] For instance, a court-martial agreed on a legal sentence which included forfeiture of pay of $58.80 *each* month for thirty-six months. The president announced that the accused was to forfeit $58.80. The error was discovered after adjournment but before any of the principals in the trial left the court room. The president immediately opened court and corrected the error which he made in announcing the sentence. The Court approved[139] his action and indicated such errors could be corrected up to the time the accused began serving his sentence.

XVII. Records of Trial

Paragraph 82*b* of the *Manual* requires that the record in a general court-martial trial set forth a verbatim transcript of all proceedings in open sessions of the court-martial and any consultation between the court-martial and the law officer in closed session.[140] Articles 54 (b) and 19 of the Code and paragraph 15*b* of the *Manual* require a *complete* record in cases tried before a special court-martial in which a bad conduct discharge was adjudged. A complete record, according to the Court, need not be verbatim so long as it constitutes an accurate account of the essential substance of the proceedings.[141] But paragraph 83*a* of the *Manual* states that a *verbatim* record must be kept in special court-martial cases in which a bad conduct discharge is included in the sentence. The Court decided[142] paragraph 83*a* should prevail and it is prejudicial error to impose a bad conduct discharge without recording the proceedings verbatim. Thus a verbatim record is required not only in all trials by general court-martial but also in

[137] Art. 62 (b); United States v. Long, 4 USCMA 101, 15 CMR 101 (1954). For a discussion of the correction of these errors by reviewing authorities see Chapter 9.

[138] United States v. Robinson, 4 USCMA 12, 15 CMR 12 (1954).

[139] *Ibid.* The Court indicated that the accused might be considered to have started his sentence either when he was returned to the stockade after trial or when the record is authenticated. It did not make a selection in this case.

[140] The Code Committee has recommended that Article 54 of the Code be amended to permit a summarized record in those cases tried by a general court-martial where the accused is acquitted or the proceedings otherwise terminated in his favor, or where the sentence does not extend to death, dismissal, dishonorable or bad conduct discharge, or to confinement for 1 year or more. It was further recommended, however, that an accused may under these circumstances, at his own expense, be permitted to obtain a verbatim record of the trial. Annual Report, June 1, 1952, to December 31, 1953, p. 10.

[141] United States v. Whitman, 3 USCMA 179, 11 CMR 179 (1953).

[142] *Ibid.*

those before a special court-martial in which a bad conduct discharge is included in the sentence.

The Court refuses to adhere rigidly to a "word for word" test in determining if a transcript is verbatim. If the record is sufficient to present all material evidence bearing on the issues, omissions will not constitute prejudicial error.[143]

Revision proceedings may serve in some cases as a means to supply omissions in a transcript which is required to reflect a verbatim account of the trial proceedings.[144]

XVIII. Arrest after Conviction

A commanding officer may, upon probable cause to believe restraint is necessary, order a convicted accused in arrest pending final action on the case.[145]

XIX. Disagreement between Convening Authority and Staff Judge Advocate or Legal Officer

If a convening authority takes action different from that recommended by his staff judge advocate or legal officer in connection with the review of the case, the *Manual* states that in cases forwarded to The Judge Advocate General the convening authority should give reasons for his action. Apparently the Court regards this provision as an administrative requirement not of sufficient importance to affect the rights of the accused.[146]

XX. Computation of Time Limits

The Code does not except Sundays and holidays in computing periods of time. The Court suggested,[147] as a working rule to be used under normal conditions, that the services might adopt the federal rule and except these days when the period prescribed for the action is less than seven days.

[143] United States v. Nelson, 3 USCMA 482, 13 CMR 38 (1953).

[144] United States v. Self, 3 USCMA 568, 13 CMR 124 (1953). United States v. Galloway, 2 USCMA 433, 9 CMR 63 (1953). Revision proceedings permit a court-martial to reconvene for the purpose of making corrections. All proceedings in open court must be in the presence of the law officer, the accused, and counsel for both sides. Since the action which may be taken is entirely corrective, a case cannot be reopened by the calling or recalling of witnesses or otherwise. Manual for Courts-Martial, United States, 1951, par. 80.

[145] United States v. Teague, 3 USCMA 317, 12 CMR 73 (1953).

[146] United States v. Sippel, 4 USCMA 50, 15 CMR 50 (1954).

[147] United States v. Nichols, 2 USCMA 27, 6 CMR 27 (1952). See Rule 26, *Rules of Practice and Procedure*, United States Court of Military Appeals, 1 USCMA xxix.

CHAPTER 9

Appellate Review—Action by Reviewing Authorities

I. General

In addition to the court-martial[1] (trial court) there are two other judicial bodies in the military legal system: the board of review (appellate forum) and the Court of Military Appeals (appellate court[2]). The President, Secretary of a Department and a convening authority are included among the reviewing authorities. Sentences of death or involving a general or flag officer may not be executed until they are approved by the President.[3] Sentences dismissing officers other than a general or flag officer may not be executed until approved by the Secretary of a Department.[4]

The convening authority must make an initial review of every record of trial by courts-martial.[5] He cannot go outside the record for evidence of guilt.[6] Further he cannot alter a finding of not guilty or in-

[1] Judge Brosman concurring in United States v. Long, 2 USCMA 60, 6 CMR 60 (1952) stated that in his view courts-martial are not part of the federal judiciary. However, he did not express an opinion on the status of the Court of Military Appeals.

[2] United States v. Reeves, 1 USCMA 388, 3 CMR 122 (1952). The Court stated: "For all practical purposes, the Code sets up three judicial or quasi-judicial bodies: The court-martial (trial court), the board of review (appellate forum), and the Court of Military Appeals (appellate court)."

The Court of Military Appeals has been characterized as a "specialized legislative court." Begalke v. United States, 209 F. 2d 811 (D. C. Cir. 1954).

It has been strongly suggested that all doubts concerning the status of the Court should be resolved by action of Congress to give life tenure to the judges. Walker, *An Evaluation of the United States Court of Military Appeals,* 48 N. W. L. Rev. 714 (1954); Thornton, *Military Law,* 1953 Annual Surv. Am. L. 125.

[3] Code, Art. 71(a).

[4] Code, Art. 71(b).

[5] Code, Arts. 60-65. Manual for Courts-Martial, United States, 1951, Chs. 17-19. The commanding officer of an accused may lawfully order him into restriction pending notice of the action of the convening authority on a sentence imposed by a special court-martial. United States v. Howard, 2 USCMA 519, 10 CMR 17 (1953).

[6] United States v. Duffy, 3 USCMA 20, 11 CMR 20 (1953).

crease any sentence. He has the power to approve only such findings of guilt and so much of the sentence as he finds to be correct in law and fact. And he may decrease or suspend a sentence other than a death sentence, or order a rehearing or dismiss the charges. It is impossible for an accused to suffer detriment because of action taken by a convening authority.[7]

The Judge Advocate General of each service performs important functions in the operation of the system of appellate review.[8] Moreover, in certain cases involving minor sentences[9] a review is made by the Examination Branch in his office but his powers of review do not extend to cases involving more serious sentences. In the review of the latter, which go to a board of review, his office performs certain administrative duties but it is not regarded as a separate appellate forum.

II. Boards of Review

A board of review is composed of not less than three qualified lawyers who may be either officers or civilians.[10] A Judge Advocate General is required by Article 66(b) of the Code to refer to a board of review the record in every case of trial by a court-martial in which the sentence, as approved by the convening authority, affects a general or flag officer or extends to death, dismissal of an officer, cadet, or midshipman, dishonorable or bad conduct discharge, or confinement for one year or more.[11] A board has authority to weigh the evidence,

[7] In a review of a special court-martial case a supervisory authority may disapprove the sentence and order a rehearing even though the sentence includes a bad conduct discharge. United States v. Frisbee, 2 USCMA 293, 8 CMR 93 (1953); United States v. Wyatt, 2 USCMA 647, 10 CMR 145 (1953); United States v. Freeman, 3 USCMA 71, 11 CMR 71 (1953).

[8] A Judge Advocate General may certify questions to the Court and he assists boards of review administratively. Code, Art. 66 (e), (f). For additional provisions concerning the duties of a Judge Advocate General see Articles 73, 74 (a) and Section 12 of the Code.

[9] Code, Art. 69. (No punitive discharge and less than one year of confinement.) Also records in cases resulting in acquittals are reviewed for jurisdiction.

[10] Code, Art. 66 (a).

[11] Cases reviewed by The Judge Advocates General under Article 69 of the Code must be referred to a board of review if any part of the findings and sentence are unsupported in law. The Code Committee has recommended that in cases covered by Article 69 a Judge Advocate General be given authority to take such corrective action as boards of review now exercise under the authority granted to them by Article 66 of the Code. Annual Report, June 1, 1950, to December 31, 1953, p. 8. The Code Committee has further recommended:

> ". . . that in cases involving pleas of guilty before a special or general court-martial, there be no review by a board of review of the same; that in such cases the accused be required within 5 days from the date sentence is adjudged to file notice of appeal to a board of review. *Provided,* that the same be limited to questions of law, and that it affirmatively appears of record that the accused was advised of his appellate rights at the time of sentence." Annual Report, June 1, 1952, to December 31, 1953, p. 6.

judge the credibility of witnesses, and determine controverted questions of fact.[12] If it sets aside the findings and sentence, it may order a rehearing except where the setting aside is based on a lack of sufficient evidence in the record to support the findings.[13] If the findings and sentence are set aside and a rehearing is not ordered, the board shall order the charges dismissed.

A board must confine its deliberations to the record in the case. With the exception[14] of evidence as to sanity, consideration of matter outside the record, even if favorable to the accused, is not authorized.[15] The Code provides in the event of a rehearing that an "accused shall not be tried for any offense of which he was found not guilty by the first court-martial, and no sentence in excess of or more severe than the original sentence shall be imposed unless the sentence is based upon a finding of guilty of an offense not considered upon the merits in the original proceedings or unless the sentence prescribed for the offense is mandatory."[16]

A. *Motion for reconsideration*

After an accused has received notice of an unfavorable decision by a board of review, he has a choice of seeking reconsideration before the board[17] or petitioning the Court.[18] The authority of a board of review to reconsider its action is not divested until jurisdiction of the case has been acquired by the Court[19] or until The Judge Advocate General[20] has returned the case to the convening authority for further action in accordance with the board's decision.

If an accused files a motion for reconsideration before a board of

[12] CODE, Art. 66 (d).
[13] *Ibid.*
[14] United States v. Burns, 2 USCMA 400, 9 CMR 30 (1953). See in this connection MANUAL FOR COURTS-MARTIAL, UNITED STATES, 1951, par. 124.
[15] United States v. Whitman, 3 USCMA 179, 11 CMR 179 (1953); United States v. Gordon, 2 USCMA 632, 10 CMR 130 (1953).
[16] CODE, Art. 63.
[17] United States v. Reeves, 1 USCMA 388, 3 CMR 122 (1952); United States v. Weeden, 3 USCMA 405, 12 CMR 161 (1953). Sometimes a board of review will grant another hearing. If defense counsel requests that this hearing be before a different board of review, it should be granted. But it is not error if some of the members of the board who initially heard the case also compose part of the membership of the board which reheard the case. United States v. Thomas, 3 USCMA 798, 14 CMR 216 (1954).
[18] See United States v. Jackson, 2 USCMA 179, 7 CMR 55 (1953) for a discussion of what constitutes a petition and the filing thereof.
[19] United States v. Corbin, 3 USCMA 99, 11 CMR 99 (1953). The board loses jurisdiction to reconsider when a petition is filed for a grant of review or a certificate of a Judge Advocate General has been filed or a record of trial in a case involving an automatic appeal has reached the Court. United States v. Reeves, 1 USCMA 388, 3 CMR 122 (1952).
[20] United States v. Reeves, 1 USCMA 388, 3 CMR 122 (1952). United States v. Sell, 3 USCMA 202, 11 CMR 202 (1953).

review and also petitions the Court, the first in time is paramount. If the motion is first, the board retains jurisdiction until it has disposed of the motion.[21] If the petition is first, the Court acquires jurisdiction. However, the Court in this situation has remanded the case to The Judge Advocate General for transmittal to the board of review in order that the motion might be considered.[22] A motion for reconsideration, if granted, gives an accused a possible advantage over review by the Court inasmuch as the board may pass on the credibility of witnesses and reappraise the facts.

An accused has thirty days from the time he is notified of the decision of a board of review to petition the Court for a grant of review.[23] The Court has made it clear that the thirty-day period does not begin to run until a board has completed action on a motion to reconsider.[24] Although these motions may delay the final disposition of a case, a board is thereby given an opportunity to correct its own errors.

A board cannot reconsider its action on the request of a Judge Advocate General.[25]

III. Court of Military Appeals

The Court of Military Appeals, consisting of three civilian judges, officially began its duties on July 25, 1951 and its first written opinion was published on November 8, 1951.[26] Since that time it has been busily engaged in its dual but related roles of undertaking to insure that essential justice is had in individual cases and to establish a sound decisional framework for operation under the Code and *Manual.* Ordinarily the act of Congress (the Code) and the act of the Executive (the *Manual*) are on the same level and a violation of either constitutes error. If, however, a *Manual* provision is in conflict with the Code, the latter must control.[27] The Court has not yet undertaken to decide the "delicate and difficult" question concerning whether it has the power to declare any part of the Code in conflict with the Constitution of the United States.[28]

The Code provides in substance that the Court shall review the record in the following cases:

[21] United States v. Weeden, 3 USCMA 405, 12 CMR 161 (1953).
[22] United States v. Jackson, 2 USCMA 179, 7 CMR 55 (1953).
[23] Code, Art. 67 (c).
[24] United States v. Sell, 3 USCMA 202, 11 CMR 202 (1953).
[25] United States v. Reeves, 1 USCMA 388, 3 CMR 122 (1952).
[26] United States v. McCrary, 1 USCMA 1, 1 CMR 1 (1951).
[27] United States v. Clark, 1 USCMA 201, 2 CMR 107 (1952); United States v. Wappler, 2 USCMA 393, 9 CMR 23 (1953).
[28] United States v. Sutton, 3 USCMA 220, 11 CMR 220 (1953). See Judge Quinn's dissenting opinion.

(1) All cases in which the sentence, as affirmed by a board of review, affects a general or flag officer or extends to death;

(2) All cases reviewed by a board of review which The Judge Advocate General orders to the Court of Military Appeals for review; and

(3) All cases reviewed by a board of review in which, upon petition of the accused and on good cause shown, the Court of Military Appeals has granted a review.[29]

The extent of review to be exercised by the Court in each of these three categories is further defined by Congress:

(1) The Court of Military Appeals shall act only with respect to the findings and sentence as approved by the convening authority and as affirmed or set aside as incorrect in law by the board of review.

(2) In a case which a Judge Advocate General orders forwarded to the Court of Military Appeals, such action need be taken only with respect to the issues raised by him.

(3) In a case reviewed upon petition by the accused, such action need be taken only with respect to issues specified in the grant of review.[30]

All cases coming before the Court must have been first reviewed by a board of review.[31] Unlike a convening authority[32] or a board of review,[33] the Court is not authorized to review questions of fact. Congress specifically provided that the Court "shall take action only with respect to matters of law."[34] If there is insufficient evidence in the record to support the findings, the Court will dismiss the charges. Occasionally the Court will dismiss[34a] the charges in cases involving prejudicial error, but the usual procedure in this situation is to order a rehearing. As discussed in the previous chapter, the Court, in certain limited circumstances, will purge instructional errors by affirming a finding of guilty of an appropriate lesser included offense.

[29] CODE, Art. 67 (b).

[30] CODE, Art. 67 (d).

[31] CODE, Art. 67 (b). The board must have acted with regard to both the findings and sentence. United States v. Best, 4 USCMA 581, 16 CMR 155 (1954).

[32] CODE, Art. 64.

[33] CODE, Art. 66 (c).

[34] CODE, Art. 67 (d).

[34a] United States v. Perna, 1 USCMA 438, 4 CMR 30 (1952); United States v. James, 1 USCMA 379, 3 CMR 113 (1952).

A. *Mandatory review*

The Court has decided a few cases on mandatory review[35] but the exercise of this jurisdiction has produced little, if any, difficulty insofar as the operation of the appellate system is concerned.

B. *Certified questions*

Questions certified by The Judge Advocates General have been substantial in number, and many problems concerning the extent and scope of this jurisdiction have been resolved by the Court. The Court has recognized that there are at least two limitations on its certificate jurisdiction:

(1) A finding of fact made by a board of review cannot be overturned by the Court;[36]

(2) The Court will not render an advisory opinion.[37]

In connection with the first limitation, difficulty has been encountered by the Court in deciding whether a particular decision of a board of review was based on the board's fact finding powers or on a matter of law or both. Should a board of review base its decision on both law and fact, the Court will review the questions of law.[38] The Court has observed that review would be expedited if boards of review would express "clearly" when they are exercising their fact-finding powers.[39] On the other hand, a statement by a board of review that its ruling is based on a finding of fact does not preclude review by the Court if actually it is a question of law.[40]

The majority of the Court continues to adhere to its original view[41] that the Court cannot be required to render an advisory opinion even though presented in the form of a certified question.[42] But the Court does not appear to object to considering moot questions[43] or going beyond[44] the question certified if in its judgment this would be helpful

[35] Illustrative cases are: United States v. O'Brien, 3 USCMA 105, 11 CMR 105 (1953) (death penalty); United States v. Grow, 3 USCMA 77, 11 CMR 77 (1953) (General officer).

[36] United States v. Sell, 3 USCMA 202, 11 CMR 202 (1953); United States v. Thompson, 2 USCMA 460, 9 CMR 90 (1953).

[37] United States v. Thompson, 2 USCMA 460, 9 CMR 90 (1953).

[38] United States v. Engle, 3 USCMA 41, 11 CMR 41 (1953). The legality of a search presented a question of law. United States v. Wilcher, 4 USCMA 215, 15 CMR 215 (1954).

[39] United States v. Sell, 3 USCMA 202, 208, 11 CMR 202, 208 (1953).

[40] United States v. Benson, 3 USCMA 351, 12 CMR 107 (1953).

[41] United States v. Thompson, 2 USCMA 460, 9 CMR 90 (1953).

[42] United States v. Engle, 3 USCMA 41, 11 CMR 41 (1953). Judge Latimer believes the Court must answer all certified questions.

[43] United States v. Blue, 3 USCMA 550, 13 CMR 106 (1953).

[44] United States v. Frisbee, 2 USCMA 293, 8 CMR 93 (1953); United States v. O'Neal, 1 USCMA 138, 2 CMR 44 (1952). See also United States v. Smith, 3 USCMA 336, 12 CMR 92 (1953).

to the services. In *Prescott*[45] certified questions concerning the case of the accused reached the Court after he had served his period of confinement and had been restored to duty. The Court rejected an argument advanced by the Government that the questions in this case had become moot. It pointed out that several rights of the accused, including computation of leave, longevity increases in pay and re-enlistment allowances, were involved in the outcome.

If the decision of a board of review had prevailed in *Zimmerman*,[46] there would have been a third limitation on the exercise of certificate jurisdiction. In that case the accused was convicted of two offenses by a special court-martial. A board of review found procedural errors and dismissed the charges. Notwithstanding the dismissal, The Judge Advocate General of the Navy certified the case to the Court. The rulings of the board were reversed, but because of improper presentation of previous convictions at the trial the Court found error in the sentence. When the Court remanded the case, it did so in the belief that the board of review would affirm so much of the sentence as it deemed appropriate in the absence of the improperly considered previous convictions. This time the board, one member dissenting, ruled that its prior dismissal must stand and that to reinstate the conviction would violate the prohibition against double jeopardy.[47]

This action squarely raised the question of the effect to be given to a dismissal by a board of review based on a ruling of law. Would it result in curtailing the certificate jurisdiction of the Court? On a second certification the Court held that it could review a case after dismissal by a board of review where its ruling was based on an error of law. Such ruling, according to the Court, does not have the same effect as a finding of not guilty by a trial court. The Court arrived at this result after characterizing appellate review in the military system as being "unitary." Even though boards of review are empowered to render "decisions," this action is interlocutory until the case has either been presented to the Court or the time in which it could be done has expired. Regardless of the number of times a case may pass between a board of review and the Court—the "sum" constitutes only one appellate review. Jeopardy, therefore, does not attach until all action has been completed in the "unitary" appellate system.

The Court also considered the contention that a certificate by a Judge Advocate General after a board of review had dismissed the

[45] 2 USCMA 122, 6 CMR 122 (1952). The same result was reached on petition of the accused in a case in which the discharge had been remitted. United States v. Murgaw, 2 USCMA 369, 8 CMR 169 (1953).

[46] 2 USCMA 12, 6 CMR 12 (1952).

[47] See Chapter 8.

charges was, in a sense, a prosecution appeal. It concluded that the accused was not deprived of any of his fundamental rights. Certification of a question by a Judge Advocate General does not necessarily reflect his views on the "decision" rendered by the board of review inasmuch as his interest may be solely to obtain an answer to questions of law not otherwise available.

When a court-martial concludes there is insufficient evidence to sustain a finding and returns a verdict of not guilty, there is no appeal by the Government from that finding and the record of the case never reaches the Court.[48] In *Zimmerman* the Court reserved decision on whether a dismissal by a board of review based on insufficiency of the evidence as a matter of law would have the same finality. Later, the Court considered this question[49] and stated that it was a matter of law and the action of the board of review was not final. Therefore, the Court will review on certificate jurisdiction a case dismissed by a board of review because of insufficiency of the evidence the same as it will review any other dismissal of a case based on errors of law.

The Court, with the exception of the limitations on the review of findings of fact and rendering advisory opinions, has taken a liberal attitude in regard to its certificate jurisdiction. If more than one certified question is submitted to the Court in a case, it may answer several or all of them notwithstanding that the answer of one may be sufficient to dispose of the case.[50] Moreover, it does not hesitate to consider questions other than those contained in the certificate if it deems that justice would be better served.[51]

Certificate jurisdiction provides a means whereby the Court may review a few cases involving persons not subject to the Code. Pursuant to Article 18 of the Code a general court-martial has jurisdiction to try any person who by the law of war is subject to trial by a military tribunal. The Court has held that it is authorized to review a decision of a general court-martial sitting as a military tribunal if the case comes to the Court on questions certified by a Judge Advocate General.[52]

C. *Petition of the accused*

The most numerous group of cases reviewed by the Court is comprised of those in which it exercises its discretion and grants a petition

[48] United States v. Sell, 3 USCMA 202, 11 CMR 202 (1953).
[49] *Ibid.*
[50] United States v. O'Neal, 1 USCMA 138, 2 CMR 44 (1952).
[51] United States v. Zimmerman, 1 USCMA 160, 2 CMR 66 (1952).
[52] United States v. Schultz, 1 USCMA 512, 4 CMR 104 (1952). The Court expressly reserved the question of whether it would exercise this jurisdiction on petition of an accused.

on good cause shown by the accused.[53] The right of an accused to petition the Court for review is not subject to waiver except through failure actually to exercise the right. An agreement executed by an accused purporting to waive his right to petition is a "legal nullity."[54] The Court has manifested a willingness to depart from a rigid application of its rules in order to insure that the rights of an accused in exceptional cases are fully protected. In this connection the Court adopted the language of a federal case[55] which states, in part:

> "The admitted normal rule is that an appellate court will not consider matters which are alleged as error for the first time on appeal, and this is true of criminal as well as civil cases. However, an exception exists in criminal cases where the alleged error would result in a manifest miscarriage of justice, or would 'seriously affect the fairness, integrity, or public reputation of judicial proceedings.' "[56]

For example, in a murder case the petition of an accused was specifically limited by the Court to certain issues, yet because of the seriousness of the offense it subsequently decided to deal with other matters raised in the brief of appellate defense counsel.[57] And, further, the Court has agreed in a few exceptional cases to consider points raised in a supplemental brief filed after argument.[58] Perhaps of even more significance is the fact that the Court will consider errors in the record not urged at all either at the trial or appellate level.[59] This is especially true in cases involving serious instructional errors.[60] Diligence in searching for errors does not mean that the Court is overzealous in rendering decisions in favor of the accused. In a substantial number of cases in which the Court has reversed a decision of a board of review the reversal has been to the detriment of the accused.[61] As in certified

[53] CODE, Art. 67 (b) (3); United States v. Harvey, 2 USCMA 609, 10 CMR 107 (1953). The simplest general court-martial case; i.e., one involving a sentence of six months or less and partial forfeitures or, in the case of an officer, a reprimand and forfeitures, will not get to a board of review unless it is forwarded by a Judge Advocate General. The accused in such cases does not have a right to petition the Court for review after the decision of the board of review. A Judge Advocate General could send the case to the Court. If he does so, the accused is entitled to counsel the same as he was before the board of review. LEGAL AND LEGISLATIVE BASIS, MANUAL FOR COURTS-MARTIAL, UNITED STATES, 1951, p. 150.

[54] United States v. Ponds, 1 USCMA 385, 387, 3 CMR 119, 121 (1952).

[55] Smith v. United States, 173 F. 2d 181, 184 (9 Cir. 1949).

[56] United States v. Masusock, 1 USCMA 32, 34, 1 CMR 32, 34 (1951).

[57] United States v. Bigger, 2 USCMA 297, 8 CMR 97 (1953).

[58] United States v. Cooper, 2 USCMA 333, 8 CMR 133 (1953).

[59] United States v. Crusoe, 3 USCMA 793, 14 CMR 211 (1954) (error in previous convictions).

[60] United States v. Cromartie, 1 USCMA 551, 4 CMR 143 (1952).

[61] In 377 cases checked (the first 377) the Court affirmed the board in 202. It reversed the board in the remaining 175 cases. Of the 175 reversals 65 were detrimental to the accused and the remainder were beneficial to him.

question cases, the Court will extend its opinion beyond the grant of review in petition cases if it considers it would be helpful to the services to do so.[62]

Some cases reach the Court through a combination of certified questions and petition.[63]

The accused has thirty days from the time he is notified of the decision of a board of review to petition the Court for a grant of review.[64]

IV. Action on a Sentence

A. *Suspension*

A court-martial is not authorized to suspend a sentence. If it undertakes to do so, the attempted suspension is void and the sentence remains in effect.[65] The power of suspension is expressly given by the Code[66] to a convening authority, Secretary of a Department and the President. Although a board of review is permitted to remit[67] a punitive discharge, it does not have the authority to suspend one. The Court has observed: ". . . it seems anomalous that a board should have the power to remit a disciplinary discharge entirely, but not to suspend it for a probationary period."[68] Perhaps the reason a board is not granted the authority to suspend a sentence is that, unlike a convening authority, it cannot go outside the record to secure information upon which to determine the wisdom of granting a suspension.

The Court cannot suspend a sentence or direct that it be suspended.

A convening authority may suspend a bad conduct discharge and order into execution the remaining part of the sentence, which may include forfeiture of pay and a period of confinement in excess of six months. Such action does not violate the *Manual* provision[69] which prohibits a court-martial from adjudging confinement and forfeitures in excess of six months without including in the sentence a punitive discharge. The Court has ruled that the punitive discharge remains a part of the sentence after it has been suspended.[70]

[62] United States v. Williams, 4 USCMA 241, 15 CMR 241 (1954).

[63] For example: United States v. Bigger, 2 USCMA 297, 8 CMR 97 (1953); United States v. Hopf, 1 USCMA 584, 5 CMR 12 (1952).

[64] Rule 22 of the Court provides that a petition is deemed filed upon the date postmarked on the envelope containing the petition, or upon the date when the petition is deposited in military channels for transmittal. I USCMA xxviii.

The Code Committee has recommended that this period be reduced to fifteen days. This should be sufficient time. Annual Report, June 1, 1952, to December 31, 1953, p. 8.

[65] United States v. Marshall, 2 USCMA 342, 8 CMR 142 (1953) (punitive discharge).

[66] Art. 71. Historically the suspension power has been vested solely in those reviewing authorities possessing the power to execute a sentence.

[67] Code, Art. 66.

[68] United States v. Simmons, 2 USCMA 105, 106, 6 CMR 105, 106 (1952).

[69] Par. 127*b*.

[70] United States v. Phillips, 1 USCMA 349, 3 CMR 83 (1952).

B. *Remitting a discharge*

In *Brasher*[71] the question for decision was whether a board of review was bound by the *Manual* provision previously mentioned which states, in part, that a court-martial shall not, by a single sentence which does not include a punitive discharge, adjudge against an accused confinement or forfeitures in excess of six months. The court-martial had imposed a sentence of bad conduct discharge, confinement for ten months and appropriate forfeitures for ten months. Could the board of review remit the discharge without reducing the confinement and forfeitures to six months or less? A divided Court decided that the sentence as approved by a board of review must be one which could be legally imposed by a court-martial; therefore in this case it was necessary to reduce the confinement and forfeitures to six months.

C. *Commutation*

The Code[72] authorizes the Secretary of a Department and the President to commute (i.e., to change a punishment to one of a different nature) a sentence but no provision is made for a board of review to exercise this power. In *Bigger*[73] the trial court rendered a verdict of guilty of premeditated murder and adjudged the death penalty. A board of review concluded that the evidence would support only the lesser included offense of unpremeditated murder and reduced the death sentence to life imprisonment. A change in the sentence was necessary inasmuch as the death penalty is not authorized for unpremeditated murder. But the change, in effect, was a commutation. The Court decided that Congress intended to permit a board of review to substitute a lesser legal sentence in cases in which its action had been to affirm a lesser included offense. To hold otherwise, according to the Court, would restrict the board "where benevolence is most needed."[74] This decision is a restricted one and its effect is to permit a board of review to commute when the death sentence has been imposed and there is a finding that the evidence is sufficient to support only an offense which cannot be punished by death. The Court does

[71] 2 USCMA 50, 6 CMR 50 (1952). Judge Latimer dissented because he believed that a board of review should be permitted to affirm any part of a sentence.

[72] Art. 71 (a), (b). MANUAL FOR COURTS-MARTIAL, UNITED STATES, 1951, par. 88*c* provides, in part: "The convening authority, may, subject to the limitations in 88*a*, approve a part of a sentence adjudged by a court-martial, but unless he is empowered to commute a sentence, . . . the sentence approved by him must be included in the sentence adjudged by the court and must be one that the court might have imposed in the case. However, when a court has adjudged a mandatory sentence to imprisonment for life (Art. 118 (1) and (4)), the convening authority may approve any sentence included in that adjudged by the court."

[73] 2 USCMA 297, 8 CMR 97 (1953).

[74] *Id.* at 305, 8 CMR at 105.

not appear inclined to undertake to extend the power of a board of review to commute a sentence beyond necessity of the kind exemplified in the *Bigger* case.[75]

A lack of power to suspend and commute (except as permitted in *Bigger*) does not preclude a board from making recommendations to proper authorities to exercise commutation or clemency in a particular case. Such a recommendation, however, should not be used in lieu of the exercise by a board of its own authority to reduce a sentence it deems excessive. The Court has frowned on an attempt to "pass the buck" in the following language:

> "All persons who have any responsibility in fixing, affirming, or reviewing sentences should meet their responsibility by adjudging or affirming a fair and just sentence without regard to any further reductive action that might be taken by others who will subsequently act on the record."[76]

D. *Sentence after findings altered on review*

It is customary practice in the military system for practical reasons of dispatch to join all known offenses against an accused and to dispose of all of them at a single trial. A single sentence is adjudged for all of the offenses on which the accused was convicted. Regardless of the merits of the single sentence for some purposes, it creates serious problems when a reviewing authority approves the findings as to some but not all of the offenses considered by the court-martial in imposing the single sentence.

In *Strong*[77] the accused was convicted of voluntary manslaughter and absence without leave for which he was given a single sentence. On review the voluntary manslaughter conviction was reversed and that of absence without leave was affirmed. In this case the conviction of absence without leave was legally sufficient to support the sentence adjudged. The Government contended that the entire sentence must stand if supported by a valid conviction under a single charge regardless of whether the trial court would, in fact, have imposed that sentence had it known of the infirmities in the other charge. The Court rejected this contention. Proper procedure demands that the sentence be reviewed to determine if it is *appropriate* as well as legal. The Court does not possess the authority to pass on the appropriateness of a sentence. Moreover, in the military system, it is not usually

[75] United States v. Freeman, 4 USCMA 76, 15 CMR 76 (1954).

[76] United States v. Cavallaro, 3 USCMA 653, 656, 14 CMR 71, 74 (1954).

[77] 1 USCMA 627, 5 CMR 55 (1952); *accord,* United States v. Keith, 1 USCMA 442, 4 CMR 34 (1952); United States v. Peterson, 2 USCMA 645, 10 CMR 143 (1953); United States v. Horst, 1 USCMA 452, 4 CMR 44 (1952).

practicable to return a case to the trial court for reconsideration of the sentence;[78] therefore, the Court remanded the case to The Judge Advocate General of the Army for reference to the board of review. A board of review is authorized to determine the adequacy of a sentence. The same procedure is employed when the Court affirms only a lesser included offense to the offense charged—even though the lesser offense is legally sufficient to support the sentence imposed by the court-martial.[79]

If the accused is found guilty of multiple offenses and one or more is set aside on review, it may be that the sentence would then exceed legal limits. A board of review may resolve this difficulty by reducing the sentence.[80]

In exceptional cases the Court has departed from the usual procedure and has declined to have a board of review reconsider the sentence after the findings were changed by the Court. For example, in *Hunter*[81] the court-martial had adjudged the death penalty after finding the accused guilty of rape, two unpremeditated murders, and four separate specifications of assault with a dangerous weapon to do bodily harm. On review the Court reduced three of the assault offenses at least one degree because of improper instructions but the more serious offenses were affirmed. The Court did not believe that any board of review would commute the death sentence in this case (assuming it had power to do so[82]) and for this reason declined to return the case to a board of review for further action on the sentence.[83]

E. *Correction of errors*

A court-martial may not reconsider a legal sentence with a view to increasing its severity after the sentence has been announced.[84] If it undertakes to do so, reviewing authorities may correct the error by

[78] See CODE, Art. 62 for provision permitting a convening authority to return a record to a court-martial for reconsideration and revision.

[79] United States v. Goddard, 1 USCMA 475, 4 CMR 67 (1952).

[80] United States v. Horst, 1 USCMA 452, 4 CMR 44 (1952).

[81] 2 USCMA 37, 6 CMR 37 (1952).

[82] See United States v. Bigger, 2 USCMA 297, 8 CMR 97 (1953).

[83] In United States v. Murgaw, 2 USCMA 369, 8 CMR 169 (1953) the Court set aside a punitive discharge because the law officer had incorrectly informed the court-martial regarding the maximum confinement which could be given without imposing a punitive discharge. Although the punitive discharge was legal in form, the Court considered it a product of an error of law. The case was not returned to the board of review because it would constitute "purely formal action, unnecessarily prolonging final disposition of the case." Judge Latimer dissented because he did not think the Court had been granted power to modify a sentence by setting aside a part and affirming a part of a legal sentence.

[84] CODE, Art. 62, United States v. Long, 4 USCMA 101, 15 CMR 101 (1954). See Chapter 8, Section XVI.

disapproving the illegal portion of the sentence.[85] It is error for a law officer to advise a court-martial that the maximum sentence is greater than that permitted by law notwithstanding the imposition of a sentence within the legal limits. This error may be purged by action of a convening authority or board or review in specifically passing on the appropriateness of the sentence.[86] If a board of review sets aside a punitive discharge[87] or all[88] of a sentence because of its own misinterpretation of the legality of the findings or sentence, it is not precluded from restoring the findings and sentence on remand of the case to it from the Court.

V. New Trial

Article 73 of the Code deals with the subject of new trials for offenses committed on or after May 31, 1951 which involve a sentence extending to death, dismissal, dishonorable or bad conduct discharge, or confinement for one year or more. The petition must be filed within one year after approval of the sentence by the convening authority.[89] The grounds for relief are limited to newly discovered evidence or fraud[90] on the court-martial. A mere showing of error is not sufficient. The *Manual*[91] requires the accused to show an injustice plus an indication that a new trial probably would produce for him a substantially more favorable result.

Usually the petition is acted upon by a Judge Advocate General, but if the case of the accused is pending before a board of review or the Court, the petition must be referred to the board or the Court respectively for action.[92] Although the Court cannot entertain a petition while the case is before a board of review, it can review the action taken by such board. This review, on petition of the accused, will be confined to a determination whether the board abused its discretion in the action it took.[93]

[85] United States v. Castner, 3 USCMA 466, 13 CMR 22 (1953); *cf.* United States v. Flood, 2 USCMA 114, 6 CMR 114 (1952). See also United States v. Smith, 2 USCMA 119, 6 CMR 119 (1952) (board of review required to correct its own error).

[86] United States v. Crusoe, 3 USCMA 793, 14 CMR 211 (1954); United States v. Cooper, 2 USCMA 333, 8 CMR 133 (1953); United States v. Williams, 4 USCMA 69, 15 CMR 69 (1954).

[87] United States v. Wappler, 2 USCMA 393, 9 CMR 23 (1953).

[88] United States v. Zimmerman, 2 USCMA 12, 6 CMR 12 (1952) (not former jeopardy).

[89] Different rules apply to offenses committed prior to May 31, 1951. Manual for Courts-Martial, United States, 1951, par. 110.

[90] United States v. McCarthy, 4 USCMA 385, 15 CMR 385 (1954).

[91] Par. 109*d;* United States v. Thomas, 3 USCMA 161, 11 CMR 161 (1953).

[92] Code, Art. 73, United States v. Borner, 3 USCMA 313, 12 CMR 69 (1953) (Court denied the petition); United States v. Thomas, 3 USCMA 161, 11 CMR 161 (1953) (board of review denied the petition).

[93] United States v. Thomas, 3 USCMA 161, 11 CMR 161 (1953).

The Court stated[94] that it is not authorized to consider newly discovered evidence as a part of its review of a case in which it granted a petition of the accused on good cause shown "on the basis of the entire record." The appropriate procedure in this situation is for the accused to also petition for a new trial on the basis of the newly discovered evidence. The Court mentioned[95] the possibility of making an exception to this rule in cases in which to do so will prevent a miscarriage of justice, but it has not found it necessary to decide this point.[96]

[94] United States v. Harvey, 2 USCMA 609, 10 CMR 107 (1953).

[95] *Ibid.*

[96] The Code Committee made two recommendations concerning petitions for a new trial:

"It is recommended that Article 73 of the Code be amended so that the time within which a petition for a new trial may be filed be extended to 2 years from the date of imposition of sentence. This will be in accord with the present federal practice."

"It is recommended that Article 73 of the Code be further amended to provide that in all cases involving a petition for new trial, authority be given to order a new trial, in whole or in part, or to take corrective action as provided for under Article 66 (c) and (d) of the Code, and to extend similar authorization to The Judge Advocates General in those cases acted upon by them under the Article in question."

The last recommendation was made because the Committee found substantial uncertainty existed in the services as to whether a new trial is required for an entire case involving multiple offenses even though the petition for a new trial may attack less than all of the findings of guilty—and when the unassailed findings would legally support the approved sentence. The recommended change would permit the dismissal of the particular findings attacked and thereafter permit appropriate sentence reductions on the review level without requiring a retrial on valid findings. ANNUAL REPORT, June 1, 1952, to December 31, 1953, pp. 8-9.

CHAPTER 10

Prejudicial Error vs. "Military Due Process"*

I. A Label or Catch Phrase

On November 27, 1951, the United States Court of Military Appeals, then some five months old, fashioned in the *Clay* case[1] what is characterized as a label. It embellished this label with quotation marks at least twice in the course of the opinion. This label, which was, in the language of the Court, used "for lack of a more descriptive phrase," was "military due process." This, and later use of the term by the Court in other opinions,[2] has caused some students of military law to speculate as to whether there is occurring the emergence of a new doctrine of law. Others incline to the view that old wine is being purveyed in a new bottle. The opinions of the Court up to now seem to indicate a trend to consider the term as alternative nomenclature for the process of finding and declaring reversible error.

The words "due process" are perhaps the outstanding contribution of the law to the dialectics of *Alice in Wonderland*. Fundamental, solid and useful though the general doctrine of due process is, the civil courts have repeatedly adverted to the difficulty encountered in endeavoring to define it,[3] Of the innumerable attempts to do so[4] perhaps

* This chapter originally appeared in 6 Vanderbilt Law Review 251 (1953). Copyright, 1953, by the Vanderbilt University Press, and reprinted by permission of the copyright proprietor.

[1] United States v. Clay, 1 USCMA 74, 77, 1 CMR 74, 77 (1951).

[2] United States v. Welch, 1 USCMA 402, 3 CMR 136 (1952), discussed in Sec. III *infra.;* United States v. Bartholomew, 1 USCMA 307, 3 CMR 41 (1952); United States v. Carter, 1 USCMA 108, 2 CMR 14 (1952); United States v. Davis, 1 USCMA 102, 2 CMR 8 (1952).

[3] *Ex parte* MacDonald, 76 Ala. 603 (1884); Davis v. State, 68 Ala. 58, 62, 63 (1880); People v. Tilkin, 13 Cal. 2d 89, 90 P. 2d 148, 152 (1939); Gilmer v. Bird, 15 Fla. 410, 421 (1875); Hodge v. Muscatine County, 121 Iowa 482, 96 N. W. 968, 971 (1903); Bardwell v. Collins, 44 Minn. 97, 46 N. W. 315, 317 (1890); *In re* Fuller's Estate, 34 Misc. 752, 70 N. Y. Supp. 1050, 1051 (Surr. Ct. 1901); Stuart v. Palmer, 74 N. Y. 183, 191 (1878); Jones v. Franklin County, 130 N. C. 451, 42 S. E. 144, 149 (1902); Hallenbeck v. Hahn, 2 Neb. 377, 403 (1872); Gaffney v. Jones, 44 Wash. 158, 87 Pac. 114, 116 (1906); State v. Sponaugle, 45 W. Va. 415, 32 S. E. 283, 284 (1898).

[4] See case excerpts collected in 13 Words and Phrases 488-593.

one of the best so far as criminal law is concerned is that of the United States Court of Appeals for the Ninth Circuit which declared:

> "Due process of law in a criminal proceeding has been defined as consisting of 'a law creating or defining the offense, an impartial tribunal of competent jurisdiction, accusation in due form, notice and opportunity to defend, trial according to established procedure, and discharge unless found guilty.' "[5]

Speaking through Justice Holmes, the Supreme Court has said, "that what is due process of law depends on circumstances. It varies with the subject matter and the necessities of the situation."[6]

Fortunately, our inquiry here need not extend over the entire scope of due process. It is limited not only to criminal proceedings, but has been drastically confined by definition by the United States Supreme Court which has said, "To those in the military or naval service of the United States the military law is due process."[7]

The addition by the Court of Military Appeals of the adjective "military" to the words due process does not necessarily bring their thought content into sharp focus. Whether "military due process" is simply

[5] Simons v. United States, 119 F. 2d 539, 544 (9th Cir.), *cert. denied,* 314 U. S. 616 (1941).

[6] In Moyer v. Peabody, 212 U. S. 78, 82, 84, 86, 29 Sup. Ct. 235, 53 L. Ed. 410 (1909), the Supreme Court declared: "This is an action brought by the plaintiff in error against the former governor of the State of Colorado, the former adjutant general of the national guard of the same state and a captain of a company of the national guard, for an imprisonment of the plaintiff by them while in office. . . .

"The complaint alleges that the imprisonment was continued from the morning of March 30, 1904, to the afternoon of June 15, and that the defendants justified under the Constitution of Colorado, making the governor commander in chief of the state forces, and giving him power to call them out to execute laws, suppress insurrection, and repel invasion. It alleges that his imprisonment was without probable cause. . . .

"In such a situation we must assume that he had a right, under the state constitution and laws, to call out troops, as was held by the supreme court of the state. The constitution is supplemented by an act providing that 'when an invasion of or insurrection in the state is made or threatened, the governor shall order the national guard to repel or suppress the same.' Laws of 1897, chap. 63, art. 7, sec. 2, p. 204. That means that he shall make the ordinary use of the soldiers to that end; that he may kill persons who resist, and, of course, that he may use the milder measure of seizing the body of those whom he considers to stand in the way of restoring peace. Such arrests are not necessarily (85) for punishment, but are by way of precaution, to prevent the exercise of hostile power.... the plaintiff's position is that he has been deprived of his liberty without due process of law. But it is familiar that what is due process of law depends on circumstances. It varies with the subject-matter and the necessities of the situation. Thus, summary proceedings suffice for taxes, and executive decisions for exclusion from the country. . . .

". . . the declaration does not disclose a 'suit authorized by law to be brought to redress the deprivation of any right secured by the Constitution of the United States.' "

[7] Reeves v. Ainsworth, 219 U. S. 296, 304, 31 Sup. Ct. 230, 55 L. Ed. 225 (1911).

the violation label which the Court will paste upon any error which it has already determined "materially prejudices the substantial rights of the accused,"[8] or whether the words possess in their own right some separate specific significance, is an open question which should be put at rest. Some of the considerations involved are presented in this chapter.

II. Does the Court of Military Appeals Need a "Military Due Process" Concept to Dispatch Its Business?

With rare exceptions[9] the business of the United States Court of Military Appeals is to examine records of trial in court-martial cases to determine whether they contain reversible error which has not been corrected by action of the convening authority or by a board of review[10] While the factual situations and legal problems thus presented are widely varied and highly complex the cases as ultimately resolved by the Court fall into five classifications. These are: First, cases in which there is no error except for the absence of substantial evidence to support the findings; Second, cases supported by substantial evidence in which there is no error present; Third, cases supported by substantial evidence in which error is present but is found by the Court to be not materially prejudicial to the substantial rights of the accused; Fourth, cases supported by substantial evidence in which error is present and is found by the Court to be materially prejudicial to the substantial rights of the accused; and Fifth, cases in which the court-martial was without jurisdiction. Cases determined to be in classification two or three must be affirmed, those determined to be in classification one or five must be resolved in favor of the accused,[11] and those

[8] 50 U. S. C. A. § 646 (1951).

[9] Such exceptions normally deal with appellate powers. Representative are the cases of United States v. Martin, 1 USCMA 82, 1 CMR 82 (1951), and United States v. Sonnenschein, 1 USCMA 64, 1 CMR 64 (1951), in which the Court declared itself to be without jurisdiction to entertain the appeals since the Judicial Council had undertaken their appellate determination prior to May 31, 1951, the effective date of the creation of the Court. In United States v. Reeves, 1 USCMA 388, 392, 3 CMR 122, 126 (1952), it was held that "a board of review has the authority, when the application (for reconsideration) is not made by The Judge Advocate General, to reconsider its decision prior to the time a petition for review has been served and filed by an accused, or a certificate by a Judge Advocate General has been filed, or a record of trial in a case involving an automatic appeal has reached this Court." In United States v. Keith, 1 USCMA 442, 4 CMR 34 (1952), where it was necessary to reverse one of two convictions for different offenses and the original sentence imposed was still within the authorized limit for the single offense approved, the Court held it had no authority to determine as a matter of fact the appropriateness of the sentence and remanded the case to the board of review to make this determination. The same technique was used in United States v. Shepard, 1 USCMA 487, 4 CMR 79 (1952).

[10] 50 U. S. C. A. § 654 (1951).

[11] 50 U. S. C. A. § 654 (1951).

determined to be in classification four must be reversed and either remanded for further appropriate proceedings or dismissed.[12]

Some of the cases falling within the classification of groups one and two are mentioned at this point for purposes of placing the other groups in context. However, the subject of sufficiency of the evidence as a matter of law is given detailed treatment in Chapter 11.

The number of cases reaching the Court which fall into the first group in which the only vice is insufficiency of the evidence is small. Typical of these are *United States v. O'Neal*[13] and *United States v. Shull*,[14] both decided by a divided Court. In the former Air Force case the evidence was found insufficient to sustain a finding of guilty under Article of War 94[15] of making a false writing in furtherance of a claim against the United States. In the latter Army case the evidence was found insufficient to sustain a finding of guilty under Article of War 58[16] of absence without leave with intention to shirk important service. In each case Judge Latimer felt the evidence was sufficient to sustain the findings. These cases present no classification problem. The Court has not discussed due process in these opinions and it seems clear that the

[12] 50 U. S. C. A. § 654 (1951). In United States v. James, 1 USCMA 379, 3 CMR 113 (1952), the accused pleaded guilty to failure to obey a lawful order and not guilty to petty theft, was found guilty of both and the finding as to failure to obey was disapproved by the reviewing authority. The Navy Board of Review affirmed without opinion, noting that accused had pleaded guilty to the charge of theft. This moved the Court to take the Navy Board of Review to task in these words, "We are unable to understand this action. The record is perfectly clear that petitioner pleaded not guilty to this charge. There is little excuse for such obvious errors on the part of an appellate reviewing agency where the liberty and reputation of one convicted of a serious crime is at stake." This, and a failure of the president of the special court-martial to instruct on the elements of the offense to which the accused pleaded not guilty, so disturbed the Court that it not only reversed but, exercising its prerogative under Art. 67(e), 50 U. S. C. A. § 654 (1951), dismissed the charge, thus returning to the Navy immune from prosecution a person prima facie guilty of theft. In United States v. Perna, 1 USCMA 438, 4 CMR 30 (1952), also a theft case, the Court goaded by at least five different substantially prejudicial errors committed by a Navy special court-martial simply dismissed the charges saying, "The numerous errors committed . . . render undesirable any further proceedings." It would indeed be most unfortunate if the Court should make it a practice to vent its exasperation at the legal inaptitude of some court-martial personnel by returning suspect thieves to the services cloaked with immunity. Such is not the practice of the federal courts where error, even in flagrant form, is dealt with dispassionately and with due regard for the rights of the Government as well as those of the accused.

[13] 1 USCMA 138, 2 CMR 44 (1952). This case raises the important and interesting question of the quantum of evidence required by the Court to restrain it from reversing for insufficient evidence. Followed in United States v. Horst, 1 USCMA 452, 4 CMR 44 (1952), where conviction for cowardly conduct in the presence of the enemy was reversed for lack of evidence of cowardice.

[14] 1 USCMA 177, 2 CMR 83 (1952).

[15] 41 STAT. 805 (1920).

[16] 41 STAT. 800 (1920).

familiar doctrine of insufficiency of the evidence is alone adequate for their determination without resort to due process considerations.

The second group of cases, supported by substantial evidence and in which the Court finds no error, is a large one. It embraces two principal situations. In one of these the sole question is the sufficiency of the evidence. The court has experienced considerable difficulty in determining its position as to its powers and limitations in reviewing evidence for sufficiency. Its first pronouncement on the subject was in the *McCrary* case in which Judge Latimer in the majority opinion of a divided Court found the evidence sufficient and held:

> ". . . if there is any substantial evidence in the record to support a conviction an appellate court . . . will not set aside the verdict. . . . In stating this rule we have not overlooked the converse principle that where there is no substantial evidence in the record to sustain the conviction the appellate court will set it aside.... [However], this [second] rule neither precludes those tribunals from drawing reasonable inferences from the evidence presented nor does it permit this court to set aside a conviction because we might have inferred differently."[17]

Judge Brosman concurred in this opinion but three months later apparently shifted his view and, writing for the changed majority in the *O'Neal* case, said, "we must not reverse unless we believe that reasonable men would be in accord in holding that a rational hypothesis other than that of guilt may be drawn from the evidence."[18] In a strong dissent Judge Latimer adhered to the position taken in the *McCrary* case.[19] A few days later in the *Shull* case Judge Brosman, again representing the majority of a divided court, wrote:

> ". . . it is clearly allowable that we weigh the evidence for the limited purpose of testing for substance and determining the

[17] United States v. McCrary, 1 USCMA 1, 3-4, 1 CMR 1, 3-4 (1951). Followed in United States v. Goodman, 1 USCMA 170, 2 CMR 76 (1952).

[18] United States v. O'Neal, 1 USCMA 138, 148, 2 CMR 44, 54 (1952).

[19] In United States v. O'Neal, 1 USCMA 138, 149, 2 CMR 44, 55 (1952), Judge Latimer, in dissent, wrote: "In view of the fact that I believe the opinion of the Court announces a rule which permits us to invade the province of the court-martial and weigh the evidence to arrive at a result, or function which Congress specifically denied us, I am compelled to dissent. . . ." He continued, "If we hold that we can weigh the evidence on scales tilted in favor of the accused then we become the third fact-finding body in the military justice system and legislate unto ourselves powers which a fully informed Congress specifically refused to grant." *Id.* at 151, 2 CMR at 57. The reference here is to the last sentence of Art. 67(d) of the Code, 50 U. S. C. A. § 654 (1951), which provides, "The Court of Military Appeals shall take action only with respect to matters of law." The view expressed by Judge Latimer appears to possess superior merit.

> reasonableness as a matter of law of inferences drawn by the fact-finders. . . . This action [setting aside the finding as based on insufficient evidence] is predicated on the position that the evidence before the court-martial did not permit a determination of the possession of such an intent on the part of the accused beyond a reasonable doubt and within the fair operation of reasonable minds."[20]

Judge Latimer again dissented. Less than a month later the Court achieved judicial harmony on this issue in the *Jacobs* case by saying:

> ". . . we find adequate evidence—the 'substantial evidence' regarded by us as necessary—to support the court-martial's conclusion that petitioner intended to and did in fact participate in the felony here charged. See *United States v. McCrary,* 1 USCMA 1, decided November 8, 1951; *United States v. O'Neal,* 1 USCMA 138, decided February 7, 1952; *United States v. Shull,* 1 USCMA 77, decided February 18, 1952. In the first of these cited cases the following language was used, which is here repeated with approval: [The Court then repeated the exact language from the *McCrary* case, quoted above.]"[21]

This bears all the earmarks of a *sub silentio* strategic retreat from the *O'Neal* case. A month later however in upholding a Navy desertion case the Court through Judge Brosman was still citing the *O'Neal* case:

> "Our inquiry, then, becomes one of whether the complex of evidence in this case permitted a determination, beyond a reasonable doubt and within the fair operation of reasonable minds, that the accused, at the inception of, or at some time during his unauthorized absence, possessed the intention permanently to abandon the naval service. See *United States v. O'Neal,* 1 USCMA 138, decided February 7, 1952; *United States v. Shull,* 1 USCMA 77, decided February 18, 1952; *United States v. Peterson, supra.* We are convinced that it did."[22]

Judge Latimer pointedly concurred in the result only. Then less than a week later a reconciled and unanimous Court speaking through Judge Latimer in an involuntary manslaughter case opined:

> "We are satisfied that any fair minded person could conclude the accused was guilty of culpable negligence and . . .

[20] United States v. Shull, 1 USCMA 177, 180, 183, 2 CMR 83, 86, 89 (1952).
[21] United States v. Jacobs, 1 USCMA 209, 212, 2 CMR 115, 118 (1952).
[22] United States v. Ferretti, 1 USCMA 323, 325, 3 CMR 57, 59 (1952). See also United States v. Peterson, 1 USCMA 317, 3 CMR 51 (1952).

> there was sufficient evidence before the court to permit the members to find his conduct was reckless and in wanton disregard of the rights of the deceased."[23]

No attempt was made to define the required quantum of evidence, but after a careful review of the facts the Court simply stated its ultimate conclusion that the evidence was sufficient. Finally in a murder case we have a unanimous court declaring:

> "It is familiar learning that the guilt of an accused person may be established through circumstantial evidence. It is also recognized that the jurisdiction of this Court extends only to matters of law. See Uniform Code of Military Justice, Article 67(d), 50 U. S. C., Sec. 654. Our task, therefore, is to determine whether the findings of guilty in the case at bar . . . are based on some substantial evidence, as that term has been interpreted by us in previous decisions. We entertain no doubt that they are so based under the test applied in such cases as *United States v. McCrary,* 1 USCMA 1, decided November 8, 1951, and *United States v. O'Neal,* 1 USCMA 138, decided February 7, 1952. We are quite unwilling to disturb the findings in the present case."[24]

This magical and belated twinning of the *McCrary* and *O'Neal* cases is possibly an invitation to the military practitioner to take his choice or perhaps a caveat that things have changed and that the talisman has now become "some substantial evidence." This latter test has been applied in holding the evidence sufficient to support a conviction of a civilian employee in Japan for conduct bringing discredit upon the military service,[25] and to support a conviction of assault with a dangerous weapon.[26] That this issue is in foment is indicated by the fact that in June, 1952, a bill was introduced in the House of Representatives to change Article 67 (d) of the Uniform Code of Military Justice to read:

> "In any case reviewed by it, the Court of Military Appeals shall have authority to weigh the evidence, judge the credibility

[23] United States v. Riggleman, 1 USCMA 336, 341, 3 CMR 70, 75 (1952).
[24] United States v. Jarvis, 1 USCMA 368, 371, 3 CMR 102, 105 (1952).
[25] United States v. Marker, 1 USCMA 393, 3 CMR 127 (1952).
[26] United States v. Norton, 1 USCMA 411, 4 CMR 3 (1952). In United States v. Sperland, 1 USCMA 661, 5 CMR 87 (1952), the evidence was held sufficient to sustain a conviction of misbehavior before the enemy by running away.

of witnesses, and determine controverted questions of fact, recognizing that the trial court saw and heard the witnesses."[27]

Should this become law the Court, within its sphere, would exercise powers not possessed by the Supreme Court of the United States nor other appellate tribunals. The significant fact for our present inquiry is that in none of these cases raising the sufficiency of the evidence has the Court felt any question of due process is involved. Nor has the Court used the term due process in any of these opinions, heavily laden with legal travail though they are.

The other cases falling in group two as being supported by substantial evidence and without error, are usually those in which the issue of the admissibility of a confession has been raised and determined adversely to the accused. In the *Monge* larceny case the Court held admissible a second voluntary confession given eleven hours after a first involuntary statement had been forcibly taken from the accused without warning him of his right against self-incrimination.[28] The Court said:

> "If the fact-finders could reasonably conclude that the confession was voluntary, then we must affirm. . . . The question remains one of fact. . . . The relationship between the earlier and later confession is not so close that we must say the facts of the former control the character of the latter."[29]

Appellant further contended that failure to warn him at the time of the second statement that any prior involuntary confession could not be used against him itself required exclusion of the latter statement. The Court in rejecting this contention declared:

> "Congress has specifically required that an accused, before being questioned, must be warned of his right to say nothing and of the fact that anything he says may be used against him at trial. The effect of the defense argument is to require an additional warning, not provided by Congress. We are not disposed to add judicially to the warning deemed adequate by Congress unless there are impelling reasons for so doing. We find none here. . . . While the presence of a warning such as contended for

[27] H. R. 8395 reported in JAG Chronicle No. 29, page 125, July 18, 1952. This proposed wording, from "shall" on, is taken verbatim from Art. 66(c) of the Uniform Code which vested this power in boards of review. Congress not only has not conferred such power upon the Court, but in Art. 67(d) expressly provided, "The Court of Military Appeals shall take action only with respect to matters of law."

[28] United States v. Monge, 1 USCMA 95, 2 CMR 1 (1952).

[29] *Id.* at 98-100, 2 CMR at 4-6.

by defense may well be a factor in deciding that subsequent confessions are, in fact, voluntary, and while we may feel that such a warning is desirable, we cannot conclude that its absence must result in exclusion of a confession."[30]

In the *Sapp* larceny case the Court held proper the admission of a second voluntary confession which followed by only four hours a first confession of another offense which had been obtained by coercion.[31] In the *Creamer* case, after finding the record contained substantial independent evidence of the *corpus delicti* of the offense of absence without leave, the Court in these words held a spontaneous confession admissible:

> "It is urged that the original declaration was involuntary because made to a uniformed air policeman, who identified himself as such, and who had not at the time warned the accused of his rights [against self-incrimination] under Article of War 24, *supra*. We are not impressed by these arguments. The testimony of Corporal Lewis that the accused's initial remark was volunteered and unsolicited was . . . wholly uncontradicted. . . . Thus we are required to ask whether an unrequested disclosure freely made during the course of a friendly and aimless conversation by an accused person to one of the same military grade is necessarily inadmissible as involuntary by virtue of the fact that the latter is a member of the military police. We think that it is not."[32]

The Court takes the position that if "the accused fairly possessed, at the time of the confession, 'mental freedom' to confess or to deny participation in the crime charged,"[33] then the confession is admissible. No resort to the language of "due process" was made by the Court in determining these confession admissibility cases nor does the application of legal principles other than the normal rules of evidence appear to be required.

The third category of cases in which error is present but is found to be "harmless" is a wide one. Not all error necessitates reversal. Congress has expressly provided that, "A finding or sentence of a court-martial shall not be held incorrect on the ground of an error of law

[30] *Id.* at 100, 2 CMR at 6.

[31] United States v. Sapp, 1 USCMA 100, 2 CMR 6 (1952).

[32] United States v. Creamer, 1 USCMA 267, 273, 3 CMR 1, 7 (1952).

[33] United States v. Webb, 1 USCMA 219, 222, 2 CMR 125, 128 (1952). In this larceny case it was held that a statement made by the investigating agent in the same conversation in which the accused confessed, but afterwards, to the effect that another person who had confessed had received a relatively light sentence, did not make the confession inadmissible.

unless the error materially prejudices the substantial rights of the accused."[34] The Court painstakingly applies this rule to each error which is paraded before it. In a given case if no error is found to be "materially prejudicial" it is affirmed, but if any one error is considered to be "materially prejudicial" to the substantial rights of the accused it is reversed and normally remanded for further proceedings. By way of definition the Court has said, "'Substantial rights' means not seeming or imaginary, not illusive, but real, solid and firm rights."[35] The following array of situations is illustrative of those declared by the Court to constitute error but not materially prejudicial error:

1. The charges were not sworn to as required by Article 30(a) of the Uniform Code.[36]

2. The admission of hearsay evidence, where apart from the hearsay there is ample evidence to support the conviction.[37]

3. The failure of the president of a special court-martial, after a a plea of guilty, to instruct the court as to the elements of the offense and failure to vote upon the findings as distinguished from the sentence.[38]

4. The attempt of trial counsel in an embezzlement case to elicit from a government witness testimony concerning a separate offense of absence without leave committed by the accused, to which objection was sustained.[39]

[34] 50 U. S. C. A. § 646 (1951).

[35] United States v. Lucas, 1 USCMA 19, 23, 1 CMR 19, 23 (1951).

[36] United States v. May, 1 USCMA 174, 2 CMR 80 (1952).

[37] United States v. Doyle, 1 USCMA 545, 550, 4 CMR 137, 142 (1952); United States v. Flores, 1 USCMA 42, 1 CMR 42 (1951); United States v. Isbell, 1 USCMA 131, 2 CMR 37 (1952). In the latter case the Court stated: "We would not permit a finding to stand if it were based solely on hearsay evidence, but when, as here, each finding is based on substantial evidence and at the best the hearsay is either repetitious of the competent evidence, bolstered by cross-examination, fortified in part by defense testimony, or admissible as in exception to the hearsay rule, we cannot say that it prejudiced the defendant within the meaning of Article 59, Uniform Code of Military Justice, 50 U. S. C. A. Sec. 646, which provides that the finding or sentence of a court-martial shall not be held incorrect on the grounds of an error of law unless the error materially prejudices the substantial rights of the accused. We must place some burden on counsel for the accused to police the record, know the issues, and object to incompetent evidence, unless they believe it to be beneficial. If it can be considered as either favorable or unfavorable and a gamble is taken on its effect, then the accused must accept the consequences." *Id.* at 137, 2 CMR at 43. For a case in which the admission of hearsay was held to be prejudicial error see United States v. Kellum, 1 USCMA 482, 4 CMR 74 (1952).

[38] See also United States v. Jones, 1 USCMA 276, 3 CMR 10 (1952); United States v. Lucas, 1 USCMA 19, 1 CMR 19 (1951); United States v. O'Brassill, 1 USCMA 27, 1 CMR 27 (1951); United States v. Bishop, 1 USCMA 29, 1 CMR 29 (1951); United States v. Goodrich, 1 USCMA 26, 1 CMR 26 (1951). These were all Navy cases. In the Lucas case the court astutely observed, "An accused is not presumed innocent after he has pleaded guilty." 1 USCMA at 24, 1 CMR at 24.

[39] United States v. Valencia, 1 USCMA 415, 4 CMR 7 (1952). The Court said: "Trial counsel is entitled to try a case as he sees it, and it would be ridicu-

5. In a case controlled by the law effective before the Uniform Code of Military Justice, in which the accused pleaded guilty, where neither trial counsel nor defense counsel were admitted to practice law, the fact that trial counsel held a law degree and defense counsel did not.[40]

6. The appointment of a noncommissioned warrant officer to serve as trial counsel of a Navy special court-martial in which the accused pleaded guilty.[41]

7. The appointment of a noncommissioned warrant gunner as assistant defense counsel in a Navy special court-martial case in which the accused pleaded guilty and in which the assistant defense counsel did not participate.[42]

8. Where the evidence clearly established intent to avoid hazardous service rather than ordinary desertion, and the accused was charged with desertion with intent to avoid hazardous service, the giving of an instruction regarding intent to remain away permanently which is not an element of the offense charged.[43]

9. The admission in evidence of a confession not affirmatively shown to be voluntary.[44]

---

lous to argue that he is guilty of misconduct in every instance where an offer of evidence or the answer to a question in [*sic*] excluded by the law officer. Mistakes of judgment as to the law often occur, and such mistakes do not show an intention to deliberately flout established law in order to persuade the court to convict. The test to be applied must, therefore, have two branches. First, does the conduct indicate an intent to deliberately disregard the rules of evidence in order to influence the court, and, second, could the improper remarks have reasonably affected the court's deliberations on the findings and sentence? Or, to put it another way, we should reverse only for prejudicial misconduct on the part of the trial counsel. A mere error of judgment will not reach the level of misconduct; the erroneous statement or question may be such as to carry no prejudicial effect; and even if both of these tests are satisfied, there may be convincing evidence of guilt, which would also negate the effect of prejudice." *Id.* at 418, 4 CMR at 10.

[40] United States v. Phillips, 1 USCMA 316, 3 CMR 50 (1952).

[41] United States v. Goodson, 1 USCMA 298, 3 CMR 32 (1952).

[42] United States v. Hutchison, 1 USCMA 291, 3 CMR 25 (1952).

[43] United States v. Moynihan, 1 USCMA 333, 3 CMR 67 (1952); United States v. Jenkins, 1 USCMA 329, 3 CMR 63 (1952). See also United States v. Boone, 1 USCMA 381, 3 CMR 115 (1952), in which the accused was charged with and found guilty of ordinary desertion and the court held the giving of instructions which also covered desertion to avoid hazardous duty and to shirk important service, was, under the evidence of that case, nonprejudicial error. The Court said: "Because of the lack of evidence to support an inference of intent to shirk important service or avoid hazardous duty and the preponderance of evidence upon which to base an inference of intent to abandon the service, we believe this case falls within the rule announced in United States v. Jenkins, *supra,* and United States v. Moynihan, *supra.*" *Id.* at 385, 3 CMR at 119.

[44] United States v. Doyle, 1 USCMA 545, 4 CMR 137 (1952). The Court stated: "We are not here called upon to decide whether the improper reception in evidence of an involuntary confession will vitiate the proceedings regardless of other compelling evidence of guilt. Here, there is no indication that the confession was actually involuntary. The policy considerations which have led some courts to reverse convictions solely because of the use of involuntary confessions in evidence has no application here. We are aware of no similar

10. Where the accuser also served as trial counsel.[45]

11. The imposing of a sentence reading, "to forfeit two-thirds pay per month for two months" instead of in specific terms of dollars and cents.[46]

12. Failure to afford defense counsel a formal opportunity for inspection of service record entries of previous convictions before their admission in evidence.[47]

The foregoing are representative examples of nonprejudicial error.

In at least one case the Court has held, by a two-to-one decision, that prejudicial error committed by a court-martial in considering evidence of a previous conviction which the law officer had erroneously excluded was purged by subsequent substantial reductions in the period of confinement by both the convening authority and the board of review.[48] The fact that the prior conviction in question was as a matter of law properly admissible perhaps influenced the Court considerably in this case.

The Court in its unanimous decision in the *Jenkins* case has well stated its approach to the problem of error:

> "Having determined that error is present, we are compelled to test the record for prejudice as Congress has decreed that we shall not reverse a finding of guilty for an error of law unless it prejudicially affects the substantial rights of petitioner. See Article 59(a), Uniform Code of Military Justice, 50 U. S. C. Sec. 646. In each previous desertion case involving the same error in instructions we have analyzed the facts to determine whether the impact of the error would in any way influence the court to the prejudice of the accused. Because in the previous cases the evidence on each type of intent was substantial and almost in equipoise, we concluded it was probable that reasonable men might be led to render a finding on an element of intent

policy consideration which requires that a failure to follow the prescribed procedure in introducing confessions should be, *per se,* fatal to the proceedings. In such a case, it is appropriate that we should be bound by the rule which prohibits reversal for error unless it is substantially prejudicial to the accused. Here, there is other and convincing proof of guilt." *Id.* at 550, 4 CMR at 142.

[45] In United States v. Lee, 1 USCMA 212, 218, 2 CMR 118, 124 (1952), the Court ruled, "[T]he inquiry conducted by the accuser here did not constitute him an investigating officer and thus disqualify him."

[46] United States v. Gilgallon, 1 USCMA 263, 2 CMR 170 (1952). The Court here reversed a Navy Board of Review.

[47] United States v. Castillo, 1 USCMA 352, 3 CMR 86 (1952). In reversing a Navy Board of Review the Court said, "At most a procedural irregularity transpired, which could have been rectified immediately upon application." *Id.* at 357, 3 CMR at 91.

[48] United States v. Jones, 1 USCMA 302, 3 CMR 36 (1952).

not framed by the specification and that a fair risk of substantial prejudice was present. In this instance, we arrive at a contrary conclusion.

"While we desire to protect adequately the rights of an accused, we can not found prejudice on every inaccuracy in instructions. Technical errors and minor irregularities will creep into the trial of law suits and appellate courts can not administer justice fairly by failing to appreciate that the trial of criminal cases is a practical business, which can not be carried on with perfection. The best we can do is to place our stamp of disapproval on the error and then affirm only those cases where the irregularity does not touch the merits of the findings."[49]

Another illuminating statement of the Court's thinking on this point is found in the *Lee* case:

"It is clear, however, that Article 59(a), as well as other similar Federal and State legislation, grew out of a widespread and deep conviction concerning the general course of review in American criminal cases, and the fear that our appellate courts in criminal cases had become in truth 'impregnable citadels of technicality.' See *Kotteakos v. United States,* 328 U. S. 750, 759-760, notes 11-14. The object of 'harmless error' legislation, we are told by Mr. Justice Rutledge in the *Kotteakos* case *supra,* is: 'To substitute judgment for automatic application of rules; to preserve review as a check upon arbitrary action and essential unfairness in trials, but at the same time to make the process perform that function without giving men fairly convicted the multiplicity of loopholes which any highly rigid and minutely detailed scheme of errors, especially in relation to procedure, will engender and reflect in a printed record' [p. 760]."[50]

The Court has served notice on counsel that timely objection must be made to the admission of evidence. In the *Masusock* case it said:

". . . before this court will review an assignment of error based on the inadmissibility of evidence, where it clearly appears that the defense understood its right to object, except in those instances of manifest miscarriage of justice, there must be an appropriate objection or protest lodged before the trial court so that the court and opposing counsel will be put on notice that the admissibility is in dispute. Otherwise we will consider the ob-

[49] United States v. Jenkins, 1 USCMA 329, 331, 332, 3 CMR 63, 65, 66 (1952).
[50] United States v. Lee, 1 USCMA 212, 216, 2 CMR 118, 122 (1952).

jection waived. See paragraph 154d, Manual for Courts-Martial 1951. It should be apparent that to hold otherwise would result in an inefficient appellate system, interminable delays in the final disposition of cases, and careless trial representation."[51]

In transition from group three to group four in this analysis of the business of the Court it may be appropriate to observe that error as it comes to the Court is initially a single undifferentiated pool. Not so limpid perhaps as that located in Yellowstone Park balanced on the continental divide, but akin to it in that from the single bosom of the latter one part flows to the Pacific and the other to the Mississippi, while from the error pool the Court directs one stream through the nonprejudicial or harmless channel to the sea of Affirmed and the other through the prejudicial channel to the sea of Reversed.

Among errors which the Court has found to be prejudicial are the following:

1. Failure to put in evidence the record of two previous convictions where such previous convictions are essential to the validity of the sentence imposed. "That an excessive sentence is prejudicial is apparent."[52]

2. The refusal of the law officer in a rape case to grant the accused a continuance to obtain another witness, an interpreter, requested because of asserted surprise resulting from the exclusion of certain hearsay evidence regarding fresh complaint sought to be elicited from a witness who received the complaint through the interpreter.[53]

3. The exclusion of a dying declaration offered in evidence in behalf of the accused in a murder case.[54]

4. The admission in evidence in a sodomy case of testimony by the victim's mother as to the details told to her shortly after the event by the four-year-old twin brother of the victim. With this evidence excluded it was then prejudicial error to admit the accused's confession

[51] United States v. Masusock, 1 USCMA 32, 34, 1 CMR 32, 34 (1951).

[52] United States v. Carter, 1 USCMA 108, 114, 2 CMR 14, 20 (1952); United States v. Townsend, 1 USCMA 441, 4 CMR 33 (1952); United States v. Deweese, 1 USCMA 400, 3 CMR 134 (1952); United States v. Pruchniewski, 1 USCMA 328, 3 CMR 62 (1952); United States v. Hand, 1 USCMA, 301, 3 CMR 35 (1952); United States v. Adams, 1 USCMA 275, 3 CMR 9 (1952); United States v. Schabel, 1 USCMA 275, 3 CMR 9 (1952); United States v. Trimiar, 1 USCMA 262, 2 CMR 169 (1952); United States v. Zimmerman, 1 USCMA 160, 2 CMR 66 (1952). These are all Navy cases.

[53] United States v. Plummer, 1 USCMA 373, 3 CMR 107 (1952). Judge Latimer dissenting, said, "I would not scrutinize diligence so closely if the record showed substantial prejudice to the accused, but it does not. Prejudice ties in with the factor that accused must show the evidence was necessary for a just determination of the cause. The burden to establish both is on accused." *Id.* at 379, 3 CMR at 113.

[54] United States v. De Carlo, 1 USCMA 90, 1 CMR 90 (1951).

since no valid evidence remained tending to establish the *corpus delicti*.[55]

5. The proof before findings of prior offenses entirely unrelated to the offenses charged, and reference to other offenses not charged.[56]

6. Where the accused had burglarized the residence of two general officers, for one general to act as convening and reviewing authority in the case based upon the burglary of the residence of the other general.[57]

7. The failure of the president of a Navy special court-martial to instruct as to the presumption of innocence, burden of proof and the elements of an offense to which the accused had pleaded not guilty.[58]

8. The failure to instruct as to the elements of a lesser included offense where the evidence tended to establish guilt of the lesser included offense.[59]

[55] United States v. Mounts, 1 USCMA 114, 2 CMR 20 (1952).

[56] United States v. Yerger, 1 USCMA 288, 3 CMR 22 (1952). The Court reversed the Coast Guard Board of Review and returned the record to the General Counsel for the Treasury Department for further proceedings.

[57] United States v. Gordon, 1 USCMA 255, 2 CMR 161 (1952). The Court stated, "the test should be whether the appointed authority was so closely connected to the offense that a reasonable person would conclude that he had a personal interest in the matter." *Id.* at 261, 2 CMR at 157. The Court disposed of the case on the ground of prejudicial error, rather than jurisdiction.

[58] United States v. Clay, 1 USCMA 74, 81, 1 CMR 74, 81 (1951). Although the square holding was that this failure to instruct was "error materially prejudicial to the substantial rights of the accused," this is the first opinion in which the Court discussed military due process. This aspect of the case will be considered later. The *Clay* case has been followed as to failure to instruct in United States v. Shepard, 1 USCMA 487, 4 CMR 79 (1952), and United States v. Keith, 1 USCMA 442, 4 CMR 34 (1952). In United States v. Rhoden, 1 USCMA 193, 2 CMR 99 (1952), the Court reversed for prejudicial error where the instructions given adequately covered only the elements of lesser included offenses and omitted necessary elements of the greater offenses of which accused was both charged and convicted. No objection was interposed on behalf of the accused at the time of the trial.

[59] United States v. Williams, 1 USCMA 231, 2 CMR 137 (1952). Accused was charged with assault with intent to commit murder and no instruction was given as to the elements of the offense of assault with a dangerous weapon. Followed in United States v. Avery, 1 USCMA 533, 4 CMR 125 (1952), and United States v. Drew, 1 USCMA 471, 4 CMR 63 (1952). Also United States v. Clark, 1 USCMA 201, 2 CMR 107 (1952), in which the accused, charged with voluntary manslaughter, was found guilty of negligent homicide and no instruction was given as to the elements of negligent homicide. Judge Quinn dissented, saying that the name of the crime of negligent homicide supplies its own definition. The majority said: "Correct procedure under military law requires that, unless the evidence excludes any reasonable inference that a lesser crime was committed, the duty of the law officer is to carve out instructions concerning the offense. He is the judge in the military system and he must furnish to the court the legal framework of all offenses which the evidence tends to establish. Unless he does so the accused has been denied a right which we conclude was granted by Congress and error as a matter of law follows." *Id.* at 205, 206, 2 CMR at 111, 112. See, however, United States v. Ginn, 1 USCMA 453, 4 CMR 45 (1952), where the accused was charged with premeditated murder but was found guilty of voluntary manslaughter. The evidence did not raise the issue of self-defense and no instruction on self-defense was requested by

9. The failure to instruct as to the elements of murder where accused was charged with the offense of assault with intent to commit murder.[60]

10. Where the accused, in Korea, was charged only with ordinary desertion, the giving of instructions which included the elements of desertion to avoid hazardous duty and to shirk important service, in a case where the evidence might have established any of the three offenses. This result was reached even though no objection was made to the instruction at the trial.[61]

The *ratio decidendi* of all these cases was the presence of error materially prejudicial to the substantial rights of the accused which necessitated reversal.

The fifth group of cases into which the business of the Court falls are those in which attack is made upon the jurisdiction of the court-martial. If jurisdiction is lacking the entire proceeding falls. The question of jurisdiction may, of course, be raised at any stage of the proceeding including appeal. Furthermore, jurisdiction is the sole aspect of a court-martial proceeding which may be considered in the regular Federal courts and this only by way of collateral attack in a habeas corpus proceeding,[62] and then only after all military remedies of appeal and motion for new trial have first been exhausted.[63] The Supreme Court of the United States has succinctly stated court-martial jurisdictional requisites in these words:

> "The single inquiry, the test, is jurisdiction. . . . In this case the court-martial had jurisdiction of the person of accused and

---

defense counsel. The evidence supported the charge of murder and not the finding of voluntary manslaughter. In this case it was held not error not to have instructed on self-defense nor on the elements of the lesser included offense of voluntary manslaughter. See also, United States v. Quisenberry, 1 USCMA 670, 5 CMR 98 (1952), where the accused was charged with and convicted of unpremeditated murder, and under the facts of the case the absence of instructions as to the elements of lesser included offenses was held not to be error.

[60] United States v. Williams, 1 USCMA 231, 234, 2 CMR 137, 141 (1952). See also United States v. Drew, 1 USCMA 471, 4 CMR 63 (1952), and United States v. Banks, 1 USCMA 479, 4 CMR 71 (1952).

[61] United States v. Williams, 1 USCMA 186, 2 CMR 92 (1952). The Court declared, "When a substantial right is denied we will not speculate as to the extent of the damage done. . . ." It went on to state, "We cannot emphasize too strongly the necessity of objection at the proper time." *Id,* at 188, 189, 2 CMR at 94, 95. To the same effect, on the instruction issue, see United States v. Justice, 1 USCMA 643, 5 CMR 71 (1952); United States v. Shepard, 1 USCMA 487, 4 CMR 79 (1952); United States v. Goddard, 1 USCMA 475, 4 CMR 67 (1952); United States v. Hemp, 1 USCMA 290, 3 CMR 14 (1952).

[62] Hiatt v. Brown, 339 U. S. 103, 111, 70 Sup. Ct. 495, 94 L. Ed. 691 *rehearing denied,* 339 U. S. 939 (1950); *Ex parte* Reed, 100 U. S. 13, 23, 25 L. Ed. 538 (1879). For a detailed discussion of military habeas corpus see Chapter 15, *post.*

[63] Gusick v. Schilder, 340 U. S. 128, 132-33, 71 Sup. Ct. 149, 95 L. Ed. 146 (1950).

the offense charged, and acted within its lawful powers. The correction of any errors it may have committed is for the military authorities which are alone authorized to review its decisions."[64]

The question of whether the court-martial was duly constituted, *i.e.*, "acted within its lawful powers," was before the Court in the following five cases. In the *Merritt* case,[65] the accused was brought to trial on June 6, 1951, before a summary court convened under the old Articles for the Government of the Navy and not in accordance with the requirements for a special court-martial, its successor, as set forth in the Uniform Code of Military Justice which became effective May 31, 1951. The Court held the Naval summary court was without jurisdiction. This situation was peculiar to the change-over period and presumably will not arise again.

In the *Emerson* case,[66] charges against the accused were referred for trial by indorsement to Navy special court "A". The case was in fact tried by special court "B," an entirely different court, convened however by the same convening authority. The Court held this procedural irregularity in bringing the case before the special court-martial did not divest it of jurisdiction.

In the *Hutchison* case,[67] the Court held that where the appointed assistant defense counsel of a Navy special court was a noncommissioned warrant gunner and thus not an officer as defined by Article 1(5) of the Uniform Code of Military Justice,[68] this did not operate to deprive the Court of jurisdiction and that if it did constitute procedural error it was harmless.[69] The question before the Court in the *Goodson* case[70] was whether the appointment of a noncommissioned warrant officer pay clerk, not an officer within the meaning of the Code, as trial coun-

[64] Hiatt v. Brown, 339 U. S. 103, 111, 70 Sup. Ct. 495, 94 L. Ed. 691, *rehearing denied,* 339 U. S. 939 (1950).

[65] United States v. Merritt, 1 USCMA 56, 1 CMR 56 (1951).

[66] United States v. Emerson, 1 USCMA 43, 1 CMR 43 (1951).

[67] United States v. Hutchison, 1 USCMA 291, 3 CMR 25 (1952).

[68] 50 U. S. C. A. § 551 (1951).

[69] United States v. Hutchison, 1 USCMA 291, 3 CMR 25 (1952). "Congress has not . . . conferred upon an accused an explicit and absolute right to have any assistant defense counsel appointed, nor to have such counsel, if appointed, be an officer. This case presents, therefore, no violation of a statutory right. Congress has laid out in the Uniform Code of Military Justice the framework within which military courts-martial must function, and a court must step outside that framework before it will lose jurisdiction already properly acquired under the statute. . . .

"There is here no violation of a mandatory requirement of the Code, and therefore no jurisdictional defect. . . . Even assuming that the appointment of Warrant Officer Chew constituted error, we fail to see how this error in any way harmed the accused." *Id.* at 292, 293, 3 CMR at 26, 27.

[70] United States v. Goodson, 1 USCMA 298, 3 CMR 32 (1952).

sel of a Navy special court-martial deprived it of jurisdiction. The Court answered this in the negative.[71]

The two joint accused in the *LaGrange* case[72] were hospitalmen assigned to the USS Haven. The commander of this ship, a Navy captain, personally formally accused them of violation of ship regulations in misusing drugs and forwarded the charges to his superior, the Commander of Naval Forces, Far East, who in turn referred the charges for trial to a naval base at Pusan, Korea, commanded by a Naval commander. The Court held under these circumstances that this special court was without jurisdiction since an officer junior to the accuser and one not in the normal chain of command did not have authority to appoint it. "Congress intended that if an officer authorized to convene a court is disqualified, a superior must assume the responsibility and convene the court."[73] The jurisdictional question in all of these cases was whether the court was duly constituted.

The issue of jurisdiction of the person was presented in the *Marker* case,[74] in which the accused was a GS-11 civilian employee of the Army in Japan convicted under Article of War 96 of conduct of a nature to bring discredit upon the military service by exacting substantial gifts from Japanese employees subordinate to him. The Court held the accused was "accompanying or serving with the armies of the United States without the territorial jurisdiction of the United States" and so subject to court-martial jurisdiction under Article of War 2(d).[75]

Jurisdiction of the offenses was challenged in the *Snyder* case,[76] where the accused marine contended that his actions in attempting three times on a base to entice others to engage in intercourse with a female and of bringing her into a barracks in violation of a general order constituted no violation of the Uniform Code of Military Justice.

[71] The Court said: "Congress did not intend to make otherwise valid court-martial judgments wholly void merely because of a technical non-compliance with a provision of the Code which is not an 'indispensible prerequisite' to concepts of military justice and a fair trial.

"Even though the defect we are considering is not jurisdictional . . . error was committed by the appointment of a noncommissioned warrant officer as trial counsel. Paragraph 6 of the Manual prohibits this action. As we have constantly reiterated, it is not every error which will cause reversal—prejudice must be shown. It is difficult to see how an accused in any case could be harmed by a noncommissioned warrant officer serving as counsel for the Government." United States v. Goodson, 1 USCMA 298, 299, 300, 3 CMR 32, 34, 35 (1952).

[72] United States v. LaGrange and Clay, 1 USCMA 342, 3 CMR 76 (1952).

[73] United States v. LaGrange and Clay, 1 USCMA 342, 345, 3 CMR 76, 79 (1952).

[74] United States v. Marker, 1 USCMA 393, 3 CMR 127 (1952).

[75] 41 STAT. 787 (1920).

[76] United States v. Snyder, 1 USCMA 423, 4 CMR 15 (1952). See also United States v. Herndon, 1 USCMA 461, 4 CMR 53 (1952). United States v. Wade, 1 USCMA 459, 4 CMR 51 (1952).

The Court held the former to be an offense under Article 134[77] and the latter an offense under Article 92.[78]

The final facet of jurisdiction was before the Court in *Carter*[79] and its companion cases[80] in which, due to erroneous consideration of prior convictions not properly in evidence, sentences including bad conduct discharges were imposed where the court-martial only had jurisdiction to impose three days' confinement and forfeiture of two-thirds pay for a like period for each day of the short unauthorized absence with which the accused were charged. As to that portion of a sentence imposed in excess of the maximum authorized by law a court is without jurisdiction.[81] In these cases the Court did not discuss lack of jurisdiction but contented itself with finding that the erroneous consideration of the prior convictions was prejudicial.

The preceding sampling of the business of the Court of Military Appeals is by no means exhaustive of the specific questions that have arisen, and will hereafter arise, but it is broad enough to establish the pattern made by the impact of that business. In this litigation the Court did not find it necessary to resort to due process considerations to reach a just result. The sturdy baskets labeled "insufficient evidence," "substantial evidence," "harmless error," "materially prejudicial error" and "with or without jurisdiction" served adequately to carry off these cases to their proper destinations. The question remains, is a "military due process" basket required?

III. "Military Due Process" as Defined by the Court of Military Appeals

The case chosen by the Court for its initial excursion into the field of due process was one in which a sailor named Clay was charged with wearing an improper uniform and with disorder.[82] To the first charge Clay pleaded guilty, to the second, not guilty. The president of the special court-martial failed to instruct at all as to the elements of the offense of disorder or as to the presumption of innocence or the burden of proof. Conviction followed, which was affirmed by the board of review and reversed by the Court. The Court, very properly, expressly found this failure to instruct constituted error materially prejudicial to the substantial rights of the accused.[83] Having done so it was its duty to reverse.[84] The Court was not content, however, to do this and

[77] 50 U. S. C. A. § 728 (1951). [78] 50 U. S. C. A. § 686 (1951).
[79] United States v. Carter, 1 USCMA 108, 2 CMR 14 (1952).
[80] Collected in footnote 52, *supra*.
[81] See *Ex parte* Reed, 100 U. S. 13, 23, 25 L. Ed. 538 (1879).
[82] United States v. Clay, 1 USCMA 74, 1 CMR 74 (1951).
[83] *Ibid.*
[84] 50 U. S. C. A. § 646 (1951).

no more. Perhaps having in mind the justice of the peace commissions which gave rise to *Marbury v. Madison*[85] and feeling that no set of facts is too trivial to provide the vehicle for expounding a judicial doctrine, it elected in this typical police court case to state, by way of dicta, its views regarding military due process. Since these views are the focal point of this discussion it is appropriate to set them forth at length.

> "There are certain standards in the military accusatorial system which have been specifically set by Congress and which we must demand be observed in the trials of military offenses. Some of these are more important than others, but all are of sufficient importance to be a significant part of military law. We conceive these rights to mold into a pattern similar to that developed in Federal civilian cases. For lack of a more descriptive phrase, we label the pattern as 'military due process' and then point up the minimum standards which are the framework for this concept and which must be met before the accused can be legally convicted. The Uniform Code of Military Justice, *supra,* contemplates that he be given a fair trial and it commands us to see that the proceedings in the courts below reach that standard.
>
> "Generally speaking, due process means a course of legal proceedings according to those rules and principles which have been established in our system of jurisprudence for the enforcement and protection of private rights. For our purposes, and in keeping with the principles of military justice developed over the years, *we do not bottom those rights and privileges on the Constitution. We base them on the laws as enacted by Congress.* But, this does not mean that we can not give the same legal effect to the rights granted by Congress to military personnel as do civilian courts to those granted to civilians by the Constitution or by other Federal Statutes.
>
> "A cursory inspection of the Uniform Code of Military Justice, *supra,* discloses that Congress granted to an accused the following rights which parallel those accorded to defendants in civilian courts; to be informed of the charges against him; to be confronted by witnesses testifying against him; to cross-examine witnesses for the Government; to challenge members of the court for cause or peremptorily; to have a specified number of members compose general and special courts-martial; to be repre-

[85] 1 Cranch 137, 2 L. Ed. 60 (U. S. 1803).

sented by counsel; not to be compelled to incriminate himself; to have involuntary confessions excluded from consideration; to have the court instructed on the elements of the offense, the presumption of innocence, and the burden of proof; to be found guilty of an offense only when a designated number of members concur in a finding to that effect; to be sentenced only when a certain number of members vote in the affirmative; and to have an appellate review.

"By mentioning the foregoing rights and benefits, we have not intended to make the list all-inclusive, nor to imply others might not be substantial. We have merely enumerated those which are of such importance as to be readily catalogued in that category. In addition, *we disclaim any intent to classify these as jurisdictional or nonjurisdictional. Under our powers as an appellate court we can reverse for errors of law which materially prejudice the substantial rights of the accused, and we need go no further than to hold that the failure to afford to an accused any of the enumerated rights denied him military due process* and furnishes grounds for us to set aside the conviction.

"Previously adjudicated Federal court cases are a source from which we can test the *prejudicial effect* of denying an accused the rights we have set out as our pattern of 'military due process.'

"True, we need not concern ourselves with the constitutional concepts, but if the denial of these benefits to a defendant is of sufficient importance to justify a civilian court in holding that it denied him due process, it should be apparent to a casual reader that denial of a similar right granted by Congress to an accused in the military service constitutes a violation of military due process. By adopting these principles we impose upon military courts the duty of jealously safeguarding those rights which Congress has decreed are an integral part of military due process.

"Aside from the constitutional due process concept threading its way through Federal cases, *we find Federal appellate courts passing directly on the prejudicial error of failure of trial judges properly to instruct a jury.*

"It was for Congress to set the rules governing military trials. It legislated on the subject and not without adequate consideration. We are not concerned with the wisdom of the enactment, but we might suggest that there are many reasons which may have prompted Congress to demand that instructions be given to members of courts-martial. . . .

"We cannot better set out reasons why the error materially prejudiced the substantial rights of the accused than did Mr. Justice Frankfurter in the case of *Bruno v. United States,* 308 U. S. 297. Speaking for the Court, he stated (pp. 293-294):

"'A subsidiary question remains for determination. It derives from the Act of February 26, 1919, 40 Stat. 1181, 28 U. S. C. Sec. 391, whereby appellate courts are under duty in criminal as well as civil cases to disregard 'technical errors, defects, or exceptions which do not affect the substantial rights of the parties.' Is the disregard of the right which Congress gave to Bruno an error, the commission of which we may disregard? We hold not. It would be idle to predetermine the scope of such remedial provision as Sec. 391 by anticipating the myriad varieties of rulings made in trials and attempting an abstract, inclusive definition of 'technical errors.' Suffice it to indicate, what every student of the history behind the Act of February 26, 1919, knows, that that Act was intended to prevent matters concerned with the mere etiquette of trials and with the formalities and minutiae of procedure from touching the merits of a verdict. Of a very different order of importance is the right of an accused to insist on a privilege which Congress has given him.'

"What we have previously stated goes with like effect to the failure of the court to instruct on the presumption of innocence and the burden of proof. We are not impressed with the argument made by the board of review that it was clothed with authority to determine the sufficiency of the evidence and that it found the failure to instruct was not prejudicial because the evidence overcame the presumptions of innocence; that the elements were established beyond a reasonable doubt; and that it was satisfied the court or the board of review could not have made a finding other than that of guilty. Assuming without deciding that the evidence compels such a finding, we are, nevertheless, required to hold the error materially prejudiced the substantial rights of the accused, for the reason that we can not say one of the historic cornerstones of our system of civil jurisprudence is merely a formality of military procedure. If Congress specifically grants what it considers to be a substantial right, we can not deny the authoritative requirement by refusing to recognize it. . . .

"In applying the concepts we have discussed to this case we find the trial of the accused far short of what is deemed essential to military justice. In the final analysis, the record as a whole convinces us that the accused was denied those necessary elements of military due process by which *Congress* sought to protect him."[86] (Emphasis supplied.)

A moment's reflection discloses that, by its own analysis, the due process of which the Court speaks is not that of the due process clause of the Fifth Amendment nor is it constitutional due process at all. Rather, it derives solely from the laws enacted by Congress and all of its component requisites are to be found by an inspection of the provisions of the Uniform Code of Military Justice. The absence of one or more of these components is not necessarily jurisdictional and such absence can be adequately dealt with by the Court exercising its power to reverse for errors of law which materially prejudice the substantial rights of the accused. The Court relies on the quotation from the *Bruno* case[87] in which Mr. Justice Frankfurter was concerned with the difference between technical error and prejudicial error and not at all with due process. From the *Clay* opinion there emerges our old friend, prejudicial error. Significantly, whereas Congress, in fashioning the Uniform Code of Military Justice, did not once use the words "due process" it most emphatically did say in Article 59(a) "A finding or sentence . . . shall not be held incorrect . . . unless the error materially prejudices the substantial rights of the accused."

The next appearance of the term due process was again in the roll of dictum. In the *Davis* case,[88] tried before the effective date of the Uniform Code of Military Justice, none of the counsel were members of the bar and the record contained no affirmative statement that no officers so qualified were available. The Court rejected the contention that the absence of such a statement was fatal error, resting its decision on *Hiatt v. Brown*[89] and *Whelchel v. McDonald*,[90] two Supreme Court habeas corpus cases which had squarely held that the absence of an affirmative showing of nonavailability presented no jurisdictional defect. The Court of Military Appeals said:

"It is recognized, of course, that the Federal authorities referred to in foregoing paragraphs were concerned with questions of jurisdiction, while we are not limited to review of this nature. It is certainly true in the present case that, without holding the court-martial to have been without jurisdiction to try Davis, it

[86] United States v. Clay, 1 USCMA 74, 77-82, 1 CMR 74, 77-82 (1951).

[87] Bruno v. United States, 308 U. S. 287, 293, 294, 60 Sup. Ct. 198, 84 L. Ed. 257 (1939).

[88] United States v. Davis, 1 USCMA 102, 2 CMR 8 (1952).

[89] 339 U. S. 103, 70 Sup. Ct. 495, 94 L. Ed. 691, *rehearing denied*, 339 U. S. 939 (1950).

[90] 340 U. S. 122; 71 Sup. Ct. 146, 95 L. Ed. 141 (1950).

is legally and logically open to us to conclude that the failure of the record to reflect affirmatively the unavailability of lawyers under Article of War 11, 10 U. S. C. A., Sec. 1482, is reversible error. However, we are unwilling to do this."[91]

Having thus disposed of the only issue raised by the case, one which can no longer arise under the Uniform Code of Military Justice, the Court, apparently by way of afterthought, in the last paragraph of its opinion declared:

"Apart from the matters dealt with in preceding paragraphs, it should be said that we find no substantial evidence of neglect of the interests of the accused by defense counsel—much less that arising to the level of a denial of due process. Indeed, appellant's case has been presented to us solely on the basis of the general considerations discussed, and no slightest suggestion of specific neglect has been made."[92]

Under these circumstances this casual use of the term adds little to the literature of due process.

The third dictum use of the term military due process was in the *Carter* case in which trial counsel had read to the court-martial detailed information concerning two previous convictions of the accused without ever placing this data in evidence. In reversing, the Court used this language:

"The question of prejudice can be disposed of with little comment. If, as we hold, the accused neither waived his right to assign insufficiency of the evidence as error, nor stipulated that the statement made by trial counsel could be considered as evidence of the previous convictions, then it follows that the sentence exceeds the limits permitted by the Manual. That an excessive sentence is prejudicial is apparent.

"Our attention has been called to several service cases which have directly or indirectly considered this question. Without reviewing them in detail, we believe the rationale expressed in the case of *United States v. Arizona* (ACM S-1681), 1 CMR 725, of October 5, 1951, is more consistent with our views of military due process and trial procedure."[93]

Here the court found prejudicial error and proceeded to speak of military due process as roughly synonymous to proper trial procedure. The finding of prejudicial error alone had fully disposed of the case.

[91] United States v. Davis, 1 USCMA 102, 2 CMR 8, 13 (1952).
[92] *Id.* at 108, 2 CMR at 14.
[93] United States v. Carter, 1 USCMA 108, 114, 2 CMR 14, 20 (1952).

In the *Bartholomew* case[94] tried under the 1948 Articles of War, the Court affirmed a conviction of voluntary manslaughter. The principal ground upon which reversal was urged was that while neither counsel was a lawyer the trial judge advocate held a law degree and defense counsel had no formal legal training. In disposing of this contention the Court declared:

> "A clear violation of the express terms of Article of War 11 would certainly raise serious questions of military due process, if not of jurisdiction. Cf. *United States v. Clay,* 1 USCMA 74, decided November 27, 1951; *United States v. Berry,* 1 USCMA 235, decided March 18, 1952; *United States v. Bound,* 1 USCMA 224, decided March 13, 1952; *United States v. Lee,* 1 USCMA 212, decided March 13, 1952. We have, however, been reminded that 'courts sit as well to convict the guilty as to acquit the innocent, and complaint alone, without a showing that a fair trial has been denied, will not support a reversal.' *Couchois v. United States,* 142 F. 2d. 1, 2 (C. A. 5th Cir.). Congress has implicitly recognized, through the Article of War so frequently cited herein, that an accused person may obtain adequate representation by a non-lawyer. Indeed, line officers have long been permitted to defend such persons before military courts-martial. *This background is persuasive that prejudice cannot be inferred solely from the fact that the prosecutor was legally trained, whereas defense counsel was not.* In view of these factors, and recalling that we find here at least a literal and technical compliance with the command of Congress, it is appropriate that we should scan the record to determine whether the accused's want of legally-trained counsel materially prejudiced him in this case. . . .
>
> *"After a painstaking search of the entire record, we find nothing whatever which would indicate that the accused was not accorded full, fair, and competent representation by his counsel. This being the case we cannot at all say that he was materially prejudiced in any substantial right."*[95]

Once more the reference to military due process is pure dictum. Again the Court based its decision on the absence of material prejudice and inferred that before there can be a want of military due process there must be a finding of prejudicial error.

The *Welch* case, which evoked military due process language,

[94] United States v. Bartholomew, 1 USCMA 307, 3 CMR 41 (1952).
[95] *Id.* at 311, 3 CMR at 45.

was one in which the accused, a lieutenant, was convicted under Article of War 95 of cheating on an examination. In reversing, the majority opinion of the Court contained this statement:

> "At the outset of the investigation, the officer conducting it did not fully advise petitioner of his rights under Article of War 24, *supra*. This was a clear violation of that Article. Nor did he advise petitioner of the nature of the investigation, or of the charges against him. This officer then conducted a searching and inquisitorial examination, utilizing all the devices of an expert prosecutor cross-examining a hostile witness, accompanied by shouting, accusations of falsehood, reprimands, and castigations of character. All these factors inevitably lead to the conclusion that petitioner was, in effect, compelled to incriminate himself. This smacks too much of Star Chamber proceedings. Petitioner did not have a free choice to admit or deny his guilt or to refuse to answer the questions asked.
>
> "It follows automatically that the testimony given at this investigation should not have been received in evidence at the trial. Article of War 24, *supra*, and Article 31 of the Uniform Code of Military Justice, 50 U. S. C. Sec. 602, so command. Further, it matters not that there may be other evidence of guilt. The right here violated flows, through Congressional enactment, from the Constitution of the United States. Military due process requires that courts-martial be conducted not in violation of these constitutional safeguards which Congress has seen fit to accord to members of the Armed Forces, *United States v. Clay*, 1 USCMA 74, decided November 27, 1951. These safeguards are for the protection of all who are brought within the military disciplinary system, and are not to be disregarded merely in order to inflict punishment on one who is believed to be guilty."[96]

The majority here indicated that so far as military justice is concerned constitutional benefits are switched on and off by the legislative action of Congress. Technically, this differs from the position taken by the Court in the *Clay* opinion that military due process derives not at all from the Constitution but solely from Congress. Practically the result is the same under either concept since without the affirmative action of Congress no right exists. Judge Latimer, who authored the extended discussion of due process in *Clay* felt it necessary in *Welch*

[96] United States v. Welch, 1 USCMA 402, 407, 3 CMR 136, 142 (1952).

to file a separate concurring opinion setting forth reservations. He said:

> "I concur in the result. I do not concur outright because I have certain reservations concerning some of the concepts developed in the Court's opinion and, therefore, prefer to base my reversal on different grounds. . . .
>
> ". . . the provisions of both the Articles of War and the paragraph from the Manual . . . were violated. . . . Accordingly, the ruling of the law member in admitting the statement in evidence was error as a matter of law. This, then, poses the question of whether the error was prejudicial. . . .
>
> "One fundamental difference between civilian practice and military practice which is of importance in this instance is that in the former the jury does not ordinarily sentence the defendant, while in the military system the members of the court-martial do. In testing prejudice in military tribunals consideration must be given to the probable impact on the minds of the members of the court both as to the findings and the sentence; and if the error itself substantially influenced the court, or if there is grave doubt as to its prejudicial effect, the findings and sentence should not be permitted to stand. . . .
>
> "Keeping in mind the considerations mentioned, there are at least three ways in which I believe the inadmissible evidence prejudiced the accused. . . ."[97]

Thus Judge Latimer expressly found a violation of the rights of the accused under Article of War 24, as indeed did the majority, that this error was prejudicial, and rested the reversal on prejudicial error and not at all on lack of due process.

Another reference to due process by the Court was in the *Lucas* case[98] where its task in hand was a definition of the "substantial rights" of the accused, which if materially prejudiced necessitate reversal under Article 59(a). There the Court quoted from Section 87(c) of the *Manual for Courts-Martial 1951:*

> "The test to be applied in determining whether an error materially prejudiced the substantial rights of the accused is this: An error prejudicial to the rights of the accused must be held to require the disapproval of a finding of guilty of an offense, or the part thereof, to which it relates unless the competent evidence of record is of such quantity and quality that a

[97] *Id.* at 408, 3 CMR at 138.
[98] United States v. Lucas, 1 USCMA 19, 1 CMR 19 (1951).

court of reasonable and conscientious men would have made the same finding had the error not been committed.

"Regardless, however, of the test in the subparagraph above, if the error is such a flagrant violation of a fundamental right of the accused as to amount to a denial of due process (e.g., when the disloyalty of defense counsel directly aids the prosecution) the finding must be disapproved regardless of the compelling nature of the competent evidence of record."[99]

It will be remembered that in the *Lucas* case not only did the Court not pursue due process, but, in view of the plea of guilty of the accused, found that no prejudicial error existed, reversed the board of review and affirmed the court-martial conviction. It is significant that the only mention of due process in the *Manual for Courts-Martial* is contained in a discussion of materially prejudicial error. In passing it might be noted that disloyalty of defense counsel, cited as an example of denial of due process would be an express violation of defense counsel's oath to perform his duties faithfully as required by Article 42(a)[100] and would constitute materially prejudicial error.

This examination of these opinions points to the conclusion that the Court, on those occasions where it employs the term "military due process" does so interchangeably with, and cumulative to, its application of the test of the presence or absence of "error materially prejudicial to the substantial rights of the accused."[101]

IV. What Military Due Process Is Not

First of all the concept of military due process, and even the concatenation of the words themselves, is not new. Currently there is some slight tendency to think that military justice originated on May 31, 1951, the effective date of the Uniform Code of Military Justice.[102] Such was not the case. British Articles of War reach back to the time of Glanvil and antedate Magna Charta itself by some twenty-five

[99] *Id.* at 23, 1 CMR at 23.

[100] 50 U. S. C. A. § 617 (1951).

[101] This conclusion is supported by United States v. Hunter, 2 USCMA 37, 6 CMR 37 (1952), in which the Court affirmed a death sentence murder case. In disallowing an appellate contention that legal representation afforded accused at his trial lacked the quality necessary to insure a fair trial, the Court said: "We believe the requirements of the applicable provisions of the Code and Manual, and of military due process were fully met. Those require that accused be afforded the help and guidance of military counsel with certain specified qualifications or of counsel of his own choice. Here he had both." This statement, with the words "and of military due process" deleted, correctly declares the applicable law. *Id.* at 41, 6 CMR at 41.

[102] 50 U. S. C. A., note preceding § 551 (1951).

years.[103] If by military due process we mean procedural safeguards for the fundamental rights of the accused, this was a matter of concern in the Articles issued in 1621 by King Gustavus Adolphus of Sweden,[104] in 1672 by Prince Rupert,[105] in 1686[106] and in 1688[107] in the English Military Disciplines of James II, and by Parliament in the Mutiny Act of 1689.[108] Procedural protection was given the accused in Articles adopted by the Provisional Congress of Massachusetts Bay on April 5, 1775,[109] and by those adopted by the Second Continental Congress on June 30, 1775,[110] and amended by it in 1776.[111] Thus, preconstitutionally, consideration was given to a fair system of military justice. The Constitution itself vested in Congress the power "To make Rules for the Government and Regulation of the land and naval forces."[112]

Congress has consistently discharged this duty from the very beginning. The first Congress recognized the existing military establishment and provided that it should "be governed by the rules and articles of war which have been established by the United States in Congress assembled or by such rules and articles of war as may hereafter by law be established."[113] Congress adopted new articles of war in 1806,[114] 1874,[115] 1916,[116] 1920,[117] and 1948,[118] and has repeatedly voted amend-

[103] Ordinance of Richard I, 1190. Reprinted in 2 WINTHROP, MILITARY LAW, Appendix 3 (1886).

[104] Reprinted in 2 WINTHROP, MILITARY LAW, Appendix 8-23 (1886). See Chapter 1, note 23.

[105] Reprinted in DAVIS, A TREATISE ON THE MILITARY LAW OF THE UNITED STATES, Appendix A, 567-80 (3d ed. 1915). See Chapter 1, note 24.

[106] Reprinted in 2 WINTHROP, MILITARY LAW, Appendix 24-25 (1886). See Chapter 1, note 25.

[107] Reprinted in 2 WINTHROP, MILITARY LAW, Appendix 26-37 (1886). See Chapter 1, note 26.

[108] Statutes of the Realm 55, 1 W. & M., c. 5, Reprinted in 2 WINTHROP, MILITARY LAW, Appendix 38-39 (1886). See Chapter 1, note 27.

[109] Reprinted in 2 WINTHROP, MILITARY LAW, Appendix 61-67 (1886).

[110] Reprinted in 2 WINTHROP, MILITARY LAW, Appendix 68-76 (1886).

[111] WINTHROP, MILITARY LAW AND PRECEDENTS 22 (2d ed. 1920). Art. 8 of § XIV of these Articles of War of 1776, reprinted at page 968, provided: "No sentence of a general court-martial shall be put in execution, till after a report shall be made of the whole proceedings to Congress, or to the general or commander in chief of the forces of the United States, and their or his directions be signified thereon." Art. 2 of § XVIII, reprinted at page 970, provided: "The general, or commander in chief for the time being, shall have full power of pardoning or mitigating any of the punishments ordered to be inflicted, for any of the offenses mentioned in the foregoing articles; and every offender convicted as aforesaid, by any regimental court-martial, may be pardoned, or have his punishment mitigated by the colonel, or officer commanding the regiment."

[112] U. S. CONST. Art. 1, § 8, cl. 14.

[113] 1 STAT. 95-96 (1789).

[114] 2 STAT. 359 (1806).

[115] REV. STAT. § 1342 (1878).

[116] 39 STAT. 650-70 (1916).

[117] 41 STAT. 787 (1920), 10 U. S. C. A. §§ 1471-1593a (1946).

[118] 62 STAT. 627-44 (1948), 10 U. S. C. A. c. 36 (1950 Supp.).

ments thereto. When in 1950 Congress enacted the Uniform Code of Military Justice,[119] it engaged in no legislative innovation but simply discharged a recurring historic constitutional obligation.

As early as 1911 the United States Supreme Court was called upon to determine whether an Army officer had been deprived of due process in the manner in which his commission had been terminated. In reversing a writ of mandate issued by the trial court, and upholding the action taken by military authorities, the Supreme Court said, "To those in the military or naval service of the United States the military law is due process."[120] The Supreme Court has twice had occasion to reaffirm this view of due process as applied to the military in officer elimination cases.[121] Furthermore, in the only two military justice cases to reach the Supreme Court in which it was contended that the accused had been denied due process and in which such a finding had been made by the United States Courts of Appeal, the Supreme Court reversed, refused habeas corpus relief, and found that although extensive error had been committed there was no denial of due process.[122] Thus, consistently, through the years, the United States Supreme Court has refused to recognize that there is any such thing as military due process apart from the acts of Congress declaring what the military law is. Stated another way, although the concept of military due process is not new, it has never been subscribed to by the Supreme Court.

As a pertinent parallel it should be observed that the essence of the provision of Article 59(a) of the Uniform Code of Military Justice that "a finding . . . shall not be held incorrect . . . unless the error [of law] materially prejudices the substantial rights of the accused," is not new to military law. Article of War 37 of the 1920 Articles in pertinent part provided that "proceedings . . . shall not be held invalid . . .

[119] Act of May 5, 1950, 64 STAT. 108, 50 U. S. C. A. c. 22 (1951).

[120] Reeves v. Ainsworth, 219 U. S. 296, 304, 31 Sup. Ct. 230, 55 L. Ed. 225 (1911).

[121] French v. Weeks, 259 U. S. 326, 335, 42 Sup. Ct. 505, 66 L. Ed. 965 (1922), where the Supreme Court said, "As a Colonel in the Army, the relator was subject to military law and the principles of that law, as provided by Congress, constituted for him due process of law in a Constitutional sense. *Reeves v. Ainsworth*, 219 U. S. 296, 304." Also Creary v. Weeks, 259 U. S. 336, 344, 42 Sup. Ct. 509, 66 L. Ed. 973 (1922), "Without pursuing the subject further it is sufficient to repeat what was said by this Court in *Reeves v. Ainsworth*, 219 U. S. 296, 304: 'To those in the military or naval service of the United States the military law is due process. The decision, therefore, of a military tribunal acting within the scope of its lawful powers cannot be reviewed or set aside by the courts.'"

[122] Smith v. Hiatt, 170 F. 2d 61 (3d Cir. 1948), *rev'd sub nom.* Humphrey v. Smith, 336 U. S. 695, 69 Sup. Ct. 830, 93 L. Ed. 986, *rehearing denied*, 337 U. S. 934 (1949); and Hiatt v. Brown, 175 F. 2d 273 (5th Cir. 1949), *reversed*, 339 U. S. 103, 70 Sup. Ct. 495, 94 L. Ed. 691, *rehearing denied*, 339 U. S. 939 (1950). See Chapter 15, *post*.

for any error as to any matter of pleading or procedure unless . . . it shall appear that the error . . . has injuriously affected the substantial rights of the accused."[123] Its successor, Article of War 37 of the 1948 Articles, contained exactly the same language. Thus for over thirty years Army boards of review have been reversing convictions where the record disclosed that error "injuriously affected the substantial rights of the accused." Whether under the present test of "materially prejudices," more serious error must be found to warrant reversal than was necessary under the old test of "injuriously affected" is conjectural. As a practical matter the legal result under either yardstick would probably be substantially the same, and the Court has so indicated.[124]

A second thing military due process is not, and hence is to be distinguished from, is jurisdiction. The Court has drawn this distinction. In the *Clay* case it said:

> ". . . we disclaim any intent to classify these [rights] as jurisdictional or non jurisdictional. Under our powers as an appellate court we can reverse for errors of law which materially prejudice the substantial rights of the accused, and we need go no further than to hold that the failure to afford to an accused any of the enumerated rights denied him military due process. . . ."[125]

In the *Davis* case it stated,[126] "It is recognized . . . that the federal authorities . . . were concerned with . . . jurisdiction, while we are not limited to review of this nature." Finally in the *Bartholomew* case the Court, declared,[127] "A clear violation of . . . Article of War 11 would certainly raise serious questions of military due process, if not of jurisdiction." Furthermore, when the Court has been confronted with real jurisdictional issues it has treated them as such without reference to due process. This comports with the steadfast refusal of the Supreme Court to exalt asserted due process violations to the stature of jurisdictional defects in military habeas corpus cases.[128]

Thirdly, military due process is not constitutional due process. The

[123] 41 STAT. 794 (1920).
[124] United States v. Berry, 1 USCMA 235, 2 CMR 141 (1952).
[125] United States v. Clay, 1 USCMA 74, 78, 1 CMR 74, 78 (1951).
[126] United States v. Davis, 1 USCMA 102, 107, 2 CMR 8, 13 (1952).
[127] United States v. Bartholomew, 1 USCMA 307, 311, 3 CMR 41, 45 (1952).
[128] Humphrey v. Smith, 336 U. S. 695, 700-01, 69 Sup. Ct. 830, 93 L. Ed. 986 (1949), *rehearing denied,* 337 U. S. 934 (1949); Hiatt v. Brown, 339 U. S. 103, 110-11, 70 Sup. Ct. 495, 94 L. Ed. 691, *rehearing denied,* 339 U. S. 939 (1950); Burns v. Wilson, 346 U. S. 137, 73 Sup. Ct. 1045, 97 L. Ed. 1508 (1953), *rehearing denied,* 346 U. S. 884, 74 Sup. Ct. 3, 98 L. Ed. 51 (1953).

Court of Military Appeals speaking of due process has said,[129] ". . . [We] do not bottom those rights and privileges on the Constitution. We base them on the laws as enacted by Congress," and further,[130] ". . . we need not concern ourselves with the constitutional concepts. . . ." This conforms to the holding of the Supreme Court in *Creary v. Weeks*[131] that the due process clause of the Fifth Amendment does not apply to military tribunals.

Nor do the other provisions of the Bill of Rights apply to military law. The Court of Military Appeals has recognized this in holding that the Fourth Amendment prohibition "against unreasonable searches and seizures" does not in the military service require a search warrant, and does not make unlawful, searches conducted by a military commander or his authorized representatives where there is probable cause to believe an offense has been committed.[132] This result is quite different from that reached in civil life under the Fourth Amendment.

The Supreme Court has held that not only does the Fifth Amendment right to grand jury indictment, from which "cases arising in the land or naval forces" are expressly excepted, not apply to military prosecutions, but that the Sixth Amendment guaranty of the right to trial by jury is equally inapplicable to military prosecutions, even though the exception is not there spelled out. It has also held that the constitutional provision of Article III, Section 2, that, "The trial of all crimes, except in Cases of Impeachment, shall be by Jury" has no application to military tribunal prosecutions.[133] Even more sweepingly

[129] United States v. Clay, 1 USCMA 74, 77, 1 CMR 74, 77 (1951).

[130] *Id.* at 79, 1 CMR at 79.

[131] 259 U. S. 336, 343, 42 Sup. Ct. 509, 66 L. Ed. 973 (1922). "Thus is presented for decision the question whether the due process clause of the Fifth Amendment required that the relator should be given an opportunity to be heard before the finding was made by the board which required his discharge from the Army.

"The power given to Congress by the Constitution to raise and equip armies and to make regulations for the government of the land and naval forces of the country (Art. I, Sec. 8) is as plenary and specific as that given for the organization and conduct of civil affairs; military tribunals are as necessary to secure subordination and discipline in the army as courts are to maintain law and order in civil life; and the experience of our Government for now more than a century and a quarter, and of the English Government for a century or more, proves that a much more expeditious procedure is necessary in military than is thought tolerable in civil affairs (2 STAT. 359; *Dynes v. Hoover*, 20 How. 65). It is difficult to imagine any process of government more distinctively administrative in its nature and less adapted to be dealt with by the processes of civil courts than the classification and reduction in number of the officers of the Army, provided for in Sec. 24b. In its nature it belongs to the executive and not to the judicial branch of the Government."

[132] United States v. Doyle, 1 USCMA 545, 549, 4 CMR 137, 141 (1952). The Court stated, "[T]he action of the master-at-arms in searching petitioner's locker was, according to existing military and naval law, reasonable."

[133] *Ex parte* Quirin, 317 U. S. 1, 39-45, 63 Sup. Ct. 1, 87 L. Ed. 3 (1942). In 317 U. S. at page 40 the Supreme Court said, "[W]e must conclude that Sec. 2 of

the Supreme Court has said, "the power of Congress, in the government of the land and naval forces and the militia, is not at all affected by the fifth or any other amendment."[134]

Citations are unnecessary for the proposition that the due process clause of the Fourteenth Amendment, directed at state action, has no application to the federal instrumentality of military justice.

Military due process, fourthly, is not a totality of error doctrine, and cannot be brought into play by the cumulation of a number of nonprejudicial errors in a single case. The Court of Military Appeals so held in the *Zimmerman* case:

> "Appellate defense counsel, admitting *arguendo* that, considered individually, none of the errors listed above prejudiced the accused, argues that their cumulative effect was such as to warrant a finding of prejudice. Counsel refers to several Federal cases in support of this proposition. Without analyzing those decisions in detail, we note that the individual errors in each of them contained some, although slight, possibility of prejudice. Such is not the case here. The errors discussed above are formal in nature and we fail to see how, individually or collectively, they could have in any way materially harmed the accused. Since we find no substantial prejudice, we are bound by Article 59 of the Uniform Code of Military Justice, 50 USCA Sec. 646, to hold that the errors considered by the board of review do not require disapproval of the findings and sentence."[135]

Finally, military due process does not stem from a segregation of general prejudice as distinguished from specific prejudicial errors. This differentiation has been undertaken by the Court of Military Appeals but in its treatment of general prejudice no reference has been made to due process.

The development of the doctrine of general prejudice has pursued a curious course. Judge Brosman first spoke of it in a case in which the question certified was whether the fact that the accuser later served as trial counsel divested the court-martial of jurisdiction. The square holding on this single issue, in the language of the Court, was:

> "We have searched the record with care and find no suggestion whatever of *specific* prejudice—that is, of prejudice operating against the accused in this particular case. . . . We find, in

Article III and the Fifth and Sixth Amendments cannot be taken to have extended the right to demand a jury trial by military commission. . . ." Also Kahn v. Anderson, 255 U. S. 1, 8, 41 Sup. Ct. 224, 65 L. Ed. 469 (1920).

[134] *Ex parte* Milligan, 4 Wall. 2, 138, 18 L. Ed. 281 (U. S. 1866).

[135] United States v. Zimmerman, 1 USCMA 160, 162, 2 CMR 66, 68 (1952).

short, no shadow of showing in the record that the accused in this case was or could have been prejudiced by the fact that the interests of the Government therein were represented by the accuser who had perforce conducted an informal presignature inquiry into its facts. . . .

". . . the inquiry conducted by the accuser here did not constitute him an investigating officer, and thus disqualified him—and we explicitly so hold."[136]

Having thus disposed of the case, Judge Brosman then wrote:

"Nor do we find a basis for the belief that what might be described as *general* prejudice should be deemed to exist by virtue of the fact that Lieutenant Barton, the accuser, also served as trial counsel. We are confident that our meaning in the use of this standard will not be misapprehended. Report has already been made of the limitations on the 'harmless error' formula set up in the *Kotteakos* case, *supra.* At this point it should be said that we are not at all sure that equal caution should not be exercised in the invocation of this otherwise wholesome principle in perhaps one further setting. We have in mind here a situation in which the error consists not in a violation of constitutional or legislative provisions, but involves instead an overt departure from some 'creative and indwelling principle'—some critical and basic norm operative in the area under consideration. Such a compelling criterion we find within the sphere of this Court's effort in the sound content of opposition to command control of the military judicial process to be derived with assurance from all four corners of the Uniform Code of Military Justice. Is this criterion violated by permitting the accuser to serve as trial counsel? We think not.

"It has been suggested, however, that departure from a specific requirement of the Manual should, of itself, constitute 'general prejudice' of the type we are here discussing. We have no doubt that this may be true in a proper case if, but *only* if, the policy underlying the Manual requirement is so overwhelmingly important in the scheme of military justice as to elevate it to the level of a 'creative and indwelling principle.' The previous discussion should be persuasive that no such policy consideration exists here."[137]

[136] United States v. Lee, 1 USCMA 212, 216, 218, 2 CMR 118, 122, 124 (1952).
[137] *Id.* at 217, 218, 2 CMR at 123, 124.

Thus "general prejudice," like "military due process," was conceived in dicta. Judge Latimer concurred only in the result,[138] based patently upon a different premise.

In another case decided the same day, Judge Brosman quoted from the *Lee* case and then said:

> "Because of the finding of a probability of specific prejudice against the accused, it is unnecessary that we inquire into the presence of general prejudice growing out of the membership in the court-martial under the facts of the instant case [accused pleaded guilty] of one who was an investigating officer within the meaning of paragraph 64, Manual for Courts-Martial, United States, 1951. For this reason we express no conclusion on the subject at this time."[139]

This time the straw man does not even get to assume an upright position before being stricken down, but general prejudice is nurtured by a dictum.

In the *Berry* case[140] the accused was tried in Korea on May 4, 1951, under the procedure established by the 1948 Articles of War. The President of the Court usurped the duties of the law member by ruling on motions to dismiss a specification, to exclude a confession and for findings of not guilty, and by advising the accused as to his rights. The Court addressed itself to the question of whether this error was prejudicial, and Judge Brosman writing the majority opinion said:

> "We have recently examined the content of the phrase 'material prejudice' in our opinion in the *Lee* case, *supra*. There we enunciated two approaches to the question of prejudice. The first and more obvious of these was denominated *specific* prejudice and described as that to be derived from the facts and circumstances of the particular case before the court and either more or less demonstrably operative against the accused there. . . . The second concept we termed *general* prejudice. This was characterized as the product of an 'overt departure from some "creative and indwelling principle"—some critical and basic norm operative in the area under consideration.' *United States v. Lee, supra.* Such a compelling criterion—we there suggested by way of example—is to be found within the sphere of this Court's efforts in the 'sound content of opposition to command control of the military judicial process to be derived with

[138] *Id.* at 218, 2 CMR at 124.
[139] United States v. Bound, 1 USCMA 224, 230, 2 CMR 130, 136 (1952).
[140] United States v. Berry, 1 USCMA 235, 2 CMR 141 (1952).

assurance from all four corners of the Uniform Code of Military Justice.' The complete independence of the law member and his unshackled freedom from direction of any sort or nature are, we entertain no doubt, vital, integral, even crucial, elements of the legislative effort to minimize opportunity for the exercise of control over the court-martial process by any agency of command. It follows that any abdication by the law member of his statutory duties and an attendant usurpation of those functions by the president—much more directly a representative of the convening authority—must be viewed with stern suspicion. . . ."[141]

Here, the majority resolutely turned its back upon its tried and true prejudicial error formula of the specific variety and elected to base its decision on the general prejudice dictum from the *Lee* case. Judge Latimer, concurring in the result only, filed a separate opinion in which he ably and vigorously espoused, as the basis of decision, common garden variety prejudicial error. He wrote:

"I agree that the cause should be reversed, but do so on the narrow ground that the trial before the court-martial was so lacking in the essentials of military judicial procedure that the rights of this accused were substantially prejudiced. The court's opinion goes much further and rationalizes on general prejudice, which appears to me unnecessary in this setting, and contrary to the clear mandate of Congress. It is to reserve from my concurrence an approval of that concept which leads me to file this opinion.

"Congress commanded that an accused have questions of law and preliminary questions of fact decided by a law member who possessed certain qualifications. Here that command was ignored. To say that bypassing the law member is not prejudicial to the man on trial is to say that any reviewer of trial or trier of fact can be eliminated without harm to the individual on trial.

"I believe that when Congress authorized preliminary rulings by a legally trained person and that right is refused there is involved a prejudicial denial of a right of substance. It is more than a belief that some over-arching principle of general prejudice permeates the atmosphere of the court room. It is the refusal to grant to the accused a fundamental right guaranteed to him by the Articles of War. If we are permitted to reason by analogy with the civilian practice this, to me, smacks of a judge

[141] *Id.* at 240, 2 CMR at 146.

allowing the foreman of a jury to decide questions of law and admissibility of confessions. . . ."[142]

The very next day the Court in the *Gordon* case[143] held it was prejudicial error for a General whose quarters had been burglarized by the accused to be the convening authority of a general court-martial to try even another offense committed by this accused. Judge Brosman in a separate concurring opinion wrote:

> "I concur fully in the result in this case.
>
> "I do not understand Judge Latimer to evaluate the error it contains as jurisdictional—whatever exactly this term may mean. I do understand him to have concluded that the substantial rights of the accused were materially prejudiced. I am sure he is correct in this determination. Without, however, inquiring whether the record reflects a basis for a finding of specific prejudice as developed in *United States v. Lee,* 1 USCMA 212, decided March 13, 1952, I prefer to bottom my concurrence on the concept of general prejudice, as applied by this Court in *United States v. Berry,* 1 USCMA 235, decided March 18, 1952. See also *United States v. Bound,* 1 USCMA 224, decided March 13, 1952."[144]

This separate opinion relies on a dictum to reach by a separate route a result already arrived at by the Court by an application of the well-established prejudicial error doctrine.

From these four cases it is apparent that Judge Brosman is the progenitor of "general prejudice" and that Judge Latimer has refused to subscribe to it. The congressional mandate is "error materially prejudicial," without subdivision. It would seem that material prejudice, no matter how thinly sliced, would continue to be material prejudice and that multiplying the adjectives in front of prejudice is not helpful. In none of the cases in which it has been mentioned was it necessary to a finding of prejudicial error, to resort to the heady elixir of an "overt departure from some 'creative and indwelling principle'—some critical and basic norm operative in the area under consideration."[145] Congress is not so esoteric. The prose employed in the Uniform Code of Military Justice is quite specific, and in a given case, its provisions either are or are not violated, and where violated, the resulting error either is or is not materially prejudicial to the accused. As Judge Latimer has said, the finding of prejudice involves "more

[142] *Id.* at 242, 243, 2 CMR at 148-150.
[143] United States v. Gordon, 1 USCMA 255, 2 CMR 161 (1952).
[144] *Id.* at 262, 2 CMR at 168.
[145] United States v. Lee, 1 USCMA 212, 218, 2 CMR 118, 123 (1952).

than a belief that some overarching principle of general prejudice permeates the atmosphere of the court room."[146]

In any event it is clear that when the Court speaks of due process it does not mean general, as distinguished from specific, prejudice, nor does it have reference to an "overt departure from some 'creative and indwelling principle'—some critical and basic norm operative in the area under consideration."

V. What Military Due Process Probably Is

"To those in the military or naval service of the United States the military law is due process."[147] "The Congress shall have power . . . to make rules for the government and regulation of the land and naval forces. . . ."[148] This "power of Congress . . . is not at all affected by the fifth or any other amendment."[149] "It was for Congress to set the rules governing military trials."[150] "[T]he only way by which Congress can make certain what it deems important is by saying so in its legislative pronouncement."[151] "[W]e are unable to escape the express mandate from Congress that we should not reverse except for an error materially prejudicing the substantial rights of the accused."[152]

Military due process is not jurisdictional, it is not constitutional due process, it is not violated by a cumulation of nonprejudicial error, it is not general prejudice and it has not once been mentioned by Congress in the Uniform Code of Military Justice. By process of elimination then, any violation of a provision of the Uniform Code of Military Justice resulting in error which the Court finds materially prejudiced the substantial rights of an accused constitutes a want of military due process. Conversely, any military tribunal action, within its jurisdiction, supported by "some substantial evidence" in which the Court finds no error materially prejudicial to the substantial rights of the accused is one complying with military due process.

The formulas of the Court then become, "The case is reversed because of error materially prejudicial to the substantial rights of the accused, a failure to comply with military due process," and, "The case is affirmed because there is no error materially prejudicial to the substantial rights of the accused, a compliance with military due process." It is submitted that the addition of the final clause, in each

146 United States v. Berry, 1 USCMA 235, 243, 2 CMR 141, 149 (1952).
147 Reeves v. Ainsworth, 219 U. S. 296, 304, 31 Sup. Ct. 230, 55 L. Ed. 225 (1911).
148 U. S. Const., Art. I, § 8, cl. 14.
149 *Ex parte* Milligan, 4 Wall. 2, 138, 18 L. Ed. 281 (U. S. 1866).
150 United States v. Clay, 1 USCMA 74, 80, 1 CMR 74, 80 (1951).
151 *Ibid.*
152 United States v. Lucas, 1 USCMA 19, 25, 1 CMR 19, 25 (1951).

case, to the formulas, adds nothing to their thought content. Accordingly, they should be deleted, unless one fully subscribes to the position taken by Judge Brosman in the *O'Neal* case that, "Words mean nothing in themselves; we have no desire to bog down in a morass of verbalism; and we regard the semantic aspect of the matter as of little importance into the bargain."[153]

VI. What to Do About It

The Court of Military Appeals may make what it will of "military due process." So long as that Court avoids jurisdictional error adverse to an accused there is no judicial agency which can review its opinions.[154] It could, if it chose, say, "We find prejudicial error which violates the doctrine of '*ex bono et aequo*' and therefore reverse." A court with this practically unlimited power may, in appropriate cases, exercise the doctrine of self correction, even as does the Supreme Court.

Delicacy dictates discreetly decorous dissent from the use the Court has made of the words military due process. The writer would not go quite so far as did the Court when in speaking of *res gestae* it characterized it as "the bastard and unhelpful catchphrase *res gestae* of nebulous meaning. . . ."[155] Without casting aspersions upon the venerable ancestry of the words military due process, they may be aptly characterized as "the . . . unhelpful catchphrase *military due process* of nebulous meaning." If they have a separate significance the Court has not removed their nebulosity and this should be done. If they are simply another way of saying "no prejudicial error" they are tautological and should be excised.

It is hoped the Court will work out the destiny of military justice within the prescribed Uniform Code framework by continuing the very fine start it has made in applying to each case the congressionally imposed test of the presence or absence of error materially prejudicial to the substantial rights of the accused. This places the Court in no strait-jacket. Rather it permits the Court to engage in each case in unlimited inquiry and in painstaking analysis as it has ably done in the many cases in which it has applied the prejudicial error rule. In the course of time the Court of Military Appeals will, in the words of Mr. Justice Holmes, "prick . . . out by the gradual approach and contact

[153] United States v. O'Neal, 1 USCMA 138, 143, 2 CMR 44, 49 (1952).

[154] Hiatt v. Brown, 339 U. S. 103, 111, 70 Sup. Ct. 495, 94 L. Ed. 691, *rehearing denied,* 339 U. S. 939 (1950); Burns v. Wilson, 346 U. S. 137, 73 Sup. Ct. 1045, 97 L. Ed. 1508 (1953), *rehearing denied,* 346 U. S. 884, 74 Sup. Ct. 3, 98 L. Ed. 51 (1953); Shaw and Begalke v. United States (D. C. Cir. 1954), 209 F. (2d) 811.

[155] United States v. Mounts, 1 USCMA 114, 118, 2 CMR 20, 24 (1952).

of decisions on the opposing sides"[156] the lines delimiting the boundaries of prejudicial error.

VII. Conclusion

The foregoing analysis of "military due process" was written in the fall of 1952 and originally published in February 1953.[157] In December 1953 the Court of Military Appeals itself furnished the epilogue. Judge Brosman, as spokesman for the majority of a sharply divided Court,[158] wrote:

> "This Court has held that error deemed reversible through the doctrine of general prejudice may be the subject of purgation. *United States v. Ferry,* 2 CMR 129. Certainly, we are aware of no reason why *at least certain* violations of military due process may not likewise be cured. This conclusion may give pause to one familiar only with the procedures and thinking of the civilian—as distinguished from the military—practice. However, the approach upon which it is predicated is in no sense a product of the imagination of this Court or of any member of it. Rather, it is firmly rooted in the unequivocal language of Congress in Article 59 of the Code, *supra.*"[159]

A fitting conclusion to "military due process." The Court has boxed the compass and come full circle. Its "due process" and "general prejudice" powers, at last, have been traced by the Court to their Congressional fountainhead in Article 59 of the Uniform Code of Military Justice and are there dispelled. In the apothecary shop of appellate review the Court is likely, from time to time, to paste on a given bottle a "due process" label, until the stock on hand is used up, but, following its own prescription laid down in *Gibson,* the contents in every case will have been weighed in the scale of Article 59 and the label affixed will not alter the contents nor the measurement process.[160]

[156] Noble State Bank v. Haskell, 219 U. S. 104, 31 Sup. Ct. 186, 55 L. Ed. 112 (1911).

[157] 6 Vand. L. Rev. 251 (1953).

[158] See the fourteen page dissenting opinion of Judge Latimer in United States v. Gibson, 3 USCMA 512, 523, 13 CMR 68, 79 (1953). It appears to be this dissenting opinion to which Judge Brosman has reference when, at page 523 of the decision, he said: "This unselective criticism, in truth, is compact of the very stuff of which bugaboos are made; and to express it is to talk through one's hat. . . . We accord the mercy of silence."

[159] United States v. Gibson, 3 USCMA 512 at 517, 13 CMR 68 at 73 (1953).

[160] A case which illustrates this trend is United States v. Josey, 3 USCMA 767, 14 CMR 185 (1954). The Court reversed a board of review and unanimously upheld a larceny conviction in which the independent evidence of guilt was clear. This was done although a confession had been admitted in evidence in the ab-

It must be here observed that Article 59, in pertinent part, provides, and has always provided: "A finding or sentence of a court-martial shall not be held incorrect on the ground of an error of law unless the error materially prejudices the substantial rights of the accused."[161]

---

sence of any showing that the accused had been warned of his right under Article 31 to remain silent and in the face of strong evidence that accused's statement had been induced by a promise of immunity. Judge Brosman, who wrote the opinion of the Court, at 775, said: "We are and must ever be especially concerned with demanding a proper factual basis for application of the strong medicine implicit in the doctrines of general prejudice and military due process—that is, with demanding something more than a mere 'indication.' . . ." Judge Latimer in a separate concurring opinion, at 778, 781, astutely observed:

"I concur in the result.

"I do not concur outright because I am unwilling to join my associates in deciding cases on a rationale which seems to rely on the strength of the medicine to be administered. . . .

"I can understand why there should be an effort made to narrow the doctrine of general prejudice, and while I have never subscribed to it, I am in full accord with any restriction which will limit its application. However, in this instance, it is not necessary that we probe further in that field as this case can be disposed of by adopting the compelling evidence rule, a concept which is recognized in most jurisdictions and one which the Court concedes has long been the service rule. In essence that rule is expressed in Article 59(a), 50 USC Sec. 646, which states we should not reverse a case in the absence of prejudice, . . .

"All I need say is that the error did not materially prejudice a substantial right of the accused."

[161] 50 U. S. C. A. Sec. 646 (1951).

CHAPTER 11

Sufficiency of the Evidence as a Matter of Law

I. General

The Court, as is usual with appellate tribunals in criminal cases, is limited to correction of errors of law.[1] Within this concept appellate courts in varying degrees concern themselves with deciding whether the evidence in a given case is sufficient to support the findings as a matter of law. The Court was faced, at the outset, with the difficult task of determining the degree to which it would apply this principle.

In *McCrary*,[2] the first written opinion of the Court, Judge Latimer, writing for the majority, set forth "a few well known principles of law" which govern the scope of review. After recognizing that the Court is limited to correction of errors of law, he stated in substance:

(1) If there is *any* substantial evidence in the record to support a conviction the Court, in the absence of other error, will not set aside the verdict or conversely, the Court will set aside a conviction where there is *no* substantial evidence to sustain the finding.

(2) The principle of law requiring that the evidence must establish beyond a reasonable doubt that the defendant is guilty of the crime charged and the rule which states that the evidence must exclude every reasonable hypothesis of innocence are applicable to the trial forums and are *not* to be applied by the Court of Military Appeals.[3]

[1] Code, Art. 67(d), (e).
[2] 1 USCMA 1, 1 CMR 1 (1951).
[3] *Ibid.* Manual for Courts-Martial, United States, 1951, par. 74*a* (3) provides that the following rule is to be observed by a court-martial: "When the only competent evidence of the commission of an offense is circumstantial in nature, the inference to be drawn from such evidence must not only prove all the elements of the offense, but must at the same time exclude every reasonable hypothesis of innocence." See also Manual for Courts-Martial, United States, 1951, par. 28*a* (3): "A specification must exclude every reasonable

Judge Quinn registered his disagreement with such a restricted view. Although he conceded that the Court was limited to correction of errors of law, he believed that the proper rule to invoke in reviewing cases involving circumstantial evidence was as follows:

> ". . . There must be substantial evidence consistent with guilt and inconsistent with any reasonable hypothesis of innocence. This rule has been laid down even more strongly to the effect that the evidence must exclude every reasonable hypothesis but that of guilt. . . ."[4]

Unlike Judge Latimer, he did not regard this test in either of its versions as being confined to the trial forums but rather as an appropriate test to be applied by the Court.

The issue in *McCrary* was whether the court-martial was justified in finding an intent to desert. Judges Latimer and Brosman concluded that the finding should be affirmed on the basis of the following facts which they considered were in evidence before the court-martial:

(1) The accused was stationed at Camp Stoneman, California;
(2) The station of the accused was in use as a staging area;
(3) The station of the accused was approximately forty-five miles from the San Francisco Port of Embarkation;
(4) The accused was a member of an overseas replacement unit;
(5) The absence without leave had lasted sixty days;
(6) This absence had terminated by surrender at a point approximately two thousand miles from the station of the accused;
(7) A state of armed conflict existed in Korea involving United States forces.

Judge Quinn's dissent does not reveal how he would apply the "reasonable hypothesis" rule which he favored inasmuch as he disagreed with the majority on the facts which he considered were in the record. He concluded there was ". . . no legal competent evidence to indicate that the accused intended permanently to abandon the military service."[5]

The issue regarding the test to be applied by the Court in determining whether circumstantial evidence was sufficient as a matter of law

---

hypothesis of innocence." Compare par. 71 which deals with ruling on a motion for a finding of not guilty. It states in part: "If there is any substantial evidence which, together with all proper inferences to be drawn therefrom and all applicable presumptions, reasonably tends to establish every essential element of an offense charged or included in any specification to which the motion is directed, the motion will not be granted." Par. 71 is discussed in United States v. Toms, 3 USCMA 435, 12 CMR 191 (1953).

[4] United States v. McCrary, 1 USCMA 1, 12, 1 CMR 1, 12 (1951).

[5] *Id.* at 16.

was raised but not settled in *McCrary*. This question was again considered in *O'Neal*.[6] In this case, Judge Brosman set forth his views, which received the concurrence of Judge Quinn,[7] as follows:

> "Among other principles of law relevant to the problem before us is that providing in substance that the evidence in a criminal case must establish beyond a reasonable doubt that the accused is guilty of the offense charged. To this must be added, of course, the related proposition, often clothed in varying verbiage, to the effect that the evidence in such a case must exclude every reasonable hypothesis save that of guilt. All of these considerations were recognized by us in United States v. McCrary, . . . together with the observation that [these] . . . rules exist *primarily* for the guidance of trial forums. However, we should not have said there, we did not intend to say there, nor did we say there, that their administration by such agencies is above and beyond the supervision of an appropriate appellate tribunal—by this Court, in fact, although limited to 'action only with respect to matters of law.' To hold the converse would effectively deprive appellate courts, including this one, of any sort of effective control over subordinate elements of the judicial scheme in an important area of law administration."[8] (Emphasis supplied.)

Having established the authority of the Court to supervise trial forums in the execution of the duty to determine if the evidence is consistent with the hypothesis that the accused is guilty, and at the same time inconsistent with the hypothesis of innocence, and with every other rational hypothesis except that of guilt, the Court was still confronted with the question of whose judgment was to be applied in making this determination. The answer was ". . . our judgment, as such, is not the standard for application, but rather our conception of the judgment of reasonable men."[9]

Judge Latimer did not approve of the idea of supervising the fact-finding powers of the court-martial. He adhered to the view he expressed in the *McCrary* case:

[6] 1 USCMA 138, 2 CMR 44 (1952).

[7] Judge Quinn stated: "I have some slight reservation about the distinction made between this case and the McCrary case. The result reached appears to support my position in the McCrary case." *Id.* at 149, 2 CMR at 55. The difference appears to be that in *McCrary* Judge Quinn spoke in terms not of supervising but of applying the reasonable hypothesis rule.

[8] United States v. O'Neal, 1 USCMA 138, 143-144, 2 CMR 44, 49-50 (1952).

[9] *Id.* at 148, 2 CMR at 54.

"If there is some substantial evidence in the record which permits the court-martial to conclude the accused is guilty beyond a reasonable doubt then we are not permitted to reverse because we might or can draw a different conclusion.[10]

In order more fully to understand the quantum of evidence required by the Court it is necessary to examine the facts of selected cases. In *O'Neal* the court-martial found the accused guilty of making a false writing in furtherance of a claim against the United States. The facts were complicated but the issue was simple. Did the accused make the entry which resulted in his receiving money for separate rations to which he was not entitled? Judges Brosman and Quinn agreed that the evidence showed the accused had opportunity and motive for making the false writing. There was also a possible inference of guilt arising from the "quite loose similarity" between the method of adding the name of the accused to a document admittedly made by him and the manner in which the name of the accused was placed on the document in question. Beyond this, however, there was according to these two judges little to support the findings save "suspicion, conjecture and speculation." Further it was concluded that the opportunity was open to others to commit the offense and there was possibly a motive for at least one of these persons. The conviction was reversed because the Court's conception of the judgment of reasonable men was that such men would find a reasonable inference other than that of guilt could be drawn from the evidence.

Judge Latimer, dissenting, found the evidence sufficient to sustain the conviction. Although he objected to the majority's seeking out some hypothesis upon which the accused might be found innocent, he made it clear that his dissent was not based solely on his differing with the theory of review. In his opinion ". . . the facts and circumstances do exclude every reasonable hypothesis of innocence."[11] He further voiced his objection to the technique adopted by the majority, for it permitted the Court to ". . . invade the province of the court-martial and weigh evidence to arrive at a result . . ."[12] On the other hand, the majority does not believe that to supervise the inferences of a court-martial violates the "clear legislative directive away from the fact-finding power."[13]

In testing for sufficiency the Court will consider all of the evidence in the record, and not merely that which is adduced by the prosecution. According to the Court, there will be instances where the evi-

[10] *Id.* at 152, 2 CMR at 58.
[11] *Id.* at 155, 2 CMR at 61.
[12] *Id.* at 149, 2 CMR at 55.
[13] *Id.* at 144, 2 CMR at 50.

dence presented by the defense will be such that reasonable men simply cannot disbelieve it.[14]

If the Court finds the evidence insufficient to support the verdict, it will either order the charges dismissed[15] or in an appropriate case find the accused guilty of a lesser included offense. For example, in most desertion cases where there is a failure to prove the required intent there is usually sufficient evidence to prove the accused was guilty of the lesser included offense of absence without leave.[16] A rehearing may not be ordered if there is a lack of evidence to support the offense charged or any lesser included offense. However, if proof of guilt consisted of *inadmissible* evidence rather than insufficient evidence, a rehearing may be ordered if there is available an admissible substitute.[17]

II. Sufficiency of the Evidence in Desertion Cases

Desertion is usually committed in one of the three following ways:

(1) absence without leave with intent to remain away permanently;

(2) absence without leave with intent to shirk important service; or

(3) absence without leave with intent to avoid hazardous duty.[18]

Although these offenses are not identical, each requires proof of an unauthorized absence and the requisite intent. Proof of the unauthorized absence is usually accomplished by introducing in evidence a duly authenticated extract copy of a morning report or service record. If the original document and the extract copy were correctly prepared,[19] they constitute sufficient evidence to prove the element of unauthorized absence. But, as previously revealed in the *McCrary* case, the real difficulty is to prove the element of *intent* to desert.

A. *Permanent desertion*

The Court heard oral arguments in *Peterson*[20] and *Ferretti*[21] the same day. In each case the accused had been found guilty of desertion

[14] United States v. Williams, 4 USCMA 69, 15 CMR 69 (1954). The Court cited Legal and Legislative Basis, Manual for Courts-Martial, United States, 1951, pp. 168, 211, but did not cite any specific examples.

[15] United States v. Dodd, 2 USCMA 94, 6 CMR 94 (1952) (larceny); United States v. Ryan, 3 USCMA 735, 14 CMR 153 (1954) (damaging military vehicle through neglect). A United States Court of Appeals can dismiss or order a new trial. Bryan v. United States, 338 U. S. 552 (1950).

[16] United States v. Peterson, 1 USCMA 317, 3 CMR 51 (1952).

[17] Manual for Courts-Martial, United States, 1951, par. 92; United States v. Eggers, 3 USCMA 191, 11 CMR 191 (1953).

[18] Code, Art. 85, Manual for Courts-Martial, United States, 1951, par. 164.

[19] See Chapter 13.

[20] 1 USCMA 317, 3 CMR 51 (1952).

[21] 1 USCMA 323, 3 CMR 57 (1952).

by a court-martial and a board of review had affirmed the finding. The prosecution presented evidence of an unauthorized absence of forty-six days in one case and forty-eight in the other. In each case the accused took the stand and undertook to explain his absence. The only issue before the Court in the two cases was whether the evidence was sufficient to support a finding of intent to desert the military service. The Court reversed the conviction in *Peterson.* The majority found *some* evidence but it was insufficient because it was as consistent with innocence as with guilt. Judge Latimer concurred in the result because he found the inference drawn by the court-martial was "wholly unsupported by any evidence."

In *Ferretti* the Court affirmed the conviction. The majority stated that they could not believe that reasonable minds, as triers of fact, would be in agreement that "reasonable hypotheses" other than guilt could be drawn from the evidence. Judge Latimer concurred in the result without opinion.

The difference in result in these two cases can be explained by a difference in the facts. The Court had announced in *Peterson* that ". . . in this area . . . the presence or absence of facts—or perhaps even a single fact—may lead to divergent results."[22] Judge Brosman wrote the opinion for the Court in both cases and stated the essential differences of fact were as follows:

> "In the Peterson case, the accused assigned as the explanation for his unauthorized absence the fact that his parents had received news of the death of his brother in Korea, and that he wished to be near them in their grief. In the present case [*Ferretti*] however, petitioner admitted that he was without reason for his failure to return. His only explanation of the lengthy absence was that it was 'just one of those things.' Secondly, Peterson remained at his home of record during the entire period of the offense, and thus could have been apprehended with ease and returned to military control. On the other hand—although his home was in California—this accused [Ferretti] spent the period of his misconduct at various points along the eastern seaboard. Finally, Peterson voluntarily returned to his station and surrendered himself, whereas Ferretti was arrested by civilian authorities for vagrancy at a considerable distance from his duty station. Accused stated that he was 'heading for base' when picked up for vagrancy in Miami, Florida—apparently en route

[22] 1 USCMA 317, 321, 3 CMR 51, 55 (1952).

from the northeast to Camp Lejeune [North Carolina] via Miami!"[23]

In *Oliver*[24] the majority of the Court undertook specifically to show how, on the facts in that case, reasonable minds, as triers of fact, must be in agreement that reasonable hypotheses other than guilt could be drawn from the evidence. The accused went home during a delay en route granted when he received orders to report to Fort Lawton, Washington, for shipment to the Far East Command. He was apprehended at home after an unauthorized absence of thirty-three days. The testimony of the accused gave the illness of his daughter as the reason for his unauthorized absence. Hospital records in evidence corroborated his statement concerning the illness of his child. Further evidence revealed that he wore his uniform at all times but that he did not request an extension of his delay en route. The accused testified that he did not make a request because he had no reasonable expectation that an extension would have been granted, if sought, and that he intended to return the same week he was apprehended. On the basis of this complex evidence the majority of the Court believed that two general interpretations were possible:

> "On the one hand is that apparently adopted by the court [martial]: a soldier, fresh from basic training and ordered to important service, wants no more of the Army, and chooses to absent himself with no intention of returning voluntarily. On the other, the canvas reveals a young father, similarly fresh from basic training and ordered to foreign duty, who, upon his authorized arrival at home, finds his infant daughter, his only child whom he had not hitherto seen, ill. Subsequently the child's condition became serious enough to require hospitalization. The young man's intention was to remain absent from his unit only so long as was necessary to ascertain that the baby was out of danger. Although the first picture clearly shows an accused who is guilty of desertion, the second with equal force suggests criminal responsibility for mere absence without leave, a much less serious offense. The accused's straight-forward and consistent testimonial account of his conduct and promptings certainly is not inherently improbable; moreover it was reliably corroborated in a critical particular."[25]

[23] 1 USCMA 323, 325-326, 3 CMR 57, 59-60 (1952).
[24] 2 USCMA 613, 10 CMR 111 (1953).
[25] United States v. Oliver, 2 USCMA 613, 615, 10 CMR 111, 113 (1953).

Judge Latimer expressed a preference for the view adopted by the court-martial[26] but the majority reduced the offense to absence without leave.

The Court has stated that "each sufficiency case rests on its own bottom."[27] Nevertheless, certain factors which frequently appear in the desertion cases are helpful on the issue of intent. Evidence that the unauthorized absence was preceded by a breach of arrest[28] or imminent overseas duty,[29] or that the accused expected court-martial proceedings to be instituted against him for some prior offense[30] is, in the absence of strong countervailing factors, sufficient to support a court-martial finding of an intent to desert. Likewise, a purpose to return, conditioned on the happening of some uncertain event[31] is more harmful than beneficial to the accused. The manner of termination, the length of the unauthorized absence and the testimony of the accused are recurrent factors which require more detailed consideration. (1.) *Manner of termination of unauthorized absence*—Apprehension means that the accused was taken into custody by proper authorities without voluntarily surrendering himself in good faith to the custody of such authorities for the purpose of being returned to military control.[32] A prompt repentence by a deserter resulting in a voluntary return, while material in extenuation, is no defense.[33] A voluntary return from an unauthorized absence does not compel a finding that

[26] *Id.* at 616, 10 CMR at 114. Judge Latimer regarded this case similar to *United States v. Knoph,* 2 USCMA 108, 6 CMR 108 (1952) in which a contrary result was reached. He stated: "What appears to me to be inconsistent holdings will continue so long as we weigh evidence and determine the credibility of witnesses." The majority frequently states, along with Judge Latimer, that the credibility of witnesses is a determination within the province of the triers of fact and not a proper function for the Court. United States v. Washington, 2 USCMA 177, 7 CMR 53 (1953) and cases therein cited.

[27] United States v. Peterson, 1 USCMA 317, 322, 3 CMR 51, 56 (1952).

[28] United States v. Barrett, 3 USCMA 294, 12 CMR 50 (1953). Other evidence was a twenty-seven day unauthorized absence terminated by apprehension at a point remote from his place of duty.

[29] United States v. West, 1 USCMA 590, 5 CMR 18 (1952); *cf.* United States v. Logas, 2 USCMA 489, 9 CMR 119 (1953).

[30] United States v. West, 1 USCMA 590, 5 CMR 18 (1952).

[31] United States v. Knoph, 2 USCMA 108, 6 CMR 108 (1952); *cf.* United States v. Oliver, 2 USCMA 613, 10 CMR 111 (1953). See MANUAL FOR COURTS-MARTIAL, UNITED STATES, 1951, par. 164(a) for additional examples. See also United States v. Rushlow, 2 USCMA 641, 10 CMR 139 (1953) (use of language in the *Manual* held prejudicial).

[32] If the greater punishment authorized by the Table of Maximum Punishments is to be imposed, the Government must allege and prove beyond a reasonable doubt that the accused was apprehended. United States v. Nickaboine, 3 USCMA 152, 11 CMR 152 (1953) (evidence insufficient).

[33] MANUAL FOR COURTS-MARTIAL, UNITED STATES, 1951, par. 164*a*; United States v. Cirelli, 1 USCMA 568, 4 CMR 160 (1952). During times of peace the maximum punishment for desertion is greater when the absence is terminated by apprehension. MANUAL FOR COURTS-MARTIAL, UNITED STATES, 1951, par. 127*c*.

the accused did not intend to desert[34] but it is a factor which will in most instances be favorable to the accused. A court-martial must decide whether a voluntary return means that the accused never intended to desert or that he had decided to turn himself in and accept the consequences of his desertion. In two cases in which the accused voluntarily returned to the service the Court upheld a finding of desertion.[35] Evidence of desertion has been found sufficient in most of the cases in which the absence without leave was terminated by apprehension.[36]

(2.) *Length of unauthorized absence*—If the period of unauthorized absence is much prolonged and there is no satisfactory explanation of it, the court-martial may be justified in inferring from that alone an intention to remain away permanently.[37] How long is much prolonged? Twenty-seven days aggravated by breach of arrest at the inception thereof plus apprehension a considerable distance from the unit of the accused has been held sufficient.[38] The Government was successful in a "borderline" case involving a sixty-day absence without leave in which the accused voluntarily surrendered 2000 miles from his post on the West coast during the Korean War;[39] another involving a seventy-one day unauthorized absence in Korea terminated by apprehension some distance from the unit of the accused;[40] and a third involving a forty-eight day unauthorized absence on the East coast of the United States during the Korean War in which the accused took the stand but failed to give any reason for his absence.[41] An equal number of borderline cases have been ultimately decided in favor of the accused. Unauthorized absences of thirty-three,[42] forty-six[43] and thirty-three[44] days, respectively, accompanied by testimony of the accused explaining these absences, have resulted in an affirmance of a finding of only an absence without leave in each case.

(3.) *Testimony of the accused*—Testimony by an accused to the effect

[34] United States v. McCrary, 1 USCMA 1, 1 CMR 1 (1951).

[35] *Ibid.;* United States v. Whitley, 3 USCMA 639, 14 CMR 57 (1954).

[36] For an exception see United States v. Oliver, 2 USCMA 613, 10 CMR 111 (1953).

[37] United States v. Cirelli, 1 USCMA 568, 4 CMR 160 (1952); United States v. Uzzo, 3 USCMA 563, 13 CMR 119 (1953) (seven and one-half months).

[38] United States v. Barrett, 3 USCMA 294, 12 CMR 50 (1953). See also United States v. Schuler, 2 USCMA 611, 10 CMR 109 (1953).

[39] United States v. McCrary, 1 USCMA 1, 1 CMR 1 (1951).

[40] United States v. Cirelli, 1 USCMA 568, 4 CMR 160 (1952). *Cf.* United States v. Powell, 3 USCMA 64, 11 CMR 64 (1953). Proving previous convictions of absence without leave strengthened the prima facie case arising from a showing of an unauthorized absence of fifty-three days, and the apprehension of the accused in civilian clothes.

[41] United States v. Ferretti, 1 USCMA 323, 3 CMR 57 (1952).

[42] United States v. Oliver, 2 USCMA 613, 10 CMR 111 (1953).

[43] United States v. Peterson, 1 USCMA 317, 3 CMR 51 (1952).

[44] United States v. Logas, 2 USCMA 489, 9 CMR 119 (1953).

that his child was sick[45] or that his brother was killed in Korea[46] and that he was needed at home for such reason may be helpful in supporting a denial that he intended to desert. On the other hand, his testimony may be beneficial to the prosecution.[47] For example, the testimony of the accused revealed that just prior to his unauthorized absence he had assaulted a sergeant and that he anticipated court-martial proceedings.[48] In others it appeared to carry little weight inasmuch as it was disbelieved by the court-martial.[49] Some significance may be given to the fact that the Court has upheld the sufficiency of the evidence in apparently all of the permanent desertion cases in which the accused elected not to testify.[50]

B. *Intent to shirk important service*

In *Shull*[51] a court-martial found the accused guilty of absence without leave with intent to shirk important service, to wit, shipment to the Far East Command. Accused was stationed at Fort Campbell, Kentucky, and had volunteered for overseas duty. He was informed that he would be transferred to the replacement pool at that station. His request for a three-day pass to go home and deal with a "family difficulty" was granted with a warning of the seriousness involved if he should overstay his pass. Approximately two weeks after the expiration of the pass he was apprehended in his home town. During this period of absence, orders had been issued transferring him to the replacement pool and a contingent of enlisted men had departed from the pool to Camp Stoneman, California. Judges Brosman and Quinn concluded that the evidence before the court-martial did not permit a determination of an intent on the part of the accused to shirk important service in the Far East Command beyond a reasonable doubt and within the fair operation of reasonable minds. They further observed that beyond the transfer order to the pool "there is little to support the findings save suspicion, conjecture, and speculation."[52]

[45] United States v. Oliver, 2 USCMA 613, 10 CMR 111 (1953).
[46] United States v. Peterson, 1 USCMA 317, 3 CMR 51 (1952).
[47] United States v. West, 1 USCMA 590, 5 CMR 18 (1952); United States v. Whitley, 3 USCMA 639, 14 CMR 57 (1954); United States v. Knoph, 2 USCMA 108, 6 CMR 108 (1952).
[48] United States v. West, 1 USCMA 590, 5 CMR 18 (1952).
[49] United States v. Rushlow, 2 USCMA 641, 10 CMR 139 (1953); United States v. Schuler, 2 USCMA 611, 10 CMR 109 (1953); United States v. Ferretti, 1 USCMA 323, 3 CMR 57 (1952); United States v. Uzzo, 3 USCMA 563, 13 CMR 119 (1953).
[50] United States v. McCrary, 1 USCMA 1, 1 CMR 1 (1951); United States v. McNeill, 2 USCMA 383, 9 CMR 13 (1953); United States v. Barrett, 3 USCMA 294, 12 CMR 50 (1953); United States v. Cirelli, 1 USCMA 568, 4 CMR 160 (1952) (accused made a limited pretrial statement).
[51] 1 USCMA 177, 2 CMR 83 (1952).
[52] *Id.* at 182, 2 CMR at 88.

Judge Latimer, dissenting, found the evidence sufficient to permit the court-martial to find that accused knew "or should have known" that any absence over and beyond the leave period probably would result in his missing the shipment; and that an absence of from ten days to two weeks would, with reasonable certainty, bring that result.

In this case the company commander testified that earmarked contingents ordinarily cleared the pool within "ten days, two weeks or so." The value placed on this testimony by the majority and the dissenter divulges an essential point of difference between them. The majority stated that they found no evidence in the record to show that the *accused* was aware of this procedure; whereas the dissenting judge was of the opinion that one who had been at Fort Campbell for some time, as had the accused, and who had volunteered for overseas duty and had been partially processed for such duty, knew or should have known the maximum time he could rely on between the time of selection for overseas duty and departure from the pool.

Another point of difference which developed in the Court was that the majority did not regard shipment to the Far East Command as having its "measurable origin" in the order transferring accused to a replacement pool at Fort Campbell, Kentucky, but believed that necessary subsequent steps for one to be sent overseas provided a lane in which "there are just too many possible turnings."[53] The dissenting judge felt that once the journey was started there was little likelihood that there would be any permanent interruption.

In *Taylor*[54] the facts were a little stronger in favor of the prosecution and the outcome was different. The unauthorized absence occurred while the accused was on orders to transfer from his unit in Camp Breckinridge, Kentucky, to the Personnel Center, Camp Stoneman, California, for shipment to the Far East Command. Two questions involving the sufficiency of the evidence were raised: (1) Was transfer to a port of embarkation for shipment to the Far East Command important service? (2) Did the accused have knowledge of the orders making the transfer?

On the question of important service the Court quoted the following from *Hemp*:[55]

> "It is well established in military law that absence without leave with knowledge of immediate overseas movement is sufficient from which a court may find desertion predicated on the intent to shirk important service."

[53] *Id.* at 181, 2 CMR at 87.
[54] 2 USCMA 389, 9 CMR 19 (1953); *accord,* United States v. Willingham, 2 USCMA 590, 10 CMR 88 (1953).
[55] 1 USCMA 280, 287, 3 CMR 14, 21 (1952).

In regard to the second question the Court stated that a court-martial may take judicial notice of regulations which require that individuals be furnished a copy of transfer orders.[56] Moreover, there is a rebuttable presumption that Army officials perform their administrative affairs in accordance with regulations. Here this presumption was unrebutted. In addition, other items of evidence showed that the accused was available for reassignment: the orders stated a delay en route and the address of the accused during the delay; the accused was in camp for two weeks after the date the orders were issued; and he left camp on the effective date of the orders. The Court concluded that the facts and circumstances were sufficient to justify the court-martial in finding that he knew of his transfer and intended to remain absent until such time as would be necessary to escape shipment to the Far East Command.

C. *Intent to avoid hazardous duty*

An accused must have knowledge of the hazardous duty. The Court reversed a conviction of desertion with intent to avoid hazardous duty because there were insufficient facts in the record to support a finding that the accused heard his platoon leader state that the accused "was to go on a listening post."[57]

In *Squirrell*[58] the accused was charged with desertion with intent to avoid hazardous duty, namely, combat with the enemy. After accused was informed that his unit would attack the following morning and after some preparations for combat had been completed, the accused absented himself to visit a friend for "ten minutes." Twelve hours later he turned himself in at a stockade many miles in the rear. Four days elapsed before he was finally returned to his unit. A divided Court, Judge Quinn dissenting, found the evidence sufficient. The dissenting judge stated: "The majority here decides that proof alone of absence without leave while in the face of prospective combat duty will support a conviction for desertion with intent to avoid hazardous duty."[59] In a later decision,[60] Judge Quinn wrote the opinion for a unanimous Court in which a conviction for this offense was upheld when the evidence appeared to show only absence without leave (fifteen

[56] In United States v. Vick, 3 USCMA 288, 12 CMR 44 (1953) the Government established delivery of orders to the accused. However, he could not read and it was not shown that the orders had been read to him. Nevertheless, the Court affirmed the conviction because there was a sufficient basis on which the triers of fact could find that the accused knew the contents of the orders.

[57] United States v. Tilton, 4 USCMA 120, 15 CMR 120 (1954). See also MANUAL FOR COURTS-MARTIAL, UNITED STATES, 1951, par. 164*a*.

[58] 2 USCMA 146, 7 CMR 22 (1953).

[59] *Id.* at 152, 7 CMR at 28.

[60] United States v. Cook, 2 USCMA 223, 8 CMR 23 (1953).

days) while under orders to perform medical aid duty with a combat unit.

III. Sufficiency of the Evidence in Cases Other than Desertion

A. *Larceny*[61]

Weakness in prosecution evidence is common in larceny cases. It is the only offense in which reversals[62] for an insufficiency of the evidence are almost as numerous as cases in which the Court found the evidence sufficient.[63] Some of the weaknesses appearing in the cases are: in an alleged larceny and sale of a government vehicle it was not shown that the "jeep" belonged to the Government;[64] and in an alleged larceny and wrongful sale of oil belonging to the Government it was not shown that any oil was illegally taken.[65] A mere showing that the accused was present at the scene and had knowledge of the larceny of a vehicle is insufficient to establish that he aided and abetted in the commission of the offense.[66]

B. *Other offenses*

The remaining "sufficiency" cases: (1) are considerable in number; (2) cover a wide variety of offenses; (3) have not often divided the Court.

Cases in which the evidence has been found to be insufficient involve the following offenses: absence without leave,[67] willful disobedience of a lawful order,[68] damaging government vehicle by neglect,[69] unpremeditated murder,[70] cowardly conduct,[71] premeditated murder,[72] and misbehavior before the enemy.[73] A discussion of the misbehavior

[61] Art. 121 includes larceny, embezzlement, false pretenses and wrongful appropriation.

[62] United States v. Dodd, 2 USCMA 94, 6 CMR 94 (1952); United States v. Duffy, 3 USCMA 20, 11 CMR 20 (1953); United States v. Guest, 3 USCMA 147, 11 CMR 147 (1953); United States v. Brown, 3 USCMA 242, 11 CMR 242 (1953).

[63] United States v. Wooten, 1 USCMA 358, 3 CMR 92 (1952); United States v. Grueschow, 1 USCMA 367, 3 CMR 101 (1952) (companion case); United States v. O'Brien, 3 USCMA 325, 12 CMR 81 (1953) (wrongful appropriation). United States v. Valencia, 1 USCMA 415, 4 CMR 7 (1952) (embezzlement).

[64] United States v. Dodd, 2 USCMA 94, 6 CMR 94 (1952).

[65] United States v. Brown, 3 USCMA 242, 11 CMR 242 (1953) (Judge Latimer dissented).

[66] United States v. Guest, 3 USCMA 147, 11 CMR 147 (1953).

[67] United States v. Harjo, 2 USCMA 9, 6 CMR 9 (1952).

[68] United States v. Martin, 1 USCMA 674, 5 CMR 102 (1952).

[69] United States v. Ryan, 3 USCMA 735, 14 CMR 153 (1954).

[70] United States v. Burts, 3 USCMA 418, 12 CMR 174 (1953). The government conceded that the evidence was insufficient.

[71] United States v. Horst, 1 USCMA 452, 4 CMR 44 (1952). Judge Latimer did not participate.

[72] United States v. Wilson and Harvey, 2 USCMA 248, 8 CMR 48 (1953) (Judge Latimer dissented).

[73] United States v. Yarborough and Marshall, 1 USCMA 678, 5 CMR 106 (1952).

before the enemy charge will serve to illustrate the occasional but continued reappearance of the difference in views of the judges as expressed in the *O'Neal* case.

In *Yarborough* and *Marshall*[74] the basis of the charges was that the two accused had carried out an agreement whereby Marshall had deliberately shot himself in the hand and Yarborough had deliberately and knowingly allowed himself to be hit on the foot by the same bullet. The Court was in agreement that accused Marshall was guilty of the charge of conspiracy to malinger and malingering, and that the evidence was insufficient to support the third charge of misbehavior before the enemy. The Court disagreed as to accused Yarborough. Judge Quinn, writing for the majority, applied the reasonable hypothesis test of the *O'Neal* case and concluded that the evidence tending to show that Yarborough deliberately allowed himself to be shot was equivocal. The majority assumed that Yarborough did seriously intend, at some undefined date in the future, to inflict self-injury. However, because at the time of the shooting he did nothing to co-operate with Marshall, did not know the gun was loaded, acted like a normal person just before the gun was fired and was surprised when he was hit, the majority concluded that reasonable men would be in accord in saying that it is reasonable to assume from the circumstances surrounding the shooting that Yarborough was unaware of any intention on the part of Marshall to carry out the previous threats of self-injury. Therefore, the majority believed that there was a reasonable hypothesis other than that of guilt, and for this reason they could not say that the findings as to Yarborough were based on sufficient circumstantial evidence. Judge Latimer, in his partial dissent, reiterated his objection to the rationale of *O'Neal* and concluded that the court-martial could reasonably find from the evidence beyond a reasonable doubt that Yarborough was a willing victim to the shooting.

Cases in addition to desertion and larceny in which the evidence has been found sufficient involved the following offenses: rape,[75] robbery,[76] premeditated murder,[77] unpremeditated murder,[78] assault with

[74] *Ibid.*

[75] United States v. Slozes, 1 USCMA 47, 1 CMR 47 (1951); United States v. Houghtaling, 2 USCMA 230, 8 CMR 30 (1953); United States v. Washington, 2 USCMA 177, 7 CMR 53 (1953); United States v. Borner, 3 USCMA 306, 12 CMR 62 (1953); United States v. Henderson, 4 USCMA 268, 15 CMR 268 (1954).

[76] United States v. Jacobs, 1 USCMA 209, 2 CMR 115 (1952).

[77] United States v. O'Brien, 3 USCMA 105, 11 CMR 105 (1953); United States v. Sechler, 3 USCMA 363, 12 CMR 119 (1953).

[78] United States v. Jarvis, 1 USCMA 368, 3 CMR 102 (1952); United States v. Bigger, 2 USCMA 297, 8 CMR 97 (1953); United States v. McDonald, 4 USCMA 130, 15 CMR 130 (1954).

intent to commit murder,[79] manslaughter,[80] negligent homicide,[81] willful disobedience of an order of a superior officer,[82] failure to obey lawful order,[83] cowardly conduct in the presence of the enemy,[84] misbehavior before the enemy,[85] sodomy,[86] assault with a dangerous weapon,[87] bigamy,[88] scandalous conduct tending to the destruction of good morals,[89] conduct unbecoming an officer and a gentleman,[90] absence without leave,[91] breach of arrest,[92] carrying a concealed weapon,[93] wrongfully using morphine,[94] making a false official statement,[95] escape from confinement,[96] misbehavior of a sentinel,[97] housebreaking,[98] and unlawful entry.[99]

C. *Matters other than offenses*

A question of sufficiency of the evidence may also arise in connection with the imposition of a sentence. This may be illustrated by a case in which the accused was found guilty of the theft of military payment certificates in the sum of forty dollars from one deceased soldier's estate and thirty dollars from the estate of another. The court-martial combined the two sums and found a total value in excess

[79] United States v. Floyd, 2 USCMA 183, 7 CMR 59 (1953); United States v. Holman, 3 USCMA 396, 12 CMR 152 (1953).

[80] United States v. Riggleman, 1 USCMA 336, 3 CMR 70 (1952); United States v. Fox, 2 USCMA 465, 9 CMR 95 (1953) (reversed on other grounds).

[81] United States v. Schultz, 1 USCMA 512, 4 CMR 104 (1952). United States v. Russell, 3 USCMA 696, 14 CMR 114 (1954).

[82] United States v. Stout, 1 USCMA 639, 5 CMR 67 (1952); United States v. Benders, 2 USCMA 620, 10 CMR 118 (1953); United States v. Majia, 2 USCMA 616, 10 CMR 114 (1953); United States v. Vansant, 3 USCMA 30, 11 CMR 30 (1953) (superior warrant officer).

[83] United States v. Horst, 1 USCMA 452, 4 CMR 44 (1952); United States v. Sell, 3 USCMA 202, 11 CMR 202 (1953).

[84] United States v. King, 2 USCMA 397, 9 CMR 27 (1953); United States v. Smith, 3 USCMA 25, 11 CMR 25 (1953).

[85] United States v. Smith, 2 USCMA 197, 7 CMR 73 (1953); United States v. Sperland, 1 USCMA 661, 5 CMR 89 (1952); United States v. Carey, 4 USCMA 112, 15 CMR 112 (1954).

[86] United States v. Phillips, 3 USCMA 137, 11 CMR 137 (1953).

[87] United States v. Norton, 1 USCMA 411, 4 CMR 3 (1952).

[88] United States v. Patrick, 2 USCMA 189, 7 CMR 65 (1953).

[89] United States v. Schumacher, 2 USCMA 134, 7 CMR 10 (1953).

[90] United States v. Stewart, 1 USCMA 648, 5 CMR 76 (1952); United States v. Gomes, 3 USCMA 232, 11 CMR 232 (1953).

[91] United States v. Strong, 1 USCMA 627, 5 CMR 55 (1952); United States v. Cliette, 2 USCMA 240, 8 CMR 40 (1953).

[92] United States v. Barrett, 3 USCMA 294, 12 CMR 50 (1953).

[93] United States v. Thompson, 3 USCMA 620, 14 CMR 38 (1954).

[94] United States v. Smith, 3 USCMA 803, 14 CMR 221 (1954).

[95] United States v. Cliette, 2 USCMA 240, 8 CMR 40 (1953).

[96] United States v. Wilson, 4 USCMA 3, 15 CMR 3 (1954).

[97] United States v. Williams, 4 USCMA 69, 15 CMR 69 (1954).

[98] United States v. Williams, 4 USCMA 241, 15 CMR 241 (1954); United States v. Armstrong, 4 USCMA 248, 15 CMR 248 (1954); United States v. Crunk, 4 USCMA 290, 15 CMR 290 (1954).

[99] United States v. Love, 4 USCMA 260, 15 CMR 260 (1954).

of fifty dollars. A sentence of five years' confinement was adjudged. If the two sums had not been combined the maximum confinement permitted would have been one year for each theft. The Court held[100] there was no evidence that the accused "pilfered" the two estates at substantially the same time; therefore, the sentence was excessive. On the other hand, the Court overruled a board of review and held the evidence was sufficient to support a finding that the accused consented to a search of his person and effects.[101]

Sufficiency of the evidence on the issues of intoxication and insanity are discussed in Chapter 7.

IV. Conclusion

The Court had been criticized[102] for its failure to adopt the substantial evidence rule which prevails[103] in many, but not all, of the federal appellate courts. The majority of the Court unquestionably intended, in deciding to supervise the application of the reasonable hypothesis rule by the triers of fact, to adopt a rigid test for making a determination of the sufficiency of the evidence. It is equally clear that Judge Latimer favors a more lenient test. It is difficult to be more precise. In fact, it is unlikely that in more than a paucity of cases the individual judges would have voted any differently had they all been in agreement that they were applying either the substantial evidence rule or the reasonable hypothesis rule.[104] If it can be shown that the Court has reversed or affirmed cases because it has become a jury rather than an appellate Court confined to reviewing questions of law, there is a sound basis for criticism. Such criticism does not appear to be warranted.

[100] United States v. Florence, 1 USCMA 620, 5 CMR 48 (1952).

[101] United States v. Wilcher, 4 USCMA 215, 15 CMR 215 (1954). See Chapter 13 on Search and Seizure.

[102] Note; *The United States Court of Military Appeals and Sufficiency of the Evidence,* 42 Geo. L. J. 108 (1953).

[103] Note; *Rules of Proof Employed by Federal Appellate Courts in Reviewing Criminal Convictions,* 38 Geo. L. J. 285 (1950).

[104] For example, Judge Quinn would have dissented in *McCrary,* as he did, even though he had agreed that the substantial evidence rule of Judge Latimer was the proper one for the Court to apply. Likewise, Judge Latimer would have dissented in *O'Neal,* as he did, even though he had agreed that the rule applied by the majority was the proper one for the Court.

CHAPTER 12

Punishments

I. General Limitations

A. *Forfeitures*

Paragraph 127*c* of the *Manual* requires that loss of pay in a sentence be stated in dollars and cents. The Court regards this provision as one to simplify bookkeeping. A sentence imposing forfeiture of two-thirds pay per month for two months is a legal sentence inasmuch as it can be reduced to dollars and cents by easy computation.[1] The Court held[2] valid a provision in a sentence which required the accused "to forfeit all pay and allowances during confinement and until release therefrom." Although this provision was somewhat uncertain at the time imposed (i.e., confinement may be reduced by good conduct time), it is one that would be made certain by an event which must happen.

Unless the convening authority in his action expressly defers the effective date, forfeitures will apply to pay and allowances becoming due on and after[3] the date such sentence is approved by the convening authority in all cases in which the approved sentence also includes confinement not suspended.[4] All other forfeitures become effective on the date the sentence is ordered executed.

The Court has settled questions which have arisen in connection with the effective date of forfeitures when the sentence contains a bad conduct discharge. If the convening authority suspends the punitive discharge, he can order execution of that part of a sentence adjudging partial forfeitures.[5] If he does not suspend the discharge, he can, nevertheless, take action which will insure collection of the forfeitures from

[1] United States v. Gilgallon, 1 USCMA 263, 2 CMR 170 (1952).

[2] United States v. Smith, 3 USCMA 336, 12 CMR 92 (1953).

[3] It is error for the order merely to state "forfeiture of all pay and allowances." This is greater punishment than a forfeiture on and after the date the sentence is ordered executed. United States v. O'Neal, 1 USCMA 138, 2 CMR 44 (1952).

[4] Manual for Courts-Martial, United States, 1951, par. 126*h* (5).

[5] United States v. Watkins, 2 USCMA 287, 8 CMR 87 (1953).

the date he approved the sentence when the sentence is ordered executed on completion of appellate review. In this connection the Court stated:

> "We believe that Article 57 of the Code is expressly worded to authorize a sentence which will permit an orderly, and at the same time, a fair method of collecting forfeitures. It may amount to no more than a bookkeeping entry but there is a difference between applying forfeitures and executing them. Application can commence on the date the convening authority acts even though execution must be deferred until completion of appellate review."[6]

It would be contrary to the customs of the service to suspend both the execution of a punitive discharge and confinement and order total forfeitures into execution.[7] This would, in effect, require an accused to perform his duties without any compensation whatever. On the other hand, if the sentence includes partial forfeitures and no confinement, the forfeitures may become effective on the date the convening authority orders them into execution.[8]

B. *Close order drill*

A court-martial is not authorized to adjudge close order drill as punishment, but a commanding officer may order additional drill as a corrective for apparent want of discipline and lack of self-control as long as the real purpose of such drill is training and not punishment.[9]

C. *Restriction*

The Court held that the authority of a court-martial to impose restriction as a punishment was not limited by the application of the Table of Equivalent Punishments.[10] The only limitation on a court-martial in adjudging this punishment is that it must not exceed two months. Therefore, a special court-martial may in the same sentence impose a bad conduct discharge and a restriction for two months. Likewise, a convening authority may mitigate a sentence of confinement to one of restriction in a case in which a punitive discharge was adjudged.[11]

[6] United States v. Smith, 3 USCMA 336, 340, 12 CMR 92, 96 (1953).

[7] MANUAL FOR COURTS-MARTIAL, UNITED STATES, 1951, par. 88*e* (1).

[8] United States v. Watkins, 2 USCMA 287, 8 CMR 87 (1953).

[9] United States v. Trani, 1 USCMA 293, 3 CMR 27 (1952); MANUAL FOR COURTS-MARTIAL, UNITED STATES, 1951, par. 125 does not specifically mention close order drill.

[10] United States v. Benson, 3 USCMA 351, 12 CMR 107 (1953); MANUAL FOR COURTS-MARTIAL, UNITED STATES, 1951, par. 127*c*.

[11] United States v. Austin, 3 USCMA 433, 12 CMR 189 (1953); United States v. O'Shea, 3 USCMA 434, 12 CMR 190 (1953).

D. *Bread and water*

Discussed in Chapter 5.

II. Maximum Punishments

Punishments authorized by the Code are subject to limitations which are stated in the Table of Maximum Punishments.

A. *In time of war*

The Court held that forces of the United States in Korea were engaged in the prosecution of a war within the meaning of the Code.[12] In explaining this conclusion the Court stated:

> "The factors which make certain offenses— . . . more heinous and reprehensible in time of war depend upon the existence *in fact* of substantial armed hostilities—regardless of whether those hostilities have been formally declared to constitute 'war' by action of the Executive and Congress."[13]

This decision would have been sufficient to authorize the death penalty for certain offenses which are not capital in time of peace except for the fact that the Table of Maximum Punishments contained in the *Manual* is automatically suspended only on a *declaration* of war.[14] However, an Executive Order specifically removed the limitations imposed by the Table of Maximum Punishments on certain offenses committed in the Far East.[15]

B. *Offenses related to those in the Table of Maximum Punishments*

Paragraph 127*c* of the *Manual* refers to the Table of Maximum Punishments and provides:

> "If an offense not listed in the table is included in an offense which is listed and is also closely related to some other listed

[12] Subsequently the Court held that an absence without leave committed in continental United States during the Korean conflict (December 23, 1950) was committed "in time of war" within the meaning of Article 43(a) of the Code (statute of limitations). United States v. Ayers, 4 USCMA 220, 15 CMR 220 (1954). See also United States v. Anderten, 4 USCMA 354, 15 CMR 354 (1954).

[13] United States v. Gann, 3 USCMA 12, 13, 11 CMR 12, 13 (1953); United States v. Bancroft, 3 USCMA 3, 11 CMR 3 (1953), 2 J. Public L. 459. See also United States v. Ayers, 4 USCMA 220, 15 CMR 220 (1954) (discussed in Chapter 8, Sec. XII A).

[14] Manual for Courts-Martial, United States, 1951, par. 127*c*.

[15] Executive Order 10247 May 29, 1951 suspended the limitations upon punishments for violations of Articles 82, 85, 86 (3), 87, 90, 91 (1) and (2), 113 and 115 by persons under the command of, or within any area controlled by, the Commander-in-chief, Far East, or any of his successors in command. See United States v. Christensen, 4 USCMA 22, 15 CMR 22 (1954). Offering violence to a commissioned officer in the execution of his office is a capital offense when committed in Korea during hostilities. United States v. Gann, 3 USCMA 12, 11 CMR 12 (1953) (desertion).

offense, the lesser punishment prescribed for either the included or closely related offense will prevail as the maximum limit of punishment."

Using a Government vehicle for private gain is not a listed offense, however, both graft and simple disorder are listed in the Table of Maximum Punishments. The Court decided that the use of a Government vehicle for private gain more closely resembled graft than a simple disorder; therefore, the former and not the latter was a related offense.[16]

The Table of Maximum Punishments does not list the offense of negligent forwarding of mail. The Court decided that the offense of being derelict in the performance of duties, a violation of Article 92, was closely related to the offense charged. Consequently, the maximum of three months' confinement for Article 92 applied to the offense of negligent forwarding of mail.[17]

Wrongful possession of a false pass violates Article 134 and may be punished by confinement not in excess of three years. The Table of Maximum Punishments does not distinguish between wrongful possession *with* and *without* intent to deceive. The Court decided the three year provision applied only to wrongful possession *with* intent to deceive.[18] Wrongful possession without an intent to deceive is a neglect or disorder which cannot be punished in excess of four months.[19]

C. *Offenses unrelated to and not included in the offenses listed*

If an offense is neither listed in the Table of Maximum Punishments, nor included within an offense listed, nor closely related to a listed or included offense, it is punishable as authorized by the United States Code or the Code of the District of Columbia, whichever is lesser. The offense of obstructing justice is not listed in the Table, or included within any offense listed, or closely related thereto. The sentence adjudged for this offense was held legal because the Court found that it did not exceed that authorized by the United States Code.[20] If neither Code prescribes a punishment, the court-martial must be guided by the customs of the service.

[16] United States v. Alexander, 3 USCMA 346, 12 CMR 102 (1953). The law officer actually used the maximum sentence for bribery but the error was not prejudicial because it was the same for graft. Judge Quinn dissented because he did not think there was a marked similarity between graft and the offense charged.

[17] United States v. Beach, 2 USCMA 172, 7 CMR 48 (1953).

[18] United States v. Blue, 3 USCMA 550, 13 CMR 106 (1953).

[19] *Ibid.*

[20] United States v. Long, 2 USCMA 60, 6 CMR 60 (1952).

D. *Expiration of enlistment*

Although an enlistment expires while the accused is absent without leave, the absence is not thereby terminated and the accused may be punished for the entire period of the absence.[21]

E. *Desertion terminated by apprehension*

In order to impose the greater punishment authorized in the Table of Maximum Punishments for desertion terminated by *apprehension,* the Government must allege and prove *apprehension.*[22]

F. *Offenses before the Code*

Discussed in Chapter 5.[23]

III. Offenses Arising out of the Same Transaction

Paragraph 76*a* (8) of the *Manual* provides that the maximum authorized punishment may be imposed for each of two or more *separate* offenses arising out of the same act or transaction. Thus, if an accused during the same night forcibly enters three buildings and steals money from vending machines located in each building, he may be found guilty of six offenses—three for housebreaking and three for larceny. The maximum sentence which could be adjudged in a trial of all six offenses would be the total of the maximums for each of the six offenses.[24]

The *Manual* test to be applied in determining if offenses are separate is whether each offense requires proof of an element not required to prove the other.[25] This test was intended to be in conformity with the so-called Blockburger rule adopted by the federal courts.[26] This rule was stated by the Supreme Court of the United States as follows:

> "The applicable rule is that where the same act or transaction constitutes a violation of two distinct statutory provisions, the test to be applied to determine whether there are two offenses or only one, is whether each provision requires proof of a fact which the other does not."[27]

One of the effects of the adoption of this rule may be illustrated by the following example: If one cuts wire and thereby escapes from a stock-

[21] United States v. Klunk, 3 USCMA 92, 11 CMR 92 (1953).

[22] United States v. Nickaboine, 3 USCMA 152, 11 CMR 152 (1953).

[23] United States v. Downard, 1 USCMA 346, 3 CMR 80 (1952); United States v. Sippel, 4 USCMA 50, 15 CMR 50 (1954).

[24] United States v. Gibson, 3 USCMA 746, 14 CMR 164 (1954) (apparently three transactions with two offenses each).

[25] Paragraph 76*a* (8); United States v. Yarborough, 1 USCMA 678, 5 CMR 106 (1952).

[26] United States v. Larney, 2 USCMA 563, 10 CMR 61 (1953); United States v. McVey, 4 USCMA 167, 15 CMR 167 (1954).

[27] Blockburger v. United States, 284 U. S. 299, 304 (1932).

ade, he has committed two offenses—escape from confinement and willful destruction of Government property—even though cutting the wire was an aspect of the escape. According to the 1949 *Manual*[28] (Army) an accused could be punished only for the offense in its most important aspect. Under the current rule the maximum authorized punishment may be imposed for each of these two separate offenses.[29] The Court rejected[30] an interpretation advanced by the Government that if offenses alleged may theoretically and conceivably be established by evidence which is not the same, cumulative sentences are sustainable.

In *Soukup*[31] the accused, who had been stationed with his company at the front, was discovered three or four miles to the rear. Although ordered to return to the front, he refused to do so. He was charged with cowardly conduct and willful disobedience of a lawful order. The Court held there was no unwarranted multiplication of charges growing out of the same transaction because two duties were breached—the one to *remain* at the front with his company, and the other to obey the direct and specific order to *return* thereto. In rendering this decision the Court stated that the *Manual* test requiring proof of an element not required to prove the other was an appropriate test in this case. However, it went further and stated that this test may not serve accurately and safely in all situations.

The "duty" approach as distinguished from the "facts" approach to the separateness test was discussed in the concurring opinion in *Larney*.[32] The accused, while under Naval control, was ordered to report to a specified station on a certain date. He did not comply. Because of this conduct he was charged with both absence without leave and failure to obey a lawful order. The Court held that the offenses were separate because each required the proof of a fact which the other did not. Judge Brosman, concurring, found two orders violated—the order to report to the new station and some different general order, regulation, or other directive to remain at the new station. But he contended that where the duty to be present arises only from a specific order, one could not be sentenced separately for the absence *and* for a violation of the order.

In *Redenius*[33] the Court applied the "facts" approach and the "duty"

[28] Par. 80.

[29] United States v. Vaughan, 3 USCMA 121, 11 CMR 121 (1953).

[30] United States v. Davis, 2 USCMA 505, 10 CMR 3 (1953). The Court was discussing felony murder and unpremeditated murder. See also United States v. Beene, 4 USCMA 177, 15 CMR 177 (1954).

[31] 2 USCMA 141, 7 CMR 17 (1953); *accord,* United States v. Wallace, 2 USCMA 595, 10 CMR 93 (1953).

[32] 2 USCMA 563, 10 CMR 61 (1953).

[33] 4 USCMA 161, 15 CMR 161 (1954).

approach and found unwarranted multiplicity existed under either test. In that case the accused failed to comply with orders to report to Camp Stoneman, California, for shipment to the Far East. His unauthorized absence of more than two months was terminated by apprehension. For this misconduct he was charged with both permanent desertion and desertion with an intent to shirk important service. He was convicted of each offense and sentenced on both. In view of some of its previous statements[34] the Court was somewhat concerned whether desertion was a single offense which may be committed by any one of several different acts or whether the various types of desertion constituted separate offenses. However, the Court found it unnecessary to grapple with this puzzling question because even if separate the requirements of the "facts" test were not met. In this connection the Court stated:

> ". . . in desertion, imminent overseas shipment may supply an inference of two different intents, either of which is sufficient to complete the offense. As inferences, the different intents are not self-sustaining facts; instead, they find support only in the overt act. Under the allegations and proof here, the single overt act is identical for both specifications. Hence, the intent which can be inferred from it may be one or the other of two possibilities but it cannot properly be split into fractions of each. . . . This is quite different from establishing separate intents as independent facts. In the latter instance, if it is assumed that Article 85 establishes different offenses of desertion, there may well be two offenses of desertion committed in one period of unauthorized absence. Under the circumstances of allegation and proof in this case the specifications are not separate according to the Blockburger rule, or the Manual test approved by the Court in . . . Larney. . . ."[35]

In regard to the "duty" test the Court held that the accused had only one duty and that was to remain with his organization until reassignment. Since only one duty was breached, there was only one offense.

An accused may commit the offenses of drunken driving resulting in personal injury and involuntary manslaughter in the same transaction. In deciding that these offenses were separate the Court suggested that it would be helpful in applying the test of separateness to try to determine whether Congress intended to punish drunken driving

[34] United States v. Aldridge, 2 USCMA 330, 8 CMR 130 (1953). Article 85, according to the dictum of the Court in this case, spells out three very different offenses.

[35] United States v. Redenius, 4 USCMA 161, 166-167, 15 CMR 161, 166-167 (1954).

and involuntary manslaughter.[36] Obviously a drunken driver should not be excused for that offense simply because he also committed the offense of involuntary manslaughter while driving drunk. The *Manual*[37] states that an accused may not be punished for both a principal offense and for an offense included therein. Assault with a dangerous weapon and robbery may be separate offenses but in some situations the former may be a lesser offense of the latter. If the use of a dangerous weapon constitutes the force and violence in the robbery charge, and the robbery specification is broad enough to permit proof of the use of a dangerous weapon—then the assault with a dangerous weapon offense, although separately charged, is a lesser included offense to robbery. In such case it is prejudicial error for the law officer to instruct that the maximum sentence is the sum of the maximum sentences for the two offenses.[38]

Although multiplicity should be avoided,[39] the prejudicial effect thereof is confined to the sentence.[40] If the accused is found guilty of two offenses arising out of the same transaction and they are not separate, the law officer should instruct that the maximum sentence is that of the greater offense. If he does so, there is no prejudice.[41] It is only when an accused is sentenced on the basis of the maximum penalty for each nonseparate offense arising out of a single transaction that prejudice results.[42] The fact that in this situation a court-martial imposed a sentence less than the legal maximum does not remove the prejudice because the sentence was based on a potential sentence greater than the legal maximum.[43]

IV. Permissible Additional Punishments

Section B, paragraph 127*c* of the *Manual* provides in part:

> "If an accused is found guilty of an offense or offenses for none of which dishonorable or bad conduct discharge is authorized, proof of two or more previous convictions will authorize bad conduct discharge *and* forfeiture of all pay and allowances *and,* if the confinement otherwise authorized is less than three months,

[36] United States v. Beene, 4 USCMA 177, 15 CMR 177 (1954).

[37] Par. 76*a* (8).

[38] United States v. McVey, 4 USCMA 167, 15 CMR 167 (1954); United States v. Coughlin, 4 USCMA 175, 15 CMR 175 (1954).

[39] Manual for Courts-Martial, United States, 1951, par. 26*b*.

[40] Manual for Courts-Martial, United States, 1951, pars. 74*b*, 76*a*(8); United States v. Yarborough, 1 USCMA 678, 5 CMR 106 (1952); United States v. Soukup, 2 USCMA 141, 7 CMR 17 (1953).

[41] United States v. Nelson, 3 USCMA 482, 13 CMR 38 (1953).

[42] United States v. Redenius, 4 USCMA 161, 15 CMR 161 (1954); United States v. Christensen, 4 USCMA 22, 15 CMR 22 (1954).

[43] United States v. McVey, 4 USCMA 167, 15 CMR 167 (1954); United States v. Coughlin, 4 USCMA 175, 15 CMR 175 (1954).

> confinement at hard labor for three months. In such a case no forfeiture shall be imposed for any period in excess of the period of confinement so adjudged." (Emphasis supplied.)[44]

In *Prescott*[45] the Court was requested to determine whether a punitive discharge is a necessary condition precedent to the imposition of increased confinement and forfeitures permitted under this paragraph. Army and Air Force boards of review had concluded that it was, whereas a Navy board had taken the other view. The Court agreed with the Navy interpretation and stated that the word "and" means "or," thus authorizing the listed punishments severally.[46]

A sentence imposing the maximum confinement and a fine is not excessive if it further provides for additional confinement if the fine is not paid. The Court regards the provisional confinement as a means of coercing the collection of the fine and not as additional punishment.[47]

V. Footnote 5 to Article 92

The first part of Article 92 denounces the offense of violating or failing to obey any lawful general order or regulation, the maximum punishment for which is a dishonorable discharge, confinement at hard labor not to exceed two years and forfeitures. The second part states the offense of knowingly failing to obey any other lawful order, which is punishable by a bad conduct discharge, confinement at hard labor for six months and forfeitures. The maximum punishment for these offenses is subject to footnote 5 to Article 92 in the Table of Maximum Punishments which states:

> "The punishment for [these] offense[s] does not apply in those cases wherein the accused is found guilty of an offense which, although involving a failure to obey a lawful order, is specifically listed elsewhere in this table."

The Court has characterized this language as being "exceedingly ambiguous." The authors of the *Manual* had the following to say about this footnote:

[44] The Court upheld the validity of Section B stating that it was not an unreasonable or arbitrary exercise of executive power and that it did not amount to an habitual criminal statute. United States v. Prescott, 2 USCMA 122, 6 CMR 122 (1952).

[45] 2 USCMA 122, 6 CMR 122 (1952).

[46] *Cf.* United States v. Watkins, 2 USCMA 287, 8 CMR 87 (1953). This section does not apply if the sentence includes only forfeitures and no confinement.

[47] United States v. DeAngelis, 3 USCMA 298, 12 CMR 54 (1953). See Manual for Courts-Martial, United States, 1951, par. 126*h* (3). The provision in the 1949 *Manual* considered by the Court was to the same effect.

> "It is designed to eliminate the confusion which could result from a contention that a violation of other specifically listed offenses, for example, disobedience of a superior officer under Article 90, or willful disobedience of the lawful order of a warrant officer or non commissioned or petty officer under Article 91, or wrongfully appearing in civilian clothing under Article 134, should be punished as a violation of Article 92."[48]

In *Buckmiller*[49] quite a different interpretation of the footnote appeared. The accused failed to obey a direct order of a non-commissioned officer to report to the ration breakdown section for duty. He was found guilty of violating Article 92 (failure to obey the lawful order of a noncommissioned officer) and was sentenced to a bad conduct discharge and confinement at hard labor for six months with partial forfeitures for the same period. A board of review decided that the offense which was charged as a failure to obey under Article 92 constituted a violation of Article 86 (failure to go to the appointed place of duty) and, since the maximum punishment for the latter offense was confinement at hard labor for one month and forfeiture of two-thirds pay for one month, the application of footnote 5 was proper and it required that the sentence be reduced accordingly. The Court conceded that a "technical and entirely literal" interpretation of the footnote leads to a conclusion that:

> "... in no case can an accused be convicted of knowingly failing to obey a lawful order under Article 92..., if the circumstances of the offense also involve, in any way 'failing to go to ... the appointed place of duty' under Article 86."[50]

However, the Court decided that this cannot be an intended result. After holding that the board of review erred in its interpretation, the Court said the proper test is to compare the *gravamen*[51] of the offense set out in the specification with the charge it is laid under and with other Articles under which it might have been laid. In determining the punishment to be assessed, the controlling element is whether the failure to obey involved a direct personal order of a superior or mere failure to perform some duty ordinarily considered routine. If the failure to obey indicates disrespect for authority by the flaunting of a direct order of a superior, the footnote is inapplicable and the greater

[48] LEGAL AND LEGISLATIVE BASIS, MANUAL FOR COURTS-MARTIAL, UNITED STATES (1951), p. 196.
[49] 1 USCMA 504, 4 CMR 96 (1952).
[50] *Id.* at 505, 4 CMR at 97.
[51] Compare the equivocal language of Judge Quinn in United States v. Yunque-Burgos, 3 USCMA 498, 13 CMR 54 (1953).

punishment may be imposed.[52] Since the accused in *Buckmiller*[53] violated a direct personal order of a superior he was subject to the greater punishment permitted by Article 92.[54]

The Table of Maximum Punishments provides a punishment for appearing in other than the prescribed uniform but it does not contain a specific provision for appearing in civilian clothing without authority. The Court held[55] that a violation of a general order by appearing in civilian clothing in Germany was a serious offense and was neither lesser included in, nor closely related to, appearing in improper uniform. For these reasons footnote 5 was held inapplicable.

VI. Conclusion

The rules governing punishments in the military legal system are numerous and complex. There are pitfalls for the careful and experienced military lawyers and bewilderment for the uninitiated. These rules have evolved over the years in a haphazard fashion. Continued patchwork on an ancient and perhaps antiquated system appears to have reached the point of diminishing returns. A complete inventory is in order. A reappraisal[56] of the entire subject of punishment, with

[52] Judge Latimer concurred in the result. He would apply footnote 5 in those cases in which there is a fair probability that the accused was guilty of a listed offense, but was charged with failure to obey an order as a device to permit imposition of a greater sentence.

[53] *Accord,* United States v. Larney, 2 USCMA 563, 10 CMR 61 (1953); United States v. McNeely, 1 USCMA 510, 4 CMR 102 (1952). The accused knowingly failed to obey a direct personal order to report for kitchen police at the mess hall.

[54] United States v. McKnight, 4 USCMA 190, 15 CMR 190 (1954). The Court assumed footnote 5 properly applied because of facts which might have been judicially noticed by the court-martial.

[55] United States v. Yunque-Burgos, 3 USCMA 498, 13 CMR 54 (1953).

[56] The Code Committee made several valuable recommendations to Congress regarding punishment and sentence in its Annual Report, June 1, 1952, to December 31, 1953, pp. 5, 7, 10. Among the recommendations are:

> ". . . in general court-martial cases, where the accused with the consent of his counsel requests and the convening authority approves, a one-officer court, whose identity must be known to the accused in advance, be permitted to accept a plea of guilty and adjudged a sentence in all, except capital cases. . . ."
>
> ". . . where the accused, with the consent of his counsel, requests, and the convening authority approves, and where the identity of a one-officer court is known to the accused in advance, such officer be permitted to accept pleas of guilty, to conduct the trial of contested special court-martial cases, and to adjudge sentences. . . ."
>
> ". . . Article 71 of the Code be amended to provide that a convening authority should be empowered to order all parts of a sentence into execution when approved by him except that portion involving dismissal, or a dishonorable or a bad-conduct discharge. This recommendation is not intended to affect sentences involving death or a general or flag officer. . . ."
>
> ". . . the Code be amended by providing that in the case of a prisoner in confinement under sentence of death, no pay and allowances would accrue to him as a matter of law after the date the convening authority approves such sentence, subject, of course, to his rights under Article 75 in the event such sentence is disapproved or set aside."

a view to discarding the obsolete while preserving the best which has been produced by years of experience, should result in a more efficient system. A complete survey should include consideration of many changes such as placing the responsibility of imposing sentence on the law officer or a legally trained president of a special court-martial; adjudging a separate sentence for each separate offense in which the court-martial returns a finding of guilty; a simplified table of maximum punishments; and more effective ways of expediting the execution of various types of sentences.

". . . Congress give consideration to increasing the permissive punishments imposable under Article 15 of the Code, the maximum not to exceed the forfeiture of one-half of 1 month's basic pay per month for a period of two months in the case of officers, and the loss of one-half month's pay for a period of 1 month, or confinement up to 7 days, in the cases of enlisted personnel."

CHAPTER 13

Rules of Evidence

The rules of evidence prescribed by the President pursuant to Article 36 of the Code[1] appear in the *Manual.*[2] This is the primary source of authority for rules of evidence for courts-martial. If a particular situation is not covered in the *Manual,* the rules of evidence generally recognized in the trial of criminal cases in the United States district courts should be applied. If neither of these sources provides sufficient guidance, resort may be had to common-law rules of evidence.

I. Identity

A Korean doctor, unacquainted with the deceased, heard neighbors of the victim identify him by a particular name during a post mortem investigation. Later, while a witness, the doctor was permitted to testify that Jong Ku Suop was the name of the person he examined. The Court held[3] it was not error to admit this testimony. In doing so it went beyond the practice of courts that restrict testimony as to the name of an individual to witnesses who know the name through personal familiarity with the community reputation of the deceased.

A limited user of a habit-forming drug may express an opinion as to the identity of the solution injected in his arm.[4]

II. Character Evidence

The *Manual*[5] provides that character may be proved by the testimony of a person who has personal knowledge of the character of the

[1] The President is not required to adopt any particular rule but ordinarily he is expected to follow the rules generally recognized in the trial of criminal cases in the United States district courts. Legal and Legislative Basis, Manual for Courts-Martial, United States, 1951, p. 210. For an example of a departure from the rules of the federal district courts see United States v. White, 3 USCMA 666, 14 CMR 84 (1954).

[2] Chapter XXVII.

[3] United States v. Jarvis, 1 USCMA 368, 3 CMR 102 (1952). See also Manual for Courts-Martial, United States, 1951, par. 144*d*.

[4] United States v. Smith, 3 USCMA 803, 14 CMR 221 (1954).

[5] Par. 138*f*.

individual in question *or* by proving his reputation in the community in which he lives *or* pursues his business or profession. However, testimony involving reputation must come from a person whose knowledge of such reputation was gained from having himself been a member of the community in question. These liberal provisions enable a person in the military service to prove his reputation in the civilian community or at his duty station or both. The Court held that a military person living in a civilian community may properly undertake to prove his reputation in the civilian community by the testimony of his pastor who lived in the same community.[6]

In order to show the probability of his innocence, an accused may introduce evidence of his own good character. This includes evidence of his military record. Character evidence is particularly important in most cases involving sex offenses.[7] The Court has reversed[8] several convictions because law officers excluded general character evidence for consideration on the issue of guilt or innocence. The *Manual* provides that the prosecution may, in rebuttal, introduce evidence as to the bad character of the accused. However, it must be limited by the scope of the character evidence introduced by the accused.[9]

III. Evidence of Other Offenses or Acts of Misconduct of the Accused

Evidence of other misconduct is generally not admissible against an accused. Proof of other crime, collateral to the issues in the case being tried, supplies no legal presumption or inference relevant to the offenses charged. Therefore, such proof can only tend to prejudice the court-martial against the accused because it may produce an impression that the accused is guilty simply because he has previously demonstrated a criminal tendency.[10] The problem of confining the proof to particular offenses is more difficult in court-martial proceedings than in civilian courts inasmuch as it is customary for the accused to be tried for all offenses charged against him at the same time even though such offenses may be entirely unrelated to each other.[11]

Several exceptions to this rule of exclusion of proof of other of-

[6] United States v. Johnson, 3 USCMA 709, 14 CMR 127 (1954).

[7] United States v. Phillips, 3 USCMA 137, 11 CMR 137 (1953).

[8] United States v. Browning, 1 USCMA 599, 5 CMR 27 (1952); United States v. Presley, 2 USCMA 414, 9 CMR 44 (1953); United States v. Johnson, 3 USCMA 709, 14 CMR 127 (1954); United States v. Phillips, 3 USCMA 137, 11 CMR 137 (1953). The law officer refused to give the requested or any other instruction on character evidence in a case involving the offense of sodomy.

[9] Par. 138*f* (2).

[10] Manual for Courts-Martial, United States, 1951, par. 138*g*. United States v. Yerger, 1 USCMA 288, 3 CMR 22 (1952).

[11] United States v. Jones, 2 USCMA 80, 6 CMR 80 (1952).

fenses are outlined in the *Manual*.[12] One of these is other offenses or misconduct which tend to show motive or intent. After recognizing this exception, the Court held[13] that in proving desertion with an intent to remain away permanently it is permissible in some cases to admit evidence of previous convictions of absence without leave. If such evidence is offered, the law officer should examine the record of previous offenses with care and reject them should they fail to shed some light on the mental attitude of the accused. In this situation the Court regards as important the manner in which the unauthorized absences were terminated. If the manner in which the unauthorized absences were terminated is not revealed in the prosecution evidence, the Court has indicated that it may be incumbent on the accused to show that he was not apprehended.[13a] Evidence of periods spent by the accused in confinement is admissible where avoidance of training is a vital element in the offense charged; for instance, where the offense alleged is desertion with intent to shirk important service and basic training[14] was the service the accused was trying to avoid.

Evidence that an accused was involved in an attempted robbery earlier in the evening of the alleged killing was properly admissible inasmuch as it tended to show motive or intent with respect to the homicide.[15] In another case an accused was found not guilty of larceny of two outboard motors. Nevertheless, evidence that he was in possession of two stolen motors was admissible in a subsequent trial in which he was accused of stealing a third motor because this evidence tended to establish the scienter of the accused.[16] Occasionally, members of a court-martial hear evidence of other misconduct which is subsequently ruled inadmissible by the law officer. The Court will not reverse in this situation unless the statements were so prejudicial that, notwithstanding the exclusionary and admonitory rulings of the law officer, the effect of the statements could not be erased from the minds of the members of the court-martial.[17] In this situation the Court is also concerned whether the trial counsel was deliberately violating the rules of evidence.[18]

12 Par. 138*g*.

13 United States v. Powell, 3 USCMA 64, 11 CMR 64 (1953); United States v. Deller, 3 USCMA 409, 12 CMR 165 (1953); United States v. O'Neil, 3 USCMA 416, 12 CMR 172 (1953).

13a United States v. Powell, 3 USCMA 64, 11 CMR 64 (1953).

14 United States v. Deller, 3 USCMA 409, 12 CMR 165 (1953); United States v. O'Neil, 3 USCMA 416, 12 CMR 172 (1953).

15 United States v. Vigneault, 3 USCMA 247, 12 CMR 3 (1953).

16 United States v. Petty, 3 USCMA 87, 11 CMR 87 (1953).

17 United States v. Johnson, 3 USCMA 447, 13 CMR 3 (1953).

18 United States v. Valencia, 1 USCMA 415, 4 CMR 7 (1952).

IV. Hearsay Rule

The *Manual* provides:

> "A statement which is offered in evidence to prove the truth of the matters therein stated, but which is not made by the author when a witness before the court at the particular trial in which it is so offered is heresay (*sic.*)."[19]

The well established rule is that hearsay is not competent evidence. It is error to admit it but isolated minor violations will not be a basis for reversal. The Court, however, will not condone repeated violations of the hearsay rule.[20] And a single violation may be prejudicial to the accused. A conviction was reversed[21] because an agent of the Criminal Investigation Division and a sergeant were permitted to testify to a matter which another witness (also an accused) had told them concerning the accused. The Court concluded that for all practical purposes these witnesses were permitted to pyramid into great importance the version offered by another accused. This was prejudicial where the facts, as in that case, were in dispute. Likewise, the receipt in evidence of unauthenticated photostats of a payroll in a forgery case was held prejudicial inasmuch as the facts were in sharp dispute and the effect was to permit inadmissible evidence to corroborate the evidence of the Government.[22]

A mechanical recording of statements of the accused if duly identified and authenticated, may be introduced in evidence and the sound reproduced for members of the court-martial for purposes of impeachment of the accused by proving that certain questions were asked and answers were made in a pretrial investigation. The Court went further and held that a typewritten transcript of the recording may be introduced in evidence for the same purpose if it is properly identified and authenticated. The hearsay rule was not involved in that case because the sole purpose in introducing the evidence was impeachment.[23]

Defense counsel should object to the admission of hearsay testimony. However, his failure to do so does not make hearsay competent evidence.[24] The Court has indicated[25] that a failure to object will not

[19] Par. 139.

[20] United States v. Yerger, 1 USCMA 288, 3 CMR 22 (1952). There were several violations in United States v. Isbell, 1 USCMA 131, 2 CMR 37 (1952), but each finding was based on substantial evidence. The defense counsel offered no objection. The Court held the admission of hearsay evidence was not prejudicial under these circumstances.

[21] United States v. Kellum, 1 USCMA 482, 4 CMR 74 (1952).

[22] United States v. Field, 3 USCMA 182, 11 CMR 182 (1953).

[23] United States v. Jewson, 1 USCMA 652, 5 CMR 80 (1952).

[24] Manual for Courts-Martial, United States, 1951, par. 139.

[25] United States v. Smith, 3 USCMA 15, 11 CMR 15 (1953). The trial was commenced before the effective date of the Code.

foreclose an examination on appeal to determine whether its admission materially prejudiced the substantial rights of the accused.

V. Exceptions to Hearsay Rule

A. *Confessions and admissions*

The *Manual* provides that a confession is an acknowledgment of guilt, whereas an admission is a self-incriminatory statement falling short of an acknowledgment of guilt.[26] The requirements for admission in evidence are not always the same for confessions and admissions. Generally, the requirements for either a valid confession or admission may be divided into three categories: (1) advising an accused of his rights; (2) voluntariness; (3) corpus delicti. These three categories will be discussed separately.

(1) *Advising of rights*—Article 31 of the Code provides in part:

> "(*a*) No person subject to this code shall compel any person to incriminate himself or to answer any question the answer to which may tend to incriminate him.
>
> (*b*) No person subject to this code shall interrogate, or request any statement from, an accused or a person suspected of an offense without first informing him of the nature of the accusation and advising him that he does not have to make any statement regarding the offense of which he is accused or suspected and that any statement made by him may be used as evidence against him in a trial by court-martial."

The Court stated[27] that distinctions between subsections (a) and (b) are:

(1) subsection (a) deals with compulsion whereas subsection (b) does not; (2) subsection (a) is not confined to testimonial utterances whereas (b) is confined to oral and written statements. Because of these important differences in the two sub-sections it is advisable to treat them separately although the close relationship between them is obvious. Subsection (a) is discussed under the topic "Self-incrimination" Section VII *infra*. Subsection (b) is appropriately discussed here in connection with the subject of confessions and admissions.

Subsection (b) conveniently may be broken down as follows:

An accused or person suspected of an offense must be informed:

(1) of the nature of the accusation;

(2) that he need not make any statement regarding the offense;[28]

[26] Par. 140*a*.

[27] United States v. Booker, 4 USCMA 335, 15 CMR 335 (1954).

[28] The protection here goes further than a literal prevention of compulsory self-incrimination. United States v. Phillips, 2 USCMA 534, 10 CMR 32 (1953).

(3) that any statement made by him may be used as evidence against him at a subsequent trial by courts-martial.

The Court has indicated that the person obtaining the statement need not personally advise the accused or suspect of his rights provided it was done by some other person.[29] A verbatim reading of Article 31 is desirable. But it is not essential—the requirement is that the accused or suspect be *informed* of his rights.[30]

An accused or suspect must be offered a free choice between making a statement and remaining silent—not merely the opportunity between oral or written exculpation and incrimination.[31] Thus it is reversible error to admit into evidence a statement taken by an interrogator who advised the suspect that he could refuse to answer only incriminating questions.[32]

Although failure to inform an accused of the nature of the offense may be error, the Court will not reverse unless there is a showing of a fair risk of prejudice.[33] Usually it is sufficient that the accused or suspect know generally the subject of the inquiry.[34]

Suppose a pretrial statement is secured from an accused or suspect without informing him of his rights—what are the consequences? Article 31 (d) provides that any statement obtained in violation of the requirement that an accused be warned of his rights shall not be received in evidence against him in a trial by court-martial. Must the prosecution show the statement was secured after proper warning as a prerequisite to admissibility or is it admissible unless the accused shows he was not warned of his rights? The Court has provided the answer as follows:

(1) A confession is admissible in evidence only if there is an affirmative showing that it was secured after proper warning had been given;[35]

(2) An admission ordinarily may be received in evidence without the necessity of showing the accused was warned of his rights;[36]

[29] United States v. Smith, 4 USCMA 369, 15 CMR 369 (1954).

[30] United States v. O'Brien, 3 USCMA 325, 12 CMR 81 (1953).

[31] United States v. Josey, 3 USCMA 767, 14 CMR 185 (1954). Mere silence of an accused during an investigation cannot, of course, constitute an admission. United States v. Armstrong, 4 USCMA 248, 15 CMR 248 (1954).

[32] United States v. Williams, 2 USCMA 430, 9 CMR 60 (1953). But the mere fact that an accused does not recite to the interrogator all the provisions of Article 31 does not in itself cast doubt on his statement that he understood all of his rights. United States v. Molette, 3 USCMA 674, 14 CMR 92 (1954).

[33] United States v. O'Brien, 3 USCMA 105, 11 CMR 105 (1953).

[34] United States v. O'Brien, 3 USCMA 325, 12 CMR 81 (1953).

[35] United States v. Josey, 3 USCMA 767, 14 CMR 185 (1954).

[36] *Ibid.*

(3) An admission indicated to be *involuntary* must be preceded by an affirmative showing of both warning and voluntariness before it may be received in evidence;[37]

(4) An admission shown by the record to have been secured without warning the accused of his rights should not be admitted.[38]

(5) An admission may properly be received in evidence if the record is *silent* regarding whether the accused was informed of his rights.[39]

A pretrial statement secured in violation of the rights of an accused should not be admitted in evidence. If admitted, it should be stricken by the reviewing authorities. The Court further has considered whether the entire case should be reversed even though the record contains sufficient competent evidence to support the finding of guilty. In *Wilson v. Harvey*[40] a military police sergeant investigating the shooting of a Korean was informed by another military policeman that the two accused had been identified by a group of Koreans as the men who had done the shooting. The sergeant then approached a group of soldiers, which included the accused, and while looking directly at the accused asked who had done the shooting. The accused responded with the statement that they "had shot at the man." The *record showed that the accused had not been advised of their rights* before they made this admission. The Court held this statement was not properly received in evidence. Since there was a lack of other evidence to support the conviction the Court had no alternative but to reverse. This was sufficient to dispose of the case but the majority of the Court went further to state:

> "Where—as here—an element of officiality attended the questioning which produced the admissions, there is more than a violation of the naked rule of Article 31 (b). . . . there is an abridgment of the policy underlying the Article which must—we think—be regarded as 'so overwhelmingly important in the scheme of military justice as to elevate it to the level of a creative and indwelling principle.' "[41]

[37] *Ibid.*

[38] United States v. Wilson and Harvey, 2 USCMA 248, 8 CMR 48 (1953).

[39] United States v. Seymour, 3 USCMA 401, 12 CMR 157 (1953).

[40] 2 USCMA 248, 8 CMR 48 (1953). A confession of one accused cannot be considered against another accused. United States v. Wooten, 1 USCMA 358, 3 CMR 92 (1952).

[41] United States v. Wilson and Harvey, 2 USCMA 248, 255, 8 CMR 48, 55 (1953). The offense occurred before Article 31 became effective, and Judge Latimer dissented because he objected not only to the application of the doctrine of general prejudice but also to applying it *ex post facto*.

This is the language of the general prejudice rule which, when invoked, goes beyond the requirement of the Code and results in a reversal even though there is reflected in the record other sufficient evidence to sustain the conviction. The Court has interpreted this dictum in a restrictive manner. For instance, the Court has stated that the doctrine will not apply in a situation in which the record is silent whether the accused was advised of his rights before making an admission.[42] It further appears that the Court will reverse for a lack of warning only when there is a *positive* showing that the accused was not warned of his rights before making a pretrial statement.[43]

In addition, the Court has held that the waiver doctrine is applicable in these cases. In the absence of special circumstances, a failure to object at the trial to the receipt in evidence of a pretrial statement (confession or admission) obtained from an accused who was not warned of his rights in accordance with Article 31 precludes the accused from raising the error for the first time on appeal.[44]

It was held reversible error to admit in evidence statements made by an accused in a "line of duty" investigation when it was shown that the accused was not informed of his rights. This was true even though the statements were admitted for purposes of impeachment.[45]

Article 31 (b) states broadly that *no person subject to the Code* shall interrogate or request any statement from an accused or person suspected of an offense without first informing him of his rights. Notwithstanding the express words of this Article, the Court held that a confession made to a fellow prisoner by an accused was admissible even though he had not been warned of his rights.[46] The fellow prisoner was "a good reliable rat" for the Criminal Investigation Division. The accused made statements regarding his criminal activities in response to a question by his fellow prisoner to the effect: "What are you in for?" The Court concluded that Congress was concerned principally with eliminating the possibility of implied coercion due to military discipline and superiority, rather than with suppressing the use of statements obtained by trickery. Thus the Court appears to have adopted the civilian rule that deceit and fraud would negative admissibility only when the nature of the deceit or fraud was calculated to elicit an untrue statement.

[42] United States v. Seymour, 3 USCMA 401, 12 CMR 157 (1953).
[43] United States v. Josey, 3 USCMA 767, 14 CMR 185 (1954).
[44] United States v. Fisher, 4 USCMA 152, 15 CMR 152 (1954); United States v. Henry, 4 USCMA 158, 15 CMR 158 (1954).
[45] United States v. Pederson, 2 USCMA 263, 8 CMR 63 (1953).
[46] United States v. Gibson, 3 USCMA 746, 14 CMR 164 (1954). *Cf.* United States v. Creamer, 1 USCMA 267, 3 CMR 1 (1952). (A. W. 24.)

In another case the Court held that the "element of officiality" required by Article 31 was present in a case in which a Criminal Investigation Division agent was present and cooperating in the negotiations carried out by another soldier which led to the making of incriminatory statements by the accused.[47]

Paragraph 140*a* of the *Manual* provides that mere silence on the part of an accused when questioned as to his supposed offense is not to be treated as a confession. However, it further states that when an accused is not in arrest or custody or under investigation, there are circumstances under which his failure to utter a denial of an accusation that he had participated in an offense may be regarded as incriminating evidence. For example, when an accused remains silent after a friend has stated to the accused that he saw him commit an offense. No warning is required in this situation. But it is sometimes difficult to determine whether the accused was under investigation at the time of the accusation.[47a]

(2) *Voluntariness*—It is not always possible to make clear-cut distinctions between the concepts of advising an accused of his rights, voluntariness, and self-incrimination. For instance, the *Manual*[48] provides that one of the bases for a finding of involuntariness is that the accused was not advised of his rights. If an interrogator does not advise an accused of his rights pursuant to Article 31 and also promises the accused immunity from prosecution, there are both questions of advising the accused of his rights and voluntariness involved in making determination of the validity of an admission or confession secured under these circumstances.[49] It is possible that an accused may be advised of his rights and then induced to make an incriminatory statement because of hope or fear. Moreover, an accused may be advised of his rights and then forced to talk at the point of a bayonet. In such case, because of the coercion involved the Court may hold that such statements were secured in violation of the privilege against self-incrimination. An involuntary statement is not admissible in evidence. A statement secured by coercion sufficient to constitute a violation of the privilege against self-incrimination may not only be inadmissible but it may also be the basis for reversal of a conviction notwithstanding the existence of other evidence in the record sufficient to support a finding of guilty.[50]

[47] United States v. Josey, 3 USCMA 767, 14 CMR 185 (1954).
[47a] United States v. Armstrong, 4 USCMA 248, 15 CMR 248 (1954).
[48] Par. 140*a*.
[49] United States v. Josey, 3 USCMA 767, 14 CMR 185 (1954).
[50] *Ibid;* United States v. Welch, 1 USCMA 402, 3 CMR 136 (1952). Discussed in Section VII this chapter.

A confession must be established by an affirmative showing that it was voluntary, unless the defense expressly consents to the omission of such a showing, but an admission may be introduced without such preliminary proof if there is no indication that it was involuntary.[51] A confession or admission following inducements calculated to arouse either hope[52] or fear is just as untrustworthy in a court-martial as it is in a civilian criminal court. The issue of voluntariness is usually one of fact. The basic question is "whether the accused possessed, at the time of the confession, 'mental freedom' to confess or deny participation in the crime."[53] Mere nervousness plus the presence of officers does not alone amount to unlawful mental compulsion.[54] The Court has outlined its scope of review on the question of voluntariness as follows:

> "To fulfill our appellate responsibility, it is incumbent upon us to review independently the circumstances surrounding the allegedly involuntary confession. But where there is disagreement as to whether claimed improper acts actually occurred or where admitted facts permit different inferences, the trial forum is not only better equipped but has the legal duty to weigh the evidence and decide whether the confession is, in fact, voluntary. We must accept the determination of the triers of fact on the question of voluntariness whenever it is supported by substantial evidence, regardless of whether we, as individuals, might resolve the conflict otherwise, or draw different inferences from the facts. If the fact finders could reasonably conclude that the confession was voluntary, then we must affirm."[55]

In *Colbert*[56] the accused confessed to the larceny of a typewriter. There was no indication of the "third degree" but there was evidence of an alleged "threat" to the effect that the accused could be prosecuted for perjury and sentenced to five additional years in the penitentiary should he persist in denying any part in the theft and subsequently

[51] MANUAL FOR COURTS-MARTIAL, UNITED STATES, 1951, par. 140*a*. United States v. Doyle, 1 USCMA 545, 4 CMR 137 (1952). The confession was not affirmatively shown to be voluntary but the Court refused to reverse because there was other compelling evidence of guilt.

[52] United States v. Webb, 1 USCMA 219, 2 CMR 125 (1952).

[53] United States v. Monge, 1 USCMA 95, 2 CMR 1 (1952). The mere fact the accused was in custody or confined at the time of giving the statement does not render it inadmissible. United States v. Vigneault, 3 USCMA 247, 12 CMR 3 (1953).

[54] United States v. Hagelberger, 3 USCMA 259, 12 CMR 15 (1953).

[55] United States v. Monge, 1 USCMA 95, 98, 2 CMR 1, 4 (1952); *accord,* United States v. Sapp, 1 USCMA 100, 2 CMR 6 (1952); United States v. Webb, 1 USCMA 219, 2 CMR 125 (1952).

[56] 2 USCMA 3, 6 CMR 3 (1952).

be convicted for it. The Court refused to adopt the rule of the Court of Appeals for the Fifth Circuit[57] that no confession induced by official threat of prosecution is voluntary. Instead, the Court adhered to the view that voluntariness is a question of fact and that the result in each case must depend upon its own peculiar circumstances. The test to be applied was stated by the Court to be as follows:

> "Was the nature of the statement such that there is any reasonable likelihood that it would so constrict the will of petitioner that he might have been induced to confess guilt of a serious crime which he did not commit?"[58]

It was held that the "threat" in the *Colbert* case did not have such effect, nor did the use of the confession violate military due process.

In *Fair and Boyce*[59] one of the accused gave information as to the location of the stolen gun. During the trial it was determined that this admission was freely given even though there was evidence that the accused had been put into segregated confinement, subjected to repeated questioning, and on one occasion water had been thrown in his face. The Court, after observing that the segregated confinement was not coercive, that the questioning periods were very short and extended over a period of eight days, and that the water throwing incident occurred seven days before the admission was made, concluded that the circumstances fell "far short" of establishing the "lack of free will" that is required before the Court could upset the determination of voluntariness made by the triers of fact.

An unrequested disclosure freely made during the course of a friendly and aimless conversation by an accused person to one of the same military grade is not involuntary simply because the latter is a member of the military police.[60] If an investigator informs an accused that a statement would probably help him and nothing more, such is insufficient to destroy voluntariness.[61]

(3) *Effect of previous involuntary confessions*—The Court has also been concerned with the voluntariness of a confession where it was preceded by another clearly involuntary confession.

[57] Cannan v. United States, 19 F. 2d 823, 824 (5th Cir. 1927).
[58] United States v. Colbert, 2 USCMA 3, 6, 6 CMR 3, 6 (1952).
[59] 2 USCMA 521, 10 CMR 19 (1953).
[60] United States v. Creamer, 1 USCMA 267, 3 CMR 1 (1952).
[61] United States v. Borner, 3 USCMA 306, 12 CMR 62 (1953). See also United States v. Jackson, 3 USCMA 646, 14 CMR 64 (1954). In that case the Court held that the triers of fact reasonably could conclude that the confession was induced solely by his consultation with the chaplain, and not by deprivation of sleep or shoes or by lengthy interrogation.

In *Monge*[62] two soldiers, acting on suspicion, entered the barracks of the accused and pulled him from bed at four o'clock in the morning. He was forced to lie on the floor; a bayonet was held at his back and, after being questioned, he admitted the theft of money. During the questioning one of the soldiers searched the clothes of the accused and found large sums of money. On the afternoon of the same day, the accused, after being advised of his right to remain silent, made a written confession to Criminal Investigation Division agents. None of those who were present at the time of the oral confession were present at these interrogations. Four days later the accused executed a second written confession in more detail.

The court-martial admitted the written confession and the accused was found guilty of larceny. The Court affirmed the conviction and in doing so it relied on *United States v. Bayer*,[63] a decision of the United States Supreme Court, dealing with the rule, which, in effect, states that the influence of a prior improper inducement is presumed to continue during the subsequent confession until the prosecution establishes the contrary. According to the Court, the issue was still one of fact and the prior confession was a "weighty" factor to be considered with other things such as the mental character of the accused, the nature and degree of the influence, the time intervening between the confessions and all circumstances surrounding the subsequent confession. For this reason the Court observed that it was "deceptive" to say that the prosecution must establish that the improper influences have been dissipated. On the basis of all the facts it was concluded that the triers of fact in *Monge* had a reasonable basis for finding that the prior improper influences had been dispelled.

The Court refused to require, as had several prior decisions of boards of review, that the accused be warned that prior involuntary confessions could not be used against him. On this point, it is sufficient that the accused be warned of his right to remain silent.

(4) *Who determines voluntariness*—When a law officer admits a confession in evidence, he should advise the court-martial that his ruling is not conclusive on the issue of voluntariness inasmuch as each member of the court-martial may, during the court-martial's deliberations, arrive at his own conclusions concerning the voluntary nature of the confession. This instruction is not mandatory, but it is error for the law officer to leave the court-martial with the impression that his

[62] 1 USCMA 95, 2 CMR 1 (1952); *accord*, United States v. Sapp, 1 USCMA 100, 2 CMR 6 (1952) (four hours between first and second confessions).

[63] 331 U. S. 532, 540-541 (1947) (six months between first and second confessions).

ruling is final.[64] Such error may or may not be reversible depending on the existence of the required prejudice.

The usual procedure is to determine the voluntariness of a confession before dealing with its substance. In *Davis*[65] the prosecution undertook to introduce an alleged *oral* confession. The law officer ruled that the defense could not contest the voluntary nature of the alleged confession until *after* it had been related by the witness. The Court recognized that it was not possible to contest it until disclosed and refused to hold the procedure erroneous. However, a preferable procedure suggested was for the law officer to determine out of the presence of the members of the court-martial the substance of the prospective testimony, after which the court-martial could be recalled and informed that relevant evidence bearing on the question of voluntariness of an alleged oral confession was going to be heard.[66]

(5) *Corpus delicti*—A conviction may not be sustained if it rests upon an uncorroborated admission or confession made by the accused.[67] Corroborating evidence (corpus delicti), whether direct or circumstantial, must be independent of the admission or confession and according to the *Manual* it must show that the offense charged has probably been committed by someone.[68] However, it need not tend to connect the accused with the offense.[69]

In *Uchihara*[70] the Court considered the problem of corroborating evidence. In this case Government counsel had argued that proof of absence without leave was sufficient to corroborate the confession of the accused of desertion with intent to avoid hazardous duty. Judge Brosman in writing the majority opinion, in which Judge Latimer concurred, did not deal with this contention. Instead, he assumed that proper admission of the confession required evidence, other than the

[64] United States v. Davis, 2 USCMA 505, 10 CMR 3 (1953) (not reversible error).

[65] *Ibid.*

[66] United States v. Smith, 3 USCMA 680, 14 CMR 98 (1954). An out of court hearing was held on accused's alleged motive for making a confession. United States v. Cooper, 2 USCMA 333, 8 CMR 133 (1953). Defense counsel waived the right to have members of the court-martial hear the evidence on involuntariness.

[67] MANUAL FOR COURTS-MARTIAL, UNITED STATES, 1951, par. 140*a*. United States v. Mounts, 1 USCMA 114, 2 CMR 20 (1952); United States v. Bryson, 3 USCMA 329, 12 CMR 85 (1953). The 1949 *Manual* required "substantial evidence." For cases applying provisions of the 1949 *Manual* see United States v. Brooks, 1 USCMA 88, 1 CMR 88 (1951); United States v. Goodman, 1 USCMA 170, 2 CMR 76 (1952); United States v. Evans, 1 USCMA 207, 2 CMR 113 (1952).

[68] United States v. Jones, 2 USCMA 80, 6 CMR 80 (1952).

[69] United States v. Dolliole, 3 USCMA 101, 11 CMR 101 (1953).

[70] 1 USCMA 123, 2 CMR 29 (1952).

confession itself, of every element of the charge of desertion. Looking at the record, he concluded that sufficient evidence was present in this case inasmuch as the morning report (properly in evidence) revealed that the camp and unit to which the accused was assigned was in Japan. The court-martial with knowledge of the camp and unit could take judicial notice that such unit was a "pipeline" for Korean combat. Judge Latimer thought evidence in the record concerning efforts of the accused to remain in Japan was sufficient in itself to establish probable intent not to go back to Korea.

Chief Judge Quinn in a strong dissent met the contention of Government counsel squarely and stated that the *Manual* and the better reasoned federal decisions are "irreconcilable with the government claim that the corpus delicti of desertion is made out solely by a showing of the unauthorized absence alleged." He referred to the majority opinion as only "timidly" intimating instead of clearly recognizing that the *Manual* requires corroboration of a pretrial confession. Moreover, he strongly reiterated an objection, previously made,[71] to stretching "the record to plug loop-holes in deficient prosecution cases by the expedient of judicial notice."

In *Isenberg*[72] the Court examined both federal civilian and military cases regarding the question of corroborating evidence. The cases were not in agreement whether a showing that the offense had probably been committed by someone was sufficient, or whether it was necessary to go further and produce some evidence tending to establish the probability of the existence of each element of the offense charged. The Court appeared to lean in favor of the latter requirement but decided the case on the ground there was no evidence that the offense had probably been committed. The accused was charged with desertion with the intent to remain away from the service permanently. The only evidence presented by the prosecution was testimony that the accused was absent without leave for about ten days and a confession of the accused that he intended to desert. The Court held that mere absence without leave of short duration is insufficient to show that the offense of permanent desertion probably has been committed, and the finding of guilty of desertion was reduced to absence without leave. A unanimous Court in *Petty*[73] referred to *Isenberg* as follows:

[71] United States v. McCrary, 1 USCMA 1, 1 CMR 1 (1951).

[72] 2 USCMA 349, 8 CMR 149 (1953), 29 N. Y. U. L. Q. Rev. 513 (1954).

[73] 3 USCMA 87, 11 CMR 87 (1953). See dictum in *accord,* United States v. Williams, 4 USCMA 241, 245, 15 CMR 241, 245 (1954). *Cf.* United States v. Manuel, 3 USCMA 739, 14 CMR 157 (1954).

> "In our recent decision in the Isenberg case . . . we sought to make plain that present military practice requires, as corroboration of a confession, some evidence tending to establish the probability of the existence of each element of the offense charged—thus adopting, at least in substance, the rule announced in Forte v. United States, 94 F. 2d 236 (CA DC Cir.), and Ercoli v. United States, 131 F. 2d 354 (CA DC Cir.)."[74]

This appears to go beyond the *Manual* provision which states that it must be shown that the offense charged probably had been committed by someone.[75]

In a forgery[76] case the corpus delicti was supplied by the signature of the accused in his confession inasmuch as it resembled the writing on the alleged forged instrument. Permitting the corpus delicti to be shown in this manner indicates that the majority of the Court regards corpus delicti as a protection against the occasional case where one confesses to a non-existent crime and that it will not result in the exclusion from evidence of any substantial number of confessions. Other cases decided by the Court appear to support this conclusion even though it is not yet clear whether the corpus delicti requirement is met by showing that the crime has probably been committed by someone or whether it must tend to establish each element of the offense.[76a]

In other cases the Court has found the corroborating evidence sufficient to support a confession of murder,[77] larceny,[78] and of receiving stolen property[79] and insufficient to support a confession of wrongful possession of marihuana.[80]

(6) *A confession may be oral or written*—The *Manual*[81] provides that a voluntary oral confession or admission of the accused may be proved by the testimony of anyone who heard him make it, even though it was reduced to writing and the writing was unaccounted for. An unsigned statement, part of which was denied by the accused, was admitted in

[74] United States v. Petty, 3 USCMA 87, 89, 11 CMR 87, 89 (1953).

[75] Par. 140*a*. In *Isenberg* the Court pointed out that a provision in previous *Manuals* expressly stating that there was no need to cover every element of the offense charged had been deleted in the MANUAL FOR COURTS-MARTIAL, UNITED STATES, 1951.

[76] United States v. Manuel, 3 USCMA 739, 14 CMR 157 (1954).

[76a] *Cf.* United States v. Petty, 3 USCMA 87, 11 CMR 87 (1953) *with* United States v. Dolliole, 3 USCMA 101, 11 CMR 101 (1953).

[77] United States v. Long, 2 USCMA 45, 6 CMR 45 (1952).

[78] United States v. Colbert, 2 USCMA 3, 6 CMR 3 (1952).

[79] United States v. Petty, 3 USCMA 87, 11 CMR 87 (1953).

[80] United States v. Jones, 2 USCMA 80, 6 CMR 80 (1952). The corroborating evidence was sufficient in two of the four specifications and insufficient in the other two.

[81] Par. 140*a*.

evidence to show prior consistent statements of the interrogator following his impeachment as a witness, and to impeach the accused as a witness by showing previous inconsistent statements.[82] The Court found it unnecessary to decide whether a document prepared for the accused's signature, with his concurrence in the preparation, is admissible regardless of whether he finally signed the document.

(7) *Exculpatory Statements in a Confession or Admission*—Exculpatory statements contained in an admission or confession are not binding on the Government but for instructional necessities such statements are on par with other evidence. Unless the exculpatory statements are inherently improbable and unworthy of belief, they should be accepted by the law officer to frame his issues.[83]

B. *Statements of accomplices*

Although a statement of one accused may implicate his co-accused, this factor alone does not require severance. Usually an instruction by the law officer that the court-martial may consider the statement as evidence only against the accused who made it will provide adequate safeguard against prejudice to the co-accused.[84]

C. *Statements made through interpreters*

The general rule is that statements made through an interpreter may be proved only by the testimony of the interpreter. The Court recognized an exception where the interpreter may be considered the agent of the person making the statement.[85] Moreover, the Court indicated that under some circumstances it may be proper to regard an interpreter as an agent for both parties;[86] thus implying that it would in appropriate cases give recognition to a broad view of the agency doctrine.

D. *Dying Declarations*

In *DeCarlo*[87] the accused asked a Korean boy, employed in the service of supply, for some candy. He was told there was none and a "good-natured argument in bantering words with no serious overtones" ensued. Finally the accused stated, "If you don't give me

[82] United States v. Molette, 3 USCMA 674, 14 CMR 92 (1954). But see Judge Brosman's opinion in which he concurred in the result.

[83] United States v. Johnson, 3 USCMA 209, 11 CMR 209 (1953); United States v. Lee, 3 USCMA 501, 13 CMR 57 (1953) (unworthy of belief).

[84] United States v. Borner, 3 USCMA 306, 12 CMR 62 (1953); MANUAL FOR COURTS-MARTIAL, UNITED STATES, 1951, par. 140*b*.

[85] United States v. Day, 2 USCMA 416, 9 CMR 46 (1953).

[86] United States v. Plummer, 1 USCMA 373, 3 CMR 107 (1952). See also MANUAL FOR COURTS-MARTIAL, UNITED STATES, 1951, par. 141.

[87] 1 USCMA 91, 1 CMR 90 (1951).

some candy, I'll shoot you," or words to that effect. A shot from the rifle of the accused hit the Korean. While *in extremis,* the boy stated that it was an "accident." This statement was offered in evidence as a dying declaration, but upon objection was excluded on the grounds that it was opinion evidence and of such nature that the deceased could not have so testified had he been living. The Court concluded that the opinion rule was not violated because the testimony was a "collective statement of fact" based on the observations of the deceased who was in a position to know the circumstances of the shooting. Accordingly, it was error not to have admitted the statement as a dying declaration.

E. *Spontaneous Exclamations*

To qualify a spontaneous exclamation as an exception to the hearsay rule, there must be other evidence of the event. In *Mounts*[88] the mother of two small children testified concerning what her sons had told her about the alleged offense of sodomy committed against one of them. Her testimony was hearsay and it was not admissible as an exception to the rule on the ground that the statements were spontaneous exclamations because the record was totally devoid of other evidence of the shocking event. Further, the statements made by the alleged victim did not constitute a fresh complaint inasmuch as they were made in response to questioning by his mother. In order for a fresh complaint to be admissible to prove directly the truth of the matters stated it must qualify under the spontaneous exclamation exception to the hearsay rule.

F. *Best Evidence Rule*

A writing is the best evidence of its own contents, and the original thereof must be introduced to prove its contents.[89] Carbon copies of longhand letters taken from an accused are duplicate originals and not secondary evidence.[90] But had these carbon copies been declared to be secondary evidence, they nevertheless would have been admissible under an exception to the best evidence rule inasmuch as the co-conspirator who received the originals had destroyed them.[91] A party must exercise his right to object to the introduction of secondary evidence. Failure to do so will waive the right.[92] However, the *Manual* provides

[88] 1 USCMA 114, 2 CMR 20 (1952).
[89] MANUAL FOR COURTS-MARTIAL, UNITED STATES, 1951, par. 143*a*.
[90] United States v. Rhodes, 3 USCMA 73, 11 CMR 73 (1953); *accord,* United States v. Jewson, 1 USCMA 652, 5 CMR 80 (1952).
[91] United States v. Rhodes, 3 USCMA 73, 11 CMR 73 (1953).
[92] United States v. Deller, 3 USCMA 409, 12 CMR 165 (1953); United States v. McNeill, 2 USCMA 383, 9 CMR 13 (1953). Accused's own testimony removed any prejudicial effect of the alleged secondary evidence.

that a waiver adds nothing to the weight to be given to, or the evidentiary nature of, the particular writing so received.[93] The Court has indicated approval of admission of secondary evidence when the matter contained therein is collateral to the main issues. For instance, it is admissible for purposes of impeachment by self-contradiction of the accused at least when it involves only a very small portion of his testimony.[94]

(1) *Exception—Fingerprints*—The Court upheld[95] a provision in paragraph 143*a* of the *Manual* which permits the custodian of personnel records, under certain prescribed circumstances, to certify to the result of an examination of fingerprint records in his office. If identity is the question involved, such a certificate constitutes only prima facie evidence. The *Manual* further provides that fingerprints forwarded to an appropriate office for comparison may be identified by the testimony of the person who took them or by someone who was present at the time they were taken. The Court approved this provision but held that the Government was not confined to it. Indirect testimony can be used to prove the fingerprints taken were those of a particular person.[96]

G. *Official Records*

Whenever there is a duty to record official events, the record thus kept is official and if properly prepared, it falls within the exceptions to the hearsay rule.[97] The basic tests for the admissibility of a document in evidence as an official record are: (1) was it made by one whose duty it was to make it? (2) did he know or ascertain, through appropriate and trustworthy channels of information, the truth of the matter recorded?[98]

A commanding officer may designate an officer[99] or warrant officer[100] not a member of the reporting unit to sign the morning report. It is presumed this delegation is properly accomplished and therefore it is unnecessary affirmatively to show in the record the manner in

[93] MANUAL FOR COURTS-MARTIAL, UNITED STATES, 1951, par. 143*a*.
[94] United States v. Jewson, 1 USCMA 652, 5 CMR 80 (1952).
[95] United States v. White, 3 USCMA 666, 14 CMR 84 (1954).
[96] United States v. Taylor, 4 USCMA 232, 15 CMR 232 (1954).
[97] MANUAL FOR COURTS-MARTIAL, UNITED STATES, 1951, par. 144; United States v. Parlier, 1 USCMA 433, 4 CMR 25 (1952); United States v. Creamer, 1 USCMA 267, 3 CMR 1 (1953). United States v. Patrick, 2 USCMA 189, 7 CMR 65 (1953) (marriage license). United States v. Self, 3 USCMA 568, 13 CMR 124 (1953) (receipts as business entries).
[98] United States v. Hagen, 2 USCMA 324, 8 CMR 124 (1953).
[99] United States v. Masusock, 1 USCMA 32, 1 CMR 32 (1951). It was signed by the personnel officer of the regiment rather than by the company commander.
[100] United States v. Clements, 1 USCMA 39, 1 CMR 39 (1951).

which it was done. An officer who has a duty to record events concerning personnel of a unit, is not restricted to events occurring at his own station. For instance, an entry in the service record of a sailor is admissible in evidence even though the events recorded concerned his apprehension and escape at an Air Force Base.[101]

The events which should be recorded in an official record are prescribed by regulations. A Navy service record can be used to prove that an unauthorized absence was terminated by apprehension because the recording official has a duty to state the circumstances of a return to duty.[102] However, a morning report cannot be used to prove apprehension because there is no duty imposed by regulations on the official to make this determination.[103] But a morning report is competent to establish prima facie proof of an alleged escape because regulations require the recordation of this event.[104] For the same reason evidence of breach of arrest from Navy service records has been held admissible.[105] Likewise, a Marine service record can be used to show the nature and content of a special order.[106] A document prepared in accordance with regulations is official although some of the data contained therein is inaccurate. Thus a morning report which incorrectly states the initial date of the unauthorized absence is admissible. The inaccuracy of entries affects the weight to be given to the evidence and not its admissibility.[107]

An entry in an official record is not necessarily inadmissible because it was not made within the time prescribed by the regulation. The Court holds that it is sufficient if the entry is made within a reasonable time. Entries made forty-six days,[108] eighty-nine days,[109] and even four and one-half months[110] after the occurrence of the event have been admitted in evidence. There is no time limit on the duty to correct an entry. A correction made in a morning report nineteen months after the original entry was held to be properly admitted in evidence.[111]

[101] United States v. Coates, 2 USCMA 625, 10 CMR 123 (1953).
[102] *Ibid.* *Cf.* United States v. Bennett, 4 USCMA 309, 15 CMR 309 (1954).
[103] *Ibid.*
[104] United States v. Wilson, 4 USCMA 3, 15 CMR 3 (1954).
[105] United States v. Lowery, 2 USCMA 315, 8 CMR 115 (1953); United States v. Barrett, 3 USCMA 294, 12 CMR 50 (1953).
[106] United States v. Bennett, 4 USCMA 309, 15 CMR 309 (1954).
[107] United States v. Phillips, 3 USCMA 557, 13 CMR 113 (1953).
[108] United States v. Barrett, 3 USCMA 294, 12 CMR 50 (1953).
[109] United States v. Hagen, 2 USCMA 324, 8 CMR 124 (1953).
[110] United States v. Phillips, 3 USCMA 557, 13 CMR 113 (1953).
[111] United States v. Wilson, 4 USCMA 3, 15 CMR 3 (1954); United States v. Williams, 1 USCMA 186, 2 CMR 92 (1952) (four months). See also United States v. Strong, 1 USCMA 627, 5 CMR 55 (1952).

The Army and the Air Force customarily use morning report entries to show prima facie an unauthorized absence; whereas the Navy relies on the service record for prima facie proof of this offense.[112]

Extract or photostatic copies of official records authenticated by the officer having custody thereof are admissible in evidence as duplicates of the original records.[113] But an extract copy which fails to reveal that the original was properly authenticated is inadmissible.[114] The presumption of regularity simply does not extend to a situation in which there is no indication in the extract copy that the original was signed.

As previously stated the Court usually will not review an assignment of error based on the inadmissibility of evidence where it clearly appears that the defense understood the right to object and the right was not exercised,[115] except in those instances in which there would be a manifest miscarriage of justice. There is a substantial miscarriage of justice when the sole evidence of guilt is an extract copy of a morning report which fails to show that the original was ever authenticated.[116] However, the Court is aware that defense counsel deliberately may avoid an objection to a defective exhibit and it has stated that defective documentary evidence will not result in a *dismissal* if the record discloses an available substitute.[117]

Although paragraph 143*b* of the *Manual* provides that proof of authenticity can be waived by a failure to object, the Court has held[118] that morning report extracts unsigned and uninitialed cannot support a finding of guilty of an unauthorized absence even though defense counsel failed to object to the introduction in evidence of these extracts.

On one occasion[119] the law officer directed that certain extracts from a service record be marked as exhibits. No objection was made by the defense counsel; in fact, there was express consent. A Navy

[112] MANUAL FOR COURTS-MARTIAL, UNITED STATES, 1951, par. 164*a*. The personnel diary of a construction battalion was held insufficient to show the inception of an alleged unlawful absence. United States v. Harjo, 2 USCMA 9, 6 CMR 9 (1952).

[113] United States v. Parlier, 1 USCMA 433, 4 CMR 25 (1952); United States v. Masusock, 1 USCMA 32, 1 CMR 32 (1951); United States v. Harris, 1 USCMA 430, 4 CMR 22 (1952) (photostatic copies). United States v. Bennett, 4 USCMA 309, 15 CMR 309 (1954) (extracts from service record).

[114] United States v. Parlier, 1 USCMA 433, 4 CMR 25 (1952); United States v. Collier, 1 USCMA 439, 4 CMR 31 (1952); United States v. Teal, 3 USCMA 404, 12 CMR 160 (1953).

[115] United States v. Masusock, 1 USCMA 32, 1 CMR 32 (1951).

[116] United States v. Teal, 3 USCMA 404, 12 CMR 160 (1953).

[117] United States v. Phillips, 3 USCMA 557, 13 CMR 113 (1953).

[118] United States v. Smith, 2 USCMA 121, 6 CMR 121 (1952). See also United States v. Bryson, 3 USCMA 329, 12 CMR 85 (1953). There was no waiver of the authentication of a check which was a part of a deposition even though defense counsel offered no objection to the deposition.

[119] United States v. Harris, 1 USCMA 430, 4 CMR 22 (1952).

board of review excluded the evidence on the ground that the record did not show it actually was introduced in evidence. The Court reversed this ruling after deciding that the statement of the law officer could be construed to be a reception in evidence of the questioned documents. To hold otherwise, according to the Court, would be "to unduly emphasize form over substance."

The Court approved the following method of introducing documents in evidence as meeting minimal standards without the necessity for the trial counsel to be sworn as a witness at the time he read from the documents.

> "TRIAL COUNSEL: The prosecution offers in evidence a Special Order from the Marine Corps Forwarding Depot, Portsmouth, Virginia, dated 15 January 1953 which is in the current service record of the accused. It is offered to the defense for inspection and possible objection with the request that a true copy be substituted for the record. This exhibit which is offered is a true copy appearing in the current service record of the accused.
>
> "DEFENSE COUNSEL: No objection.
>
> "LAW OFFICER: A true copy of a special order in the current service record of the accused dated 15 January 1953 will be received in evidence as Prosecution Exhibit 1, and a true copy may be substituted therefor. The trial counsel read Prosecution Exhibit 1."[120]

H. *Photographs*

A photograph may be admitted in evidence for the purpose of identifying a person, even though it possesses a "shocking" aspect which might conceivably tend to excite the members of the court-martial.[121]

I. *Depositions*

Article 49 provides in part:

> "A duly authenticated deposition taken upon reasonable notice to the other party, so far as otherwise admissible under the rules of evidence, may be read in evidence before any military court or commission in any case not capital . . . if it appears—
>
> (1) that the witness resides or is beyond the State, Territory, or District in which the court . . . is ordered to sit, or

[120] United States v. Wellman, 4 USCMA 348, 350, 15 CMR 348, 350 (1954); *accord*, United States v. Shelton, 4 USCMA 352, 15 CMR 352 (1954).

[121] United States v. Bartholomew, 1 USCMA 307, 3 CMR 41 (1952).

beyond the distance of one hundred miles from the place of trial . . . or

(2) that the witness by reason of death, age, sickness, bodily infirmity, imprisonment, military necessity, nonamenability to process, or other reasonable cause, is unable or refuses to appear and testify in person at the place of trial or

(3) that the present whereabouts of the witness is unknown."

The most significant feature in these liberal provisions for deposition testimony is the authorization for their use by the prosecution in all non-capital cases. Moreover, deposition testimony may be introduced by the prosecution in capital cases if (1) the convening authority prior to trial directs that the case be treated as non-capital, in which event the death penalty may not be imposed,[122] or (2) the accused expressly consents to its admission in evidence.[123] The mere statement by defense counsel of "no objection" to a deposition offered as evidence by the prosecution in a capital case does not meet the requirements of express consent.[124] It must be shown that the accused and counsel were aware that the evidence was inadmissible and they nevertheless were willing to have it used against the accused.[125] If the prosecution introduces deposition testimony in a capital case and there is no waiver, the error will be tested for prejudice. In some cases the Court has found that this error was not prejudicial[126] but in at least one case the deposition evidence was prejudicial because it supplied an essential element of proof.[127]

The *Manual*[128] provides that the prosecution may use deposition testimony in proving a non-capital offense which is tried with a capital offense. The Court held this provision was not inconsistent with Article 49 of the Code.[129]

Testimony taken by deposition may be introduced by the defense in

[122] Art. 49 (f). The proper manner to direct that a case be treated as non-capital is to include an indorsement to that effect in the charge sheet. But this can be accomplished in other ways. For instance, in United States v. Anderten, 4 USCMA 354, 15 CMR 354 (1954) the Court approved a direction that a case be treated as non-capital when it appeared in the form of written approval by the convening authority of a recommendation by the staff judge advocate that the case be treated as non-capital. This approved recommendation was a part of the record in the case.

[123] Manual for Courts-Martial, United States, 1951, par. 145*a*.

[124] United States v. Aldridge, 4 USCMA 107, 15 CMR 107 (1954).

[125] United States v. Young, 2 USCMA 470, 9 CMR 100 (1953).

[126] *Ibid.; accord,* United States v. Horner, 2 USCMA 478, 9 CMR 108 (1953).

[127] United States v. Aldridge, 4 USCMA 107, 15 CMR 107 (1954).

[128] Par. 145*a*. If the non-capital offense is relevant to the capital offense the law officer must give appropriate instructions to the court-martial regarding the extent to which the deposition properly can be considered.

[129] United States v. Gann, 3 USCMA 12, 11 CMR 12 (1953).

capital cases if otherwise admissible.[130] Admissibility of evidence contained in a deposition is governed by the same rules which apply to other evidence produced at the trial.[131]

Depositions may be taken on oral examination or upon written interrogatories. In *Sutton*[132] the accused was tried in California. The prosecution introduced in evidence a deposition taken in Korea by written interrogatories. Counsel for the accused had been given an opportunity, but declined, to prepare cross-interrogatories before the deposition was taken. A board of review set aside the finding of guilty on the ground that the accused had been denied his right of confrontation because he was not present at the taking of the deposition used against him. Thus the Court was presented a difficult question. Had Congress authorized the use of depositions on written interrogatories in the absence of the accused at the taking thereof? The majority were certain that Congress had no intention of limiting the use of depositions to cases in which an accused could be present at the time of its taking. And further, they considered that it was implicit in the specific provision for written depositions that it is contemplated that an accused will not be present. Judge Quinn dissented. He did not read Article 49 as doing more than authorizing the use of depositions by the Government. But more significantly he stated:

> "I have absolutely no doubt in my mind that accused persons in the military service of the Nation are entitled to the rights and privileges secured to all under the Constitution of the United States, unless excluded directly or by necessary implication, by the provisions of the Constitution itself. . . . On that basis, I cannot agree with the majority opinion which lightly deprives the accused in this case of a basic constitutional privilege."[133]

This dissent provides the first outright indication by any of the judges that he would go beyond interpreting an act of Congress and undertake to determine whether Congress had exceeded its powers in enacting a provision of the Code.

[130] Manual for Courts-Martial, United States, 1951, par. 145*a*.
[131] United States v. Bryson, 3 USCMA 329, 12 CMR 85 (1953).
[132] 3 USCMA 220, 11 CMR 220 (1953), 22 Geo. Wash. L. Rev. 502 (1954).
[133] *Id.* at 228. On this same page Judge Quinn further stated:
"Under the express exception, set out in the Fifth Amendment, an accused in the armed forces may be held to answer for a capital, or otherwise infamous crime, without presentment or indictment of a grand jury . . . To this express exception may be added the implied limitation of the right of trial by jury, as protected by the Sixth Amendment, to the extent that a jury trial is required only where presentment or indictment is necessary . . . No other recognized exceptions have been cited and I know of none."

It is not necessary that the officer representing the accused at the taking of the deposition also represent him at trial.[134]

The prosecution cannot introduce depositions in evidence except in case of death, sickness and other situations specifically authorized by the Code. A deposition taken in contemplation that the witness would not be present at the trial is not admissible if the witness is present. This is true even though the witness was not co-operative on the stand and the law officer found it necessary to hold her in contempt. The admission of the deposition was found prejudicial because it contained damaging evidence against the accused in a bitterly contested case.[135]

J. *Former Testimony*

The *Manual*[136] provides that testimony given by a witness at a former trial, "in which the issues were substantially the same," with some exceptions, may be read in evidence if the witness is not available to give oral testimony. Neither the *Manual* nor the Code[137] makes any specific reference to the use of reported testimony secured in the course of a pretrial investigation. The Court held[138] if the testimony at the pretrial examination had been subject to cross-examination and the issues were substantially the same as those in the trial the tests for trustworthiness were met and the reported testimony therefore was admissible.

Somewhat related to the subject of former testimony is whether testimony at a hearing before a board of inquiry may be used in a subsequent court-martial trial. The Court dealt with this question to the extent that it involves testimony given by the accused. If he is warned of his rights and then voluntarily testifies before a board of inquiry, his statements may be introduced in evidence in a subsequent trial by court-martial.[139]

K. *Memoranda*

The *Manual*[140] provides that if a witness does not remember the facts or events but relies on a memorandum "exclusively" it may be admitted in evidence if it can further be shown that the memorandum was ac-

[134] United States v. Sutton, 3 USCMA 220, 11 CMR 220 (1953). See MANUAL FOR COURTS-MARTIAL, UNITED STATES, 1951, par. 117. The officer representing the accused does not have to be a lawyer unless the officer representing the prosecution is so qualified.

[135] United States v. Barcomb, 2 USCMA 92, 6 CMR 92 (1952).

[136] Par. 145*b*.

[137] CODE, Art. 50 (a) (courts of inquiry).

[138] United States v. Eggers, 3 USCMA 191, 11 CMR 191 (1953).

[139] United States v. Sippel, 4 USCMA 50, 15 CMR 50 (1954).

[140] Par. 146.

curate and correct in stating the knowledge of the witness. The Court rejected[141] an argument that the witness must have forgotten all of the facts contained in the memorandum before it could be introduced in evidence. The rule is not so limited. Instead the memorandum may be received in evidence if the witness is unable to recall all of the material facts provided, of course, other requirements are met including a showing that the memorandum was made when the facts were fresh in the memory of the witness. In this regard, a statement made a few hours after the occurrence of an alleged murder is sufficient.[142]

L. *Mechanical Recordings*

The Court has announced that the exigencies of the service imperatively require extensive resort to recordings of interviews held in the field, and to subsequent typewritten transcriptions made by or under the supervision of the interviewing officers. A mechanical recording or a transcript thereof may be introduced in evidence if identified positively by one informationally equipped to do so.[143]

VI. Witnesses

A. *Competency*

The determination of a child's competency to testify is within the discretion of the law officer. The weight to be given such testimony is for the court-martial.[144]

In *Slozes*[145] a thirteen year old Korean girl upon being questioned about her religion replied, "I have no religion." She was apparently required to take an oath rather than an affirmation. The Court took the view that the purpose of the oath was primarily a solemn reminder to the witness of a special obligation to tell the truth and concluded that the oath administered was sufficient to include the required affirmation. In respect to the competency of children as witnesses the Court stated that the true test was intelligence and not age. The determination of competency is for the trial court and such finding will not

[141] United States v. Day, 2 USCMA 416, 9 CMR 46 (1954). The Court was dealing with par. 132 of the 1949 *Manual* but there is no significant difference in that provision and paragraph 146 of the Manual for Courts-Martial, United States, 1951. Legal and Legislative Basis Manual for Courts-Martial, United States, 1951, p. 233.

[142] United States v. Day, 2 USCMA 416, 9 CMR 46 (1953).

[143] United States v. Jewson, 1 USCMA 652, 5 CMR 80 (1952).

[144] United States v. Hunter, 2 USCMA 37, 6 CMR 37 (1952); United States v. Marshall, 2 USCMA 54, 6 CMR 54 (1952).

[145] 1 USCMA 47, 1 CMR 47 (1951). Although the Court was not "entirely satisfied" with the manner in which the court-martial dealt with the questions of competency and qualifications, it finally concluded that the record sufficiently revealed the witness had an appreciation of the moral responsibility to speak the truth.

be disturbed on review unless it clearly appears that there was an abuse of discretion or that the action was based on a mistake of law.

B. *Hostile Witness*

If a witness appears to be hostile to the party calling him, or is manifestly unwilling to give evidence, the law officer may be justified in granting permission to treat him as a hostile witness.[146] This would permit the use of leading questions[147] and impeachment[148] of the witness.

VII. Self-Incrimination

Article 31 (a) of the Code provides that no person subject to the Code shall compel any person to incriminate himself or to answer any question the answer to which may tend to incriminate him. The privilege is not limited to a person on trial but extends to any person who may be called as a witness. Unlike Article 31 (b), this subsection is not confined to oral or written statements of the accused. The Court observed that Congress intended in Article 31 (a) to secure to persons subject to the Code the same rights against compulsion as secured to those of the civilian community under the Fifth Amendment.[149]

Paragraph 150*b* of the *Manual* limits the prohibition of Article 31 (a) to compulsion in obtaining verbal or other communications in which an individual expresses his knowledge of the matter.[150] To require a person to place his foot in tracks, submit to fingerprinting, give a sample of handwriting and to utter words for the purpose of voice identification are not, according to the *Manual,* in violation of Article 31 (a). However, the Court has disapproved some of the *Manual* provisions because they do, in fact, conflict with Article 31 (a). Thus requiring a person to print the alphabet,[151] give a sample of his handwriting[152] and read for voice[153] identification violate the prohibition against self-incrimination. It makes no difference whether the compulsion occurred before[154] or during[155] trial. In regard to handwriting the Court stated:

[146] United States v. Armstrong, 4 USCMA 248, 15 CMR 248 (1954).
[147] Manual for Courts-Martial, United States, 1951, par. 149*c*.
[148] *Ibid.,* par. 153*b*.
[149] United States v. Eggers, 3 USCMA 191, 11 CMR 191 (1953); United States v. Rosato, 3 USCMA 143, 11 CMR 143 (1953).
[150] In United States v. Dupree, 1 USCMA 665, 5 CMR 93 (1952) the Court apparently agreed with the view expressed in par. 150*b* of the Manual for Courts-Martial, United States, 1951.
[151] United States v. Rosato, 3 USCMA 143, 11 CMR 143 (1953).
[152] United States v. Eggers, 3 USCMA 191, 11 CMR 191 (1953), 7 Vand. L. Rev. 147.
[153] United States v. Greer, 3 USCMA 576, 13 CMR 132 (1953).
[154] United States v. Eggers, 3 USCMA 191, 11 CMR 191 (1953).
[155] United States v. Greer, 3 USCMA 576, 13 CMR 132 (1953).

> "The compulsory production of a handwriting specimen goes far beyond taking of a fingerprint, placing a foot in a track, an examination for scars, forcibly shaving a man or trimming his hair, requiring him to grow a beard, or try on a garment. Such instances do not involve an affirmative conscious act on the part of the individual affected by the demand. Whereas the printing of the alphabet involves a conscious exercise of both mind and body, an affirmative action."[156]

The test applied is whether the compulsion calls only for "passive cooperation" or goes so far as to require "affirmative conduct."[157]

Extraction of body fluids does not require affirmative conduct on the part of the accused. Thus the Court held that taking urine from an accused by proper use of a catheter while the accused was unconscious did not violate the privilege.[158] An analysis of the urine was admitted in evidence to show the presence of morphine. Further, such evidence was held admissible in a case in which the accused cooperated in securing urine by the same method.[159] The Court made it clear that it was not dealing with a situation in which the urine was obtained by force and violence or brutal methods or where proper medical safeguards were not provided.

The most obvious violation of the right against self-incrimination to come before the Court occurred in *Welch.*[160] In that case a lieutenant was suspected of cheating on an examination because his paper indicated that he had access to the official answer sheet. A lieutenant-colonel was appointed to make an official investigation. He proceeded to place the lieutenant under oath and, without informing him of the possible charges and the nature of the investigation, inquired whether he understood his rights under Article of War 24 (now Article 31). The lieutenant replied: "Yes, sir. Anything you ask me I am supposed to tell you the truth." The investigating officer did not explain to the suspect either his right to remain silent or his right to refuse to answer questions which might tend to incriminate him. Instead the lieutenant was questioned, accused of lying and, in effect, was in-

[156] United States v. Rosato, 3 USCMA 143, 146, 11 CMR 143, 146 (1953).
[157] United States v. Eggers, 3 USCMA 191, 11 CMR 191 (1953).
[158] United States v. Williamson, 4 USCMA 320, 15 CMR 320 (1954).
[159] United States v. Booker, 4 USCMA 335, 15 CMR 335 (1954).
[160] 1 USCMA 402, 3 CMR 136 (1952). The Court could have reached the same result by applying the general prejudice rule because the record showed the accused was not warned of his rights. United States v. Wilson, 2 USCMA 248, 8 CMR 48 (1953) (discussed in Section V A (1) *supra*). Another possible course would have been to exclude the statement because it was not voluntarily given. MANUAL FOR COURTS-MARTIAL, UNITED STATES, 1951, par. 140*a*.

formed that he was unworthy of being an officer. Finally, he admitted he had cheated.

This testimony was received in evidence notwithstanding an objection made by the defense counsel. The Court chose to dispose of this case on the ground that the conduct of the investigating officer had deprived the accused of his right against self-incrimination.[161] This investigation, although not made pursuant to Article 32, was nevertheless an official one. The lieutenant did not claim the privilege but the Court found compulsion inasmuch as the investigating officer was in a position to initiate disciplinary proceedings against the lieutenant. The Court described the investigation in the following manner:

> "At the outset of the investigation, the officer conducting it did not fully advise petitioner of his rights under Article of War 24, *supra*. This was a clear violation of that Article. Nor did he advise petitioner of the nature of the investigation or of the charges against him. This officer then conducted a searching and inquisitorial examination, utilizing all the devices of an expert prosecutor cross-examining a hostile witness, accompanied by shouting, accusations of falsehood, reprimands, and castigations of character. All these factors inevitably lead to the conclusion that petitioner was, in effect, compelled to incriminate himself. This smacks too much of Star Chamber proceedings. Petitioner did not have a free choice to admit or deny his guilt or to refuse to answer the questions asked."[162]

As foreshadowed in *Clay*[163] the Court invoked military due process and reversed. And, according to the Court, it did not matter that there was other evidence of guilt.

The Court usually regards violations of the privilege against self-incrimination as so serious in nature that it will not affirm a finding of guilt tainted therewith. But the accused's own conduct may operate to alter the attitude of the Court toward the protection of this right.[164] Thus the Court may refrain from applying the concept of military due process where there was a violation of the right against self-incrimination in a case in which the accused voluntarily confessed.[165] This

[161] United States v. Wilson and Harvey, 2 USCMA 248, 8 CMR 48 (1953). See section V A *supra* on Confessions and Admissions.

[162] United States v. Welch, 1 USCMA 402, 407-408, 3 CMR 136, 141-142 (1952).

[163] 1 USCMA 74, 1 CMR 74 (1951).

[164] United States v. Morris, 4 USCMA 209, 15 CMR 209 (1954). The Court referred to United States v. Lucas, 1 USCMA 19, 1 CMR 19 (1951) and United States v. McElroy, 3 USCMA 606, 14 CMR 24 (1954) (concurring opinion) as supporting this concept.

[165] *Ibid.*

departure from the usual rule was made easier for the Court because the confession provided essentially the same evidence obtained by securing samples of handwriting by illegal means. And further, it was apparent to the Court that the violation was not an intentional disregard of the rights of the accused.

The Court considered several cases involving questions of self-incrimination in which it was reasonably clear that there was no intention to deprive the accused of his rights. In *Collier*[166] the law officer, while performing his duty of determining whether the accused understood a stipulation offered in evidence, phrased some of his questions so that the accused, in effect, orally admitted that he did not voluntarily return to the service. A majority of the Court conceded that the law officer used an "ill chosen" phrase when he asked the accused if the contents of the stipulation were true. However, it was concluded that the privilege had not been violated.

In *Hatchett,*[167] a later case, the accused took the stand for the limited purpose of giving evidence on the question of the voluntariness of a confession. The law officer asked the accused several questions which a board of review concluded violated the accused's right against self-incrimination. The Court was not at all sure that the questions went beyond the possible bounds of inquiry even though the accused had taken the stand for a limited purpose. However, it was held that if error had been committed, the accused waived his rights when he subsequently took the stand and voluntarily testified as to the same matters involved in the earlier questioning. The Court made it clear that it was adopting the waiver rule announced by Judge Brosman in his concurring opinion in *Collier.*

A question, carelessly phrased by the law officer, deprived the accused in *Phillips*[168] of his right against self-incrimination. A knife, supposedly used in the alleged assault, was received in evidence over defense counsel's objection that the chain of custody had not been established. The trial counsel undertook to describe the knife for the record. The law officer then made the following statement to the accused:

[166] 1 USCMA 575, 5 CMR 3 (1952).

[167] 2 USCMA 482, 9 CMR 112 (1953). In United States v. Jackson, 3 USCMA 646, 14 CMR 64 (1954) the accused took the stand for the limited purpose of supporting his contention that his confession was involuntary. A member of the court-martial asked the accused if the shoes taken from him were those exhibited to the court-martial. The Court was not certain the question was incriminating under the circumstances but, if so, the law officer repaired any possible damage by instructing the court-martial to disregard the question and the answer.

[168] 2 USCMA 534, 10 CMR 32 (1953).

Law Officer: "Phillips, is that satisfactory to you? Does that describe *your* knife all right?"
Accused: "Yes, sir."
Law Officer: "Any objection by the defense counsel?"
Defense: "No objection."

The Court, although somewhat puzzled at the statement of defense counsel, held that it did not constitute a waiver. The decision of the board of review to reverse was affirmed.

VIII. Search and Seizure

The subject of search and seizure is not dealt with in the Code but the *Manual*[169] lists examples of searches which are considered lawful for the purpose of admitting the evidence thereby obtained. Specifically mentioned are searches authorized or directed by a commanding officer, searches pursuant to a lawful apprehension, searches required to prevent removal of criminal goods, those made in accordance with military custom, and those made with consent or with a warrant. Evidence is inadmissible if it was obtained as a result of an unlawful search conducted or instigated by persons acting under the authority of the United States.[170] Likewise, all evidence obtained through information supplied by such illegally obtained evidence is inadmissible.[171] The Court has stated that the military rule is "nothing more nor less than an evidentiary rule of exclusion."[172] In applying the rule the fundamental inquiry is whether the search is unreasonable, and, if so, it is unlawful.[173] Although the military rule carries out the policy of the Fourth Amendment, it is not commanded by that Amendment; therefore, the accused is required to raise the issue of unlawful search and seizure in the trial court.[174] Only in extreme circumstances will

[169] Par. 152. Note, 101 U. of Pa. L. Rev. 851 (1953); JAG Journal (July-August, 1953), p. 3.

[170] Par. 152 of the Manual for Courts-Martial, United States, 1951, further provides: ". . . or if it was obtained under such circumstances that the provisions of Section 605 of the Communications Act of 1934 . . . pertaining to the unauthorized divulgence of communications by wire or radio, would prohibit its use against the accused were he being tried in a United States district court."

[171] Compare with Manual for Courts-Martial, United States, 1951, par. 140*a* where it is provided: "Although a confession or admission may be inadmissible because it was not voluntarily made, nevertheless, the circumstance that it furnished information which led to the discovery of pertinent facts will not be a reason for excluding evidence of such pertinent facts."

[172] United States v. Dupree, 1 USCMA 665, 668, 5 CMR 93, 96 (1952).

[173] United States v. Doyle, 1 USCMA 545, 4 CMR 137 (1952). See also United States v. Marrelli, 4 USCMA 276, 15 CMR 276 (1954) (documents in possession of civilian attorney).

[174] United States v. Dupree, 1 USCMA 665, 5 CMR 93 (1952). The Court in referring to the federal civilian rule states: "Although it was derived originally

the Court consider a question of search and seizure if it is raised for the first time subsequent to trial. Since the purpose of the rule is to protect an individual's right to privacy in his personal property and effects, it has no relation to the trustworthiness of the evidence.

A. *Powers of the commanding officer*

There has long existed in the services a rule to the effect that a military commander has the power to search military property within his jurisdiction.[175] This power may be delegated[176] but it is not clear that it automatically devolves on a subordinate during a momentary absence of the commanding officer.[177] The Court has observed that the power of a commanding officer to search has been stated broadly by some boards of review.

> "Authority to make, or order, an inspection, or search of a member of the military establishment, or of a public building *in a place under military control,* even though occupied as an office or living quarters by a member of the military establishment, always has been regarded as indispensable to the maintenance of good order and discipline in any military command . . . such a search is not unreasonable and therefore not unlawful."[178]

The Court appears to have recognized the need for the exercise of extensive powers of search and seizure by a commanding officer. However, it has warned that there may be some limitations[179] inasmuch as the Court desires, wherever possible, to carry out the congressional intent to grant to military personnel the same rights and privileges accorded civilians.[180]

---

from the Fourth Amendment, it appears today that it is a rule of evidence, based primarily on the desirability of providing a means for enforcing the protections afforded by the Amendment." *Cf.* United States v. Swanson, 3 USCMA 671, 14 CMR 89 (1954) and United States v. Rhodes, 3 USCMA 73, 11 CMR 73 (1953). The Court stated in the latter case that it need not decide if the Fourth Amendment applied with full force and effect to the military establishment.

[175] United States v. Doyle, 1 USCMA 545, 4 CMR 137 (1952); United States v. Florence, 1 USCMA 620, 5 CMR 48 (1952).

[176] United States v. Doyle, 1 USCMA 545, 4 CMR 137 (1952).

[177] United States v. Swanson, 3 USCMA 671, 14 CMR 89 (1954).

[178] United States v. Wilson, CM 248379, 31 BR 231 (quoted by the Court in United States v. Florence, 1 USCMA 620, 622, 5 CMR 48, 50 (1952)).

[179] United States v. Doyle, 1 USCMA 545, 4 CMR 137 (1952).

[180] United States v. Florence, 1 USCMA 620, 5 CMR 48 (1952). In this case the Court stated that the MANUAL FOR COURTS-MARTIAL, UNITED STATES, 1951, may be the foundation for curtailing the power of commanding officers in searches and seizures. Par. 152 provides: "A search of property which is owned or controlled by the United States and is under the control of an armed force, or of property which is located within a military installation or in a foreign country or in occupied territory and is owned, used, or occupied by persons subject to military law or to the law of war, which search has been authorized by a commanding officer (including an officer in charge) having jurisdiction over the place where the property is situated or, if the property is in a foreign country

In *Doyle*[181] the master-at-arms, after receiving a report from a member of the unit that his shoes were missing and that he had seen them in the locker of the accused, made a search and found the shoes in the locker. The Court approved this search. The master-at-arms was supposed to protect government property and he acted after having had reasonable and probable cause to believe that an offense had been committed by the accused. The Court found it unnecessary to determine whether the master-at-arms possessed the inherent search powers of a commanding officer but indicated it doubted the propriety, in the absence of express authorization, of allowing such a person to make general exploratory searches without a showing of good cause.

Subsequently, the Court approved[182] a search of an officer's military desk by his superior. The search was made after Criminal Investigation Division agents had warned the superior officer that the accused was engaged in illegal practices and that a diary in his desk contained information of his misconduct. The superior officer (not a commanding officer) made photostatic copies of the diary before it was returned to the desk. The Court observed that the search was not general or exploratory but instead was narrowly restricted in scope, purpose and physical area. The Court stated that this decision was not to be understood as "laying down the broad rule that any military person possesses inherent authority to search the effects of another who is his subordinate in rank or grade."[183]

B. *Search incidental to lawful apprehension*

The *Manual* provides for a search of an individual's person, of the clothing he is wearing, and of the property in his immediate possession or control when the search is conducted as an incident of lawfully *apprehending*[184] him. In *Florence*[185] a company commander had information which gave him reason to believe that a member of his command had committed an offense. He sent for the suspect and on arrival asked him to produce his wallet. The wallet was produced and it contained some of the stolen military payment certificates. The Court concluded that the search was permissible because it was made as an incident to a lawful arrest.[186] It then made the following statement concerning the status of the accused:

---

or in occupied territory, over personnel subject to military law or to the law of war in the place where the property is situated" is lawful.

[181] 1 USCMA 545, 4 CMR 137 (1952).

[182] United States v. Rhodes, 3 USCMA 73, 11 CMR 73 (1953).

[183] United States v. Rhodes, 3 USCMA 73, 75, 11 CMR 73, 75 (1953).

[184] Par. 152.

[185] 1 USCMA 620, 5 CMR 48 (1952).

[186] The Court apparently finds it unnecessary to distinguish apprehension and arrest in this setting.

> "Under military procedure arrest may be the final step in a series of disassociated acts from receipt of information of a supposed offense to confinement, or it may be the end of a sequence of events so closely interrelated that it is impossible to fix the point of actual deprivation of liberty. In this case it appears the latter situation existed and that the initiatory step in the arrest was the order directing the accused to report."[187]

Since the order directing the accused to report was made on reasonable belief that an offense had been committed by him, it was made on probable cause and the search was reasonable under these circumstances.

C. *Search to prevent removal of criminal goods*

The Court has approved an "exploratory search" on the theory it was made to prevent the removal of criminal goods. In *Swanson*[188] the field first sergeant, during the absence of his superiors, called a formation after he was informed that a wallet had been stolen. He announced at the formation that if the person responsible for the theft would throw the money to the ground as the group dispersed the matter would not be pursued further. This procedure was unsuccessful. An immediate inspection of the men revealed the stolen money in the helmet liner of the accused. The Court in approving the search stated:

> "In the instant case, money had in fact been stolen from a member of an organization in bivouac. No other organization was in the area. Therefore, an inference that the theft was committed by some member of that organization was clear. An opportunity to return the money without detection and with complete impunity was offered and refused. The thief was then aware that further action to discover the fruits of the crime would probably follow. Concealing his connection with the offense was his primary objective, and this could be accomplished only by concealing the money. Delay afforded him greater opportunity to effectuate his purpose, and necessarily worked to the disadvantage of the victim, as well as to the prejudice of discipline. If successful action was to be taken at all, it had to be taken immediately."[189]

D. *Search with consent*

A search made with the consent of the person whose property is searched is not unlawful.[190] However, mere acquiescence, by peace-

[187] United States v. Florence, 1 USCMA 620, 625, 5 CMR 48, 53 (1953).
[188] 3 USCMA 671, 14 CMR 89 (1954).
[189] *Id.* at 673, 14 CMR at 91.
[190] United States v. Marrelli, 4 USCMA 276, 15 CMR 276 (1954).

fully submitting to the demands of a person acting under color of office does not make an otherwise illegal search a lawful one. The Court disagreed with a board of review and held[191] the testimony of a Criminal Investigation Division agent was sufficient to permit a finding that the accused consented. The agent stated that he "requested" the accused to permit a search of his person and premises. This "request" was made in the presence of the first sergeant. The accused took him to his room for the purpose of permitting the search. And some of the missing money was found in the possession of the accused. The Court was somewhat concerned because the agent's testimony revealed that he was unable to recall exactly how the accused expressed his consent; nevertheless, it concluded that it could not hold, as a matter of law, that the evidence was insufficient to support a finding of consent.

E. *Other items*

The Court adopted[192] the rule of *Harris v. United States,*[193] which permits officers who are making a lawful search to seize items readily apparent, even though the original purpose of the search did not relate to those items.

Although the Court will continue to determine the legality of searches and seizures on the basis of the facts in each case, it is apparent from the foregoing decisions that it will not unduly restrict searches in the armed forces.

IX. Credibility of Witnesses

The *Manual* provides:

> "If a witness testifies as to the identity of the *accused* as the person who committed, or did not commit, the offense in question, such testimony may be corroborated, even though the credibility of the witness has not been directly attacked, by showing that the witness made a similar identification with respect to the *accused* on a previous occasion. In such a case the identifying witness himself and any person who has observed the previous identification may testify concerning it."[194] (Emphasis supplied.)

The Court held[195] that although the quoted paragraph speaks in terms of identification of one accused of crime that it was not so confined.

[191] United States v. Wilcher, 4 USCMA 215, 15 CMR 215 (1954).
[192] United States v. Doyle, 1 USCMA 545, 4 CMR 137 (1952).
[193] 331 U. S. 145 (1947).
[194] Par. 153*a*.
[195] United States v. Tobita, 3 USCMA 267, 12 CMR 23 (1953); United States v. Parker, 3 USCMA 272, 12 CMR 28 (1953).

Instead it extends to any other person whose identity might become important in a case.

Thus it was held proper for a prosecution witness immediately prior to identifying the complaining witness to testify that two days earlier he had identified the same person as the complaining witness.

X. Ignorance of Fact

Paragraph 154*a* (3) of the *Manual* provides:

> "Unless otherwise provided (expressly or by implication) by the law denouncing the offense in question, ignorance or mistake of fact will exempt a person from criminal responsibility if it is an honest ignorance or mistake and not the result of carelessness or fault on his part."

The Court has condemned[196] an instruction based on this paragraph in "possession" cases (for example, wrongful possession of marijuana) because it permits a court-martial to base a finding of knowledge on a lack of due care on the part of the accused. The Court has expressed doubt regarding the use of this *Manual* provision in some other situations but has not found it necessary further to express its views.[197]

XI. Stipulations

Stipulations frequently serve to avoid delay and expense in the trial, as they are accepted substitutes for other competent sources of proof or the direct testimony of witnesses.[198] They are especially useful in proving the fact of apprehension as the means whereby an unauthorized absence was terminated.[199] Some stipulations prepared for this purpose have been rejected because they did not contain sufficient information to prove the accused was actually apprehended.[200] For example, a stipulation that a certain chief of police would testify in substance as follows: "I know the accused in this case. I apprehended the accused at 1130 hours, 22 September 1953, at Fayette, Missouri" is insufficient to show apprehension.[201] The accused might have been freed by the civilian authorities and thereafter surrendered himself to the military.

[196] United States v. Lampkins, 4 USCMA 31, 15 CMR 31 (1954).

[197] *Ibid.*, United States v. Perruccio, 4 USCMA 28, 15 CMR 28 (1954) (negligent homicide). See also United States v. Furney, 2 USCMA 270, 8 CMR 70 (1953). The law officer was not required to instruct on mistake of fact.

[198] Manual for Courts-Martial, United States, 1951, par. 154*b*.

[199] United States v. White, 3 USCMA 666, 14 CMR 84 (1954).

[200] United States v. Nickaboine, 3 USCMA 152, 11 CMR 152 (1953); United States v. Beninate, 4 USCMA 98, 15 CMR 98 (1954); United States v. Salter, 4 USCMA 338, 15 CMR 338 (1954).

[201] United States v. Cowans, 4 USCMA 308, 15 CMR 308 (1954).

In a rehearing it is often necessary to rely on the testimony of witnesses given at the previous trial. Better procedure is for counsel to stipulate to the authenticity of the original, or a copy, of the record of the former trial, and to have it formally received in evidence before reading it to the members of the court-martial.[202] However, the Court has approved[203] a less formal procedure in which the former testimony is read into the record without actually introducing the original or a copy in evidence.

It is not essential that the accused be made to stand up in open court and give his express, personal assent before a stipulation can be accepted by a court-martial.[204] This is true notwithstanding language which appears to the contrary in Appendix 8*a* of the *Manual.* An accused is bound by the stipulations entered into by his counsel.[205] But better practice requires the law officer to assure himself that the accused joined in the stipulation.

XII. Res ipsa Loquitur

The Court rejected the use of res ipsa loquitur in a case involving a charge of damaging a government vehicle through neglect because it thought too many possible explanations for the damage were available. The Court made the following statement about res ipsa loquitur:

> "Although we tend to question the availability of the doctrine of *res ipsa loquitur* for use as a crutch to courts-martial trial counsel, the present problem does not require that the matter be dealt with as to all cases—and we seek to supply no definitive answer."[206]

[202] United States v. Cambridge, 3 USCMA 377, 12 CMR 133 (1953).

[203] United States v. Niolu, 4 USCMA 18, 15 CMR 18 (1954); United States v. Cambridge, 3 USCMA 377, 12 CMR 133 (1953).

[204] United States v. Cambridge, 3 USCMA 377, 12 CMR 133 (1953).

[205] *Ibid.*

[206] United States v. Ryan, 3 USCMA 735, 738, 14 CMR 153, 156 (1954). See also Manual for Courts-Martial, United States, 1951, par. 187*b*.

CHAPTER 14

Punitive Articles

Punitive Articles

The offenses under the Code appear in fifty-eight punitive articles. The Court has considered a substantial number of these articles and the interpretations given them provide the subject-matter for this chapter. All persons concerned with military justice consider the meaning given the language of these substantive offenses of great importance. This is especially true of law officers inasmuch as they must in some cases, and should in all, take cognizance of the opinions of the Court in preparing instructions on the principal offense charged and on any appropriate lesser* included offenses.

Article 77—*Principals*

This Article provides that a principal is one who commits an offense, or aids, abets, counsels, commands or procures its commission. This statutory definition, in effect, incorporates into one Article the common law concepts of principals, aiders and abettors and accessories before the fact.

In *Wooten*[1] the accused was not present at the time the larceny and subsequent sale of Government property occurred. However, by words and conduct he had brought together two other individuals with a view to promoting or instigating the commission of larceny. And he demanded a specified sum of money—presumably a share of the fruits of the wrongdoing. The Court held that the evidence was sufficient to permit the triers of fact reasonably to infer that the accused incited or promoted the performance of criminal acts by his partners and that he had such a stake in the outcome that he would have been an accessory before the fact at common law and hence a principal under the Code.

* See Chapter 7 for law officer's instructions on lesser included offenses.

[1] 1 USCMA 358, 3 CMR 92 (1952). The provision in the 1949 *Manual* was substantially unchanged in the 1951 *Manual*.

Mere presence at the scene of an offense is not enough to constitute one an aider or abettor. The accused must associate himself with the venture. In this connection the Court stated:

> "The standard of relationship to the offense by which conviction as an aider and abettor must be measured, therefore, lies somewhat between proof of participation as a paramount agent, on the one hand, and speculative inference based on mere presence at the scene of the crime, on the other, and is made definite by the requirement of evidence of specific intent."[2]

In *Jacobs*[3] the accused accompanied others in breaking and entering a Japanese home and he participated in an assault which immediately preceded the robbery. The act of participating in the assault was, according to the Court, sufficient to associate the accused with the venture even though personally he may not have committed the robbery. Further, it was concluded that the act of housebreaking was sufficient to justify the court-martial in reaching a conclusion that the accused and his associates *intended* to commit the act of robbery. The accused was, therefore, an aider and abettor to the robbery offense and guilty as a principal under Article 77.

Article 78—*Accessory after the fact*

The Court has recognized that the general rule is that the offense of an accessory after the fact is a crime separate from that of the substantive offense.[4] Consequently, in cases other than those in which the substantive offense and the action of the accessory after the fact constitutes a single continuous criminal transaction[5] (for instance, to agree as part of a conspiracy to be an accessory after the fact), the law officer may correctly instruct that being an accessory after the fact is not a lesser included offense of the substantive offense charged. If an accused is charged with a substantive offense, and it develops that his activities were those of an accessory after the fact, proper procedure should require an amendment in the charges and specifications.

Article 80—*Attempts*

In a charge of wrongful attempt to introduce marihuana into a certain station for sale, the Court found it unnecessary to discuss what

[2] United States v. Jacobs, 1 USCMA 209, 211, 2 CMR 115, 117 (1952). No substantial change in this provision was made in the 1951 *Manual*.

[3] 1 USCMA 209, 2 CMR 115 (1952).

[4] United States v. London, 4 USCMA 90, 15 CMR 90 (1954).

[5] *Ibid.* The Court stated: "Under certain conditions, the acts of a principal to a substantive offense and those of an accessory after the fact may properly be charged as a single continuous criminal transaction. See Skelly v. United States, 76 F. 2d 483 (CA 10 Cir. 1935), cert. den. 295 U. S. 757, 79 L. ed. 1699, 55 S. Ct. 914."

is required to constitute an overt act because the evidence was sufficient to show that the accused actually introduced it into the station.[6]

Article 81—*Conspiracy*

The Court approved the *Manual*[7] provision which states that an accused properly may be convicted of both a conspiracy to commit an offense and the substantive offense itself. This is true even when the overt act alleged in support of the conspiracy charge consists of the commission of the offense. Thus, it is proper to convict an accused of conspiring with another to malinger by inflicting self-injury, and with malingering by shooting himself in the finger with a carbine. The Court recognized the rule that a charge of conspiracy will not lie where the substantive offense itself involves concert of action such as dueling, adultery, bribery and bigamy, but found it inapplicable when the substantive offense (shooting himself) did not require concert of action.[8]

Article 85—*Desertion*

The existence or non-existence of a state of hostilities is not a necessary element in the offense of desertion and need not be alleged.[9]

As stated in Chapter 11, three of the several and distinct ways in which the offense of desertion might be committed are:[10]

(1) absence without leave with *intent* to desert the military service,

(2) absence without leave with an *intent* to avoid hazardous duty, and

(3) absence without leave with an *intent* to shirk important service.

Although each is based on a different mental attitude, a board of review held[11] that a specification which alleged that the accused "deserted the service and remained absent in desertion until apprehended" permitted a court-martial to return a verdict of guilty of any of the three types of desertion proved by the facts. The Court rejected[12] this view, and

[6] United States v. Jones, 2 USCMA 80, 6 CMR 80 (1952).

[7] Par. 160; United States v. Yarborough, 1 USCMA 678, 5 CMR 106 (1952).

[8] *Ibid.* Presumably this rule would not apply if A and B conspired to bribe C insofar as A and B are concerned.

[9] United States v. Brooks, 1 USCMA 88, 1 CMR 88 (1951) (AW 58).

[10] Others are listed in Art. 85. The Court has not decided whether desertion is one offense which may be committed in several different ways or several offenses. United States v. Redenius, 4 USCMA 161, 15 CMR 161 (1954) (multiplicity of charges). However, in cases involving law officers' instructions the Court refers to separate offenses and in this setting treats them as such.

[11] United States v. Hemp, 1 USCMA 280, 3 CMR 14 (1952) (citing specifically CM 245568, United States v. Clancy, 29 BR 215).

[12] *Ibid.*

stated that it was better practice to place the burden on the prosecution to allege specifically the type of mental attitude to be used as a basis for a finding of guilt rather than to require the accused to meet any or all of the three mental attitudes embraced by a specification alleging general intent. Therefore, according to the Court, a specification which alleges that "the accused deserted the service and remained absent in desertion until apprehended" is not a general allegation. It will be construed to allege only (1) *supra,* i.e., absence without leave with intent to desert the military service.

In addition to requiring the prosecution to allege specifically the type of intent it will try to prove, the Court decided it was error for the law officer to instruct that the elements of proof include an intent other than the one alleged.[13] Proper procedure requires that the instruction be "tailored" to fit the intent charged.

The Court, after finding error, is still concerned whether it is prejudicial. To decide this question it must analyze the facts of each case to determine if it was probable that reasonable men might be led to render a finding on an element of intent not framed by the specification. If so, the instruction constitutes error which is materially prejudicial to the substantial rights of the accused and, therefore, reversible error. The manner in which the Court has determined this question of prejudice may be understood more clearly by considering one case in which the Court found prejudice and another in which it did not.

In *Hemp*[14] the specification under which the accused was tried follows:

> "In that [accused] did, while enroute [*sic*] from Westover Air Force Base, Massachusetts, to McAndrew Air Force Base, Newfoundland, on or about 19 October 1950, desert the service of the United States, and did remain absent in desertion until he was apprehended at Springfield, Massachusetts, on or about 2 June 1951."

As previously indicated a specification phrased in this manner is regarded by the Court as charging only desertion with an intent not to return. The law officer instructed the court-martial that the elements of proof were as follows:

> "Proof: (a) that the accused absented himself without leave from his place of service, organization, or place of duty, as alleged; (b) that he intended, at the time of absenting himself, or at some time during his absence, to remain away permanently

[13] United States v. Williams, 1 USCMA 186, 2 CMR 92 (1952).
[14] 1 USCMA 280, 3 CMR 14 (1952).

> from such place *or* to avoid hazardous duty, *or* to shirk important service, as alleged. . . ."[15] (Emphasis supplied.)

The accused was found guilty of desertion by the court-martial. After examining the facts, the Court found that two possible intents were "interwoven inextricably" in the case. It said:

> "The evidence may preponderate in favor of an intent to abandon the service permanently, but the accused testified and denied that he so intended. No one contends that the court was bound to believe his testimony, and that it was therefore required to find some other intent or return a finding of not guilty. *But the very fact that he left while on orders to report to a post outside the continental United States brings into prominence an intent to shirk important service.*"[16] (Emphasis supplied.)

Here, according to the Court, the evidence was not "weighted overwhelmingly" in favor of an intent not to return as alleged in the specification, and further, the Court felt that the scales might tilt in favor of intent to shirk important service. Consequently, the law officer in his instruction interjected in the trial an intent not contained in the specification. Under these circumstances the court-martial might have concluded that proof of either intent was sufficient, and could have convicted the accused of an offense beyond the fair confines of the pleadings. The result was an erroneous instruction which "may have affected the findings" and, therefore, materially prejudiced the substantial rights of the accused. The conviction was reversed.

In *Jenkins*[17] the specification on which accused was tried and convicted alleged:

> "In that [accused] did, in the vicinity of Packtong-Ni Yongdu-Ri Area Korea on or about 7 March 1951, desert the service of the United States by absenting himself without leave from his organization, with intent to avoid hazardous duty, to wit; service with his unit in a combat area, and did remain absent in desertion until he was apprehended at Pusan, Korea, on or about 19 March 1951."[18]

The law officer committed the same error as in *Hemp* by instructing the court-martial on three types of desertion although only one type was alleged in the specification. The record showed that the accused

[15] *Id.* at 281-282, *Id.* at 15-16.
[16] *Id.* at 287, *Id.* at 21.
[17] 1 USCMA 329, 3 CMR 63 (1952).
[18] *Id.* at 331, *Id.* at 65.

had been sent from his unit, which occupied a defensive position, to assist a litter team in carrying a wounded soldier to an aid station. The following morning he was discovered in the rear area and ordered forward with a food-carrying party. He fled the first time the party was exposed to mortar and artillery fire. The Court observed that the specification and the theory of both the prosecution and defense were all directed toward one intent; i.e., to avoid hazardous duty. Although the Court conceded that an inference of an intent to remain away permanently might be drawn from the fact that the accused was apprehended two hundred miles from his unit, it felt that to draw such an inference would require the court-martial to overlook the obvious intent involved in the case. The Court found the error was not prejudicial and distinguished this case from the *Hemp* case in the following language:

> In the *Hemp*[19] case . . . "the pleadings, evidence, arguments and the entire proceedings weighted almost equally on both issues of intent. Reasonable minds might have determined that there was substantial evidence on both sides of the scale, and might have chosen either as a base [*sic*] for an inference or intent. Not so here. This whole proceeding is weighted so overwhelmingly with evidence indicating an intent to avoid hazardous duty that a reasonable mind would have to ignore one side of the scale which was heavily loaded to choose the other which held barely a scintilla. Our understanding of human behavior leads us to believe that when the scales are so obviously out of balance reasonable minds would not be confused or misled as to which intent could be inferred from the facts."[20]

Instructional errors of this type have been considered by the Court in several other cases. Those in which the error was deemed prejudicial[21] and those in which it was held harmless[22] are approximately equal in number.

These three types of desertion are sufficiently distinct to preclude any one from being regarded as a lesser included offense of any other.[23]

[19] The Court was also distinguishing United States v. Williams, 1 USCMA 186, 2 CMR 92 (1952).

[20] United States v. Jenkins, 1 USCMA 329, 333, 3 CMR 63, 67 (1952).

[21] United States v. Johnson, 1 USCMA 536, 4 CMR 128 (1952); United States v. Justice, 1 USCMA 643, 5 CMR 71 (1952); United States v. Williams, 1 USCMA 186, 2 CMR 92 (1952); United States v. Shepard, 1 USCMA 487, 4 CMR 79 (1952).

[22] United States v. Moynihan, 1 USCMA 333, 3 CMR 67 (1952); United States v. Boone, 1 USCMA 381, 3 CMR 115 (1952); United States v. Cooke, 1 USCMA 421, 4 CMR 13 (1952); United States v. McIntyre, 2 USCMA 559, 10 CMR 57 (1953).

[23] United States v. Jenkins, 1 USCMA 329, 3 CMR 63 (1952).

A. *Permanent desertion*

Although a court-martial may infer an intent to desert from a prolonged[24] absence, it is prejudicial error for the law officer to instruct, in effect, that desertion is proved as a matter of law if the alleged absence (three months) is proved.[25]

The law officer may admit evidence of previous convictions of absence without leave for the purpose of showing intent if he finds that such evidence sheds some light on the mental attitude of the accused.[26]

Paragraph 164*a* (1) of the *Manual* includes the following statement concerning permanent desertion:

> ". . . a purpose to return, provided a particular but uncertain event happens in the future, may be considered as an intent to remain away permanently . . ."

The Court, conceding this may be a correct statement of the law under some circumstances, regards it as inartfully drawn and believes its use could be prejudicial to the accused in some cases. For instance, if an accused testifies that he intended to return as soon as his brother was released from the service, the court-martial, by following an instruction based on this *Manual* provision, could transform this defense evidence into a judicial confession.[27] The Court concluded that it was inadvisable to incorporate this *Manual* provision into an instruction.

B. *Desertion with intent to shirk important service*

There are two elements in this offense: (1) an absence without leave; (2) characterized by a purpose to avoid through absence service which, as a matter of law, may properly be regarded as important. The accused must have actual knowledge that he was required to perform important service.[28] However, the required knowledge may be proved by circumstantial evidence.

A transfer to a port of embarkation for shipment overseas is important service.[29] Likewise, an absence without leave with knowledge

[24] For a discussion of "prolonged" see Chapter 11, Section II A 2.

[25] United States v. Goddard, 1 USCMA 475, 4 CMR 67 (1952).

[26] United States v. Powell, 3 USCMA 64, 11 CMR 64 (1953) (the leading case). See Chapter 13, Section III for a further discussion.

[27] United States v. Rushlow, 2 USCMA 641, 10 CMR 139 (1953). *Cf.* United States v. Knoph, 2 USCMA 108, 6 CMR 108 (1952).

[28] United States v. Stabler, 4 USCMA 125, 15 CMR 125 (1954). On page 129 the Court stated: "Whether in most situations evidence of a failure to comply with overseas orders would permit an inference that an accused knew of the impending duty and intended to shirk it, we need not now decide." See the provisions in MANUAL FOR COURTS-MARTIAL, UNITED STATES, 1951, par. 164*a*, p. 314.

[29] United States v. Taylor, 2 USCMA 389, 9 CMR 19 (1953); United States v. Willingham, 2 USCMA 590, 10 CMR 88 (1953).

of "immediate" overseas movement is sufficient to permit a finding by a court-martial that the accused intended to shirk important service.[30] The Court stated that it likely would take "judicial notice that all duty in a theater of operations, if not actually hazardous, would certainly involve important service."[31] This does not mean that a member of the military establishment already at an overseas base automatically commits desertion by going absent without leave. The Court stated specifically that it does not regard absence without leave and desertion as synonymous charges when there is an unauthorized absence committed outside the United States.[32]

The Universal Military Training and Service Act of 1951[33] prohibits the assignment of military personnel to service outside the continental limits of the United States until after the completion of four months' basic training. For this reason, the Court ruled that basic training is important service within the meaning of Article 85 of the Code.[34] Proof of previous convictions for absence without leave, together with a statement of periods spent in confinement as a result of these absences is relevant on the issue of intent in a case in which the avoidance of basic training is a vital element in the offense charged.[35]

C. *Desertion with intent to avoid hazardous duty*

The accused must have actual knowledge that he was required to perform hazardous duty. The Court reversed[36] a finding of guilty of this type of desertion because the Government failed to produce evidence of facts sufficient to raise a proper inference that the accused knew with reasonable certainty that he would be required for duty at a "listening post" during the Korean conflict.

Hazardous duty is not confined to front-line combat but it has been defined to include, at the least, such duty as would be covered by the term (in Article 99) "before or in the presence of the enemy."[37]

The word "quit" in Article 85 is a word of art legally synonymous with "goes absent without authority." Hence absence without leave is a lesser included offense in desertion with intent to avoid hazardous duty or desertion with intent to shirk important service.[38]

[30] United States v. Hemp, 1 USCMA 280, 3 CMR 14 (1952).
[31] United States v. Williams, 1 USCMA 186, 2 CMR 92 (1952).
[32] United States v. Boone, 1 USCMA 381, 3 CMR 315 (1952) (offense occurred at Clark Field, Philippine Islands, in 1949).
[33] 62 STAT. 605, 622, 50 USC appendix, Supp. V, Section 462.
[34] United States v. Deller, 3 USCMA 409, 12 CMR 165 (1953); United States v. O'Neil, 3 USCMA 416, 12 CMR 172 (1953).
[35] *Ibid.* See also Chapter 13, Section III.
[36] United States v. Tilton, 4 USCMA 120, 15 CMR 120 (1954).
[37] United States v. Cook, 2 USCMA 223, 8 CMR 23 (1953).
[38] United States v. Bondar, 2 USCMA 357, 8 CMR 157 (1953).

D. *Apprehension*

Apprehension is in the nature of an aggravating circumstance and not an element of the offense of desertion. However, in order to impose the greater punishment authorized when a desertion is terminated by apprehension, it is essential that the fact of apprehension be (1) alleged in the specification; (2) included in the instructions; and (3) established as a part of the Government's proof.[39] A stipulation[40] is frequently the means by which the court-martial is apprised of the fact that an unauthorized absence was terminated by apprehension.

Service record entries, as official records, may be used by the Navy to show the fact of apprehension.[41]

If the accused discloses his military status only after he has been taken into custody on a criminal charge, the court-martial may reject a contention that he voluntarily surrendered; instead, it may justifiably infer that the accused revealed his military status solely to avoid prosecution by the civilian authorities.[42]

An unauthorized absence is legally ended by return to any military control, including control exercised only temporarily by a service other than that of the offender.[43]

Article 86—*Absence without Leave*

There are two elements in the offense of unauthorized absence: the absence, and the want of authority. Unless a specification alleges both directly or by clear implication, it states only an innocent act. Therefore, a plea of guilty by the accused to a specification which does not allege that the absence was without authority is not a waiver of the defect and the specification can be attacked on appeal. Moreover, alleging that an absence was a violation of Article 86 does not cure the defect for the reason that the nature of an offense depends upon the facts set out in the specification, and not upon the Article under which it is alleged.[44]

An accused[45] was tried by a summary court-martial in Taegu, Korea, for a minor offense. During the trial he did not disclose that he was absent without leave. Subsequently, the accused was tried for absence without leave and it was contended on his behalf that the

[39] United States v. Nickaboine, 3 USCMA 152, 11 CMR 152 (1953).

[40] United States v. White, 3 USCMA 666, 14 CMR 84 (1954); *cf.* United States v. Beninate, 4 USCMA 98, 15 CMR 98 (1954).

[41] United States v. Coates, 2 USCMA 625, 10 CMR 123 (1953).

[42] United States v. White, 3 USCMA 666, 14 CMR 84 (1954); United States v. Clayborne, 4 USCMA 105, 15 CMR 105 (1954).

[43] United States v. Coates, 2 USCMA 625, 10 CMR 123 (1953). But see case cited in note 45 *infra.*

[44] United States v. Fout, 3 USCMA 565, 13 CMR 121 (1953).

[45] United States v. Jackson, 1 USCMA 190, 2 CMR 96 (1952).

temporary exercise of military control by the summary court-martial terminated the unlawful absence. The Court decided that the unlawful absence would not terminate unless the accused disclosed his status or the military authorities could by reasonable diligence obtain knowledge that he was absent without leave from his organization. Since neither had occurred in this case the conviction was affirmed.

The expiration of an enlistment while the accused is absent without leave does not in itself terminate the absence.[46]

Article 87—*Missing Movement*

This offense has presented many problems.[47] The *Manual*[48] states that proof of this offense must consist of the following:

(a) That the accused actually missed the movement of a ship, aircraft, or unit with which he was required in the course of duty to move; and

(b) that he missed the movement of the ship, aircraft, or unit through neglect or design.

The Court does not regard this as sufficient proof. In addition it must be shown that the accused knew or should have known of the prospective movement and that such movement was a substantial one.[49] Paragraph 166 of the *Manual* provides in part:

> "Knowledge of the exact hour or even of the exact date of the scheduled movement is not required. It is sufficient if the approximate date is known to the accused. However, there must always be a causal connection between the conduct of the accused and the missing of the scheduled movement."

The Court interpreted this provision to require proof of causal connection only under certain circumstances. It said:

> "We think that, by this sentence, the drafters intended to cover the situation where, for example, a sailor is told that his ship is scheduled to sail about the 7th of July. The sailor's leave expires at midnight on the 6th, but he does not return until 8:00 a.m. on the 7th. The ship sails at midnight on the 6th. In

[46] United States v. Klunk, 3 USCMA 92, 11 CMR 92 (1953); United States v. Downs, 3 USCMA 90, 11 CMR 90 (1953) (desertion); United States v. Barrett, 3 USCMA 294, 12 CMR 50 (1953) (desertion).

[47] JAG JOURNAL (January 1954), p. 11.

[48] Par. 166.

[49] United States v. Jones, 1 USCMA 276, 3 CMR 10 (1952). This is consistent with the "discussion" of this offense as distinguished from the "proof" in the MANUAL FOR COURTS-MARTIAL, UNITED STATES, 1951, par. 166. In *Jones* the Court indicated that the word "movement" should be defined.

> such a situation, it would be difficult to say that there is a causal connection between the conduct of the accused and the missing of the scheduled movement. In other words, because of the uncertainty in the mind of the sailor as to the precise time of departure, he could not reasonably have foreseen that staying over leave for eight hours would result in missing his ship. . . . Where a definite movement is set and known to the accused, who thereupon remains absent without authority beyond the scheduled date of departure, we can see no necessity for any special proof of causal connection. . . . It is our conclusion that the drafters of the Manual intended to require causal connection between the conduct of the accused and the missing of the movement as an affirmative element of the offense only where an approximate date of movement is known to the accused."[50]

The Court rejected a board of review decision which limited this Article to situations in which an accused must either be assigned to duty with the ship or aircraft or he must be a member of a "unit" to be transported. A person, not a member of the crew, ordered to travel individually to another post via a certain aircraft may violate this Article.[51]

If a member of the armed forces is through his own fault not at the place where he is required to be at a prescribed time, he may have possibly violated one or more of the following Articles: 85 (desertion), 86 (absence without leave), 87 (missing movement). Article 134 (General Article) does not include this type of offense. Moreover, if the prosecution fails to prove all elements of a charge of missing movement, a court-martial cannot punish the accused under Article 134 on the ground that the elements of missing movement which were proved constituted a neglect to the prejudice of good order and discipline.[52]

Article 89—*Disrespect towards a Superior Officer*

The *Manual* does not specify that "knowledge" that the victim was a superior officer is an element of this offense. However, if knowledge is reasonably raised as a factual issue, the law officer must instruct the members of a court-martial that they are required to find, as a basis for conviction, that the accused knew that the person to whom the disrespect was directed was a superior officer.[53] The question of proof

[50] United States v. Thompson, 2 USCMA 460, 463-464, 9 CMR 90, 93-94 (1953).
[51] United States v. Johnson, 3 USCMA 174, 11 CMR 174 (1953).
[52] *Ibid.*
[53] United States v. Etchon, 3 USCMA 394, 12 CMR 150 (1953).

of knowledge in connection with Articles 89 and 90 has been discussed in Chapter 7. This discussion should be equally applicable to offenses alleged under Article 91 (noncommissioned officer).

Threatening language to a military superior such as offering to fight him is per se disrespect and a violation of this Article.[54]

Article 90—*Assaulting or Willfully Disobeying Officer*

The command of a superior officer is clothed with a presumption of legality and the burden of establishing the converse is on the defense.[55] Willful disobedience of an order constitutes a violation regardless of whether it is accompanied by an "arrogant" manner, or is attended by the most respectful demeanor.[56] An intentional defiance of authority may be manifest by deliberately omitting to do that which is ordered, by an express refusal to obey, by simple noncompliance or by doing the opposite.[57] The form of an order is immaterial, so long as it is understood by the accused, and, furthermore, the mere fact that it is phrased in precatory form does not necessarily render it less than a positive command.[58]

Initially, the Court appeared to have decided to require that the accused have "knowledge" that the person was his superior officer as an essential element of this offense.[59] Subsequent decisions have not done so. Instead, the Court has refused to label "knowledge" as an element of the offense or a lack thereof as an affirmative defense.[60] The Court stated that the difficulty in determining the proper category in which to place knowledge may be attributed to the equivocal language in the *Manual*.[61] Usually the Court is not so hesitant in clarifying a *Manual* provision. Nevertheless, it has provided guidance on the basic issue. The crucial question, according to the Court, is whether there is a factual issue of knowledge raised by the evidence.[62] If so, the law

[54] United States v. Richardson, 2 USCMA 88, 6 CMR 88 (1952).
[55] United States v. Trani, 1 USCMA 293, 3 CMR 27 (1952).
[56] United States v. Soukup, 2 USCMA 141, 7 CMR 17 (1953).
[57] United States v. Vansant, 3 USCMA 30, 11 CMR 30 (1953).
[58] United States v. Glaze, 3 USCMA 168, 11 CMR 168 (1953) (order given by a noncommissioned officer).
[59] United States v. Simmons, 1 USCMA 691, 5 CMR 119 (1952). The Court in a dictum suggested that the services correct the *Manual* to show "knowledge is an element which must be included in the proof."
[60] United States v. Wallace, 2 USCMA 595, 10 CMR 93 (1953); United States v. Majia, 2 USCMA 616, 10 CMR 114 (1953); United States v. St. Pierre, 3 USCMA 33, 11 CMR 33 (1953); *cf.* United States v. Eagleson, 3 USCMA 685, 14 CMR 103 (1954). Lack of knowledge is definitely an affirmative defense to a charge of leaving the scene of an accident.
[61] United States v. Eagleson, 3 USCMA 685, 14 CMR 103 (1954).
[62] The Court held there was no issue of knowledge in the following cases: United States v. Wallace, 2 USCMA 595, 10 CMR 93 (1953); United States v. Majia, 2 USCMA 616, 10 CMR 114 (1953); United States v. St. Pierre, 3 USCMA 33, 11 CMR 33 (1953).

officer must instruct the members of the court-martial that to return a finding of guilty it is necessary that they find the accused had the requisite knowledge.[63]

Physical incapacity to carry out the order is an affirmative defense to a charge of willful disobedience of an order of a superior officer, noncommissioned officer or warrant officer. If physical incapacity is fairly raised by the evidence, the law officer, with or without a request, is required to give appropriate instructions. Failure to do so has been held prejudicial error.[64]

Article 91—*Insubordinate Conduct towards Noncommissioned Officer*

This Article is violated when a warrant officer or enlisted person strikes or assaults a warrant officer, noncommissioned officer or petty officer, while such officer is *in the execution of his office*. The Court adopted[65] the broad definition of the phrase *in the execution of his office* given in *Winthrop's Military Law and Precedents*.[66]

Cases involving willful disobedience and disrespect decided under this Article appear in the discussion of Articles 89 and 90 *supra*.[67]

Article 92—*Failure to Obey Order or Regulation*

Article 92 (1) makes it an offense to violate or fail to obey any lawful general order or regulation. Directives and regulations coming within the purview of this provision include "orders ranging from those issued by a Department down to those promulgated by the commander of a post, ship or station."[68] However, the services may restrict the authority to issue general orders and regulations to commanders of the higher ranks.[69]

The Code fails to state whether it is necessary to allege and prove knowledge of the order as an element of this offense. The Court has supplied the answer in two installments: (1) If the order emanated

[63] United States v. Benders, 2 USCMA 620, 10 CMR 118 (1953). Knowledge was in issue and a failure to instruct thereon was prejudicial error.

[64] United States v. Heims, 3 USCMA 418, 12 CMR 174 (1953). An order to tie sandbags was given by a superior noncommissioned officer.

[65] United States v. Glaze, 3 USCMA 168, 11 CMR 168 (1953).

[66] (2d ed. 1920 Reprint, p. 571, any legal and appropriate act whether strictly duty in a military sense).

[67] United States v. Richardson, 2 USCMA 88, 6 CMR 88 (1952); United States v. Glaze, 3 USCMA 168, 11 CMR 168 (1953); United States v. Heims, 3 USCMA 418, 12 CMR 174 (1953). A specification which stated, "I can't do anything about it now, but I'll use my fists on you later, or words to that effect . . ." sufficiently alleged an offense under Article 4 (Third) A. G. N., United States v. Sturmer, 1 USCMA 17, 1 CMR 17 (1951).

[68] United States v. Snyder, 1 USCMA 423, 4 CMR 15 (1952); United States v. Simpson, 2 USCMA 493, 9 CMR 123 (1953) (sufficiency of specification).

[69] United States v. Bunch, 3 USCMA 186, 11 CMR 186 (1953). See Naval Supplement to the MANUAL FOR COURTS-MARTIAL, UNITED STATES, 1951.

from a Department, or territorial, theater, or similar area command, knowledge is conclusively presumed and it need not be proved; (2) If the general order was issued by an inferior commander such as a camp, post or ship commander, it is not necessary to allege[70] knowledge but it is an element which must be proved.[71] Thus it is prejudicial error for the law officer to omit from his instructions a statement that knowledge is an essential element in an alleged violation of a general order of a post commander.[72]

Cases involving Department regulations considered by the Court under Article 92 (1) involve a failure to classify military information[73] and possession of intoxicating beverages in an unauthorized place.[74] Camp or post regulations concerned with possession of firearms,[75] bringing civilians in barracks,[76] and payment of financial obligations before departing from the station[77] also have been before the Court.

If an order or regulation was issued by a commander who is not authorized to promulgate general orders or regulations, it is appropriate to charge a violation under Article 92 (2). Knowledge is made an element of this branch of Article 92 and it must be alleged and proved.[78]

If there are exceptions in a general order, it is unnecessary for the prosecution to allege or prove that the accused, who is charged with violating the general order, is not within the exceptions specified in the order. The accused must carry the burden of proving himself within an exception.[79]

[70] United States v. Obligenhart, 3 USCMA 627, 14 CMA 45 (1954).

[71] United States v. Snyder, 1 USCMA 423, 430, 4 CMR 15, 22 (1952). In this regard the Court stated:

> "Indeed there is nothing inconsistent with a requirement that a certain element of an offense be established by proof, even though the element need not be alleged specifically in the specification. Examples of this phenomenon are found in murder (malice aforethought); rape (against the will of the victim); larceny (intent permanently to deprive the owner of the property); and willful disobedience of an officer's order (knowledge that person is officer)."

[72] United States v. Arnovits, 3 USCMA 538, 13 CMR 94 (1953). See also United States v. Greenlee, 3 USCMA 284, 12 CMR 40 (1953) for an error in the instruction because the law officer stated: ". . . violating or failing to obey *any* lawful general order or regulation."

[73] United States v. Grow, 3 USCMA 77, 11 CMR 77 (1953).

[74] United States v. Greenlee, 3 USCMA 284, 12 CMR 40 (1953).

[75] United States v. Wade, 1 USCMA 459, 4 CMR 51 (1952).

[76] United States v. Snyder, 1 USCMA 423, 4 CMR 15 (1953).

[77] United States v. Arnovits, 3 USCMA 538, 13 CMR 94 (1953). For violation of a military brig regulation see United States v. Sell, 3 USCMA 202, 11 CMR 202 (1953).

[78] MANUAL FOR COURTS-MARTIAL, UNITED STATES, 1951, p. 476; United States v. Bunch, 3 USCMA 186, 11 CMR 186 (1953) (dictum).

[79] United States v. Gohagen, 2 USCMA 175, 7 CMR 51 (1953); United States v. Berry, 2 USCMA 374, 9 CMR 4 (1953); United States v. Christophe, 2 USCMA 375, 9 CMR 5 (1953); United States v. Welborne, 2 USCMA 378, 9 CMR 8 (1953).

Article 94—*Mutiny or Sedition*

The Court stated that the offense of mutiny may be committed in either one of two ways:

> "First, if the necessary intent to override military authority and concerted action are present, it may be committed by refusal to obey orders from a proper authority.
> Second, it may be committed by a person, with a similar intent, acting either alone or in concert with others, creating a violence or disturbance."[80a]

Law officers have experienced some difficulty in determining whether riot, an offense under Article 116, is lesser included within the offense of mutiny. In this connection the Court expressly stated that riot is not a lesser included offense in those instances in which a mutiny is alleged to have been committed by a passive refusal to obey orders or where one person committed a violent mutiny.[80b] On the other hand, riot may be an included offense within a specification which alleges a mutiny committed in concert with others through violence. In cases involving such a specification the law officer must instruct that riot is a lesser included offense if the facts in evidence reasonably show that the offense of riot is in issue. In two cases concerned with the question of whether the evidence raised such an issue the Court held that it did[80c] in one case and did not[80d] in the other.

Article 99—*Misbehavior before the Enemy*

The offense of misbehavior before the enemy is committed when any member of the armed forces who before or in the presence of the enemy

> "(1) runs away; or
> (3) through disobedience, neglect or intentional misconduct endangers the safety of any such command, unit, place or military property; or
> (5) is guilty of cowardly conduct; or
> (8) willfully fails to do his utmost to encounter, engage, capture or destroy any enemy troops . . . or any other thing, which it is his duty so to encounter. . . ."

Altogether this offense consists of nine subdivisions; however, only the four above enumerated have been involved in cases considered by the

[80a] United States v. Duggan, 4 USCMA 396, 398, 15 CMR 396, 398 (1954).
[80b] *Ibid.*
[80c] United States v. Watson, 4 USCMA 557, 16 CMR 131 (1954).
[80d] United States v. Duggan, 4 USCMA 396, 15 CMR 396 (1954).

Court. The clause "before or in the presence of the enemy" is applicable to each of the nine subdivisions. The Court has given the following definition to this clause:

> "It may not be possible to carve out a general rule to fit all situations, but if an organization is in a position ready to participate in either an offensive or defensive battle, and, its weapons are capable of delivering fire on the enemy and in turn are so situated that they are within effective range of the enemy weapons, then that unit is before the enemy."[80]

A member of a front line platoon,[81] or machine gun platoon,[82] or mortar unit[83] supporting front line troops has been held to be before the enemy. Likewise, an accused was "before the enemy" when he ran away while near friendly artillery units less than six miles from the front lines.[84]

In defining subsection (1) which involves the offense of "running away" the Court stated:

> "This term must connote some form of fleeing from an ensuing or impending battle. It seems unrealistic to assume that every unauthorized absence from any unit which might be considered in the presence of the enemy constituted misbehavior. On the other hand it appears that to limit the phrase to flight from fear or cowardice is too restricted. It would appear to be more in keeping with the offense, if an intent to avoid combat, with its attending hazards and dangers is considered as an essential part of running away."[85]

The Court then concluded that "runs away" must be interpreted as an absence under conditions from which it may be reasonably inferred that the leaving was *with intent to avoid some form of combat action by or with the enemy.* An adequate instruction on this subdivision of Article 99 requires the law officer to explain the meaning of "runs away" in accordance with the interpretation given that term by the Court.[86]

Subdivision (3) of this Article was violated by a tank commander who became intoxicated while he occupied a position in the main line of resistance and was under a duty to render fire support.[87]

[80] United States v. Sperland, 1 USCMA 661, 663, 5 CMR 89, 91 (1952).
[81] United States v. Smith, 3 USCMA 25, 11 CMR 25 (1953).
[82] United States v. King, 2 USCMA 397, 9 CMR 27 (1953).
[83] United States v. Sperland, 1 USCMA 661, 5 CMR 89 (1952).
[84] United States v. Smith, 2 USCMA 197, 7 CMR 73 (1953).
[85] United States v. Sperland, 1 USCMA 661, 664, 5 CMR 89, 92 (1952).
[86] United States v. Parker, 3 USCMA 541, 13 CMR 97 (1953).
[87] United States v. Carey, 4 USCMA 112, 15 CMR 112 (1954).

Several cases involving subdivision (5) i.e., misbehavior before the enemy through cowardly conduct, have been decided by the Court. Fear is an essential element of this offense.[88] An admission by the accused that he was afraid to go forward is perhaps the best evidence of fear.[89] Fear is sufficiently indicated when an accused refuses to proceed toward the front lines when he hears nearby artillery fire and there is evidence that his hands were trembling and he had the appearance of being nervous.[90] However, the Court warned that evidence of intent to avoid combat duty does not itself impel a court-martial to infer fear—a brave man may get tired of fighting without being afraid of the enemy.[91] It is error for a law officer to omit the element of fear from his instructions.[92] Although several cases have been reversed[93] because this element was omitted from the instructions, the language in some of the opinions[94] of the Court can be construed to mean that this error may not be prejudicial except in those cases in which the evidence indicates that it is possible that the action of the accused may have been motivated by something other than fear.

The following specification was held to allege an offense either under subdivision (1) or (5):

> "On or about 2210 hours, 16 September 1952, in the presence of the enemy, [the accused] was guilty of *cowardly conduct,* in that he *ran away* from his combat outpost."[95]

If the accused was motivated by fear, he violates either (1) or (5), but if the motivation was something other than fear, the running away must be under (1).

If the accused objects to a single specification stating an offense under two subdivisions of the same Article, he must file his objections during trial or else there is a waiver.[96]

A law officer does not adequately instruct on the element of "willfully" included in subdivision (8) by use of the term "wrongfully."[97]

[88] United States v. Soukup, 2 USCMA 141, 7 CMR 17 (1953).
[89] United States v. Smith, 3 USCMA 25, 11 CMR 25 (1953).
[90] United States v. Smith, 2 USCMA 197, 7 CMR 73 (1953).
[91] United States v. Yarborough, 1 USCMA 678, 5 CMR 106 (1952).
[92] *Ibid; accord,* United States v. Soukup, 2 USCMA 141, 7 CMR 17 (1953).
[93] United States v. Soukup, 2 USCMA 141, 7 CMR 17 (1953); United States v. Smith, 2 USCMA 197, 7 CMR 73 (1953); United States v. Wallace, 2 USCMA 595, 10 CMR 93 (1953); United States v. Brown, 3 USCMA 98, 11 CMR 98 (1953); United States v. McCormick, 3 USCMA 361, 12 CMR 117 (1953).
[94] United States v. Wallace, 2 USCMA 595, 10 CMR 93 (1953); United States v. McCormick, 3 USCMA 361, 12 CMR 117 (1953).
[95] United States v. Parker, 3 USCMA 541, 544, 13 CMR 97, 100 (1954).
[96] *Ibid.*
[97] United States v. Hallett, 4 USCMA 378, 15 CMR 378 (1954).

The Court made the following statement regarding the scope of Article 99:

"Congress meant that Article 99 of the Code should cover the gamut of offenses closely allied to misbehavior before the enemy. In short, an offense characterized by improper conduct 'before the enemy' is to be alleged within the terms of Article 99, or else the circumstance that the misconduct occurred 'in the presence of the enemy' becomes irrelevant in determining its nature. Article 134, we decided, was not intended by Congress to constitute a catch-all for combat offenses not specifically proscribed elsewhere."[98]

Article 108—*Military Property of the United States—Loss, Damage, Destruction, or Wrongful Disposition*

Under this Article the damaging of military property of the United States through neglect is a lesser included offense in a charge of willfully damaging such property by force.[99]

Article 113—*Misbehavior of Sentinel*

It is unlawful for any sentinel or lookout to be found drunk or sleeping upon his post, or to leave it before he is properly relieved.

A. *Sleep*

The Court has described what constitutes sleep within the meaning of this Article as follows:

". . . [it] does not require a showing beyond reasonable doubt that the accused was in a wholly comatose condition. Many persons are light sleepers who seldom, if ever, fall into that deep state. Instead, we believe that the standard to be applied is roughly analogous to that which might be utilized for purposes of prosecution for drunkenness on post. All that is required by way of evidence in the case at bar, we believe, is the showing of a condition of insentience which is sufficient sensibly to impair the full exercise of the mental and physical facilities of the sentinel. In framing Article 113, the draftsmen of the Code were, in our view, seeking to assure—through the imposition of penal sanctions—the alert and rational performance of duty as a sentinel. Other lives are at stake in this situation much too frequently

[98] United States v. Hamilton, 4 USCMA 383, 384, 15 CMR 383, 384 (1954).

[99] United States v. Wright, 3 USCMA 431, 12 CMR 187 (1953). See also United States v. Groves, 2 USCMA 541, 10 CMR 39 (1953). A charge of willful destruction was reversed because the law officer should have instructed on intoxication.

to permit the adoption of other than the most rigorous standards of enforcement of this duty. . . . the accused must be asleep in some proper meaning of the term—and this requirement is not met by a mere dulling of the perceptions through say, physical exhaustion not amounting to slumber."[100]

B. *Leaving post*

The Court upheld [101] a finding of guilty in the case of an accused who left his post which covered a particular avenue of approach by the enemy and went with his weapon to an adjacent post about 100 feet away. He remained at the adjacent post without justification until found by the officer of the guard.

The Court held the following instruction was not prejudicial under the facts of the case before it:

> ". . . any evidence regarding why the accused left his post without authority is immaterial to the issue of guilt or innocence; and that in determining guilt or innocence the court must disregard it . . ."[102]

The Court found it unnecessary to decide whether a sentry may have a good reason to leave his post. Should it do so, such a sweeping instruction might become the basis for reversal in a case in which it was found that the accused left his post because of a good reason.

Article 118—*Murder*

This Article specifically defines as murder four categories of homicide. These include premeditated murder, unpremeditated murder (two types), and felony murder. Although not phrased in terms of degrees of murder, there are nevertheless distinctions in these categories. For instance, punishment for premeditated murder and felony murder must be death or life imprisonment, whereas there is no such requirement for unpremeditated murder.

A. *Premeditated murder*

Premeditation is a question of fact for the court-martial. It may be inferred from the circumstances attending the killing.[103] The Court made the following statement regarding the length of time required for deliberation:

[100] United States v. Williams, 4 USCMA 69, 74, 15 CMR 69, 74 (1954).
[101] United States v. Hattley, 3 USCMA 114, 11 CMR 114 (1953).
[102] *Id.* at 115.
[103] United States v. Sechler, 3 USCMA 363, 12 CMR 119 (1953).

"... it has been almost universally held, that the deliberation and premeditation may be almost instantaneous, though, generally, the authorities require some appreciable lapse of time."[104]

In *Sechler*[105] the accused was upset because of A's alleged association with his girl. He knocked *A* down and loaded his carbine with the announced intention of killing *A*. When *B*, one of *A's* companions, reached to extinguish a cigarette, the accused turned toward him and fired a burst from his carbine. *C*, another companion of *A*, nearer to the accused than *B*, fell to the floor mortally wounded. The Court held that a court-martial was justified in finding premeditation. This was not a sudden and startling event which would bring spontaneous reaction into play inasmuch as the accused had been in this room just previously and had observed the presence of others in the small restaurant—the scene of the killing.

The Court has stated that it is desirable for the law officer to define premeditation. However, failure to do so will not be regarded as reversible error unless there is a specific request by the defense counsel which apparently must be based on special circumstances showing the need for such an instruction.[106]

B. *Unpremeditated murder*

Article 118 (2) and (3) provide definitions of unpremeditated murder. Clause (2) deals with the unlawful killing of a human being when the accused *intends to kill or inflict great bodily harm*. Clause (3) deals with the unlawful killing of a human being when the accused is engaged in *an act which is inherently dangerous to others and evinces a wanton disregard for human life*.

A conviction may not lawfully be rendered under clause (3) in a setting in which only one person is endangered by the conduct of the accused.[107] If the acts of the accused are directed at one person and no other person is endangered, an instruction on unpremeditated murder should be confined to clause (2).[108] Several convictions for unpremeditated murder have been reversed[109] because the Court found

[104] United States v. Goodman, 1 USCMA 170, 173, 2 CMR 76, 79 (1952) (A. W. 92).

[105] 3 USCMA 363, 12 CMR 119 (1953).

[106] United States v. Amdahl, 3 USCMA 199, 11 CMR 199 (1953); United States v. Day, 2 USCMA 416, 9 CMR 46 (1953); United States v. Felton, 2 USCMA 630, 10 CMR 128 (1953).

[107] United States v. Dacanay, 4 USCMA 263, 15 CMR 263 (1954).

[108] United States v. Davis, 2 USCMA 505, 10 CMR 3 (1953).

[109] *Ibid; accord*, United States v. Holsey, 2 USCMA 554, 10 CMR 52 (1953); United States v. Johnson, 3 USCMA 209, 11 CMR 209 (1953); United States v. Decanay, 4 USCMA 263, 15 CMR 263 (1954). Judge Quinn dissented because he did not regard the error as prejudicial in the latter case.

prejudicial error in instructions which permitted the court-martial to find the accused guilty under clause (2) or (3) even though the facts showed the acts of the accused were aimed at and endangered only one person.

The Court held[110] that even though the accused may have intended to kill one particular person, his action in firing in the dark, in a house occupied by more than one person, was inherently dangerous to others. No instructional problems arose in this case because trial counsel and defense counsel agreed that the Government would proceed only on the theory that the accused was guilty of engaging in inherently dangerous acts as defined in Article 118 (3). On the other hand, both types of this crime may be involved. For instance, the accused may direct his acts at one person but if his deliberate firing of a pistol is done in a tent filled with soldiers it is also an act inherently dangerous to others and evinces a wanton disregard of human life in general. In a fact situation such as this the alternative instruction is proper.[111]

C. *Felony murder*

Felony murder as defined in Article 118 (4) does not require that perpetration or an attempted perpetration of burglary, sodomy, rape, robbery, or aggravated arson *and* the death coincide in point of time.[112] All that is required is the establishment of a causal connection between the crime or attempt and the death.

Notwithstanding the language of paragraph 158 of the *Manual* to the contrary, the Court held[113] that unpremeditated murder can be a lesser included offense in felony murder if the evidence establishes it as a reasonable alternative to a charge of felony murder. In this situation the intent to kill or inflict grievous bodily harm must be found in the evidence independent of that tending to show that the accused was engaged in a robbery, burglary, sodomy, rape or aggravated arson at the time of the killing.

Article 119—*Manslaughter*

This Article undertakes to define both voluntary and involuntary manslaughter. The *Manual* provides the following as a guide for instructing a court-martial on these offenses:

"Proof.—(a) That the victim named or described is dead;
(b) that his death resulted from the act or omission of the accused, as alleged; and

[110] United States v. Sandoval, 4 USCMA 61, 15 CMR 61 (1954).
[111] United States v. McDonald, 4 USCMA 130, 15 CMR 130 (1954).
[112] United States v. Borner, 3 USCMA 306, 12 CMR 62 (1953).
[113] United States v. Davis, 2 USCMA 505, 10 CMR 3 (1953).

(c) facts and circumstances showing that the homicide amounted in law to the degree of manslaughter alleged."[114]

The Court has criticized (b) and (c) for the reason they do not provide a court-martial with sufficient standards by which to measure the conduct of the accused. Further, it has condemned instructions confined to this language in cases in which involuntary manslaughter was either the principal offense charged[115] or was the subject of an instruction because it was properly in issue as a lesser included offense.[116] Involuntary manslaughter is committed when a person, without an intent to kill or inflict great bodily harm, unlawfully kills a human being—

(1) by culpable negligence; or
(2) while perpetrating or attempting to perpetrate an offense other than burglary, sodomy, rape, robbery, or aggravated arson, directly affecting the person.[117]

If an accused is charged with involuntary manslaughter based on an act of culpable negligence, the law officer should include in his instructions that the conduct of the accused was a negligent act (or omission). Further, it is desirable to define culpable negligence—but generally a failure to do so, especially in the absence of a request by the defense, is not prejudicial error.[118]

If involuntary manslaughter is based on perpetration of other offenses (part (2)), the law officer should advise the court-martial of the elements of the offense involved in the perpetration (or attempt). If an attempt as distinguished from a perpetration is alleged, it is necessary to define attempt.

An instruction involving either branch of the offense of involuntary manslaughter should, of course, include a statement that the victim named (or described) is dead.

Article 120—*Rape and Carnal Knowledge*

The Court endorsed[119] a *Manual* provision which states that "a conviction cannot be based upon the uncorroborated testimony of an al-

[114] Par. 198*b*.
[115] United States v. Grosman, 2 USCMA 406, 9 CMR 36 (1953).
[116] United States v. Johnson, 3 USCMA 209, 11 CMR 209 (1953).
[117] Art. 119.
[118] United States v. Cobb, 2 USCMA 339, 8 CMR 139 (1953). The majority appeared to view as important the fact that *counsel* defined these words. United States v. Felton, 2 USCMA 630, 10 CMR 128 (1953) (dictum).
[119] United States v. Henderson, 4 USCMA 268, 15 CMR 268 (1954). If corroboration was essential, it sufficiently appeared in the evidence.

leged victim in a trial for a sexual offense, . . . if such testimony is self-contradictory, uncertain, or improbable."[120] However, the Court does not demand that there be a showing that the victim resisted to the "uttermost" in determining whether corroboration of her testimony is essential. In this regard the Court stated:

> "We are content to adhere to the view that a rape victim's resistance need only be such as to make a want of consent and actual resistance reasonably manifest—having regard to her age, her strength, and the surrounding circumstances. . . . If there be such resistance in the face of sufficient force to create in the mind of the victim a real apprehension of dangerous consequences—and if her will is in fact overcome—we are willing to regard the evidence as sufficient to make out the crime of rape."[121]

The fact that the prosecutrix may have been a prostitute does not establish consent.[122]

Unless requested to do so, the law officer is not required to define carnal knowledge, use of force, or lack of consent.[123]

Article 121—*Larceny and Wrongful Appropriation*

Congress in enacting Article 121 eliminated the often subtle and confusing distinctions between common-law larceny, embezzlement and false pretenses. Any of the various acts denounced as larceny in this Article may be charged and proved under a specification alleging the accused stole the property in question.[124] The consolidation of these crimes under the larceny label did not purport to extend the scope of any of these three offenses. Therefore, conduct which did not constitute either common-law larceny, embezzlement, or false pretenses prior to the Code, is not punishable as a violation of "larceny" under Article 121.[125]

In *Aldridge*[126] the accused was charged with a violation of this

[120] Par. 153*a*.
[121] United States v. Henderson, 4 USCMA 268, 273, 15 CMR 268, 273 (1954).
[122] United States v. Washington, 2 USCMA 177, 7 CMR 53 (1953). The testimony was not self-contradictory, uncertain, nor improbable and not without corroboration.
[123] United States v. Long, 2 USCMA 45, 6 CMR 45 (1952); United States v. Marshall, 2 USCMA 54, 6 CMR 54 (1952) (carnal knowledge); United States v. Parker, 3 USCMA 272, 12 CMR 28 (1953) (carnal knowledge). This is consistent with the Court's view that a law officer need not elaborate on the meaning of a commonly understood term unless requested to do so. United States v. Soukup, 2 USCMA 141, 7 CMR 17 (1953).
[124] Manual for Courts-Martial, United States, 1951, par. 200*a*.
[125] United States v. Buck, 3 USCMA 341, 12 CMR 97 (1953).
[126] 2 USCMA 330, 8 CMR 130 (1953).

Article in that he did "steal" specified sums of money from named individuals. The instructions given to the members of the court-martial embodied the common-law offenses of "larceny," "embezzlement" and "false pretenses." Defense counsel contended that these instructions, as in desertion cases, should have been "tailored" specifically to fit the theory of the Government's case.[127] The Court rejected this contention because in this connection there is an important difference in Article 121 (larceny) and Article 85 (desertion). Only one intent is involved in Article 121 (1)—i.e., to deprive the owner *permanently* of the property. The method of "taking" is not material. Consequently, instructions in the alternative are not erroneous. On the other hand, Article 85 (desertion) creates separate offenses (at least for instructional purposes[128]) with *different* intents. Although "stole" is sufficient to allege larceny, it is not a satisfactory substitute in the instructions of a law officer for the element of intent to deprive the owner permanently of his property.[129]

The difference between larceny and wrongful appropriation under Article 121 is that the former requires that the wrongful taking, obtaining, or withholding must be with intent to deprive, defraud, or appropriate *permanently;* whereas the latter is concerned with an intent *temporarily* to do these things.[130] A person may be guilty of larceny even though he intends to return the property ultimately, if the execution of that intent depends on a future condition or contingency which is not likely to happen within a reasonably limited and definite period of time. The time of return is not uncertain or indefinite to such a degree as to justify a demand that wrongful appropriation be excluded from consideration in a case in which an accused pawns property of another without authority intending to redeem it upon receipt of his pay and allowances at the end of the month or when his wife receives her allotment check.[131] The Court upheld[132] the following provision in the *Manual:*

[127] Counsel for the Government were in agreement with the contentions of defense counsel that the president of the special court-martial had erred in giving this instruction.

[128] See the equivocal language of the Court in United States v. Redenius, 4 USCMA 161, 15 CMR 161 (1954).

[129] United States v. Rios, 4 USCMA 203, 15 CMR 203 (1954).

[130] Art. 121; MANUAL FOR COURTS-MARTIAL, UNITED STATES, 1951, par. 200. United States v. Krawczyk, 4 USCMA 255, 15 CMR 255 (1954); United States v. Norris, 2 USCMA 236, 8 CMR 36 (1953); United States v. May, 3 USCMA 703, 14 CMR 121 (1954). In United States v. McCarthy, 4 USCMA 385, 15 CMR 385 (1954) the Court held that "stolen," within the meaning of the Dyer Act, does not include appropriation of a vehicle with the intent temporarily to deprive the rightful owner or possessor of its use.

[131] United States v. Johnson, 3 USCMA 709, 14 CMR 127 (1954).

[132] United States v. Krull, 3 USCMA 129, 11 CMR 129 (1953).

"An intention to pay for the property stolen or otherwise to replace it with an equivalent is not a defense, even though such an intention existed at the time of the theft, and, once a larceny is committed, a return of the property or payment for it is no defense."[133]

In order to put the lesser included offense of wrongful appropriation in issue a showing must be made that the accused intended to return the identical property misappropriated. In this connection money is regarded as property. Thus if misappropriated money has been spent, the fact that the accused intended to return the amount taken by him does not reduce the offense from larceny to wrongful appropriation.[134]

Whether the taking is with an intent permanently or temporarily to deprive the owner or other person of the property, it is necessary that the property have some value. Value, in some instances, may be inferred from the nature and description of the property. Thus a specification which describes a motor vehicle carries with it a sufficient showing of value.[135] If a specification alleges the value of the truck at $750.00, the action of the convening authority in approving so much of the specification as alleged that the accused wrongfully appropriated a motor vehicle which was described in the specification (without stating a sum) does not have the effect of eliminating the element of value.[136] However, an instruction is inadequate if it may be construed by a court-martial as not requiring a finding of value.[137]

Cases involving each of the common-law offenses now consolidated under Article 121 have been considered by the Court.[138]

Although it has not specifically passed on the question, the Court has intimated that the bare possession of recently stolen goods is not

[133] Par. 200*a* (6).

[134] United States v. Krawczyk, 4 USCMA 255, 15 CMR 255 (1954).

[135] United States v. Johnson, 3 USCMA 706, 14 CMR 124 (1954).

[136] United States v. May, 3 USCMA 703, 14 CMR 121 (1954). The Court in a dictum stated: "An omission of an allegation of specific value may preclude punishment greater than that for the least degree of the offense irrespective of the proven value. . . ."

[137] United States v. Peterson, 2 USCMA 645, 10 CMR 143 (1953); *cf.* United States v. Johnson, 3 USCMA 706, 14 CMR 124 (1954).

[138] United States v. Buck, 3 USCMA 341, 12 CMR 97 (1953) (larceny of chevrons); United States v. Valencia, 1 USCMA 415, 4 CMR 7 (1952) (embezzlement); United States v. Beasley, 3 USCMA 111, 11 CMR 111 (1953); United States v. Marrelli, 4 USCMA 276, 15 CMR 276 (1954) (false pretense—bad checks). Giving bad checks under less serious circumstances may be punished under Article 134. See MANUAL FOR COURTS-MARTIAL, UNITED STATES, 1951, par. 200 and model specifications pp. 489-490. The Code Committee has recommended that an additional punitive statute having provisions similar to the District of Columbia bad-check law be added to the Code to meet the particular needs of the services. ANNUAL REPORT, June 1, 1952, to December 31, 1953, p. 9.

sufficient to justify a conviction of larceny. But the exclusive and unexplained possession of recently stolen property might be regarded by the Court as justifying an inference that the possessor is the thief.[139]

Article 122—*Robbery*

The very "touchstone" of robbery is that it constitutes an offense against the person. Accordingly, a specification which alleges the accused did "by means of putting in fear, steal" from the victim is insufficient inasmuch as it fails to allege that the accused stole *from the person or in the presence of the victim.*[140]

Article 125—*Sodomy*

In the absence of a request, it is not error for the law officer to fail to instruct on the meaning of the words "unnatural carnal copulation."[141] This is in accordance with the rule that a failure to clarify commonly understood words used in an instruction is not reversible error unless a request has been made for such clarification.[142]

Character evidence is very important in a trial involving sodomy. Evidence of good general character may be of great value to the accused. Therefore, it was prejudicial error for a law officer in a trial involving this offense to refuse the following instruction or its equivalent:

> "The Court is instructed that evidence of good character, when considered in connection with the other evidence in the case, may generate a reasonable doubt; and the circumstances may be such that an established reputation of good character would alone create a reasonable doubt, although without it the other evidence would be convincing."[143]

Article 128—*Assault*

A. *Simple assault*

Simple assault is defined in the Code as an attempt or offer with unlawful force or violence to do bodily harm to another person, whether or not the attempt or offer is consummated. The *Manual*[144] states:

[139] United States v. Johnson, 3 USCMA 447, 13 CMR 3 (1953).
[140] United States v. Rios, 4 USCMA 203, 15 CMR 203 (1954).
[141] United States v. Phillips, 3 USCMA 137, 11 CMR 137 (1953).
[142] United States v. Day, 2 USCMA 416, 9 CMR 46 (1953).
[143] United States v. Phillips, 3 USCMA 137, 141, 11 CMR 137, 141 (1953).
[144] Par. 207. See also United States v. Simmons, 1 USCMA 691, 5 CMR 119 (1952). The specification was sufficient to allege simple assault. It failed to state whether the pistol was loaded. Par. 207*a* MANUAL FOR COURTS-MARTIAL, UNITED STATES, 1951, further provides: "To aim a pistol at a man at such distance that it clearly could not injure would not be an assault." The Court has indicated that this particular provision is, in reality, a departure from the subjective test stated in the *Manual.* United States v. Smith, 4 USCMA 41, 15 CMR 41 (1954).

"An offer to do bodily harm to another, as distinguished from an attempt to do such harm, is a putting of the other in reasonable fear that force will at once be applied to his person. Pointing an unloaded pistol which the assailant knows to be unloaded at another is not an attempt to do bodily harm with the pistol, for the assailant is cognizant of his inability to shoot the victim; yet such an act may be an assault if the victim is aware of the attack and is put in reasonable fear of bodily injury."

Notwithstanding this distinction, assault is regarded as a term of art; therefore, an allegation of assault permits proof either that the accused actually intended to commit a battery upon another, or that he put another in reasonable fear of immediate bodily harm.[145]

B. *Aggravated assault*

Section (b) of Article 128 defines two types of aggravated assault:

(1) Assault with a dangerous weapon or other means or force likely to produce death or grievous bodily harm; or

(2) An assault in which grievous bodily harm is intentionally inflicted with or without a weapon.

(1) *Subsection* (1)—The first subsection does not require a specific intent but the second demands that the injury be intentionally inflicted.[146] The Court dealt with the question whether the subjective test of apparent ability applied to these aggravated assaults. The *Manual*[147] indicates that an unloaded pistol, when presented as a firearm and not as a bludgeon, is not a dangerous weapon or a means or force likely to produce grievous bodily harm, and this would be so whether or not the assailant knew it was unloaded. This, according to the Court,[148] is unqualified objectivity, for it entirely omits the possible presence of reasonable apprehension.

In *Smith*[149] the accused and the alleged victim were involved in an argument while participating in a football game. After a physical encounter, the two were separated. The accused immediately extracted

[145] LEGAL AND LEGISLATIVE BASIS, MANUAL FOR COURTS-MARTIAL, UNITED STATES, 1951, p. 284. MANUAL FOR COURTS-MARTIAL, UNITED STATES, 1951, specification 99, appendix 6*c*.

[146] United States v. Woodson, 3 USCMA 372, 12 CMR 128 (1953). Article of War 93 made it an offense to assault with an intent to do bodily harm with a dangerous weapon, instrument or thing. A specific intent to do bodily harm was required. United States v. Cromartie, 1 USCMA 551, 4 CMR 143 (1952); United States v. Hunter, 2 USCMA 37, 6 CMR 37 (1952); United States v. Long, 2 USCMA 45, 6 CMR 45 (1952); United States v. Day, 2 USCMA 416, 9 CMR 46 (1953), United States v. Hopf, 1 USCMA 584, 5 CMR 12 (1952).

[147] Par. 207*b* (1).

[148] United States v. Smith, 4 USCMA 41, 15 CMR 41 (1954).

[149] *Ibid.*

a pocket knife with a five-inch blade from his clothing and began swinging it as he started toward the victim. Initially, there was a distance of approximately ten yards between the two. The victim ran as soon as the accused had advanced two or three steps. The accused stopped when an officer ordered him to do so. He had advanced only a few yards. The issue before the Court was whether—in view of the distance of several yards which at all times separated the participants—a finding of aggravated assault was sustainable. The Court applied the subjective test and affirmed the finding of guilty of an aggravated assault. In doing so, the Court did not purport to overrule the objective test provision in the *Manual* regarding pistols; instead, the Court simply refused to extend the provision to include a knife. The Court agreed that to brandish a knife from afar, without effort to establish contact, would fail in most cases to constitute any sort of assault, simple or aggravated but it proceeded to make the following statement:

> "Yet, once the prospect of uninvited contact develops to the point at which a reasonable man would be compelled to retreat, we believe that an assault has been committed. And if that prospective contact assumes the form of a cutting or stabbing with a knife—in most uses a dangerous weapon—we conclude that an aggravated assault has been committed. The form of the foreseeable contact—that is, whether it in fact involves a means likely to produce 'death or grievous bodily harm'—is the determinant as to aggravation. The element of distance is material in these premises only in deciding whether any assault was committed."[150]

The dangerous character of a weapon is tested not only by the weapon itself but also by the manner in which it is used.[151]

In this class of aggravated assaults fall all those accomplished not simply by means of instrumentalities normally considered "weapons," but also by means which, according to the manner of their use, are potentially dangerous. Thus the fists can be a means or force likely to produce grievous bodily harm.[152]

(2) *Subsection* (2)—Since an assault in which grievous bodily harm is intentionally inflicted with a weapon requires a specific intent, the law officer must determine in a case in which there is some allegation

[150] *Id.* at 46-47. Judge Latimer dissented. He was of the opinion that only a simple assault had been proved.

[151] United States v. Norton, 1 USCMA 411, 4 CMR 3 (1952) (knife).

[152] United States v. Vigil, 3 USCMA 474, 13 CMR 30 (1953). The victim was asleep and the blows from the fist of the accused fractured his cheek bones and his jaws and in addition caused the loss of eleven teeth.

of intoxication if it is shown to have been of such a degree that it may have prevented the accused from forming a specific intent. If so, an appropriate assault (or assaults) not requiring a specific intent must be included in the instructions. For instance, if an intoxicated accused sticks a bayonet in the leg of another in a manner to cause serious injury, the law officer should instruct on the lesser offense of assault with a dangerous weapon.[153]

In the absence of a request the law officer does not commit error if he does not define "grievous bodily harm."[154] It may be error to refuse a request, but whether this error is prejudicial may depend on the facts of a particular case. If the evidence that the victim suffered a fractured jaw is clear and unrebutted, it will establish "grievous bodily harm" as a matter of law.[155]

The vitally distinguishing feature between the aggravated assaults in subsections (1) and (2) is that in the latter bodily harm must be intentionally inflicted. Consequently, if an accused is charged with violating subsection (2) and the law officer confines his instructions to subsection (1), the court-martial commits prejudicial error[156] if it returns a finding that the accused was guilty under subsection (2)—the more serious offense. On the other hand, if an accused is charged with violating subsection (2), the court-martial by exceptions and substitutions may convict of an assault under subsection (1). This is permissible because subsection (1) is lesser included in subsection (2).[157]

C. *Summary*

In *Williams*[158] the accused after complaining of a headache was given aspirin and sent back to duty. When his company was ordered into formation, he went into a trench in a nearby hill. He fired several shots at his officer and a non-commissioned officer who had approached within 175 to 200 yards of his position. Subsequently the accused made his presence known and surrendered his rifle. The accused testified that he remembered only one shot; that he was not shooting at anybody; and that he had never had any trouble with the officer or non-commissioned officer. The accused was charged with an assault with intent to murder—a violation of Article 134. Because there was evidence that the accused did not intend to kill, the Court concluded that the law officer erred in failing to instruct on some lesser offense.

[153] United States v. Backley, 2 USCMA 496, 9 CMR 126 (1953).
[154] United States v. Dejewski, 3 USCMA 53, 11 CMR 53 (1953).
[155] *Ibid.*
[156] United States v. Wright, 1 USCMA 602, 5 CMR 30 (1952).
[157] United States v. Vigil, 3 USCMA 474, 13 CMR 30 (1953).
[158] 1 USCMA 231, 2 CMR 137 (1952).

The Court analyzed the evidence and the various types of assault and drew the following conclusions:

(1) Simple assault was not in issue because the firing of the weapon under the circumstances was of the aggravated type;
(2) Assault in which grievous bodily harm was inflicted was not in issue because all the bullets missed;
(3) Assault with a dangerous weapon was in issue and should have been the subject of instruction.

The Court also ruled out the necessity of instructing on an assault with intent to commit voluntary manslaughter. There was no evidence of heat or passion brought about by provocation. If the accused had killed the officer or noncommissioned officer, the offense would have been murder and not manslaughter.

Although the Court, for the purpose of illustrating a point stated that an assault with an intent to inflict grievous bodily harm would support a finding of aggravated assault under Article 128,[159] it has subsequently indicated that this is not an offense under the Code. In a dictum in another case the Court said:

> "The intent used in the instruction was an intent to inflict great bodily harm and while an assault based on that intent is no longer defined as an offense, if it were, we believe it would be less serious than the one proscribed by Article 128 (b) (2) and more serious than the one defined in Article 128 (b) (1). We further believe Congress concluded that Articles 128 and 134 of the Code carved out the necessary gradations of assault and that further refinement was not desirable as the previous offense of assault with intent to inflict great bodily harm was eliminated from the 1951 Code."[160]

It is not yet clearly settled whether an allegation of an assault with intent to inflict grievous bodily harm will support a finding of an aggravated assault under Article 128 (b) (1).

Article 130—*Housebreaking*

The Code states this offense is committed when there is an unlawful entry into a building or structure of another with an intent to commit a criminal offense therein. The Court rejected[161] a contention by

[159] United States v. Floyd, 2 USCMA 183, 7 CMR 59 (1953).

[160] United States v. Woodson, 3 USCMA 372, 375, 12 CMR 128, 131 (1953). There is no apparent difference in "grievous" bodily harm used in Article 128 and "great" bodily harm used in Article 118 (2). LEGAL AND LEGISLATIVE BASIS, MANUAL FOR COURTS-MARTIAL, UNITED STATES, 1951, p. 286.

[161] United States v. Williams, 4 USCMA 241, 15 CMR 241 (1954).

Government counsel that the entry was per se unlawful when undertaken with an intent to commit a crime in the building or structure. Instead, it held[162] that a trespass is an essential element of this offense. Consequently, it is necessary to allege and prove the entry was unlawful. And this element must be the subject of an instruction to the members of the court-martial. The Court stated that the *Manual*[163] description of this element was adequate except in those cases in which an accused justifiably requested more detailed instructions.[164] In the event of such a request, the law officer must include in his instructions additional information. The adequacy of the instruction will depend on the complexity of the facts in a particular case. The reviewing authorities must be satisfied that the members of the court-martial were sufficiently informed to act intelligently on the issue.

The Court has decided cases in which a tent,[165] a barracks[166] and a post exchange[167] were unlawfully entered.

Article 131—*Perjury*

Proof of perjury or false swearing cannot, without corroboration by other testimony or by circumstances tending to prove such falsity, be proved by the testimony of a single witness.[168] The Court held[169] that it is desirable for a law officer to instruct the court-martial on this rule requiring corroboration, but a failure to do so will not, in the absence of a request by the defense, constitute prejudicial error.

Article 132—*Frauds against the Government*

A. *Subsection* (1) (A)

Some of the several ways in which this Article may be violated have been considered by the Court. Subsection 1 (A) makes it an offense for the accused to make any claim against the United States knowing it to be false *or* fraudulent. Although a model specification in the *Manual*[170] permits an allegation that the conduct was false, fraudulent, or false and fradulent, the Court held there was only one offense. Consequently, an instruction that the claim was false *or* fraudulent is not prejudicial though the specification is phrased false *and* fraudulent.[171]

[162] *Ibid.*

[163] Par. 209.

[164] United States v. Williams, 4 USCMA 241, 15 CMR 241 (1954).

[165] United States v. Crunk, 4 USCMA 290, 15 CMR 290 (1954); United States v. Love, 4 USCMA 260, 15 CMR 260 (1954).

[166] United States v. Williams, 4 USCMA 241, 15 CMR 241 (1954).

[167] United States v. Armstrong, 4 USCMA 248, 15 CMR 248 (1954).

[168] MANUAL FOR COURTS-MARTIAL, UNITED STATES, 1951, pars. 210, 213*d* (4).

[169] United States v. Gomes, 3 USCMA 232, 11 CMR 232 (1953).

[170] Specification 106, appendix 6*c*.

[171] United States v. Ariola, 2 USCMA 637, 10 CMR 135 (1953).

The mere writing of a pretended claim, unknown to others, does not constitute a crime. Some further act is required in order to make a false claim. This act does not have to amount to presentment[172] for payment. It is sufficient that the act be one which would start the claim in circulation in official channels.[173]

B. *Subsection* (2) (B)

This subsection is violated when an accused, for the purpose of obtaining the approval, allowance, or payment of any claim against the United States or any officer thereof, makes any oath to any fact or to any writing or other paper knowing such oath to be false. The purpose of this provision is to punish a false oath when performed for the purpose of obtaining payment, approval or allowance of a claim. It is not material that a false claim may never be made or presented or that the accused may be entitled to the claim if established by proper means. The Court emphasized that a specification is sufficient if it alleges a false oath directed to obtaining pay for the accused regardless of his right to that pay if he had claimed it in a proper manner.[174]

C. *Subsection* (2) (C)

This subsection makes it unlawful to forge or counterfeit any signature upon any writing or paper for the purpose of obtaining payment of any claim against the United States. Signing the payroll is more than an acknowledgement of receipt of the money. It is a prerequisite to receiving it; therefore, if an accused signs the name of another and receives money to which he is not entitled, he violates this subsection.[175]

Article 133—*Conduct Unbecoming an Officer and Gentleman*

This Article is not confined to conduct punishable by other Articles. However, an act which violates another Article may, in addition, violate this one provided such act also amounts to conduct unbecoming an officer and a gentleman.[176] But if the act charged as conduct unbecoming an officer and gentleman constitutes a separate offense, the

[172] For the difference in making a claim and presenting it see MANUAL FOR COURTS-MARTIAL, UNITED STATES, 1951, par. 211*a*, and LEGAL AND LEGISLATIVE BASIS, MANUAL FOR COURTS-MARTIAL, UNITED STATES, 1951, p. 292.

[173] United States v. Steele, 2 USCMA 379, 9 CMR 9 (1953). The Court made these statements in connection with deciding whether the specification alleged an offense.

[174] United States v. Lawrence, 3 USCMA 628, 14 CMR 46 (1954). The accused made a knowingly false statement that he did not have an "overpaid balance" at the time he opened a temporary pay record.

[175] United States v. Field, 3 USCMA 182, 11 CMR 182 (1953).

[176] MANUAL FOR COURTS-MARTIAL, UNITED STATES, 1951, par. 212.

particular requirements of proof of such offense must be met in order to establish the charge.[177]

The Court has considered cases involving a violation of this Article (or its predecessors) which include the following charges: an accused with intent to deceive made a false statement to two special agents of the Federal Bureau of Investigation;[178] wrongfully and knowingly permitting and assisting in the showing of lewd and obscene motion pictures;[179] wrongfully and knowingly instructing a soldier to deny knowledge of lewd and obscene films he had procured should he be called to testify in connection with an investigation then pending;[180] cheating on a written examination;[181] assaulting and using obscene language toward his wife in a semi-public place;[182] and misappropriation of food belonging to an enlisted men's mess.[183]

Article 134—*General Article*

Jurisdictional aspects of the various offenses included in this Article have been considered in Chapter 4. Other aspects warrant discussion in this section. Article 134 contains three different clauses:

(1) All disorders and neglects to the prejudice of good order and discipline in the armed forces;

(2) All conduct of a nature to bring discredit upon the armed forces; and

(3) Crimes and offenses not capital.

Assaults committed with the intent to commit certain of the more serious crimes such as murder, voluntary manslaughter, rape, robbery and sodomy are specifically included in the *Manual*[184] discussion of this Article. The list is not exclusive. Others not enumerated may be punishable thereunder. A study of the various service predecessors of Article 134 will be helpful in identifying other assaults of this type which have been recognized as offenses in the past.

An assault with intent to murder has been the source of some difficulty and will be discussed separately.

[177] United States v. Gomes, 3 USCMA 232, 11 CMR 232 (1953) (perjury and false swearing).

[178] *Ibid.* Manual for Courts-Martial, United States Coast Guard, 1949, Art. 212.

[179] United States v. Jewson, 1 USCMA 652, 5 CMR 80 (1952) (A. W. 95). There was also a charge that accused made a false statement under oath that he had no prior knowledge of the film.

[180] United States v. Stewart, 1 USCMA 648, 5 CMR 76 (1952) (A. W. 95).

[181] United States v. Welch, 1 USCMA 402, 3 CMR 136 (1952) (reversed because of a violation of accused's right against self-incrimination).

[182] United States v. Downard, 1 USCMA 346, 3 CMR 80 (1952) (reversed because of errors in the instructions given by the law officer).

[183] United States v. Krull, 3 USCMA 129, 11 CMR 129 (1953).

[184] Par. 213*d*.

A. *Assault with intent to murder*

Actual infliction of injury is not a necessary element of this offense and it need not be alleged or proved.[185] When a substantive offense, as here, is the basis of one of the forms of aggravated assault, the law officer must include a definition of the substantive offense in his instructions.[186] The logical place to find a definition of murder is Article 118 of the Code, but not all of the definitions of murder contained in that Article are suitable for this purpose. This may be explained by the fact that the Court regards the offense of assault with intent to murder, if the alleged victim is one person, as an assault with intent to kill.[187] In this connection the Court stated that the crime of assault with intent to murder is reserved exclusively for those instances in which the accused "genuinely, albeit unsuccessfully, proposed to produce the death of his victim."[188] However, Article 118 does not confine the definition of murder to situations in which the accused has an intent to kill. For instance, Article 118 (2) provides in substance:

> Any person subject to this code who, without justification or excuse, unlawfully kills a human being when he—intends to kill *or inflict great bodily harm* . . . is guilty of murder.

Should a law officer include both these definitions of murder in his instructions, he commits error because he permits the court-martial to convict the accused of an intent to kill (i.e., assault with intent to murder) when the instruction required only a finding that he intended to inflict great bodily harm.[189] Whether the error is prejudicial depends on the facts of a particular case. The Court appears to have adopted the technique employed by it in determining the prejudicial effect of erroneous instructions in desertion cases. Accordingly, the error is prejudicial if one of the "rational possibilities" is that the accused intended seriously to disable rather than to kill his victim. On the other hand, the Court has indicated that if the evidence is such that the court-martial must find the accused intended to kill, the words "inflict great bodily harm" in an instruction will be regarded as harm-

[185] United States v. Shelton, 4 USCMA 116, 15 CMR 116 (1954).

[186] United States v. Williams, 1 USCMA 231, 2 CMR 137 (1952); United States v. Banks, 1 USCMA 479, 4 CMR 71 (1952); United States v. Floyd, 2 USCMA 183, 7 CMR 59 (1953).

[187] United States v. Floyd, 2 USCMA 183, 7 CMR 59 (1953); United States v. Bentley, 3 USCMA 625, 14 CMR 43 (1954).

[188] United States v. Holman, 3 USCMA 396, 399, 12 CMR 152, 155 (1953).

[189] United States v. Floyd, 2 USCMA 183, 7 CMR 59 (1953); United States v. Bentley, 3 USCMA 625, 14 CMR 43 (1954); United States v. Christensen, 4 USCMA 22, 14 CMR 22 (1954).

less error.[190] Similar instructional problems may arise should the law officer employ other definitions of murder in Article 118 which do not require an intent to kill.[191]

An assault with intent to commit murder requires a specific and not a general intent to kill.[192] An assault of such nature and under such circumstances as might reasonably be expected to result in death does not establish an intent to murder as a matter of law. However, such a showing may in itself, in some cases, constitute sufficient evidence of a purpose to kill to permit the triers of fact to conclude as a matter of fact that the accused had the intent to kill.[193]

A definition of murder which states that a court-martial may find the accused guilty if he acted in a way inherently dangerous to others without any intent to cause death of, or great bodily harm to, any particular person is likewise incorrect if the acts of the accused are directed solely at one person.[194] The Court has stated, without explanation, that under certain circumstances the offense of an assault with intent to murder may be extended to "acts inherently dangerous which show a wanton disregard for the lives of more than one."[195]

B. *Negligent homicide*

Negligent homicide is an unlawful killing coupled with simple negligence.[196] It is lesser included in involuntary manslaughter. Imposing criminal liability for negligent homicide is a relatively new concept in criminal law.[197] Although not specifically mentioned in the Code, this offense is definitely included in the *Manual.*[198] The Army

[190] United States v. Christensen, 4 USCMA 22, 14 CMR 22 (1954). Judge Quinn apparently first suggested this technique be applied to this offense in his dissent in United States v. Woodson, 3 USCMA 372, 12 CMR 128 (1953). He regarded the intent to kill as the only intent in issue in these two cases.

[191] United States v. Woodson, 3 USCMA 372, 12 CMR 128 (1953). Three types of murder were included in the instruction.

[192] United States v. Holman, 3 USCMA 396, 12 CMR 152 (1953). See MANUAL FOR COURTS-MARTIAL, UNITED STATES, 1951, par. 213*d* (1), (c), (d), (e) for specific intent to rape, rob and commit sodomy.

[193] United States v. Holman, 3 USCMA 396, 12 CMR 152 (1953).

[194] United States v. Woodson, 3 USCMA 372, 12 CMR 128 (1953). This is consistent with the murder cases. See Article 118 *supra.*

[195] *Id.* at 375, 12 CMR at 131. See Art. 118 (3). For a discussion of a lesser included offense to a charge of assault with intent to commit murder, see United States v. Williams, 1 USCMA 231, 2 CMR 137 (1952).

[196] United States v. Kirchner, 1 USCMA 477, 4 CMR 69 (1952); United States v. Russell, 3 USCMA 696, 14 CMR 114 (1954).

[197] Since negligent homicide has not been given universal recognition as a criminal offense it is not regarded by the Court as an offense under the laws of war. A military tribunal may impose punishment for negligent homicide if it was an offense under the penal code of an occupied country, provided the occupying power has decreed that such code is a part of the "law in effect" in the occupied country. United States v. Schultz, 1 USCMA 512, 4 CMR 104 (1952).

[198] Appendix 6, sample specification 144; par. 198*b*, appendix 12, Table of Maximum Punishments.

and the Air Force recognized this offense prior to the Code, but the Navy did not.[199] In two cases[200] the Court appeared to assume that negligent homicide was punishable as conduct of a nature to bring discredit upon the armed forces, or a disorder and neglect to the prejudice of good order and discipline in the armed froces. Then, in a Navy case,[201] it was argued that since Article 134 must be interpreted in the light of existing service customs and usages there were no grounds to make this an offense for that service. The Court agreed that it must look to customs and usages but in this situation decided it would examine the manner in which all the services had treated this problem. The Court concluded that the *Manual,* Army and Air Force precedents, and its own decisions recognizing the offense, should be followed and that it would apply to sailors as well as to soldiers and airmen.[202]

The Court approved a definition of negligent homicide which stated, in substance, that it is unlawfully causing the death of another by simple negligence—that is, an act or omission not negligent to such a degree as to justify a charge of voluntary manslaughter—but nevertheless one which exhibits a lack of that degree of care for the safety of others which a reasonably prudent person would have exercised under the circumstances.[203]

When an accused shoots and kills a fellow guard, he may be tried for the offense of negligent homicide on the ground that he did not use reasonable means to determine the identity of the victim before he fired. The law officer is not required to give a separate instruction on a defense based on a mistake of fact in this situation in the absence of a request. The very nature of the offense, of necessity, requires the court-martial to consider an alleged mistake in making its determination on the issue of negligence.[204]

C. *Wrongful possession of habit-forming drugs*

If an accused is charged with wrongful possession of a habit-forming drug, he may defend on the ground of ignorance of the presence of the drug. In this situation, an instruction which permits a court-martial to find an accused guilty of this offense based on negligence in not dis-

[199] United States v. Kirchner, 1 USCMA 477, 4 CMR 69 (1952).

[200] United States v. Roman, 1 USCMA 244, 2 CMR 150 (1952); United States v. Clark, 1 USCMA 201, 2 CMR 107 (1952).

[201] United States v. Kirchner, 1 USCMA 477, 4 CMR 69 (1952).

[202] *Ibid.* The Court recognized that some offenses may be peculiarly limited to one or more of the services.

[203] United States v. Bull, 3 USCMA 635, 14 CMR 53 (1954). Negligence of a higher degree than simple negligence will, of course, support a conviction of negligent homicide if the homicide was unlawfully caused by such negligence. For a full instruction in a negligent homicide case involving a shooting, see United States v. Perruccio, 4 USCMA 28, 15 CMR 28 (1954).

[204] United States v. Perruccio, 4 USCMA 28, 15 CMR 28 (1954).

covering the presence of the drug is prejudicial error.[205] If the words of the *Manual*[206] relating to ignorance of fact are followed too literally a law officer may commit this error. The Court indicated there may be a difference between a person who knows that he possesses an article which may or may not be contraband and one who honestly, although negligently, is ignorant of the presence of the article. In the case of the former, there may be some duty to determine its characteristics and if an accused unreasonably fails to do so he may be convicted for having it in his possession.[207] The Court further stated that the authorities uniformly hold that a conscious possession must be affirmatively shown, either by direct or circumstantial evidence.[208]

D. *Leaving scene of accident*

Leaving the scene of an accident is an offense in which there is no requirement that knowledge that there had been an accident be set out in the specification or established by the prosecution as a part of its case.[209] Lack of knowledge is an affirmative defense and instructions thereon are required only when it is reasonably raised by the evidence.[210]

E. *Willful discharge of a firearm*

Willfulness is an essential element of the offense of willful discharge of a firearm under circumstances such as to endanger human life and it is reversible error to omit it from instructions.[211]

F. *Taking indecent liberties with a child*

This offense may be committed without any physical contact or touching if it involves an indecent exposure with intent to gratify the lust, passions, or sex desires of either the person committing the act or of the child. This is a more serious offense than indecent exposure.[212]

[205] United States v. Lampkins, 4 USCMA 31, 15 CMR 31 (1954).

[206] Par. 154*a* (3). "Unless otherwise provided (expressly or by implication) by the law denouncing the offense in question, ignorance or mistake of fact will exempt a person from criminal responsibility if it is an honest ignorance or mistake and not the result of carelessness or fault on his part. . . ."

[207] United States v. Lampkins, 4 USCMA 31, 15 CMR 31 (1954) (dictum in part).

[208] *Ibid.*

[209] United States v. Eagleson, 3 USCMA 685, 14 CMR 103 (1954); United States v. Russell, 3 USCMA 696, 14 CMR 114 (1954). Judge Latimer considers knowledge as an essential element.

[210] *Cf.* United States v. Majia, 2 USCMA 616, 10 CMR 114 (1953) and other cases involving willful disobedience of a superior officer discussed under Article 90 this chapter.

[211] United States v. Nidy, 3 USCMA 408, 12 CMR 164 (1953); United States v. Simmons, 1 USCMA 691, 5 CMR 119 (1952).

[212] United States v. Brown, 3 USCMA 454, 13 CMR 10 (1953).

G. *Other offenses under Article 134*

In addition to the foregoing the Court found the following types of conduct constituted a violation of this Article:

(1) Carrying a concealed weapon;[213]

(2) Wrongfully and unlawfully accepting from another enlisted man a specified sum of money to transport a Korean female in a Government vehicle;[214]

(3) Wrongful sale of military passes;[215]

(4) Deceitful possession of a false liberty pass;[216]

(5) Solicitation to make a false statement in a pretrial investigation;[217]

(6) Receiving property stolen from the United States with knowledge of its character;[218]

(7) Wrongfully and unlawfully attempting to entice another to engage in sexual intercourse with a female to be directed to him by the accused;[219]

(8) Civilian employee subject to Code using his official position to secure gifts;[220]

(9) Negligent failure to deliver mail by one entrusted with this duty;[221]

(10) Obstructing justice[222] (i.e., assault and battery on a person on account of her having testified as a witness in a summary court-martial);

(11) Impersonating an officer;[223]

(12) Unlawful entry in a tent;[224]

(13) Wrongful use of a habit-forming narcotic drug (morphine).[225]

H. *Crimes and Offenses Not Capital*

This clause, unlike the other two, is very definite in the limits of

[213] United States v. Bentley, 3 USCMA 625, 14 CMR 43 (1954).

[214] United States v. Alexander, 3 USCMA 346, 12 CMR 102 (1953).

[215] United States v. Karl, 3 USCMA 427, 12 CMR 183 (1953). The Court was considering the sufficiency of the specifications.

[216] United States v. Frantz, 2 USCMA 161, 7 CMR 37 (1953).

[217] United States v. Isbell, 1 USCMA 131, 2 CMR 37 (1952).

[218] United States v. Herndon, 1 USCMA 461, 4 CMR 53 (1952).

[219] United States v. Snyder, 1 USCMA 423, 4 CMR 15 (1952). A board of review had decided it was not an offense.

[220] United States v. Marker, 1 USCMA 393, 3 CMR 127 (1952).

[221] United States v. Beach, 2 USCMA 172, 7 CMR 48 (1953).

[222] United States v. Long, 2 USCMA 60, 5 CMR 60 (1952).

[223] United States v. Messenger, 2 USCMA 21, 6 CMR 21 (1952); Criticized in Note, 22 Geo. Wash. L. Rev. 76 (1953).

[224] United States v. Love, 4 USCMA 260, 15 CMR 260 (1954).

[225] United States v. Williamson, 4 USCMA 320, 15 CMR 320 (1954).

its application. It is concerned with those crimes and offenses denounced by Congress and triable in federal courts.[226]

An act of misconduct which *may* be charged under this clause, does not necessarily have to be so charged. If the conduct violates other clauses it is permissible to proceed on the theory that other clauses were violated.[227]

When a specification alleges a crime or offense not capital, a failure to prove every element of the federal offense does not preclude punishment of the misconduct under the other clauses in this Article if the requirements of either of these other clauses are met by the proof.[228]

Section 643 of Title 18, United States Code provides:

> "Whoever, being an officer, employee or agent of the United States or of any department or agency thereof, having received public money which he is not authorized to retain as salary, pay or emolument, fails to render his accounts for the same as provided by law is guilty of embezzlement, and shall be fined in a sum equal to the amount of the money embezzled or imprisoned not more than ten years, or both; but if the amount embezzled does not exceed $100, he shall be fined not more than $1,000 or imprisoned not more than one year, or both."

The majority of the Court do not regard the mere filing or rendering of the account according to the requirements of the law as to time, manner and place as sufficient to prevent conviction under this statute. Instead, they interpret the statute as requiring a true accounting of the stewardship.[229]

In preparing a specification under this statute, it is better to allege a "willful" violation and then the law officer should instruct that "willful" is an essential element of the offense. The substitution of "wrongful"[230] in a specification is acceptable in this particular situation, but it is doubtful that an *instruction* would meet the approval of the majority of the Court unless it included "willful."[231] However,

[226] MANUAL FOR COURTS-MARTIAL, UNITED STATES, 1951, 213*c*. The Court is required under this section to interpret Acts of Congress other than the Code. See United States v. McCarthy, 4 USCMA 385, 15 CMR 385 (1954) (Dyer Act).

[227] United States v. Herndon, 1 USCMA 461, 4 CMR 53 (1952).

[228] United States v. Long, 2 USCMA 60, 6 CMR 60 (1952). The same principle operates if an offense is charged under one Article and it proves to be a violation of another Article. United States v. O'Neil, 3 USCMA 416, 12 CMR 172 (1953).

[229] United States v. Doyle, 3 USCMA 585, 14 CMR 3 (1954); United States v. McElroy, 3 USCMA 606, 14 CMR 24 (1954).

[230] See Judge Brosman's concurrence in the result in United States v. McElroy, 3 USCMA 606, 14 CMR 24 (1954).

[231] *Ibid.*

the absence of the use of "willful" may not be prejudicial if the accused's sworn testimony is construed as an admission of willfulness.[232]

I. *Offenses which are not punishable under Article 134*

The Court has made it clear that there are some well-defined limitations on the application of this Article. For example, the Court has held that Congress intended Article 121 of the Code to preempt the field of misappropriation of another's property with the result that courts-martial are not free under Article 134 to convict an accused of any wrongful taking which fails to fall within the prohibitions of Article 121.[233] Moreover, the Court decided that new varieties of desertion may not be derived from Article 134.[234] All instances in which any member of the Armed Forces is, through his own fault, not at the proper place at the required time is covered by Articles 85, 86 and 87 and the Court refused to permit an offense sounding in unauthorized absence to be made the subject of punishment under Article 134.[235] And further, the Court held[236] that Congress proposed to cover the entire range of offenses which are assimilable to misbehavior before the enemy under Article 99 and therefore any misconduct before the enemy not covered by Article 99 cannot be punished under Article 134.

[232] *Ibid.* Judge Quinn stated the admission did not cover the period in which the violation was alleged to have occurred. Judge Latimer considered that proving the elements in the statute presented a prima facie case.

[233] United States v. Norris, 2 USCMA 236, 8 CMR 36 (1953).

[234] United States v. Deller, 3 USCMA 409, 12 CMR 165 (1953).

[235] United States v. Johnson, 3 USCMA 174, 11 CMR 174 (1953).

[236] United States v. Hallett, 4 USCMA 378, 15 CMR 378 (1954); United States v. Hamilton, 4 USCMA 383, 15 CMR 383 (1954).

CHAPTER 15

Military Habeas Corpus

Preliminary Considerations

The mobilization of over twelve million persons into the armed forces in World War II made necessary a vastly expanded resort to court-martial proceedings to enforce criminal law. The trial by military tribunals of civilian employees of the military establishment in overseas areas and of prisoners of war and war crimes defendants added substantially to the number confined by military authority. On January 31, 1950, there remained in federal penal institutions 2508[1] prisoners serving civilian type felony sentences imposed by military tribunals. Those sentenced to serve terms of more than one year for felonies involving moral turpitude are sent to federal penal institutions. All other military prisoners including those guilty of purely military offenses are confined in post guardhouses, rehabilitation centers or United States Disciplinary Barracks. Before World War II, legal problems arising from attempts to invoke the remedy of habeas corpus by military prisoners were rare and were primarily of historical and academic interest. Since 1945 the quantitative pressure of this military prisoner population, augmented by the product of the Korean operation has produced a substantial volume of case law in the field of military habeas corpus, has caused the United States Supreme Court to review the subject, and has made it one of practical interest to the private practitioner as well as the military lawyer.

Accuracy requires expansion of the concise chapter title "Military Habeas Corpus" to "A Brief Study of the History and Scope of Habeas Corpus Review of Detention Imposed by Military Authority." The material lends itself to the following organizations: I. Historical Background; II. Habeas Corpus Jurisdiction; III. Habeas Corpus Pre-

[1] From official records compiled by the Corrections Branch, Adjutant General's Office, Department of the Army, from periodic wardens' reports.

requisites; IV. Types of Military Detention Reviewable; V. Grounds for Habeas Corpus Relief; and VI. Conclusions.

I

Historical Background of the Writ of Habeas Corpus

"The writ of habeas corpus is of immemorial antiquity. It is deduced by the standard writers on the English law from the great charter of King John. It is unquestionable, however, that it is substantially of much earlier date; and it may be referred without improbability, to the period of the Roman invasion. Like the trial by jury, it entered into the institutions of Rome before the Christian era, if not as early as the times of the republic. Through the long series of political struggles which gave form to the British constitution, it was claimed as the birthright of every Englishman, and our ancestors brought it with them as such to this country. At the common law, it issued whenever a citizen was denied the exercise of his personal liberty, or was deprived of his rightful control over any member of his household, his wife, his child, his ward, or his servant. It issued from the courts of the sovereign, and in his name, at the instance of any one who invoked it, either for himself or another. It commanded, almost in the words of the Roman edict,—'De libero homine exhibendo' (D. 43, T. 29),—that the party under detention should be produced before the court, there to await its decree. It left no discretion with the party to whom it was addressed. He was not to constitute himself the judge of his own rights or of his own conduct; but to bring in the body, and to declare the cause wherefore he had detained it; and the judge was then to determine whether that cause was sufficient in law or not. Such in America, as well as England, was the well known, universally recognized writ of habeas corpus."[2]

Blackstone traced the ancestry of the writ of habeas corpus back through Coke and Bracton to the ancient writ *de odio et atia.*[3] Radin

[2] This succinct statement of the historical aspect of the writ of habeas corpus was made in 1855 by Judge John K. Kane of the Federal District Court for the Eastern District of Pennsylvania in United States v. Williamson, 28 Fed. Cas. 686 at 688 no. 16, 721 (E. D. Pa. 1855).

[3] 3 Blackstone, Commentaries, Cooley, 4th ed., 128-129 (1899):

"The writ de odio et atia was anciently used to be directed to the sheriff, commanding him to inquire whether a prisoner charged with murder was committed upon just cause of suspicion, or merely *propter odium et atium,* for hatred and ill-will; and if upon the inquisition due cause of suspicion did not appear, then there issued another writ for the shiriff to admit him to bail. This writ, according to Bracton, (*i*) ought not to be denied to any man, it being expressly ordered to be made out *gratis,* without any denial, by *magna carta,* c. 26, and has established that it was this writ *de odio et atia* which Magna Carta provided should "be denied to no man,"[4] but also has shown that it differed in material respects from the modern writ of habeas corpus.[5]

Habeas corpus in the form pertinent to this study is spoken of by Blackstone in this language:

> ". . . the great and efficacious writ, in all manner of illegal confinement, is that of *habeas corpus ad subjiciendum;* directed to the person detaining another, and commanding him to produce the body of the prisoner, with the day and cause of his caption and detention, *ad faciendum, subjiciendum, et recipiendum,* to do, submit to, and receive whatsoever the judge or court awarding such writ shall consider in that behalf.
>
> ". . . THIS IS A HIGH PREROGATIVE WRIT, and therefore by the common law issuing out of the court of king's bench not only in term-time, but also during the vacation by a *fiat* from the chief justice or any other of the judges, and running into all parts of the king's dominions; for the king is at all times entitled to have an account, why the liberty of any of his subjects is restrained wherever that restraint may be inflicted."[6]

Judge-made law in the reign of Charles I held that a prisoner committed by special command of the king or by the lords of the privy council could not be granted either release or bail upon habeas corpus even though held without any cause assigned. The oppressive denial by King's Bench of habeas corpus relief to Jenks, who was in 1676 committed by the king in council for a turbulent speech at Guildhall, resulted in the Habeas Corpus Act of 31 Charles II, c. 2.[7] Interestingly enough this famous act excepted treason and felony and addressed itself

statute West. 2, 13 Edw. 1, c. 29. But the statute of Gloucester, 6 Edw. I, c. 9, restrained it in the case of killing by misadventure or self-defense, and the statute 28 Edw. III, c. 9, abolished it in all cases whatsoever: but as the statute 42 Edw. III, c. 1, repealed all statutes then in being, contrary to the great charter, Sir Edward Coke is of opinion . . . that the writ *de odio et atia* was thereby revived."

[4] Radin, Anglo-American Legal History 209 (1936).

[5] *Id.* at 209-211 for a discussion of the writ *de odio et atia.*

[6] 3 Blackstone, Commentaries, 131 (Cooley ed., 1899).

[7] *Id.* at 134-136. In part this Act provided:

"That on complaint and request in writing by or on behalf of any person committed and charged with any *crime* (unless committed for treason or felony expressed in the warrant . . .); the lord chancellor or any of the twelve judges, in vacation, upon viewing a copy of the warrant, or affidavit that a copy is denied, shall . . . award a *habeas corpus* for such prisoner, returnable immediately before himself or any other of the judges; and upon the return made shall discharge the party, if bailable, upon giving security to appear and answer to the accusation in the proper court of judicature. . . . 3. That the writ shall be returned and the prisoner brought up, within a limited time according to the distance, not exceeding in any case twenty days."

to granting bail rather than testing jurisdiction. Today it would no doubt be considered a most inadequate remedy. The Habeas Corpus Act did not change the nature of the common law proceeding or the practice of the courts in granting the writ.[8] *Bushell's* case,[9] decided before the Habeas Corpus Act, firmly established that the Court of Common Pleas in England, although it possessed no criminal jurisdiction, had the common law power to issue writs of habeas corpus.

The American colonists brought with them the writ of habeas corpus.[10] The Articles of Confederation contained no provision concerning habeas corpus and the only Constitutional treatment of the subject was in Article I, Section 9, Clause 2, which requires that "the Privilege of the Writ of Habeas Corpus shall not be suspended unless when in Cases of Rebellion or Invasion the public Safety may require it." Thus it may be said that the Constitution simply assumed the existence of the remedy of habeas corpus.[11] Chief Justice Marshall expressed the opinion in 1807, in *Ex parte Bollman*,[12] that the exceptional power to suspend the writ vested in Congress and not the President, and this was reaffirmed by Chief Justice Taney on circuit in 1861 in *Ex parte Merryman*.[13]

The earliest pronouncement of the United States Supreme Court on habeas corpus was made in 1795 in an original proceeding in which the Court admitted to bail in the sum of $4000 a defendant charged

[8] Simmons v. Georgia Iron & Coal Co., 117 Ga. 305, 43 S. E. 780 (1903). This case contains an interesting statement of the history of the writ of habeas corpus.

[9] Reported in Sir Thomas Jones 18, 84 Eng. Rep. 1123; stated in Wood's case, 3 Wils. 175, 95 Eng. Rep. 996 (1771); restated in *Ex parte* Bollman, 4 Cranch *75 at *80-81 (U. S. 1807).

[10] *Ex parte* Yerger, 8 Wall. 85 at 95 (U. S. 1868). See LONGSDORF, HABEAS CORPUS—A PROTEAN WRIT AND REMEDY, 8 F. R. D. 179 (1948).

[11] United States v. Williamson, 28 Fed. Cas. 686 at 688, No. 16,726 (E. D. Pa. 1855), contains the following account of the deliberations of the Constitutional convention on this matter: "When the federal convention was engaged in framing a constitution for the United States, a proposition was submitted to it by one of the members, that 'the privileges and benefits of the writ of habeas corpus shall be enjoyed in this government in the most expeditious and ample manner; and shall not be suspended by the legislature except upon the most urgent and pressing occasions.' See the Madison Papers (vol. 3, 1365). The committee to whom this was referred for consideration, would seem to have regarded the privilege in question as too definitely implied in the idea of free government to need any formal assertion or confirmation; for they struck out that part of the proposed article in which it was affirmed, and retained only so much as excluded the question of its suspension from the ordinary range of congressional legislation. The convention itself must have concurred in their views; for in the constitution, as digested, and finally ratified, and as it stands now, there is neither enactment nor recognition of the privilege of this writ, except as it is implied in the provision that it shall not be suspended. It stands then under the constitution of the United States, as it was under the common law of English America, an indefeasible privilege, above the sphere of ordinary legislation."

[12] 4 Cranch *75 at *101 (U. S. 1807).

[13] 17 Fed. Cas. 144, No. 9487 (D. Mo. 1861).

with treason in the federal district court for Pennsylvania.[14] In an original proceeding in 1806 the Supreme Court again granted habeas corpus, to a person committed in Alexandria, Virginia, upon failure to post a peace bond in the sum of $4000, upon the ground that the warrant did not state an offense. In spite of his own momentous decision in *Marbury v. Madison,*[15] that the Supreme Court under the Constitution did not have original jurisdiction to issue a writ of mandate, Chief Justice Marshall speaking for the Court granted the writ of habeas corpus.[16] The following year in 1807 in *Ex parte Bollman and Swartwout, supra,* Chief Justice Marshall, as spokesman for the majority of a divided Court, again granted an original application for habeas corpus. That this was an original application by these petitioners, who were co-conspirators with Aaron Burr,[17] is made clear from the statement in the dissenting opinion of Justice Johnson, that, "the prisoners are in confinement under a commitment ordered by the superior court of the District of Columbia, upon a charge of high treason. This motion has for its object their discharge or admission to bail, under an order of this court. . . ."[18] In granting the writ Marshall made the singular pronouncement that, "The decision that the individual shall be imprisoned, must always precede the application for a writ of *habeas corpus,* and this writ must always be for the purpose of revising that decision, and therefore, appellate in its nature."[19] The hold-

[14] United States v. Hamilton, 3 Dall. 17 (U. S. 1795).

[15] 1 Cranch 137 (U. S. 1803).

[16] *Ex parte* Burford, 3 Cranch 448 (U. S. 1806). The Chief Justice said: "There is some obscurity in the act of congress, and some doubts were entertained by the court as to the construction of the constitution. The court, however, in favor of liberty, was willing to grant the *habeas corpus.* But the case of *United States v. Hamilton,* 3 Dall. 17, is decisive. It was there determined, that this court could grant a *habeas corpus;* therefore, let the writ issue, returnable immediately, together with a certiorari, as prayed."

[17] *Ex parte* Bollman and Swartwout, 4 Cranch *75 at *118 (U. S. 1807).

[18] *Id.* at 101.

[19] *Id.* at 100. At page 100 the Chief Justice said:

"If the act of Congress gives this court the power to award a writ of *habeas corpus* in the present case, it remains to inquire whether that act be compatible with the constitution. In the *mandamus case* (*Marbury v. Madison,* 1 Cr. 175), it was decided, that this court would not exercise original jurisdiction, except so far as that jurisdiction was given by the constitution. But so far as that case has distinguished between original and appellate jurisdiction, that which the court is now asked to exercise is clearly appellate. It is the revision of a decision of an inferior court, by which a citizen has been committed to jail.

"It has been demonstrated at the bar, that the question brought forward on a *habeas corpus,* is always distinct from that which is involved in the cause itself. The question whether the individual shall be imprisoned, is always distinct from the question whether he shall be convicted or acquitted of the charge on which he is to be tried, and therefore, these questions are separated, and may be decided in different courts. The decision that the individual shall be imprisoned, must always precede the application for a writ of *habeas corpus,* and this writ must always be for the purpose of revising that decision, and therefore, appellate in its nature."

ing was that all habeas corpus petitions are addressed to the appellate jurisdiction of the Court and hence properly lie. That the Court so intended was highlighted by the powerful dissent of Associate Justice William Johnson who said, ". . . the principle in *Marbury v. Madison* applies as much to the issuing of a *habeas corpus* in a case of treason, as to the issuing of a *mandamus* in a case not more remote from the original jurisdiction of this court."[20]

This interesting controversy of original versus appellate jurisdiction simmered for sixty-one years until reviewed in 1868 in *Ex parte Yerger*.[21] In that case a private citizen held upon a charge of murder for trial by a military commission applied to a federal circuit court for habeas corpus relief and the writ being there dismissed petitioned the Supreme Court for certiorari to grant the writ denied below. The contention was that the Congressional Act of March 27, 1868, passed to divest the Supreme Court of jurisdiction in *McCardle's Case*[22] had deprived it of all habeas corpus jurisdiction. The Court in rejecting the assertion said:

[20] *Id.* at *105. In dissent Justice Johnson said, at *104-5:

"It appears to my mind, that the case of *Hamilton* bears upon the face of it evidence of its being entitled to little consideration, and that the authority of it was annihilated by the very able decision in *Marbury v. Madison.* In this case, it was decided, that Congress could not vest in the supreme court any original powers beyond those to which this court is restricted by the constitution. That an act of Congress vesting in this court the power to issue a writ of *mandamus,* in a case not within their original jurisdiction, and in which they were not called upon to exercise an appellate jurisdiction, was unconstitutional, and void. In the case of *Hamilton,* the court does not assign the reasons on which it founds its decision, but it is fair to presume, that they adopted the idea which appears to have been admitted by the district-attorney in his argument, to wit, that this court possessed a concurrent power with the district court in admitting to bail. Now, a concurrent power in such a case must be an original power, and the principle in *Marbury v. Madison* applies as much to the issuing of a *habeas corpus* in a case of treason, as to the issuing of a *mandamus* in a case not more remote from the original jurisdiction of this court. Having thus disembarrassed the question from the effect of precedent, I proceed to consider the construction of the two sections of the judiciary act above referred to.

"It is necessary to premise, that the case of treason is one in which this court possesses neither original nor appellate jurisdiction. The 14th section of the judiciary act, so far as it has relation to this case, is in these words: 'All the before-mentioned courts (of which this is one) of the United States shall have power to issue writs of *scire facias, habeas corpus,* and all other writs not specially provided for by statute, which may be necessary for the exercise of their respective jurisdictions, and agreeable to the principles and usages of law.' I do not think it material to the opinion I entertain, what construction is given to this sentence. If the power to issue the writs of *scire facias* and *habeas corpus* be not restricted to the cases within the original or appellate jurisdiction of this court, the case of *Marbury v. Madison* rejects the clause as unavailing; and if it relate only to cases within their jurisdiction, it does not extend to the case which is now moved for."

[21] 8 Wall. 85 at 98 (U. S. 1868).

[22] 7 Wall. 506 (U. S. 1868).

"We are obliged to hold, therefore, that in all cases where a Circuit Court of the United States has, in the exercise of its original jurisdiction, caused a prisoner to be brought before it, and has, after inquiring into the cause of detention, remanded him to the custody from which he was taken, this court, in the exercise of its appellate jurisdiction, may, by the writ of *habeas corpus,* aided by the writ of *certiorari,* revise the decision of the Circuit Court, and if it be found unwarranted by law, relieve the prisoner from the unlawful restraint to which he has been remanded."[23]

This pronouncement established what has ever since been the law on this jurisdictional issue.

The amazing thing about the otherwise able opinion of Chief Justice Solomon Portland Chase in *Ex parte Yerger* was its complete misconstruction of Marshall's decision in *Ex parte Bollman and Swartwout.* Chase deemed the Court bound by *Ex parte Bollman and Swartwout* to limit its habeas corpus activities to its appellate jurisdiction only and indicated that if the matter were one of first impression he would favor extending the original jurisdiction of the Supreme Court to petitions for habeas corpus.[24] The unanimous Court in the *Yerger* case while purporting to follow the decision in *Bollman and Swartwout* actually rejected it and adopted the minority views expressed by Justice Johnson. In this curious situation the Court while professing adherence to the doctrine of stare decisis was unwittingly pursuing the doctrine of self correction. That Chief Justices Marshall and Chase,

[23] 8 Wall. 85 at 103 (U. S. 1868).

[24] *Id.* at 97. Chief Justice Chase said:

"If the question were a new one, it would, perhaps, deserve inquiry whether Congress might not, under the power to make exceptions from this appellate jurisdiction, extend the original jurisdiction to other cases than those expressly enumerated in the Constitution; and especially, in view of the constitutional guaranty of the writ of *habeas corpus,* to cases arising upon petition for that writ.

"But in the case of *Marbury v. Madison,* it was determined, upon full consideration, that the power to issue writs of mandamus, given to this court by the 13th section of the Judiciary Act, is, under the Constitution, an appellate jurisdiction, to be exercised only in the revision of judicial decisions. And this judgment has ever since been accepted as fixing the construction of this part of the Constitution.

"It was pronounced in 1803. In 1807 the same construction was given to the provision of the 14th section relating to the writ of *habeas corpus,* in the case of *Bollman and Swartwout.*

"The power to issue the writ had been previously exercised in *Hamilton's case* (1795), and in *Burford's case* (1806), in neither of which cases does the distinction between appellate and original jurisdiction appear to have been made.

"In the case of *Bollman and Swartwout,* however, the point was brought distinctly before the court; the nature of the jurisdiction was carefully examined, and it was declared to be appellate. The question then determined has not since been drawn into controversy."

of all people, should have been the contrivers of this double legal legerdemain calls to mind that "to err is human."

Chief Justice Chase in *Ex parte Yerger* either ignored or overlooked two cases which followed the original rule of the *Hamilton* case. The first of these is *Ex parte Kearney*[25] decided in 1822 in which the Court through Justice Joseph Story affirmed its jurisdiction to entertain original applications for habeas corpus, but disclaimed any appellate jurisdiction at all in criminal cases and denied the writ.[26] The other case is *Ex parte Watkins*,[27] decided in 1830. Chief Justice Marshall in the *Watkins* opinion again reviewed and affirmed the doctrine of Supreme Court habeas corpus jurisdiction as contained in the *Hamilton, Burford,* and *Bollman and Swartwout* cases, distinguishing them only to the extent of pointing out that in each the prisoner had not yet been confined under the judgment of a court. In denying the writ in the *Watkins* case Marshall rested his decision on the ground that as the statutes then stood the Supreme Court had no appellate power to revise circuit court decisions in criminal cases and could not usurp that power by the instrumentality of habeas corpus.[28] The ratio decidendi

[25] 7 Wheat. 37 (U. S. 1822).

[26] *Id.* at *41. ". . . Upon the argument of this motion, two questions have been made: first, whether this court has authority to issue a *habeas corpus,* where a person is in jail, under the warrant or order of any other court of the United States; secondly, if it have, whether, upon the facts stated, a fit case is made out, to justify the exercise of such an authority.

"As to the first question, it is unnecessary to say more, than that the point has already passed *in rem judicatam* in this court. In the case of *Bollman and Swartwout* (4 Cranch 75), it was expressly decided, upon full argument, that this court possessed such an authority, and the question has ever since been considered at rest.

"The second point is of much more importance. It is to be considered, that this court has no appellate jurisdiction confided to it in criminal cases, by the laws of the United States. It cannot entertain a writ of error, to revise the judgment of the circuit court, in any case where a party has been convicted of a public offense. And, undoubtedly, the denial of this authority proceeded upon great principles of public policy and convenience. If every party had a right to bring before this court every case, in which judgment had passed against him, for a crime, or misdemeanor or felony, the course of justice might be materially delayed and obstructed, and in some cases, totally frustrated. If, then, this court cannot directly revise a judgment of the circuit court in a criminal case, what reason is there to suppose, that it was intended to vest it with the authority to do it indirectly?"

[27] 3 Pet. *193 (U. S. 1830).

[28] *Id.* at *207: "The cases are numerous, which decide, that the judgments of a court of record, having general jurisdiction of the subject, although erroneous, are binding, until reversed. It is universally understood, that the judgments of the courts of the United States, although their jurisdiction be not shown in the pleadings, are yet binding on all the world; and that this apparent want of jurisdiction can avail the party only on a writ of error. This acknowledged principle seems to us, to settle the question now before the court. The judgment of the circuit court, in a criminal case, is, of itself, evidence of its own legality, and requires for its support, no inspection of the indictment on which it is founded. The law trusts that court with the whole subject, and has not confided to this court the power of revising decisions. We cannot usurp that power, by the in-

was that the Court might not do by indirection what it could not do directly, not that it lacked original jurisdiction in habeas corpus.

In *Ex parte Dorr,*[29] the Court held that it could not issue a habeas corpus to bring up a prisoner in custody under a sentence of a state court since this power was not given to it under section 14 of the Judiciary Act of 1789, but did not go into the question of appellate as distinguished from original jurisdiction.[30]

The cases of *Metzger,*[31] *Kaine,*[32] and *Wells,*[33] cited in the *Yerger* case, serve only to emphasize the confusion of the Court as to the nature of its habeas corpus jurisdiction. In *Kaine,* an eight judge Court split three ways in extended and inconclusive opinions. Four judges, without squarely meeting the issue of jurisdiction, denied the writ of habeas corpus on the merits.[34] Justice Curtis concurred, but only upon

strumentality of the writ of *habeas corpus.* The judgment informs us, that the commitment is legal, and with that information, it is our duty to be satisfied."

[29] 3 How. 103 (U. S. 1845).

[30] *Id.* at 105: "Neither this nor any other court of the United States, or judge thereof, can issue a *habeas corpus* to bring up a prisoner, who is in custody under a sentence or execution of a state court, for any other purpose than to be used as a witness. And it is immaterial whether the imprisonment be under civil or criminal process. As the law now stands, an individual, who may be indicted in a Circuit Court for treason against the United States, is beyond the power of federal courts and judges, if he be in custody under the authority of a state.

"Dorr is in confinement under the sentence of the Supreme Court of Rhode Island, consequently this court has no power to issue a *habeas corpus* to bring him before it. His presence here is not required as a witness, but to signify to the court whether he desires a writ of error to bring before this tribunal the record of his conviction."

[31] 5 How. 176 (U. S. 1847).

[32] 14 How. 103 (U. S. 1852).

[33] 18 How. 307 (U. S. 1855).

[34] *In re* Kaine, 14 How. 103 at 116 (U. S. 1852) four judges through Justice Catron said: "After Kaine had been committed by the Commissioner, the Circuit Court was applied to, by petition, for writs of *habeas corpus* and *certiorari,* to bring up the prisoner and proceedings before that court. The writs were issued, and a very thorough examination had of the law and the facts. The court decided that the commitment was, in all respects, legal and proper, concurred with the Commissioner's decision, and ordered the prisoner to be remanded to the custody of the marshal, under the commitment of the Commissioner. . . .

"After this careful consideration of the case, in open court, the Circuit Judge granted a second writ of *habeas corpus,* and thereby stayed the warrant for Kaine's extradition, awarded by the Secretary of State, and which had been delivered to the British authorities; and the matter was again brought before that judge, at chambers, but not deeming it proper to act, he adjourned the proceeding, as presented to him, into this court; and of the case thus presented, we are called to take jurisdiction. Cognizance could only be taken of the matter, on the assumption that original jurisdiction existed in the Circuit Judge to act, but on which he did not act; and the case comes here as one of original jurisdiction, which we are called on to exercise; and as the Constitution declares that this court shall only have appellate powers in cases like this, it follows that the transfer made by the Circuit Judge is of no validity, and must be rejected. Foreseeing that we might thus hold, the counsel for the prisoner, Kaine, also moved this court, on petition, with the papers and proceedings presented to the Circuit Judge annexed thereto, for writs of *habeas corpus* and *certiorari,* to bring up the defendant, and the record from the Circuit Court, to the end of having the decision of the court examined here."

the ground that the Court did not have jurisdiction to entertain the application, and in so doing shed some new factual light on the *Burford* case but challenged even the appellate jurisdiction of the Supreme Court in habeas corpus.[35] Three judges dissented on the ground that the petition should be granted on the merits and because the Court had jurisdiction under the *Hamilton* case without regard to whether the circuit court had passed upon a petition for habeas corpus.[36]

In *Ex parte Wells,* by a six to three decision, the Court assumed true appellate jurisdiction in a habeas corpus proceeding. Wells had been convicted of murder in the District of Columbia and sentenced to be hanged. President Fillmore granted a pardon conditioned upon

[35] *Id.* at *124:

"There are two cases which have been chiefly relied on at the bar. The first is *Ex parte Burford,* 3 Cranch 448. As this case has many facts in common with the case at bar, it is necessary carefully to examine it. Without detailing the preliminary proceedings, it will be sufficient to say, that Burford was committed to the jail of the county of Washington, in the District of Columbia, by a warrant of certain justices of the peace, which was defective, because it did not state 'some good cause certain, supported by oath.' That he was brought before the Circuit Court for the District of Columbia, upon a writ of *habeas corpus,* and, after a hearing, [was by that court remanded to jail, appears] . . . from the original record in this court. . . .

"This case is relied upon as a decision to show, that although this court cannot, as was held in *Metzger's case,* issue a writ of *habeas corpus* to examine the validity of the warrant of the Commissioner; yet, if the Circuit Court, has, by such a writ, examined its validity, pronounced it valid, and therefore dismissed the writ, and ordered the prisoner to be continued in the custody of the marshal, this court may, upon a writ of *habeas corpus,* examine that decision, and reverse it, if found erroneous.

"Before considering whether the decision in *Burford's case,* goes this length, I think it consistent with the profoundest respect for the very eminent judges who sat in that case, to say, that it does not appear that the question now made, was by them examined and considered, or that they themselves would have deemed it foreclosed by that decision.

". . . I cannot doubt, therefore, that if at that time the further question had arisen whether the court had also jurisdiction to examine a cause of commitment by a Commissioner, after the Circuit Court had reviewed that cause, and pronounced it sufficient, the court would have though it necessary to consider that question also *de novo,* upon all its grounds, and would not have treated *Burford's* case as a sufficient basis on which to rest their decision."

[36] *Id.* at *146, Justice Nelson, with whom Chief Justice Taney and Justice Daniel concurred, said: ". . . I cannot but think the denial of the power to grant to writ of *habeas corpus,* in this case, is calculated to shake the authority of a long line of decisions in this court, from *Hamilton's case,* decided in 1795, down to the present one. That case, as understood and expounded in the case of Bollman and Swartwout, in 1807, which received the most deliberate consideration of the court, and to which the doctrine in *Hamilton's case* was applied, held that this great writ was within the cognizance of the court, under the 14th section of the Judiciary Act, in all cases where the prisoner was restrained of his liberty, 'under, or by color of the authority of the United States,' and no case has held the contrary since that decision, with the exception of that of Metzger, decided in 1847, which, I have already stated, stands alone, but which distinctly admits the power and jurisdiction of the court in the case before us. . . .

"Upon the whole, I am satisfied, that the prisoner is in confinement under the treaty and act of Congress, without any lawful authority. I am of opinion, therefore, that the writ of *habeas corpus* should issue in the case, to bring up the prisoner."

Wells' being imprisoned for life. Wells petitioned the Circuit Court of the District of Columbia for a writ of habeas corpus which was denied, and appealed from this decision. After considering the validity of the conditional pardon the Court affirmed the order of the court below. The majority did not discuss the jurisdiction issue, but two judges dissented on the ground that the Court had no jurisdiction.[37]

From this review of the state of the authorities at the time the *Yerger* case came before the Court it is apparent that Chief Justice Chase rendered a great service by his opinion. Since he brought authority out of chaos in a field where certainty was imperative his treatment of the earlier cases should be cheerfully condoned. Since the *Yerger* case courts have been content to cite it as the basic authority on the point.[38] The rule proscribing original jurisdiction (except as to ambassadors, public ministers and consuls) was from 1946 to 1950 repeatedly reaffirmed in denying, to over two hundred persons convicted of war crimes by American Military Government Courts in Germany, motions for leave to file petitions for original writs of habeas corpus in

[37] *Ex parte* Wells, 18 How. 307 at 330 (U. S. 1855). In the dissenting opinion Justice McLean at 330, said: ". . . the petitioner is imprisoned under a criminal sentence of the circuit court, either as originally pronounced, or as modified by the order of the circuit court made under the writ of *habeas corpus*. That original or modified criminal sentence is the cause of his commitment. Though this court has no jurisdiction by writ of error to revise such a sentence, and has deliberately decided, in *ex parte Watkins,* that a writ of *habeas corpus* cannot be made a writ of error for such a purpose, yet by a writ of *habeas corpus* we do revise such a sentence in this case.

"It seems to me that the refusal of a writ of error in criminal cases is not only idle, but mischievous, if a writ of *habeas corpus,* which is certainly a very clumsy proceeding for the purpose, may be resorted to, to bring the record of every criminal case, of whatever kind, before this court.

"With deference for the opinions of my brethren, in my judgment, it goes very little way towards avoiding the difficulty to hold that, before one under a criminal sentence of a circuit court can thus attack his sentence collaterally, in a court which cannot review it by any direct proceeding, he must first apply to the circuit court for a writ of *habeas corpus;* and if the writ, or his discharge under it, be refused, he may then bring into action the appellate power of this court, and by a writ of *habeas corpus* out of this court stop the execution of a sentence, which we have no power to reverse. Few questions come before this court which may affect the general course of justice more deeply than questions of jurisdiction. This great remedial writ of *habeas corpus,* so efficacious and prompt in its action, and so justly valued in our country, may become an instrument to unsettle the nicely adjusted lines of jurisdiction, and produce conflict and disorder. If the true sphere of its action, and the precise limits of the power to issue it, should become in any degree confused or indistinct, serious consequences may follow—consequences not only affecting the efficient administration of the criminal laws of the United States, but the harmonious action of the divided sovereignties by which our country is governed. For these reasons, though sensible of the bias, which, I suppose, every one has in favor of this process, I have heretofore felt, and now feel, constrained to examine with care the question of our jurisdiction to issue it; and being of opinion that this court has not power to inquire into the validity of the cause of commitment stated in this petition, I think it should be dismissed for that reason."

[38] For example, *Ex parte* Parks, 93 U. S. 18 at 23 (1876).

the Supreme Court.[39] That the point still is not without difficulty is demonstrated by the four to four division of the Court in these cases. Justice Jackson having disqualified himself, half of the balance of the court felt that the doctrine of lack of original jurisdiction should be reexamined.

Although the Supreme Court at an earlier date had addressed itself to the subject of military habeas corpus in the case of military commission prisoners[40] it was not until 1879 that the Court first had before it a habeas corpus proceeding involving detention resulting from a court-martial conviction.[41] That these two ancient elements of Anglo-American law, a court-martial sentence and a habeas corpus petition each in its own right antedating Magna Carta, should have continued in their respective separate courses without meeting in Supreme Court litigation until after ninety years of American constitutional government is indeed remarkable. It is indicative of the fundamental autonomy of the American courts-martial system.

At this point the reader may have in mind *Martin v. Mott,*[42] and *Dynes v. Hoover,*[43] and be preparing to do battle against the propo-

[39] Milch v. United States, 332 U. S. 789, 68 Sup. Ct. 92 (1947); Brandt v. United States, 333 U. S. 836, 68 Sup. Ct. 1801 (1948); *In re* Krautwurst, 334 U. S. 826, 68 Sup. Ct. 1328 (1948); *In re* Ehlen, 334 U. S. 836, 68 Sup. Ct. 1431 (1948); *In re* Gronwald, 334 U. S. 857, 68 Sup. Ct. 1522 (1948). Full citations of all these petitions are collected in footnote 1 to the opinion in Johnson v. Eisentrager, 339 U. S. 763 at 768, 70 Sup. Ct. 936 (1950).

[40] *Ex parte* Milligan, 4 Wall. 2 (U. S. 1866) and *Ex parte* Yerger, 8 Wall. 85 (U. S. 1868). It is beyond the scope of this chapter to pursue the niceties of distinction between various types of military jurisdiction other than to set forth here the classic definition given by Chief Justice Chase in his separate concurring opinion in *Ex parte* Milligan at page 141:

"There are under the Constitution three kinds of military jurisdiction: one to be exercised both in peace and war; another to be exercised in time of foreign war without the boundaries of the United States, or in time of rebellion and civil war within states or districts occupied by rebels treated as belligerents; and a third to be exercised in time of invasion or insurrection within the limits of the United States, or during rebellion within the limits of states maintaining adhesion to the National Government, when the public danger requires its exercise. The first of these may be called jurisdiction under MILITARY LAW, and is found in acts of Congress prescribing rules and articles of war, or otherwise providing for the government of the national forces; the second may be distinguished as MILITARY GOVERNMENT, superseding, as far as may be deemed expedient, the local law, and exercised by the military commander under the direction of the President, with the express or implied sanction of Congress; while the third may be denominated MARTIAL LAW PROPER, and is called into action by Congress, or temporarily, when the action of Congress cannot be invited, and in the case of justifying or excusing peril, by the President, in times of insurrection or invasion, or of civil or foreign war, within districts or localities where ordinary law no longer adequately secures public safety and private rights." The extension of the President's military government jurisdiction to tribunals established in the United States occupation zone of Germany by the State Department, as distinguished from Department of Defense tribunals, was approved in Madsen v. Kinsella, 343 U. S. 341, 72 Sup. Ct. 699 (1952).

[41] *Ex parte* Reed, 100 U. S. 13 (1879).

[42] 12 Wheat. 19 (U. S. 1827).

[43] 20 How. 65 (U. S. 1857).

sition above stated. True, in earlier cases the Supreme Court had passed upon other collateral attacks against courts-martial proceedings but never by habeas corpus.

The earliest case with a military background to engage the attention of the Supreme Court was that of *Wise v. Withers*,[44] in which Marshall wrote the opinion in 1806. Wise, a federal justice of the peace, sued Withers, the collector of military fines, in an action of trespass vi et armis for entering Wise's house and removing his goods. The Circuit Court of the District of Columbia sustained a demurrer and upon writ of error the Supreme Court reversed the lower court. The Chief Justice said:

> ". . . the court must, in conformity with that import, declare that a justice of the peace, within the District of Columbia, is exempt from the performance of militia duty. It follows . . . that a court-martial has no jurisdiction over [him] as a militiaman; he could never be legally enrolled; and it is a principle, that a decision of such a tribunal, in a case clearly without its jurisdiction, cannot protect the officer who executes it. The court and the officer are all trespassers."

The point of decision was that since the court-martial did not have jurisdiction of the person its decision was a nullity.

In *Houston v. Moore*,[45] in 1820, the Court on writ of error to the Supreme Court of Pennsylvania affirmed that court's judgment upholding the constitutionality of a sentence of a state court-martial punishing disobedience to the call of the President. The majority of the Court held:

> "The state court-martial had a concurrent jurisdiction with the tribunal pointed out by the acts of congress, to try a militiaman who had disobeyed the call of the president, and to enforce the laws of congress against such delinquent; and that this authority will remain to be so exercised, until it shall please congress to vest it exclusively elsewhere, or until the state of Pennsylvania shall withdraw from their court-martial the authority to take such jurisdiction."

In *Martin v. Mott, supra,* Mott had been convicted and fined by a court-martial for failing to enter the service as a militiaman in the War of 1812 after having been required so to do by the President of the United States. The defendant Martin, deputy marshal, had levied

[44] 3 Cranch 330 at 337 (U. S. 1806).
[45] 5 Wheat. 1 at 31 (U. S. 1820).

execution on goods of Mott to satisfy the court-martial fine. Mott brought a possessory action in the New York Supreme Court to recover these goods and was given judgment on the pleadings which was affirmed by the New York Court of Errors. On writ of error the Supreme Court reversed the judgment and upheld the jurisdiction of the court-martial to try militiamen lawfully called into the service of the United States. It also sustained the unlimited constitutional power of the President to call forth the militia to repel invasion by extending this power to the threat of invasion. This attempted collateral attack of the court-martial sentence was in replevin. It did not involve habeas corpus since Mott was not in custody.

In *Ex parte Vallandigham,*[46] in 1863 the Court held it did not have jurisdiction to review by certiorari the proceedings of a military commission. In *Dynes v. Hoover, supra,* a sailor convicted by a navy court-martial of attempting to desert brought a civil action in the Circuit Court for the District of Columbia against the United States Marshal for damages for false imprisonment. The Supreme Court on writ of error affirmed the judgment of the circuit court in favor of the defendant.[47]

As already indicated the historical threads of courts-martial and habeas corpus proceedings first met in *Ex parte Reed, supra.* The petitioner, a navy paymaster's clerk, contested the jurisdiction of a naval court-martial convened on board the United States ship "Essex" at Rio de Janeiro to try, convict and sentence him for malfeasance. The

[46] 1 Wall. 243 (U. S. 1863).

[47] Dynes v. Hoover, 20 How. 65 at 81-82 (U. S. 1857). In speaking of a court-martial sentence the Court said:

". . . When confirmed, it is altogether beyond the jurisdiction or inquiry of any civil tribunal whatever, unless it shall be in a case in which the court had not jurisdiction over the *subject-matter or charge,* or one in which having jurisdiction over the subject-matter, it has failed to observe the rules prescribed by the statute for its exercise. . . .

"When we speak of *proceedings* in a cause, or for the organization of the court and for trials, we do not mean mere irregularity in practice on the trial, or any mistaken rulings in respect to evidence or law, but of a disregard of the essentials required by the statute under which the court has been convened to try and to punish an offender for an imputed violation of the law. . . .

"With the sentences of courts martial which have been convened regularly, and have proceeded legally, and by which punishments are directed, not forbidden by law, or which are according to the laws and customs of the sea, civil courts have nothing to do, nor are they in any way alterable by them. If it were otherwise, the civil courts would virtually administer the rules and articles of war, irrespective of those to whom that duty and obligation has been confided by the laws of the United States, from whose decisions no appeal or jurisdiction of any kind has been given to the civil magistrate or civil courts. But we repeat, if a court martial has no *jurisdiction over the subject-matter of the charge* it has been convened to try, or shall inflict a punishment *forbidden by the law,* though its sentence shall be approved by the officers having a revisory power of it, *civil courts* may, on an action by a party aggrieved by it, inquire into the want of the court's jurisdiction, and give him redress."

Circuit Court of the United States for the District of Massachusetts denied the writ and remanded the petitioner to naval custody. The Supreme Court in denying Reed's petition for certiorari laid down the narrow limits of habeas corpus inquiry into confinement adjudged by courts-martial in this language:

> "The court had jurisdiction over the persons and the case. It is the organism provided by law and clothed with the duty of administering justice in this class of cases. Having had such jurisdiction, its proceedings cannot be collaterally impeached for any mere error or irregularity, if there were such, committed within the sphere of its authority. Its judgments, when approved as required, rest on the same basis, and are surrounded by the same considerations which give conclusiveness to the judgments of other legal tribunals including as well the lowest as the highest, under like circumstances. The exercise of discretion, within authorized limits, cannot be assigned for error and made the subject of review by an appellate court.
>
> "We do not overlook the point that there must be jurisdiction to give the judgment rendered, as well as to hear and determine the cause. If a magistrate having authority to fine for assault and battery should sentence the offender to be imprisoned in the penitentiary, or to suffer the punishment prescribed for homicide, his judgment would be as much a nullity as if the preliminary jurisdiction to hear and determine had not existed. Every act of a court beyond its jurisdiction is void, *Cornett v. Williams,* 20 Wall. 226; *Windsor v. McVeigh,* 93 U. S. 274; 7 Wait's Actions and Defences, 181. Here there was no defect of jurisdiction as to anything that was done. Beyond this we need not look into the record. Whatever was done, that the court could do under any circumstances, we must presume was properly done. If error was committed in the rightful exercise of authority, we cannot correct it.
>
> "A writ of *habeas corpus* cannot be made to perform the functions of a writ of error. To warrant the discharge of the petitioner, the sentence under which he is held must be, not merely erroneous and voidable, but absolutely void. *Ex parte Kearney,* 7 Wheat, 38; *Ex parte Watkins,* 3 Pet. 193; *Ex parte Milligan,* 4 Wall. 2.
>
> "The application of the petitioner is, therefore, denied."[48]

[48] 100 U. S. 13, 23 (1879).

The above language made directly applicable to habeas corpus proceedings the limitations already imposed by the Court in *Dynes v. Hoover, supra,* on collateral attacks against courts-martial sentences in general.

Although a few inferior federal courts have wavered, the Supreme Court has never departed from the original forthright pronouncement in *Ex parte Reed.* As we shall see in Part V, the Court had occasion in 1950[49] to reaffirm with force and clarity this doctrine. Thus history merges into current problems in the field of military habeas corpus.

II

Habeas Corpus Jurisdiction

The next subject for consideration is what courts have habeas corpus jurisdiction to inquire into confinement imposed by military authority.

A. State Courts

In 1871 in *Tarble's Case,*[50] the Court, through Justice Stephen J. Field, established the rule that a state court has no jurisdiction to test the validity of the confinement of a person pursuant to color of federal military authority. Tarble had, while under eighteen years of age, enlisted in the Army representing his age as twenty-one. Shortly thereafter he deserted, was later apprehended, and confined under charges of desertion awaiting trial by court-martial. A Wisconsin court commissioner on petition of Tarble's father issued a writ of habeas corpus, conducted a hearing, and ordered Tarble released. The Supreme Court of Wisconsin affirmed this order and the Supreme Court on writ of error reversed the state court.[51] The Court simply applied to federal

[49] Hiatt v. Brown, 339 U. S. 103, 70 Supt. Ct. 495 (1950), *rehearing denied,* 339 U. S. 939, 70 Sup. Ct. 672 (1950).

[50] 13 Wall. 397 (U. S. 1871).

[51] *Id.* at 411:

". . . the State judge or State court should proceed no further when it appears, from the application of the party, or the return made, that the prisoner is held by an officer of the United States under what, in truth, purports to be the authority of the United States; that is, an authority, the validity of which is to be determined by the Constitution and laws of the United States. If a party thus held be illegally imprisoned it is for the courts or judicial officers of the United States, and those courts or officers alone, to grant him release.

"This limitation upon the power of State tribunals and State Officers furnishes no just ground to apprehend that the liberty of the citizen will thereby be endangered. The United States are as much interested in protecting the citizen from illegal restraint under their authority, as the several States are to protect him from the like restraint under their authority, and are no more likely to tolerate any oppression. Their courts and judicial officers are clothed with the power to issue the writ of *habeas corpus* in all cases, where a party is illegally restrained of his liberty by an officer of the United States, whether such illegality consist in the character of the process, the authority of the officer, or the invalidity of the law under which he is held. And there is no just reason

military confinement the general rule previously announced in *Ableman v. Booth.*[52] Chief Justice Chase alone dissented. The decision in *Tarble's* case has never since been challenged in the Supreme Court and is controlling today.

B. Federal Courts

That in proper cases and within proper limits the federal courts have habeas corpus jurisdiction to examine detention imposed by military authority was definitely established at least as early as *Ex parte Milligan, supra.* This was discussed at some length in Part I, and need not be here elaborated. The question as to what federal court shall exercise this jurisdiction requires some inquiry. The statute[53] alone is not crystal clear and resort must be had to the case authority.

It may be safely said that the normal tribunal for an original habeas corpus petition is the federal district court of the district in which the military prisoner is confined,[54] that the courts of appeal decline such

---

to believe that they will exhibit any hesitation to exert their power, when it is properly invoked. Certainly there can be no ground for supposing that their action will be less prompt and efficient in such cases than would be that of State tribunals and State officers.

"It follows, from the views we have expressed, that the court commissioner of Dane County was without jurisdiction to issue the writ of *habeas corpus* for the discharge of the prisoner in this case, it appearing, upon the application presented to him for the writ, that the prisoner was held by an officer of the United States, under claim and color of the authority of the United States, as an enlisted soldier mustered into the military service of the National government; and the same information was imparted to the commissioner by the return of the officer. The commissioner was, both by the application for the writ and the return to it, apprised that the prisoner was within the dominion and jurisdiction of another government, and that no writ of *habeas corpus* issued by him could pass over the line which divided the two sovereignties."

[52] 21 How. 506 (U. S. 1858).

[53] Title 28, United States Code, § 2241, in pertinent part provides:

"(a) Writs of habeas corpus may be granted by the Supreme Court, any justice thereof, the district courts and any circuit judge within their respective jurisdictions. The order of a circuit judge shall be entered in the records of the district court of the district wherein the restraint complained of is had.

"(b) The Supreme Court any justice thereof and any circuit judge may decline to entertain an application for a writ of habeas corpus and may transfer the application for hearing and determination to the district court having jurisdiction to entertain it.

"(c) The writ of habeas corpus shall not extend to a prisoner unless—

(1) he is in custody under or by color of the authority of the United States or is committed for trial before some court thereof."

[54] Ahrens v. Clark, 335 U. S. 188, 68 Sup. Ct. 1443 (1948); United States v. Hayman, 342 U. S. 205, 213, 220, 72 Sup. Ct. 263 (1952). In this latter case the Court concisely said, at p. 213, "a habeas corpus action must be brought in the district of confinement," and at p. 220, "in Ahrens v. Clark... we held that the phrase 'within their respective jurisdictions' in the habeas corpus statute required the presence of the prisoner within the territorial jurisdiction of the District Court as a prerequisite to his filing an application for habeas corpus."

Ahrens v. Clark, *supra,* has been followed as controlling in Dorsch v. Hunter, 101 F. Supp. 751 (W. D. Pa. 1951) and Orloff v. Lovett, 101 F. Supp. 750, 751 (D. D. C. 1951). In the latter, a military habeas corpus case, Orloff, on leave from his Army duty assignment elsewhere, voluntarily came to the District of

original jurisdiction and that the Supreme Court denies that it has such jurisdiction.[55] Beyond these basic principles interesting problems arise.

In *Hirota, Dohihara, Kido, et al. v. MacArthur,* the Court in a per curiam, six to one, opinion denied prisoners sentenced by the International Military Tribunal sitting in Tokyo, Japan, leave to file petitions for writs of habeas corpus on the ground that no United States court had power to set aside a judgment of an international tribunal.[56] Justice Murphy dissented; Justice Jackson disqualified himself; Justice Rutledge reserved decision, which he did not render prior to his death; and six months later Justice Douglas filed a separate concurring opinion.[57] He expressed the view that the acts of an American general

---

Columbia and there filed a petition for habeas corpus release from military service. The court said, "petitioner . . . is not restrained in the District of Columbia, but is here voluntarily. Therefore, this court has no jurisdiction to entertain this writ."

When such jurisdiction has once been acquired it is retained although the petitioner is thereafter removed from the district. United States v. Neelly, 115 F. Supp. 615 at 621 (N. D. Ill. 1953).

[55] See authorities collected in footnote 39, *supra.*

[56] 338 U. S. 197, 69 Sup. Ct. 1238 (1949). The per curiam opinion at page 198, read: "The petitioners, all residents and citizens of Japan, are being held in custody pursuant to the judgments of a military tribunal in Japan. Two of the petitioners have been sentenced to death, the others to terms of imprisonment. They filed motions in this Court for leave to file petitions for *habeas corpus. . . .*

"We are satisfied that the tribunal sentencing these petitioners is not a tribunal of the United States. The United States and other allied countries conquered and now occupy and control Japan. General Douglas MacArthur has been selected and is acting as the Supreme Commander for the Allied Powers. The military tribunal sentencing these petitioners has been set up by General MacArthur as the agent of the Allied Powers.

"Under the foregoing circumstances the courts of the United States have no power or authority to review, to affirm, set aside or annul the judgments and sentences imposed on these petitioners and for this reason the motions for leave to file petitions for writs of *habeas corpus* are denied."

[57] Justice Douglas said, in part at page 204: "I assume that we have no authority to review the judgment of an international tribunal. But, if as a result of unlawful action, one of our Generals holds a prisoner in his custody, the writ of *habeas corpus* can effect a release from that custody. It is the historic function of the writ to examine into the cause of restraint of liberty. We should not allow that inquiry to be thwarted merely because the jailer acts not only for the United States but for other nations as well." At page 207: ". . . To this court the Supreme Commander appointed from names submitted by the respective nations eleven judges—one each from the United States, China, United Kingdom, Russia, Australia, Canada, France, The Netherlands, New Zealand, India, and the Philippines. So I think there can be no serious doubt that, although the arrangement is in many respects amorphous and though the tribunal is dominated by American influence it is nonetheless international in character. But it should be noted that the chain of command from the United States to the Supreme Commander is unbroken. It is he who has custody of petitioners. It is through that chain of command that the writ of *habeas corpus* can reach the Supreme Commander." At page 215: "The conclusion is therefore plain that the Tokyo Tribunal acted as an instrument of military power of the Executive branch of government. It responded to the will of the Supreme Commander as expressed in the military order by which he constituted it. It took its law

wherever performed and regardless of their international character should be subject to the scrutiny of United States courts since the superiors of all American generals are physically present and subject to such jurisdiction and may be required to issue orders controlling the conduct of their subordinates. His concurrence was based on the ground that the control of enemy prisoners was a political question exclusively within the foreign affairs powers of the President and hence not subject to judicial review. These views of Justice Douglas did not receive the concurrence of any other member of the Court.

The Court of Appeals for the District of Columbia followed the *Hirota* case as controlling in affirming an order of the district court denying a petition for habeas corpus made on behalf of a German citizen held in custody by American Army forces in Germany while serving a sentence imposed by "Military Tribunal IV."[58] Upon finding that this was an international tribunal it was held that the district court had no jurisdiction.

This same court of appeals, however, in *Eisentrager v. Forrestal*[59] elected to follow the Douglas dictum in *Hirota* that the federal district courts for the District of Columbia have habeas corpus jurisdiction over persons scattered over the world in foreign countries if held in American military custody because the superiors in the chain of command of all American generals are to be found within the jurisdiction of the District of Columbia and so may be required by that court to issue orders releasing persons so held. Eisentrager and the other petitioners were German nationals in United States Army custody in Germany, pursuant to conviction in China by an exclusively United States Military Com-

---

from its creator and did not act as a free and independent tribunal to adjudge the rights of petitioner under international law. As Justice Pal said, it did not therefore sit as a judicial tribunal. It was solely an instrument of political power. Insofar as American participation is concerned, there is no constitutional objection to that action. For the capture and control of those who were responsible for the Pearl Harbor incident was a political question on which the President as Commander-in-Chief, and as spokesman for the nation in foreign affairs, had the final say."

[58] Flick v. Johnson, 174 F. (2d) 983 at 986 (D. C. Cir. 1949); "Concededly, the International Military Tribunal, established under the London Agreement, was a court of international character. How, then, can it be said that Military Tribunal IV was not of the same character, with its existence and jurisdiction rooted in the sovereignity of the Four Powers, exercised jointly through the supreme governing authority of the Control Council? We think, therefore, that the tribunals established under its authority were legitimate and appropriate instruments of judicial power for the trial of war criminals. (See 39 Am. J. Int'l Law at pg. 525, 1945).

"Accordingly, we are led to the final conclusion that the tribunal which tried and sentenced Flick was not a tribunal of the United States. Hence the District Court was without power to review its judgment and sentence. Hirota case, supra."

[59] 174 F. (2d) 961 (D. C. Cir. 1949).

mission, for law of war violations committed in China. The court of appeals reversed the district court dismissal for lack of jurisdiction, and remanded for consideration on the merits. The Supreme Court granted certiorari.[60]

This presented a choice between the conflicting views of Justices Douglas and Black, on the one hand, and on the other, those expressed by the majority of the Court in *Ahrens v. Clark, supra,* that only the district court of the district in which the petitioner is confined has habeas corpus jurisdiction. The former view ignores the limited and wholly statutory nature of federal district court jurisdiction. Moreover, this reasoning, if valid, would apply equally to petitions by all federal prisoners both civil and military, wherever held, since the Attorney General, the superior of all federal prison wardens, is personally subject to the jurisdiction of the District Court for the District of Columbia. The latter view, as here applied, is consistent with *Downes v. Bidwell* doctrine,[61] that the Constitution does not, per se, follow the flag. Since constitutional benefits do not flow to those in territory permanently acquired by the United States, unless and until Congress formally incorporates such territory, it is difficult to work out a legal right for an enemy alien in foreign, albeit occupied, territory to invoke such constitutional benefits. Congress, assuredly, has taken no steps to incorporate Western Germany, or other foreign areas where American forces are stationed, as territory of the United States.

The Court in its six to three *Eisentrager* decision[62] reversed the court of appeals and affirmed the judgment of the district court that it was without jurisdiction. Justices Black, Douglas and Burton dissented. The majority expressly reserved decision in event the petitioner were an American citizen since that state of facts was not before the Court. Justice Jackson speaking for the Court did say, "Citizenship as a head of jurisdiction and a ground of protection was old when Paul invoked it in his appeal to Caesar." The decision differentiated not only between citizens and aliens, but between aliens of friendly and enemy countries, and further divided the latter into resident and non-

[60] *Sub nominee* Johnson v. Eisentrager, 338 U. S. 877, 70 Sup. Ct. 158 (1949). Fairman, "Some New Problems of the Constitution Following the Flag," 1 Stan. L. Rev. 587 at 631-643 (1949), presents a detailed discussion of the problem involved in the Eisentrager case.

[61] 182 U. S. 244, 21 Sup. Ct. 770 (1901). Also Hawaii v. Mankichi, 190 U. S. 197, 23 Sup. Ct. 787 (1903); Dorr v. United States, 195 U. S. 138, 24 Sup. Ct. 808 (1904); Rasmussen v. United States, 197 U. S. 516, 25 Sup. Ct. 514 (1905). The district court in Madsen v. Kinsella, 93 F. Supp. 319 (S. D. W. Va. 1950), follows the Dorr case in denying relief to an American citizen; *affd.,* 343 U. S. 341 (1952).

[62] Johnson v. Eisentrager, 339 U. S. 763, 70 Sup. Ct. 936 (1950). Followed in Nash v. MacArthur 184 F. (2d) 606 at 608 (D. C. Cir. 1950).

resident enemy aliens. The door was left ajar for all but the non-resident enemy alien. The Court also adverted to the fact that except for the English-speaking peoples the writ of habeas corpus is generally unknown and that no reciprocity could be expected, and concluded that such extraterritorial application of organic law would be opposed to the practice of every modern government. It held that the Constitution does not confer immunity from military trial and punishment upon an alien enemy engaged in the service of a government at war with the United States, and that it was within the jurisdiction of a military commission to try these prisoners.

Among the sturdy foundation timbers relied upon in the construction of the majority opinion were included *Ahrens v. Clark, supra; Downes v. Bidwell, supra;* and the rule of *United States v. Curtis-Wright Corp.*,[63] that the President is exclusively responsible for the conduct of foreign affairs.

The *Eisentrager* decision is not only sound in principle, but is of great practical importance to the Department of Defense in the discharge of those portions of its combat and occupational missions which fall within the jurisdiction of military commissions. The Court aptly said, "The obvious importance of these holdings to both judicial administration and military operations impelled us to grant certiorari." It also, with commendable realism declared, "The writ, since it is held to be a matter of right, would be equally available to enemies during active hostilities as in the present twilight between war and peace. Such trials would hamper the war effort and bring aid and comfort to the enemy."

The problem of whether American citizens tried, convicted and sentenced by American military tribunals, and confined as a result thereof in places of American military detention in foreign countries are within the habeas corpus jurisdiction of a federal district court for the District of Columbia, or elsewhere, has not yet been made the subject of authoritative judicial consideration. In *Burns v. Lovett* the district court for the District of Columbia said, ". . . petitioner . . . is held under authority of respondents by the Japan Logistical Command . . . ," did not consider the question of its own jurisdiction, and dismissed the petition upon the ground that the military court had jurisdiction over the petitioner.[64] The court of appeals in this case likewise failed to inspect its own jurisdiction or that of the district court, con-

[63] 299 U. S. 304, 57 Sup. Ct. 216 (1936).

[64] Burns v. Lovett, 104 F. Supp. 312 (D. D. C. 1952). Also Dennis v. Lovett, 104 F. Supp. 310 at 311 (D. D. C. 1952). See *Ex parte* Albertson, 103 F. Supp. 617 at 618 (D. D. C. 1951).

tented itself with saying, "Appellants are presently confined in the custody of Headquarters of the Japan Logistical Command," and affirmed the district court after finding no failure of due process.[65] The Supreme Court in affirming denial of the writ did not at all concern itself with whether the district court had habeas corpus jurisdiction over petitioners confined in foreign countries.[66]

The same issue was tendered in a recent military habeas corpus case, initiated in the district court for the District of Columbia.[67] Toth, a former airman, the petitioner, was held in custody in Korea by the Air Force under a murder charge for an offense allegedly committed while in service in Korea. The district court first "assumed" it had jurisdiction, noted respondent did not raise this issue, and then proceeded to grant the writ based on a finding that the arrest procedure was illegal. Why the Department of Justice did not contest the jurisdiction of the district court is not apparent. Jurisdiction is not a commodity to be "assumed" by a federal district court nor conferred by the charity of counsel.[68] This case was reversed on appeal on another point by the Court of Appeals for the District of Columbia, the same court which in the *Eisentrager* case[69] erroneously felt habeas corpus jurisdiction existed in behalf of nonresident enemy aliens. It is to be hoped this troublesome point of district court habeas corpus jurisdiction will be given definitive treatment in the final disposition of the *Toth* case. To uphold jurisdiction here would be to establish a new doctrine of implied federal jurisdiction and would constitute a drastic deviation from the clear rule of *Ahrens v. Clark*.[70] To deny jurisdiction under these circumstances would be consistent with *Ahrens v. Clark* and would present to Congress the issue whether it desires to extend the habeas corpus jurisdiction of one or all district courts to cases where a petitioner is confined within the geographical area of none.

C. Foreign Courts

The current foreign policy of the United States, including as it does military alliances and military assistance agreements, results in the con-

[65] Burns and Dennis v. Lovett, 202 F. (2d) 335 at 338 (D. C. Cir. 1952).

[66] Sub nominee Burns and Dennis v. Wilson, *cert. granted,* 344 U. S. 903 (1952); *affd.,* 346 U. S. 137, 73 Sup. Ct. 1045 (1953); *rehearing denied,* 346 U. S. 844, 74 Sup. Ct. 3 (1953). At 346 U. S. 851, Justice Frankfurter noted the failure of the Court to consider this basic jurisdictional issue.

[67] Toth v. Talbott, 113 F. Supp. 330 (D. D. C. 1953) and 114 F. Supp. 468 (D. D. C. 1953), *reversed,* 215 F. (2d) 22 (D. C. Cir. 1954).

[68] Commanding Officer Camp Breckenridge v. Bumanis, 207 F. (2d) 499 at 501 (6th Cir. 1953); Penwell v. Newland, 180 F. (2d) 551 (9th Cir. 1950); Marten v. Hess, 176 F. (2d) 834 (6th Cir. 1952); Quinn v. Hunter, 162 F. (2d) 644 (7th Cir. 1947); Belardi v. Day, 50 F. (2d) 816 (3d Cir. 1931); Circella v. Neelly, 115 F. Supp. 615 at 621 (N. D. Ill. 1953).

[69] See note 59, *supra.*

[70] See note 54, *supra.*

tinuing presence of American military forces within the sovereign territory of friendly foreign nations. The international law problems as to the exercise of criminal and civil jurisdiction over such visiting forces present a broad and interesting field of inquiry beyond the scope of this chapter. The basic rule as to trial jurisdiction so far as American courts are concerned, was established by Chief Justice Marshall in 1812, in the leading case of *Schooner Exchange v. M'Faddon*[71] and has been followed at least by the American writers on international law.[72] It is to the effect that where a foreign army, or fleet, marches through, sails over, or is stationed in the territory of another state, with whom the foreign sovereign to whom they belong is in amity, its members are exempt from the civil and criminal jurisdiction of the place and are subject to the military law of their own government.

A practical difficulty however may arise from the fact that the international law view of the guest sovereign on this point may be in conflict with the American view. The author was confronted with this situation in New Guinea in 1948 in a case involving American graves registration military personnel. The wartime agreement by which Australia and the United States had expressly and reciprocally vested jurisdiction over armed force members in the nation which they served had expired. The volume containing the report of *Schooner Exchange v. M'Faddon,* brought in by air from Manila, was submitted to the one and only judge of the civil court for all of Papua and the portion of New Guinea mandated to Australia. After a careful reading of the opinion, this jurist in substance said, "Very interesting, but not the British rule, and of course not binding on this court." Practical action ultimately resulted in the United States exercising jurisdiction in this case but this disposition did not flow from any meeting of the minds of the representatives of the two sovereignties as to a controlling international rule of jurisdiction. Express reciprocal legislation, or at least a definitive reciprocal agreement, is essential wherever forces are to be maintained in foreign countries.[73]

[71] 7 Cranch 116 (U. S. 1812).

[72] 1 HYDE, INTERNATIONAL LAW CHIEFLY AS INTERPRETED AND APPLIED BY THE UNITED STATES, § 247, 819-820 (2d rev. ed., 1945); LAWRENCE, PRINCIPLES OF INTERNATIONAL LAW, § 107, 246 (6th ed., 1915); OPPENHEIM, INTERNATIONAL LAW, § 445, 662-663 (5th ed., 1937); WOOLSEY, INTERNATIONAL LAW, § 68 (5th ed., 1891); WILSON, HANDBOOK OF INTERNATIONAL LAW, § 50, 148-149 (1910); Panama v. Schwartzfiger, 21 AM. J. INT. L. 182 (1927); MCNAIR AND LAUTERPACHT, ANNUAL DIGEST, Case No. 114 (1927-1928).

[73] Examples of such agreements are: 82d Congress, 2d Session, Senate Documents, EXECUTIVES Q and R, June 2, 1952, pp. 89-130, CONVENTION ON THE RIGHTS AND OBLIGATIONS OF FOREIGN FORCES AND THEIR MEMBERS IN THE FEDERAL REPUBLIC OF GERMANY; 82d Congress, 2d Session, Senate Document, EXECUTIVE T, June 16, 1952, pp. 7-9, Article VII of AGREEMENT BETWEEN THE PARTIES TO THE NORTH ATLANTIC TREATY REGARDING THE STATUS OF THEIR FORCES;

Philippine Republic independence on July 4, 1946 gave rise to the first occasions for a foreign court to be petitioned to exercise habeas corpus inquiry over American courts-martial sentences. The Military Bases Agreement[74] which became effective on March 14, 1947 contained complicated jurisdictional provisions making the same individual subject to the jurisdiction of the Philippine civil courts or American courts-martial depending on the place and nature of the act.[75] This situation gave rise to three original habeas corpus proceedings in the Supreme Court of the Philippines. The first of these cases arose early in 1947 after Philippine independence and before the effective date of

ADMINISTRATIVE AGREEMENT UNDER ARTICLE III OF THE SECURITY TREATY BETWEEN THE UNITED STATES OF AMERICA AND JAPAN, February 28, 1952, pamphlet, General Headquarters, Far East Command.

[74] Agreement Between the United States of America and the Republic of the Philippines concerning Military Bases. This Agreement was executed on behalf of the United States by American Ambassador Paul V. McNutt pursuant to Congressional authority vested in the President of the United States to enter into an executive agreement, and on behalf of the Philippine Republic by its President, Manuel Roxas, and was subsequently ratified by the Philippine Senate. U. S. DEPT. OF STATE TREATIES AND OTHER INTERNATIONAL ACTS SERIES 1775.

[75] Article XIII in part provided:

"1. The Philippines consents that the United States shall have the right to exercise jurisdiction over the following offenses:

(a) Any offense committed by any person within any base except where the offender and the offended parties are both Philippine citizens (not members of the armed forces of the United States on active duty) or the offense is against the security of the Philippines;

(b) Any offense committed outside the bases by any member of the armed forces of the United States in which the offended party is also a member of the armed forces of the United States; and

(c) Any offense committed outside the bases by any member of the armed forces of the United States against the security of the United States.

"2. The Philippines shall have the right to exercise jurisdiction over all other offenses committed outside the bases by any member of the armed forces of the United States.

"3. Whenever for special reasons the United States may desire not to exercise the jurisdiction reserved to it in paragraphs 1 and 6 of this Article, the officer holding the offender in custody shall so notify the fiscal (prosecuting attorney) of the city or province in which the offense has been committed within ten days after his arrest, and in such a case the Philippines shall exercise jurisdiction.

"4. Whenever for special reasons the Philippines may desire not to exercise the jurisdiction reserved to it in paragraph 2 of this Article, the fiscal (prosecuting attorney) of the city or province where the offense has been committed shall so notify the officer holding the offender in custody within ten days after his arrest, and in such a case the United States shall be free to exercise jurisdiction. If any offense falling under paragraph 2 of this Article is committed by any member of the armed forces of the United States

(a) While engaged in the actual performance of a specific military duty, or

(b) During a period of national emergency declared by either government and the fiscal (prosecuting attorney) so finds from the evidence, he shall immediately notify the officer holding the offender in custody that the United States is free to exercise jurisdiction. In the event the fiscal (prosecuting attorney) finds that the offense was not committed in the actual performance of a specific military duty, the offender's commanding officer shall have the right to appeal from such finding to the Secretary of Justice within ten days from the receipt of the decision of the fiscal and the decision of the Secretary of Justice shall be final."

the Military Bases Agreement. It was then decided in Washington as a policy matter that the representatives of the United States in the Philippines should not plead sovereign immunity and should submit to the jurisdiction of the Philippine courts.

The Philippine Supreme Court, not at all embarrassed by any distinctions between original and appellate jurisdiction, proceeded to exercise original jurisdiction. The first of these cases[76] was brought by two American civilian employees of the United States Army, then being held in confinement awaiting trial by court-martial for misappropriation of United States Government property, claiming that as civilians they could be prosecuted only in the civil courts of the Philippines. So far as American law was concerned, these civilian employees of the Army overseas were, under Article of War 2, subject to military law. The Philippine Supreme Court by a ten to one decision in an opinion written by Chief Justice Moran dismissed the writ, held that the petitioners were persons subject to American military law, and expressly affirmed the doctrine of *Schooner Exchange v. M'Faddon* without any consideration of the effect of the provisions of the Military Bases Agreement.

The next petition[77] involved a Filipino civilian employee of the United States Army who had been convicted by court-martial of misappropriating United States property from the port area in the City of Manila. His contention was that under the Military Bases Agreement the United States had relinquished the exercise of all jurisdiction within the City of Manila. The Court, again speaking through its Chief Justice, construed an ambiguous provision of the Military Bases Agreement relative to jurisdiction in the port area, and granted the writ on the ground that the United States had no jurisdiction over offenses committed within the territorial limits of the City of Manila.

In the last of these unusual cases[78] a Filipino civilian employee of the United States Army had been convicted by court-martial of misappropriating United States property from an American base not within the City of Manila. He contended that the provision of Article XIII of the Military Bases Agreement vesting jurisdiction in the United States under these circumstances was violative of the Constitution of the Philippine Republic and hence void. This contention raised an issue which was considered to be exclusively one for Philippine determination and the petition was resisted by an assistant attorney general of

[76] Tubb and Tedrow v. Griess, Supreme Court of the Philippines, General Register No. L-1325, April 7, 1947.

[77] Miquiabas v. Commanding General, Supreme Court of the Philippines, General Register No. L-1988, Feb. 24, 1948.

[78] Dizon v. Commanding General, Supreme Court of the Philippines, General Register No. L-2110, July 22, 1948.

the Philippine Republic. The Philippine Supreme Court, Justice Paras writing the opinion, upheld the constitutionality of the Military Bases Agreement, dismissed the petition, and again affirmed the principle of *Schooner Exchange v. M'Faddon.*

It must be stressed that these three cases are most unusual and might never have reached decision if the United States had elected to raise the issue of sovereign immunity. The Manual[79] then in effect did not cover the situation, it presumably not previously having arisen. The new Manual provides that habeas corpus process of a foreign court will not be obeyed.[80] This gives an answer to the judge advocate in the field, but due to the delicate considerations of diplomatic policy which will inevitably be involved it is believed that the answer can be neither so simple nor so final. The new Manual provision clearly requires report to higher authority and contemplates a policy decision in each case. Pending such decision the judge advocate on the ground must seek continuance of a proceeding which is normally characterized by its summary nature. It is essential that reciprocal jurisdictional agreements be simple, clear and practical. They should cover expressly, not only trial jurisdiction but also habeas corpus or similar process where such is known to the law of the other sovereign.

D. World Court

Any discussion of habeas corpus in the sphere of the court of international justice necessarily involves academic speculation. However, it is not beyond the realm of possibility that the rule of *Hirota v. MacArthur* may someday lead to a treaty-created habeas corpus jurisdiction of the World Court to inquire into the jurisdiction of international military tribunals. On the other hand it may be urged that the resort to force implicitly prerequisite to the convening of international military tribunals is antithetical to ultimate extension of the rule of law in this particular to the international sphere. Military tribunals constituted by a single sovereign would presumably not come within the sphere of such a convention or multilateral treaty.

[79] MANUAL FOR COURTS-MARTIAL, U. S. Army (1928, revised to 1942).

[80] MANUAL FOR COURTS-MARTIAL, U. S. Army (1951), par. 216, p. 390, provides: "A court or judge of a foreign country has no authority to inquire into the legality of restraint upon any person held by United States military authority. Any process in the nature of a writ of habeas corpus issued by any foreign court or judge to any officer acting in his official capacity as an officer of the United States will not be obeyed, but its issuance will be reported to the commander of the United States force within whose command the person restrained is located and to The Judge Advocate General of the appropriate department."

III

Habeas Corpus Prerequisites

The doctrine is well established that habeas corpus is an extraordinary remedy which will not ordinarily lie where the law has provided another remedy.[81] The numerical pressure of habeas corpus petitions by all types of prisoners in recent years has reached such proportions as to constitute a major problem in the administration of justice.[82] It has engaged the administrative consideration of judicial officers[83] and been the subject of legislation both federal and state. The Chief Justice of the United States in an address before the American Bar Association on September 7, 1949 strikingly stated the problem and urged "that something should be done to stem the flow."[84]

Something has in fact been done in at least one state,[85] and by Congress in the federal jurisdiction as to both civil[86] and military

[81] Sunal v. Large, 332 U. S. 174, 67 Sup. Ct. 1588 (1947); Adams v. United States, 317 U. S. 269 at 274-275, 63 Sup. Ct. 236 (1942); Goto v. Lane, 265 U. S. 393 at 401-402, 44 Sup. Ct. 525 (1924).

[82] United States v. Hayman, 342 U. S. 205, 213, notes 13 and 14, 72 Sup. Ct. 263 (1952) and authorities therein cited.

[83] See Parker, Limiting the Abuse of Habeas Corpus, 8 F. R. D. 171 (1948). Judge Parker was chairman of the Judicial Conference Committee on Habeas Corpus Procedure.

[84] Address reported in 70 Supreme Court Reporter, Nov. 15, 1949, p. xiii at xvi-xvii. Chief Justice Vinson in discussing habeas corpus petitions arising out of state convictions said:

". . . the fact that the volume of such petitions has reached the six-hundred mark in each of the past three or four years and that ninety-six out of every one hundred have little or no legal merit suggests that something should be done to try to stem the flow. . . .

"If a state provides a well-defined method by which prisoners can challenge their convictions, and if their allegations are aired in open hearings, most of the charges are either not proved or are found to be far outside the protection of the Due Process Clause. Faced with these facts, the prisoner sees little advantage in further appeal. But until he receives such a hearing, his allegations remain unchallenged and his persistence knows no bounds. I feel safe in estimating that over 75% of the *in forma pauperis* petitions filed last term were cases in which the petitioner had not received a post-conviction hearing in a state court. . . .

"To be concrete, the states should aid in the solution of this problem in several ways. In the first place, they should set up clearly defined post-trial procedures by which prisoners may obtain hearings into the legality of their detention. If the blind alleys are eliminated and the procedure is made definite and precise, the prisoner knows how to challenge his conviction, and he is put to the proof. If his allegations are not borne out by the facts, that is the end of the matter. If his allegations are proved true, the question of unfairness or illegality of his conviction is one of primary importance to the state. It should be to the state's advantage to have that question of law fully and fairly developed in the state courts."

[85] Jenner, The Illinois Post-Conviction Hearing Act, 9 F. R. D. 347 (1949). See Schilder v. Gusik, 180 F. (2d) 662 (6th Cir. 1950) and Frankel, Federal Habeas Corpus Jurisdiction to Review State Convictions, 14 F. R. D. 99 (1953).

[86] 28 U. S. C. § 2255 (M 52) which in pertinent part provides:

"A prisoner in custody under sentence of a court established by Act of Congress claiming the right to be released upon the ground that the sentence was imposed in violation of the Constitution or laws of the United States, or that the

prisoners.[87] These recent statutory remedies, which have been defined and made prerequisites to habeas corpus, do not constitute a departure

court was without jurisdiction to impose such sentence, or that the sentence was in excess of the maximum authorized by law, or is otherwise subject to collateral attack, may move the court which imposed the sentence to vacate, set aside or correct the sentence.

"A motion for such relief may be made at any time.

". . . If the court finds that the judgment was rendered without jurisdiction, or that the sentence imposed was not authorized by law or otherwise open to collateral attack, or that there has been such a denial or infringement of the constitutional rights of the prisoner as to render the judgment vulnerable to collateral attack, the court shall vacate and set the judgment aside and shall discharge the prisoner or resentence him or grant a new trial or correct the sentence as may appear appropriate. . . .

"The sentencing court shall not be required to entertain a second or successive motion for similar relief on behalf of the same prisoner.

"An appeal may be taken to the court of appeals from the order entered on the motion as from a final judgment on application for a writ of habeas corpus.

"An application for a writ of habeas corpus in behalf of a prisoner who is authorized to apply for relief by motion pursuant to this section, shall not be entertained if it appears that the applicant has failed to apply for relief, by motion, to the court which sentenced him, or that such court has denied him relief, unless it also appears that the remedy by motion is inadequate or ineffective to test the legality of his detention."

See LONGSDORF, THE FEDERAL HABEAS CORPUS ACTS ORIGINAL AND AMENDED, 13 F. R. D. 407 (1953).

[87] 10 U. S. C. § 1525 (Supp. 1950) Article of War 53, read:

"Under such regulations as the President may prescribe, the Judge Advocate General is authorized, upon application of an accused person, and upon good cause shown, in his discretion to grant a new trial, or to vacate a sentence, restore rights, privileges, and property affected by such sentence, and substitute for a dismissal, dishonorable discharge, or bad conduct discharge previously executed a form of discharge authorized for administrative issuance, in any court-martial case in which application is made within one year after final disposition of the case upon initial appellate review: *Provided,* That with regard to cases involving offenses committed during World War II, the application for a new trial may be made within one year after termination of the war, or after its final disposition upon initial appellate review as herein provided, whichever is the later: *Provided,* That only one such application for a new trial may be entertained with regard to any one case; *And provided further,* That all action by the Judge Advocate General pursuant to this article, and all proceedings, findings, and sentences on new trials under this article, as approved, reviewed, or confirmed under articles 47, 48, 49, and 50, and all dismissals and discharges carried into execution pursuant to sentences adjudged on new trials and approved, reviewed, or confirmed, shall be final and conclusive and orders publishing the action of the Judge Advocate General or the proceedings on new trial and all action taken pursuant to such proceedings, shall be binding upon all departments, courts, agencies, and officers of the United States."

Article of War 50-(h), 10 U. S. C. § 1521 (Supp. 1950), in part provided: ". . . orders publishing the proceedings of courts-martial and all action taken pursuant to such proceedings shall be binding upon all departments, courts, agencies, and officers of the United States, subject only to action upon application for a new trial as provided in Article 53."

Article 73 of the Uniform Code of Military Justice, 50 U. S. C. § 660 (1954), reads:

"At any time within one year after approval by the convening authority of a court-martial sentence which extends to death, dishonorable or bad conduct discharge, or confinement for one year or more, the accused may petition The Judge Advocate General for a new trial on the grounds of newly discovered evidence or fraud on the court. If the accused's case is pending before the board of review or before the Court of Military Appeals, The Judge Advocate General

from established principles but rather evidence legislative recognition and extension of established Supreme Court doctrine. That a petitioner must first exhaust all other court[88] and administrative remedies[89] before he will be permitted to resort to habeas corpus in a federal court was well established before the enactment of section 2255 of the United States Code, Article of War 53, and Article 73.

The provision of section 2255 which requires a prisoner convicted in a federal court to exhaust his remedy to move for a new trial in the federal district court in which convicted before he may petition for habeas corpus has been held to be constitutional,[90] and in the normal case mandatory.[91] Not only must the section 2255 remedy be pursued in the district court but if the decision there is adverse to the prisoner he must exhaust his remedy by appeal from the adverse decision upon his section 2255 motion before he may resort to habeas corpus.[92] This includes the requirement of application for certiorari to the Supreme Court from a denial of section 2255 relief.[93] In the *Meyers* case, while appeal was pending from the district court in which the prisoner had been originally convicted, he petitioned for habeas corpus in the District Court for the Eastern District of Virginia in which district he was con-

---

shall refer the petition to the board or court, respectively, for action. Otherwise, The Judge Advocate General shall act upon the petition."

Article 76, 50 U. S. C. § 663 (1951) provides:

"The appellate review of records of trial provided by this code, the proceedings, findings, and sentence of courts-martial as approved, reviewed, or affirmed as required by this code, and all dismissals and discharges carried into execution pursuant to sentences by courts-martial following approval, review, or affirmation as required by this code, shall be final and conclusive, and orders publishing the proceedings of courts-martial and all action taken pursuant to such proceedings shall be binding upon all departments, courts, agencies, and officers of the United States, subject only to action upon a petition for a new trial as provided in Article 73 and to action by the Secretary of a Department as provided in article 74, and the authority of the President."

[88] *Ex parte* Hawk, 321 U. S. 114, 64 Sup. Ct. 448 (1944).

[89] Yakus v. United States, 321 U. S. 414 at 434-435, 64 Sup. Ct. 660 (1944); United States v. Sing Tuck, 194 U. S. 161, 167-168, 170, 24 Sup. Ct. 621 (1904); Falbo v. United States, 320 U. S. 549, 64 Sup. Ct. 346 (1944); Lee Fong Fook v. Wixon, 170 F. (2d) 245, 246 (9th Cir. 1948), *cert. denied,* 336 U. S. 914, 69 Sup. Ct. 604 (1949); Trinler v. Carusi, 166 F. (2d) 457 (3d Cir. 1948).

[90] United States v. Hayman, 342 U. S. 205, 72 Sup. Ct. 263 (1951); Martin v. Hiatt, 174 F. (2d) 350 (5th Cir. 1949); Barrett v. Hunter, 180 F. (2d) 510 (10th Cir. 1950), *cert. denied,* 340 U. S. 897, 71 Sup. Ct. 234; United States v. Anselmi, 207 F. (2d) 312, 314 (3d Cir. 1953).

[91] Pinkerton v. Steele, 181 F. (2d) 536 (8th Cir. 1950); Armstrong v. Steele, 181 F. (2d) 763 (8th Cir. 1950); Higgins v. Steele, 195 F. (2d) 366 (8th Cir. 1952); Duquesne v. Steele, 197 F. (2d) 56 (8th Cir. 1952); Taylor v. United States, 177 F. (2d) 194 (4th Cir. 1950); Barnes v. Hunter, 188 F. (2d) 86 (10th Cir. 1951), *cert. denied,* 342 U. S. 920, 72 Sup. Ct. 368 (1951).

[92] Meyers v. Welch, 179 F. (2d) 707 (4th Cir. 1950). This case has a military flavor, though wry, by reason of the fact that the prisoner Meyers, prior to his civil court conviction for subornation of perjury, was a retired Air Force major general.

[93] Weber v. Steele, 185 F. (2d) 799 (8th Cir. 1950).

fined. The court of appeals in affirming the order of the district court dismissing the habeas corpus petition held:

". . . The prisoner has no right to relief by habeas corpus where there exists the right to relief under 28 U. S. C. A., Sec. 2255; and the fact that the motion has been denied does not give the right to resort to habeas corpus, even if the movant is entitled to relief, since the remedy in such case is by appeal. Only where the remedy by motion with appeal therefrom is inadequate or ineffective to test the legality of the detention may there be resort to habeas corpus."[94]

When the Supreme Court first focused its attention upon section 2255 it said:

> "Section 2255 . . . was passed at the instance of the Judicial Conference to meet practical difficulties that had arisen in administering the habeas corpus jurisdiction of the federal courts. Nowhere in the history of Section 2255 do we find any purpose to impinge upon prisoners' rights of collateral attack upon their convictions. On the contrary, the sole purpose was to minimize the difficulties encountered in habeas corpus hearings by affording the same rights in another and more convenient forum.[95]
>
> "In a case where the Section 2255 procedure is shown to be 'inadequate or ineffective,' the Section provides that the habeas corpus remedy shall remain open to afford the necessary hearing. (Note 40, at this point, reads: "If Section 2255 had not expressly required that the extraordinary remedy of habeas corpus be withheld pending resort to established procedures providing the same relief, the same result would have followed under our decisions. . . .") Under such circumstances we do not reach constitutional questions."[96]

[94] Meyers v. Welch, 179 F. (2d) 707 at 708 (4th Cir. 1950). When this material was first published, prior to the decision of United States v. Hayman, 342 U. S. 205, 72 Sup. Ct. 263 (1951), the text, at this point, observed: "The court here, by way of dictum, seems to say that even after a prisoner exhausts his appellate remedies following a section 2255 hearing he is not eligible to seek habeas corpus relief except in rare cases where the section 2255 remedy is inadequate or ineffective. The question arises, does this result in suspending the writ of habeas corpus in contravention of article I, section 9 of the Constitution? On this the Supreme Court has not yet spoken. However, it seems most probable the answer is no. It is entirely possible to view the section 2255 proceeding itself as a wholly remedial extension of the function of the writ of habeas corpus which enlarges rather than restricts the constitutional guaranty. In any event the extraordinary writ is still available in situations where a section 2255 proceeding is in fact inadequate or ineffective."

[95] United States v. Hayman, 342 U. S. 205, 219, 72 Sup. Ct. 263 (1952).

[96] *Id.* at 223, 72 Sup. Ct. at 274.

Not only must the section 2255 remedy be fully exhausted as a prerequisite to seeking habeas corpus relief, but, except for the unusual case where "the remedy by motion is inadequate or ineffective," the section itself is a bar to a petition for habeas corpus.[97] However, habeas corpus petition remains open to a prisoner contending he is confined without any judgment of a court or after fully serving the sentence for which committed.[98]

It is important to remember the extraordinary nature of habeas corpus, the basic doctrine of the necessity of full exhaustion of all other remedies first, the vast administrative burden that abusive resort to the writ has cast upon the courts and the desire of both the courts and Congress to establish post-conviction hearing procedures which are both more adequate and more conclusive than the traditional writ of habeas corpus *ad subjiciendum*. An evaluation of the effect of Article of War 53 upon military habeas corpus is simplified by having those facts in mind. Article of War 53, and its Uniform Code successor, Article 73, constitute the congressional solution to the problem in military cases just as section 2255 is its solution in civil cases. Federal courts will effectuate the purpose "to stem the flow" by insisting that military prisoners fully exhaust this post-trial proceeding as to all issues before permitting habeas corpus proceedings.

Habeas corpus has been abused by military as well as civil prisoners. For example, William Jackson, a previously convicted felon in civil life, served three years in the Atlanta penitentiary for the burglary of a post exchange. In this one case in three years Jackson filed sixteen different petitions for habeas corpus in the District Court for the North-

[97] United States v. Hayman, 342 U. S. 205, 219, 72 Sup. Ct. 263 (1953); Meyers v. Welch, 179 F. (2d) 707 (4th Cir. 1950); Whiting v. Hunter, 204 F. (2d) 471, 472 (10th Cir. 1953); Jones v. Squier, 195 F. (2d) 179, 180 (9th Cir. 1952); Smith v. Reid, 191 F. (2d) 491 (D. C. Cir. 1951); United States v. Gallagher, 183 F. (2d) 342 (3d Cir. 1951); Robinson v. Swope, 197 F. (2d) 633 (9th Cir. 1952); Crow v. United States, 186 F. (2d) 704 (9th Cir. 1951); Barrett v. Hunter, 180 F. (2d) 510 (10th Cir. 1950); Clough v. Hunter, 186 F. (2d) 516 (10th Cir. 1951); Hallowell v. Hunter, 186 F. (2d) 837 (10th Cir. 1951); Martin v. Hiatt, 174 F. (2d) 350 (5th Cir. 1950); Weber v. Steele, 185 F. (2d) 799 (8th Cir. 1951); McIntosh v. Steele, 184 F. (2d) 721, 722 (8th Cir. 1951); Decatur v. Hiatt, 184 F. (2d) 719, 720 (5th Cir. 1951); Tacoma v. Hiatt, 184 F. (2d) 569 (5th Cir. 1951); Winhoven v. Swope, 195 F. (2d) 181, 183 (9th Cir. 1952); Josey v. Humphrey, 210 F. (2d) 826, 827 (3d Cir. 1954).

[98] Mills v. Hunter, 204 F. (2d) 468, 470 (10th Cir. 1953). See also Talbott v. Toth, —— F. (2d) —— (D. C. Cir. 1954). Furthermore, since there is no jurisdiction to grant section 2255 relief where the applicant is no longer in custody, United States v. Lavelle, 194 F. (2d) 202 (2d Cir. 1952), the Supreme Court has held that, even since the enactment of section 2255, federal district courts, in proper cases, have jurisdiction to grant relief to such applicants upon petition for writ of error *coram nobis*. United States v. Morgan, 346 U. S. 502, 74 Sup. Ct. 247 (1954).

ern District of Georgia,[99] six times lost appeals to the Court of Appeals for the Fifth Circuit,[100] unsuccessfully petitioned the Supreme Court six times,[101] twice sought and was denied declaratory judgment relief in the District Court for the District of Columbia and upon his conditional release at the expiration of his term had pending before the district court his sixteenth petition for habeas corpus. All this was *in propria persona* without benefit of counsel. One of Jackson's relatively early efforts evoked this comment from the court of appeals: "We think it clear too that applicant, in continually filing groundless applications for writs of habeas corpus has greatly abused the process of the courts. . . ."[102] Jackson was returned to custody for parole violation and sought, and was denied, habeas corpus relief from this action of the parole board in *Jackson v. Humphrey*.[103] The rule that the doctrine of res judicata has no formal application to habeas corpus[104] makes possible this abuse of the writ.

Article of War 53 became effective on February 1, 1949 and was implemented in detail by chapter 22 of the *Manual for Courts-Martial,* U. S. Army, 1949 as promulgated by Executive Order No. 10020. It in substance provided that a military prisoner may, within one year after initial appellate review or after the official termination of World War II, apply to the Judge Advocate General for a new trial, to vacate sentence, and/or restore rights in the court-martial case and that all action taken by the Judge Advocate General pursuant to such proceedings, shall be binding upon all departments, courts, agencies and officers of the United States. The first court to take notice of this article was the District Court for the District of Columbia on June 14, 1949, in an unreported case denying a petition on the merits.[105] The issue was next

[99] See Jackson v. Sanford, 79 F. Supp. 74 (1947) (Habeas Corpus Nos. 2198, 2234, 2261, 2308, 2358, 2399, 2407, 2409, 2445 and seven other petitions dismissed in the lower court without filing and without case numbers).

[100] Nos. 12,111 and 12,113 combined, Jackson v. Sanford, 163 F. (2d) 875 (5th Cir. 1947); 12,402 and 12,452 combined, Jackson v. Gough, 170 F. (2d) 630 (5th Cir. 1948); 12,678, Jackson v. Hiatt, 173 F. (2d) 760 (5th Cir. 1947); and 12,981, Hiatt v. Jackson, 179 F. (2d) 680 (5th Cir. 1950).

[101] Nos. 12,111 and 12,113 combined, *cert. denied,* 332 U. S. 848; Nos. 12,402, and 12,462 combined, *cert. denied,* 336 U. S. 938, *motion for leave to file petition for writ of habeas corpus denied,* 335 U. S. 805; and No. 12,678, *cert. denied,* 339 U. S. 968.

[102] Jackson v. Sanford, 170 F. (2d) 630, 632 (5th Cir. 1948).

[103] 92 F. Supp. 635 (M. D. Pa. 1950).

[104] Innes v. Hiatt, 141 F. (2d) 664 (3d Cir. 1944). See also Dolenz v. Shaunessy, 206 F. (2d) 392 (2d Cir. 1953) and United States v. Shaunessy, 115 F. Supp. 165 (S. D. N. Y. 1953).

[105] Case No. 3530, Browell v. Johnson. The court said: "The Court further finds, upon consideration of the provisions of Article of War 50(h) and 53 (Public Law 759, 80th Congress, Title II), that the petitioner has failed to exhaust his remedies in that he has not applied to The Judge Advocate General for a new trial or other relief under the provisions of Article of War 53, as amended (Public Law 759, 80th Congress, Title II, Sec. 230) and Chapter XXII of the

raised in three cases[106] in the Northern District of Georgia in which the judge held that a military petitioner need not comply with Article of War 53 but might immediately resort to habeas corpus. These three cases are the only ones in which a court has so ruled and all were reversed and the petitioners remanded to custody in per curiam opinions by the Court of Appeals for the Fifth Circuit.[107]

The first appellate court decision on the point was rendered by the Fifth Circuit in a case in which the District Court for the Southern District of Texas had denied a writ on January 10, 1949, before the effective date of Article of War 53. In this case the appellate court affirmed the district court on the merits and then said:

> "Habeas corpus to review the action of another court is in its nature extraordinary, and will not be used, if available at all, till other remedies have been exhausted, Goto v. Lane, 265 U. S. 393, 401. . . . See also Ex parte Hawk, 321 U. S. 114. . . . On Feb. 1, 1949, the amended Articles of War, Act of June 24, 1948, 62 Stats. 627 went into effect. Article 53, 10 U. S. C. A. § 1525, provides for the grant of a new trial or the vacation of a sentence for a good cause shown within one year after final disposition of a court-martial case; and in cases involving offenses committed during World War II, the application may be made within one year after termination of the war. The action taken on such application is expressly made binding on all courts of the United States. This remedy is much better adapted to reach justice than any within the power of the district court on habeas corpus. That it has not been sought here is within itself a sufficient reason for noninterference."[108]

The *Whelchel* case was decided on July 22, 1949, just one week after the district judge in the Northern District of Georgia, in the three cases above, had reached the opposite conclusion. It was upon the authority of the *Whelchel* decision that these three cases were reversed on appeal. The district judge who had originally decided them, after the publication of the *Whelchel* decision, proceeded to dismiss at least thirty-four other pending petitions as premature because no compliance with Article of War 53 was alleged by the petitioner.[109]

Manual for Courts-Martial, U. S. Army, 1949, which remedy is readily available to him."

[106] Burchfield v. Hiatt, 86 F. Supp. 18 (N. D. Ga. 1949); Fugate v. Hiatt, 86 F. Supp. 22 (N. D. Ga. 1949); Jackson v. Hiatt, not reported.

[107] Hiatt v. Burchfield, Hiatt v. Fugate, Hiatt v. Jackson, 179 F. (2d) 679-680 (5th Cir. 1950).

[108] Whelchel v. McDonald, 176 F. (2d) 260, 262 (5th Cir. 1949).

[109] Typical of these cases are Sinclair v. Hiatt, 86 F. Supp. 828 (N. D. Ga. 1949), and Lindsey v. Hiatt, H. C. No. 2470 (N. D. Ga.), unreported. In the

The *Whelchel* decision, affirmed by the Supreme Court, has been followed by an unbroken line of cases approving and following its doctrine.[110] *Whelchel* assumed, without discussing the point, that even though the prisoner's petition had been filed and acted upon in the district court before the effective date of Article of War 53 it was incumbent upon the court of appeals to invoke the rule of exhaustion of remedies when the case came before it. This rule was expressly applied under these circumstances in *McMahan v. Hunter,*[111] after de-

former the district court said at 832: "My conclusion is that, upon authority of Whelchel v. McDonald, *supra,* compliance with Article of War 53 is a condition precedent to the institution of habeas corpus proceedings, except in 'exceptional circumstances where need for the remedy afforded by the writ of habeas corpus is apparent'; and that in the absence here of such showing, the petition should be dismissed without prejudice." In the latter the district court held: "The petition does not allege compliance with Article of War 53 or any exceptional circumstances which would excuse such compliance. . . . The motion to dismiss . . . is sustained, and the petition dismissed as premature, without prejudice, however, to the right to present a new application after compliance with Article of War 53."

[110] Whelchel v. McDonald, 340 U. S. 122, 71 Sup. Ct. 146 (1950) ; Spencer v. Hunter, 177 F. (2d) 370 (10th Cir. 1949) ; McMahan v. Hunter, 179 F. (2d) 661 (10th Cir. 1950) ; Simmons v. Hunter, 179 F. (2d) 664 (10th Cir. 1950) ; Hiatt v. Burchfield, 179 F. (2d) 679-680 (5th Cir. 1950) ; Evans v. Hunter, 180 F. (2d) 354, 355 (10th Cir. 1950) ; Giese v. Chamberlin, 184 F. (2d) 404 (7th Cir. 1950) ; Hunter v. Beets, 180 F. (2d) 101 (10th Cir. 1951) ; Schilder v. Gusik, 180 F. (2d) 662 (6th Cir. 1950) ; Massey v. Humphrey, 85 F. Supp. 534 (M. D. Pa. 1949) ; Smith v. Humphrey, 89 F. Supp. 948 (M. D. Pa. 1949) ; Cochrane v. Zuppan, 89 F. Supp. 329 (M. D. Pa. 1950) ; and a number of recent unreported cases in the District Court for the Northern District of Georgia. Most of these authorities are cited and followed in Giese v. Chamberlin, 184 F. (2d) 404 (7th Cir. 1950). Whelchel v. McDonald was cited with approval in Burns v. Wilson, 346 U. S. 137, 73 Sup. Ct. 1045 (1953), *rehearing denied,* 346 U. S. 844, 74 Sup. Ct. 3 (1953). *Cf.* McKinney v. Finletter, 205 F. (2d) 761, 762 (10th Cir. 1953).

[111] 179 F. (2d) 661 (10th Cir. 1950), *cert. denied,* 339 U. S. 968, 70 Sup. Ct. 985 (1950). At page 663 the court of appeals said:

"Appellant contends, however, that since the judgment in this case in the United States District Court was entered prior to the effective date of Article of War 53, it cannot retroactively be made to apply to him. . . .

"On October 10, 1949, the Supreme Court denied the petition for certiorari in seven cases (70 S. Ct. 37-50), all filed against Joseph E. Ragen, a warden of an Illinois penal institution, without consideration of the question presented therein and without prejudice to the right of the petitioners to institute proceedings in the state court under the new act passed by the State of Illinois, entitled: 'An Act to provide a remedy for persons convicted and imprisoned in the penitentiary, who assert that rights guaranteed them by the Constitution of the United States or the State of Illinois, or both, have been denied or violated, in proceedings in which they were convicted.' Smith-Hurd Stats. c. 38, § 826 *et seq.* In six of these seven cases, the petition for certiorari had been filed in the Supreme Court prior to the passage of the new Illinois Statute. Thus, the Supreme Court, in effect, held that petitioners were required to exhaust their remedies under the new Statute notwithstanding that it had been passed after their petitions for certiorari were lodged in the Supreme Court.

"We, accordingly, conclude that appellant must first exhaust his remedies under Article of War 53 before he may raise these questions in a Federal District Court, or in this case, on appeal to this court."

tailed consideration by the court. In *Schilder v. Gusik*[112] the contention was made that Article of War 53 could have no retroactive effect with respect to court-martial sentences imposed, reviewed and approved prior to its effective date and this contention was held to be without merit since the article in question is remedial. Finally in *Hunter v. Beets,*[113] the court of appeals remanded the prisoner to custody and held compliance with Article 53 to be essential in a case where a writ had been granted by a district court and the prisoner discharged from custody before the effective date of the article.

In none of these cases had the petitioner exhausted his remedies under Article 53 at the time of decision, so the courts did not have before them for determination the effect of the language in the article which purports to make all action taken thereunder by the Judge Advocate General final and conclusive and binding upon all courts. However, three of the cases have discussed this question. *McMahan* simply reserved opinion on the point. *Gusik* read the article so as to give it finality upon the merits only and not so as to preclude ultimate

[112] 180 F. (2d) 662, 664 (6th Cir. 1950): "The contention is without merit. Article 53 is a remedial measure. It creates no new offenses, increases no penalties and is not in any respect punitive. It does not, therefore, come within the constitutional condemnation of an *ex post facto* law. It would be an unfortunate result and one clearly not intended, either by amended Articles or the Presidential proclamation, to deny to soldiers convicted before their effective date, while granting to others a review now deemed necessary to protect them against erroneous convictions.

"Rather is it a more salutary principle that now governs this situation. Since the decision in Vandenmark v. Owens-Illinois Glass Co., 311 U. S. 538, . . . there is no longer doubt that the law to be applied by a reviewing court is the law in force when decision is made and not the law as it existed at the time of the trial and judgment. It is a principle that evolves from the earlier case of U. S. v. Schooner Peggy, 1 Cranch 103, . . . and has now been applied by the Courts of Appeal in many cases. Specifically it has been applied by the Fifth Circuit to cases involving convicted soldiers in Whelchel v. McDonald, 176 F. 2d 260, and by the Tenth Circuit in McMahan v. Hunter, Warden, 179 F. 2d 661 and Simmons v. Hunter, Warden, 179 F. 2d 664 and Hunter v. Beets, 180 F. 2d 101."

[113] 180 F. (2d) 101 (10th Cir. 1950), *cert. denied,* 339 U. S. 963, 70 Sup. Ct. 997 (1950). At 102-103 the court of appeals said:

"That administrative remedy has been available to petitioner at all times since the amended Articles of War became effective, and it has not been invoked. But it is argued that petitioner should not be compelled to exhaust such remedy for the reason that the judgment discharging him from custody was entered before the amended Articles of War went into effect and that Article 53 cannot apply retroactively to him. The contention is not well-founded. Even though the post-conviction administrative remedy contained in Article 53 became effective after entry of the judgment in the district court, the exhaustion of that remedy is a prerequisite in a case of this kind to the right to final discharge in habeas corpus. McMahan v. Hunter, *supra.*

"The judgment is reversed and the cause remanded with directions to restore petitioner to the custody of the warden, without prejudice to the right of petitioner to proceed under Article of War 53, and without prejudice to his right, if any exists, to institute a proceeding in habeas corpus after the exhaustion of the administrative remedy provided in Article 53." The Beets case is cited with approval in Goldstein v. Johnson, 184 F. (2d) 342 (D. C. Cir. 1950).

habeas corpus attack in a proper case after unsuccessful resort to the article.[114] Finally, in a per curiam opinion denying a motion for rehearing in *Whelchel v. McDonald,* the court of appeals refused to allow the petitioner to amend his motion to show unsuccessful compliance with Article 53 after the original appellate decision, refused to permit the petitioner to assert a new ground of attack upon the judgment of conviction not presented in the district court, and said, "Moreover the last words of the amended Article of War 53, seem to make the action of the Judge Advocate General refusing a new trial binding upon the courts of the United States."[115]

In the *McMahan, Simmons, Beets, Burchfield* and *Jackson* cases, petitions for certiorari were denied by the Supreme Court,[116] thus approving the square holding in those cases that the Article 53 remedy must first be exhausted even though not available at the time the district court passed upon the habeas corpus petition.

The other interesting issue as to whether the finality provision of Article 53 involved constitutional complications arrested the attention of the Court and it granted certiorari in the *Whelchel* and *Schilder* cases.[117] On principle, the most critical treatment likely to be accorded to this aspect of Article 53 is that, suggested by the court of appeals in the *Schilder* case, of construing it as simply reaffirming finality on the

[114] 180 F. (2d) 662, 665 (6th Cir. 1950). The court said:

"Another contention of the appellee is that because Article 53 provides that action taken thereunder upon application for a new trial or vacation of sentence is expressly made binding on all of the courts of the United States, the remedy provided by that Article is available to Gusik only upon condition that he surrender his right to challenge the jurisdiction of the military court and his deprivation of constitutional rights by applying for a writ of habeas corpus. This provision, he says, is unconstitutional and he should not be compelled to avail himself of an unconstitutional process. The Tenth Court of Appeals disposes of a similar contention in McMahan v. Hunter, *supra,* by the observation that it will be time enough to answer the question of finality when it is necessarily involved in an appeal before the court. It seems to us, however, that we meet one aspect of that question now, for it would seem unsound to relegate the appellee to an application for review under Article 53 at the hazard of surrendering important constitutional rights if such hazard exists. Whether the finality provision, literally read, is constitutional or not, we need not decide, for applying the principle of decision so often availed of, that an issue of constitutionality will not be considered if an act may reasonably be so read that constitutional validity appears, it would seem that all that is meant by the finality provision in Article 53 is that decision upon the merits is final and does not go to those contentions which attack decision collaterally. So read the finality created by Article 53 differs in no wise from the finality, in the absence of or after futile appeal, accorded to trial decisions upon consideration of a writ of habeas corpus."

[115] 178 F. (2d) 760 (5th Cir. 1949). *Cf.* Olsen v. Hiatt, 89 F. Supp. 174, 176 (N. D. Ga. 1950).

[116] McMahan v. Hunter, 339 U. S. 968, 70 Sup. Ct. 985 (1950); Simmons v. Hunter, 339 U. S. 968, 70 Sup. Ct. 984 (1950); Beets v. Hunter, 339 U. S. 963, 70 Sup. Ct. 997 (1950); Burchfield v. Hiatt, 339 U. S. 987, 70 Sup. Ct. 1009 (1950); Jackson v. Hiatt, 339 U. S. 968, 70 Sup. Ct. 985 (1950).

[117] Whelchel v. McDonald, 339 U. S. 977, 70 Sup. Ct. 1019 (1950); Gusik v. Schilder, 339 U. S. 977, 70 Sup. Ct. 1014 (1950).

merits, and not as precluding habeas corpus proceedings after exhaustion of the Article 53 remedy. The intimation, in the *Whelchel* opinion on rehearing, that Article 53 action is binding on the courts in habeas corpus should be considered along with the decision in *Myers v. Welch,*[118] that section 2255 action precludes subsequent resort to habeas corpus except where it can be shown that the section 2255 remedy is inadequate or ineffective. Also pertinent is the decision in *Barrett v. Hunter*[119] that the order made by the sentencing court under section 2255 is res judicata. In any event such habeas corpus review as may survive after exhausting the Article 53 remedy should be confined to the narrow traditional inquiry into jurisdiction only, that is, the rule laid down in *Ex parte Reed*[120] from which the Supreme Court has never departed.

The preceding paragraph, written before, and hence without benefit of, the Supreme Court decisions in *Whelchel, Gusik,*[121] *Hayman*[122] and *Burns v. Wilson,*[123] continues to square with the Supreme Court thinking therein announced. The constitutionality, and mandatory prerequisite nature, of Article of War 53 proceedings was upheld in Gusik.[124]

[118] 179 F. (2d) 707 (4th Cir. 1950). See note 92, *supra.*

[119] 180 F. (2d) 510, 516 (10th Cir. 1950). See also Tacoma v. Hiatt, 184 F. (2d) 569 (5th Cir. 1950).

[120] See discussion, commencing p. 327, *supra.*

[121] On December 4, 1950, the Supreme Court unanimously affirmed denial of habeas corpus relief in Whelchel v. McDonald, 340 U. S. 122, 71 Sup. Ct. 146 (1950). On the same day in Gusik v. Schilder, 340 U. S. 128, 71 Sup. Ct. 149 (1950), a unanimous Court, speaking through Justice Douglas, upheld the constitutionality of Article 53, employing this unequivocal language (at 132-133):

"An argument is woven around the finality clause of Article 53 as a foundation to a claim of unconstitutionality. The provision is that all action by the Judge Advocate General under Article 53 shall be 'final and conclusive' and shall be 'binding upon all departments, agencies, and officers of the United States.' It is argued that this clause deprives the courts of jurisdiction to review these military judgments and therefore amounts to a suspension of the writ. We do not so read Article 53. Congress was legislating as respects tribunals over which the civil courts have traditionally exercised no power of supervision or review. See *In re Grimley,* 137 U. S. 147, 150. These tribunals have operated in a self-sufficient system, save only as habeas corpus was available to test their jurisdiction in specific cases. We read the finality clause of Article 53 as doing no more than describing the terminal point for proceedings within the court-martial system. If Congress had intended to deprive the civil courts of their habeas corpus jurisdiction, which has been exercised from the beginning, the break with history would have been so marked that we believe the purpose would have been made plain and unmistakable. The finality language so adequately serves the more restricted purpose that we would have to give a strained construction in order to stir the constitutional issue that is tendered.

"Petitioner says that resort to Article 53 will be futile. If it proves to be, no rights have been sacrificed. Habeas corpus will then be available to test any questions of jurisdiction which petitioner may offer."

[122] United States v. Hayman, 342 U. S. 205, 72 Sup. Ct. 263 (1952).

[123] 346 U. S. 137, 73 Sup. Ct. 1045 (1953); *rehearing denied,* 346 U. S. 844, 74 Sup. Ct. 3 (1953).

[124] 340 U. S. 128, 71 Sup. Ct. 149 (1950). See Easley v. Hunter, 209 F. (2d) 484, 485 (10th Cir. 1953).

In *Whelchel* the finality of factual determinations, not jurisdictional, made in such proceedings was affirmed.[125] The Court in *Burns v. Wilson* has again reaffirmed these views in these words:

> "Congress has provided a special post-conviction remedy within the military establishment, apart from ordinary appellate review, whereby one convicted by a court-martial, may attack collaterally the judgment under which he stands convicted. (Note 8, at this point, reads: "62 Stat. 639, 10 U. S. C. (Supp. III) sec. 1525. See *Gusik v. Schilder,* 340 U. S. 128 (1950). This provision was also made a part of the Uniform Code of Military Justice. 64 Stat. 131, 50 U. S. C. (Supp. V) sec. 660; 64 Stat. 147, 50 U. S. C. (Supp. V) sec. 740.")[126]
>
> ". . . Congress has provided that these determinations are 'final' and 'binding' upon all courts. . . . We have held before that this does not displace the civil courts' jurisdiction over an application for habeas corpus from the military prisoner. *Gusik v. Schilder,* 340 U. S. 128 (1950). But these provisions do mean that when a military decision has dealt fully and fairly with an allegation raised in that application, it is not open to a federal civil court to grant a writ simply to re-evaluate the evidence. *Whelchel v. McDonald,* 340 U. S. 122 (1950).[127]
>
> "Petitioners have failed to show that this military review was legally inadequate to resolve the claims which they have urged upon the civil courts. They simply demand an opportunity to make a new record, to prove *de novo* in the District Court precisely the case which they failed to prove in the military courts. We think, under the circumstances, that due regard for the limitations on a civil court's power to grant such relief precludes such action. We think that although the Court of Appeals may have erred in reweighing each item of relevant evidence in the trial record, it certainly did not err in holding that there was no need for a further hearing in the District Court."[128]

Thus, a finality, precluding habeas corpus review as a post-trial

[125] "Any error by the military in evaluating the evidence on the question of insanity would not go to jurisdiction, the only issue before the court in habeas corpus proceedings." Whelchel v. McDonald, 340 U. S. 122 at 126, 71 Sup. Ct. 146 (1950).

[126] Burns v. Wilson, 346 U. S. 137, 141, 73 Sup. Ct. 1045, 1048 (1953); *rehearing denied,* 346 U. S. 844, 74 Sup. Ct. 3 (1953).

[127] *Id.* at 142, 73 Sup. Ct. at 1049.

[128] *Id.* at 146, 73 Sup. Ct. at 1050.

remedy, is ascribed to Article of War 53 and Article 73 proceedings, akin to that possessed by section 2255 proceedings.[129]

The value of requiring exhaustion of Article 53 relief to the orderly administration of justice has been thoroughly demonstrated. The same district judge who was reversed after granting four writs of habeas corpus,[130] because of alleged disqualification of the law members of the convicting general courts, had before him at least thirty-four other cases involving substantially the same proposition of law. It is reasonable to suppose that the decision on the substantive point would have been the same in all, had not the district court felt bound to follow the court of appeals *Whelchel* decision and dismissed these cases for non-compliance with Article 53.[131] In view of the reversal of the district court by the Supreme Court in *Hiatt v. Brown* these thirty-four prisoners, if discharged, would have had to be recommitted and the term of their sentences extended by the time they had been at large. The interposition of Article 53 prevented the occurrence of this disservice to both the government and the individuals concerned.

Article 53 relief is not a mere will-of-the-wisp and has in fact been more successful from the petitioning prisoners' point of view than have been habeas corpus proceedings. From February 1, 1949 to February 15, 1950, the Judge Advocate General of the Army and Air Force received 245 applications under Article 53. Of this number 66, or 27 per cent, had been determined by February 15, 1950. Relief was granted in 9 cases, or almost 13 per cent of the applications completed, and 4 per cent of the total filed.[132] A large number of the applications on which action had not been completed involved the point decided by the Supreme Court in *Hiatt v. Brown* in March, 1950, and these were naturally deferred until the Supreme Court had spoken. This is a considerably more liberal result than that produced by the federal courts. At least 324 military prisoners sought habeas corpus relief

[129] For a discussion of the due process aspects of Burns v. Wilson see pp. 369-370, *post*.

[130] Brown v. Hiatt, 81 F. Supp. 647 (N. D. Ga. 1948), 175 F. (2d) 273 (5th Cir. 1949), *reversed,* 339 U. S. 103, 70 Sup. Ct. 495 (1950), *rehearing denied,* 339 U. S. 939, 70 Sup. Ct. 672 (1950); Burchfield v. Hiatt, 86 F. Supp. 18 (N. D. Ga. 1949), *reversed,* 179 F. (2d) 679-680 (5th Cir. 1950); Jackson v. Hiatt, (not reported in F. Supp.), *reversed,* 179 F. (2d) 679-680 (5th Cir. 1950). The last three cases were reversed for non-compliance with Article of War 53.

[131] Sinclair v. Hiatt, (D. C. Ga. 1949) 86 F. Supp. 828 and the following unreported habeas corpus case numbers, all in the Northern District of Georgia: 2391, 2410, 2411, 2414, 2415, 2430, 2416, 2429, 2427, 2421, 2433, 2418, 2455, 2482, 2446, 2470, 2417, 2456, 2458, 2469, 2479, 2451, 2452, 2453, 2454, 2460, 2463, 2464, 2466, 2474, 2477, 2478 and 2481.

[132] Official figures prepared in the office of the Judge Advocate General of the Army. After Feb. 15, 1950, AW 53 relief was granted in a number of additional cases.

from January 1, 1945, up to May 1, 1950. Of that number only one was finally granted release,[133] and in that case the office of the Solicitor General administratively determined not to appeal from the decision of the district court. The record of 4 per cent relief by Article 53 as against one-third of one per cent relief by habeas corpus gives meaningful assent to the *Whelchel* decision statement that, "This remedy [Article 53] is much better adapted to reach justice than any within the power of the district court on habeas corpus."[134]

There was great reluctance on the part of some military prisoners to apply for a new trial under Article of War 53 even where associated with the possibility of other relief. This particularly applied to those convicted of murder or rape and originally given death sentences later reduced by post-trial procedures to terms of years. The fate of Palko[135] seems to be well known in penitentiary circles. It will be recalled that Mr. Palko was convicted of murder and sentenced to life imprisonment. From this conviction he sought, and was granted, a new trial, at which he was again convicted and sentenced to death. The Supreme Court approved the death sentence finding it to constitute due process of law. Those who wanted "out," rather than justice, felt there were possible hazards connected with Article 53 not present in habeas corpus. Such feeling patently did not cause Article 53 relief to be inadequate or ineffective. This risk to the petitioner is no longer present in exhausting the successor remedy afforded by Article 73 of the Uniform Code. Congress did not intervene in this matter, but the new Manual, as promulgated by the President, expressly provides: "Upon a new trial . . . no sentence in excess of or more severe than the original sentence as approved or affirmed shall be adjudged."[136] Thus this otherwise possible hazard is eliminated.

Some prisoners have attempted "hit and run" compliances by filing a petition under Article 53 and then within a few days petitioning for habeas corpus alleging that the Article 53 petition has been ignored. The district courts have consistently dismissed such petitions, holding that the Article 53 remedy must be not only initiated, but exhausted, as a prerequisite to habeas corpus.[137]

The general rule that in habeas corpus the petitioner has the burden both to allege and prove all facts necessary to entitle him to relief[138] has

[133] Anthony v. Hunter, 71 F. Supp. 823 (D. Kan. 1947).

[134] 176 F. (2d) 260 at 263 (5th Cir. 1949).

[135] Palko v. Connecticut, 302 U. S. 319, 58 Sup. Ct. 149 (1937).

[136] MANUAL FOR COURTS-MARTIAL, UNITED STATES, 1951, p. 179, ¶ 109 (g).

[137] Typical of these unreported cases are Stevenson v. Hiatt and Gorham v. Hiatt, both G. I. No. 24084, and Fisher v. Hiatt, No. 2523, all in the Northern District of Georgia.

[138] Christakos v. Hunter, 161 F. (2d) 692 at 694 (10th Cir. 1947). Addi-

been expressly applied to military prisoners[139] and held to require of them allegation and proof of compliance with Article 53.[140]

One may safely conclude that Article of War 53 is constitutional, is a substantial right, is remedial in nature, is a mandatory condition precedent to habeas corpus relief, was designed to, and in fact does, "stem the flow" of groundless habeas corpus petitions and affords a remedy "much better adapted to reach justice than any within the power of the district court upon habeas corpus."[141] The same is true of its successor, Article 73 of the Uniform Code.[142]

IV

TYPES OF MILITARY DETENTIONS REVIEWABLE

A. *Physical Confinement*

The general rule that only a prisoner in actual custody may maintain a petition for habeas corpus[143] has been expressly applied to those with a military status. Accordingly an appeal from a judgment denying habeas corpus was dismissed where a military prisoner was paroled dur-

---

tionally, where the allegations of a return to a habeas corpus writ are not denied by the petitioner, in his traverse, they must be taken as true. Doyle v. Shaughnessy, 112 F. Supp. 143, 144 (S. D. N. Y. 1953).

[139] Duval v. Humphrey, 83 F. Supp. 457, 461 (M. D. Pa. 1949); McClelland v. Humphrey, 83 F. Supp. 510, 514 (M. D. Pa. 1949); Hayes v. Hunter, 83 F. Supp. 940 at 945 (D. Kan. 1948).

[140] Typical are the following unreported cases, all in the Northern District of Georgia: Lindsey v. Hiatt, H. C. No. 2470; Tate v. Hiatt, H. C. No. 2494; Suber v. Hiatt, H. C. No. 2496. This point was presented in the brief and in the argument and was necessary to the decision in Hiatt v. Jackson, 179 F. (2d) 679-680 (5th Cir. 1950).

[141] Whelchel v. McDonald, 176 F. (2d) 260 at 263 (5th Cir. 1949).

[142] See note 87, p. 341, *supra*. The fact that Article 73 limits consideration to cases involving newly discovered evidence or fraud upon the court, and hence is less sweeping in scope than its predecessor, Article of War 53, has not yet expressly engaged the attention of the courts. It does not seem probable that jurisdictional error, or other materially prejudicial error, would be permitted to go unremedied, on military post-conviction hearing, even under the more restrictive language of Article 73. The respective Judge Advocates General have under consideration a proposal to recommend to Congress amending Article 73 to widen the scope of review and relief afforded by it. In any event, it is clear from Burns v. Wilson that exhausting Article 73 relief is mandatory before a habeas corpus petition may be undertaken.

[143] McNally v. Hill, 293 U. S. 131, 25 Sup. Ct. 24 (1934). At page 136, Chief Justice Stone said: "The purpose of the proceeding defined by the statute was to inquire into the legality of the detention, and the only judicial relief authorized was the discharge of the prisoner or his admission to bail, and that only if his detention were found to be unlawful. In this, the Statute conformed to the traditional form of the writ, which put in issue only the disposition of the custody of the prisoner according to law. There is no warrant in either the statute or the writ for its use to invoke judicial determination of questions which could not affect the lawfulness of the custody and detention, and no suggestion of such a use has been found in the commentaries on the English common law." *Cf.* Adams v. Ellis, 197 F. (2d) 483 (5th Cir. 1952).

ing its pendency.[144] In *Wales v. Whitney* the Supreme Court held that the then Surgeon General of the Navy, who had been placed under arrest by the Secretary of the Navy and ordered to confine himself to the limits of the City of Washington pending trial by court-martial, was under only moral restraint, and, since not in actual confinement, could not obtain habeas corpus relief. The Court said:

> "But neither the Supreme Court of the District nor this court has any appellate jurisdiction over the naval court-martial, nor over offenses which such a court has power to try. Neither of these courts is authorized to interfere with it in the performance of its duty, by way of a writ of prohibition or any order of that nature. The civil courts can relieve a person from imprisonment under order of such court only by writ of *habeas corpus,* and then only when it is made apparent that it proceeds without jurisdiction. If there is no restraint, there is no right in the civil court to interfere. Its power *then* extends no further than to release the prisoner. It cannot remit a fine, or restore to an office, or reverse the judgment of the military court. Whatever effects the decision of the court may have on the proceedings, orders or judgments of the military court, is incidental to the order releasing the prisoner. Of course, if there is no prisoner to release, if there is no custody to be discharged, if there is no such restraint as requires relief, then the civil court has no power to interfere with the military court or other tribunal over which it has by law no appellate jurisdiction."[145]

Assuming, then, actual physical restraint, what different types of military prisoners may seek habeas corpus relief? The inquiry at the moment is limited to the bare right to seek such relief and does not extend to the grounds which warrant granting such relief. This latter questions will be considered in Part V. Resort to habeas corpus, after full compliance with prerequisites, is open, in extraordinary cases, to prisoners confined by sentence of Navy courts-martial,[146] Army courts-

[144] Murray v. Wedemeyer, 179 F. (2d) 963 (9th Cir. 1950), *cert. denied,* 339 U. S. 980, 70 Sup. Ct. 1025 (1950). *Cf.* Brewster v. Swope, 180 F. (2d) 984, 986 (9th Cir. 1950).

[145] 114 U. S. 564, 570, 5 Sup. Ct. 1050, 1052 (1885). Followed in Goldstein v. Johnson, 184 F. (2d) 342 (D. C. Cir. 1950), which held federal courts have no jurisdiction to grant either declaratory judgment or mandatory injunctive relief to a court-martial convict not in custody. *Contra: Ex parte* Fabiani, 105 F. Supp. 139, 148 (E. D. Pa. 1952).

[146] *Ex parte* Reed, 100 U. S. 13 (1879); Wales v. Whitney, 114 U. S. 564, 5 Sup. Ct. 1050 (1885); Johnson v. Sayre, 158 U. S. 109, 15 Sup. Ct. 773 (1895); *cf.* Smith v. Whitney, 116 U. S. 167, 6 Sup. Ct. 570 (1886).

martial,[147] Air Force courts-martial,[148] United States military commissions,[149] and State Department operated executive tribunals.[150]

B. *Military Status*

Under certain circumstances, habeas corpus has been used to test the validity of required military status without any question of confinement being involved. Relief has been denied where the petitioner was: an enlisted man seeking to avoid completing a voluntary enlistment;[151] a reserve officer trying to terminate, during the Korean emergency, his active duty under a reserve commission, claiming the commission had expired;[152] and a doctor of medicine, inducted under the Doctors Draft Act,[153] demanding a commission on his own terms or, alternatively, release from enlisted service. In the latter case, Orloff, who had received his professinoal training at government expense during World War II, was called under selective service and tendered a commission as a Captain, Medical Corps, Air Force Reserve, but upon his refusal to state whether he was or ever had been a member of the

[147] *Ex parte* Mason, 105 U. S. 696 (1882); Carter v. McClaughry, 183 U. S. 365, 22 Sup. Ct. 181 (1902); Kahn v. Anderson, 255 U. S. 1, 41 Sup. Ct. 224 (1921); Givens v. Zerbst, 255 U. S. 11, 41 Sup. Ct. 227 (1921); Wade v. Hunter, 336 U. S. 684, 69 Sup. Ct. 834 (1949); Humphrey v. Smith, 336 U. S. 695, 69 Sup. Ct. 830 (1949); Hiatt v. Brown, 339 U. S. 103, 70 Sup. Ct. 495 (1950).

[148] Burns v. Wilson, 346 U. S. 137, 73 Sup. Ct. 1045 (1953), *rehearing denied,* 346 U. S. 844, 74 Sup. Ct. 3 (1953).

[149] *Ex parte* Milligan, 4 Wall. 2, 107 (U. S. 1866); *Ex parte* Yerger, 8 Wall. 85 (U. S. 1869); *Ex parte* Quirin, 317 U. S. 1, 63 Sup. Ct. 1 (1942) (this is the case of the seven German saboteurs who landed in the United States from a submarine); *In re* Yamashita, 327 U. S. 1, 66 Sup. Ct. 340 (1946) (certiorari to the Supreme Court of the Philippines). *Cf.* Johnson v. Eisentrager, 339 U. S. 763, 70 Sup. Ct. 158 (1950).

[150] The jurisdiction of the "United States Court of the Allied High Commission for Germany, Fourth Judicial District," was upheld against habeas corpus attack in Madsen v. Kinsella, 343 U. S. 341 (1952).

[151] McCord v. Page, 124 F. (2d) 68 (5th Cir. 1941). Petitioner's rejected contention was that after voluntarily enlisting he became an ordained minister of the Watch Tower Bible Society and that his religious tenets were incompatible with his military duties to salute the flag and his superiors.

[152] Miley v. Lovett, 193 F. (2d) 712, 714 (4th Cir. 1952), *affirming,* 100 F. Supp. 1012, *cert. denied,* 342 U. S. 919, 72 Sup. Ct. 366 (1952). "Reserve officers of the Army and Air Force were appointed for terms of 5 years subject to continuation until 6 months after the legal termination of World War II. Since World War II has not been legally terminated for that purpose, these officers continue to be Reserve officers even though 5 years have elapsed since their appointments.

"We are convinced that Section 127a, paragraph 7 of the National Defense Act is applicable and controlling to officers of the Reserve Corps of the Army appointed during wartime under Section 37. Accordingly, petitioner's term of office must be held to continue until six months after the termination of war."

[153] Universal Military Training and Service Act, 64 STAT. 826, 828, 50 U. S. C. App. § 454 (i) (1) (A) (1950). In pertinent part it provided: "any person... on . . . active duty as a physician or dentist in the Armed Forces . . . *may* . . . be promoted to such . . . rank as may be commensurate with his medical or dental . . . experience. . . ." (Italics added.)

Communist party was not commissioned and was retained in the Medical Corps in an enlisted status. In denying relief the Supreme Court said:

> "We cannot comply with the appellant's insistence that we order him to be commissioned or discharged. . . .
>
> "The petitioner appears to be under the misconception that a commission is not only a matter of right, but is to be had upon his own terms. . . .
>
> ". . . the commissioning of officers . . . is a matter of discretion within the province of the President as Commander in Chief. . . . Courts . . . have never assumed by any process to control the appointing power either in civilian or military positions. . . .
>
> "Petitioner, like every conscript, was inducted as a private. . . .
>
> ". . . the President . . . before . . . appointing him to commissioned rank, has the right to learn whatever facts the President thinks may affect his fitness. . . . Whether Orloff deserves appointment is not for judges to say. . . .
>
> "This leaves the question as to whether one lawfully inducted may have habeas corpus to obtain a judicial review of his assignment to duty. . . . The very essence of compulsory service is the subordination of the desires and interests of the individual to the needs of the service.
>
> ". . . Orloff is now assigned to medical duties. . . .
>
> ". . . it is not within the power of this Court by habeas corpus to determine whether specific assignments to duty fall within the basic classification of petitioner.
>
> ". . . Judges are not given the task of running the Army. . . . We have found no case where this Court has assumed to revise duty orders as to one lawfully in the service."[154]

After the *Orloff* decision, an opposite conclusion, based upon an intervening change in wording of the Doctors Draft Law, was reached by the Court of Appeals for the Fourth Circuit. Nelson, a dentist of six years' practice, with Communist affiliations, who was thirty-seven years old and not subject to military service under the general provisions of the Universal Military Training and Service Act, was ordered released from service unless accorded commissioned status. The court said:

[154] Orloff v. Willoughby, 342 U. S. 83, 88, 90, 91, 92, 93, 94, 72 Sup. Ct. 998 (1953).

> ". . . The courts are without power to direct the granting of a commission to appellant; and, in the absence of the change made in the language of the Doctors Draft Law by the amendment of 1953, we would unhesitatingly hold, in line with *Orloff v. Willoughby, supra,* that the appellant was without any ground of relief. We think that it was the clear intention of Congress, however, by the change of language made in the amendment, to require that a physician or dentist held to service thereunder shall be granted a rank or grade 'commensurate with his professional education, experience, or ability,' and that this must be construed as a condition of the right to hold him to service. While the courts cannot direct or control the granting of rank or grade, they can direct that a physician or dentist be released from service when this condition of the law is not complied with. Because of appellant's Communist affiliations, the officials of the Army were acting within the proper scope of their authority in refusing to grant him a commission carrying the rank and grade of an officer; but they could not deny him this rank and grade and at the same time hold him to service under the statute as we think it must be interpreted. If not fit to be an officer, he should be held not fit for the services for which he has been drafted and should be dismissed."[155]

The general principle is clear. One lawfully in the service may by habeas corpus obtain neither a discharge nor a change of his duty assignment.

C. *Selective Service Induction*

The Selective Service and Training Acts of 1940, and 1948 and 1951 amendments thereto,[156] have produced a number of cases in which

[155] Nelson v. Peckham, 210 F. (2d) 574, 577 (4th Cir. 1954). As amended by the Act of June 29, 1953, 67 STAT. 86, the Doctors Draft Law required: ". . . any person . . . ordered to active duty as a . . . dentist . . . *shall* . . . be appointed . . . to such . . . rank as may be commensurate with his professional . . . experience." (Italics added.)

[156] 54 STAT. 885 (1940), 50 U. S. C. App. §§ 301-318 (1946). The operation of the system established by this legislation has been thus described by the Supreme Court:

"The selective service process begins with registration with a local board composed of local citizens. The registrant then supplies certain information on a questionnaire furnished by the board. On the basis of that information and, where appropriate, a physical examination, the board classifies him in accordance with standards contained in the Act and the Selective Service Regulations. It then notifies him of his classification. The registrant may contest his classification by a personal appearance before the local board, and if that board refuses to alter the classification, by carrying his case to a board of appeal, and thence, in certain circumstances, to the President.

"Only after he has exhausted this procedure is a protesting registrant ordered

the issue raised was the validity of the classification of the petitioner made by the selective service system. Section 11 of the act imposes penal sanctions for wilful failure to perform any duty thereby required, including that of reporting for service. In affirming a conviction for wilful violation of an order directing a registrant to report for assignment to work of national importance the Supreme Court held that Congress had not "authorized judicial review of the propriety of a board's classification in a criminal prosecution."[157] This ruling was soon followed by a decision that an inductee who reported to and was accepted by the military authorities, but refused to take the oath and to perform military service, was not, by reason of such refusal, subject to trial by court-martial, but was subject to criminal prosecution in the federal civil courts for violation of the Selective Service Act.[158]

The next question to arise was whether, in a civil court criminal prosecution for refusal to submit to induction after reporting, having exhausted his administrative remedies, the accused was entitled to judicial review of the selective service action taken in his case. The Court reversed a conviction below, held the accused, under these circumstances, was entitled to a limited judicial review, and said:

> ". . . The courts are not to weigh the evidence to determine whether the classification made by the local boards was justified. The decisions of the local boards made in conformity with

to report for service. If he has been classified for military service, his local board orders him to report for induction into the armed forces. If he has been classified a conscientious objector opposed to noncombatant military service, as was petitioner, he ultimately is ordered by the local board to report for work of national importance. In each case the registrant is under the same obligation to obey the order. But in neither case is the order to report the equivalent of acceptance for service. Completion of the functions of the local boards and appellate agencies, important as are these functions, is not the end of the selective service process. The selectee may still be rejected at the induction center and the conscientious objector who is opposed to noncombat duty may be rejected at the civilian service camp. The connected series of steps into the national service which begins with registration with the local board does not end until the registrant is accepted by the army, navy, or civilian public service camp. Thus a board order to report is no more than a necessary intermediate step in a united and continuous process designed to raise an army speedily and efficiently." Falbo v. United States, 320 U. S. 549 at 552, 553, 64 Sup. Ct. 346 (1944).

This procedure, though somewhat altered, has remained substantially the same under the Selective Service Act of 1948, 62 Stat. 604 (1948) and the Universal Military Training and Service Act of 1951, 65 Stat. 75, 50 U. S. C. A. App. §§ 451-473 (1951).

[157] Falbo v. United States, 320 U. S. 549, 554, 64 Sup. Ct. 346, 349 (1944). A subsequent petition for habeas corpus release from confinement under this conviction was denied to Falbo in United States v. Kennedy, 141 F. (2d) 689 (4th Cir. 1944).

[158] Billings v. Truesdale, 321 U. S. 542, 64 Sup. Ct. 737 (1944). *Cf.* Corrigan v. Secretary, 211 F. (2d) 293 (9th Cir. 1954) in which it was held that a selectee who did not take one step forward at the induction ceremony, and who thereafter refused service, was not subject to military law.

the regulations are final even though they may be erroneous. The question of jurisdiction of the local board is reached only if there is no basis in fact for the classification which it gave to the registrant."[159]

A registrant who was deprived of a fair and impartial hearing by selective service agencies may defeat criminal prosecution on this ground.[160]

In *Cox v. Wedemeyer*[161] the habeas corpus petitioner was an inductee who had reported to the military, moved on orders from one training camp to another, wore the uniform, accepted his first pay check and then deserted. The Court of Appeals for the Ninth Circuit released this petitioner from military custody, in which he was being held pending trial for desertion, saying, "We believe it immaterial whether he did or did not submit to the induction oath."[162] The court seized upon a dictum in *Gibson v. United States,*[163] which was not a military case at all, where the Supreme Court, citing as authority therefore *Billings v. Truesdale,*[164] said:

> "It has been clearly established that the remedy by way of habeas corpus is open to the wrongfully inducted member of the armed forces to secure his release."[165]

[159] Estep v. United States, 327 U. S. 114 at 122, 66 Sup. Ct. 423 (1946). Followed in Cox v. United States 332 U. S. 442 at 453, 68 Sup. Ct. 115 (1948) in which the contention of Jehovah's Witnesses, that a local draft board had improperly classified them as conscientious objectors rather than exempt ministers of religion, was rejected and their civil court conviction for absence without leave from a civilian public service camp affirmed. Also, United States v. Burnett, 115 F. Supp. 141 (W. D. Mo. 1953). *Cf.* Gibson v. United States, 329 U. S. 338, 67 Sup. Ct. 301 (1946). See also Niznik v. United States, 184 F. (2d) 972 (6th Cir. 1950); Imboden v. United States, 194 F. (2d) 508 (6th Cir. 1952); Annett v. United States, 205 F. (2d) 689, 692 (10th Cir. 1953); United States v. Pekarski, 207 F. (2d) 930 (2d Cir. 1953); Head v. United States, 199 F. (2d) 337 (10th Cir. 1953), ". . . In no event is classification a jury question"; United States v. Hartman, 209 F. (2d) 366, 371 (2d Cir. 1954); Taffs v. United States, 208 F. (2d) 329 (8th Cir. 1953); Schuman v. United States, 208 F. (2d) 801, 805 (9th Cir. 1953); United States v. Rumsa, 212 F. (2d) 927, 933 (7th Cir. 1954); Weaver v. United States, 210 F. (2d) 815, 823 (8th Cir. 1954); United States v. Simmons, 213 F. (2d) 901, 904 (7th Cir. 1954); United States v. Lynch, 115 F. Supp. 735 (S. D. Cal. 1953); United States v. Rodriguez, 119 F. Supp. 111 (D. P. R. 1954).

[160] United States v. Nugent, 346 U. S. 1, 73 Sup. Ct. 991 (1953); United States v. Zieber, 161 F. (2d) 90 (3d Cir. 1947); United States v. Stiles, 169 F. (2d) 455 (3d Cir. 1948); *In re* Abramson, 196 F. (2d) 261 (3d Cir. 1952); Knox v. United States, 200 F. (2d) 398 (9th Cir. 1952); United States v. Fry, 203 F. (2d) 638 (2d Cir. 1953); United States v. Wider, 119 F. Supp. 676 (E. D. N. Y. 1954). *Cf.* United States v. Witmer, 115 F. Supp. 19 (M. D. Pa. 1953).

[161] 192 F. (2d) 920 (9th Cir. 1951).

[162] *Id.* at 924. Followed on this point in Weidman v. Sweeney, 117 F. Supp. 739 (E. D. Pa. 1954).

[163] 329 U. S. 338, 359, 67 Sup. Ct. 301, 311 (1946).

[164] 321 U. S. 542, 64 Sup. Ct. 737 (1944).

[165] Gibson v. United States, 329 U. S. 338, 359, 67 Sup. Ct. 301, 311 (1944), quoted in Cox v. Wedemeyer, 192 F. (2d) 920, 924 (9th Cir. 1951).

After reviewing the entire selective service action in the case the court held:

> "What leads us to the conclusion that the induction order was void is not that the evidence compelled a IV-E classification, but that the board of appeals refused to consider the question of registrant's right to such classification."[166]

The *Cox* decision, while consistent with the scope of judicial review as announced in *Estep,* appears to be wholly inconsistent with the *Billings* rule that once the oath is taken military jurisdiction attaches.[167] *Cox* is similar to *Billings* only in that in each the petitioner was in actual military confinement at the time the writ was granted. In *Cox,* however, the court appeared to brush off this fact of confinement under charges, and treated the case essentially as one challenging the legality of imposing any military status at all upon petitioner.

There remains for consideration, whether, short of inviting military prosecution and confinement in order to challenge by habeas corpus the jurisdiction of the military, there is any way for one already inducted to test the validity of the selective service process which resulted in his induction. Although without express Supreme Court sanction, habeas corpus has emerged as a means of obtaining a limited judicial review of disputed selective service classification and induction even where no confinement is involved beyond the normal restriction of action which is inherent to military status. Habeas corpus was granted in at least three World War I draft cases releasing petitioners from involuntary military service,[168] and a few were similarly released during World War II.[169]

More recently lower federal courts have granted habeas corpus release from compulsory military service to inductees who claimed exemption as: a married man,[170] a medical student,[171] a theological student,[172] a Latvian citizen,[173] a prospective father,[174] and a con-

[166] Cox v. Wedemeyer, 192 F. (2d) 920, 923 (9th Cir. 1951).

[167] For a discussion as to when military jurisdiction attaches, see page 40, *supra.*

[168] Arbitman v. Woodside, 258 Fed. 441 (4th Cir. 1919); *Ex parte* Cohen, 254 Fed. 711 (E. D. Va. 1918); *Ex parte* Beck, 245 Fed. 967 (D. Mont. 1917). World War I cases are collected and discussed in Note, 10 GEO. WASH. L. REV. 287 (1942) and Note, 129 A. L. R. 1171, 1186 (1940).

[169] World War II cases are collected and discussed in Notes, 147 A. L. R. 1313, 1324 (1943); 148 A. L. R. 1388, 1389 (1944); 149 A. L. R. 1457, 1458 (1944); 154 A. L. R. 1448, 1449 (1945); 155 A. L. R. 1452 (1945); 156 A. L. R. 1450 (1945).

[170] *Ex parte* Barrial, 101 F. Supp. 348 (S. D. Cal. 1951).

[171] *Ex parte* Fabiani, 105 F. Supp. 139 (E. D. Pa. 1952).

[172] United States v. Craig, 107 F. Supp. 529, 532 (D. N. J. 1952) *affd.,* 207 F. (2d) 888 (3d Cir. 1953).

[173] Commanding Officer v. Bumanis, 207 F. (2d) 499 (6th Cir. 1953).

[174] *In re* Abramson, 196 F. (2d) 261 (3d Cir. 1952); Mintz v. Howlett, 207

scientious objector inducted into the Marine Corps.[175]

If the inductee was denied any part of the series of hearings given to him by the law[176] or if there was no evidence at all presented which could support the classification made,[177] and all administrative remedies were exhausted and petitioner submitted to induction [178] the writ will be granted. Judicial review is limited, however, to ascertaining whether all authorized hearings were granted and to determining whether the record contains any evidence at all to support the classification made. If these two conditions are met the writ will be denied[179] and it makes no difference that the court would have arrived at a different factual conclusion than that reached by the draft and appeal boards.[180] Certiorari is not the proper remedy.[181]

D. *Prisoner Status*

Habeas corpus is a proper remedy for one who has recovered his sanity to obtain release from a naval mental institution.[182] A detained "sexual psychopath" may test the question of his recovery by habeas

---

F. (2d) 758 (2d Cir. 1953). *Contra:* United States v. Bullock, 110 F. Supp. 698 (N. D. Ill. 1953).

[175] Weidman v. Sweeney, 117 F. Supp. 739 (E. D. Pa. 1953).

[176] Mintz v. Howlett, 207 F. (2d) 758 (2d Cir. 1953); Berman v. Craig, 207 F. (2d) 888, 890 (3d Cir. 1953); Cox v. Wedemeyer, 192 F. (2d) 920, 923 (9th Cir. 1951).

[177] Cox v. Wedemeyer, 192 F. (2d) 920 (9th Cir. 1951); *Ex parte* Fabiani, 105 F. Supp. 139 (E. D. Pa. 1952); *cf.* United States v. Lynch, 115 F. Supp. 735, 738 (S. D. Cal. 1953).

[178] Phillips v. Downer, 135 F. (2d) 521 (2d Cir. 1943); *Ex parte* Catanzaro, 138 F. (2d) 100 (3d Cir. 1943); *Ex parte* Stanziale, 138 F. (2d) 312 (3d Cir. 1943); Mintz v. Howlett, 205 F. (2d) 758, 760 (2d Cir. 1953); *Ex parte* Hanning, 106 F. Supp. 715, 717 (N. D. Cal. 1952). *Cf.* Bronemann v. United States, 138 F. (2d) 333 (8th Cir. 1943); United States v. Rumsa, 212 F. (2d) 927, 938 (7th Cir. 1954); United States v. Bullock, 110 F. Supp. 698, 701 (N. D. Ill. 1953). However, see *Ex parte* Fabiani, 105 F. Supp. 139, 143 (E. D. Pa. 1952), where the district court without citing authority for its action granted habeas corpus to a medical student registrant although he had reported neither for preinduction physical examination nor for induction.

[179] Eagles v. Samuels, 329 U. S. 304, 67 Sup. Ct. 313 (1946). Petitioner's unsuccessful contention was that the New York City Selective Service Advisory Panel on theological classifications had improperly concluded that petitioner was not "preparing in good faith for a career of service in the practicing rabbinate." Eagles v. Horowitz, 329 U. S. 317, 67 Sup. Ct. 320 .(1946); Sunal v. Large, 332 U. S. 174, 67 Sup. Ct. 1588 (1947); *Ex parte* Stanziale, 138 F. (2d) 312 (3d Cir. 1943); *Ex parte* Albertson, 105 F. Supp. 617 (D. D. C. 1951); *Ex parte* Hanning, 106 F. Supp. 715, 717 (N. D. Cal. 1952); Tomback v. Bullock, 110 F. Supp. 698, 703 (N. D. Ill. 1953).

[180] *Ex parte* Stanziale, 138 F. (2d) 312, 316 (3d Cir. 1943); Trainin v. Cain, 144 F. (2d) 944, 947 (2d Cir. 1944); *cf.* Cox v. United States, 332 U. S. 442, 68 Sup. Ct. 115 (1947); Smith v. United States, 157 F. (2d) 176, 178 (4th Cir. 1946); Dickinson v. United States, 203 F. (2d) 336, 343 (9th Cir. 1953).

[181] Drumheller v. Board, 130 F. (2d) 610, 611 (3d Cir. 1942); *cf.* United States v. Mancuso, 139 F. (2d) 90 (3d Cir. 1943); United States v. Rumsa, 212 F. (2d) 927, 938 (7th Cir. 1954).

[182] Overholser v. Boddie, 184 F. (2d) 240 (D. C. Cir. 1950), *expressly overruling* Overholser v. Treibly, 147 F. (2d) 705 (D. C. Cir. 1945).

corpus.[183] However, whether a federal prisoner is a suitable subject for hospitalization at the United States Medical Center for Federal Prisoners is a question for the Attorney General and the prison authorities and not for the courts.[184]

Habeas corpus cannot be used to correct alleged mistreatment by prison authorities of prisoners subject to valid judgment and commitment,[185] nor to test the legality of previous confinement no longer continuing,[186] nor to challenge prospective future confinement not yet occurring,[187] nor to determine eligibility for parole,[188] nor, except in the case of arbitrary or capricious action, to review the revocation of parole.[189] A prisoner, confined in a place not authorized by law, is not thereby entitled to enlargement by habeas corpus, but only to the designation of a proper place of confinement.[190] Furthermore, a prisoner serving a sentence in excess of that which the law permits is not entitled to habeas corpus release if the excess is separable from the residue and may be reached without disturbing the portion which is legal.[191]

Prisoners convicted by military tribunals confined in civil federal penal institutions are subject to all the statutes and regulations governing other persons so confined.[192]

[183] A detained "sexual psychopath" may test the question of his recovery by habeas corpus. Miller v. Oberholser, 206 F. (2d) 415, 421 (D. C. Cir. 1953), and Malone v. Overholzer, 93 F. Supp. 647, 648 (D. D. C. 1950). See Higgins v. McGrath, 98 F. Supp. 670, 675 (W. D. Mo. 1951).

[184] Rosheisen v. Steele, 193 F. (2d) 273, 275 (8th Cir. 1951); Garcia v. Steele, 193 F. (2d) 276, 278 (8th Cir. 1951).

[185] McNally v. Hill, 293 U. S. 131, 136, 55 Sup. Ct. 24, 26 (1934); Adams v. Ellis, 197 F. (2d) 483, 485 (5th Cir. 1952); Powell v. Hunter, 172 F. (2d) 330, 331 (10th Cir. 1949); Bowe v. Skeen, 107 F. Supp. 879, 880 (N. D. W. Va. 1952); *cf. Ex parte* Pickens, 101 F. Supp. 285, 289 (D. Alaska 1951).

[186] Lopez v. Swope, 205 F. (2d) 8, 10 (9th Cir. 1953); Green v. Maine, 113 F. Supp, 253, 256 (D. Me. 1953).

[187] Hollowell v. Looney, 207 F. (2d) 433, 434 (10th Cir. 1953); Pope v. Huff, 204 F. (2d) 468, 470 (D. C. Cir. 1953).

[188] Wing v. Commonwealth, 90 F. Supp. 208, 212 (W. D. Pa. 1950).

[189] Hiatt v. Compagna, 178 F. (2d) 42 (5th Cir. 1949); Jackson v. Humphrey, 92 F. Supp. 635 (M. D. Pa. 1950).

[190] Givens v. Zerbst, 255 U. S. 11, 41 Sup. Ct. 227 (1921); Jones v. Looney, 107 F. Supp. 624, 627 (E. D. Mich. 1952).

[191] United States v. Pridgeon, 153 U. S. 48, 14 Sup. Ct. 746 (1894); McKinney v. Finletter, 205 F. (2d) 761, 763 (10th Cir. 1953).

[192] ". . . Petitioner, whose original designation of a place of confinement pursuant to his conviction . . . by court-martial . . . was a Federal institution is subject to all the provisions of Chapter 309, Title 18 United States Code, and to other laws applying to Federal prisoners, to the same extent as though he had been confined in such institution as the result of a conviction by civil court, . . . and accordingly . . . is subject . . . to all the statutes and regulations governing the good time allowances and parole of other persons confined in Federal penal or correctional institutions." Jones v. Looney, 107 F. Supp. 624, 627 (E. D. Mich. 1952). Article 58 (a) of the Uniform Code of Military Justice, 64 STAT. 107, 50 U. S. C. § 645 (1951), in pertinent part, expressly provides, "persons so confined in a penal or correctional institution not under the

E. *Miscellaneous Status*

Resort to the writ by persons of Japanese ancestry detained during World War II in relocation centers did not strictly fall within the scope of military habeas corpus. These relocation centers were operated by the War Relocation Authority, a civilian agency, in which was vested control over the ingress and egress of such evacuees.[193]

In re Territo[194] presented an interesting petition by a prisoner of war who was an American citizen. Born in the United States of Italian parents, Territo was taken to Italy, later impressed into the Italian Army, captured by United States forces during World War II, and removed to the United States as a prisoner of war where he joined the Italian service unit to perform labor for the United States for pay. It was held that neither the petitioner's American citizenship nor Italy's surrender changed his prisoner of war status and that he was not entitled to release.

In at least one case an unusual use was made of habeas corpus to obtain the release, back to military authority for trial, of a soldier who was being held by state civil authorities under indictment for murder of a civilian policeman.[195] In granting his release the district court held that in time of war the military authorities had superior jurisdiction of the offense charged.

Normally the petition is brought by the prisoner who seeks his own release. Not more than one applicant may join in a single petition.[196] Where the prisoner is a minor, as a procedural matter, the petition for habeas corpus may be maintained by a parent.[197] However, it has been held that a corporate employer had no standing to petition on its own behalf for habeas corpus release of a minor employee from military service under the Selective Service Act.[198] The contention was that

---

control of one of the armed forces shall be subject to the same discipline and treatment as persons confined or committed by the courts of the United States or of the State, Territory, District, or place in which the institution is situated." See also Fitch v. Hiatt, 48 F. Supp. 388 (M. D. Pa. 1942); Innes v. Hiatt, 57 F. Supp. 17 (M. D. Pa. 1944); Johnson v. Hiatt, 71 F. Supp. 865 (M. D. Pa. 1947), *affirmed,* 163 F. (2d) 1018 (3d Cir. 1947).

[193] *Ex parte* Endo, 323 U. S. 283, 65 Sup. Ct. 193 (1944).

[194] 156 F. (2d) 142 (9th Cir. 1946).

[195] *Ex parte* King, 246 Fed. 868 (E. D. Ky. 1917).

[196] *In re* Kosopud, 272 Fed. 330 (N. D. Ohio 1920); United States v. Skeen, 107 F. Supp. 879, 881 (N. D. W. Va. 1952).

[197] Goodman v. Hearn, 153 F. (2d) 186 (5th Cir. 1946); *Ex parte* Lewkowitz, 163 Fed. 646 (C. C. S. D. N. Y. 1908); *Ex parte* King, 246 Fed. 868 (E. D. Ky. 1917). *Cf. In re* Morrissey, 137 U. S. 157, 11 Sup. Ct. 57 (1890). See also cases collected at pages 270-271, MANUAL FOR COURTS-MARTIAL, UNITED STATES, ARMY, 1949. A petition may be signed and verified on behalf of another, but the person in custody is the only real party in interest, Nash v. MacArthur, 184 F. (2d) 606 (D. C. Cir. 1950).

[198] Sisquoc Ranch Co. v. Roth, 153 F. (2d) 437, 441 (9th Cir. 1946).

the draft board and appeal board had wrongfully refused further deferment as an agricultural worker. In affirming an order denying the writ the court held:

> "The petition here is solely a recital of hardship to the Ranch Company with the prayer, in effect, that Green be ordered back into its service. . . .
>
> "We hold that the Ranch Company cannot plead its sufferings as a basis for its claim that Green is under illegal restraint. . . ."

The court however considered the case on its merits since the petition also recited that it was brought on behalf of H. S. Green, the person inducted. Petitions by a wife on behalf of her husband[199] and by a sister on behalf of her brother have been entertained.[200]

While the unusual resorts to habeas corpus above discussed are of interest, it should be emphasized that the vast bulk of military habeas corpus petitions are those of prisoners seeking release from confinement imposed by court-martial sentence. These cases, based on alleged invalidity of courts-martial proceedings, will be discussed in the following section.

V

Grounds for Habeas Corpus Relief

A. *Lack of Jurisdiction*

The only ground for habeas corpus relief from confinement imposed by either a civil or military court is that the sentencing court lacked jurisdiction. The inquiry in military habeas corpus may extend to these questions: (1) Was the military court legally constituted? (2) Did it have jurisdiction of the person tried? (3) Did it have jurisdiction of the offense charged? (4) Was the sentence imposed within the maximum limit for the offense? Once these questions are answered in the affirmative the habeas corpus inquiry may go no further. The Supreme Court has never deviated from this fundamental limitation upon the scope of military habeas corpus and has reaffirmed the rule in an unbroken line of cases.[201] Nor may the civil courts, by habeas cor-

[199] *Ex parte* Stanziale, 138 F. (2d) 312, 313 (3d Cir. 1943); *Ex parte* Albertson, 103 F. Supp. 617, 618 (D. D. C. 1951); *Ex parte* Hanning, 106 F. Supp. 715, 716 (N. D. Cal. 1952).

[200] Talbott v. Toth, 215 F. (2d) 22 (D. C. Cir. 1954).

[201] Dynes v. Hoover, 20 How. 65, 83 (U. S. 1857); *Ex parte* Reed, 100 U. S. 13, 23 (1879); *Ex parte* Mason, 105 U. S. 696, 697 (1882); Smith v. Whitney, 116 U. S. 167, 177-179, 6 Sup. Ct. 570 (1886); *In re* Grimley, 137 U. S. 147, 150, 11 Sup. Ct. 54 (1890); Johnson v. Sayre, 158 U. S. 109, 118, 15 Sup. Ct. 773 (1895); Swaim v. United States, 165 U. S. 553, 561, 17 Sup. Ct. 448 (1897); Carter v. Roberts, 177 U. S. 496, 498, 20 Sup. Ct. 713 (1900); *In re* Vidal, 179 U. S. 126, 127, 21 Sup. Ct. 48 (1900); Carter v. McClaughry, 183 U. S. 365, 401,

pus or otherwise, exercise any supervisory, correcting, appellate or writ of error powers over either court-martial[202] or military commission proceedings.[203] These two basic propositions were clearly and succinctly reaffirmed by the Supreme Court in March 1950, in this language.[204]

> "It is well settled that 'by *habeas corpus* the civil courts exercise no supervisory or correcting power over the proceedings of a court-martial. . . . The single inquiry, the test, is jurisdiction.' *In re Grimley,* 137 U. S. 147, 150 (1890). In this case the court-martial had jurisdiction of the person accused and the offense charged, and acted within its lawful powers. The correction of any errors it may have committed is for the military authorities which are alone authorized to review its decision."

To one not familiar with recent inferior court litigation in this field these points probably appear clearly to be, not only decided law, but correct law. The Supreme Court has always so held and the whole matter might be dropped right here so far as a proper academic statement of the law is concerned. However, the insistent clamors of the petitioners, and their counsel, and a few erroneous decisions by inferior federal courts have obscured the fundamental law of the subject to the point where it is of practical value to catalogue those contentions which have been held not to affect the jurisdiction of military courts and hence not to constitute grounds for habeas corpus relief. When district courts, in releasing habeas corpus petitioners, depart from the fundamental issue of jurisdiction, reversal results.[205]

---

22 Sup. Ct. 181 (1902); McClaughry v. Deming, 186 U. S. 49, 69, 22 Sup. Ct. 786 (1902); Grafton v. United States, 206 U. S. 333, 347, 27 Sup. Ct. 749 (1907); Mullan v. United States, 212 U. S. 516, 520, 29 Sup. Ct. 330 (1909); Collins v. McDonald, 258 U. S. 416, 418, 42 Sup. Ct. 326 (1922); *In re* Yamashita, 327 U. S. 1, 8, 66 Sup. Ct. 340 (1946); Humphrey v. Smith, 336 U. S. 695, 696, 69 Sup. Ct. 830 (1949); Hiatt v. Brown, 339 U. S. 103, 111, 70 Sup. Ct. 495 (1950); Whelchel v. McDonald, 340 U. S. 122, 126, 71 Sup. Ct. 146 (1950); Gusik v. Schilder, 340 U. S. 128, 133, 71 Sup. Ct. 149 (1950); Madsen v. Kinsella, 343 U. S. 341, 72 Sup. Ct. 699 (1952); Burns v. Wilson, 346 U. S. 137, 73 Sup. Ct. 1045 (1953), *rehearing denied,* 346 U. S. 884, 74 Sup. Ct. 3 (1953).

[202] Dynes v. Hoover, 20 How. 65, 83 (U. S. 1857); *Ex parte* Reed, 100 U. S. 13, 23 (1879); *In re* Grimley, 137 U. S. 147, 150, 11 Sup. Ct. 54 (1890); Swaim v. United States, 165 U. S. 553, 562, 17 Sup. Ct. 448 (1897); McClaughry v. Deming, 186 U. S. 49, 69, 22 Sup. Ct. 786 (1902); Hiatt v. Brown, 339 U. S. 103, 111, 70 Sup. Ct. 495 (1950); *rehearing denied,* 339 U. S. 939, 70 Sup. Ct. 672 (1950).

[203] *In re* Yamashita, 327 U. S. 1, 66 Sup. Ct. 340 (1946).

[204] Hiatt v. Brown, 339 U. S. 103, 111, 70 Sup. Ct. 495, 498 (1950).

[205] For example, from November, 1935, to February, 1950, 38 appeals were taken from orders of one of the judges of the District Court for the Northern District of Georgia granting release to habeas corpus prisoners both civil and

B. *Due Process Considerations*

The extent, if any, to which habeas corpus inquiry may extend to due process of law considerations, not actually jurisdictional, presents an interesting facet of the general problem of defining the boundaries of due process of law. Seven court of appeals decisions have stated that in a habeas corpus proceeding civil courts may consider whether the manner in which a court-martial proceeding was conducted denied due process of law. This proposition was best stated in *Innes v. Hiatt*[206] in which the court found there had been no denial of due process. In *Schita v. King,*[207] where the case was remanded for consideration on the merits of the due process issue, the allegations were not borne out by the proof. In *Kuykendall v. Hunter*[208] the court, by way of dictum, said: "Due process of law must be observed in military trials the same as trials in civil courts," but found no lack of due process, and affirmed denial of the writ.

---

military. Twenty-eight were reversed by the court of appeals: 80 F. (2d) 258 (5th Cir. 1935); 80 F. (2d) 259 (5th Cir. 1935); 84 F. (2d) 543 (5th Cir. 1936); 84 F. (2d) 559 (5th Cir. 1936); 92 F. (2d) 671 (5th Cir. 1937); 97 F. (2d) 253 (5th Cir. 1938); 99 F. (2d) 1014 (5th Cir. 1938); 99 F. (2d) 1020 (5th Cir. 1938); 99 F. (2d) 1020 (5th Cir. 1938); 99 F. (2d) 1021 (5th Cir. 1938) (3 cases); 99 F. (2d) 1022 (5th Cir. 1938) (4 cases); 99 F. (2d) 1023 (5th Cir. 1938) (4 cases); 99 F. (2d) 1024 (5th Cir. 1938); *115 F. (2d) 435 (5th Cir. 1940); 136 F. (2d) 54 (5th Cir. 1943); *148 F. (2d) 376 (5th Cir. 1945); 170 F. (2d) 473 (5th Cir. 1948); *179 F. (2d) 679-680 (5th Cir. 1950) (3 cases); 180 F. (2d) 453 (5th Cir. 1950). Nine others affirmed by the court of appeals, but reversed by the Supreme Court, were Zerbst v. Kidwell, 304 U. S. 359, 58 Sup. Ct. 872 (1938) (8 cases) and *Hiatt v. Brown, 339 U. S. 103, 70 Sup. Ct. 495 (1950). One was affirmed, 136 F. (2d) 106 (5th Cir. 1943). (* denotes military cases.) Net result: 37 reversals, 1 affirmance.

[206] 141 F. (2d) 664 (3d Cir. 1944). At page 666 the court of appeals said:

"We think that this basic guarantee of fairness afforded by the due process clause of the fifth amendment applies to a defendant in criminal proceedings in a federal military court as well as in a federal civil court. . . .

"This is not to say that members of the military forces are entitled to the procedure guaranteed by the Constitution to defendants in the civil courts. As to them due process of law means the application of the procedure of the military law. Many of the procedural safeguards which have always been observed for the benefit of defendants in the civil courts are not granted by the military law. In this respect the military law provides its own distinctive procedure to which the members of the armed forces must submit. But the due process clause guarantees to them that this military procedure will be applied to them in a fundamentally fair way. We conclude that it is open for a civil court in a habeas corpus proceeding to consider whether the circumstances of a court-martial proceeding and the manner in which it was conducted ran afoul of the basic standard of fairness which is involved in the constitutional concept of due process of law and, if it so finds, to declare that the relator has been deprived of his liberty in violation of the fifth amendment and to discharge him from custody." Cited in White v. Humphrey, 212 F. (2d) 503, 507 (3d Cir. 1954) in which the court found there was no violation of due process.

[207] 133 F. (2d) 283 (8th Cir. 1943), *second appeal,* 139 F. (2d) 971 (8th Cir. 1944), *cert. denied,* 322 U. S. 761, 64 Sup. Ct. 1273 (1944).

[208] 187 F. (2d) 545 (10th Cir. 1951).

Two cases, *Smith v. Hiatt*[209] and *Hiatt v. Brown*,[210] in which the petitioners had been released, were both reversed by the Supreme Court. In the *Smith* case on this point the Supreme Court said:

> "We hold that a failure to conduct pre-trial investigations as required by Article 70 does not deprive general courts-martial of jurisdiction so as to empower courts in habeas corpus proceedings to invalidate court-martial judgments. . . .
>
> "This court-martial conviction resulting from a trial fairly conducted cannot be invalidated by a judicial finding that the pre-trial investigation was not carried on in the manner prescribed by the 70th Article of War."[211]

This certainly precludes any habeas corpus due process inquiry into pre-trial proceedings and seems to limit due process relief to such circumstances at the trial itself as in themselves would deprive the court-martial of jurisdiction. This position harmonizes with the classic jurisdiction doctrine of *Ex parte Reed*.[212] In the *Brown* case, the Supreme Court even more explicitly stated.[213]

> "The Court of Appeals also concluded that certain errors committed by the military tribunal and reviewing authorities had deprived respondent of due process.
>
> "The following instances of error in the military proceedings were cited by the Court of Appeals:
>
> '(1) Accused was convicted on the theory that although he was on duty as a sentry at the time of the offense, it was incumbent upon him to retreat from his post of duty.
>
> '(2) Accused has been convicted of murder on evidence that does not measure to malice, premeditation, or deliberation.
>
> '(3) The record reveals that the law member appointed was grossly incompetent.
>
> '(4) There was no pre-trial investigation whatever upon the charge of murder.
>
> '(5) The record shows that counsel appointed to defend the accused was incompetent, gave no preparation to the case, and submitted only a token defense.

[209] 170 F. (2d) 61 (3d Cir. 1948), *reversed sub nom.* Humphrey v. Smith, 336 U. S. 695, 69 Sup. Ct. 830 (1949).

[210] 175 F. (2d) 273 (5th Cir. 1949), *reversed,* 339 U. S. 103, 70 Sup. Ct. 495 (1950).

[211] Humphrey v. Smith, 336 U. S. 695, 700-701, 69 Sup. Ct. 830, 833 (1949), *rehearing denied,* 337 U. S. 934, 69 Sup. Ct. 942 (1949).

[212] See discussion at p. 328, *supra*.

[213] Hiatt v. Brown, 339 U. S. 103, 110-111, 70 Sup. Ct. 495, 498 (1950), *rehearing denied,* 339 U. S. 939, 70 Sup. Ct. 642 (1950). The enumeration of errors (small type) appears in the Court's footnote number 6, at 110.

'(6) The appellate reviews by the Army reviewing authorities reveal a total misconception of the applicable law.' 175 F. 2d at 277.

"We think the court was in error in extending its review for the purpose of determining compliance with the due process clause, to such matters as the propositions of law set forth in the staff judge advocate's report, the sufficiency of the evidence to sustain respondent's conviction, the adequacy of the pretrial investigation, and the competence of the law member and defense counsel. *Cf. Humphrey v. Smith,* 336 U. S. 695 (1949). It is well settled that 'by *habeas corpus* the civil courts exercise no supervisory or correcting power over the proceedings of a court-martial. . . . The single inquiry, the test, is jurisdiction.' *In re Grimley,* 137 U. S. 147, 150 (1890). In this case the court-martial had jurisdiction of the person accused and the offense charged, and acted within its lawful powers. The correction of any errors it may have committed is for the military authorities which are alone authorized to review its decision."

The persistence of petitioners' counsel in asserting alleged failures of due process as ground for habeas corpus relief in military cases, the tendency of some inferior federal courts to adopt this view and the adamant refusal of the Supreme Court to grant habeas corpus release to military prisoners for alleged want of due process are all strikingly illustrated in the *Burns* and *Dennis* proceedings, the last of this group of cases. The district court promptly denied these petitions and said:

"It is for this Court, on a petition for a writ of habeas corpus, only to inquire into and determine whether or not the court-martial before which a petitioner is tried was lawfully constituted, had jurisdiction of the person and offense, and imposed a sentence authorized by law. Beyond that the civil courts should not and cannot go. The Congress has constituted the system by which military law shall be administered, and it is not given to the civil courts, beyond the jurisdiction of a military court, to inquire into the regularity of its proceedings for the correction of errors committed therein. Hiatt v. Brown, 339 U. S. 103."[214]

A divided court of appeals affirmed, but not until it had said:

"(1) An accused before a court-martial is entitled to a fair trial within due process of law concepts. (2) The responsibility

[214] Dennis v. Lovett, 104 F. Supp. 310, 311 (D. D. C. 1952); and Burns v. Lovett, 104 F. Supp. 312, 313 (D. D. C. 1952).

for insuring such fairness and for determining debatable points is upon the military authorities, and their determinations are not reviewable by the courts, except (3) that, in the exceptional case when a denial of a constitutional right is so flagrant as to affect the 'jurisdiction' (i.e. the basic power) of the tribunal to render judgment, the courts will review upon petition for *habeas corpus*. To support issuance of a writ of *habeas corpus* the circumstances shown by the papers before the court must so seriously affect the fundamental fairness of the trial and the validity of the appellate and later determinations as to deprive the military authorities of jurisdiction, i.e., power to act.

"As is our frequent practice in capital cases, we have examined the whole of both of these long records. Accused were vigorously defended at all points. Actions of the military authorities appear to have conformed meticulously to the rules of procedure, and the reviews were exhaustive. We conclude . . . that the facts alleged in the petitions . . . do not supply grounds upon which the relief sought can be granted."[215]

Had the Supreme Court agreed with the due process views expressed by the court of appeals a simple denial of certiorari would have sufficed. It chose to grant certiorari, affirmed denial of habeas corpus, and, in its prevailing opinion, proceeded to approve the view of the district court and to disapprove the approach of the court of appeals, in this significant language:

"The District Court dismissed the applications without hearing evidence, and without further review, after satisfying itself that the courts-martial which tried petitioners had jurisdiction over their persons at the time of the trial and jurisdiction over the crimes with which they were charged as well as jurisdiction to impose the sentences which petitioners received. . . . The Court of Appeals affirmed the District Court's judgment, after expanding the scope of review by giving petitioners' allegations full consideration on their merits, reviewing in detail the mass of evidence to be found in the transcripts of the trial and other proceedings before the military court.

". . . We think that although the Court of Appeals may have erred in reweighing each item of relevant evidence in the trial record, it certainly did not err in holding that there was no need for a further hearing in the District Court."[216]

[215] Burns v. Lovett, 202 F. (2d) 335, 342, 347 (D. C. Cir. 1952).
[216] Burns v. Wilson, 346 U. S. 137, 139, 146, 73 Sup. Ct. 1045, 1051 (1953);

Thus the record of the Supreme Court of never having sanctioned the granting of a writ of habeas corpus in a military case on due process, as distinguished from jurisdictional, grounds, remains intact.[217] In the *Smith, Brown, Whelchel, Gusik* and *Burns* cases the Court does not blaze a new trail but stands on familiar ground. It but repeats what it has said before: "To those in the military or naval service of the United States the military law is due process."[218]

C. *Alleged Errors Held Insufficient to Support Habeas Corpus Relief*

A habeas corpus court is not at all concerned with the guilt or innocence or sanity of the accused and will not review the record to determine these issues.[219] It is not the function of a federal civil court to

---

rehearing denied, 346 U. S. 884, 74 Sup. Ct. 3 (1953). Followed in McKinney v. Finletter, 205 F. (2d) 761, 762 (M. D. Pa. 1953), and White v. Humphrey, 115 F. Supp. 317, 323 (M. D. Pa. 1953) *affd.,* 212 F. (2d) 503 (3d Cir. 1954). For a discussion of the impact of the Burns case upon problems of military jurisdiction, see pp. 97-101, *supra.*

[217] At the time the Court denied a rehearing in Burns v. Wilson, 346 U. S. 844, 73 Sup. Ct. 1045 (1953), Mr. Justice Frankfurter expressed a personal opinion that Johnson v. Zerbst, 304 U. S. 458, 58 Sup. Ct. 1019 (1938) is authority for permitting habeas corpus attack of military court convictions to extend to due process considerations, as distinguished from jurisdictional inquiry only. No other member of the Court joined in this view.

Johnson v. Zerbst at page 468 held only that, "A court's jurisdiction . . . may be lost . . . due to failure to complete the court . . . by providing counsel for an accused who is unable to obtain counsel who has not intelligently waived this constitutional guaranty . . ." and remanded to give petitioner an opportunity to prove he had not intelligently waived counsel. Under military law, UNIFORM CODE OF MILITARY JUSTICE, Article 27, 50 U. S. C. 591 (Supp. 1952), it is mandatory that a qualified defense counsel be appointed for each accused tried by a general or special court-martial. Not to do so would constitute jurisdictional error in failing properly to constitute the court. (See discussion of Counsel eligibility at pp. 27-31, *supra.*) If not corrected on appeal, within the military justice system, such failure would come within the traditional ambit of military habeas corpus as a jurisdictional defect. Due process, as distinguished from jurisdiction, would not be involved.

[218] Reeves v. Ainsworth, 219 U. S. 296, 304, 31 Sup. Ct. 230, 1 (1911); French v. Weeks, 259 U. S. 326, 42 Sup. Ct. 505 (1922); Creary v. Weeks, 259 U. S. 336, 344, 42 Sup. Ct. 509 (1922).

[219] Carter v. McClaughry, 183 U. S. 365, 381, 22 Sup. Ct. 181 (1902). *Ex parte* Quirin, 317 U. S. 1 at 25, 63 Sup. Ct. 1 (1942): "We are not here concerned with any question of the guilt or innocence of petitioners." *In re* Yamashita, 327 U. S. 1 at 8, 17, 66 Sup. Ct. 340 (1946): ". . . on application for habeas corpus we are not concerned with the guilt or innocence of petitioners. . . . We do not here appraise the evidence on which petitioner was convicted. . . . These are questions within the peculiar competence of the military officers composing the commission and were for it to decide." Humphrey v. Smith, 336 U. S. 695 at 698, 69 Sup. Ct. 830 (1949): "But our authority in habeas corpus proceedings to review court-martial judgments does not permit us to pass on the guilt or innocence of persons convicted by courts-martial." Whelchel v. McDonald, 176 F. (2d) 260 at 262 (5th Cir. 1949): "It is no more appropriate for a habeas corpus court to try the sanity of an accused convicted by a court-martial than to try his guilt. Both questions are the responsibility of the court-martial and the reviewing authorities including the President." *Affd.,* 340 U. S.

grant habeas corpus simply to evaluate the evidence.[220]

The following are illustrative of allegations of fact which have been held not to constitute grounds for habeas corpus relief in military cases:

1. That a reserve officer was on terminal leave at the time charges were preferred;[221]

2. That there was substantial or complete failure to comply with the pre-trial investigative procedure required by Article of War 70 of 1920;[222]

3. That accused was not represented by counsel at the pre-trial investigation;[223]

4. That, under the 1920 Articles of War, the officer appointed as defense counsel of a general court was not a lawyer;[224]

5. That, under the 1920 Articles of War, assigned counsel was ordered away during the course of the trial and appellant assumed his own defense after stating in court that he had no objection;[225]

6. That civilian defense counsel was excluded from court while secret maps were placed in evidence but regularly appointed defense counsel was present;[226]

7. That assistant defense counsel was absent where regularly appointed defense counsel was present at all times and accused stated he desired to be defended by the regularly appointed defense counsel and made no objection to the absence of the assistant defense counsel;[227]

122, 124, 71 Sup. Ct. 149 (1950). Schilder v. Gusik, 195 F. (2d) 657, 659 (6th Cir. 1952); McClellan v. Humphrey, 181 F. (2d) 757 (3d Cir. 1950); Bigrow v. Hiatt, 70 F. Supp. 826, 830 (M. D. Pa. 1947); White v. Humphrey, 115 F. Supp. 317, 322 (M. D. Pa. 1953), *affd.,* 212 F. (2d) 503 (3d Cir. 1954).

[220] Burns v. Wilson, 346 U. S. 137, 142, 73 Sup. Ct. 1045, *rehearing denied,* 346 U. S. 884; White v. Humphrey, 115 F. Supp. 317, 323 (M. D. Pa. 1953), *affd.,* 212 F. (2d) 503 (3d Cir. 1954).

[221] Hironimus v. Durant, 168 F. (2d) 288 (4th Cir. 1948), *reversing,* 73 F. Supp. 79 (S. D. W. Va. 1947); *cert. denied,* 335 U. S. 818, 69 Sup. Ct. 40 (1948); Durant v. Hiatt, 177 F. (2d) 373 (5th Cir. 1949), *affirming,* 81 F. Supp. 948 (N. D. Ga. 1948).

[222] Humphrey v. Smith, 336 U. S. 695 at 700-701, 69 Sup. Ct. 830 (1949); Hiatt v. Brown, 339 U. S. 103 at 110, 70 Sup. Ct. 495 (1950); Schilder v. Gusik, 195 F. (2d) 657, 659 (6th Cir. 1952); Rougt v. Steele, 184 F. (2d) 188 (8th Cir. 1950); Evans v. Hunter, 94 F. Supp. 837, 840 (D. Kan. 1951); Lucas v. Matthews, 90 F. Supp. 21 (D. Me. 1950).

[223] Romero v. Squier, 133 F. (2d) 528 at 532 (9th Cir. 1943), *cert. denied,* 318 U. S. 785, 63 Sup. Ct. 982 (1943).

[224] Altmayer v. Sanford, 148 F. (2d) 161 at 162 (5th Cir. 1945), where the court said: "The appointed counsel, being a commissioned officer admitted to practice before courts-martial, was a competent attorney within the purview of the Sixth Amendment. Romero v. Squier, 9 Cir. 133 F. (2d) 528, *certiorari denied,* 318 U. S. 785." *Cf.* Evans v. Hunter, 94 F. Supp. 837, 842 (D. Kan. 1951).

[225] Innes v. Crystal, 131 F. (2d) 576 (2d Cir. 1943), *cert. denied,* 319 U. S. 755, 63 Sup. Ct. 1321 (1943).

[226] Romero v. Squier, 133 F. (2d) 528 at 532 (9th Cir. 1943), *cert. denied,* 318 U. S. 785, 63 Sup. Ct. 982 (1943).

[227] Flackman v. Hunter, 75 F. Supp. 871 (D. Kan. 1948).

8. That, under the 1920 Articles of War, the law member of the court-martial was not a Judge Advocate General's Department officer even though such officers did serve on the court in other capacities;[228]

9. That accused was deprived of a jury trial;[229]

10. That, prior to February 1, 1949, no member of the court was an enlisted person;[230]

11. That no Negro was a member of the court which tried a Negro;[231]

12. That the investigating officer was not present at the trial;[232]

13. That there was improperly admitted into evidence a pre-trial confession of the accused;[233]

14. That, under the 1920 Articles of War, no copy of the staff judge advocate review nor of the opinion of the board of review was supplied to the accused or his counsel;[234]

15. That the court failed to find from the evidence that accused had been subjected to entrapment;[235]

16. That secret Army maps which formed the basis of conviction of an officer were not included in the record which was forwarded to the Secretary of War and upon which the sentence was confirmed by the President;[236]

17. That in the absence of bad faith a commanding general decided

[228] Hiatt v. Brown, 339 U. S. 103, 70 Sup. Ct. 495 (1950); Henry v. Hodges, 171 F. (2d) 401 at 403 (2d Cir. 1948), *cert. denied,* 336 U. S. 968, 69 Sup. Ct. 937 (1949) expressly approved in Hiatt v. Brown, *supra;* Whelchel v. McDonald, 340 U. S. 122, 126, 71 Sup. Ct. 146 (1950); Schilder v. Gusik, 195 F. (2d) 656, 660, *cert. denied,* 344 U. S. 844 (1952); McClellan v. Humphrey, 181 F. (2d) 757, 759 (3d Cir. 1950).

[229] *Ex parte* Milligan, 4 Wall. 2 at 123, 138 (U. S. 1866); *Ex parte* Mason, 105 U. S. 696 (1882); *Ex parte* Quirin, 317 U. S. 1 at 40-43, 63 Sup. Ct. 1 (1942); Reilly v. Pescor, 156 F. (2d) 632 at 635 (8th Cir. 1946), *cert. denied,* 329 U. S. 790, 67 Sup. Ct. 353 (1946); Innes v. Crystal, 131 F. (2d) 576 (2d Cir. 1943), *Cert. denied* 319 U. S. 755, 63 Sup. Ct. 1321 (1943); DeWar v. Hunter, 170 F. (2d) 993 (10th Cir. 1948), *cert. denied,* 337 U. S. 908, 69 Sup. Ct. 1048 (1949); Whelchel v. McDonald, 340 U. S. 122, 127, 71 Sup. Ct. 146 (1950).

[230] Whelchel v. McDonald, 176 F. (2d) 260 at 261 (5th Cir. 1949), *affd.,* 340 U. S. 122, 71 Sup. Ct. 146 (1950); DeWar v. Hunter, 170 F. (2d) 993 at 997 (10th Cir. 1948), *cert. denied,* 337 U. S. 908, 63 Sup. Ct. 1048 (1949).

[231] Jackson v. Gough, 170 F. (2d) 630 at 631 (5th Cir. 1948), *cert. denied,* 336 U. S. 938, 69 Sup. Ct. 1502 (1949).

[232] *Ibid.*

[233] Hironimous v. Durant, 168 F. (2d) 288 at 294 (4th Cir. 1948); Brown v. Sanford, 170 F. (2d) 344 (5th Cir. 1944). *Cf.* Burns v. Wilson, 346 U. S. 137, 73 Sup. Ct. 1045 (1953), *rehearing denied,* 346 U. S. 884, 74 Sup. Ct. 3 (1953); White v. Humphrey, 115 F. Supp. 317, 321 (M. D. Pa. 1953), *affd.,* 212 F. (2d) 503 (3d Cir. 1954).

[234] Weintraub v. Sevenson, 165 F. (2d) 756 (2d Cir. 1948).

[235] Romero v. Squier, 133 F. (2d) 528 at 532 (9th Cir. 1943), *cert. denied,* 318 U. S. 785, 63 Sup. Ct. 982 (1943).

[236] *Ibid.*

that the tactical situation required discontinuance of a trial and the transfer of the charges to another headquarters;[237]

18. That a civilian cook on an Army transport who deserted the vessel just as it was leaving a United States port to take troops overseas had not agreed to be subject to Army orders and did not know that he was subject to military law;[238]

19. That charges were not stated with the precision of a common-law indictment;[239]

20. That an identification line-up was improperly conducted;[240]

21. That the accused was insane either at the time of the offense or at the time of trial;[241]

22. That the accused was at the time of the pre-trial investigation denied an opportunity to cross examine, because they were not available, two witnesses who at the time were one hundred miles away;[242]

23. That accused was mistreated by guards and prisoners while being held in a stockade awaiting trial, in the absence of any evidence that a confession was so obtained;[243]

24. That accused was prevented from preparing his defense by being refused the privilege of referring to law books;[244]

25. That the same officer served as both president and law member of the court;[245]

26. That there was considerable delay in completing the pre-trial investigation and the trial;[246]

27. That the accused was illegally arrested;[247]

[237] Wade v. Hunter, 336 U. S. 684, 69 Sup. Ct. 834 (1949), *rehearing denied,* 337 U. S. 921, 69 Sup. Ct. 1152 (1949).

[238] McCune v. Kilpatrick, 53 F. Supp. 80 (E. D. Va. 1943).

[239] Bigrow v. Hiatt, 70 F. Supp. 826 (M. D. Pa. 1947), 168 F. (2d) 992 (3d Cir. 1948).

[240] White v. Humphrey, 115 F. Supp. 317, 321 (M. D. Pa. 1953), *affd.,* 212 F. (2d) 503 (3d Cir. 1954).

[241] Whelchel v. McDonald, 176 F. (2d) 260 at 262 (5th Cir. 1949): "It is no more appropriate for a habeas corpus court to try the sanity of an accused convicted by a court-martial than to try his guilt." *Affd.,* 340 U. S. 122, 124, 71 Sup. Ct. 146 (1950). *Cf.* Brown v. Sanford, 170 F. (2d) 344 at 345 (5th Cir. 1948).

[242] DeWar v. Hunter, 170 F. (2d) 933 at 996 (10th Cir. 1948), *Cert. denied,* 337 U. S. 908, 69 Sup. Ct. 1048 (1949), *rehearing denied,* 337 U. S. 934, 69 Sup. Ct. 1493 (1949).

[243] Benjamin v. Hunter, 75 F. Supp. 775 (D. Kan. 1947), 169 F. (2d) 512 (10th Cir. 1948). *Cf.* Durant v. Hiatt, 81 F. Supp. 948 (N. D. Ga. 1948), 177 F. (2d) 373 (10th Cir. 1948). (The Hesse crown jewel theft case.)

[244] *Ibid.*

[245] Benjamin v. Hunter, 75 F. Supp. 775 at 781 (D. Kan. 1947), 169 F. (2d) 512 (10th Cir. 1948).

[246] Durant v. Hiatt, 81 F. Supp. 948 at 954 (N. D. Ga. 1948), 177 F. (2d) 373 (5th Cir. 1949); *In re* Wrublewski, 71 F. Supp. 143, 145 (S. D. Cal. 1947).

[247] *Ibid.*

28. That officers from other commands were made available to sit as members of the court and were so detailed;[248]

29. That during the course of the trial the court sat in Germany, reconvened in Washington, D. C., and again reconvened in Germany;[249]

30. That defense counsel did not call available witnesses;[250]

31. That a Board of Review took its appellate action on petitioner's case the same day that it received his brief;[251]

32. That instructions given to the court-martial by the law member (law officer) were erroneous;[252]

33. That four charges of rape against accused were consolidated into one set of charges and one trial;[253]

34. That the sentence imposed, although authorized, was severe;[254]

35. That in time of war, less than five days elapsed from the service of charges until trial;[255]

36. That at the time the court-martial sat, one member had been appointed by verbal order only.[256]

The above list, while representative, is by no means exhaustive of the grounds asserted for habeas corpus relief from court-martial sentences. Often such allegations have not been supported by evidence. None has prevailed. Under the Articles of War effective February 1, 1949, item eight of the foregoing list has been made a jurisdictional requisite to the extent that the law member (law officer) must be an officer of the Judge Advocate General's Corps or a lawyer officer certified by the Judge Advocate General to be qualified.[257] As to item ten, where requested by him, an enlisted accused is entitled to have at least one-third of the court membership consist of enlisted personnel.[258] As to items four and five, if the trial counsel of a special court-martial is a Judge Advocate General's Corps officer or a lawyer, the defense counsel must also be so qualified and in every general court-martial case the defense counsel must be so qualified and certified by the Judge Advocate General as competent to perform such duties and must actually serve.[259]

[248] *Id.* at 955. Lucas v. Matthews, 90 F. Supp. 21, 27 (D. Me. 1950).

[249] *Ibid.*

[250] Schilder v. Gusik, 195 F. (2d) 657, 660 (6th Cir. 1952).

[251] White v. Humphrey, 115 F. Supp. 317, 322 (M. D. Pa. 1953), *affd.*, 212 F. (2d) 503 (3d Cir. 1954).

[252] *Id.* at 321.

[253] Kuykendall v. Hunter, 187 F. (2d) 545, 547 (10th Cir. 1951).

[254] *Ibid.*

[255] Bigrow v. Hiatt, 70 F. Supp. 826, 831 (M. D. Pa. 1947) and 168 F. (2d) 992 (3d Cir. 1948).

[256] McClellan v. Humphrey, 181 F. (2d) 757, 758 (3d Cir. 1950).

[257] 10 U. S. C. § 1479 (1946), Article of War 8 and 50 U. S. C. § 590 (a) (1951), Article 26 (a).

[258] 10 U. S. C. § 1475 (1946), Article of War 4 and 50 U. S. C. § 589 (c), Article 25 (c).

[259] 50 U. S. C. § 591 (b) and (c), Article 27 (b) and (c).

Wherever the Articles of War vest a discretion in the officer appointing a court-martial to select its members, the Supreme Court has consistently refused to review the exercise of that discretion.[260] This rule was reaffirmed in *Hiatt v. Brown*.[261] In that case the contention was advanced that the court-martial was without jurisdiction because, in violation of Article of War 8, [262] a Judge Advocate General's Department officer had been designated trial judge advocate while the law member was a colonel of Field Artillery. The Court said:[263]

> "We are unable to agree with the Court of Appeals that this record discloses any disregard of the 8th Article of War in the appointment of the tribunal which convicted respondent. . . .
>
> ". . . the availability of an officer as law member was intended by Congress to be a matter within the sound discretion of the appointing authority. Ordinarily the 'availability' of military personnel who are subject to assignment by an appointing authority is understood to depend upon a discretionary determination by the superior. . . . Moreover, the phrase adopted in the 8th Article, 'available *for the purpose*,' expresses a clear intent that the concept of availability should include the exercise of discretion by the appointing authority.
>
> "The 8th Article has also been consistently interpreted and applied by the Army as vesting a discretion in the appointing authority, which when exercised is conclusive in determining not only the accessibility of personnel but also the suitability of the officer detailed as the law member of a general court-martial. CM 231963, *Hatteberg*, 18 B. R. 349, 366-369 (1943); CM ETO 804, *Ogletree*, 2 B. R. (ETO) 337, 346 (1943); CM 209988, *Cromwell*, 9 B. R. 169, 196 (1938); Digest of Opinions of The Judge Advocate General (1912-1940) § 365(9). This established interpretation is entitled to great weight in our de-

[260] Mullan v. United States, 140 U. S. 240 at 245, 11 Sup. Ct. 788 (1891); Bishop v. United States, 197 U. S. 334, 340, 25 Sup. Ct. 440 (1905); Swaim v. United States, 165 U. S. 553 at 560, 17 Sup. Ct. 448 (1897); Kahn v. Anderson, 255 U. S. 1 at 8, 41 Sup. Ct. 224 (1921); Hiatt v. Brown, 339 U. S. 103 at 110, 70 Sup. Ct. 495 (1950). *Cf.* Martin v. Mott, 12 Wheat. 19 at 30, 34, 35 (U. S. 1827).

[261] 339 U. S. 103, 70 Sup. Ct. 495 (1950).

[262] Article of War 8 of 1920, 41 STAT. L. 788, 10 U. S. C. § 1479 (1946), in pertinent part provided: "The authority appointing a general court martial shall detail as one of the members thereof a law member, who shall be an officer of the Judge Advocate General's Department, except that when an officer of that department is not available for the purpose the appointing authority shall detail instead an officer of some other branch of the service selected by the appointing authority as specially qualified to perform the duties of law member."

[263] 339 U. S. 103 at 107-110, 70 Sup. Ct. 495 (1950).

termination of the meaning of the article. *Cf. United States ex rel. Hirshberg v. Cooke,* 336 U. S. 210, 216 (1949).

"The exercise of the discretion thus conferred on the appointing authority may be reviewed by the courts only if a gross abuse of that discretion would have given rise to a defect in the jurisdiction of the court-martial. However, we need not determine at this time whether the provision of the 8th Article relied upon below imposed a requirement going to the jurisdiction of the court-martial, for nothing in the record here involved indicates that the discretion of the appointing authority was improperly exercised. Clearly no abuse is disclosed by the appointment of an officer from the Judge Advocate General's Department to a capacity other than law member on the detail, or by reassignment of that officer to other duty at the time of trial, or by the standard of competence in legal matters shown by the law member at the trial."

The Supreme Court has spoken the first and last word on grounds for granting habeas corpus in military cases. In 1879 it said, "Here there was no defect of jurisdiction as to anything that was done. Beyond this we need not look into the record. . . . If error was committed in the rightful exercise of authority, we cannot correct it.[264] In 1950 it said, "The single inquiry, the test, is jurisdiction. . . . In this case the court-martial had jurisdiction of the person accused and the offense charged, and acted within its lawful powers. The correction of any errors it may have committed is for the military authorities which are also authorized to review its decision."[265]

Again in 1950, it said, "Any error by the military in evaluating the evidence on the question of insanity could not go to jurisdiction, the only issue before the court in habeas corpus proceedings."[266] Also in 1950 it said, "Congress was legislating as respects (military) tribunals over which the civil courts have traditionally exercised no power of supervision or review. . . . Military tribunals have operated in a self sufficient system, save only as habeas corpus was available to test their jurisdiction in specific cases."[267] In 1953, it approved action by the district court which it characterized in these words, "The District Court dismissed the applications without hearing evidence, and without further review, after satisfying itself that the courts-martial which tried petitioners had jurisdiction over the crimes with which they were

[264] *Ex parte* Reed, 100 U. S. 13 at 23 (1879).

[265] Hiatt v. Brown, 339 U. S. 103 at 111, 70 Sup. Ct. 495 (1950). Followed in McClellan v. Humphrey, 181 F. (2d) 757 at 759 (3d Cir. 1950).

[266] Whelchel v. McDonald, 340 U. S. 122, 126, 71 Sup. Ct. 146 (1950).

[267] Gusik v. Schilder, 340 U. S. 128, 132, 71 Sup. Ct. 149 (1950).

charged as well as jurisdiction to impose the sentences which petitioners received."[268] It has never said otherwise.

Nor has the Supreme Court ever sanctioned granting a writ of habeas corpus to a petitioner convicted by a military court except where it found the military tribunal which imposed the confinement was without jurisdiction.[269]

VI

Conclusions

The authorities here collected sustain the following military habeas corpus conclusions: (1) That independent military tribunals are as old as the civil courts and are as well rooted in antiquity as the writ of habeas corpus; (2) that military justice comprises a wholly separate system of jurisprudence blessed with both United States Constitutional and Supreme Court sanction; (3) that normally the only court possessing original habeas corpus jurisdiction is the federal district court of the district in which the military prisoner is confined; (4) that all other remedies, including application to the Judge Advocate General for relief under Article of War 53, or its successor, Article 73, must be exhausted before resort to habeas corpus is open, if at all; (5) that, except in involuntary induction cases, actual confinement must exist to invoke habeas corpus; (6) that the only remedy obtainable in habeas corpus is release from confinement or involuntary service; (7) that a habeas corpus court may not properly inquire into the guilt, innocence, or sanity of a petitioner; (8) that the test in habeas corpus is jurisdiction; and finally (9) that if a duly constituted military court had jurisdiction of the person, the offense and the sentence, habeas corpus must be denied.

[268] Burns and Dennis v. Lovett, 346 U. S. 137, 138, 73 Sup. Ct. 1045 (1953), *rehearing denied,* 346 U. S. 844, 74 Sup. Ct. 3 (1953).

[269] *Ex parte* Milligan, 4 Wall. 2 (U. S. 1866); Billings v. Truesdale, 321 U. S. 542, 64 Sup. Ct. 737 (1944); Hirschberg v. Cooke, 336 U. S. 210, 69 Sup. Ct. 530 (1949).

Table of Cases

Note: Unless otherwise indicated the United States was the other party.

Index

Table of Articles of War and the Uniform Code

APPENDIX

Uniform Code of Military Justice

ARTICLE 1. Definitions.

The following terms when used in this code shall be construed in the sense indicated in this article, unless the context shows that a different sense is intended, namely:

(1) "Department" shall be construed to refer, severally, to the Department of the Army, the Department of the Navy, the Department of the Air Force, and, except when the Coast Guard is operating as a part of the Navy, the Treasury Department;

(2) "Armed force" shall be construed to refer, severally, to the Army, the Navy, the Air Force, and, except when operating as a part of the Navy, the Coast Guard;

(3) "Navy" shall be construed to include the Marine Corps and, when operating as a part of the Navy, the Coast Guard;

(4) "The Judge Advocate General" shall be construed to refer, severally, to The Judge Advocates General of the Army, Navy and Air Force and except when the Coast Guard is operating as a part of the Navy, the General Counsel of the Treasury Department;

(5) "Officer" shall be construed to refer to a commissioned officer including a commissioned warrant officer;

(6) "Superior officer" shall be construed to refer to an officer superior in rank or command;

(7) "Cadet" shall be construed to refer to a cadet of the United States Military Academy or of the United States Coast Guard Academy;

(8) "Midshipman" shall be construed to refer to a midshipman at the United States Naval Academy and any other midshipman on active duty in the naval service;

(9) "Enlisted person" shall be construed to refer to any person who is serving in an enlisted grade in any armed force;

(10) "Military" shall be construed to refer to any or all of the armed forces;

(11) "Accuser" shall be construed to refer to a person who signs and swears to charges, to any person who directs that charges nominally be signed and sworn by another, and to any other person who has an interest other than an official interest in the prosecution of the accused;

(12) "Law officer" shall be construed to refer to an official of a general court-martial detailed in accordance with article 26;

(13) "Law specialist" shall be construed to refer to an officer of the Navy or Coast Guard designated for special duty (law);

(14) "Legal officer" shall be construed to refer to any officer in the Navy or Coast Guard designated to perform legal duties for a command.

ART. 2. Persons subject to the code.

The following persons are subject to this code:

(1) All persons belonging to a regular component of the armed forces, including those awaiting discharge after expiration of their terms of enlistment; all volunteers from the time of their muster or acceptance into the armed forces of the United States; all inductees from the time of their actual induction into the armed forces of the United States, and all other persons lawfully called or ordered into, or to duty in or for training in, the armed forces, from the dates they are required by the terms of the call or order to obey the same;

(2) Cadets, aviation cadets, and midshipmen;

(3) Reserve personnel while they are on inactive duty training authorized by written orders which are voluntarily accepted by them which orders specify that they are subject to this code;

(4) Retired personnel of a regular component of the armed forces who are entitled to receive pay;

(5) Retired personnel of a reserve component who are receiving hospitalization from an armed force;

(6) Members of the Fleet Reserve and Fleet Marine Corps Reserve;

(7) All persons in custody of the armed forces serving a sentence imposed by a court-martial;

(8) Personnel of the Coast and Geodetic Survey, Public Health Service, and other organizations, when assigned to and serving with the armed forces of the United States;

(9) Prisoners of war in custody of the armed forces;

(10) In time of war, all persons serving with or accompanying an armed force in the field;

(11) Subject to the provisions of any treaty or agreement to which the United States is or may be a party or to any accepted rule of international law, all persons serving with, employed by, or accompanying the armed forces without the continental limits of the United States and without the following territories: That part of Alaska east of longitude one hundred and seventy-two degrees west, the Canal Zone, the main group of the Hawaiian Islands, Puerto Rico, and the Virgin Islands;

(12) Subject to the provisions of any treaty or agreement to which the United States is or may be a party or to any accepted rule of international law, all persons within an area leased by or otherwise reserved or acquired for the use of the United States which is under the control of the Secretary of a Department and which is without the continental limits of the United States and without the following Territories: That part of Alaska east of longitude one hundred and seventy-two degrees west, the Canal Zone, the main group of the Hawaiian Islands, Puerto Rico, and the Virgin Islands.

ART. 3. Jurisdiction to try certain personnel.

(a) Subject to the provisions of article 43, any person charged with having committed, while in a status in which he was subject to this code, an offense against this code, punishable by confinement of five years or more and for which the person cannot be tried in the courts of the United States or any State or Territory thereof or of the District of Columbia, shall not be relieved from amenability to trial by courts-martial by reason of the termination of said status.

(b) All persons discharged from the armed forces subsequently charged with having fraudulently obtained said discharge shall, subject to the provisions of article 43, be subject to trial by court-martial on said charge and shall after apprehension be subject to this code while in the custody of the armed forces for such trial. Upon conviction of said charge they shall be subject to trial by court-martial for all offenses under this code committed prior to the fraudulent discharge.

(c) Any person who has deserted from the armed forces shall not be relieved from amenability to the jurisdiction of this code by virtue of a separation from any subsequent period of service.

ART. 4. Dismissed officer's right to trial by court-martial.

(a) When any officer, dismissed by order of the President, makes a written application for trial by court-martial, setting forth, under oath, that he has been wrongfully dismissed, the President, as soon as practicable, shall convene a general court-martial to try such officer on the charges on which he was dismissed. A court-martial so convened shall have jurisdiction to try the dismissed officer on such charges, and he shall be held to have waived the right to plead any statute of limitations applicable to any offense with which he is charged. The court-martial may, as part of its sentence, adjudge the affirmance of the dismissal, but if the court-martial acquits the accused or if the sentence adjudged, as finally approved or affirmed, does not include dismissal or death, the Secretary of the Department shall substitute for the dismissal ordered by the President a form of discharge authorized for administrative issuance.

(b) If the President fails to convene a general court-martial within six months from the presentation of an application for trial under this article, the Secretary of the Department shall substitute for the dismissal ordered by the President a form of discharge authorized for administrative issuance.

(c) Where a discharge is substituted for a dismissal under the authority of this article, the President alone may reappoint the officer to such commissioned rank and precedence as in the opinion of the President such former officer would have attained had he not been dismissed. The reappointment of such a former officer shall be without regard to position vacancy and shall affect the promotion status of other officers only insofar as the President may direct. All time between the dismissal and such reappointment shall be considered as actual service for all purposes, including the right to receive pay and allowances.

(d) When an officer is discharged from any armed force by administrative action or is dropped from the rolls by order of the President, there shall not be a right to trial under this article.

ART. 5. Territorial applicability of the code.

This code shall be applicable in all places.

ART. 6. Judge advocates and legal officers.

(a) The assignment for duty of all judge advocates of the Army and Air Force and law specialists of the Navy and Coast Guard shall be made upon the recommendation of The Judge Advocate General of the armed force of which they are members. The Judge Advocate General or senior members of his staff shall make frequent inspections in the field in supervision of the administration of military justice.

(b) Convening authorities shall at all times communicate directly with their staff judge advocates or legal officers in matters relating to the administration of military justice; and the staff judge advocate or legal officer of any command is authorized to communicate directly with the staff judge advocate or legal officer of a superior or subordinate command, or with The Judge Advocate General.

(c) No person who has acted as member, law officer, trial counsel, assistant trial counsel, defense counsel, assistant defense counsel, or investigating officer in any case shall subsequently act as a staff judge advocate or legal officer to any reviewing authority upon the same case. . . .

ART. 7. Apprehension.

(a) Apprehension is the taking into custody of a person.

(b) Any person authorized under regulations governing the armed forces to apprehend persons subject to this code or to trial thereunder may do so upon reasonable belief that an offense has been committed and that the person apprehended committed it.

(c) All officers, warrant officers, petty officers, and noncommissioned officers shall have authority to quell all quarrels, frays, and disorders among persons subject to this code and to apprehend persons subject to this code who take part in the same.

ART. 8. Apprehension of deserters.

It shall be lawful for any civil officer having authority to apprehend offenders under the laws of the United States or of any State, District, Territory, or possession of the United States summarily to apprehend a deserter from the armed forces of the United States and deliver him into the custody of the armed forces of the United States.

ART. 9. Imposition of restraint.

(a) Arrest is the restraint of a person by an order not imposed as a punishment for an offense directing him to remain within certain specified limits. Confinement is the physical restraint of a person.

(b) An enlisted person may be ordered into arrest or confinement by any officer by an order, oral or written, delivered in person or through other persons subject to this code. A commanding officer may authorize warrant officers, petty officers, or noncommissioned officers to order enlisted persons of his command or subject to his authority into arrest or confinement.

(c) An officer, a warrant officer, or a civilian subject to this code or to trial thereunder may be ordered into arrest or confinement only by a commanding officer to whose authority he is subject, by an order, oral or written, delivered in person or by another officer. The authority to order such persons into arrest or confinement may not be delegated.

(d) No person shall be ordered into arrest or confinement except for probable cause.

(e) Nothing in this article shall be construed to limit the authority of persons authorized to apprehend offenders to secure the custody of an alleged offender until proper authority may be notified.

ART. 10. Restraint of persons charged with offenses.

Any person subject to this code charged with an offense under this code shall be ordered into arrest or confinement, as circumstances may require; but when charged only with an offense normally tried by a summary court-martial, such person shall not ordinarily be placed in confinement. When any person subject to this code is placed in arrest or confinement prior to trial, immediate steps shall be taken to inform him of the specific wrong of which he is accused and to try him or to dismiss the charges and release him.

ART. 11. Reports and receiving of prisoners.

(a) No provost marshal, commander of a guard, or master at arms shall refuse to receive or keep any prisoner committed to his charge by an officer of the armed forces, when the commiting officer furnishes a statement, signed by him, of the offense charged against the prisoner.

(b) Every commander of a guard or master at arms to whose charge a prisoner is committed shall, within twenty-four hours after such commitment or as soon as he is relieved from guard, report to the commanding officer the name of such prisoner, the offense charged against him, and the name of the person who ordered or authorized the commitment.

ART. 12. Confinement with enemy prisoners prohibited.

No member of the armed forces of the United States shall be placed in confinement in immediate association with enemy prisoners or other foreign nationals not members of the armed forces of the United States.

ART. 13. Punishment prohibited before trial.

Subject to the provisions of article 57, no person, while being held for trial or the results of trial, shall be subject to punishment or penalty other than arrest or confinement upon the charges pending against him, nor shall the arrest or confinement imposed upon him be any more rigorous than the circumstances require to insure his presence, but he may be subjected to minor punishment during such period for infractions of discipline.

ART. 14. Delivery of offenders to civil authorities.

(a) Under such regulations as the Secretary of the Department may prescribe, a member of the armed forces accused of an offense against civil authority may be delivered, upon request, to the civil authority for trial.

(b) When delivery under this article is made to any civil authority of a person undergoing sentence of a court-martial, such delivery, if followed by conviction in a civil tribunal, shall be held to interrupt the execution of the sentence of the court-martial, and the offender after having answered to the civil authorities for his offense shall, upon the request of competent military authority, be returned to military custody for the completion of the said court-martial sentence. . . .

ART. 15. Commanding officer's non-judicial punishment.

(a) Under such regulations as the President may prescribe, any commanding officer may, in addition to or in lieu of admonition or reprimand, impose one of the following disciplinary punishments for minor offenses without the intervention of a court-martial—

(1) upon officers and warrant officers of his command:

(A) withholding of privileges for a period not to exceed two consecutive weeks; or

(B) restriction to certain specified limits, with or without suspension from duty, for a period not to exceed two consecutive weeks; or

(C) if imposed by an officer exercising general court-martial jurisdiction, forfeiture of not to exceed one-half of his pay per month for a period not exceeding one month;

(2) upon other military personnel of his command:

(A) withholding of privileges for a period not to exceed two consecutive weeks; or

(B) restriction to certain specified limits, with or without suspension from duty, for a period not to exceed two consecutive weeks; or

(C) extra duties for a period not to exceed two consecutive weeks, and not to exceed two hours per day, holidays included; or

(D) reduction to next inferior grade if the grade from which demoted was established by the command or an equivalent or lower command; or

(E) if imposed upon a person attached to or embarked in a vessel, confinement for a period not to exceed seven consecutive days; or

(F) if imposed upon a person attached to or embarked in a vessel, confinement on bread and water or diminished rations for a period not to exceed three consecutive days.

(b) The Secretary of a Department may, by regulation, place limitations on the powers granted by this article with respect to the kind and amount of punishment authorized, the categories of commanding officers authorized to exercise such powers, and the applicability of this article to an accused who demands trial by court martial.

(c) An officer in charge may, for minor offenses, impose on enlisted persons assigned to the unit of which he is in charge, such of the punishments authorized to be imposed by commanding officers as the Secretary of the Department may by regulation specifically prescribe, as provided in subdivisions (a) and (b).

(d) A person punished under authority of this article who deems his punishment unjust or disproportionate to the offense may, through the proper channel, appeal to the next superior authority. The appeal shall be promptly forwarded and decided, but the person punished may in the meantime be required to undergo the punishment adjudged. The officer who imposes the punishment, his successor in command, and superior authority shall have power to suspend, set aside, or remit any part or amount of the punishment and to restore all rights, privileges, and property affected.

(e) The imposition and enforcement of disciplinary punishment under authority of this article for any act or omission shall not be a bar to trial by court-martial for a serious crime or offense growing out of the same act or omission, and not properly punishable under this article; but the fact that a disciplinary punishment has been enforced may be shown by the accused upon trial, and when so shown shall be considered in determining the measure of punishment to be adjudged in the event of a finding of guilty. . . .

ART. 16. Courts-martial classified.

There shall be three kinds of courts-martial in each of the armed forces, namely:

(1) General courts-martial, which shall consist of a law officer and any number of members not less than five;

(2) Special courts-martial, which shall consist of any number of members not less than three; and

(3) Summary courts-martial, which shall consist of one officer.

ART. 17. Jurisdiction of courts-martial in general.

(a) Each armed force shall have court-martial jurisdiction over all persons subject to this code. The exercise of jurisdiction by one armed force over personnel of another armed force shall be in accordance with regulations prescribed by the President.

(b) In all cases, departmental review subsequent to that by the officer with authority to convene a general court-martial for the command which held the trial, where such review is required under the provisions of this code, shall be carried out by the armed force of which the accused is a member.

ART. 18. Jurisdiction of general courts-martial.

Subject to article 17, general courts-martial shall have jurisdiction to try persons subject to this code for any offense made punishable by this code and may, under such limitations as the President may prescribe, adjudge any punishment not forbidden by this code, including the penalty of death when specifically authorized by this code. General courts-martial shall also have jurisdiction to try any person who by the law of war is subject to trial by a military tribunal and may adjudge any punishment permitted by the law of war.

ART. 19. Jurisdiction of special courts-martial.

Subject to article 17, special courts-martial shall have jurisdiction to try persons subject to this code for any noncapital offense made punishable by this code and, under such regulations as the President may prescribe, for capital offenses. Special courts-martial may, under such limitations as the President may prescribe, adjudge any punishment not forbidden by this code except death, dishonorable discharge, dismissal, confinement in excess of six months, hard labor without confinement in excess of three months, forfeiture of pay exceeding two-thirds pay per month, or forfeiture of pay for a period exceeding six months. A bad-conduct discharge shall not be adjudged unless a complete record of the proceedings and testimony before the court has been made.

ART. 20. Jurisdiction of summary courts-martial.

Subject to article 17, summary courts-martial shall have jurisdiction to try persons subject to this code except officers, warrant officers, cadets, aviation cadets, and midshipmen for any noncapital offense made punishable by this code. No person with respect to whom summary courts-martial have jurisdiction shall be brought to trial before a summary court-martial if he objects thereto, unless under the provisions of article 15 he has been permitted and has elected to refuse punishment under such article. Where objection to trial by summary court-martial is made by an accused who has not been permitted to refuse punishment under article 15, trial shall be ordered by special or general court-martial, as may be appropriate. Summary courts-martial may, under such limitations as the President may prescribe, adjudge any punishment not forbidden by this code except death, dismissal, dishonorable or bad-conduct discharge, confinement in excess of one month, hard labor without confinement in excess of forty-five days, restriction to certain specified limits in excess of two months, or forfeiture of pay in excess of two-thirds of one month's pay.

ART. 21. Jurisdiction of courts-martial not exclusive.

The provisions of this code conferring jurisdiction upon courts-martial shall not be construed as depriving military commissions, provost courts, or other military tribunals of concurrent jurisdiction in respect of offenders or offenses that by statute or by the law of war may be tried by such military commissions, provost courts, or other military tribunals. . . .

ART. 22. Who may convene general courts-martial.

(a) General courts-martial may be convened by—

(1) the President of the United States;

(2) the Secretary of a Department;

(3) the commanding officer of a Territorial Department, an Army Group, an Army, an Army Corps, a division, a separate brigade, or a corresponding unit of the Army or Marine Corps;

(4) the commander in chief of a fleet; the commanding officer of a naval station or larger shore activity of the Navy beyond the continental limits of the United States;

(5) the commanding officer of an air command, an air force, an air division, or a separate wing of the Air Force or Marine Corps;

(6) such other commanding officers as may be designated by the Secretary of a Department; or

(7) any other commanding officer in any of the armed forces when empowered by the President.

(b) When any such commanding officer is an accuser, the court shall be convened by superior competent authority, and may in any case be convened by such authority when deemed desirable by him.

ART. 23. Who may convene special courts-martial.

(a) Special courts-martial may be convened by—

(1) any person who may convene a general court-martial;

(2) the commanding officer of a district, garrison, fort, camp, station, Air Force base, auxiliary air field, or other place where members of the Army or Air Force are on duty;

(3) the commanding officer of a brigade, regiment, detached battalion, or corresponding unit of the Army;

(4) the commanding officer of a wing, group, or separate squadron of the Air Force;

(5) the commanding officer of any naval or Coast Guard vessel, shipyard, base, or station; the commanding officer of any Marine brigade, regiment, detached battalion, or corresponding unit; the commanding officer of any Marine barracks, wing, group, separate squadron, station, base, auxiliary airfield, or other place where members of the Marine Corps are on duty;

(6) the commanding officer of any separate or detached command or group of detached units of any of the armed forces placed under a single commander for this purpose; or

(7) the commanding officer or officer in charge of any other command when empowered by the Secretary of a Department.

(b) When any such officer is an accuser, the court shall be convened by superior competent authority, and may in any case be convened by such authority when deemed advisable by him.

ART. 24. Who may convene summary courts-martial.

(a) Summary courts-martial may be convened by—

(1) any person who may convene a general or special court-martial;

(2) the commanding officer of a detached company, or other detachment of the Army;

(3) the commanding officer of a detached squadron or other detachment of the Air Force; or

(4) the commanding officer or officer in charge of any other command when empowered by the Secretary of a Department.

(b) When but one officer is present with a command or detachment he shall be the summary court-martial of that command or detachment and shall hear and determine all summary court-martial cases brought before him. Summary courts-martial may, however, be convened in any case by superior competent authority when deemed desirable by him.

ART. 25. Who may serve on courts-martial.

(a) Any officer on active duty with the armed forces shall be eligible to serve on all courts-martial for the trial of any person who may lawfully be brought before such courts for trial.

(b) Any warrant officer on active duty with the armed forces shall be eligible to serve on general and special courts-martial for the trial of any person, other than an officer, who may lawfully be brought before such courts for trial.

(c) (1) Any enlisted person on active duty with the armed forces who is not a member of the same unit as the accused shall be eligible to serve on general and special courts-martial for the trial of any enlisted person who may lawfully be brought before such courts for trial, but he shall serve as a member of a court only if, prior to the convening of such court, the accused personally has requested in writing that enlisted persons serve on it. After such a request, no enlisted person shall be tried by a general or special court-martial the membership of which does not include enlisted persons in a number comprising at least one-third of the total membership of the court, unless eligible enlisted persons cannot be obtained on account of physical conditions or military exigencies. Where such persons cannot be obtained, the court may be convened and the trial held without them, but the convening authority shall make a detailed written statement, to be appended to the record, stating why they could not be obtained.

(2) For the purposes of this article, the word "unit" shall mean any regularly organized body as defined by the Secretary of the Department, but in no case shall it be a body larger than a company, a squadron, or a ship's crew, or than a body corresponding to one of them.

(d) (1) When it can be avoided, no person in the armed forces shall be tried by a court-martial any member of which is junior to him in rank or grade.

(2) When convening a court-martial, the convening authority shall appoint as members thereof such persons as, in his opinion, are best qualified for the duty by reason of age, education, experience, length of service, and judicial temperament. No person shall be eligible to sit as a member of a general or special court-martial when he is the accuser or a witness for the prosecution or has acted as investigating officer or as counsel in the same case.

ART. 26. Law officer of a general court-martial.

(a) The authority convening a general court-martial shall appoint as law officer thereof an officer who is a member of the bar of a Federal court or of the highest court of a State of the United States and who is certified to be qualified for such duty by The Judge Advocate General of the armed force of which he is a member. No person shall be eligible to act as law officer in a case when he is the accuser or a witness for the prosecution or has acted as investigating officer or as counsel in the same case.

(b) The law officer shall not consult with the members of the court, other than on the form of the findings as provided in article 39, except in the presence of the accused, trial counsel, and defense counsel, nor shall he vote with the members of the court.

ART. 27. Appointment of trial counsel and defense counsel.

(a) For each general and special court-martial the authority convening the court shall appoint a trial counsel and a defense counsel, together with such assistants as he deems necessary or appropriate. No person who has acted as investigating officer, law officer, or court member in any case shall act subsequently as trial counsel, assistant trial counsel, or, unless expressly requested by the accused, as defense counsel or assistant defense counsel in the same case. No person who has acted for the prosecution shall act subsequently in the same case for the defense, nor shall any person who has acted for the defense act subsequently in the same case for the prosecution.

(b) Any person who is appointed as trial counsel or defense counsel in the case of a general court-martial—

(1) shall be a judge advocate of the Army or the Air Force, or a law specialist of the Navy or Coast Guard, who is a graduate of an accredited law school or is a member of the bar of a Federal court or of the highest court of a State; or shall be a person who is a member of the bar of a Federal court or of the highest court of a State; and

(2) shall be certified as competent to perform such duties by The Judge Advocate General of the armed force of which he is a member.

(c) In the case of a special court-martial—

(1) if the trial counsel is qualified to act as counsel before a general court-martial, the defense counsel appointed by the convening authority shall be a person similarly qualified; and

(2) if the trial counsel is a judge advocate, or a law specialist, or a member of the bar of a Federal court or the highest court of a State, the defense counsel appointed by the convening authority shall be one of the foregoing.

ART. 28. Appointment of reporters and interpreters.

Under such regulations as the Secretary of the Department may prescribe, the convening authority of a court-martial or military commission or a court of inquiry shall appoint qualified court reporters, who shall record the proceedings of and testimony taken before such court or commission. Under like regulations the convening authority of a court-martial, military commission, or court of inquiry may appoint an interpreter who shall interpret for the court or commission.

ART. 29. Absent and additional members.

(a) No member of a general or special court-martial shall be absent or excused after the accused has been arraigned except for physical disability or as a result of a challenge or by order of the convening authority for good cause.

(b) Whenever a general court-martial is reduced below five members, the trial shall not proceed unless the convening authority appoints new members sufficient in number to provide not less than five members. When such new members have been sworn, the trial may proceed after the recorded testimony of each witness previously examined has been read to the court in the presence of the law officer, the accused, and counsel.

(c) Whenever a special court-martial is reduced below three members, the trial shall not proceed unless the convening authority appoints new members sufficient in number to provide not less than three members. When such new members have been sworn, the trial shall proceed as if no evidence had previously been introduced, unless a verbatim record of the testimony of previously examined witnesses or a stipulation thereof is read to the court in the presence of the accused and counsel. . . .

ART. 30. Charges and specifications.

(a) Charges and specifications shall be signed by a person subject to this code under oath before an officer of the armed forces authorized to administer oaths and shall state—

(1) that the signer has personal knowledge of, or has investigated, the matters set forth therein; and

(2) that the same are true in fact to the best of his knowledge and belief.

(b) Upon the preferring of charges, the proper authority shall take immediate steps to determine what disposition should be made thereof in the interest of justice and discipline, and the person accused shall be informed of the charges against him as soon as practicable.

ART. 31. Compulsory self-incrimination prohibited.

(a) No person subject to this code shall compel any person to incriminate himself or to answer any question the answer to which may tend to incriminate him.

(b) No person subject to this code shall interrogate, or request any statement from, an accused or a person suspected of an offense without first informing him of the nature of the accusation and advising him that he does not have to make any statement regarding the offense of which he is accused or suspected and that any statement made by him may be used as evidence against him in a trial by court-martial.

(c) No person subject to this code shall compel any person to make a statement or produce evidence before any military tribunal if the statement or evidence is not material to the issue and may tend to degrade him.

(d) No statement obtained from any person in violation of this article, or through the use of coercion, unlawful influence, or unlawful inducement shall be received in evidence against him in a trial by court-martial.

ART. 32. Investigation.

(a) No charge or specification shall be referred to a general court-martial for trial until a thorough and impartial investigation of all the matters set forth therein has been made. This investigation shall include inquiries as to the truth of the matter set forth in the charges, form of charges, and the disposition which should be made of the case in the interest of justice and discipline.

(b) The accused shall be advised of the charges against him and of his right to be represented at such investigation by counsel. Upon his own request he shall be represented by civilian counsel if provided by him, or military counsel of his own selection if such counsel be reasonably available, or by counsel appointed by the officer exercising general court-martial jurisdiction over the command. At such investigation full opportunity shall be given to the accused to cross-examine witnesses against him if they are available and to present anything he may desire in his own behalf, either in defense or mitigation, and the investigating officer shall examine available witnesses requested by the accused. If the charges are forwarded after such investigation, they shall be accompanied by a statement of the substance of the testimony taken on both sides and a copy thereof shall be given to the accused.

(c) If an investigation of the subject matter of an offense has been conducted prior to the time the accused is charged with the offense, and if the accused was present at such investigation and afforded the opportunities for representation, cross-examination, and presentation prescribed in subdivision (b) of this article, no further investigation of that charge is necessary under this article unless it is demanded by the accused after he is informed of the charge. A demand for further investigation entitles the accused to recall witnesses for further cross-examination and to offer any new evidence in his own behalf.

(d) The requirements of this article shall be binding on all persons administering this code, but failure to follow them in any case shall not constitute jurisdictional error.

ART. 33. Forwarding of charges.

When a person is held for trial by general court-martial, the commanding officer shall, within eight days after the accused is ordered into arrest or confinement, if practicable, forward the charges, together with the investigation and allied papers, to the officer exercising general court-martial jurisdiction. If the same is not practicable, he shall report in writing to such officer the reasons for delay.

ART. 34. Advice of staff judge advocate and reference for trial.

(a) Before directing the trial of any charge by general court-martial, the convening authority shall refer it to his staff judge advocate or legal officer for consideration and advice. The convening authority shall not refer a charge to a general court-martial for trial unless he has found that the charge alleges an offense under this code and is warranted by evidence indicated in the report of investigation.

(b) If the charges or specifications are not formally correct or do not conform to the substance of the evidence contained in the report of the investigating officer, formal corrections, and such changes in the charges and specifications as are needed to make them conform to the evidence may be made.

ART. 35. Service of charges.

The trial counsel to whom court-martial charges are referred for trial shall cause to be served upon the accused a copy of the charges upon which trial is to be had. In time of peace no person shall, against his objection, be brought to trial before a general court-martial within a period of five days subsequent to the service of the charges upon him, or before a special court-martial within a period of three days subsequent to the service of the charges upon him. . . .

ART. 36. President may prescribe rules.

(a) The procedure, including modes of proof, in cases before courts-martial, courts of inquiry, military commissions, and other courts-martial, courts of inquiry, military commissions, and other military tribunals may be prescribed by the President by regulations which shall, so far as he deems practicable, apply the principles of law and the rules of evidence generally recognized in the trial of criminal cases in the United States district courts, but which shall not be contrary to or inconsistent with this code.

(b) All rules and regulations made in pursuance of this article shall be uniform insofar as practicable and shall be reported to the Congress.

ART. 37. Unlawfully influencing action of court.

No authority convening a general, special, or summary court-martial, nor any other commanding officer, shall censure, reprimand, or admonish such court or any member, law officer, or counsel thereof, with respect to the findings or sentence adjudged by the court, or with respect to any other exercise of its or his functions in the conduct of the proceeding. No person subject to this code shall attempt to coerce or, by any unauthorized means, influence the action of a court-martial or any military tribunal or any member thereof, in reaching the findings or sentence in any case, or the action of any convening, approving, or reviewing authority with respect to his judicial acts.

ART. 38. Duties of trial counsel and defense.

(a) The trial counsel of a general or special court-martial shall prosecute in the name of the United States, and shall, under the direction of the court, prepare the record of the proceedings.

(b) The accused shall have the right to be represented in his defense before a general or special court-martial by civilian counsel if provided by him, or by military counsel of his own selection if reasonably available, or by the defense counsel duly appointed pursuant to article 27. Should the accused have counsel of his own selection, the duly appointed defense counsel, and assistant defense counsel, if any, shall, if the accused so desires, act as his associate counsel; otherwise they shall be excused by the president of the court.

(c) In every court-martial proceeding, the defense counsel may, in the event of conviction, forward for attachment to the record of proceedings a brief of such matters as he feels should be considered in behalf of the accused on review, including any objection to the contents of the record which he may deem appropriate.

(d) An assistant trial counsel of a general court-martial may, under the direction of the trial counsel or when he is qualified to be a trial counsel as required by article 27, perform any duty imposed by law, regulation, or the custom of the service upon the trial counsel of the court. An assistant trial counsel of a special court-martial may perform any duty of the trial counsel.

(e) An assistant defense counsel of a general or special court-martial may, under the direction of the defense counsel or when he is qualified to be the defense counsel as required by article 27, perform any duty imposed by law, regulation, or the custom of the service upon counsel for the accused.

ART. 39. Sessions.

Whenever a general or special court-martial is to deliberate or vote, only the members of the court shall be present. After a general court-martial has finally voted on the findings, the court may request the law officer and the reporter to appear before the court to put the findings in proper form, and such proceedings shall be on the record. All other proceedings, including any other consultation of the court with counsel or the law officer shall be made a part of the record and be in the presence of the accused, the defense counsel, the trial counsel, and in general court-martial cases, the law officer.

ART. 40. Continuances.

A court-martial may, for reasonable cause, grant a continuance to any party for such time and as often as may appear to be just.

ART. 41. Challenges.

(a) Members of a general or special court-martial and the law officer of a general court-martial may be challenged by the accused or the trial counsel for cause stated to the court. The court shall determine the relevancy and validity of challenges for cause, and shall not receive a challenge to more than one person at a time. Challenges by the trial counsel shall ordinarily be presented and decided before those by the accused are offered.

(b) Each accused and trial counsel shall be entitled to one peremptory challenge, but the law officer shall not be challenged except for cause.

ART. 42. Oaths.

(a) The law officer, all interpreters, and, in general and special courts-martial, the members, the trial counsel, assistant trial counsel, the defense counsel, assistant defense counsel, and the reporter shall take an oath or affirmation in the presence of the accused to perform their duties faithfully.

(b) All witnesses before courts-martial shall be examined on oath or affirmation.

ART. 43. Statute of limitations.

(a) A person charged with desertion or absence without leave in time of war, or with aiding the enemy, mutiny, or murder, may be tried and punished at any time without limitation.

(b) Except as otherwise provided in this article, a person charged with desertion in time of peace or any of the offenses punishable under articles 119 through 132 inclusive shall not be liable to be tried by court-martial if the offense was committed more than three years before the receipt of sworn charges and specifications by an officer exercising summary court-martial jurisdiction over the command.

(c) Except as otherwise provided in this article, a person charged with any offense shall not be liable to be tried by court-martial or punished under article 15 if the offense was committed more than two years before the receipt of sworn charges and specifications by an officer exercising summary court-martial jurisdiction over the command or before the imposition of punishment under article 15.

(d) Periods in which the accused was absent from territory in which the United States has the authority to apprehend him, or in the custody of civil authorities, or in the hands of the enemy, shall be excluded in computing the period of limitation prescribed in this article.

(e) In the case of any offense the trial of which in time of war is certified to the President by the Secretary of the Department to be detrimental to the prosecution of the war or inimical to the national security, the period of limitation prescribed in this article shall be extended to six months after the termination of hostilities as proclaimed by the President or by a joint resolution of Congress.

(f) When the United States is at war, the running of any statute of limitations applicable to any offense under this code—

(1) involving fraud or attempted fraud against the United States or any agency thereof in any manner, whether by conspiracy or not; or

(2) committed in connection with the acquisition, care, handling, custody, control or disposition of any real or personal property of the United States; or

(3) committed in connection with the negotiation, procurement, award, performance, payment for, interim financing, cancellation, or other termination or settlement, of any contract, subcontract or purchase order which is connected with or related to the prosecution of the war, or with any disposition of termination inventory by any war contractor or Government agency; shall be suspended until three years after the termination of hostilities as proclaimed by the President or by joint resolution of Congress.

ART. 44. Former jeopardy.

(a) No person shall, without his consent, be tried a second time for the same offense.

(b) No proceeding in which an accused has been found guilty by a court-martial upon any charge or specification shall be held to be a trial in the sense of this article until the finding of guilty has become final after review of the case has been fully completed.

(c) A proceeding which, subsequent to the introduction of evidence but prior to a finding, is dismissed or terminated by the convening authority or on motion of the prosecution for failure of available evidence or witnesses without any fault of the accused shall be a trial in the sense of this article.

ART. 45. Pleas of the accused.

(a) If an accused arraigned before a court-martial makes any irregular pleading, or after a plea of guilty sets up matter inconsistent with the plea, or if it appears that he has entered the plea of guilty improvidently or through lack of understanding of its meaning and effect, or if he fails or refuses to plead, a plea of not guilty shall be entered in the record, and the court shall proceed as though he had pleaded not guilty.

(b) A plea of guilty by the accused shall not be received to any charge or specification alleging an offense for which the death penalty may be adjudged.

ART. 46. Opportunity to obtain witnesses and other evidence.

The trial counsel, defense counsel, and the court-martial shall have equal opportunity to obtain witnesses and other evidence in accordance with such regulations as the President may prescribe. Process issued in court-martial cases to compel witnesses to appear and testify and to compel the production of other evidence shall be similar to that which courts of the United States having criminal jurisdiction may lawfully issue and shall run to any part of the United States, its Territories, and possessions.

ART. 47. Refusal to appear or testify.

(a) Every person not subject to this code who—

(1) has been duly subpenaed to appear as a witness before any court-martial, military commission, court of inquiry, or any other military court or board, or before any military or civil officer designated to take a deposition to be read in evidence before such court, commission, or board; and

(2) has been duly paid or tendered the fees and mileage of a witness at the rates allowed to witnesses attending the courts of the United States; and

(3) willfully neglects or refuses to appear, or refuses to qualify as a witness or to testify or to produce any evidence which such person may have been legally subpenaed to produce;

shall be deemed guilty of an offense against the United States.

(b) Any person who commits an offense denounced by this article shall be tried on information in a United States district court or in a court of original criminal jurisdiction in any of the Territorial possessions of the United States, and jurisdiction is hereby conferred upon such courts for such purpose. Upon conviction, such persons shall be punished by a fine of not more than $500, or imprisonment for a period not exceeding six months, or both.

(c) It shall be the duty of the United States district attorney or the officer prosecuting for the Government in any such court of original criminal jurisdiction, upon the certification of the facts to him by the military court, commission, court of inquiry, or board, to file an information against and prosecute any person violating this article.

(d) The fees and mileage of witnesses shall be advanced or paid out of the appropriations for the compensation of witnesses.

ART. 48. Contempts.

A court-martial, provost court, or military commission may punish for contempt any person who uses any menacing words, signs, or gestures in its presence, or who disturbs its proceedings by any riot or disorder. Such punishment shall not exceed confinement for thirty days or a fine of $100, or both.

ART. 49. Depositions.

(a) At any time after charges have been signed as provided in article 30, any party may take oral or written depositions unless an authority competent to convene a court-martial for the trial of such charges forbids it for good cause. If a deposition is to be taken before charges are referred for trial, such an authority may designate officers to represent the prosecution and the defense and may authorize such officers to take the deposition of any witness.

(b) The party at whose instance a deposition is to be taken shall give to every other party reasonable written notice of the time and place for taking the deposition.

(c) Depositions may be taken before and authenticated by any military or civil officer authorized by the laws of the United States or by the laws of the place where the deposition is taken to administer oaths.

(d) A duly authenticated deposition taken upon reasonable notice to the other party, so far as otherwise admissible under the rules of evidence, may be read in evidence before any military court or commission in any case not capital, or in any proceeding before a court of inquiry or military board, if it appears—

(1) that the witness resides or is beyond the State, Territory, or District in which the court, commission, or board is ordered to sit, or beyond the distance of one hundred miles from the place or trial or hearing; or

(2) that the witness by reason of death, age, sickness, bodily infirmity, imprisonment, military necessity, nonamenability to process, or reasonable cause, is unable or refuses to appear and testify in person at the place of trial or hearing; or

(3) that the present whereabouts of the witness is unknown.

(e) Subject to the requirements of subdivision (d) of this article, testimony by deposition may be adduced by the defense in capital cases.

(f) Subject to the requirements of subdivision (d) of this article, a deposition may be read in evidence in any case in which the death penalty is authorized by law but is not mandatory, whenever the convening authority shall have directed that the case be treated as not capital, and in such a case a sentence of death may not be adjudged by the court-martial.

ART. 50. Admissibility of records of courts of inquiry.

(a) In any case not capital and not extending to the dismissal of an officer, the sworn testimony, contained in the duly authenticated record of proceedings of a court of inquiry, of a person whose oral testimony cannot be obtained, may, if otherwise admissible under the rules of evidence, be read in evidence by any party before a court-martial or military commission if the accused was a party before the court of inquiry and if the same issue was involved or if the accused consents to the introduction of such evidence.

(b) Such testimony may be read in evidence only by the defense in capital cases or cases extending to the dismissal of an officer.

(c) Such testimony may also be read in evidence before a court of inquiry or a military board.

ART. 51. Voting and rulings.

(a) Voting by members of a general or special court-martial upon questions of challenge, on the findings, and on the sentence shall be by secret written ballot. The junior member of the court shall in each case count the votes, which count shall be checked by the president, who shall forthwith announce the result of the ballot to the members of the court.

(b) The law officer of a general court-martial and the president of a special court-martial shall rule upon interlocutory questions, other than challenge, arising during the proceedings. Any such ruling made by the law officer of a general court-martial upon any interlocutory question other than a motion for a finding of not guilty, or the question of accused's sanity, shall be final and shall constitute the ruling of the court; but the law officer may change any such ruling at any time during the trial. Unless such ruling be final, if any member objects thereto, the court shall be cleared and closed and the question decided by a vote as provided in article 52, viva voce, beginning with the junior in rank.

(c) Before a vote is taken on the findings, the law officer of a general court-martial and the president of a special court-martial shall, in the presence of the accused and counsel, instruct the court as to the elements of the offense and charge the court—

(1) that the accused must be presumed to be innocent until his guilt is established by legal and competent evidence beyond reasonable doubt;

(2) that in the case being considered, if there is a reasonable doubt as to the guilt of the accused, the doubt shall be resolved in favor of the accused and he shall be acquitted;

(3) that if there is a reasonable doubt as to the degree of guilt, the finding must be in a lower degree as to which there is no reasonable doubt; and

(4) that the burden of proof to establish the guilt of the accused beyond reasonable doubt is upon the Government.

ART. 52. Number of votes required.

(a) (1) No person shall be convicted of an offense for which the death penalty is made mandatory by law, except by the concurrence of all the members of the court-martial present at the time the vote is taken.

(2) No person shall be convicted of any other offense, except by the concurrence of two-thirds of the members present at the time the vote is taken.

(b) (1) No person shall be sentenced to suffer death, except by the concurrence of all the members of the court-martial present at the time the vote is taken and for an offense in this code made expressly punishable by death.

(2) No person shall be sentenced to life imprisonment or to confinement in excess of ten years, except by the concurrence of three-fourths of the members present at the time the vote is taken.

(3) All other sentences shall be determined by the concurrence of two-thirds of the members present at the time the vote is taken.

(c) All other questions to be decided by the members of a general or special court-martial shall be determined by a majority vote. A tie vote on a challenge shall disqualify the member challenged. A tie vote on a motion for a finding of not guilty or on a motion relating to the question of the accused's sanity shall be a determination against the accused. A tie vote on any other question shall be a determination in favor of the accused.

ART. 53. Court to announce action.

Every court-martial shall announce its findings and sentence to the parties as soon as determined.

ART. 54. Record of trial.

(a) Each general court-martial shall keep a separate record of the proceedings of the trial of each case brought before it, and such record shall be authenticated by the signature of the president and the law officer. In case the record cannot be authenticated by either the president or the law officer, by reason of the death, disability, or absence of such officer, it shall be signed by a member in lieu of him. If both the president and the law officer are unavailable for such reasons, the record shall be authenticated by two members.

(b) Each special and summary court-martial shall keep a separate record of the proceedings in each case, which record shall contain such matter and be authenticated in such manner as may be required by regulations which the President may prescribe.

(c) A copy of the record of the proceedings of each general and special court-martial shall be given to the accused as soon as authenticated. . . .

ART. 55. Cruel and unusual punishments prohibited.

Punishment by flogging, or by branding, marking, or tatooing on the body, or any other cruel or unusual punishment, shall not be adjudged by any court-martial or inflicted upon any person subject to this code. The use of irons, single or double, except for the purpose of safe custody, is prohibited.

ART. 56. Maximum limits.

The punishment which a court-martial may direct for an offense shall not exceed such limits as the President may prescribe for that offense.

ART. 57. Effective date of sentences.

(a) Whenever a sentence of a court-martial as lawfully adjudged and approved includes a forfeiture of pay or allowances in addition to confinement not suspended, the forfeiture may apply to pay or allowances becoming due on or after the date such sentence is approved by the convening authority. No forfeiture shall extend to any pay or allowances accrued before such date.

(b) Any period of confinement included in a sentence of a court-martial shall begin to run from the date the sentence is adjudged by the court-martial, but periods during which the sentence to confinement is suspended shall be excluded in computing the service of the term of confinement.

(c) All other sentences of courts-martial shall become effective on the date ordered executed.

ART. 58. Execution of confinement.

(a) Under such instructions as the Department concerned may prescribe, any sentence of confinement adjudged by a court-martial or other military tribunal, whether or not such sentence includes discharge or dismissal, and whether or not such discharge or dismissal has been executed, may be carried into execution by confinement in any place of confinement under the control of any of the armed forces, or in any penal or correctional institution under the control of the United States, or which the United States may be allowed to use; and persons so confined in a penal or correctional institution not under the control of one of the armed forces shall be subject to the same discipline and treatment as persons confined or committed by the courts of the United States or of the State, Territory, District, or place in which the institution is situated.

(b) The omission of the words "hard labor" in any sentence of a court-martial adjudging confinement shall not be construed as depriving the authority executing such sentence of the power to require hard labor as a part of the punishment. . . .

ART. 59. Error of law; lesser included offense.

(a) A finding or sentence of a court-martial shall not be held incorrect on the ground of an error of law unless the error materially prejudices the substantial rights of the accused.

(b) Any reviewing authority with the power to approve or affirm a finding of guilty may approve or affirm, instead, so much of the finding as includes a lesser included offense.

ART. 60. Initial action on the record.

After every trial by court-martial the record shall be forwarded to the convening authority, and action thereon may be taken by the officer who convened the court, an officer commanding for the time being, a successor in command, or by any officer exercising general court-martial jurisdiction.

ART. 61. Same—General court-martial records.

The convening authority shall refer the record of every general court-martial to his staff judge advocate or legal officer, who shall submit his written opinion thereon to the convening authority. If the final action of the court has resulted in an acquittal of all charges and specifications, the opinion shall be limited to questions of jurisdiction and shall be forwarded with the record to The Judge Advocate General of the armed force of which the accused is a member.

ART. 62. Reconsideration and revision.

(a) If a specification before a court-martial has been dismissed on motion and the ruling does not amount to a finding of not guilty, the convening authority may return the record to the court for reconsideration of the ruling and any further appropriate action.

(b) Where there is an apparent error or omission in the record or where the record shows improper or inconsistent action by a court-martial with respect to a finding or sentence which can be rectified without material prejudice to the substantial rights of the accused, the convening authority may return the record to the court for appropriate action. In no case, however, may the record be returned—

(1) for reconsideration of a finding of not guilty of any specification or a ruling which amounts to a finding of not guilty; or

(2) for reconsideration of a finding of not guilty of any charge, unless the record shows a finding of guilty under a specification laid under that charge, which sufficiently alleges a violation of some article of this code; or

(3) for increasing the severity of the sentence unless the sentence prescribed for the offense is mandatory.

ART. 63. Rehearings.

(a) If the convening authority disapproves the findings and sentence of a court-martial he may, except where there is lack of sufficient evidence in the record to support the findings, order a rehearing, in which case he shall state the reasons for disapproval. If he disapproves the findings and sentence and does not order a rehearing, he shall dismiss the charges.

(b) Every rehearing shall take place before a court-martial composed of members not members of the court-martial which first heard the case. Upon such rehearing the accused shall not be tried for any offense of which he was found not guilty by the first court-martial, and no sentence in excess of or more severe than the original sentence shall be imposed unless the sentence is based upon a finding of guilty of an offense not considered upon the merits in the original proceedings or unless the sentence prescribed for the offense is mandatory.

ART. 64. Approval by the convening authority.

In acting on the findings and sentence of a court-martial, the convening authority shall approve only such findings of guilty, and the sentence or such part or amount of the sentence, as he finds correct in law and fact and as he in his discretion determines should be approved. Unless he indicates otherwise, approval of the sentence shall constitute approval of the findings and sentence.

ART. 65. Disposition of records after review by the convening authority.

(a) When the convening authority has taken final action in a general court-martial case, he shall forward the entire record, including his action thereon and the opinion or opinions of the staff judge advocate or legal officer, to the appropriate Judge Advocate General.

(b) Where the sentence of a special court-martial as approved by the convening authority includes a bad-conduct discharge, whether or not suspended, the record shall be forwarded to the officer exercising general court-martial jurisdiction over the command to be reviewed in the same manner as a record of trial by general court-martial or directly to the appropriate Judge Advocate General to be reviewed by a board of review. If the sentence as approved by an officer exercising general court-martial jurisdiction includes a bad-conduct discharge, whether or not suspended, the record shall be forwarded to the appropriate Judge Advocate General to be reviewed by a board of review.

(c) All other special and summary court-martial records shall be reviewed by a judge advocate of the Army or Air Force, a law specialist of the Navy, or a law specialist or lawyer of the Coast Guard or Treasury Department and shall be transmitted and disposed of as the Secretary of the Department may prescribe by regulations.

ART. 66. Review by the board of review.

(a) The Judge Advocate General of each of the armed forces shall constitute in his office one or more boards of review, each composed of not less than three officers or civilians, each of whom shall be a member of the bar of a Federal court or of the highest court of a State of the United States.

(b) The Judge Advocate General shall refer to a board of review the record in every case of trial by court-martial in which the sentence, as approved, affects a general or flag officer or extends to death, dismissal of an officer, cadet, or midshipman, dishonorable or bad-conduct discharge, or confinement for one year or more.

(c) In a case referred to it, the board of review shall act only with respect to the findings and sentence as approved by the convening authority. It shall affirm only such findings of guilty, and the sentence or such part or amount of the sentence, as it finds correct in law and fact and determines, on the basis of the entire record, should be approved. In considering the record it shall have authority to weigh the evidence, judge the credibility of witnesses, and determine controverted questions of fact, recognizing that the trial court saw and heard the witnesses.

(d) If the board of review sets aside the findings and sentence, it may, except where the setting aside is based on lack of sufficient evidence in the record to support the findings, order a rehearing. If it sets aside the findings and sentence and does not order a rehearing, it shall order that the charges be dismissed.

(e) The Judge Advocate General shall, unless there is to be further action by the President or the Secretary of the Department or the Court of Military Appeals, instruct the convening authority to take action in accordance with the decision of the board of review. If the board of review has ordered a rehearing but the convening authority finds a rehearing impracticable, he may dismiss the charges.

(f) The Judge Advocates General of the armed forces shall prescribe uniform rules of procedure for proceedings in and before boards of review and shall meet periodically to formulate policies and procedure in regard to review of court-martial cases in the offices of the Judge Advocates General and by the boards of review.

ART. 67. Review by the Court of Military Appeals.

(a) (1) There is hereby established a Court of Military Appeals, which shall be located for administrative purposes in the Department of Defense. The Court of Military Appeals shall consist of three judges appointed from civilian life by the President, by and with the advice and consent of the Senate, for a term of fifteen years. Not more than two of the judges of such court shall be appointed from the same political party, nor shall any person be eligible for appointment to the court who is not a member of the bar of a Federal court or of the highest court of a State. Each judge shall receive a salary of $17,500 a year and shall be eligible for reappointment. The President shall designate from time to time one of the judges to act as Chief Judge. The Court of Military Appeals shall have power to prescribe its own rules of procedure and to determine the number of judges required to constitute a quorum. A vacancy in the court shall not impair the right of the remaining judges to exercise all the powers of the court.

(2) The terms of office of the three judges first taking office after the effective date of this subdivision shall expire, as designated by the President at the time of nomination, one of May 1, 1956, one on May 1, 1961, and one on May 1, 1966. The terms of office of all successors shall expire fifteen years after the expiration of the terms for which their predecessors were appointed, but any judge appointed to fill a vacancy occurring prior to the expiration of the term for which his predecessor was appointed shall be appointed only for the unexpired term of his predecessor.

(3) Judges of the Court of Military Appeals may be removed by the President, upon notice and hearing, for neglect of duty or malfeasance in office, or upon the ground of mental or physical disability, but for no other cause.

(4) If any judge of the Court of Military Appeals is temporarily unable to perform his duties because of illness or other disability, the President may designate a judge of the United States Court of Appeals to fill the office for the period of disability.

(b) The Court of Military Appeals shall review the record in the following cases:

(1) All cases in which the sentence, as affirmed by a board of review, affects a general or flag officer or extends to death;

(2) All cases reviewed by a board of review which The Judge Advocate General orders forwarded to the Court of Military Appeals for review; and

(3) All cases reviewed by a board of review in which, upon petition of the accused and on good cause shown, the Court of Military Appeals has granted a review.

(c) The accused shall have thirty days from the time he is notified of the decision of the board of review to petition the Court of Military Appeals for a grant of review. The court shall act upon such a petition within thirty days of the receipt thereof.

(d) In any case reviewed by it, the Court of Military Appeals shall act only with respect to the findings and sentence as approved by the convening authority and as affirmed or set aside as incorrect in law by the board of review. In a case which The Judge Advocate General orders forwarded to the Court of Military Appeals, such action need be taken only with respect to the issues raised by him. In a case reviewed upon petition of the accused, such action need be taken only with respect to issues specified in the grant of review. The Court of Military Appeals shall take action only with respect to matters of law.

(e) If the Court of Military Appeals sets aside the findings and sentence, it may, except where the setting aside is based on lack of sufficient evidence in the record to support the findings, order a rehearing. If it sets aside the findings and sentence and does not order a rehearing it shall order that the charges be dismissed.

(f) After it has acted on a case, the Court of Military Appeals may direct The Judge Advocate General to return the record to the board of review for further review in accordance with the decision of the court. Otherwise, unless there is to be further action by the President, or the Secretary of the Department, The Judge Advocate General shall instruct the convening authority to take action in accordance with that decision. If the court has ordered a rehearing, but the convening authority finds a rehearing impracticable, he may dismiss the charges.

(g) The Court of Military Appeals and The Judge Advocates General of the armed forces shall meet annually to make a comprehensive survey of the operation of this code and report to the Committees on Armed Services of the Senate and of the House of Representatives and to the Secretary of Defense and the Secretaries of the Departments the number and status of pending cases and any recommendations related to uniformity of sentence policies, amendments to this code, and any other matters deemed appropriate.

ART. 68. Branch offices.

Whenever the President deems such action necessary, he may direct The Judge Advocate General to establish a branch office, under an Assistant Judge Advocate General, with any distant command, and to establish in such branch office one or more boards of review. Such Assistant Judge Advocate General and any such board of review shall be empowered to perform for that command, under the general supervision of The Judge Advocate General, the duties which The Judge Advocate General and a board of review in his office would otherwise be required to perform in respect of all cases involving sentences not requiring approval by the President.

ART. 69. Review in the office of The Judge Advocate General.

Every record of trial by general court-martial, in which there has been a finding of guilty and a sentence, the appellate review of which is not otherwise provided for by article 66, shall be examined in the office of The Judge Advocate General. If any part of the findings or sentence is found unsupported in law, or if The Judge Advocate General so directs, the record shall be reviewed by a board of review in accordance with article 66, but in such event there will be no further review by the Court of Military Appeals except pursuant to the provisions of article 67 (b) (2).

ART. 70. Appellate counsel.

(a) The Judge Advocate General shall appoint in his office one or more officers as appellate Government counsel, and one or more officers as appellate defense who shall be qualified under the provisions of article 27 (b) (1).

(b) It shall be the duty of appellate Government counsel to represent the United States before the board of review or the Court of Military Appeals when directed to do so by The Judge Advocate General.

(c) It shall be the duty of appellate defense counsel to represent the accused before the board of review or the Court of Military Appeals—

(1) when he is requested to do so by the accused; or

(2) when the United States is represented by counsel; or

(3) when The Judge Advocate General has transmitted a case to the Court of Military Appeals.

(d) The accused shall have the right to be represented before the Court of Military Appeals or the board of review by civilian counsel if provided by him.

(e) Military appellate counsel shall also perform such other functions in connection with the review of court-martial cases as The Judge Advocate General shall direct.

ART. 71. Execution of sentence; suspension of sentence.

(a) No court-martial sentence extending to death or involving a general or flag officer shall be executed until approved by the President. He shall approve the sentence or such part, amount, or commuted form of the sentence as he sees fit, and may suspend the execution of the sentence or any part of the sentence, as approved by him, except a death sentence.

(b) No sentence extending to the dismissal of an officer (other than a general or flag officer), cadet, or midshipman shall be executed until approved by the Secretary of the Department, or such Under Secretary or Assistant Secretary as may be designated by him. He shall approve the sentence or such part, amount, or commuted form of the sentence as he sees fit, and may suspend the execution of any part of the sentence as approved by him. In time of war or national emergency he may commute a sentence of dismissal to reduction to any enlisted grade. A person who is so reduced may be required to serve for the duration of the war or emergency and six months thereafter.

(c) No sentence which includes, unsuspended, a dishonorable or bad-conduct discharge, or confinement for one year or more shall be executed until affirmed by a board of review and, in cases reviewed by it, the Court of Military Appeals.

(d) All other court-martial sentences, unless suspended, may be ordered executed by the convening authority when approved by him. The convening authority may suspend the execution of any sentence, except a death sentence.

ART. 72. Vacation of suspension.

(a) Prior to the vacation of the suspension of a special court-martial sentence which as approved includes a bad-conduct discharge, or of any general court-martial sentence, the officer having special court-martial jurisdiction over the probationer shall hold a hearing on the alleged violation of probation. The probationer shall be represented at such hearing by counsel if he so desires.

(b) The record of the hearing and the recommendations of the officer having special court-martial jurisdiction shall be forwarded for action to the officer exercising general court-martial jurisdiction over the probationer. If he vacates the suspension, the vacation shall be effective, subject to applicable restrictions in article 71 (c), to execute any unexecuted portion of the sentence except a dismissal. The vacation of the suspension of a dismissal shall not be effective until approved by the Secretary of the Department.

(c) The suspension of any other sentence may be vacated by any authority competent to convene, for the command in which the accused is serving or assigned, a court of the kind that imposed the sentence.

ART. 73. Petition for a new trial.

At any time within one year after approval by the convening authority of a court-martial sentence which extends to death, dismissal, dishonorable or bad-conduct discharge, or confinement for one year or more, the accused may petition The Judge Advocate General for a new trial on grounds of newly discovered evidence or fraud on the court. If the accused's case is pending before the board of review or before the Court of Military Appeals, The Judge Advocate General shall refer the petition to the board or court, respectively, for action. Otherwise The Judge Advocate General shall act upon the petition.

ART. 74. Remission and suspension.

(a) The Secretary of the Department and, when designated by him, any Under Secretary, Assistant Secretary, Judge Advocate General, or commanding officer may remit or suspend any part or amount of the unexecuted portion of any sentence, including all uncollected forfeitures, other than a sentence approved by the President.

(b) The Secretary of the Department may, for good cause, substitute an administrative form of discharge for a discharge or dismissal executed in accordance with the sentence of a court-martial.

ART. 75. Restoration.

(a) Under such regulations as the President may prescribe, all rights, privileges, and property affected by an executed portion of a court-martial sentence which has been set aside or disapproved, except an executed dismissal or discharge, shall be restored unless a new trial or rehearing is ordered and such executed portion is included in a sentence imposed upon the new trial or rehearing.

(b) Where a previously executed sentence of dishonorable or bad-conduct discharge is not sustained on a new trial, the Secretary of the Department shall substitute therefor a form of discharge authorized for administrative issuance unless the accused is to serve out the remainder of his enlistment.

(c) Where a previously executed sentence of dismissal is not sustained on a new trial, the Secretary of the Department shall substitute therefor a form of discharge authorized for administrative issuance and the officer dismissed by such sentence may be reappointed by the President alone to such commissioned rank and precedence as in the opinion of the President such former officer would have attained had he not been dismissed. The reappointment of such a former officer shall be without regard to position vacancy and shall affect the promotion status of other officers only insofar as the President may direct. All time between the dismissal and such reappointment shall be considered as actual service for all purposes, including the right to receive pay and allowances.

ART. 76. Finality of court-martial judgments.

The appellate review of records of trial provided by this code, the proceedings, findings, and sentences of courts-martial as approved, reviewed, or affirmed as required by this code, and all dismissals and discharges carried into execution pursuant to sentences by courts-martial following approval, review, or affirmation as required by this code, shall be final and conclusive, and orders publishing the proceedings of courts-martial and all action taken pursuant to such proceedings shall be binding upon all departments, courts, agencies, and officers of the United States, subject only to action upon a petition for a new trial as provided in article 73 and to action by the Secretary of a Department as provided in article 74, and the authority of the President. . . .

ART. 77. Principals.

Any person punishable under this code who—

(1) commits an offense punishable by this code, or aids, abets, counsels, commands, or procures its commission; or

(2) causes an act to be done which if directly performed by him would be punishable by this code;

is a principal.

ART. 78. Accessory after the fact.

Any person subject to this code who, knowing that an offense punishable by this code has been committed, receives, comforts, or assists the offender in order to hinder or prevent his apprehension, trial, or punishment shall be punished as a court-martial may direct.

ART. 79. Conviction of lesser included offense.

An accused may be found guilty of an offense necessarily included in the offense charged or of an attempt to commit either the offense charged or of an offense necessarily included therein.

ART. 80. Attempts.

(a) An act, done with specific intent to commit an offense under this code, amounting to more than mere preparation and tending but failing to effect its commission, is an attempt to commit that offense.

(b) Any person subject to this code who attempts to commit any offense punishable by this code shall be punished as a court-martial may direct, unless otherwise specifically prescribed.

(c) Any person subject to this code may be convicted of an attempt to commit an offense although it appears on the trial that the offense was consummated.

ART. 81. Conspiracy.

Any person subject to this code who conspires with any other person or persons to commit an offense under this code shall, if one or more of the conspirators does an act to effect the object of the conspiracy, be punished as a court-martial may direct.

ART. 82. Solicitation.

(a) Any person subject to this code who solicits or advises another or others to desert in violation of article 85 or mutiny in violation of article 94 shall, if the offense solicited or advised is attempted or committed, be punished with the punishment provided for the commission of the offense, but if the offense solicited or advised is not committed or attempted, he shall be punished as a court-martial may direct.

(b) Any person subject to this code who solicits or advises another or others to commit an act of misbehavior before the enemy in violation of article 99 or sedition in violation of article 94 shall, if the offense solicited or advised is committed, be punished with the punishment provided for the commission of the offense, but if the offense solicited or advised is not committed, he shall be punished as a court-martial may direct.

ART. 83. Fraudulent enlistment, appointment, or separation.

Any person who—

(1) procures his own enlistment or appointment in the armed forces by means of knowingly false representations or deliberate concealment

as to his qualifications for such enlistment or appointment and receives pay or allowances thereunder; or

(2) procures his own separation from the armed forces by means of knowingly false representations or deliberate concealment as to his eligibility for such separation;

shall be punished as a court-martial may direct.

ART. 84. Unlawful enlistment, appointment, or separation.

Any person subject to this code who effects an enlistment or appointment in or a separation from the armed forces of any person who is known to him to be ineligible for such enlistment, appointment, or separation because it is prohibited by law, regulation, or order shall be punished as a court-martial may direct.

ART. 85. Desertion.

(a) Any member of the armed forces of the United States who—

(1) without proper authority goes or remains absent from his place of service, organization, or place of duty with intent to remain away therefrom permanently; or

(2) quits his unit or organization or place of duty with intent to avoid hazardous duty or to shirk important service; or

(3) without being regularly separated from one of the armed forces enlists or accepts an appointment in the same or another one of the armed forces without fully disclosing the fact he has not been so regularly separated, or enters any foreign armed service except when authorized by the United States;

is guilty of desertion.

(b) Any officer of the armed forces who, having tendered his resignation and prior to due notice of the acceptance of the same, quits his post or proper duties without leave and with intent to remain away therefrom permanently is guilty of desertion.

(c) Any person found guilty of desertion or attempted desertion shall be punished, if the offense is committed in time of war, by death or such other punishment as a court-martial may direct, but if the desertion or attempted desertion occurs at any other time, by such punishment, other than death, as a court martial may direct.

ART. 86. Absence without leave.

Any member of the armed forces who, without proper authority—

(1) fails to go to his appointed place of duty at the time prescribed; or

(2) goes from that place; or

(3) absents himself or remains absent from his unit, organization, or other place of duty at which he is required to be at the time prescribed;

shall be punished as a court-martial may direct.

ART. 87. Missing movement.

Any person subject to this code who through neglect or design misses the movement of a ship, aircraft, or unit with which he is required in the course of duty to move shall be punished as a court-martial may direct.

ART. 88. Contempt towards officials.

Any officer who uses contemptuous words against the President, Vice President, Congress, Secretary of Defense, or a Secretary of a Department, a Governor or a legislature of any State, Territory, or other possession of the United States in which he is on duty or present shall be punished as a court-martial may direct.

ART. 89. Disrespect towards superior officer.

Any person subject to this code who behaves with disrespect towards his superior officer shall be punished as a court-martial may direct.

ART. 90. Assaulting or willfully disobeying officer.

Any person subject to this code who—

(1) strikes his superior officer or draws or lifts up any weapon or offers any violence against him while he is in the execution of his office; or

(2) willfully disobeys a lawful command of his superior officer;

shall be punished, if the offense is committed in time of war, by death or such other punishment as a court-martial may direct, and if the offense is committed at any other time, by such punishment, other than death, as a court-martial may direct.

ART. 91. Insubordinate conduct towards noncommissioned officer.

Any warrant officer or enlisted person who—

(1) strikes or assaults a warrant officer, noncommissioned officer, or petty officer, while such officer is in the execution of his office; or

(2) willfully disobeys the lawful order of a warrant officer, noncommissioned officer, or petty officer; or

(3) treats with contempt or is disrespectful in language or deportment toward a warrant officer, noncommissioned officer, or petty officer while such officer is in the execution of his office;

shall be punished as a court-martial may direct.

ART. 92. Failure to obey order or regulation.

Any person subject to this code who—

(1) violates or fails to obey any lawful general order or regulation; or

(2) having knowledge of any other lawful order issued by a member of the armed forces, which it is his duty to obey, fails to obey the same; or

(3) is derelict in the performance of his duties;

shall be punished as a court-martial may direct.

ART. 93. Cruelty and maltreatment.

Any person subject to this code who is guilty of cruelty toward, or oppression or maltreatment of, any person subject to his orders shall be punished as a court-martial may direct.

ART. 94. Mutiny or sedition.

(a) Any person subject to this code—

(1) who with intent to usurp or override lawful military authority refuses, in concert with any other person or persons, to obey orders or otherwise do his duty or creates any violence or disturbance is guilty of mutiny;

(2) who with intent to cause the overthrow or destruction of lawful civil authority, creates, in concert with any other person or persons, revolt, violence, or other disturbance against such authority is guilty of sedition;

(3) who fails to do his utmost to prevent and suppress an offense of mutiny or sedition being committed in his presence, or fails to take all reasonable means to inform his superior or commanding officer of

an offense of mutiny or sedition which he knows or has reason to believe is taking place, is guilty of a failure to suppress or report a mutiny or sedition.

(b) A person who is found guilty of attempted mutiny, mutiny, sedition, or failure to suppress or report a mutiny or sedition shall be punished by death or such other punishment as a court-martial may direct.

ART. 95. Arrest and confinement.

Any person subject to this code who resists apprehension or breaks arrest or who escapes from custody or confinement shall be punished as a court-martial may direct.

ART. 96. Releasing prisoner without proper authority.

Any person subject to this code who, without proper authority, releases any prisoner duly committed to his charge, or who through neglect or design suffers any such prisoner to escape, shall be punished as a court-martial may direct.

ART. 97. Unlawful detention of another.

Any person subject to this code who, except as provided by law, apprehends, arrests or confines any person shall be punished as a court-martial may direct.

ART. 98. Noncompliance with procedural rules.

Any person subject to this code who—

(1) is responsible for unnecessary delay in the disposition of any case of a person accused of an offense under this code; or

(2) knowingly and intentionally fails to enforce or comply with any provision of this code regulating the proceedings before, during, or after trial of an accused;

shall be punished as a court-martial may direct.

ART. 99. Misbehavior before the enemy.

Any member of the armed forces who before or in the presence of the enemy—

(1) runs away; or

(2) shamefully abandons, surrenders, or delivers up any command, unit, place, or military property which it is his duty to defend; or

(3) through disobedience, neglect, or intentional misconduct endangers the safety of any such command, unit, place, or military property; or

(4) casts away his arms or ammunition; or

(5) is guilty of cowardly conduct; or

(6) quits his place of duty to plunder or pillage; or

(7) causes false alarms in any command, unit, or place under control of the armed forces; or

(8) willfully fails to do his utmost to encounter, engage, capture, or destroy any enemy troops, combatants, vessels, aircraft, or any other thing, which it is his duty so to encounter, engage, capture, or destroy; or

(9) does not afford all practicable relief and assistance to any troops, combatants, vessels, or aircraft of the armed forces belonging to the United States or their allies when engaged in battle;

shall be punished by death or such other punishment as a court-martial may direct.

ART. 100. Subordinate compelling surrender.

Any person subject to this code who compels or attempts to compel a commander of any place, vessel, aircraft, or other military property, or of any body of members of the armed forces, to give it up to an enemy or to abandon it, or who strikes the colors or flag to an enemy without proper authority, shall be punished by death or such other punishment as a court-martial may direct.

ART. 101. Improper use of countersign.

Any person subject to this code who in time of war discloses the parole or countersign to any person not entitled to receive it or who gives to another who is entitled to receive and use the parole or countersign a different parole or countersign from that which, to his knowledge, he was authorized and required to give, shall be punished by death or such other punishment as a court-martial may direct.

ART. 102. Forcing a safeguard.

Any person subject to this code who forces a safeguard shall suffer death or such other punishment as a court-martial may direct.

ART. 103. Captured or abandoned property.

(a) All persons subject to this code shall secure all public property taken from the enemy for the service of the United States, and shall give notice and turn over to the proper authority without delay all captured or abandoned property in their possession, custody, or control.

(b) Any person subject to this code who—

(1) fails to carry out the duties prescribed in subdivision (a) of this article; or

(2) buys, sells, trades, or in any way deals in or disposes of captured or abandoned property, whereby he shall receive or expect any profit, benefit, or advantage to himself or another directly or indirectly connected with himself; or

(3) engages in looting or pillaging;

shall be punished as a court-martial may direct.

ART. 104. Aiding the enemy.

Any person who—

(1) aids, or attempts to aid, the enemy with arms, ammunition, supplies, money, or other thing; or

(2) without proper authority, knowingly harbors or protects or gives intelligence to, or communicates or corresponds with or holds any intercourse with the enemy, either directly or indirectly;

shall suffer death or such other punishment as a court-martial or military commission may direct.

ART. 105. Misconduct as a prisoner.

Any person subject to this code who, while in the hands of the enemy in time of war—

(1) for the purpose of securing favorable treatment by his captors acts without proper authority in a manner contrary to law, custom, or regulation, to the detriment of others of whatever nationality held by the enemy as civilian or military prisoners; or

(2) while in a position of authority over such persons maltreats them without justifiable cause;

shall be punished as a court-martial may direct.

ART. 106. Spies.

Any person who in time of war is found lurking as a spy or acting as a spy in or about any place, vessel, or aircraft, within the control of jurisdiction of any of the armed forces of the United States, or in or about any shipyard, any manufacturing or industrial plant, or any other place or institution engaged in work in aid of the prosecution of the war by the United States, or elsewhere, shall be tried by a general court-martial or by a military commission and on conviction shall be punished by death.

ART. 107. False official statements.

Any person subject to this code who, with intent to deceive, signs any false record, return, regulation, order, or other official document, knowing the same to be false, or makes any other official statement knowing the same to be false, shall be punished as a court-martial may direct.

ART. 108. Military property of United States—Loss, damage, destruction, or wrongful disposition.

Any person subject to this code who, without proper authority—

(1) sells or otherwise disposes of; or

(2) willfully or through neglect damages, destroys, or loses; or

(3) willfully or through neglect suffers to be lost, damaged, destroyed, sold or wrongfully disposed of;

any military property of the United States, shall be punished as a court-martial may direct.

ART. 109. Property other than military property of United States—Waste, spoil, or destruction.

Any person subject to this code who willfully or recklessly wastes, spoils, or otherwise willfully and wrongfully destroys or damages any property other than military property of the United States shall be punished as a court-martial may direct.

ART. 110. Improper hazarding of vessel.

(a) Any person subject to this code who willfully and wrongfully hazards or suffers to be hazarded any vessel of the armed forces shall suffer death or such other punishment as a court-martial may direct.

(b) Any person subject to this code who negligently hazards or suffers to be hazarded any vessel of the armed forces shall be punished as a court-martial may direct.

ART. 111. Drunken or reckless driving.

Any person subject to this code who operates any vehicle while drunk, or in a reckless or wanton manner, shall be punished as a court-martial may direct.

ART. 112. Drunk on duty.

Any person subject to this code, other than a sentinel or look-out, who is found drunk on duty, shall be punished as a court-martial may direct.

ART. 113. Misbehavior of sentinel.

Any sentinel or look-out who is found drunk or sleeping upon his post, or leaves it before he is regularly relieved, shall be punished, if the offense is committed in time of war, by death or such other punishment as a court-martial may direct, but if the offense is committed at any other time, by such punishment other than death as a court-martial may direct.

ART. 114. Dueling.

Any person subject to this code who fights or promotes, or is concerned in or connives at fighting a duel, or who, having knowledge of a challenge sent or about to be sent, fails to report the fact promptly to the proper authority, shall be punished as a court-martial may direct.

ART. 115. Malingering.

Any person subject to this code who for the purpose of avoiding work, duty, or service—

(1) feigns illness, physical disablement, mental lapse or derangement; or

(2) intentionally inflicts self-injury;

shall be punished as a court-martial may direct.

ART. 116. Riot or breach of peace.

Any person subject to this code who causes or participates in any riot or breach of the peace shall be punished as a court-martial may direct.

ART. 117. Provoking speeches or gestures.

Any person subject to this code who uses provoking or reproachful words or gestures towards any other person subject to this code shall be punished as a court-martial may direct.

ART. 118. Murder.

Any person subject to this code who, without justification or excuse, unlawfully kills a human being, when he—

(1) has a premeditated design to kill; or

(2) intends to kill or inflict great bodily harm; or

(3) is engaged in an act which is inherently dangerous to others and evinces a wanton disregard of human life; or

(4) is engaged in the perpetration or attempted perpetration of burglary, sodomy, rape, robbery, or aggravated arson;

is guilty of murder, and shall suffer such punishment as a court-martial may direct, except that if found guilty under paragraph (1) or (4) of this article, he shall suffer death or imprisonment for life as a court-martial may direct.

ART. 119. Manslaughter.

(a) Any person subject to this code who, with an intent to kill or inflict great bodily harm, unlawfully kills a human being in the heat of sudden passion caused by adequate provocation is guilty of voluntary manslaughter and shall be punished as a court-martial may direct.

(b) Any person subject to this code who, without an intent to kill or inflict great bodily harm, unlawfully kills a human being—

(1) by culpable negligence; or

(2) while perpetrating or attempting to perpetrate an offense, other than those specified in paragraph (4) of article 118, directly affecting the person;

is guilty of involuntary manslaughter and shall be punished as a court-martial may direct.

ART. 120. Rape and carnal knowledge.

(a) Any person subject to this code who commits an act of sexual intercourse with a female not his wife, by force and without her consent, in guilty of rape and shall be punished by death or such other punishment as a court-martial may direct.

(b) Any person subject to this code who, under circumstances not amounting to rape, commits an act of sexual intercourse with a female not his wife who has not attained the age of sixteen years, is guilty of carnal knowledge and shall be punished as a court-martial may direct.

(c) Penetration, however slight, is sufficient to complete these offenses.

ART. 121. Larceny and wrongful appropriation.

(a) Any person subject to this code who wrongfully takes, obtains, or witholds, by any means whatever, from the possession of the true owner or of any other person any money, personal property, or article of value of any kind—

(1) with intent permanently to deprive or defraud another person of the use and benefit of property or to appropriate the same to his own use or the use of any person other than the true owner, steals such property and is guilty of larceny; or

(2) with intent temporarily to deprive or defraud another person of the use and benefit of property or to appropriate the same to his own use or the use of any person other than the true owner is guilty of wrongful appropriation.

(b) Any person found guilty of larceny or wrongful appropriation shall be punished as a court-martial may direct.

ART. 122. Robbery.

Any person subject to this code who with intent to steal takes anything of value from the person or in the presence of another, against his will, by means of force or violence or fear of immediate or future injury to his person or property or the person or property of a relative or member of his family or of anyone in his company at the time of the robbery, is guilty of robbery and shall be punished as a court-martial may direct.

ART. 123. Forgery.

Any person subject to this code who, with intent to defraud—

(1) falsely makes or alters any signature to, or any part of, any writing which would, if genuine, apparently impose a legal liability on another or change his legal right or liability to his prejudice; or

(2) utters, offers, issues, or transfers such a writing, known by him to be so made or altered;

is guilty of forgery and shall be punished as a court-martial may direct.

ART. 124. Maiming.

Any person subject to this code who, with intent to injure, disfigure, or disable, inflicts upon the person of another an injury which—

(1) seriously disfigures his person by any mutilation thereof; or

(2) destroys or disables any member or organ of his body; or

(3) seriously diminishes his physical vigor by the injury of any member or organ;

is guilty of maiming and shall be punished as a court-martial may direct.

ART. 125. Sodomy.

(a) Any person subject to this code who engages in unnatural carnal copulation with another person of the same or opposite sex or with an animal is guilty of sodomy. Penetration, however slight, is sufficient to complete the offense.

(b) Any person found guilty of sodomy shall be punished as a court-martial may direct.

ART. 126. Arson.

(a) Any person subject to this code who willfully and maliciously burns or sets on fire an inhabited dwelling, or any other structure, movable or immovable, wherein to the knowledge of the offender there is at the time a human being, is guilty of aggravated arson and shall be punished as a court-martial may direct.

(b) Any person subject to this code who willfully and maliciously burns or sets fire to the property of another, except as providing in subdivision (a) of this article, is guilty of simple arson and shall be punished as a court-martial may direct.

ART. 127. Extortion.

Any person subject to this code who communicates threats to another person with the intention thereby to obtain anything of value or any acquittance, advantage, or immunity of any description is guilty of extortion and shall be punished as a court-martial may direct.

ART. 128. Assault.

(a) Any person subject to this code who attempts or offers with unlawful force or violence to do bodily harm to another person, whether or not the attempt or offer is consummated, is guilty of assault and shall be punished as a court-martial may direct.

(b) Any person subject to this code who—

(1) commits an assault with a dangerous weapon or other means or force likely to produce death or grievous bodily harm; or

(2) commits an assault and intentionally inflicts grievous bodily harm with or without a weapon;

is guilty of aggravated assault and shall be punished as a court-martial may direct.

ART. 129. Burglary.

Any person subject to this code who, with intent to commit an offense punishable under articles 118 through 128, inclusive, breaks and enters, in the nighttime, the dwelling house of another, is guilty of burglary and shall be punished as a court-martial may direct.

ART. 130. Housebreaking.

Any person subject to this code who unlawfully enters the building or structure of another with intent to commit a criminal offense therein is guilty of housebreaking and shall be punished as a court-martial may direct.

ART. 131. Perjury.

Any person subject to this code who in a judicial proceeding or course of justice willfully and corruptly gives, upon a lawful oath or in any form allowed by law to be substituted for an oath, any false testimony material to the issue or matter of inquiry is guilty of perjury and shall be punished as a court-martial may direct.

ART. 132. Frauds against the Government.

Any person subject to this code—

(1) who, knowing it to be false or fraudulent—

(A) makes any claim against the United States or any officer thereof; or

(B) presents to any person in the civil or military service thereof, for approval or payment, any claim against the United States or any officer thereof; or

(2) who, for the purpose of obtaining the approval, allowance, or payment of any claim against the United States or any officer thereof—

(A) makes or uses any writing or other paper knowing the same to contain any false or fraudulent statements; or

(B) makes any oath to any fact or to any writing or other paper knowing such oath to be false; or

(C) forges or counterfeits any signature upon any writing or other paper, or uses any such signature knowing the same to be forged or counterfeited; or

(3) who, having charge, possession, custody, or control of any money or other property of the United States, furnished or intended for the armed forces thereof, knowingly delivers to any person having authority to receive the same, any amount thereof less than that for which he receives a certificate or receipt; or

(4) who, being authorized to make or deliver any paper certifying the receipt of any property of the United States furnished or intended for the armed forces thereof, makes or delivers to any person such writing without having full knowledge of the truth of the statements therein contained and with intent to defraud the United States;

shall, upon conviction, be punished as a court-martial may direct.

ART. 133. Conduct unbecoming an officer and gentleman.

Any officer, cadet, or midshipman who is convicted of conduct unbecoming an officer and a gentleman shall be punished as a court-martial may direct.

ART. 134. General article.

Though not specifically mentioned in this code, all disorders and neglects to the prejudice of good order and discipline in the armed forces, all conduct of a nature to bring discredit upon the armed forces, and crimes and offenses not capital, of which persons subject to this code may be guilty, shall be taken cognizance of by a general or special or summary court-martial, according to the nature and degree of the offense, and punished at the discretion of such court. . . .

ART. 135. Courts of inquiry.

(a) Courts of inquiry to investigate any matter may be convened by any person authorized to convene a general court-martial or by any other person designated by the Secretary of a Department for that purpose whether or not the persons involved have requested such an inquiry.

(b) A court of inquiry shall consist of three or more officers. For each court of inquiry the convening authority shall also appoint counsel for the court.

(c) Any person subject to this code whose conduct is subject to inquiry shall be designated as a party. Any person subject to this code or employed by the Department of Defense who has a direct interest in the subject of inquiry shall have the right to be designated as a party upon request to the court. Any person designated as a party shall be given due notice and shall have the right to be present, to be represented by counsel, to cross-examine witnesses, and to introduce evidence.

(d) Members of a court of inquiry may be challenged by a party, but only for cause stated to the court.

(e) The members, counsel, the reporter, and interpreters of courts of inquiry shall take an oath or affirmation to faithfully perform their duties.

(f) Witnesses may be summoned to appear and testify and be examined before courts of inquiry as provided for courts-martial.

(g) Courts of inquiry shall make findings of fact but shall not express opinions or make recommendations unless required to do so by the convening authority.

(h) Each court of inquiry shall keep a record of its proceedings, which shall be authenticated by the signatures of the president and counsel for the court and forwarded to the convening authority. In case the record cannot be authenticated by the president it shall be signed by a member in lieu of the president and in case the record cannot be authenticated by the counsel for the court it shall be signed by a member in lieu of the counsel.

ART. 136. Authority to administer oaths and to act as notary.

(a) The following persons on active duty in the armed forces shall have authority to administer oaths for the purposes of military administration, including military justice, and shall have the general powers of a notary public and of a consul of the United States, in the performance of all notarial acts to be executed by members of any of the armed forces, wherever they may be, and by other persons subject to this code outside the continental limits of the United States:

(1) All judge advocates of the Army and Air Force;

(2) All law specialists;

(3) All summary courts-martial;

(4) All adjutants, assistant adjutants, acting adjutants, and personnel adjutants;

(5) All commanding officers of the Navy and Coast Guard;

(6) All staff judge advocates and legal officers, and acting or assistant staff judge advocates and legal officers; and

(7) All other persons designated by regulations of the armed forces or by statute.

(b) The following persons on active duty in the armed forces shall have authority to administer oaths necessary in the performance of their duties:

(1) The president, law officer, trial counsel, and assistant trial counsel for all general and special courts-martial;

(2) The president and the counsel for the court of any court of inquiry;

(3) All officers designated to take a deposition;

(4) All persons detailed to conduct an investigation;

(5) All recruiting officers; and

(6) All other persons designated by regulations of the armed forces or by statute.

(c) No fee of any character shall be paid to or received by any person for the performance of any notarial act herein authorized.

(d) The signature without seal of any such person acting as notary, together with the title of his office, shall be prima facie evidence of his authority.

ART. 137. Articles to be explained.

Articles 2, 3, 7 through 15, 25, 27, 31, 37, 38, 55, 77 through 134, and 137 through 139 of this code shall be carefully explained to every enlisted person at the time of his entrance on active duty in any of the armed forces of the United States, or within six days thereafter. They shall be explained again after he has completed six months of active duty, and again at the time he reenlists. A complete text of the Uniform Code of Military Justice and of the regulations prescribed by the President thereunder shall be made available to any person on active duty in the armed forces of the United States, upon his request, for his personal examination.

ART. 138. Complaints of wrongs.

Any member of the armed forces who believes himself wronged by his commanding officer, and, upon due application to such commander, is refused redress, may complain to any superior officer who shall forward the complaint to the officer exercising general court-martial jurisdiction over the officer against whom it is made. That officer shall examine into said complaint and take proper measures for redressing the wrong complained of; and he shall, as soon as possible, transmit to the Department concerned a true statement of such complaint, with the proceedings had thereon.

ART. 139. Redress of injuries to property.

(a) Whenever complaint is made to any commanding officer that willful damage has been done to the property of any person or that his property has been wrongfully taken by members of the armed forces he may, subject to such regulations as the Secretary of the Department may prescribe, convene a board to investigate the complaint. The board shall consist of from one to three officers and shall have, for the purpose of such investigation, power to summon witnesses and examine them upon oath or affirmation, to receive depositions or other documentary evidence, and to assess the damages sustained against the responsible parties. The assessment of damages made by such board shall be subject to the approval of the commanding officer, and in the amount approved by him shall be charged against the pay of the offenders. The order of such commanding officer directing charges herein authorized shall be conclusive on any disbursing officer for the payment by him to the injured parties of the damages so assessed and approved.

(b) Where the offenders cannot be ascertained, but the organization or detachment to which they belong is known, charges totaling the amount of damages assessed and approved may be made in such proportion as may be deemed just upon the individual members thereof who are shown to have been present at the scene at the time the damages complained of were inflicted, as determined by the approved findings of the board.

ART. 140. Delegation by the President.

The President is authorized to delegate any authority vested in him under this code, and to provide for the subdelegation of any such authority. . . .

86726014R00267

Made in the USA
Middletown, DE
31 August 2018